# Becoming an Outstanding Primary School Teacher

What is meant by outstanding teaching?

What makes the best teachers stand out from the rest?

How can I develop my own practice to become an outstanding teacher myself?

Whether you are training to become a primary school teacher or you are newly qualified and striving to improve your practice, this fully updated second edition of *Becoming an Outstanding Primary School Teacher* will support, inform and inspire you on your quest for excellence. Throughout, Russell Grigg draws on theory, research and case studies of real classroom practice to discuss what it takes to become an outstanding primary teacher today.

This bestselling guide has been comprehensively revised to reflect the latest changes to the curriculum, including the National Curriculum in England for 2014 and Scotland's Building Curriculum for Excellence. It has also widened its scope to appeal to trainee and serving teachers, reflecting the new Teachers' Standards in England.

Key topics include:

- defining and measuring outstanding teaching;
- understanding the theory, nature and scope of the curriculum;
- developing thinking skills in the classroom;
- understanding and meeting individual learning needs;
- using ICT to improve pedagogy;
- behaviour management;
- monitoring, assessment, recording and reporting.

*Becoming an Outstanding Primary School Teacher* will appeal to undergraduate and post-graduate students, including those on school-based programmes such as Teach First, as well as more experienced teachers seeking inspiration.

**Dr Russell Grigg** is Executive Head of Research at the Wales Centre for Equity in Education.

# Becoming an Outstanding Primary School Teacher

## Second edition

Russell Grigg

Routledge
Taylor & Francis Group

LONDON AND NEW YORK

First published 2015
by Routledge
2 Park Square, Milton Park, Abingdon, Oxon OX14 4RN

and by Routledge
711 Third Avenue, New York, NY 10017

*Routledge is an imprint of the Taylor & Francis Group, an informa business*

*British Library Cataloguing in Publication Data*
A catalogue record for this book is available from the British Library

*Library of Congress Cataloging in Publication Data*
  Grigg, Russell.
  Becoming an outstanding primary school teacher/Russell Grigg. – Second edition.
  pages cm
  Includes bibliographical references and index.
  1. Primary school teachers - In-service training. 2. Primary school teachers –
  Training of. 3. Effective teaching. 4. Successful teaching. 5. Academic achievement.
  I. Title.
  LB1062.6.G74 2014
  372.1102 – dc23
  2014012118

ISBN: 978-1-138-77923-5 (hbk)
ISBN: 978-1-138-77924-2 (pbk)
ISBN: 978-1-315-76109-1 (ebk)

Typeset in Bembo
by Florence Production Limited, Stoodleigh, Devon, UK

*To Tom and Mia*

# Contents

# Acknowledgements

I am grateful to all those who have helped to make this second edition a better book, not least the reviewers. I have been privileged to see many fine students and teachers, too many to mention but who will see something of themselves in these pages. While on secondment at Estyn, the Welsh inspectorate, I found conversations and inspections with colleagues such as Bev Jenkins and Penny Lewis particularly illuminating. I owe a big thanks to Mia, Tom, Grace and Sofie for their artwork. My mother and buddy, Helen, have provided succour when most needed. This second edition would not have been possible without their encouragement and support. I am grateful to Stuart Hay at Pearson and more recently Bruce Roberts, Natasha Ellis-Knight and others at Routledge Education for their diligence in the publication process.

# Introduction

*What marks teachers out as good, or better than good, is not only their content knowledge and pedagogical skills. It is their commitment to their teaching, their students and their learning and achievement.*

*(Day et al., 2007: 2)*

Teaching can be one of the most rewarding careers. A few years ago as part of an advertising campaign, the old Training and Development Agency for Schools reported that during a half-hour lesson, the average teacher smiled ten times, laughed three times, enjoyed a good banter five times, praised someone nine times and had an in-depth discussion on seven occasions. This was attributed to the fact that teachers 'find young people to be refreshing, different, funny, full of energy and willing to give feedback'. Another more recent small-scale survey found teachers are the happiest workers in Britain ahead of the likes of accountants, shop assistants, tradesmen and solicitors (Hall, 2013). The majority of teachers love the job that they are doing in making positive changes to children's lives (NASUWT, 2013). This is not to sidestep the challenges teachers face, for instance in managing workload, maintaining discipline and responding to initiatives. Teaching can be a testing profession and calls for many qualities, including resilience, courage and a sense of humour.

There has been a long-standing interest in the question of what it takes to become an *outstanding* teacher. In 1881 the Liverpool School Board advised its elementary school managers that 'no length of experience will make a person of poor ability into a first-rate teacher' (Liverpool School Board, 1881: 8). The managers were advised that in appointing candidates for their first post they should give preference to 'energetic teachers of good natural capacity' irrespective of their experience. In particular they should consider carefully the 'intellectual capacity' of infant schoolmistresses rather than follow the common view that 'a kindly, motherly disposition is the only qualification' necessary for teaching young children. Ultimately, the Liverpool School Board recommended that the quality of teachers should be judged on their personal qualifications, testimony from inspectors and results in the classroom.

A century later, Parliament was similarly informed in the White Paper *Teaching Quality* (1983) that the 'progress of the pupils is the measure of [teachers'] success'. This remains a powerful criterion in judging the quality of teaching. For instance, inspectors will only rate teaching outstanding in England if 'almost all pupils make rapid and sustained progress', particularly in literacy and numeracy (OFSTED, 2014: 39). While the outcomes of teaching are clearly essential in judging quality, this book seeks to explore what the best trainee and serving teachers bring to the classroom. The 'inputs' include the mix of personal qualities, values and prior experiences. Although the government-sponsored McBer Report (2000) on teacher effectiveness identified professional characteristics of outstanding teachers, it is not a question of one size fits all. Teachers are not clones – they have different styles and personalities that can prove equally effective.

Over recent years interest in outstanding teaching has increased as schools strive to improve provision and meet the expectations set by inspectorates, while governments recognize the social and economic value of becoming world leaders in education. There are an increasing number of books, reports, articles and courses for teachers pursuing the hallowed ground of 'outstanding' teaching – 2012 was an 'outstanding' year with titles such as *The Perfect Lesson* (Beere, 2012), *Outstanding Teaching, Outstanding Learning, Outstanding Leaders* (Hannan, 2012), *The Classroom X-Factor* (White and Gardner, 2012), *Outstanding Teaching: Engaging Learners* (Griffiths and Burns, 2012) and *100 Things Awesome Teachers Do* (Emeny, 2012). The field of teacher education has come under the spotlight with the government's improvement strategy, *Training our Next Generation of Outstanding Teachers* (DfE, 2011), while the House of Commons weighed in with *Great Teachers: Attracting, Training and Retaining the Best* (House of Commons Education Committee, 2012). Companies such as Osiris Educational provide Outstanding Teaching programmes and conferences, while there is a steady supply of research reports on what is known about the best performing teachers and schools produced by organizations such as The Centre for the Use of Research and Evidence in Education (Curee). Bell and Cordingley (2014), for example, report that in the highest performing schools there is a relentless focus on student achievement, consistent application of policies, and a strong commitment to professional development.

The aim of this book is to provide trainee and serving teachers with a comprehensive introduction to the notion and practices of outstanding teaching in the primary school. It is designed to bridge theory and practice and prompt deliberation through the following features:

■ *extend your understanding* – to deepen the reader's knowledge and understanding of a given subject; for instance, by reading articles in respected peer-reviewed journals or online materials;

■ *pause for reflection* – to prompt the reader to think about how the subject relates to personal values and ideas;

■ *focus on practice* – to illustrate the experiences of outstanding trainees and teachers;

■ *international view* – to draw on research from around the world so that the reader gains comparative understanding; and

■ *real-life learning challenge* – to challenge the reader to consider possible responses within an authentic learning scenario.

The focus of this book is the primary years (5–11). The Early Years is most commonly associated with pre-school education, although it can include children of statutory school age. In England, the Foundation Stage describes expectations for children from 0–5, while the Welsh Foundation *Phase* (not 'Stage') extends from 3–7 years, whereas practitioners in Northern Ireland follow the Foundation Stage for 3–5 year-olds; in Scotland, the Early Years even begins from pre-birth and ends at three, leading to a *Curriculum for Excellence* (3–18). So it is not always clear when the Early Years begins and ends. The general international consensus is to see the Early Years as a critical phase in young children's development from birth to the age of 8 (Wallace, 2008). Where appropriate, this book draws primary teachers' attention to the underlying principles of good Early Years practice for children aged between 3 and approximately 6 years old. These include:

- understanding that children develop rapidly during the Early Years – physically, intellectually, emotionally and socially;

- ensuring that all children feel included, secure and valued;

- building on what children already know and can do;

- creating enabling environments so that children can undertake activities set by adults and explore the world by themselves;

- working closely with other professionals and parents;

- planning a relevant and purposeful curriculum to stimulate and engage young children; and

- observing young children and responding appropriately.

So what sets this book apart from the rest? There are a number of reasons. First, it synthesizes what is known about high quality performance in the teacher's main areas of professional responsibility – planning, teaching, behaviour management and assessment. Second, it draws on policies and practices from different parts of the United Kingdom and, where appropriate, internationally. Third, it should appeal to teachers at different stages of their career. Finally, given the broad sweep of the book, the reader is provided with a comprehensive set of references to follow up particular areas of interest.

The first question this book considers is how outstanding teaching is defined. It is a subject that continues to attract the interest of politicians, the media and academics (Turner-Bisset, 2001; McLaughlin and Burnaford, 2007). The word itself is possibly derived from a farmer who *stood out* from the crops in the field – in other words, a distinguishable figure. Some trainee and experienced teachers are naturally worried about the notion of being outstanding because this can conjure up the idea of perfection. In reality, outstanding teaching is about being *consistently* good. As Kelley (2008: 64) acknowledges: 'Even the most dedicated teacher cannot invent excellent experiences for every child every minute of the day. Like being an absolute monarch, the position of teacher is not one that could be fulfilled to perfection by any human being.'

Chapter 1 discusses the different ways of conceptualizing outstanding teaching. For many, the best teachers are those whose personalities stand out. These charismatic teachers have an aura about them, and are often portrayed in films and literature as passionate, caring and enthusiastic individuals. The question of whether the best teachers are 'born or made' is a long-standing one (Brandt and Gunter, 1981; Scott and Dinham, 2008). Scheidecker and Freeman (1999) conclude that desirable personality traits could be fostered in *all* teachers. An alternative model of judging teaching quality adopts a more business-like framework in which teachers are judged against agreed competencies relating to such matters as planning and classroom management. The need for teachers to be reflective and self-critical underpins a third model for framing discussions about outstanding practice, one that has considerable support among tutors across higher education (Calderhead and Gates, 1993; Zeichner and Liston, 1996; Cowan, 2006; Campbell and Norton, 2007; Pollard, 2008; Paige-Smith and Craft, 2011). These models are not necessarily at odds with each other. A range of influences shape judgements on teaching. Assessors consider the technical skills demonstrated, for example in the quality of explanations and the preparation of resources (competency model). The observation is also likely to be influenced by the liveliness of the presentation, the approachability of the teacher, use of appropriate humour, general enthusiasm and deportment (charismatic model). Finally the observer may take into account the responsiveness of the teacher to feedback from the assessor, the quality of self-evaluation or the manner by which the teacher 'thinks on her feet' during the lesson, for example by changing direction because of some unexpected situation (reflective model).

We now know a great deal about what good trainee and experienced teachers think, say and do, due to the research that has accumulated over the past 30 or so years (Easterly, 1983; Gipps *et al.*, 2000; Morehead *et al.*, 2003; Moore, 2004; Hudson, 2008; Samimi, 2008). Even so, the House of Commons Education Committee has called upon the government to commission further research into the qualities shown by effective teachers and the potential link between degree class and performance (House of Commons Education Committee, 2012). This follows moves to raise the bar for entry to initial training by selecting more of the highest achieving graduates (DfE, 2011). In Wales alone, nearly half of teachers have degrees graded at a 2:2 degree or lower (*Western Mail*, 9 January 2014). Clearly, academic qualifications are important but not the only asset teachers need – the ability to communicate clearly and inspire young people is essential.

We know that teachers who perform at the highest level often learn quickly, are well organized, self-motivated, passionate, knowledgeable, caring and exceptionally skilled at what they do. Put simply, outstanding teachers do two things: they try to ensure that pupils achieve important learning objectives and they strive to arouse interest and commitment among learners over the longer term (Brundrett and Silcock, 2002). However, as Day *et al.* (2007: 2) point out, while commitment and resilience are indispensable to high quality teaching, 'we do not know much about how these are sustained or not sustained, in times of change'. The combination of personal and professional attributes demonstrated by outstanding teachers is described in Chapters 2 and 3.

Chapter 4 focuses on inspirational teaching as revealed in the manner by which learners are challenged to think for themselves. Passion and enthusiasm are often considered as the hallmarks of outstanding teachers. They are more 'learner centred' than 'curriculum centred' in their desire to draw upon pupils' interests and ideas, stimulate curiosity, and promote higher order thinking skills. They enable learners to take risks by creating a safe, supportive and challenging climate. However, the reality of some schools is that teachers feel locked into a content-driven curriculum, shaped heavily by external assessments that can demotivate (Deakin-Crick, 2005). The question of curriculum knowledge and understanding is discussed in Chapter 5. Teachers need to know about the rationale behind what they are teaching in order to explain this to others. They also need to understand how children learn and set their own practice in the wider context of fast-moving curriculum change. In recent years, throughout the United Kingdom there have been significant curriculum developments, notably the introduction of a new National Curriculum in England in 2014, and the consequences of these are still unfolding.

Chapter 6 focuses on contemporary issues in the teaching of English, mathematics and science. Literacy and numeracy have always formed the backbone of the primary curriculum. A secure knowledge of how to teach reading, writing and numeracy is critical to the success of teachers. As with mathematics, the most successful teaching of science involves pupils in undertaking investigations that enable them to see the relevance of the subject in their own lives. While subject-specific knowledge is important, outstanding teachers know how to make this accessible for learners. In recent years the focus has shifted towards understanding children's progress and learning ahead of teaching, particularly through the meta research of Professor John Hattie and colleagues (Hattie, 2009; Hattie and Yates, 2013). These findings on the 'science of learning' filter through relevant chapters.

The importance of developing a robust digital pedagogy is highlighted in Chapter 7. Teachers need to be clear about how Information and Communication Technologies (ICT) develop pupils' learning and equip them with the skills they need in the modern world. Chapter 8 looks at the challenges of providing a broad and balanced curriculum while striving for excellence across the foundation subjects and religious education. Richards (2001) uses a football analogy to describe the changing fortunes of primary curricular subjects – concluding that the 'premier league' is limited to English and mathematics, with science, religious education and ICT comprising the 'first division', the rest of the non-core subjects spread across second and third divisions, while a theme such as Education for Sustainable Development is reduced to 'non-league' status. One of the major curriculum challenges facing primary schools is what teachers should know in terms of subject breadth and depth.

Chapter 9 describes how the best teachers build upon children's experiences and ideas when planning and preparing. They take into account the varying starting positions of learners and seek to utilize their full range of resources (including additional adults) to engage learners. Thorough planning and preparation are the basis of outstanding teaching. The best teachers use plans in a flexible manner, conscious of their learning objectives but not to the extent that these squeeze out the spontaneity and dynamics of teaching. Chapter 10 has a very wide remit in considering the diverse needs of learners. It provides an overview of recent developments in the field of special and inclusive education. Teachers need to meet the needs of specific groups of learners such as those identified as gifted and talented pupils. Chapter 11 has a specific focus on communication skills, particularly how teachers can demonstrate high quality explanations, questioning and discussion.

Chapter 12 considers an area that so often concerns beginning teachers, namely how to 'manage' the behaviour of children. It discusses the causes and types of misbehaviour, the importance of motivation, developing classroom presence and how to deal with more serious issues such as bullying. Chapter 13 reviews teachers' responsibilities for monitoring, assessing, recording and reporting. It considers how teachers should use assessment to improve as well as measure learning. Finally, Chapter 14 covers the role of the teacher as researcher within the wider context of continuing professional development. It describes the tools that might be used to gain insight into what actually happens in the classroom. Educational research, specifically (action) research undertaken by practitioners themselves, can inform the direction of teaching. International evidence is clear that the most effective teachers are those who combine practical skills with the ability to understand and use research in their development of their teaching (Musset, 2010).

Education has its own language that is not always commonly shared or understood within the same school, let alone the profession. Ask a group of teachers what terms such as 'aims', 'ability' or 'assessment' mean to them. There are regional differences across the United Kingdom in how the curriculum is described and structured. To clarify terms, each chapter includes key concepts and a glossary, although readers should also consult established reference works (e.g. Hayes, 2005; Wallace, 2008; Hayes, 2009). Links to reliable and relevant websites are also included at the end of each chapter.

Any attempt to describe practice throughout the United Kingdom is ambitious and likely to do a disservice to one country at some point in the text. There are distinctive elements to the educational systems within England, Scotland, Wales and Northern Ireland. Where possible, these have been highlighted – for instance, in relation to the curriculum and assessment requirements. However, there are similarities in what is expected from trainee teachers at the end of their initial training, reflected in the respective competency or standards models. In Scotland, the Standard for Provisional Registration (SPR) set out expectations for student (trainee) teachers at the end of Initial Teacher Education who are seeking provisional registration with the General Teaching Council for Scotland (GTCS). Once student teachers gain SPR, they progress towards achieving the Standard for Full Registration (SFR) – the benchmark of teacher competence for all teachers (GTCS, 2012). In both Northern Ireland and Wales, broad professional competences or standards for Qualified Teacher Status (QTS) cover familiar ground in Professional Values, Knowledge and Understanding and Teaching, but include 27 and 35 substandards respectively (GTCNI, 2007; DCELLS, 2009). In Wales, these are likely to be revised in the near future to reflect greater coherence in teachers' professional development, following the introduction of a masters programme for newly qualified teachers in 2012. In England, trainee and serving teachers are assessed against the same set of *Teachers' Standards* (DfE, 2013). Providers are directed to assess trainees in 'a way that is consistent with what could reasonably be expected of a trainee teacher prior to the award of QTS' (DfE, 2013: 3). Recent Coalition Government discourse has focused on training 'on the job' rather than educating teachers. Hayes (2011: 20) fears that those who are 'only trained will not be able to educate'.

Undoubtedly, teacher education in the UK is under intense political scrutiny as governments respond to shortcomings in the educational system (DENI, 2010; DfE, 2010; Redford and Edwards, 2011; Tabberer, 2013; Million+, 2013). The sector is experiencing significant changes that include:

■ moves towards school-based training through programmes such as School Direct and Teach First;

■ reduction in university teacher training places and associated funding;

■ attempts to ratchet up entry qualifications;

**TABLE 0.1** Professional standards for teachers in the United Kingdom

| Country and standards | | Chapter |
|---|---|---|
| **England** | | |
| 1 | Set high expectations that inspire, motivate and challenge pupils | 4 |
| 2 | Promote good progress and outcomes by pupils | 13 |
| 3 | Demonstrate good subject and curriculum knowledge | 5–8 |
| 4 | Plan and teach well structured lesson | 9 |
| 5 | Adapt teaching to respond to the strengths and needs of all pupils | 10 |
| 6 | Make accurate and productive use of assessment | 13 |
| 7 | Manage behaviour effectively to ensure a good and safe learning environment | 12 |
| 8 | Fulfil wider professional responsibilities | 3, 14 |
| **Scotland** | | |
| 1 | Professional values and personal commitment | 2–3, 14 |
| 2 | Professional knowledge and understanding | |
| | 2.1 Curriculum | 5 |
| | 2.2 Education systems and professional responsibilities | 1, 3 |
| | 2.3 Pedagogical theories and practice | 4–8 |
| 3 | Professional skills and abilities | 9–14 |
| **Wales** | | |
| S1 | Professional values and practice | 2–3, 14 |
| S2 | Knowledge and understanding | 5–8 |
| S3 | Teaching | 1, 4, 9, 10, 11–13 |
| **Northern Ireland** | | |
| PC1 | Professional values and practice | 2–3, 14 |
| PC2–13 | Professional knowledge and understanding | 5–8 |
| PC14–27 | Professional skills and application | 9–14 |
| PC14–18 | Planning and leading | 9 |
| PC19–23 | Teaching and learning | 4, 10 |
| PC24–27 | Assessment | 13 |

Sources: DCELLS (2009); GTCS (2012); DfE (2013); GTCNI (2011)

- greater emphasis on developing trainees' literacy and numeracy skills;
- standardization of paperwork and procedures;
- reviewing the nature, extent and scope of partnership working between universities and schools; and
- ensuring greater coherence in teachers' early professional development.

Collectively these developments are designed to address the perennial twin problems of recruiting and retaining enough high-quality teachers. Short of reliable evaluative research, it is not clear whether increasing school-based training will improve the quality of teaching and learning or the preparation of teachers for their future careers. The National Association of School-Based Teacher Trainers (NASBTT) point out that school-based initial training matches the quality and importance of training provided by higher education institutions. One of the common key issues is assuring equality of opportunity through high quality placements for all those entering the profession. Schools themselves are experiencing major changes and their core business remains teaching children rather than training teachers. Most commentators agree that the way forward is to build a sustainable partnership between schools and universities but there is disagreement over how this should work in practice. What is clear from international evidence is that the quality of teachers is the most important factor in determining the effectiveness of schools. The Coalition Government acknowledges that we have the 'best generation of teachers we have ever had' (DfE, 2011: 3) and so, for many, the challenge is to move from good to outstanding. It is hoped that this book will support teachers in their journey.

## References

Beere, J. (2012) *The Perfect Lesson*, Carmarthen: Independent Thinking Press.

Bell, M. and Cordingley, P. (2014) *Characteristics of High Performing Schools*, London: Curee.

Brandt, R. and Gunter, M. (1981) 'Teachers are made, not born', *Educational Leadership*, 39(2): 149–51.

Brundrett, M. and Silcock, P. (2002) *Achieving Competence, Success and Excellence in Teaching*, London: RoutledgeFalmer.

Calderhead, J. and Gates, P. (1993) *Conceptualizing Reflection in Teacher Development*, London: Falmer.

Campbell, A. and Norton, L. (eds) (2007) *Learning, Teaching and Assessing in Higher Education*, Exeter: Learning Matters.

Cowan, J. (2006) *On Becoming an Innovative University Teacher*, Maidenhead: Open University Press.

Day, C., Sammons, P., Stobart, G., Kington, A. and Gu, O. (2007) *Teachers Matter*, Maidenhead: Open University Press.

Deakin-Crick, R. (2005) 'Learner-centred teachers', in Alexander, T. and Potter, J. (eds) *Education for a Change*, London: RoutledgeFalmer, 159–66.

DCELLS (2009) *Becoming a Qualified Teacher: Handbook of Guidance*, Cardiff: Welsh Assembly Government.

DENI (2010) *Teacher Education in a Climate of Change: The Way Forward*, Belfast: Department of Education, Northern Ireland.

DfE (2010) *The Importance of Teaching*, London: DfE.

DfE (2011) *Training our Next Generation of Outstanding Teachers*, London: DfE.

DfE (2013) *Teachers' Standards*, London: DfE.

Easterly, J.L. (1983) *Perceptions of Outstanding Elementary Teachers about Themselves and Their Profession*, Oakland, MI: School of Human and Educational Services, Oakland University.

Emeny, W. (2012) *100 Things Awesome Teachers Do*, Carmarthen: CreateSpace Independent Publishing Platform.

Gipps, C., McCallum, G. and Hargreaves, E. (2000) *What Makes a Good Primary Teacher? Expert Classroom Strategies*, London: RoutledgeFalmer.

Griffiths and Burns, M. (2012) *Outstanding Teaching: Engaging Learners*, Carmarthen: Crown House.

GTCNI (2007) *Teaching: The Reflective Profession*, Belfast: General Teaching Council for Northern Ireland.

GTCNI (2011) *Teaching: The Reflective Profession*, Belfast: General Teaching Council for Northern Ireland.

GTCS (2012) *The Standards for Registration: Mandatory Requirements for Registration with the General Teaching Council for Scotland*, Edinburgh: GTCS.

Hall, M. (2013) 'Teachers are the happiest workers in Britain, says survey', *The Telegraph*, 29 April.

Hannan, G. (2012) *Outstanding Teaching, Outstanding Learning, Outstanding Leaders*, Guildford: GHP.

Hattie, J. (2009) *Visible Learning*, Abingdon: Routledge.

Hattie, J. and Yates, G.C. (2013) *Visible Learning and the Science of How We Learn*, London: Routledge.

Hayes, D. (2005) *Primary Education: The Key Concepts*, London: Routledge.

Hayes, D. (2009) *Encyclopedia of Primary Education*, London: David Fulton.

Hayes, D. (2011) 'Who will defend teacher education?' in *In Defence of Teacher Education*, 19–20, SCETT, available at: www.scett.org.uk (accessed 14 January 2014).

House of Commons Education Committee (2012) *Great Teachers: Attracting, Training and Retaining the Best: Government Response to the Committee's Ninth Report of Session 2010–12*, London: The Stationery Office.

Hudson, D. (2008) *Good Teachers, Good Schools*, London: David Fulton.

Kelley, P. (2008) *Making Minds*, London: Routledge.

Liverpool School Board (1881) *Suggestions to the Managers of Public Elementary Schools*, London: Wm Isbister Ltd.

McBer, H. (2000) *Research into Teacher Effectiveness – A Model of Teacher Effectiveness*, London: DfEE.

McLaughlin, H.J. and Burnaford, G. (2007) 'Re-thinking the basis for "high quality" teaching: Teacher preparation in communities', in Townsend, T. and Bates, R. (eds) *Handbook of Teacher Education: Globalization, Standards and Professionalism in Times of Change*, New York: Springer, 331–42.

Million+ (2013) *Who Should Train the Teachers?* available at: www.millionplus.ac.uk (accessed 14 January 2014).

Moore, A. (2004) *The Good Teacher*, Abingdon: RoutledgeFalmer.

Morehead, M., Lyman, L. and Foyle, H. (2003) *Working with Student Teachers*, Lanham, MD: Scarecrow Education.

Musset, P. (2010) *Initial Teacher Education and Continuing Training Policies in a Comparative Perspective: Current Practices in OECD Countries and a Literature Review on Potential Effects*, OECD Education Working Papers, No. 48, Paris: OECD Publishing.

NASUWT (2013) *Teachers' Satisfaction and Wellbeing in the Workplace*, London: NASUWT.

OFSTED (2014) *School Inspection Handbook*, London: OFSTED.

Paige-Smith, A. and Craft, A. (2011) *Developing Reflective Practice in the Early Years*, Maidenhead: Open University Press.

Pollard, A. (2008) *Reflective Teaching*, London: Continuum.

Redford, M. and Edwards, R. (2011) *Scottish Teacher Education Committee (STEC): New Models of Early Career Teacher Education in Scotland*, Stirling: Univeristy of Stirling, HEA.

Richards, C. (ed.) (2001) *Changing English Primary Education*, Stoke-on-Trent: Trentham.

Samimi, S. (2008) *Qualities of Outstanding Teachers that Contribute to Student Success*, Saarbrücken, Germany: VDM Verlag Dr. Mueller E.K.

Scheidecker, D. and Freeman, W. (1999) *Bringing Out the Best in Students*, Thousand Oaks, CA: Corwin Press.

Scott, C. and Dinham, S. (2008) 'Born not made: The nativist myth and teachers' thinking', *Teacher Development*, 12(2): 115–24.

Tabberer, R. (2013) *A Review of Initial Teacher Training in Wales*, Cardiff: Welsh Government.

Turner-Bisset, R. (2001) *Expert Teaching: Knowledge and Pedagogy to Lead the Profession*, London: David Fulton.

Wallace, S. (2008) *Dictionary of Education*, Oxford: Oxford University Press.

White, J. and Gardner, J. (2012) *The Classroom X-Factor*, London: Routledge.

Zeichner, M. and Liston, P. (1996) *Reflective Teaching: An Introduction*, Hillsdale, NJ: Lawrence Erlbaum.

**1**

# How do we define and measure outstanding teaching?

## Chapter objectives

By the end of this chapter you should be able to:

- Explain why teaching is important.
- Describe how teaching quality is measured and perceived by different stakeholders.
- Summarize the main findings from research into high quality teaching.

*Evidence is clear that outstanding teachers at all phases can have a profound positive impact on pupils' performance, which in turn leads to better outcomes in further education, pay, well-being, and for society at large.*

*(House of Commons Education Committee, 2012: paragraph 41)*

## The importance of teaching

There are around 239,000 teachers in the UK's public sector primary schools (Bolton, 2012). Each of these teachers has the potential to make a significant impact on the life prospects of the 5 million or so primary children in their care. The evidence is clear. American research, which tracked 2.5 million students over 20 years, shows that children are more likely to attend college, earn more, live in comfortable surroundings and save more for retirement if they are taught by great teachers (Chetty *et al.*, 2012). One study shows that if two 8-year-olds are given different teachers – one a high performer (from the top 20 per cent) and one a low performer (from the bottom 20 per cent) – their performance diverges by 53 percentile points within three years (McKinsey, 2007). In secondary schools, the difference in a pupil's achievement between a high-performing teacher and a low-performing one could be more than three GCSE grades (Slater *et al.*, 2009).

Imagine the impact if a child has a series of good or poor teachers. American research shows that an individual pupil taught for three consecutive years by a teacher in the top

10 per cent of performance can make as much as two years more progress than a pupil taught for the same period by a teacher in the bottom 10 per cent (Sanders and Rivers, 1996). When children are taught by a series of mediocre or poor teachers, then the difficulties are compounded and it may not be possible for children to catch up. In particular, teachers can exert a powerful influence on the lives of children from disadvantaged backgrounds. A report on behalf of the Sutton Trust (2011) suggests that over a school year, disadvantaged pupils gain 1.5 years' worth of learning with good teachers, compared with 0.5 years with underperforming teachers. In other words, for these pupils the difference between a good and a poor teacher is the equivalent of a whole year's learning. High-quality teaching matters because it is recognized as the most important school-based factor in increasing students' achievement (Darling-Hammond, 2000).

Given the global financial problems of recent years, purely from an economic viewpoint teachers are important. There are strong arguments to improve the quality of teaching through strategic professional development and robust performance management. Good teachers increase the likelihood of pupils leaving school well qualified and ready to take up relevant employment or further education. Moreover, educational standards determine the wealth of nations. Economic growth is rooted in what happens in the classrooms around the UK. Professor Hanushek, a leading academic at Stanford University, has calculated the huge savings to economies if school authorities were bold enough to sack poor teachers and reward those who perform well (Hanushek, 2010a, 2010b; OECD, 2011). He has reached similar conclusions in studying the UK's educational performance, as measured by the Programme for International Student Assessment (Pisa) tests. According to Hanushek, if British children were educated to Canadian standards this would effectively mean that an average worker would receive 17 per cent more pay because the economy would be more productive (Nelson, 2013). He argues that schools would benefit by deploying their best teachers in the largest classes, where their impact will be at its greatest. Michael Wilshaw, head of OFSTED, describes the state of education in England as a tale of two nations: 'Children from similar backgrounds with similar abilities,but who happen to be born in different regions and attend different schools and colleges, can end up with widely different prospects because of the variable quality of their education' (Michael Wilshaw, OFSTED, 2013: 8). This quote appears within a section of the Annual Inspector's report for 2012–13 entitled 'a battle against mediocrity'. However, as will be discussed later, measuring the quality of teaching by a narrow set of educational outcomes is problematic on reliability grounds alone.

The importance of teaching goes beyond how well pupils do in tests and examinations. Teachers and schools have a key role to play in contributing to a just and tolerant society. Outstanding teachers continually work towards social justice by creating equal opportunities for pupils from all backgrounds. They recognize that their social obligation is to support all pupils in achieving their aspirations, rather than assuming that disadvantaged pupils do not expect much of themselves (Menzies, 2013). Above all they are driven by a moral purpose to make a positive difference to children's lives. Each year around 600,000 students pass through state schools. Of these, around 80,000 are eligible for free school meals. In 2010, just 40 out of 80,000 made it to Oxford or Cambridge. Few can disagree that more children from poorest families need the opportunity to make it into the leading universities and best jobs.

Schools are often regarded as among the frontline services that respond to wide-ranging social issues (Crowther *et al.*, 2003; Home Office, 2003). Chapter 3 discusses further the changing role of teachers as schools seek to make their facilities and expertise available to otherwise resource-poor communities. This presents significant challenges for teachers as they are sometimes perceived as social workers and the cure-all for problems such as child obesity, drug abuse and teenage pregnancy (Judd, 1994; Lipsett, 2008). However, outstanding teachers know the importance of schools working closely with parents and others in building vibrant communities and breaking down barriers:

> Where we've taken parents on trips with us, some of the parents have gone into churches for the first time ever. And they're amazed at how lovely they are, and how peaceful. And that a church can be such a calm, religious place. Because they've never been in, they didn't know anything about it. And they just love it and will then come back and talk about it and spread their awareness.
>
> (Rowe *et al.*, 2011: 18)

Teachers are important because they are cultural gatekeepers. They can literally open doors for pupils to enjoy their local and national heritage, for instance through visits to museums, galleries and libraries. Michael Gove, the former Education Secretary, said that teachers have a duty through the National Curriculum to 'introduce pupils to the best that has been thought and said' (DfE, 2013b: 5). Here, Gove is invoking the words of Matthew Arnold, the nineteenth-century writer and school inspector, who wanted schools to provide 'the best that has been thought and said in the world'. The global perspective is important. The best teachers recognize that in an increasingly diverse society, it is essential for pupils to understand how people are interconnected through trade, communication and cultural activities such as the Olympic Games.

Since schools began, one of their priorities has been to teach children to read and enjoy books. Sir Richard Steel (1672–1729), co-founder of *The Spectator* magazine, said that 'reading is to the mind what exercise is to the body'. Reading not only enables people to go about their everyday business, but also is essential for personal development. Good readers learn to appreciate the views of others, while enlarging their own identities. They question, reflect, rethink, believe, hope, trust and experience the full range of emotions. Just imagine not being able to read effectively. This is the reality facing around one in five adults in the UK who, despite attending school for ten or so years, are said to be functionally illiterate. This means that they cannot read food labels in a supermarket or complete a job application. Illiteracy is a worldwide crisis.

The American businessman and former teacher, John Corcoran, describes the shame, loneliness and fear he experienced before learning to read. He cheated his way through college and taught in a high school for 17 years before learning to read. He would carry books around to create the illusion of literacy. He compensated for his inability to read by asking students to read aloud, holding discussions and using standardized tests with hole-punched answer keys. He did not learn to read until he was nearly 50 and now presides over the John Corcoran Foundation, a non-profit organization committed to eradicating illiteracy (www.johncorcoranfoundation.org). The cost of illiteracy is around £81 billion a year (Cree *et al.*, 2012). There are clear links between illiteracy and poor health, crime and unemployment. Put simply, good readers make good citizens. Teachers then have a social responsibility to model what good readers do and inspire children to love reading.

## Defining the best

While there is widespread agreement over the importance of teaching, how to describe and measure the most effective practice is less clear. Terms include 'quality teaching' (Stones, 1992), 'expert teaching' (Turner-Bisset, 2001), 'master teachers' (Mayo, 2002), 'distinguished teachers' (Danielson, 2013), 'high quality teachers' (McLaughlin and Burnaford, 2007), 'veteran teachers' (Shulman, 1987), and 'excellent and outstanding teachers' (McBer, 2000). Outstanding and excellent are synonymous terms to describe teaching that is at the right end of the quality spectrum. Outstanding teachers are exemplary role models, demonstrating the very best practice that is around or what Zemelman *et al.* (2005) refer to as 'serious, thoughtful, informed, responsible state-of-the-art teaching' (Box 1.1).

A group of trainee teachers were asked for their views on what makes an outstanding teacher (Box 1.2). Their responses illustrate how trainees often focus on the personality of the teacher, rather than the skills of planning, classroom management, assessment and even teaching itself. Perhaps the latter are perceived as more mundane and less memorable than the dynamic, and sometimes unconventional, qualities displayed by those held aloft as outstanding teachers.

## Measuring the best

The House of Commons Education Committee (2012) acknowledges that there is no clear consensus in the existing research on how teacher quality should be measured. However, a major international review of teacher evaluation systems notes that a fair and reliable teacher evaluation model needs reference standards to evaluate teachers relatively to what is considered as 'good teaching' (OECD, 2009: 9). In England, the *Teachers' Standards* (DfE, 2013a) are the obvious benchmark and form the basis of teacher evaluations. The eight standards set out the minimum level of practice expected of all teachers:

1    set high expectations that inspire, motivate and challenge pupils;

2    promote good progress and outcomes by pupils;

3    demonstrate good subject and curriculum knowledge;

4    plan and teach well-structured lessons;

5    adapt teaching to respond to the strengths and needs of all pupils;

6    make accurate and productive use of assessment;

7    manage behaviour effectively to ensure a good and safe learning environment; and

8    fulfil wider professional responsibilities.

---

**BOX 1.1  KEY CONCEPT – OUTSTANDING TEACHING**

Outstanding teaching is the very best practice in the profession. It is instantly memorable and at the cutting edge, which others need to know about. Outstanding teachers are set apart from the rest by virtue of their *consistent* high quality work. Their in-depth professional knowledge and understanding adds confidence to their teaching, which is purposeful and engaging. Learners are at ease, motivated to learn and achieve high standards.

---

**BOX 1.2  FOCUS ON PRACTICE**

'To be an outstanding teacher you should be patient, caring and not at all biased; also, if you enjoy teaching you are half way there to being a great teacher. Once you have gained the respect of the learners you can be an excellent teacher.'

*Lisa-Marie*

'I believe that the outstanding teacher is the member of staff who every child knows about, talks about and looks forward to being taught by.'

*John*

'An outstanding teacher is someone who is able to understand each child as an individual, but also the class as a whole and be able to relate to them. They are approachable and caring. They know how to deal with unpredicted (sic) situations.'

*Fiona*

'I think it is important for an outstanding teacher to be understanding and take time to listen to children because the teacher may be the only stable person a child has in their lives.'

*Kelly*

'Outstanding teachers are those who go the extra mile and who make real connections to the kids.'

*Kathryn*

---

For initial teacher training, the Universities' Council for the Education of Teachers (UCET) has provided useful guidance on how to interpret the standards (UCET, 2012). For teachers, appraisers (such as head teachers) are required to use their professional judgement in deciding what performance is expected of a teacher in the relevant role and at the relevant stage of their career.

Beyond the *Teachers' Standards*, an independent review (Coates, 2011) has recommended the introduction of a single higher-level Master Teacher Standard (rather than standards). This sets out the characteristics of high-performing teachers:

A    knowledge – deep and extensive knowledge of their specialism, going beyond the set programmes they teach;

B    classroom performance – command the classroom, skilfully leading, encouraging and extending pupils;

C    outcomes – achieved by pupils in the context in question are outstanding;

D    environment and ethos – here is a stimulating culture of scholarship alongside a sense of mutual respect and good manners; and

E    professional context – highly regarded by colleagues, who want to learn from them. They are analytical in evaluating and developing their own craft and knowledge, making full use of continuing professional development and appropriate research.

The Coates review moves away from describing teacher progression through a stock of comparative adjectives ('good', 'outstanding') and 'tick box' assessments. Rather, it focuses on the range and depth of practice expected of a Master Teacher building on the foundations of the *Teachers' Standards*. At the time of writing, the Coalition Government had not decided whether to introduce the Master Standard, although it welcomed in principle its simplicity and clarity.

## Judging teaching

There is a significant body of literature on teacher evaluation (Campbell *et al.*, 2003; OECD, 2009; OECD, 2013). Essentially, teacher evaluation serves two purposes: either to inform decisions about hiring, promoting or sacking teachers, or to develop teaching. In short, as Koppich (2008) puts it: evaluation is about accountability and improvement. The first inevitably involves comparison against the performance of other teachers (norm-referenced) or some agreed benchmarks, such as competencies or standards (criterion-referenced). Here, evaluation needs to be both reliable and fair – the judgements are consistent for different teachers at different times – and valid – the evaluation actually measures what it is supposed to measure. For the second purpose, the evaluator needs to consider the extent to which pupils and teachers change their behaviour. Unfortunately, many of the teacher evaluation models and practices have been criticized for not bringing about any improvements in teaching or learning. One American critique suggests that this has led to a system in which 'over 90 percent of teachers are classified as top performers and only a tiny percentage are deemed unsatisfactory' (Little, 2009: vii). There is agreement, however, that any evaluations should draw upon a range of evidence, given the complexity of measuring teaching. Clearly the quality of teaching (and learning) can be judged using various sources (Figure 1.1).

### PAUSE FOR REFLECTION

A few years ago *The Times Educational Supplement* ran a series on 'My Best Teacher', interviewing famous successful people. Bradley Wiggins, the Olympic cyclist, for instance recalled his 'stone-faced, ex-military' teacher who was the only one who took a real interest in his dreams (Frankel, 2010). Who was your best teacher and what set him or her apart from the rest?

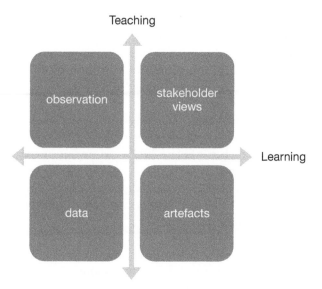

**FIGURE 1.1** Sources to judge teaching and learning

## Observations

In recent years, there has been a huge growth in the use of classroom observation for assessment purposes, backed by strong political support. In 2011 Michael Gove told the National College for School Leadership that teachers have nothing to fear from lesson observation – not only was learning from other professionals the best way to improve, confident performers should relish the opportunity to show what they can do (www.gov.uk/government/speeches/michael-gove-on-the-moral-purpose-of-school-reform).

Direct first-hand observation has traditionally been regarded as the most important source when judging the quality of learning and teaching. This includes observing assemblies, out-of-class and enrichment activities, personal and social education lessons as well as classroom sessions. However, the value of observation has been called into question by several leading educational bloggers (e.g. Bennett, 2013). Their arguments are based around the following points:

- observation is a highly skilled business;
- observers need to be at least as good as those observed if they are to offer any meaningful advice;
- observation schedules are reductionalist by nature; and
- observers tend to judge lessons by how they would have done things.

Rather than using observations as a means of judging teaching in a snapshot, alternative suggestions (not without their drawbacks) include making greater use of pupils' views and monitoring what they do and learn.

There is little doubt that the presence of an observer(s) will have some effect on those observed. At worst, observations can create considerable anxiety especially if conducted in a 'macho' or underhand manner. Unfortunately, when under stress, many teachers talk more quickly and adopt a more didactic style than usual. They take fewer 'risks' out of fear that something may go wrong while being observed. They seek to provide what they think the observer wants, creating a 'performance' rather than teaching. In sum, the psychological impact of observation can become detrimental to learning and teaching. Trade unions even report occasional stories of pupils being used covertly as 'surveillance tools to spy on their teachers' (Exley, 2012).

Clearly the purpose and focus of any lesson observation needs to be shared between parties and, if graded, then criteria made explicit at the outset. Most observers focus on the quality and nature of interactions between teacher and pupils. Observation schedules invariably include prompts relating to:

- learner outcomes – pupils' enjoyment, attitudes, responsiveness, what they know, understand and can do at the end of the session;
- teaching knowledge and skills – planning, questioning, explaining, modelling, instructing, assessing, discussing, researching, organizing, managing, relating to others; and
- the quality of the learning environment – seating arrangements, use of resources, health and safety issues, general ethos.

The skills of observing lessons should not be taken for granted. The behaviour of children, teachers and other adults in classrooms and out-of-class contexts can be complex and open to different interpretations. Observers need to be clear about their approach – are they adopting a broad sweep, searching for particular interactions, 'following' a specific child, or adopting a 'wait and see what comes up' slant? Should the observer participate in the lesson, for example by talking to pupils to gain a sense of how children are feeling, or sit quietly in the same place taking notes and scanning a range of activities? Both 'participant' and 'systematic' observer roles can increase understanding of what is happening in the lesson. Research on behalf of the Bill and Melinda Gates Foundation covering 3,000 American teachers concluded that two rather than one observers conduct the most reliable classroom observations because of the counter-checking that observer dialogue provided (Ho and Kane, 2013). To gain insight into the benefits of longer versus shorter observations, the researchers asked observers to pause and provide scores after the first 15 minutes of a video-recorded lesson and then to record their scores again at the end of the lesson. The researchers found that the reliability of a single 15-minute observation was 60 per cent as large as a full lesson observation, while requiring less than one-third of the observation time. The researchers also reported that first impressions linger. Observers who rated a teacher highly on a first observation were more likely to do so on the second occasion; similarly, if they rated a teacher poorly on the first viewing, they were more likely to do so next time around.

There is no shortage of guidance on conducting lesson observations and the mechanism for recording the outcomes. These vary considerably in quality. Observation checklists can be distracting, prescriptive and selective, resulting in a distorted record. For trainee teachers, partnership handbooks should include details of observation protocols including relevant proformas, grade descriptors (if used) and feedback arrangements.

There is some debate over whether trainee and serving teachers should offer showcase lessons when being observed. On the one hand, being observed presents an opportunity for the teacher to demonstrate their skill set and present themselves in the best light. Others, including OFSTED, argue that teachers should be seen as they would be under 'normal' circumstances and support unannounced observations. In any event, the dialogue that accompanies observations is an important indicator of a teacher's professional outlook. Outstanding teachers tend to be self-critical, keen to improve their practice and ready to absorb advice that they do not take as personal criticisms.

Observations do not have to be judgemental in tone. They can be conducted as part of a developmental process in which teachers are coached on specific skills and where teachers take the lead in self-improvement. This is a long-standing practice that is widely supported. Since the nineteenth century, teachers and teacher educators have provided model or presentation lessons to professional audiences. In modern times, some schools and universities have invested in remote viewing technology to enable managers, tutors, fellow teachers and sometimes pupils, to observe lessons. Cameras are fitted in different classrooms and outdoor areas and sessions observed remotely. Observation can also be considered in research terms, viewed as a means of collecting sample data to inform teachers on aspects of their practice.

## Artefacts

Artefacts are products resulting from a teacher's work; for instance, lesson plans, wall displays and professional development activities. Artefacts are used extensively in American state teacher evaluations. The most 'distinguished' teachers are expected to produce artefacts such as research articles and evidence of leading colleagues. Artefacts reveal messages about individual teachers and the school as a community. For instance, a bright and cheerful foyer can reflect how open and welcoming a school is perceived to be. For the purpose of gathering information about the quality of teaching, sources such as pupils' books, planning documents and reading records are valuable. Ching *et al.* (2003) classify artefacts as follows:

- concrete carriers – physical objects that convey meaning, e.g. the arrangement of classroom furniture can indicate the nature of teacher authority, expected pupil participation and use of space;
- concrete conveyors – physical objects that explicitly display representations of knowledge, e.g. interactive whiteboards, computers, televisions, blackboards, paper handouts;
- instructional artefacts – written or printed objects that focus on activity and require specialized understanding to interpret, e.g. books, films, documents, drama;
- virtual artefacts – immaterial objects that flow from the human mind or digital environment, e.g. gestures, body language, computer games; and
- ambient artefacts – physical features or forces that create an atmosphere, such as water, music, sound, temperature and lighting.

The framework is not ideal – there are factors in the learning environment that may be beyond the control of teachers, such as the condition of resources or architectural features.

## Data

Increasingly inspectors and school managers are focusing on the use of data to raise questions about the quality of learning and teaching. Data should always be used with caution, however, when linked to judgements about teaching. OFSTED (2014) acknowledge that data is often historical and relates to pupils who have left the school. Value-added data refers to the measurable improvement schools make in the education of its learners. This is compared to **attainment** data gathered from national assessments and to schools in similar circumstances. Such data is particularly important because it takes into account the starting points of learners and their actual progress, or what is sometimes referred to as 'the distance travelled'.

Schools throughout the UK use a range of data for different reasons, for example to support performance management, track pupil progress, allocate resources, identify underachieving pupils, offer challenge to staff and pupils and set targets. Data can also inform decision making at different levels, from the whole school to the individual pupil. A report on behalf of the government notes that data only becomes useful if it stimulates questions about the actual learning that is taking place and how this might be improved (Kirkup et al., 2005). Many schools in England and Wales use the Fisher Family Trust data system, which estimates what a child might be expected to attain at later key stages, based on their past performances and the average attainments of children judged by the Trust to have similar characteristics. Around 22,000 schools also use RAISEonline, which supports their in-depth analysis of performance data as part of the self-evaluation process (www.raiseonline.org). The software enables schools to compare the performance of their pupils with national averages and to track the progress and attainment of groups of learners, for instance children with special educational needs or those receiving free school meals. The inspectorates use a range of data when judging the performance of a school. OFSTED's online dashboard provides a summary of data including overall attendance at the school (percentage) and 'closing the gap' measures, which look at the attainment and expected progress of disadvantaged pupils compared with other pupils (http://dashboard. ofsted.gov.uk).

It is important to distinguish between the concepts of attainment and **achievement**. The former is particularly concerned with how well learners do in comparison to others, as evidenced in local or national tests. Schools are able to track the performance of individual pupils by different factors, such as gender, age, free schools meals and ethnicity. They can detect patterns and trends in performance. For instance, they may find that boys are not doing so well as girls in reading across Key Stage 2. They can then compare their results with other schools and national trends. Achievement is more concerned with the progress of individuals, given their respective starting points. For instance, a school may have a significantly higher proportion of children with special educational needs in Year 6. This is likely to impact on their attainment results in English and mathematics and they may fall short of national expectations. However, they may achieve well in relation to their capabilities.

There are difficulties associated with a model that measures teacher quality solely by pupil outcomes derived from data analysis. First, it is not straightforward to define 'pupil outcomes'. In Scotland, these outcomes relate to four 'capacities' of *Curriculum for Excellence* – successful learners, confident individuals, responsible citizens and effective contributors, which cannot be fully revealed by attainment results (Menter *et al.*, 2010). Second, even when standardized test results are used, there are difficulties in sorting out the relative impact of different 'input' factors – for instance, were the results due to the contribution of the teacher, peers, resources, classroom climate or other factors? Such tests are designed to measure student achievement and not teacher quality. Third, test results do not indicate what practices distinguish good teachers from poor ones. It is one thing to say that good teachers get better test scores, but the more important question is how they achieved these. Fourth, it is difficult to tease out the specific contribution of one teacher from those who taught the class in a previous year. Teaching then is a complex human activity that does not lend itself to scientific experimentation or analysis of data because it is difficult to control all the important factors that are likely to influence student outcomes. This is not to suggest that data is irrelevant in discussions about quality, but that often data raises more questions than answers.

## Stakeholder views

Discussions with teachers, parents, pupils, governors, employers and others can all contribute to a view on the quality of teaching. Over recent years the business term 'stakeholders' has entered education to describe persons, groups or organizations who have an interest in the success of the school or university in fulfilling its mission. There are internal stakeholders (e.g. teachers and senior leaders) who control what is happening in the school and external stakeholders (e.g. employers) who have a strong interest in the outcomes but who do not directly get involved in producing these outcomes. All of these parties have something at stake. Businesses, for instance, need students who are literate and numerate. So it is assumed that stakeholders should be consulted and, as a minimum, satisfied with what the school provides and its strategic direction. School inspectors and managers will often hold discussions with a range of stakeholders or survey their opinions. OFSTED also considers the views of recently qualified teachers (as former students) when judging the quality of initial teacher training.

The most important stakeholders are the learners themselves. Pupils have been asked for their views on their schooling by inspectors and others since the nineteenth century (Blishen, 1973; Wragg, 1993; Pollard and Triggs, 2000; NFER, 2011). A cross-generational wish list would be for teachers who are:

- knowledgeable;
- firm but fair;
- approachable;
- skilled at making lessons interesting;
- humorous; and
- caring.

Undoubtedly the views of learners have been taken more seriously following the rise of the children's rights agenda over recent decades. The United Nations Convention on the Rights of the Child (adopted by the UK government in 1991) legally entitles children to express their views freely. This is recognized at the UK level through government, inspectorate and professional literature (e.g. DCELLS, 2007; Aitken and Millar, 2004; Burke and Grosvenor, 2003). Despite a growing emphasis upon taking into account the views of pupils when assessing the quality of educational provision, there is a need for caution. Brundrett and Silcock (2002: 12) point out: 'Just as we cannot decide what is competent or successful teaching just by looking at what practitioners do, so we cannot decide what excellent teaching is just by talking to teachers or to pupils.' Some class teachers, head teachers and university tutors may hold the view that children are not competent enough to make judgements on such heavy matters as the quality of teaching and learning. However, in the vast majority of cases, teachers appear to have little to fear from consulting pupils whose comments are usually constructive and supportive. The more confident teacher would not see pupils' views as a threat but as a genuine source for self-reflection. It can be very challenging to change children's perceptions of teachers. One research project found that around the world mathematics teachers were seen as 'scruffy nerds' lacking style and friends, prominent for their wrinkles gained from 'thinking so hard'. Learners aged 12 and 13 from many countries, including Britain, Sweden, Germany, Romania and the United States, drew pictures of bald men with glasses and beards, who were working at a blackboard or a computer (Savill, 2001).

**FIGURE 1.2** A great teacher

Source: Sofie Lewis

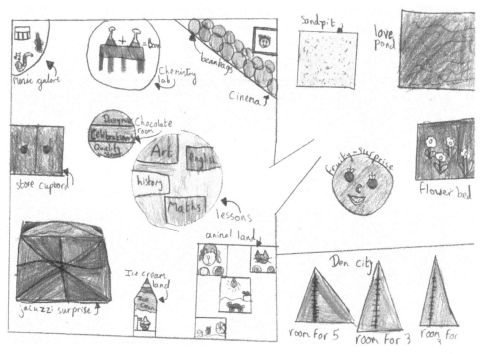

**FIGURE 1.3** A perfect classroom

Source: Grace Lewis

---

**EXTEND YOUR UNDERSTANDING**

In 2001 *The Guardian* ran a competition for children called 'The School we'd like'. The responses included voice-activated pencils, flexible timetables, chill-out rooms and quieter school bells (see www.theguardian.com/education/2001/jun/05/schools.uk7). As a group, ask some children to draw a picture of their perfect class, or write a poem or rap about their best teacher (Figures 1.2 and 1.3). Compare the views with those gained by other colleagues. How insightful do you think pupils' views can be and can these be taken too far?

---

## Views of inspectors

All inspection bodies set out their criteria for making judgements on the quality of learning and teaching (Table 1.1). OFSTED (2014) focuses on what difference this makes to learners: their motivation, engagement, pace and depth of learning, and the knowledge, skills and understanding that they develop. Significantly, under the inspection framework for 2012, unless the quality of teaching is deemed to be outstanding in most lessons, schools overall cannot be judged to be outstanding. Judgements on the quality of teaching are not based on the style adopted but by 'the amount of useful learning that takes place in lessons' (OFSTED, 2013: 9). In Wales, Estyn's grade descriptor for 'excellent' uses the expression 'significant examples of sector-leading practice' (Estyn, 2010). The term 'sector-leading' refers to innovative practice that is at the cutting edge. It has a proven impact on learners' progress and achievement. It does not have to be unique and should be capable of being adapted by others. The websites of Estyn and other inspectorates provide examples of case studies to illustrate their view of sector-leading or excellent practice. In England and Wales it is now harder to demonstrate outstanding teaching than under previous inspection frameworks. When judging the quality of teaching, the key words for inspectors are 'so what?'

The *frequency* of performance is a key factor in assessing teaching quality. The Northern Ireland inspectorate's view is that grade 1 teaching is *characterized* by excellence, while grade 2 is defined as '*consistently* good'. While the best teachers have days to forget, on balance, they operate at a *consistently* high level of performance. Similarly, the best trainee teachers are not judged by one-off lessons put on for their observing tutors or senior mentors. Rather, astute assessors consider the quality of teaching day-in and day-out over a sustained period of time; say the course of a school placement. OFSTED (2014) judges outstanding teaching by the progress and achievement of pupils with a particular teacher over time, rather than teacher performance on the day. This is a challenge for inspectors facing new, inexperienced teachers or those who have arrived from another country. OFSTED (2014) has made it clear that the inspection criteria for judging outstanding teaching should not be treated as a checklist (Box 1.3). Rather, inspectors are cautioned to use their professional judgements in reaching a 'best fit' view of teaching.

**TABLE 1.1** Descriptors of teaching quality, used by inspectorate bodies in the UK

| England | Wales | Scotland | Northern Ireland |
|---------|-------|----------|------------------|
| Outstanding | Excellent – many strengths, including examples of sector-leading practice | Excellent – outstanding, sector leading | Outstanding characterized by excellence |
| Good | Good – many strengths and no important areas requiring significant improvement | Very good – major strengths | Consistently good |
| Requires improvement | Adequate – strengths outweigh areas for improvement | Good – important strengths with some areas for improvement | Many good features but some areas for improvement that the school or organisation has the capacity to address |
| Inadequate | Unsatisfactory – important areas for improvement outweigh strengths | Weak – important weaknesses | Overall sound/satisfactory |
| | | Unsatisfactory – major weaknesses | Significant weaknesses that outweigh strengths |
| | | | Poor |

Sources: www.ofsted.gov.uk; www.estyn.gov.uk; www.educationscotland.gov.uk; www.etini.gov.uk

---

### BOX 1.3  OFSTED CRITERIA FOR OUTSTANDING TEACHING

■ Much of the teaching in all key stages and most subjects is outstanding and never less than consistently good. As a result, almost all pupils currently on roll in the school, including disabled pupils, those who have special educational needs, those for whom the pupil premium provides support and the most able, are making rapid and sustained progress.

■ All teachers have consistently high expectations of all pupils. They plan and teach lessons that enable pupils to learn exceptionally well across the curriculum.

■ Teachers systematically and effectively check pupils' understanding throughout lessons, anticipating where they may need to intervene and doing so with notable impact on the quality of learning.

■ The teaching of reading, writing, communication and mathematics is highly effective and cohesively planned and implemented across the curriculum.

■ Teachers and other adults authoritatively impart knowledge to ensure students are engaged in learning, and generate high levels of commitment to learning across the school.

■ Consistently high quality marking and constructive feedback from teachers ensure that pupils make rapid gains.

■ Teachers use well-judged and often imaginative teaching strategies, including setting appropriate homework that, together with clearly directed and timely support and intervention, match individual needs accurately. Consequently, pupils learn exceptionally well across the curriculum.

(OFSTED, 2013: 39)

---

The principle of proportionality is sometimes used to distinguish outstanding teaching. The Scottish and Welsh inspectorates quantify their comments in school reports using the phrases in Table 1.2. Although there are differences here and inspection is not a mathematical exercise, generally outstanding teachers would be expected to ensure that nearly all pupils make excellent progress relative to their starting points. In 'good' lessons, this might equate to most pupils.

Teaching and learning have a complex relationship; it is possible for one to be good and not the other. Consider a scenario where a teacher very carefully plans a lesson and provides a range of stimulating resources and activities only to see an unexpected event (a child being sick, snowfall, or a power cut) derail the lesson. Occasionally pupils can make good strides in their learning despite less than good teaching – perhaps they bring particular enthusiasm for a subject, motivated by technologies or learn from each other. Recruiting the right kind of teacher and assessing their quality are international challenges (Box 1.4).

**TABLE 1.2** Inspection quantification terms

| Scotland | Wales |
| --- | --- |
| Almost all – over 90% | Nearly all – with very few exceptions |
| Most – 75%–90% | Most – 90% or more |
| | Many – 70% or more |
| Majority – 50%–74% | Majority – over 60% |
| | Half – 50% |
| Less than half – 15%–49% | Around half – close to 50% |
| | Minority – below 40% |
| Few – up to 15% | Few – below 20% |
| | Very few – less than 10% |

Sources: www.educationscotland.gov.uk; www.estyn.gov.uk

---

### BOX 1.4  INTERNATIONAL VIEW – THE QUALITY OF TEACHING

Around the world, the quality of teachers' work is measured largely by the extent to which teachers improve pupils' outcomes. Other criteria include: teacher qualifications, how they operate in the classroom setting, personal characteristics, their knowledge and pedagogical practice. Most countries make an assessment of quality using a range of instruments, including: standardized tests, peer review, appraisals, parental ratings, classroom observations, pupils' views and self-evaluation documents (OECD, 2011). Many American states use the detailed *Framework for Teaching Evaluation Instrument* as a guide for rating effective teaching (Danielson, 2013). It covers four domains: planning and preparation, classroom environment, instruction and professional responsibilities. A teacher's performance is rated against each domain and 'scores' on components such as questioning and assessment contribute to an overall evaluation. A three-year study commissioned by the Bill and Melinda Gates Foundation recommends that equal weight should be given to criteria to create a more accurate assessment of teacher effectiveness (OECD, 2013). Unfortunately in many countries the major challenge is to recruit enough teachers, let alone train or retain outstanding ones (UNESCO, 2006). This is particularly the case in rural parts of Africa. In some countries, the reading ages of teachers are the same as those pupils in 6th grade (11–12 year-olds).

---

## What does research tell us about high-quality teaching?

There is now a substantial body of research on teacher effectiveness, spanning 30 or more years (Galton *et al.*, 1980; Gipps, 1994; Kyriacou, 1998; Dean, 2000; Muijs and Reynolds 2001; Kerry and Wilding, 2004). Most of the early research focused on identifying the personal characteristics of good teachers. More recent research has established that factors such as experience, age or qualifications do not have a direct bearing on the quality of teaching (McBer, 2000; Slater *et al.*, 2009). Researchers are faced with the difficulty of controlling many factors when measuring the impact of teaching on pupils' progress and achievement. Teacher effects tend to have a more significant impact than school differences, especially in the primary phase (where pupils tend to spend most of the day with a single teacher) and in developing countries (Mincu, 2013). Day *et al.* (2006) conducted a 4-year longitudinal study looking at variations in teachers' work, lives and effectiveness. They found that in Years 6 and 9, 15–30 per cent of the variance in pupils' progress in mathematics and English was related to the quality of teaching, taking into account pupil background and prior attainment. Similarly, Slater *et al.* (2009) reach a common-sense conclusion that having a good teacher as opposed to a mediocre or poor one does make a difference, to the effect of improving test scores by at least 25 per cent.

The McBer Report (2000) separated outstanding teachers from the rest by virtue of their consistency and commitment: they demonstrated 'professional characteristics in more circumstances and to a greater degree of intensity than effective colleagues.' Galton's (2001) review of the literature on teacher expertise shows that expert teachers tend to be more pupil-focused than novices who are more concerned with their own well-being. When viewing images of classrooms, experts were quickly able to identify meaningful *patterns*, unlike novices who tended to concentrate on discrete events. The latter found it very difficult to make sense of events that conflicted, such as explaining why some pupils were on task while others were not. Moreover, expert teachers are able to take into account contextual factors quickly when planning activities.

In recent years, Professor John Hattie (2009; 2012) has provided the most important synthesis of research on learning and teaching covering half a million studies. Hattie suggests that the biggest effects on student learning occur when students have opportunities to become their own teachers, and teachers become learners themselves. Within this, he singles out high-quality feedback as the most important factor in effective learning.

## The journey to becoming outstanding

The use of metaphor is common in teacher education as a strategy to support trainee and new teachers in their early careers. Seeing teaching as a hero's journey is among the most powerful of metaphors (Goldstein, 2005). Estyn maintains that outstanding teaching should be viewed as 'a journey rather than a fixed point' (Jensen, 1988; Estyn, 2007). Most teachers will encounter particular, and sometimes persistent, roadblocks in their careers, such as maintaining a reasonable work–life balance, clarifying role expectations and managing time effectively. Chapters 2 and 3 discuss these challenges and the importance of maintaining self-confidence and professional identity. Outstanding teachers demonstrate resilience, particularly when faced with challenging pupils and situations. As the McBer Report (2000: 21) noted: 'the very best go even further, rising to stretching challenges and expressing a belief that they will succeed against the odds.'

While research tells us something firm about what outstanding teachers do, it is less clear over the process of *becoming* an outstanding teacher. This would require substantial studies over time, for which funding is in short supply. There is, however, broad agreement across countries that the most effective way to learn to improve teaching quality is to observe good practice and to have experiences in teaching under skilled supervision. Berliner provides a theory of skill learning that charts the journey of professional development from novice to expert teacher (Table 1.3).

**TABLE 1.3** Professional development

| Stage | Teachers | Description |
|-------|----------|-------------|
| 1 Novice | Student teachers and many first-year teachers | Learns context-free rules such as 'give praise for right answers'; tends to conform to rules and procedures. |
| 2 Advanced beginner | Second and third-year teachers | Strategic knowledge is acquired, e.g. when to ignore or break rules and when to follow them. |
| 3. Competent | Third and fourth-year teachers | In more control of events, follow their own plans, respond to information that they choose, able to discern what is important. Not yet very fast or flexible in behaviour. |
| 4. Proficient | A modest number of teachers progress to this stage | Characterised by intuition where actions are 'second nature', but still analytical when necessary. Likened to the stage of most tournament chess and bridge players. |
| 5. Expert | A small number of teachers reach the last stage | Fluid performance, able to 'go with the flow' but when things do not work out as planned they analyse why. |

Source: Berliner (2001: 21–4). Reproduced with permission

This framework suggests that trainee teachers operating at the first stage generally behave in a rational and relatively inflexible manner, tending to follow what they are told and applying this advice without too much regard to context. They begin to learn and use the jargon of the profession, such as 'differentiation', 'higher-order questions' and 'learning objectives'. Many newly qualified teachers, as 'advanced beginners', recognize that they need to adapt their teaching according to the circumstances, based on their experience. For example, they learn that there are times when giving praise may not be such a good thing, if it conveys low expectations. At the 'competent' stage, teachers take greater personal responsibility for their decision making; they set their own targets and become more emotionally involved than novice or advanced beginners. Proficient teachers draw upon their intuition in the way that they act in the classroom, responding to events without seeming to think about things. They recognize patterns and make connections, for example between progress in one area of the curriculum and another.

At the final stage, expert teachers – the 'grand masters' of the profession – know where to be or what to do at the right time. They act effortlessly and with fluidity. Berliner describes their behaviour as 'arational' in that they have both an intuitive grasp of the situation and a non-deliberate sense of the appropriate response to be made. Interestingly, as with other professions such as nurses, it seems that the best teachers find it difficult to explain their decisions – 'I did it because it just felt right' (cited by Galton, 2001: 81). The general principle that Berliner is keen to highlight is the qualitative differences in the thinking and performance along the continuum.

The stage model is not without critics. Galton (2001) points out that the way expertise is defined varies – Berliner, for example, took ratings from head teachers and advisers followed by three rounds of observations before selecting a group of experts, while others

---

**BOX 1.5  REAL-LIFE LEARNING CHALLENGE**

You have a staff meeting planned to discuss what best practice looks like in different subject areas and within the Early Years. You have been given 5 minutes to make a presentation to colleagues on the subject/phase you lead in – prepare a concise and engaging presentation.

---

take experience as a guide. Galton argues that clearer criteria are needed that distinguish each stage of teaching development. He also questions the degree to which expertise is transferable – an expert in art will not necessarily be an expert in mathematics, although he concedes that in the primary school general teaching skills should have a bearing irrespective of subject content (Box 1.5).

## Models of teaching

Much of the discussion in this chapter about what it means to be outstanding depends upon how the role of the teacher is perceived (Table 1.4). If observers see teaching as establishing a special chemistry with learners, then they are likely to most value teachers' personal characteristics such as their sense of humour, openness and positive outlook. Charismatic teachers are frequently depicted in popular culture as 'carers, saviours or connectors' – particularly in relation to troubled or troublesome children (Weber and Mitchell, 1995; Moore, 2004; Ellsmore, 2005). Ultimately, most pupils learn because of connecting with their teachers as *people*, rather than what and how they teach (Day and Sachs, 2004).

On the other hand, there is a strong view that the style of teaching is far less important than the actual outcomes. Advocates of what could be described as the 'science of teaching' argue that it should be possible to identify the main building blocks of successful teaching and replicate these (Gipps *et al.*, 2000). So teachers should be able to demonstrate their technical competence in skills such as planning, explaining or questioning. This model is closely associated with performance and accountability but is seen by critics as limiting teachers' professionalism. Evidence submitted to the House of Commons (2012) does not suggest that a teacher skilled in a particular competency is more likely to be a high performer in the classroom.

Most teacher educators support a more reflective model, which sees teachers as actively involved in evaluating their own practices. It owes much to the writings of the American philosopher John Dewey in the early twentieth century. He contrasted *routine* and *reflective* action – the former guided by tradition, imitation and external authorities, while the latter involved questioning, hunting, searching and actively thinking through problems. The reflective practitioner model emphasizes teacher education rather than training, where outstanding practice is not limited to the proficient application of technical skills but includes how individuals respond to uncertain circumstances (Simco and Wilson, 2002; Pollard *et al.*, 2008). Schön (1983, 1987) highlighted the demands faced by professionals (not just teachers) as they seek to improve their work through reflection-in-action (thinking on your feet) and reflection-on-action (thinking after the event). Many writers refer to the importance of 'critical incidents' that feed into reflective evaluation (Chater, 2007: 232). These are potential turning points in the reflective process and can derive from professional conversations with colleagues, an observation of a pupil, a question or comment. Reflection is central to a cycle of planning, teaching, monitoring and evaluating. Outstanding teachers demonstrate higher-order reflection skills such as evaluating ideas and implementing change, rather than simply describing events (Nolan and Sim, 2011).

Another model values the roles teachers play as active agents of social change (Sachs, 2003). This transformative view focuses on how well teachers view pupils as co-learners in the creation of knowledge and the development of skills and dispositions to challenge the status quo. In this sense it is a more radical model than the others, but it fits in with discourses on social justice, citizenship and human rights. Outstanding teachers are rated by the extent to which they address inequalities in education and promote anti-discriminatory practices.

Finally, the enquiring teacher model values the role of teachers as researchers, discussed in Chapter 14. High-quality teachers are seen as those who regularly ask questions, explore ideas, keep up to date with research and professional development opportunities, share their insights with others, are eager to work with colleagues and external partners on research projects and seek to apply ideas in their classrooms.

These models are not mutually exclusive. Many outstanding teachers are charismatic, skilful, reflective, committed and conscientious in their outlook. The models might say more about those making assessments on teaching than the subjects themselves. The values, beliefs, theories and prior experiences of observers are important factors in the measurement of teaching, which can never be an objective process.

**TABLE 1.4** Different models of teacher professionalism

| Discourse | Summary |
| --- | --- |
| Charismatic | Teachers play on their personalities to build strong relationships with pupils. While children remember larger-than-life characters, personality factors alone do not bring about improvements in learning. |
| Reflective | Teachers continually review their planning, teaching and assessment practices and are committed to professional development. The model promotes teacher autonomy but has been criticized as being difficult to assess. |
| Technical | Teachers are viewed as technicians whose performance is measured against prescribed standards. Authorities like the measurability although critics fear that teacher creativity, risk-taking and variety are stifled. |
| Enquiring | Teachers undertake action research into their own practices with a view of improving these and sharing findings with others. The model opens up possibilities for teachers to work with colleagues in professional learning communities and to follow masters-level study. In practice, however, research is not high on many teachers' priorities. |
| Transformative | Teachers work with pupils to challenge the status quo to achieve greater social justice through education. The model highlights the urgent need for teachers to make a difference to children's lives, especially those from disadvantaged backgrounds. Caution needs to be exercised, however, in the manner by which teachers allow their personal convictions to influence children's thinking. |

This chapter has shown outstanding teachers make a significant difference to children's prospects. However, teachers can only do so much. One American study suggests that 90 per cent of the variation in student gain scores is due to factors beyond the teachers' control, such as children's prior experiences (cited by MacBeath, 2012). Children, who are able to cut through the jargon, know the great teachers who inspire, make time for them, and tell them how well they are doing. Perhaps the defining hallmark of outstanding teachers is their commitment to making a difference and establishing quality relationships.

## Glossary

**Achievement** describes the performance of learners measured against their ability and the progress they make.

**Attainment** refers to a level of learning measured against specified targets or criteria such as standardized tests.

## References

Aitken, S. and Millar, S. (2004) *Listening to Children*, Edinburgh: CALL Scotland.

Bennett, T. (2013) 'The Beaufort Wind Scale – why we need an observation revolution', *TESConnect* Blog, 24 May.

Berliner, D. (2001) 'Teacher expertise', in Banks, F. and Shelton Mayes, A. (eds) *Early Professional Development for Teachers*, London: David Fulton Books.

Blishen, E. (1973) 'Your children on their teachers', *Where*, 84, September, 253–56.

Bolton, P. (2012) *Education: Historical Statistics*, London: House of Commons.

Brundrett, M. and Silcock, P. (2002) *Achieving Competence, Success and Excellence in Teaching*, London: Routledge.

Burke, C. and Grosvenor, I. (2003) *The School I'd Like*, London: Routledge.

Campbell, R.J., Kyriakides, L., Muijs, R.D. and Robinson, W. (2003) 'Differential teacher effectiveness: Towards a model for research and teacher appraisal', in *Oxford Review of Education*, 29(3): 347–362.

Chater, M. (2007) 'Developing as a reflective practitioner', in Johnston, J., Halocha, J. and Chater, M. (eds) *Developing Teaching Skills*, Maidenhead: Open University Press, 228–49.

Chetty, R., Friedman, J. and Rockoff, J., (2012) 'Great teaching: Measuring its effect on students' future earnings', in *Education Next*, 12(3): 12–21.

Ching, C., Levin, J. and Parisi, J. (2003) 'Artifacts of knowledge and practice in university teaching and learning', Paper presented at the 2003 American Educational Research Association Annual Meeting, Chicago, IL, 22 April.

Coates, S. (2011) *Second Report of the Independent Review of Teachers' Standards*, London: DfE.

Cree, A., Kay, A. and Steward, J. (2012) *The Economic and Social Cost of Illiteracy: A Snapshot of Illiteracy in a Global Context*, Melbourne: World Literacy Foundation.

Crowther, D., Cumming, C., Dyson, A. and Millward, A. (2003) *Schools and Area Regeneration*, London: Policy Press.

Danielson, C. (2013) *Framework for Teaching Evaluation Instrument*, Princeton, NJ: The Danielson Group.

Darling-Hammond, L. (2000) 'Teacher quality and student achievement: A review of state policy evidence', in *Education Policy Analysis Archives*, 8(1): 1–44.

Day, C.W., Stobart, G., Sammons, P. and Kington, A. (2006) *Variations in Teachers' Work, Lives and Effectiveness*, London: DfES.

Day, C. and Sachs, J. (eds) (2004) *International Handbook on the Continuing Development of Teachers*, Buckingham: Open University Press.

DCELLS (2007) *Listening to Learners*, Cardiff: Welsh Assembly Government.

DfE (2013a) *Teachers' Standards*, London: DfE.

DfE (2013b) *The National Curriculum in England Key Stages 1 and 2 Framework Document*, London: DfE.

Dean, J. (2000) *Improving Children's Learning: Effective Teaching in the Primary School*, London: Routledge.

Ellsmore, S. (2005) *Carry on Teachers! Representations of the Teaching Profession in Screen Culture*, Stoke-on-Trent: Trentham Books.

Estyn (2007) *Update Training for Independent Inspectors: Primary Phase*, Cardiff: Estyn.

Estyn (2010), *Guidance on Sector-Leading Practice*, Cardiff: Estyn.

Exley, S. (2012) 'Who's watching you?', *Times Educational Supplement*, 13 July.

Frankel, H. (2010) 'My best teacher – Bradley Wiggins', *Times Educational Supplement*, 2 July.

Galton, M., Simon, B. and Croll, P. (1980) *Inside the Primary Classroom*, London: Routledge.

Gipps, C. (1994) *Beyond Testing: Towards a Theory of Educational Assessment*, London: The Falmer Press.

Gipps, C., McCallum, G. and Hargreaves, E. (2000) *What Makes a Good Primary Teacher?: Expert Classroom Strategies*, London: RoutledgeFalmer.

Goldstein, L. (2005) 'Becoming a teacher as a hero's journey: Using metaphor in pre-service education', in *Teacher Education Quarterly*, Winter, 7–24.

Hanushek, E. (2010a) 'The Economic value of higher teacher quality', Working Paper No. 56, December, Calder, available at: http://eric.ed.gov/?id=ED517170 (accessed 14 January 2014).

Hanushek, E. (2010b) *The High Cost of Low Educational Performance*, Paris: OECD.

Hattie, J. (2009) *Visible Learning*, Abingdon: Routledge.

Hattie, J. (2012) *Visible Learning for Teachers*, Abingdon: Routledge.

Ho, A.D. and Kane, T.J. (2013) *The Reliability of Classroom Observations by School Personnel*, Bill and Melinda Gates Foundation, available at: www.gatesfoundation.org/(accessed 14 January 2014).

Home Office (2003) *Respect and Responsibility: Taking a Stand Against Anti-Social Behaviour*, London: Home Office.

House of Commons Education Committee (2012) *Great Teachers: Attracting, Training and Retaining the Best: Government Response to the Committee's Ninth Report of Session 2010–12*, London: The Stationery Office.

Jensen, E, (1988) *Super Teaching*, Del Mar, CA: Turning Points.

Judd, J. (1994) 'Teachers have to be social workers', *The Independent*, 21 October.

Kerry, T. and Wilding, M. (2004) *Effective Classroom Teacher*, London: Pearson.

Kirkup, C., Sizmur, J., Sturman, L. and Lewis, K. (2005) *Schools' Use of Data in Teaching and Learning*, Nottingham: DfES.

Koppich, J. E. (2008) *Reshaping Teacher Policies to Improve Student Achievement*. Berkeley, CA: Policy Analysis for California Education.

Kyriacou, C. (1998) *Essential Teaching Skills*, Cheltenham: Nelson Thornes.

Lipsett, A. (2008) 'Teachers becoming social workers, protests union', *The Guardian*, 20 March.

Little, O. (2009) *Teacher Evaluation Systems: The Window for Opportunity and Reform*, Atlanta, CA: National Education Association.

MacBeath, J. (2012) *Future of Teaching Profession*, Cambridge: Cambridge University Press.

McBer, H. (2000) *Research into Teacher Effectiveness: A Model of Teacher Effectiveness*, London: DfEE.

McKinsey & Company (2007) *How the World's Best Performing School Systems Come Out on Top*, available at: www.mckinsey.com/clientservice/socialsector/resources/pdf/Worlds_School_Systems_Final.pdf (accessed 14 January 2014).

McLaughlin, H.J. and Burnaford, G. (2007) 'Re-thinking the basis for "high quality" teaching: Teacher preparation in communities', in Townsend, T. and Bates, R. (eds) *Handbook of Teacher Education: Globalization, Standards and Professionalism in Times of Change*, New York: Springer, 331–42.

Mayo, K.E. (2002) 'The master teacher model', *Management in Education*, 16(3): 29–33.

Menter, I., Hulme, M., Elliot, D. and Lew, J. (2010) *Literature Review on Teacher Education in the 21st Century*, Edinburgh: Scottish Government Social Research.

Menzies, L. (2013) *Educational Aspirations: How English Schools Can Work with Parents to Keep Them on Track*, York: Joseph Rowntree Foundation.

Mincu, M. (2013) *Teacher Quality and School Improvement: What is the Role of Research?* London: BERA.

Moore, A. (2004) *The Good Teacher*, London: Routledge.

Muijs, D. and Reynolds, D. (2001) *Effective Teaching: Evidence and Practice*, London: Paul Chapman.

Nelson, F. (2013) 'To transform schools, sack bad teachers and hire great ones. It'll transform education – and the economy', *The Spectator*, 15 June.

NFER (2011) *Office of the Children's Commissioner: Children and Young People's Views of Education Policy*, Slough: NFER.

Nolan, A. and Sim, J. (2011) 'Exploring and evaluating levels of reflection in pre-service early childhood teachers', *Australasian Journal of Early Childhood*, 36(3): 122–30.

OECD (2009) *Teacher Evaluation: A Conceptual Framework and Examples of Country Practices*, Paris: OECD.

OECD (2011) *Teachers Matter: Attracting, Developing and Retaining Effective Teachers*, Paris: OECD.

OECD (2013) *Teachers for the 21st Century: Using Evaluation to Improve Teaching*, Paris: OECD.

OFSTED (2013) *The Annual Report of Her Majesty's Chief Inspector of Education, Children's Services and Skills*, London: OFSTED.

OFSTED (2014) *School Inspection Handbook*, London: OFSTED.

Pollard, A. and Triggs, P. (2000) *What Pupils Say*, London: Continuum.

Pollard, A., Anderson, J., Maddock, M., Swaffield, S., Warin, J. and Warwick, P. (2008) *Reflective Teaching: Evidence-Informed Professional Practice*, London: Continuum.

Rowe, D., Horsley, N., Thorpe, T., and Breslin, T. (2011) *Teaching, Learning and Community Cohesion: A Study of Primary and Secondary Schools' Responses to a New Statutory Duty*, Reading: CfBT.

Sachs, J. (2003) *The Activist Teaching Profession*. Buckingham: Open University Press.

Sanders, W. L. and Rivers, J. C. (1996) *Cumulative and Residual Effects of Teachers on Future Students Academic Achievement*, Knoxville, TN: University of Tennessee Value-Added Research and Assessment Center.

Savill, R. (2001) 'Pupils think their maths teachers are nerds', *The Telegraph*, 3 January.

Schön, D.A. (1983) *The Reflective Practitioner*, New York: Basic Books.

Schön, D.A. (1987) *Educating the Reflective Practitioner*, San Francisco, CA: Jossey-Bass.

Shulman, L. (1987) 'Knowledge and teaching: Foundations of the new reform', *Harvard Educational Review*, 57(1): 1–22.

Simco, N. and Wilson, T. (2002) *Primary Initial Teacher Training and Education: Revised Standards, Bright Future?* Exeter: Learning Matters.

Slater, H., Davies, N., and Burgess, S. (2009) *Do Teachers Matter? Measuring the Variation in Teacher Effectiveness in England*, Bristol: University of Bristol.

Stones, E. (1992) *Quality Teaching*, London: Routledge.

Sutton Trust (2011) *Improving the Impact of Teachers on Pupil Achievement in the UK: Interim Findings*, London: Sutton Trust.

Turner-Bisset, R. (2001) *Expert Teaching: Knowledge and Pedagogy to Lead the Profession*, London: David Fulton.

UCET (2012) *Implementing the Revised Teachers' Standards in Initial Teacher Education Support materials*, London: UCET.

UNESCO (2006) *Teachers and Educational Quality: Monitoring Global Needs for 2015*, Montreal: UNESCO.

Weber, S. and Mitchell, C. (1995) *'That's Funny, You Don't Look Like a Teacher!'* London: Routledge.

Wragg, T. (1993) *Primary Teaching Skills*, London: Routledge.

Zemelman, S., Daniels, H. and Hyde, A. (2005) *Best Practice: Today's Standards for Teaching and Learning in America's Schools*, Portsmouth, NH: Heinemann.

## Websites

The Department for Education website offers teachers in England up-to-date policy news – www.education.gov.uk

Teachers in Northern Ireland should consult the Department of Education for Northern Ireland website – www.deni.gov.uk

Teachers in Wales should view the Welsh Government's Learning Wales website – http://learning.wales.gov.uk

Education Scotland is the national body supporting quality and improvement in Scottish education – www.educationscotland.gov.uk

The Office for Standards in Education (OFSTED) website provides inspection reports and other publications for England – www.ofsted.gov.uk

Estyn is the inspectorate body in Wales – www.estyn.gov.uk

The Education and Training Inspectorate for Northern Ireland website – www.etini.gov.uk

The Teaching Awards includes children's testimonies about outstanding teachers – www.teachingawards.com

The United Nations Children's Fund (UNICEF) includes publications on children's rights and well-being, including their views on what makes a good teacher – www.unicef.org/teachers/teacher/teacher.htm

The Organization for Economic Cooperation and Development (OECD) provides information on education within international contexts – www.oecd.org/education

# 2

# Know thyself

## Chapter objectives

By the end of this chapter you should be able to:

■ Explain why it is important for teachers to develop self-knowledge.
■ Understand self-efficacy and how this can be strengthened.
■ Identify appropriate strategies to handle stress and manage time.
■ Critically reflect upon personal dispositions.

*One thing is for certain – what we believe will determine what and how we teach.*

(Castle, 1961: 28)

## Introduction

The motto 'know thyself' first greeted visitors on the forecourt of the ancient temple at Delphi, the Greek mecca of wisdom. Originally this was probably a reminder of human mortality, a warning not to boast above one's station and the importance of humility before the gods. Subsequent Greek philosophers suggested that individuals needed to know themselves before knowing others and their environment. Such self-knowledge includes understanding personal goals, values, aspirations, beliefs and ideas. Today, self-knowledge is particularly relevant in a fast-changing world, which has seen a rise in emotional uncertainties within the context of profound social and economic changes. The teaching profession is often at the front end in responding to antisocial behaviour, depression and family poverty that affect significant numbers of children and young people. These can challenge even the most resilient of teachers.

The process of gaining self-knowledge centres on the fundamental question: 'Who am I?' According to Holden (2005), author of *Success Intelligence*, self-knowledge is critical in achieving a successful and contented life. He argues that without self-knowledge people end up chasing someone else's definition of success. In the context of teaching, the most successful practitioners are those who not only know their subjects and pupils, but also know themselves. They have a moral purpose that shapes what they do. They are committed but do not take things for granted and are open to change. All teachers can improve their self-knowledge through personal reflection, meditation, research and professional dialogue. The journey begins with the question prospective teachers are often asked: 'Why do you want to teach?'

## Why teach?

Studies suggest that most people join the profession because they enjoy working with children, look forward to the 'buzz' or intellectual challenge of teaching and the opportunity to make a positive difference to children's lives (Ross and Hutchings, 2003). Less impressive is the 'mattress factor' – those who join the profession as 'something to fall back on' – which is still occasionally heard.

Teaching can be one of the most rewarding careers. In one small-scale survey of 2,000 workers, teaching was considered the happiest profession, with relationships, working environment and holiday time considered the most rewarding aspects (Hall, 2013). This is a reminder of the old line about 'three reasons to be a teacher: June, July and August' and how, in reality, recovery time is essential in a high-stress profession and when few teachers take their full holiday entitlement. Morgan (2005: 5) surveyed serving teachers for their experiences and highlights the following rewards:

■  fulfilment – giving a sense of meaning and purpose to work;

■  excitement – offering variety, enjoyment and a broad range of interactions;

■  satisfaction – enabling self-development as well as the pleasure from helping young people to develop; and

■  enjoyment – interaction with young people and with colleagues was found to be a source of immediate as well as long-term pleasure (see also Box 2.1).

She found teachers experience greater work satisfaction than other careers such as banking, information technology and marketing. The highlight of the personal journey to becoming a teacher culminates in the dynamic interaction between teacher, learner and subject content; what Csikszentmihalyi (1997) calls '**flow**' and Rodgers and Raider-Roth (2006: 267) term, 'presence': 'the experience of bringing one's whole self to full attention so as to perceive what is happening in the moment.'

### EXTEND YOUR UNDERSTANDING

Discuss in small groups what attracted you to teaching and your main hopes and fears when you start to teach. When you retire, what three words would you want people to use to describe your teaching?

---

**BOX 2.1  WHY DO YOU WANT TO TEACH? THOUGHTS OF COURSE APPLICANTS**

'From an early age, I have always wanted to be a primary teacher. I want to make a difference in children's lives.'

*Sarah*

'I worked as a learning support assistant for many years and didn't think I was good enough for teaching but the head teacher encouraged me to apply and I haven't looked back since – the theoretical stuff has helped me make sense of what I saw in the classroom.'

*Jessica*

'I kind of drifted into teaching because my mother is a teacher. To be honest, it wasn't really something I was dead keen on, but it was a kind of family expectation and once I started, I enjoyed the challenge of keeping children interested.'

*John*

'There is nothing more rewarding than helping children to develop the essential skills needed for life.'

*Emma*

'I feel the opportunities are extensive once qualified. Leading to being able to teach abroad in countries where education is currently limited.'

*Mia*

---

## Learning to know yourself

Much of the literature on outstanding teachers refers to outward, observable factors such as technical skills (e.g. questioning) or attempts to measure the impact on pupils' progress in learning. This is the line taken by OFSTED (2013) in its most recent inspection framework. But important insights into the teaching–learning relationship can be gained by refocusing inwardly on the teacher as a person, or what Day and Qing Gu (2010) refer to as 'the person in the professional'. This includes considering teachers' beliefs and feelings, how they see themselves and their professional role, their personal journeys, their different personas, how motivated they are, and what they are like as *learners* themselves. Teaching is as much about *who* the teacher is, as it is about how and what is taught. Hattie (2012: 22) points out that 'teachers' beliefs and commitment are the greatest influence on student achievement *over which we can have some control*' (his italics).

The influences that shape teachers' lives are most likely to come from their own formative memories and experiences, rather than research reports, policies or school mission statements (Brookfield, 1995). Even when teachers attend the same university training programme, research shows that when they take up their teaching posts there still remains considerable variation in how they view themselves as teachers as well as how they teach (Flores and Day, 2006). Teachers' views are also influenced by the immediate environment that they work within, society at large, the media, family and friends.

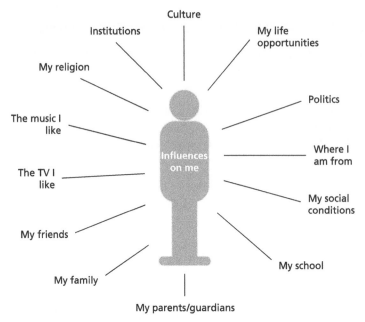

**FIGURE 2.1** The influences that shape personal development

Source: Clements and Spinks (1996: 57). Reproduced with permission

**PAUSE FOR REFLECTION**

Consider Figure 2.1 and think about who *you* are. As a teacher, does it matter what your religious or political views are? What about your musical, reading or sporting tastes? Are all of these, ultimately, private matters?

## Improving self-awareness

There are a number of specific techniques that can be used to improve self-awareness. In the 1950s two American psychologists, Joseph Luft and Harry Ingham, developed a technique that they called 'Johari', named after combining their first names, Joe and Harry (for some reason there is only ever one 'r' in 'Johari'). The intention was to improve people's understanding of their personal development, how they relate to others and team communication. The Johari window represents information about a person through four perspectives shown as quadrants or panes (Figure 2.2). The information is known or unknown by the person, and known or unknown by others in the team. In the public or open area, information about the person that is known by the person and others is recorded. This is essential for effective communication and builds trust and cooperation. The blind area or blind spot contains information unknown by the person but known

| | What you see in me | What you do not see in me |
|---|---|---|
| What I see in me | Open | Hidden |
| What I do not see in me | Blind | Unknown |

**FIGURE 2.2** Johari window

to others. The hidden area or hidden self includes information that a person knows about him/herself that others do not know. The unknown area or unknown self covers what is unknown by the person about him/herself and is also unknown by others. As more information is disclosed and team members get to know each other, the size of each quadrant changes. Hence the open area can expand at the expense of the hidden area.

The Johari window helps individuals to reflect upon their professional role, whether teacher assistant, phase leader or head teacher. It can also prompt individuals to think about the role of other people in their lives. Regular use of such exercises is useful in building self-knowledge and understanding of others in a profession where teachers are increasingly expected to work as a team. Recent research has highlighted that people have blind spots when it comes to understanding their patterns of thinking, feeling and behaving. Such blind spots in self-knowledge can lead to rash decision making, underachievement, emotional and interpersonal difficulties, and lower life satisfaction. Numerous psychologists advocate practising mindfulness techniques that involve paying attention to current thoughts and feelings in a non-judgemental manner, not assuming that thoughts such as 'I'm no good at this' are facts (Carlson, 2013). Asking for feedback can also reduce blind spots and increase open areas.

## Reflective tools

An important means of improving self-awareness is through regular reflection. As Biggs and Tang (2007) point out, the word reflection itself is rather misleading. They prefer the term 'transformative reflection':

> When you stand in front of a mirror what you see is your reflection, what you are at the time. Transformative reflection is rather like the mirror in Snow White: it tells you what you might become. The mirror uses theory to enable the transformation from the unsatisfactory what-is to the more effective what-might-be.
>
> (Biggs and Tang, 2007: 43)

Teachers can improve their self-awareness through the use of reflective tools such as journals, web-based diaries (blogs), online discussion groups, video technologies and software computer applications (Babiuk, 2007). Reflective practice can also be encouraged through 'action research' projects where teachers investigate aspects of their practice, discussed in Chapter 14.

In commenting upon the use of reflective journals, Bain *et al.* (2002: 171) warned that 'little is known about the processes and principles that need to be applied if the student journal is to become a tool for learning rather than a simple record of events'. There are challenges in sustaining enthusiasm, and avoiding superficial and unreflective writing. That said, the use of reflective journals has become standard practice in many universities. They are valued because they enable students to grow in their understanding of themselves. But effective journal writing is more than private contemplation. It moves teachers to action and to take responsibility for their decisions.

While the content and format will vary, reflective journals typically include:

- points of personal and professional interest arising from the university course or school placements;
- questions relating to background readings or experiences;
- responses to group discussions or tasks set by tutors or school mentors;
- a summary of key learning points;
- reflections on the course and how well it is meeting personal expectations; and
- emerging ideas related to existing theories.

Journals or diaries can serve the purpose of clarifying thoughts and feelings, a therapeutic way of coming to terms with one's own attitude to teaching. Ghaye (2011) points out that a commitment to journal writing is a commitment to considerable introspection, honesty with self, and a frame of mind to handle what one comes to know in a constructive way.

The quality of reflective writing can improve by focusing upon the question 'why' things happened and seeking to explain behaviour. In terms of keeping reflective journals, Kerry (2008: 81–2) provides down-to-earth advice on moving up what he considers three levels of quality:

- Level 1: Straightforward descriptive diary;
- Level 2: Diary plus analytical commentary (asking questions);
- Level 3: Diary plus analytical commentary plus the use of reading and theory.

The quality of reflection can also improve by thinking about the structure and style of writing. At the higher level, it is characterized by fluency, clarity and engagement but the nature of reflective writing is that there is room for intimacy, uncertainty and informality. This, however, brings risks in sharing one's thoughts and ideas with a relative stranger and highlights the importance of trust and transparency between the writer and the audience (Moon, 1999; Cowan and Westwood, 2006). The use of video-recordings of lessons can sharpen teachers' self-awareness and help them to see their teaching from alternative perspectives such as that of pupils (Lofthouse *et al.*, 2010).

Reflective time is critical to a teacher's well-being and can include talking to oneself, prayer, meditation, and confiding in a friend as well as keeping diaries (Holmes, 2005). Without taking time to 'stand and stare' there is a real danger that teachers, particularly the conscientious ones, will suffer burnout. Covey (2004) likens reflection to 'sharpening the saw' and suggests that if teachers do not take time to reflect then they are like the short-sighted woodcutter who refuses to stop to sharpen his blunt saw because he is too busy sawing. It is not uncommon for outstanding teachers to be too self-critical of their teaching. This is especially so when they place undue emphasis on their own shortcomings, without focusing enough on what the children have actually learned in the lesson.

## Self-efficacy

The psychologist Albert Bandura introduced the concept of self-efficacy in the 1970s to describe 'a person's sense of being able to deal effectively with a particular task' (Woolfolk *et al.*, 2008: 400). Self-efficacy is shorthand for the beliefs that people have in their own ability and capacity to do things well. It is based on social cognitive theory, which stresses that human thought and behaviour is best understood within the social system in which it operates (Bandura, 1986). In other words, how teachers think and behave can only be understood by exploring the wider environment such as what is happening in the school.

A strong self-efficacy has helped individuals address phobias, addictions and depressions. Those with confidence and strong self-belief are likely to see hard tasks as challenging rather than threatening. They do not see failures in terms of personal shortcomings, but as learning opportunities and a spur to try harder next time. On the other hand, those with low self-efficacy take time to recover their confidence when they do not succeed at first and generally display low levels of commitment and perseverance.

In teaching, self-efficacy is a teacher's belief in his or her capabilities to bring about desired outcomes in pupils' engagement and learning, even among those who may appear to be unmotivated. This includes confidence in matters such as subject knowledge, planning lessons, organizing the classroom, maintaining discipline, and seeing through activities to achieve educational goals. Studies (Skaalvik and Skaalvik, 2010) show that teachers' self-efficacy is important because it affects so much of what they do, including:

- the goals they set and the expectations they hold;
- their attitudes towards change and innovation;
- their tendency to refer children for additional support; and
- the likelihood that they will stay in the profession.

Teachers who have a strong self-efficacy tend to show greater patience with learners who are struggling and pupils generally benefit from increased motivation.

An individual teacher may also hold beliefs about the profession generally or colleagues within the school, although the relationship between individual and collective self-efficacy is an under-researched area (Goddard and Goddard, 2001). A teacher might agree with the following statement: 'When it comes right down to it, a teacher really can't do much because most of a student's motivation and performance depends on his or her home environment.' However the same teacher might believe that: 'If I really try hard, I can get through to even the most difficult or unmotivated students.'

Self-efficacy is usually measured by interviews and questionnaires. For example, Skaalvik and Skaalvik (2010) have developed a Norwegian Teacher Self-Efficacy Scale (NTSES). More than 2,000 teachers were asked to rate their confidence against each item, for instance along the lines: 'how certain are you that you can . . . motivate students who show low interest in schoolwork?' In all, NTSES uses 24 items grouped under six dimensions:

- instruction;
- adapting education to individual students' needs;
- motivating students;
- keeping discipline;
- cooperating with colleagues and parents; and
- coping with changes and challenges.

The authors found that Norwegian teachers valued their autonomy, but were concerned about increasing time spent on paperwork and the demands of parents expecting teachers to be available out of school hours.

Teachers who have a high sense of self-efficacy are motivated to achieve, tend to persist, try things out and are generally optimistic about the future. They exhibit reduced stress and outperform colleagues who have a lower level of self-efficacy (Day *et al.*, 2007). Teachers can strengthen their own self-efficacy through:

- setting realistic goals – these should be challenging but attainable;
- following good role models; for instance, observing effective teachers, listening and talking to experts and watching videos of those in similar circumstances who have succeeded;
- speaking positively about oneself, reinforcing the mantra 'I can do it';
- capitalizing on their own interests, e.g. music, travel, sport;
- accepting that success depends on effort, practice and time; and
- seeking feedback from others – taking the initiative to speak to other teachers, mentors and managers about personal strengths as well as areas for development.

Although teachers' beliefs and actions are not always the same, those who generally believe that they can make a difference to pupils' experiences in school do approach teaching in

### EXTEND YOUR UNDERSTANDING

Find and complete an online version of a teacher efficacy scale, such as the NTSES. Discuss your responses with colleagues. What do these reveal to you about your and their beliefs?

a different manner from those who think that children's success is largely beyond their control (Slavin, 2003). Above all, they do not give up on children or dismiss their chances because of factors such as the child's poor socio-economic background.

In an international study, Rollett (2001) focused on how expert teachers perceive themselves. She asked primary teachers in London, Vienna and New York to write about **critical incidents** in their teaching. Two-thirds of these were about how the teachers responded to *individual* children rather than curricular or managerial matters. Among the positive incidents were integrating an 'outsider' into a learning group and teaching something that the child had previously found difficult to grasp. The teachers were very 'child-centred' in their philosophy.

This was well illustrated when a teacher with 15 years' experience responded to a Year 6 pupil who went 'berserk' on the playground during a physical education lesson. The teacher was able to calm down the boy by removing him from the situation and discussing the incident with him. She interpreted his outbreak as a result of his anxieties over his grandmother's health and his forthcoming move to the secondary school. She attributed her success to her knowledge of the home background, her ability to sympathize with his worries, and her willingness to understand his emotions rather than punish his misbehaviour. These expert teachers revealed themselves as: 'Optimistic, outreaching, loving personalities interested in children and concerned about their needs, able and happy in relating with them and willing to put in any amount of time and effort necessary to make a success of this' (Rollett, 2001: 37–8). Furthermore, the expert teachers had a firm picture of what they wanted the individual learners to achieve academically and in social and personal growth. They were convinced that it was important to give the children the time needed to achieve these things, even when this meant departing from the prescribed curriculum.

One of the key differences between expert and novice teachers is that the former often attribute educational failure to the nature of instruction provided while novice teachers cite causes such as the pupils' home background or lack of concentration (Galton, 2001). In fact, research by Hattie (2003) shows that children's abilities are the most important variance (50 per cent) in their achievement, compared to what teachers do (30 per cent), the influence of home (5–10 per cent), school (5–10 per cent) and peers (5–10 per cent).

---

### BOX 2.2  INTERNATIONAL VIEW – TEACHERS' WELL-BEING

Teachers' self-efficacy, well-being, professionalism and professional development, are all important factors in successful schools. The OECD's Teaching and Learning International Survey (TALIS) provides important international evidence on teachers' beliefs (OECD, 2009). Among the findings, most teachers in northwest European countries, Scandinavia, Australia and Korea see themselves as facilitators of children's active learning. In southern European countries, Brazil and Malaysia, most teachers see themselves as transmitters of knowledge. TALIS reports that around 90 per cent of overall variation in teacher self-efficacy is among teachers *within* schools, suggesting that intervention is needed with individuals rather than whole schools (OECD, 2009). Most teachers work in schools that do not reward effective teachers and do not dismiss those who perform poorly.

There is a danger that teachers' self-efficacy can dip if there is little support from colleagues or managers (Woolfolk *et al.*, 2008). After five or so years in the job, most teachers tend to wane in their levels of commitment and lose the 'urgency to learn' (OECD, 2013), although this can vary considerably within schools (Box 2.2). Without the stimulus of new challenges and possibilities, they can become resigned to a business as usual mentality. This can be compounded when teachers are left out of policy decisions both at school and national level. As Bangs and Frost (2012: 3) put it, 'It is commonly assumed that the quality of what teachers do can be improved by people other than teachers themselves.'

## Stress management

Teachers with low self-efficacy struggle to cope with the stressful demands of teaching when compared to those who have strong self-belief, resilience and commitment. The management of stress has become a key issue in the profession, particularly over the last decade of a results-driven climate (Box 2.3). There are frequent reports of teachers suffering from stress induced by factors such as excessive workload, pupils' poor behaviour or school inspections (Wilson, 2002; Grey, 2005; Garner, 2005; Rothi *et al.*, 2010). In England and Wales, the introduction of the national agreement on workload in schools (2003) is an indicator of how the work–life balance has become a key issue in education. Teachers have a contractual right not to undertake certain tasks, even if requested to do so by management, such as bulk photocopying, collecting money, ICT troubleshooting and putting up classroom displays (Hartney, 2008). In 2005, teachers in England and Wales were allocated guaranteed professional time for planning, preparation and assessment (PPA), amounting to a minimum of 10 per cent of each teacher's timetabled teaching. Similar arrangements exist for teachers in maintained schools in Scotland and Northern Ireland.

Surveys often reveal that stress is a major factor in accounting for the number of teachers leaving the profession. For instance, according to a poll of 800 teachers by the National Association of Schoolmasters Union of Women Teachers (NASUWT), job satisfaction levels are falling as workload and stress increase (*The Herald*, 9 May 2013). Seven in ten teachers say that they do 'all-nighters' to prepare lessons and they typically clock up 48.3 hours a week (Gardner, 2012). There are also difficulties in recruitment that schools and

---

### BOX 2.3  KEY CONCEPT – TEACHER STRESS

The Health and Safety Executive's definition noted on its website is that stress occurs 'when the demands placed upon a person exceed the capacity to cope with them'. The concept of stress is not straightforward. Teachers and trainees require sufficient pressure to encourage them to perform creatively but excessive pressure can lead to a distressed state. Moreover, people react in different ways to pressure: one teacher may respond to a demand as a stimulus while another might see it as a source of distress.

teacher training providers face in many parts of the United Kingdom. That said, Sir Michael Wilshaw, OFSTED's chief inspector of schools, has suggested that teachers need to 'roll up their sleeves and get on with improving their schools, even in the most difficult of circumstances' (Shepherd, 2012).

Stress is clearly relative. All teachers may experience stress in their work and most are able to cope successfully with it. However, a few can experience burnout as the endpoint of chronic stress. As Figure 2.3 illustrates, when there are many demands on teachers, anxiety and other problems arise. But reasonable demands can initially spur on performance.

The concept of 'optimum stress' occupies the space between the boredom and under-stimulation of too little stress and the excessive burdens brought on by too much stress. Stress can be positive when the task is motivating and achievable.

Studies of trainee teachers' stress have tended to focus on the teaching practice placement, overlooking other causes such as: the stress brought on by assignment overload, not getting on with a roommate, homesickness, financial worries and a family crisis (Miller and Fraser, 2000). In the case of outstanding trainees and teachers, there is a danger that their talents and energies are exploited with the ultimate fear of burnout. Moreover, some teachers are very reluctant to accept advice on how to relax, seeing this as personal criticism of not being in control. Given the concerns about stress levels within the profession, there is clearly a need for initial teacher training courses to include guidance on the management of stress. Although demanding, it is important to see stress as a natural product of the school environment and modern society at large.

Teachers can benefit from expert advice on many aspects of stress management, for instance provided through trade unions and the Teacher Support Network (which has branches for England, Scotland and Wales). This includes the opportunity for teachers to communicate with professional coaches via email about any issue affecting their well-being.

Excessive stress brings huge social, health and economic costs to society. It is not surprising therefore that the anti-stress industry is flourishing. There are thousands of

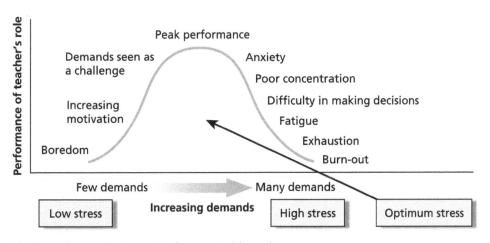

**FIGURE 2.3** Relationship between performance and demands

Source: After Paisy, 1983

websites containing 'stress-busting' advice, most of which revolves around common-sense pointers:

- keep active;
- take control;
- speak to others;
- set challenging goals;
- eat and sleep well;
- set aside personal and family time;
- be positive; and
- accept limitations.

One of the basic points to remember is that there are factors that teachers can control and others that they cannot.

The locus of control concept is attributed to Julian Rotter (1966) who based his work on Bandura's social learning theory. Individuals with an internal locus of control assume that they are personally responsible for what happens to them. Those people with an external locus of control believe that their behaviour depends more on luck, or the actions of others. Although dated, studies indicate that teachers with a belief in an external locus of control report more stress and may be more stress-prone (Kyriacou and Sutcliffe, 1979; McIntyre, 1984). Observable behaviours are either reinforced through reward or extinguished through punishment. Specific indicators have been developed for teachers and have been shown to predict their classroom behaviour. An example from the Rose and Medway (1981: 189) scale for elementary teachers is as follows:

> If the students in your class become disruptive and noisy when you left them alone in the room for five minutes, would this happen (a) because you didn't leave them interesting work to do while you were gone, or (b) because the students were more noisy that day than they usually are?

Research indicates a strong relationship between those who have internal locus of control (demonstrated by answering (a) in the above example) and children's positive outcomes.

## Time management

A particular cause of stress relates to emotional exhaustion tied to time pressures. Many teachers can equate with the scenario of having to prepare for teaching in the evenings and weekends, and having a hectic school day with little time for rest and recovery. Culture shapes attitudes towards time. According to the National Health Service website, Britons work the longest hours in Europe. Western society places a high value on speed: fast food, fast cars, fast Internet connections, speed-reading, speed-dating, power-walking – all have their followers. Education is not immune from the view that faster is better: fast-track training schemes, books for babies, 'hothouse' schemes, accelerated learning.

But there are also counter-reactionary forces at work. The Slow Movement, which began in 1989 as a protest against the opening of Italy's first MacDonald's, has expanded its interests from food to gardening, travel, education and even Slow Sex. The aim is to counter the rush and hurly-burly of the modern, materialistic age. As Honoré (2005) notes, the physical, mental, emotional and social benefits of slowing down can lead to more productive, fulfilling lives. The standards-driven educational system has been likened to a fast-food outlet, 'where packages of test-shaped knowledge are swallowed, but never properly digested' (cited by Barker, 2012). Slow education rests on the principles of nurturing creativity, enquiry-based learning and children progressing at their own pace. There are strong parallels with Steiner and Montessori schools where education is viewed as a journey rather than a race. 'Slow readers' was once a label to describe children with special educational needs. Slow reading is now an approach used in some American schools where children are encouraged to deepen their knowledge of texts using old-fashioned techniques such as reading aloud, memorizing and savouring passages, and annotating pages (Miedema, 2009). There is growing research evidence to suggest that children learn better at a slower pace. Hirsch-Pasek and Golinkoff (2003) have shown that young children develop more rounded personalities when they learn in a more relaxed, less regimented and less hurried way.

Trainee and qualified teachers often suffer from time 'poverty' – simply too much to do in the time available. Rechtschaffen (1996) refers to the concept of 'trickle down' in which most people place work first in their lives, followed by our families, then everyday chores, social life and finally whatever time is left over is given to ourselves. This is an important point for outstanding practitioners to take on board because there is a tendency for them to spend an inordinate amount of time devoted to teaching.

The only effective way of making greater use of time is first to analyse how the existing time is being used and then to consider ways of redistributing the time more efficiently. It is possible to review personally whether one is good at controlling time by answering the four questions set out in Box 2.4.

A negative response to any of these questions is said to indicate the need to rethink personal time management. It makes sense to prioritize tasks, sorting out those that require immediate attention from those that can wait until tomorrow or a few days hence.

## Establishing priorities

The abilities to prioritize and delegate are important in the repertoire of good teachers. Holmes (1999) provides guidance for newly qualified teachers on how to manage their

---

**BOX 2.4  HOW GOOD ARE YOU AT TIME MANAGEMENT SKILLS?**

| | | | |
|---|---|---|---|
| 1 | Do you have time to do what you would like to? | Yes | No |
| 2 | Do you feel there is enough time in the day? | Yes | No |
| 3 | Have you ever thought about the way you use your time? | Yes | No |
| 4 | Are you happy about the way you allocate your time? | Yes | No |

(www.channel4.com/health/microsites/0–9/4health/stress/tsg_step5.html)

time in preparation and planning. For example, teachers are encouraged to consider their 'natural' rhythms through the day, week, term and year. It is counter-productive to try and work at the same pace through the day or week. So if someone suffers a dip around 4.00 p.m. it makes sense to slow down. Each individual has an optimum level of working effectively and the key is to know what this is. Working in line with one's own biological clock is not straightforward for a teacher. But it is important to recognize personal 'prime time' – when someone feels most alert – to undertake the most thought-demanding tasks. Box 2.5 gives some pointers to help establish priorities.

Foster (2000), an expert on time management, suggests recording priority tasks using a simple A, B, C system as follows:

A = immediate attention

B = attention in the near future

C = non-essential or non-urgent items.

The ABC list should be reviewed on a daily basis. Once an A task is completed, a B task moves up to take its place. When a B task is completed, a C task also moves up the list to become a B. Following this approach, the ABC list keeps track of tasks and their relative

---

### BOX 2.5 ESTABLISHING PRIORITIES

- Ask questions such as: 'Is this necessary?', 'Can this wait?', 'How important is this?', 'What may be the impact if this isn't done today?'
- Classify tasks according to low, moderate and high priority.
- Consider workload in terms of short-, medium- and long-term goals.
- Make a 'to do' list – checklists can give a sense of control over work as tasks are ticked off.

---

### BOX 2.6 REAL-LIFE LEARNING CHALLENGE

You are a trainee teacher about to complete your final placement experience. The tutor and school have informed you that you have made good progress and they are impressed with your teaching. However, you are feeling anxious because the head teacher will observe your lesson along with an external assessor tomorrow, which is their only opportunity. The lesson is introducing decimal fractions to Year 5, which you are dreading because you lack knowledge and confidence in the subject. You have a friend who taught this lesson last week and she had good feedback – she has offered her lesson plan. You also need to update your lesson evaluations from earlier in the week and mark some work from yesterday. Meanwhile, your young son has a cold and may have to miss school tomorrow while your eldest daughter has complained that she is being bullied in school. You are a single parent. What are your priorities?

urgency. It is also possible to move a B or C task to an A if, for example, an unexpected turn of events means a formerly non-urgent task suddenly takes on greater importance. All teachers face the challenge of prioritizing workload. This is particularly so when teachers assume managerial as well as teaching responsibilities and face personal obligations (see Box 2.6). Senior leaders need to establish a culture where staff agree upon, work towards and review shared priorities.

## Developing teachers' Habits of Mind

The importance of teachers' personalities in the classroom and how they approach their work has long been recognized. The famous American philosopher John Dewey (1910: 47–8) pointed out: 'the influence of the teacher's personality is intimately fused with that of the subject; the child does not separate.' He added that most people are either unaware of or take for granted their own mental habits and yet: 'A teacher's best conscious efforts may be more than counteracted by the influence of personal traits, which he is unaware of or regards as unimportant.'

For many years there have been calls for teacher education programmes to include a stronger focus on **professional dispositions**, in addition to subject knowledge and practical skills (Katz and Raths,1985; Dottin, 2010). This has arisen in the context of huge social and technological changes in society where the role of the teacher has been recast. Teachers are now widely considered to be **facilitators** in the Google Age rather than gurus of knowledge.

To be successful, they will need to develop a frame of mind that moves them to, as a matter of routine:

- retrieve, sift and synthesize existing knowledge;
- receive, explore and create ideas with pupils;
- respond flexibly to new situations;
- model learning and good manners;
- communicate (listen, speak, read and write) effectively;
- demonstrate compassion, hope and belief in others; and
- inspire learners to do their best.

Researchers have been examining the relationship between teacher dispositions and pupils' achievement over several decades, albeit under different names; perceptions (Combs *et al.*, 1974), professional characteristics (McBer, 2000); Habits of Mind (Costa and Kallick, 2000a), thinking dispositions (Ritchhart, 2001), dispositions of character (Sockett, 2006), 'synergies' (MacDonald and Shirley, 2009); and 'habits of highly effective teachers' (Turnbull, 2013).

These models share common elements, such as the need for teachers to demonstrate open-mindedness (Table 2.1). MacDonald and Shirley (2009) consider this to be the first and most important 'synergy', or potential resource, because learners often fall prey to ingrained habitual modes of behaviour and belief that prevent them from growing. They cite the example of a commonly held belief that it is wrong for teachers to shout at children

**TABLE 2.1** Dispositions and Habits of Mind

| Dispositions of character (Sockett, 2006) | Professional characteristics (McBer, 2000) | Habits of Mind (Costa and Kallick, 2008) | Thinking dispositions (Ritchhart, 2002) | Habits (Turnbull, 2013) | Synergies (MacDonald and Shirley, 2009) |
|---|---|---|---|---|---|
| ■ Persistence<br>■ Trustworthiness<br>■ Integrity<br>■ Wisdom<br>■ Courage<br>■ Justice<br>■ Temperance<br>■ Self-knowledge | Professionalism<br>■ Confidence<br>■ Creating trust<br>■ Respect for others<br><br>Planning and setting expectations<br>■ Drive for improvement<br>■ Information seeking<br>■ Initiative<br><br>Thinking<br>■ Analytical thinking<br>■ Conceptual thinking<br><br>Relating to others<br>■ Impact and influence<br>■ Team working<br>■ Understanding others<br><br>Leading<br>■ Flexibility<br>■ Holding people accountable | ■ Persisting<br>■ Managing impulsivity<br>■ Listening and understanding with empathy<br>■ Thinking flexibly<br>■ Thinking about your thinking<br>■ Striving for accuracy and precision<br>■ Questioning and problem posing<br>■ Applying past knowledge to new situations<br>■ Thinking and communicating with clarity and precision<br>■ Gather data through all senses<br>■ Creating, imagining, innovating<br>■ Responding with awe and wonder<br>■ Taking responsible risks<br>■ Finding humour<br>■ Thinking interdependently<br>■ Remaining open to continuous learning | Creative thinking:<br>Looking out, up, around and about<br><br>Reflective thinking:<br>Looking within<br><br>Critical thinking:<br>Looking at, through and in between | Managing yourself<br>■ Thinking for yourself<br>■ Learning for life<br>■ Taking action on stress<br>■ Taking your time<br><br>Engaging with others<br>■ Creating rapport<br>■ Attentive listening<br>■ Influencing behaviour<br><br>Spreading the influence<br>■ Influencing leadership behaviours<br>■ Extending the influence | ■ Open-mindedness<br>■ Loving and caring<br>■ Stopping<br>■ Professional expertise<br>■ Authentic alignment<br>■ Integrative and harmonizing<br>■ Collective responsibility |

Sources: Socket (2006); McBer (2000); Costa and Kallick (2008); Ritchhart (2002); Turnbull (2013); MacDonald and Shirley (2009)

and support parents who are authoritarian. Findings from among African American students reveal that they would rather have teachers who hold them to high standards, even if this involves some yelling for emphasis, than teachers who are apathetic and disengaged. They add that in dangerous inner cities, authoritarian styles of parenting can be more predictive of student success because there is a small margin for error.

Teacher dispositions are habitual, enduring ways of working towards more thoughtful, intelligent teaching. Costa and Kallick's 16 Habits of Mind are based on how 'peak performers' behave when confronted with problems in all walks of life: scientists, doctors, engineers, entrepreneurs, artists and educators. These dispositions should not be seen as one-off behaviours.

According to the McBer (2000: 9) report on teacher effectiveness: 'Outstanding teachers create an excellent classroom climate and achieve superior pupil progress largely by displaying more professional characteristics at higher levels of sophistication within a very structured learning environment.' Studies of the world's best-performing educational systems show that high quality teacher education programmes underpin them, where students confront their own deep-seated beliefs and assumptions about learning and teaching (Darling-Hammond and Lieberman, 2012). For example, the Singaporean model of teacher education includes a strong focus on cultivating teachers' 'thinking dispositions' (e.g. enquiring nature, striving to improve, resilience, quest for learning) as part of their professional identity (National Institute of Education, 2009). The notion of thinking dispositions draws on the work of Ritchhart (2001) who wants educational systems to focus more on developing Habits of Mind that students will need in their lifetimes, rather than transient skills and knowledge.

Since the early 2000s, all American teacher education providers are required to develop and assess pre-service (trainee) teachers' professional dispositions. As a consequence, interest in teacher dispositions has increased considerably (LeBlanc and Gallavan, 2009). America's National Council for Accreditation of Teacher Education (NCATE) highlights two key dispositions, namely: fairness and the belief all students can learn (NCATE, 2008). On the surface these seem straightforward. However, concerns have been expressed about ideological drivers and practical matters such as how to determine the 'dispositional fit' (Wasicsko, 2007) for a career in teaching. Most American universities have responded by using multiple measures such as self-assessments, classroom observations, questionnaires, reflections and scenario-based tasks. Some distinguish between professional behaviour, such as time-keeping, and observable behaviours (dispositions), which shed light on teacher beliefs about learning and teaching.

The principle of setting out what pre-service teachers should believe and how they should behave has also proved controversial in the land of freedom. In one case, a student wrote a paper for his classroom management course advocating the use of corporal punishment. His college tried to remove him from their teacher education programme, citing differences between his personal beliefs and the programme aims. The state Court of Appeals ruled that this decision violated the student's due process rights, and he was reinstated into the programme (Wilkerson, 2006).

In the UK, teacher education providers are required to promote professional values, as discussed in Chapter 3. But teacher dispositions have not featured strongly in government policies although the Scottish Standards for Registration acknowledges: 'the educational experiences of all our learners are shaped by the values, skills and dispositions of all those who work to educate them' (GTC Scotland, 2012: 5). In England, teacher education providers have the option to assess non-cognitive attributes as part of their selection procedures using recommended assessments (National College for Teaching and Leadership, 2013). These are effectively personality tests designed to gauge applicants' abilities to keep emotions in check, manage time, relate to others and handle pressure.

## Dispositions and other aspects of learning

The metaphor of a car can be used to illustrate the relationship between teachers' dispositions (the engine) and knowledge, skills, attitudes and concepts (wheels). Knowledge includes what teachers know about themselves (self-knowledge), specific subjects, child development and learning theories, as well as general knowledge (facts relating to 'who', 'what' and 'when'). Knowledge is often provisional and contentious. Hence teachers also need to acquire the 'how' and 'why' aspects of knowing. In a narrow sense, skills are abilities to perform tasks. But they can also extend to the sensitive handling of another person's feelings and thinking strategies. Skills can be specific (e.g. using a microscope) or more general (e.g. to observe patterns). Beliefs (religious and secular) are convictions that individuals hold to be true, whether they are in reality or not. Attitudes describe how people respond to others, objects or situations, shaped by their thoughts and feelings. They are the 'overt expressions of values and personal qualities' (DES, 1985: 41). According to Katz and Raths (1985), dispositions differ from attitudes in that dispositions form 'a summary of actions observed' whereas attitudes are 'pre-dispositions to act'. Finally, concepts are general ideas derived from a process of abstraction. They enable individuals to organize knowledge and experience. Concepts can be classified as follows: spatial (location), temporal (time), quantity (number), quality (description), and social–emotional (feelings). The efficient performance of the car is dependent upon each tyre's conditions. But it is also controlled by the driver's track record (professional development), self-awareness and beliefs about the road ahead, speeding regulations, along with driving conditions generally (external environment). Dispositions, represented by the car engine, empower teachers to move forward (Figure 2.4).

When teachers are at the peak of their performance they are demonstrating Costa and Kallick's Habits of Mind each day of their lives. For instance, persistence is needed for teachers to continue each day so that they achieve their objectives. A persistent teacher may try many strategies to teach a new concept or skill and not give up if pupils do not 'get it' right away. Similarly, a persistent teacher might persevere with a conflict resolution approach to managing challenging situations, with the knowledge that pupils need time to learn and internalize these strategies.

### PAUSE FOR REFLECTION

Think further about the car metaphor. How might the driver exercise Habits of Mind in these scenarios: (a) if the car breaks down late at night on an isolated road; (b) in the middle of a traffic jam heading for an urgent appointment; (c) when driving abroad.

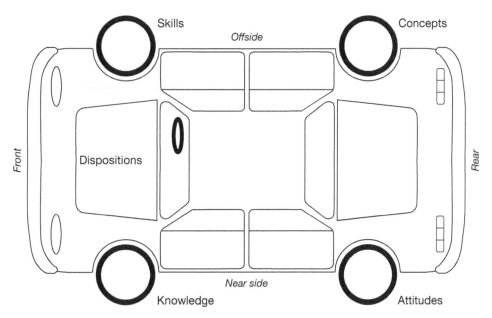

**FIGURE 2.4** Relationship between dispositions, knowledge, attitudes and skills

Traditional schooling has focused on what children know, whereas the Habits of Mind approach is interested in *how* children respond when they don't know answers. There are many opportunities for teachers to model each habit of mind and teach them across the curriculum (Costa and Kallick, 2009). For example, the habit of striving for accuracy can be promoted through these examples taken from the National Curriculum for England:

- use the first two or three letters of a word to check its spelling in a dictionary (Years 3–4, English);
- summarising the main ideas drawn from more than one paragraph (years 5–6, English);
- read, write and interpret mathematical statements involving addition (+), subtraction (−) and equals (=) signs (Year 1, mathematics);
- read relevant scales to the nearest numbered unit (Year 2, mathematics);
- using results to draw simple conclusions and suggest improvements (Years 3–4, science);
- name and locate counties and cities of the United Kingdom (Key Stage 2, geography); and
- write and test simple programs (Key Stage 1, computing)

(DfE, 2013)

Table 2.2 shows examples of how teachers can apply Habits of Mind, but these are not exhaustive. Moreover, it is not a tick-box exercise of whether teachers use Habits of

**TABLE 2.2** Applying Habits of Mind

| Habit of Mind and further cues | Examples of application |
|---|---|
| Persisting<br>■ Keep going<br>■ Never give up<br>■ Endure | ■ Try out different teaching or behaviour management strategies<br>■ Understanding what makes an individual child 'tick' |
| Managing impulsivity<br>■ Think before you act<br>■ Meditate<br>■ Self-regulate<br>■ Reflect<br>■ Count to 10<br>■ Stay calm<br>■ Take a deep breadth<br>■ Consider | ■ Gain all facts before responding to behaviour incidents<br>■ Increase use of wait time when responding to children's answers<br>■ Use of timers for starters, transitions and plenaries in lessons |
| Listening and understanding with empathy<br>■ Tune in<br>■ Concentrate<br>■ Focus<br>■ Attentive | ■ Effective use of summaries<br>■ Reducing teacher talk and increasing opportunities for pupils to speak<br>■ Setting listening exercises and games<br>■ Devising, displaying and discussing 'good listener' poster<br>■ Identifying barriers to effective listening and how these can be addressed |
| Thinking flexibly<br>■ Adapt<br>■ Consider options<br>■ Change<br>■ Lateral thinking<br>■ Alternatives<br>■ Expand | ■ Ask 'What if . . .? questions<br>■ Seek the views of others (colleagues, parents, learners)<br>■ Use SCAMPER technique (substitute, combine, adapt, modify, put to other uses, eliminate, reverse)<br>■ Explore historical interpretations<br>■ Use of 'revisionist' stories with alternative endings, e.g. *True Story of the Three Little Pigs* |
| Thinking about your thinking<br>■ Self-aware<br>■ Think aloud<br>■ Talk to yourself<br>■ Self-monitor<br>■ Self-evaluate<br>■ Inner thoughts | ■ Use concept maps, thinking maps, thinking routines, doodles, graphic organisers<br>■ Film and reflect on personal teaching style and approaches<br>■ Complete reflective journals<br>■ Model talking through problems |
| Striving for accuracy and precision<br>■ Spot on<br>■ Correct<br>■ Exact<br>■ Finished<br>■ Check and double check<br>■ Quality control | ■ Set timed targets for pupils – try to beat personal bests<br>■ Model proof reading<br>■ Use strategies such as 'three before me' – pupils hand in work only after it has been checked three times by other pupils |

**TABLE 2.2** *continued*

| Habit of Mind and further cues | Examples of application |
|---|---|
| **Questioning and problem posing**<br>■ Probe<br>■ Investigate<br>■ Inquiry<br>■ Explore<br>■ Sceptical<br>■ Doubt<br>■ Proof<br>■ Hypothesize | ■ Asking a range of purposeful questions<br>■ Setting challenges for individuals, groups, whole class, whole school and community<br>■ Undertaking real-life projects |
| **Applying past knowledge to new situations**<br>■ Recycle<br>■ Re-use<br>■ Reminders<br>■ Recall<br>■ Apply<br>■ Transfer<br>■ Use again<br>■ Just like the time when . . . | ■ Set key questions at the start of projects<br>■ Draw on and display prior knowledge using KWL (what we already know, would like to learn and have learned) grids<br>■ Use comparing and contrasting techniques |
| **Thinking and communicating with clarity and precision**<br>■ Define<br>■ Explain<br>■ Choose words<br>■ Grammatically correct<br>■ Articulate<br>■ Draft<br>■ Edit | ■ Challenge vague terms and over-generalisations in pupils' language e.g. 'Everybody has one' (everybody?)<br>■ Model provisional language in lessons e.g. 'Some people believe. . .'<br>■ Model use of dictionaries, thesaurus, reference works<br>■ Share etymology of words<br>■ Explore accuracy in sport, music and the arts<br>■ Practice speaking aloud, debates<br>■ Model writing poems, letters, emails, summaries, reports<br>■ Do crosswords, anagrams<br>■ Set word challenges e.g. how many words can you make from . . . e.g. 'Liverpool'? |
| **Gather data through all senses**<br>■ Feelings<br>■ Senses<br>■ Hands-on<br>■ Engage<br>■ Move<br>■ Experience | ■ Explore sweet, sour, salty and bitter tastes<br>■ Create nature areas indoors and outdoors<br>■ Heighten sense of touch through exercises where children close eyes and explore textures<br>■ Play sight games to develop scanning skills<br>■ Provide fragrances such as perfume, cinnamon, cloves and eucalyptus.<br>■ Use music, animals, art work, cookery and other sensory stimuli |
| **Creating, imagining, innovating**<br>■ Generate<br>■ Brainstorm<br>■ Imagine<br>■ New<br>■ Novel<br>■ Fresh<br>■ Unusual<br>■ Artistic<br>■ Innovative | ■ Use metaphors and analogies<br>■ Use audio-visual cues<br>■ Use mind maps and thinking routines |

**TABLE 2.2** *continued*

| Habit of Mind and further cues | Examples of application |
| --- | --- |
| **Responding with awe and wonder**<br>■ Wow!<br>■ Amazing<br>■ Awesome<br>■ Excited<br>■ Mysterious<br>■ Miracle<br>■ Surprise<br>■ Starry-eyed | ■ Set up dramatic experiments<br>■ Use You Tube and other facilities to show the awesome impact of the weather and nature<br>■ Celebrate human achievement using *Guinness Book of Records* and other resources<br>■ Discuss miracle of human birth<br>■ Build on children's personal interests and allow them to share regularly<br>■ Research weird and wonderful animals, people and places in the world |
| **Taking responsible risks**<br>■ Bold<br>■ Adventurous<br>■ Have a go<br>■ Live on the edge<br>■ Ice-breaker | ■ Research the lives of great explorers and risk-takers e.g. Nelson Mandela, Galileo, Columbus<br>■ Read stories of women pioneers in fields such as medicine, politics, business and sport<br>■ Plan outdoor adventure opportunities |
| **Finding humour**<br>■ Hilarious<br>■ Pun, riddle, joke<br>■ Irony<br>■ Playful<br>■ Comedy<br>■ Laugh at yourself<br>■ Cartoon | ■ Tell a joke a day<br>■ Explore humour in cartoons and comics<br>■ Smile more often<br>■ Ask children to find their favourite jokes and publish a school joke book<br>■ Participate in Comic Relief and other charities |
| **Thinking interdependently**<br>■ Cooperate<br>■ Teamwork<br>■ Support each other<br>■ Community spirit | ■ Set purposeful group activities where learners focus on teamwork as well as content<br>■ Make links with community and global projects |
| **Open to continuous learning**<br>■ Lifelong learning<br>■ Inquisitive<br>■ Self-help<br>■ Insatiable<br>■ Mastery<br>■ Committed<br>■ Forward-looking | ■ Discuss personal interests, hobbies and challenges e.g. learning a language<br>■ Research inspirational figures who continue to learn despite barriers of age, disability or finance |

Mind but how *well* they use them. So how does one become better at demonstrating Habits of Mind? Costa and Kallick (2000b) provide a framework and strategies to collect evidence for pupils' progress, such as portfolios, journals and self-evaluation rubrics or checklists. For instance, for 'Listening with Understanding and Empathy' pupils consider 'How Am I Doing?' and note the frequency (often, sometimes, not yet) of their behaviours (e.g. faces the person who is speaking) as they work along a continuum from novice to expert. Further research is needed on how Habits of Mind might be developed with trainee and serving teachers in the UK.

Habits of Mind are never fully mastered. But for outstanding teachers they become routine, automatic and spontaneous. This is particularly manifested when faced with new challenges such as the arrival of a new child in the class, planning a field visit or trying to encourage parents to take an interest in their children's school life.

## Mindsets and intelligence

The phrase Habits of Mind is important because it links actions and thought. The models outlined in Table 2.1 are all underpinned by the belief that intelligence is not fixed, comes in different forms and can be taught (Gardner, 1983; Goleman, 1996, 2007). Based on research over several decades, Carol Dweck (2006) shows that success in school and life generally is partly dependent upon holding the right mindset. Those with a 'fixed mindset' want to appear to be smart. They care more about how others perceive their intelligence, rather than a real desire to learn. Those who believe they can learn through effort and education have a 'growth mindset'. They respond readily to challenges and learn from mistakes. Having a growth mindset improves the capacity to learn. Dweck believes that mindset change is not about picking up a few pointers but seeing things in a different way, namely by moving from a 'judge-and-be-judged' to a 'learn-and-help-learn' framework.

Table 2.3 summarizes the differences between fixed and growth mindsets. It is worth noting that teachers and pupils can demonstrate a fixed mindset in one area, such as learning or teaching mathematics, and a growth mindset in another. Those teachers who demonstrate fixed mindsets do not necessarily see teaching in negative terms. But they are less willing to take risks with lessons (especially when observed) and generally undervalue their potential role as agents of change.

Over the past decade or so positive psychology has developed in response to concern that not enough attention is paid to nurturing talent and overcoming negative thinking. It is based on the principle that humans are inherently good and have a desire to achieve their creative potential. The father of modern positive psychology is Professor Martin

### PAUSE FOR REFLECTION

Think about your mindset in relation to teaching. Where would you presently locate yourself and which areas do you think you need to develop?

**TABLE 2.3** Fixed and growth mindsets in relation to teaching

| Characteristics | Fixed mindset | Growth mindset |
| --- | --- | --- |
| Beliefs | See outstanding teaching as limited to a naturally gifted few | See outstanding teaching as within grasp of all through application and learning |
| Inclination | To do enough to get by or appear capable | To strive to improve teaching |
| Risks | Avoided because they bring potential failure | Embraced because of the potential learning gains |
| Response to setbacks | Seen as permanent and a reason to give up | Seen as temporary and changeable |
| Response to criticisms | Seen as personal failure, tendency to blame others | Accepting, inquisitive, eager to learn more and how improvements could be secured |
| Views on success of colleagues | Treated with apathy, jealousy, contempt, ridicule, 'yes but . . .' attitude | Applauded and seen as a source for potential inspiration |
| Views on reading, assignments and professional development | Seen as necessary to meet expectations, but tendency to leave until last minute | Seen as opportunities to learn new ideas, exchange experiences and stimulate further growth |
| Workload | Never enough time, too high a workload | Seeks to improve time management |

**EXTEND YOUR UNDERSTANDING**

Watch the TED talk by Professor Martin Seligman on how positive psychology is more than building optimism. What, if any, are the implications for educators? www.ted.com/talks/martin_seligman_on_the_state_of_psychology.html

Seligman whose career has focused on making the lives of ordinary people more fulfilling. Seligman and his colleagues believe that pupils should be taught skills for happiness because of the worldwide prevalence of depression among young people.

Seligman introduced the concept of 'explanatory style' after analysing how people reacted differently to the same event (Table 2.4).

According to Seligman (2006), when something negative occurs, individuals either place a temporary or a permanent frame around the event. A teacher might say 'this lesson was awful and I can't teach this subject again'. On the other hand, a teacher might respond along the lines: 'I'm teaching the same lesson next week and so I can put these aspects right.' When faced with a positive experience, pessimists tend to minimize the good and say it is temporary, whereas the optimistic teacher seeks to build on the success and place this within a more permanent frame. One of the key implications of Seligman's research is the need for teachers and learners to use positive language in their everyday interactions.

**TABLE 2.4** Pessimistic and optimistic responses to situations

| Element | Questions | Pessimist response | Optimist response |
|---|---|---|---|
| Permanence (stable) | Is it permanent or temporary? | Good events are seen as infrequent and bad events as lasting | Good events are seen as likely to recur and bad events only temporary |
| Pervasiveness (global) | Is it 'specific' or 'universal'? | Bad events are seen as typical of their lives while good events limited in scope | Bad events are seen as specific to the situation while good events are seen as positive |
| Personalisation (internal) | Did I cause this to happen? | Bad events are taken personally while good news attributed to the hard work of others or factors beyond their control | Bad events may be explained by factors beyond their control or ill luck |

By using optimistic self-talk, teachers can model resilience when approaching and responding to challenges.

This chapter has introduced the importance of teacher well-being. How teachers see themselves is central to discussion over improving the performance of both teachers and pupils. A teacher with strong self-belief is likely to be resilient, able to solve problems and, above all, learn from their experience.

## Glossary

**Critical incidents** are experiences that have particular meaning to individuals – these could represent career turning points.

**Facilitators** are teachers or practitioners who guide and assist the development of young children, based on a social constructivist view of learning.

**Flow** describes a short-term peak experience at work characterized by absorption, concentration and focused motivation (Csikszentmihalyi, 1997).

**Professional dispositions** are values, beliefs and inclinations that determine how teachers behave and interact with others.

## References

Babiuk, G.E. (2007) 'Full bag of technology tools enhances the reflective process in teacher education', Conference Proceedings, WestCAST 2007, University of Manitoba.

Bain, J.D., Mills, C., Ballantyne, R. and Packer, J. (2002) 'Developing reflection on practice through journal writing: Impacts of variations in the focus and level of feedback', *Teachers and Teaching: Theory and Practice*, 8: 171–96.

Bandura, A. (1986) *Social Foundations of Thought and Action: A Social Cognitive Theory*, Englewood Cliffs, NJ: Prentice-Hall.

Bangs, J. and Frost, D. (2012) *Teacher Self-Efficacy, Voice and Leadership: Towards a Policy Framework for Education International*, Cambridge: Education International Research Institute.

Barker, I. (2012) 'Find the time for slow education', *Times Education Supplement*, 2 November.

Biggs, J. and Tang, C. (2007) *Teaching for Quality Learning at University*, Maidenhead: Open University Press.

Brookfield, S. (1995) *Becoming a Critically Reflective Teacher*, San Francisco, CA: Jossey-Bass.

Carlson, E.N. (2013) 'Overcoming the barriers to self-knowledge: Mindfulness as a path to seeing yourself as you really are', *Perspectives on Psychological Science*, 8(2): 173–86.

Castle, E.B. (1961) *Ancient Education and Today*, Harmondsworth: Penguin.

Combs, A.W., Blume, R.A., Newman, A.J. and Wass, H.L. (1974) *The Professional Education of Teachers: A Humanistic Approach to Teacher Preparation*. Boston, MA: Allyn & Bacon.

Clements, P. and Spinks, T. (1996) *The Equal Opportunities Guide*, London: Kogan Page.

Costa, A.L. and Kallick, B. (eds) (2000a) *Activating and Engaging Habits of Mind*, Alexandria, VA: ASCD.

Costa, A.L. and Kallick, B. (eds) (2000b) *Assessing and Reporting on Habits of Mind*, Alexandria, VA: ASCD.

Costa, A.L. and Kallick, B. (2009) *Habits of Mind Across the Curriculum*, Alexandria, VA: ASCD.

Covey, S. (2004) *The 7 Habits of Highly Effective People*, London: Simon & Schuster.

Cowan, J. and Westwood, J. (2006) 'Collaborative framework to guide the development of teacher reflection and decision making', *Active Learning in Higher Education*, 7(1): 63–71.

Csikszentmihalyi, M. (1997) *Finding Flow: The Psychology of Engagement with Everyday Life*, New York: Basic Books.

Darling-Hammond, L. and Lieberman, A. (eds) (2012) *Teacher Education Around the World*, London: Routledge.

Day, C. and Qing Gu (2010) *The New Lives of Teachers*, London: Routledge.

DES (1985) *The Curriculum from 5 to 16*, London: HMSO.

Dewey, J. (1910) *How We Think*, Lexington, MA: D.C. Heath.

DfE (2013) *The National Curriculum in England*, London: DfE.

Dottin, E.S. (2010) *Dispositions as Habits of Mind*, Lanham, MD: University Press of America.

Dweck, C.S. (2006) *Mind-set: The New Psychology of Success*, New York: Random House.

Flores, A. M. and Day, C. (2006) 'Contexts which shape and reshape new teachers' identities: A multi-perspective study', *Teaching and Teacher Education*, 22: 219–32.

Foster, M. (2000) *Get Everything Done and Still Have Time to Play*, London: Help Yourself.

Galton, M. (2001) 'The missing foundation of teacher education', in Cheng, Y.C. and Tsui, K.T. (eds) *New Teacher Education for the Future: International Perspectives*, Hong Kong: Hong Kong Institute of Education and Kluwer Academic Publishers, 69–88.

Gardner, H. (1983) *Frames of Mind: The Theory of Multiple Intelligences*, New York: Basic Books.

Gardner, T. (2012) '70% of teachers do an "all-nighter" to prepare for lessons', *Daily Mail*, 14 June.

Garner, R. (2005) 'Nearly half of teachers have suffered from mental illness', *The Independent*, 23 March.

Ghaye, T. (2011) *Teaching and Learning Through Reflective Practice*, Abingdon: Routledge.

Goddard, R.D. and Goddard, Y.L. (2001) 'A multilevel analysis of the relationship between teacher and collective efficacy in urban schools', *Teaching and Teacher Education*, 17: 807–18.

Goleman, D. (1996) *Emotional Intelligence: Why It Can Matter More than IQ*, London: Bloomsbury.

Goleman, D. (2007) *Social Intelligence*, London: Arrow Books.

Grey, D. (2005) *Grey's Essential Miscellany for Teachers*, London: Continuum.

GTC Scotland (2012) *The Standards for Registration: Mandatory Requirements for Registration with the General Teaching Council for Scotland* Edinburgh: GTC Scotland.

Hall, M. (2013) 'Teachers are the happiest workers in Britain, says survey', *The Telegraph*, 29 April.

Hartney, E. (2008) *Stress Management for Teachers*, London: Continuum.

Hattie, J. (2003) 'Teachers make a difference: What is the research evidence?', in *Professional Learning and Leadership Development*, NSW DET, 1–17.

Hattie, J. (2012) *Visible Learning for Teachers*, Abingdon: Routledge.

Hirsch-Pasek, K. and Golinkoff, R.M. (2003) *Einstein Never Used Flashcards: How Our Children Learn – and Why they Need to Play More and Memorize Less*, Emmaus, PA: Rodale.

Holden, R. (2005) *Success Intelligence*, London: Hodder and Stoughton.

Holmes, E. (1999) *Handbook for Newly Qualified Teachers*, London: Stationery Office.

Holmes, E. (2005) *Teacher Well-being: Looking After Yourself and Your Career in the Classroom*, London: RoutledgeFalmer.

Honoré, C. (2005) *In Praise of Slow*, London: Orion Books.

Katz, L.G. and Raths, J.D. (1985) 'Dispositions as goals for teacher education', in *Teaching and Teacher Education*, 1(4): 301–7.

Kerry, T. (2008) *How To Be a Brilliant Trainee Teacher*, London: Routledge.

Kyriacou, C. and Sutcliffe, J. (1979) 'A note on teacher stress and locus of control', in *Journal of Occupational Psychology*, 52: 227–8.

LeBlanc, P.R. and Gallavan, N.P. (2009) *Affective Teacher Education: Exploring Connections among Knowledge, Skills and Dispositions*, Plymouth: R&L Education.

Lofthouse, R. and Birmingham, P. (2010) 'The camera in the classroom: Video-recording as a tool for professional development of student teachers', *Tean Journal* 1(2) December, available at: http://bit.ly/tyfJ5M (accessed 28 October 2011).

McBer, H. (2000) *Research into Teacher Effectiveness: A Model of Teacher Effectiveness*, London: DfEE.

MacDonald, E. and Shirley, D. (2009) *The Mindful Teacher*, New York: Columbia University.

McIntyre, T. C. (1984) 'The relationship between locus of control and teacher burnout', *British Journal of Educational Psychology*, 54: 235–8.

Miedema, J. (2009) *Slow Reading*, Los Angeles, CA: Litwin Books.

Miller, D. and Fraser, E. (2000) 'Stress associated with being a student teacher: Opening out the perspective', *Scottish Educational Review*, 32(2): 142–154.

Moon, J. (1999) *Reflection in Learning and Professional Development*, London: Kogan Page.

Morgan, S. (2005) *JobLab: A Study into the Experience of Teaching*, London: TDA.

National College for Teaching and Leadership (2013) *ITT Criteria Supporting Advice*, NCTL, available at: www.gov.uk/government/publications (accessed 9 October 2013).

National Institute of Education (2009) *A Teacher Education Model for the 21st Century*, Singapore: National Institute of Education.

NCATE (2008) *Professional Standards for the Accreditation of Teacher Preparation Institutions*, Washington, DC: NCATE.

OECD (2009) *Creating Effective Teaching and Learning Environments: First Results from TALIS*, Paris: OECD.

OECD (2013) *The Innovative Learning Environments: Learning Leadership*, Paris: OECD.

OFSTED (2013) *The Framework for School Inspection*, London: OFSTED.

Rechtschaffen, S. (1996) *Time Shifting*, London: Rider Books.

Ritchhart, R. (2001) 'From IQ to IC: A dispositional view of intelligence', *Roeper Review.* 23(3): 143–50.

Rodgers, F.R. and Raider-Roth, M.B. (2006) 'Presence in teaching', *Teachers and Teaching: Theory and Practice*, 12(3): 265–87.

Rollett, B.A. (2001) 'How do expert teachers view themselves?' in Banks, F. and Shelton Mayes, A. (eds) *Early Professional Development for Teachers*, London: David Fulton, 27–40.

Rose, J. and Medway, F. (1981) 'Measurement of teachers' beliefs in their control over student outcomes', *Journal of Educational Research*, 14: 185–90.

Ross, A. and Hutchings, M. (2003) *Attracting, Developing and Retaining Effective Teachers in the United Kingdom of Great Britain and Northern Ireland*, London: London Metropolitan University.

Rothi, D., Leavey, G. and Loewenthal, K. (2010) *Teachers' Mental Health: A Study Exploring the Experiences of Teachers with Work-Related Stress and Mental Health Problems*, Birmingham: NASUWT.

Rotter, J.B. (1966) 'Generalised expectancies for internal versus external control of reinforcement', *Psychological Monographs*, 80(1): 1–28.

Seligman, M. (2006) *Learned Optimism: How to Change Your Mind and Your Life*, New York: Vintage Books.

Shepherd, J. (2012) 'Teachers don't know what stress is, says Ofsted chief', *The Guardian*, 10 May.

Skaalvik, E.M. and Skaalvik, S. (2010) 'Teacher self-efficacy and teacher burnout: A study of relations', in *Teaching and Teacher Education*, 26: 1059–69.

Slavin, R.E. (2003) *Educational Psychology*, New York: Pearson.

Sockett, H. (2006) *Teacher Dispositions: Building a Teacher Education Framework of Moral Standards*, New York: American Association of Colleges for Teacher Education.

Turnbull, J. (2013) *9 Habits of Highly Effective Teachers: A Practical Guide to Personal Development*, London: Bloomsbury.

Wasicsko, M.M. (2007) *The National Network for the Study of Educator Dispositions*, available at: www.educatordispositions.org/moodle/moodle/mod/resource/view.php?id=4 (accessed 9 October 2013).

Wilkerson, J. R. (2006) 'Measuring teacher dispositions: Standards-based or morality-based?' available at www.tcrecord.org/Content.asp?ContentID=12493 (accessed 9 October 2013).

Wilson, V. (2002) 'Feeling the Strain: An Overview of the Literature on Teachers' Stress', SCRE Research Report No. 109, Edinburgh: SCRE.

Woolfolk, A., Hughes, M. and Walkup, V. (2008) *Psychology in Education*, Harlow: Pearson.

## Websites

Teacher Support Network provides practical and emotional support to staff in the education sector – www.teacherline.org.uk

The official Habits of Mind website –www.habitsofmind.co.uk/teaching-habits.html

# 3

# Professional values in action

By the end of this chapter you should be able to:

- Understand the concept of professionalism and the core values teachers should hold.
- Explain how the role of the primary teacher has changed over time and the challenges facing teachers in the twenty-first century.
- Understand the legal responsibilities of teachers including child protection.
- Reflect upon how professional values can be demonstrated when working with other professionals, parents and carers.

## Introduction

What is the **role** of the primary teacher in the twenty-first century? An A–Z of roles performed by teachers in a typical day might include: accountant, assessor, child minder, coat finder, coach, comic, community liaison officer, co-ordinator, counsellor, crowd-control officer, diplomat, gardener, guardian angel, inspector, judge, leader, magician, manager, mentor, minister, networker, nurse, researcher, surrogate parent, and technician. These are supplementary to the main role of teaching, motivating and inspiring children to learn.

This multifaceted role has been around for some time (Redl and Wattenberg, 1951; DES, 1967). It evolved from the class teacher system introduced by the nineteenth-century founders of mass public elementary schooling. In those days what mattered most was ensuring that young children were crammed into large classes and drilled efficiently in basic knowledge and skills. It was a factory-style model appropriate for an industrial age. But the dawn of the **Knowledge Age** in the late twentieth century raises fundamental questions about the role of the teacher. Traditionally, education is based on a system in which one teacher provides information to many students. Critics argue that this 'one-for-many' Victorian model needs to shift towards a 'many-for-one' modern system in which the individual learner makes the most of the many information resources available, only one of which is the teacher. This can be seen as a movement from an emphasis on instruction to an emphasis on learning (Betts, 1992). As Gilbert (2010) ponders, through the title of his book, *Why Do I Need a Teacher When I've got Google?* To answer such questions calls for an understanding of what primary teachers should know, do and believe in the twenty-first century. In other words, what does it mean to be a professional teacher? It also requires an appreciation of how the profession has evolved, what lessons can be learned from this and where the profession is heading.

## Defining professionalism

The word 'professional' derives from medieval times when monks declared or 'professed' their vows to God. Since the 1930s sociologists have defined what it means to be professional by identifying certain traits, such as adherence to an ethical code, possessing specialist knowledge and gaining certification. This model is still widely held today. MacBeath (2012), for instance, bases teaching on such criteria as having: theoretical knowledge and skills, professional association, high quality pre-service and professional preparation, authority, self-regulation, work autonomy, a code of conduct and legal recognition. He argues that it is a lack of self-interest or profit motive that, above all, defines what it means to be a teacher (MacBeath, 2012).

The debate about professionalism has been sharpened by the Coalition Government's decision that Qualified Teacher Status (QTS) is no longer required to teach in **academies**, as is already the case with private schools. The argument runs that some of the best teachers are untrained: 'Why should a great local chef not teach cookery? Why should a great local hockey coach not teach PE? How many graduates drift into teaching without a real passion for the job? Conversely, how many people have been put off teaching by the rigid system of QTS?' (Coles, 2013).

Trade unions maintain that this is the thin end of the wedge, which aims to undermine the professional status of teachers: 'The public would be horrified if people were able to practise medicine or law without the appropriate qualifications' (Mulholland, 2012).

These views illustrate long-running dichotomies between theory and practice, university-based and school-based provision, teacher training or teacher education, and whether teaching is best seen as a craft or profession. Michael Gove preferred the term 'craft' rather than profession and focused on the 'how' of teaching more than the 'why' – teaching is learned by acquiring skills 'on the job' along apprenticeship lines. Clearly teachers need to learn practical skills and strategies to motivate pupils. At the heart of the matter is the value placed upon engagement with an academic knowledge base, a professional characteristic associated with university study.

However, if teaching is to be taken as seriously as other professions, such as medicine and law, it needs to be evidence based. In other words, in addition to drawing upon their own personal experiences, teachers need to keep up to speed with what is known about how children think, develop and relate to others. Teachers also have a professional duty to contribute to discussions on teaching and learning. Becoming a teacher means joining a community of professionals whose business is to continually refine their performance in the light of research, individual and collective experience and government policy.

In the light of disappointing UK results in international assessments of 15-year-olds, the political focus over recent times has shifted to what is known about the most effective educational systems, including teacher education programmes. Most commentators draw attention to countries such as Finland, Singapore, Taiwan and Canada as examples where teaching preparation is extensive. In these countries, the theory–practice gap is narrow because teachers are encouraged to undertake on-the-job research, are expected to commit to their own professional development and benefit from a balanced programme of subject knowledge, teaching skills and practical school experience. In short, teacher education is based on 'practical theory' (Musset, 2010).

However, it is also important to note that in such countries teachers are widely respected in society. Teaching is a high-status profession that attracts top graduates. In the UK, teachers have always been caught between high expectations and low status. Hargreaves *et al.* (2006) report that the general public's view of teachers rarely includes indicators of professional status, such as 'expertise', 'qualifications' and 'nature of work'. Whenever there are social or economic problems, ranging from teenage pregnancy to inadequate workplace skills, questions are directed towards teachers. No wonder then that the recruitment and retention of high-calibre teachers is the greatest challenge among teacher educators in the UK. Another key feature of the strongest educational systems is that teacher education is seen along a continuum. In other words, teachers' professional development is clearly mapped out from the time they begin training, through their induction period into the early years of their career.

## The changing role of the primary teacher

Sociologists, educationalists and historians have put forward different models in seeking to understand educational change. Hargreaves (2000) sees the development of the profession in terms of four overlapping ages. He suggests that teachers moved from a pre-professional age (nineteenth and early twentieth centuries) when they acquired technical skills 'on the job' (but lacked professional development), to a more autonomous era beginning in the 1960s, when they were accorded greater status. From the late 1980s, Hargreaves argues that teachers entered what he calls an 'age of the collegiate professional' where they turned to each other for professional learning, direction and mutual support. This was also driven by the need to keep pace with increased knowledge of learning and teaching developments, for instance in technologies and assessment. It was also influenced by recognition that the role of the teacher had extended (rightly or wrongly) in other directions. Teachers were expected to work closely with other professionals in responding to a range of social problems linked to family breakdown, poverty and violence. Growing multicultural diversity over the past 20 or so years has also brought into focus the need for teachers to adapt their teaching approaches to meet the needs of all pupils, if they are to provide a genuinely inclusive learning environment.

Finally, Hargreaves (2000: 167) predicted a postmodern age when 'teacher profession-alism will become diminished or abandoned'. This age is characterized by uncertainty, a time when teachers are pulled in different directions, in different places by different forces. As a consequence, teacher professionalism becomes weakened through erosion of trade union powers, a central curriculum and a gradual lowering of teacher status.

The effect of all this is to return teaching to an amateur, de-professionalized, almost premodern craft, where existing skills and knowledge are passed on practically from expert to novice, but where practice can at best only be reproduced, not improved (Hargreaves, 2000:168).

Hargreaves and Shirley (2009) have since struck a more optimistic note by referring to the *Fourth Way*, which builds on the strengths of each of the previous ages. Drawing on happiness research, they says that teachers need to have purpose, feel empowered and develop positive relationships with colleagues and others. Much of what they say fits within the narrative discussed in Chapter 2. For example, the authors describe the importance of teachers developing qualities such as resilience and 'mindful' teaching practices, such as stopping to allow time for all to reflect and think in the rush of classroom life. The new professionalism is, according to Hargreaves and Shirley, a world based on high-quality teachers, positive teacher associations and lively learning communities.

Further insight into understanding how the profession has evolved can be gained by comparing the everyday experiences of teachers since education was made compulsory in the 1870s. On the basis of a teacher's career lasting for typically 40 or so years, four generations have taught the UK's schoolchildren. As historians will readily confess, labelling ages is a dangerous business. Within each generation, teachers' experiences varied according to factors such as their backgrounds, personalities, where they taught and their relationships. However, with these caveats in mind, Table 3.1 suggests some defining characteristics for each generation.

The first generation (1870s–1914) witnessed the beginnings of the profession marked by the formation of trade unions. It was a disciplined generation where Victorian values of punctuality, obedience, respect and deference shaped what was taught and how people behaved in school. The second generation (*c.* 1914–1950) was heroic in its business-as-usual mentality through two world wars. School log books, diaries and autobiographies suggest that many teachers tried to provide practical support to poor families through the inter-war Depression years. During the chaotic evacuation of children on trains to the countryside in 1939, teachers 'achieved the impossible' by tracking down mislaid evacuees. Some children went missing for two weeks and school parties were split in different parts of the country (Dent, 1944: 19). By 1945, teachers were associated closely with the new welfare state provisions and seen as key agents in providing equality of opportunity through education.

The third generation of teachers (*c.* 1950–1988) enjoyed considerable autonomy in deciding what was taught in class. The contents page of *Exploration in the Junior School* (Philips and McInnes, 1950) summed up the spirit of the age: 'exploring the neighbourhood', 'finding out about everyday things', 'work on the farm', 'social study in a London

**TABLE 3.1** Characteristics of teachers across four generations

| | Generation | Characteristics |
|---|---|---|
| 1 | (1870–1914) | Disciplined |
| 2 | (1914–1950) | Heroic |
| 3 | (1950–1988) | Independent |
| 4 | (1988–) | Accountable |

**PAUSE FOR REFLECTION**

How would you respond to the question raised by former Prime Minister, James Callaghan: 'What do we want from the education of our children and young people?'

area', 'suggestions made by children', 'the teacher as consultant', 'pond-dipping', 'keeping animals'. The emerging mantra was 'Learning how to learn'. This is not to say that this was a golden age for primary schools. In fact, the extent to which discovery methods were adopted in schools during the 1960s is exaggerated (Jones, 2003). The 'secret garden' of teaching was unlocked by the Labour Prime Minister, James Callaghan, when he famously launched a Great Debate in 1976 on the key question: 'What do we want from the education of our children and young people?' Callaghan linked the social and economic problems of the day, including a global oil crisis, to perceived shortcomings in the educational system.

The present generation (since *c.* 1988) has experienced an era of centralized control, beginning with the National Curriculum – more than twenty education acts have been passed in the last 25 years. The cross-party House of Commons committee on school accountability acknowledged that 'the Government has continued to subject schools to a bewildering array of new initiatives' and that schools were in danger of becoming 'overwhelmed' by accountability measures (House of Commons, 2009: 3). Although historically teachers have always been held to account, as public service employees, the present generation has experienced unprecedented accountability. In England, this has included the introduction in 2012 of a fast-track scheme to sack incompetent teachers within 6 months or, in exceptional circumstances, four weeks.

Since the 1988 Education Act, teachers have generally been regarded with suspicion and not to be trusted – they are either too radical or stubborn in refusing to move with the times. Ball (2008) points out that the media, led by the *Daily Mail*, is generally quick to blame teachers and its influence on government policy cannot be ignored. The teacher reform agenda has gathered pace through calls for performance management systems to become more rigorous and, particularly in England, the undermining of university-based teacher training. Trade unions are also concerned that a 'surveillance culture' is developing in school. In one poll of 1,000 Welsh teachers, a third said they are being observed more frequently than ever before (Evans, 2012a). In 2012 the Coalition Government removed the limit of three hours formal observation of teachers (by heads) to allow schools greater flexibility in deciding what is appropriate. However, critics see this as a blunt tool to attack teachers rather than as a support mechanism.

Teachers still retain autonomy in areas such as teaching methods and, to a certain extent, curriculum content and assessment. However teachers in England have not enjoyed the professional autonomy of colleagues elsewhere in the UK and across Europe (Eurydice, 2008). Moreover, some education commentators point to the experiences of teachers in academies and free schools where the 'no excuses', results-driven culture applies to staff as well as children. Right-wing think tanks such as the Institute of Economic Affairs have lobbied the government to base education on a strong business model (Benn, 2011).

A first-generation teacher visiting a twenty-first century school would empathize with the pressures associated with meeting the demands of the National Curriculum, truancy, securing examination passes, short-notice inspections, engaging with parents, trying to establish a team spirit among colleagues and the pressures of financial management. Inside the classroom, the Victorian teacher would immediately recognize spelling tests, whole-class lessons framed around three parts (introduction, middle and conclusion), and a focus on literacy and numeracy. The 50-hour average week of modern teachers would not be surprising (DfE, 2010). The Victorian school day usually operated from 9–12 and 2–4.15 but many teachers were required to attend by 7.30 or 8.00 a.m. to prepare lessons or instruct apprentices known as pupil-teachers. The current government apprenticeship model of training teachers on site is very much an early Victorian idea. Until 1903 teachers were also contractually required to undertake 'extraneous duties' or out-of-school activities, such as playing the organ in church on Sunday or training the choir (Horn, 1989). Class sizes could reach fifty or so pupils of mixed ability and, often, mixed ages. In rural schools, resources were particularly stretched.

## Changes and continuities across the generations

There has been significant progress in the everyday experiences of teachers across the four generations. Present-day teachers are better resourced, better qualified, better paid, better supported, teach in more comfortable surroundings, are more knowledgeable about the needs of different learners, have access to more professional development opportunities and research, are better connected to the wider world and enjoy greater career prospects than previous generations.

Over recent decades teachers have faced significant social changes that have redefined childhood. These include a rise in the number of children entering school from single-parent households, from 8 per cent in 1971 to 26 per cent in 2011 (www.gingerbread. org.uk). Children from 'broken homes' are nearly five times more likely to develop emotional problems than those living with both parents. Teachers have had to develop their counselling skills in response to the rising number of children with social and emotional difficulties. Children are reportedly less independent than previous generations. This can be manifested in many ways, including the rise in the number of children who are not toilet trained when they start school, who cannot put their coats on, are unable to eat using a knife and fork and struggling to talk (Evans, 2012b). The lack of basic life skills is symptomatic of what has been described as an 'educational underclass'. According to the Centre for Social Justice, 10 per cent of those entering school are 'so unsociable that they hurt others, adults and other young children' (quoted by Withnall, 2013). The lack of personal and social skills is not confined to children brought up in poverty. Many children lacking these skills come from comfortable homes with toys, televisions and computers, but whose parents do not give enough time and energy to develop these skills (Lightfoot, 2009).

Modern-day teachers also experience children who are less fit and energetic than previous generations. The rise in child obesity is now recognized as a major health problem. The first-generation of teachers welcomed children who walked to school, up to 3 miles a day, and in rural areas sometimes across difficult terrain. Louv (2009) argues that children have lost the pleasures of riding bikes in the woods, climbing trees, collecting bugs, or picking wildflowers. They suffer from what he calls 'nature-deficit disorder', where technologies are more important than nature and parents reluctant to allow children the freedom to explore. Teachers and parents also face the greatest brand-conscious generation of children – one study reports that two-year-olds are able to recognize 8 out of 12 brands they are shown (Valkenburg and Buijzen, 2005).

Some commentators believe that modern childhood has lost its innocence and schools are facing the consequence. Many parents and teachers notice how body image and beauty matters to children, particularly girls. According to one poll in 2013, children as young as four are refusing to eat food for fear of getting fat (www.atl.org.uk). In recent years, retailers have been forced to withdraw push-up bras, saucy knickers and black lace lingerie for girls as young as 9 years old (Mayo and Nairn, 2009). One primary school head banned girls from coming to school in a G-string on the grounds that they could face possible embarrassment while changing for PE or playing out in the playground, falling over or doing handstands. One mother of an 11-year-old girl complained to the school: 'They're fed up of being treated like children' (cited by Mayo and Nairn, 2009: 72).

Teachers today are not only 'horizontally answerable' to audiences such as parents; they are also 'vertically accountable' to middle managers, head teachers and inspectors. Many teachers feel pressurized into a tick-box culture under the 'new managerialism' in education, with its emphasis upon business values, targets, measurable outcomes, league tables, customer satisfaction and securing value for money. Jeffrey (2002) argues that the performance culture has depersonalized relationships between teachers and those they are accountable to, such as inspectors. In a major literature review on teacher accountability, Levitt et al. (2008) found a growing trend of de-professionalization associated with performance measurement. Educators are concerned that this will return teachers to an age (first generation) when they implemented the curriculum rather than initiated creative approaches to meet the particular needs of learners. Michael Gove has been criticized for introducing a 'neo Victorian' curriculum, neglecting the arts and humanities (Garner, 2013).

Yet the modern teacher is also on the verge of something very exciting. At no time in history have schools had such immediate and comprehensive access to knowledge, in all its forms. For one thing, the skill of imparting knowledge has taken on a new meaning – today it is claimed that a heavyweight newspaper such as *The Telegraph* contains more information than an educated person in the eighteenth century was likely to come across in a lifetime (Baugh, 2010). Although the 'potential' of technologies to transform education has been voiced over many years, there is no doubt that teachers and children today are better connected with each other and the wider world than ever before. The progressive introduction of ICT into schools has challenged traditional patterns of teaching and learning. Virtual schools, which started in the mid 1990s, are now used successfully by local authorities to support and improve the achievement of **looked after children** (OFSTED, 2012). Some primary school teachers are remaining true to their creative urge by experimenting with innovative technologies, such as **Augmented Reality** (Kerawalla et al., 2006). Thoughtful teachers are not seduced by the hype surrounding technologies. They know that their primary role is to prepare children as best they can so they enter society as well-rounded citizens. This means that they need to be watchful of the key drivers affecting education (Table 3.2).

**TABLE 3.2**  Key drivers for change affecting educational provision in the future

| | |
|---|---|
| Demographic | ■ Younger and less experienced teaching profession<br>■ Generally people will be living and experiencing better health for longer<br>■ Greater ethnic diversity |
| Social | ■ Decline in 'traditional' family structures<br>■ Greater religious diversity<br>■ Greater proportion of children will have parents who were educated to university level<br>■ Child and adolescent mental health disorders are unlikely to diminish |
| Technological | ■ Increase in technological change such as rise in Internet-based services<br>■ Costs associated with hardware, software and data storage will decrease further<br>■ Near-universal access to personal, multi-functional devices, smarter software integrated with global standards<br>■ Increasing amount of information being available to search online (with faster search engines)<br>■ Using ICT will be natural for most pupils and for an increasing majority of teachers |
| Economic | ■ Living standards to be around 30 per cent higher, with more 'luxuries' becoming 'necessities' and a greater proportion of income spent on leisure, household services, sport and culture<br>■ Higher level skills will be emphasized within a knowledge-based economy<br>■ Working patterns will be increasingly diverse<br>■ Workplace skills will change, requiring employees to be flexible and adaptable |
| Environment | ■ Heightened awareness of environmental threats<br>■ Individuals will be expected to take personal responsibility for their impact on the environment |

Source: McBer Report (2000: 21)

The fifth generation of teachers, who should be leading in their schools by 2025, could be best described as the 'connected' generation. Already, significant numbers are participating in global education by sharing ideas through social networking and other web-based technologies. For example 'TESConnect' and its sister sites in India and America claim 50 million teachers and students in nearly 200 countries now benefit from online resources and collaboration. At its peak, there are 3.7 million downloads a week (*Times Educational Supplement*, 17 May 2013). One primary teacher in a Spanish village primary school saw her resources on the story *The Smartest Giant in Town* (Donaldson, 2003) downloaded 50,000 times in 110 countries by 13,600 users. Despite cultural differences, such online services are connecting teachers to all parts of the world. In the near future, teachers' training and professional development may well be transformed through **massive open online courses** (MOOCS) and virtual schools.

## What are the professional values expected of teachers?

**Values** are at the core of what it means to be a professional. The General Teaching Councils for Northern Ireland, Wales and Scotland identify the professional conduct and values expected of teachers, including trust, honesty, respect, and a commitment to social justice (GTCNI, 2004; GTCW, 2010; GTC Scotland, 2012a). In Scotland the values behind the *Curriculum for Excellence* are inspired by the words inscribed on the mace of the Scottish Parliament, namely wisdom, justice, compassion and integrity. The McBer Report (2000: 21) highlighted four particular professional characteristics of *outstanding* teachers (Table 3.3).

A group of thirty senior mentors was asked to sum up the kinds of professional values that they look for in all prospective teachers and if possible to note those that they considered were the hallmarks of outstanding teachers. Their collective responses are shown in Box 3.1.

Outstanding teachers often demonstrate leadership values such as a strong sense of purpose, a willingness to bring people together and a positive mind frame. Increasingly, leadership in education is seen as a collective, shared concept rather than something left to the head teacher and other senior figures. Leadership features as a strand within the professional competences expected of trainee and serving teachers in Northern Ireland.

**TABLE 3.3** The professional characteristics of outstanding teachers

| Characteristics | Description |
| --- | --- |
| Challenge and support | A commitment to do everything possible for each pupil and enable all pupils to be successful. |
| Confidence | The belief in one's ability to be effective and to take on challenges. |
| Creating trust | Being consistent and fair. Keeping one's word. |
| Respect for others | The underlying belief that individuals matter and deserve respect. |

---

**BOX 3.1  VIEWS OF SENIOR MENTORS WHO WERE ASKED WHAT PROFESSIONAL VALUES THEY LOOK FOR IN TRAINEE TEACHERS**

- Punctuality – arriving in school at least 15 minutes before the start of the school day.
- Reliability – delivering lessons, preparing resources, keeping up to date with records, and 'filling in' when asked.
- Commitment – prepared to work very hard and support children in their learning.
- Confidentiality – being sensitive to school matters and not sharing these with those who should not know.
- Respectfulness – in the manner of speaking to children and staff.
- Courage* – to defend what they believe in.
- Flexibility* – showing a willingness to adapt.
- Open-mindedness* – readiness to accept alternative ways of working.
- Initiative* – increasing independence necessary by the final school experience.

* Considered to be especially important in determining the professional values of outstanding trainees.

In England and Wales, those graduates who follow the Teach First route into the profession pursue a leadership programme throughout their two years. While effective educational leaders have different styles and qualities, they share common characteristics. For example, they have a clear vision for raising standards, are passionate about learning, prove to be astute listeners, and support others to achieve a common purpose. Above all, practitioners who show leadership skills never lose sight of the fact that teaching other people's children is a *privilege*.

In England, according to the *Teachers' Standards* (DfE, 2013a) all teachers are required to maintain high standards of ethics and behaviour, within and outside school, by:

- treating pupils with dignity, building relationships rooted in mutual respect, and at all times observing proper boundaries appropriate to a teacher's professional position;
- having regard for the need to safeguard pupils' well-being, in accordance with statutory provisions;
- showing tolerance of and respect for the rights of others by not undermining fundamental British values, including democracy, the rule of law, individual liberty and mutual respect, and tolerance of those with different faiths and beliefs; and
- ensuring that personal beliefs are not expressed in ways that exploit pupils' vulnerability or might lead them to break the law.

## Treating pupils with dignity

The word 'dignity' originally described something or someone of worth and was often associated with the nobility. Seeing all pupils as individuals worthy of respect is one of the foundation values of teaching. This requires empathy, sensitivity and a commitment to fairness. Empathy enables a teacher to recognize pupils' feelings, viewpoints and experiences. Sensitive teachers pick up the signals of how pupils feel, perhaps in what they do not say as well as their comments, or through their body language, drawings or general responsiveness. It is possible to treat children with dignity by respecting their views and developing a culture of humanity in the school. In practice this means all adults and children sharing responsibilities in developing a dignified environment.

Ultimately, a desire to be fair should underpin policies and practices. All schools are required to have an equal opportunities policy and teachers have a legal and moral duty to uphold its principles. In one city primary school in Wales, the staff sought to express their commitment to equal opportunities through a statement that included a child-friendly diagram (see Figure 3.1). Mindful of having an all-female staff, this school made a special effort to compensate by frequently inviting male, as well as female, visitors to work alongside the children. These included representatives from the media, local hospital, police, a local church and mosque. Boys and girls had the opportunity to participate in a wide range of extra-curricular clubs, older pupils acted as 'stewards' for younger ones, planning documents and displays reflected different cultures and new staff were trained in the school's commitment to anti-racism.

Figure 3.2 illustrates the transferable knowledge, skills and attitudes that teachers should seek to develop in all contexts. The boxed comments are the major skills that shape equal opportunities.

At our school we shall do our best to appreciate everyone and to show our respect for each other through the way that we:

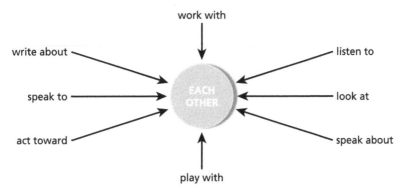

**FIGURE 3.1**  An extract from one school's equal opportunity policy

Source: ACCAC (2001: 20). Reproduced with permission

**FIGURE 3.2**  Transferable skills to promote equal opportunities

Source: Clements and Spinks (1996: 15). Reproduced with permission

The McBer Report (McBer, 2000) highlighted the importance of teachers keeping their word to children, being sincere and genuine, allowing pupils to act naturally and express themselves without fear of making mistakes. Strong modelling of these qualities helps to create a climate of trust in which children see the teacher as dependable and genuine. Hence teachers should avoid sending out 'mixed' messages by saying one thing but acting in a different way. For example, if teachers expect children to listen when others speak, they should do the same themselves.

## Observing proper boundaries and the law

The legal position of teachers is that they act *in loco parentis* (in the place of parents) by behaving reasonably in their duty of care, supervision and avoidance of negligence. Although this is not defined clearly, teachers are expected to take reasonable steps to ensure the safety of the pupils in their charge and not act in a careless or reckless way that might expose them to danger. Cohen *et al.* (2004) draw attention to legal issues that are most likely to be in the minds of student teachers while in schools. These include matters relating to discipline, detention, and confiscation of property, educational visits, accidents, child protection and data protection.

The *Teachers' Standards* expect all teachers to 'have an understanding of, and always act within, the statutory frameworks which set out their professional duties and responsibilities' (DfE, 2013: 10). The Bristol Guide (University of Bristol, 2013), updated annually, is an essential source for trainee and experienced teachers, offering current summaries and explanations of legislation and statutory guidance regulating professional work in schools. Various trade unions also provide guidance for newly qualified teachers (for example, see 'Know your Rights' available at www.nasuwt.org.uk).

Occasional stories of teachers overstepping professional boundaries are quick to make the news headlines. These have included teachers conducting inappropriate relationships with students, excessive use of physical force, and improper use of social media. In such serious cases, matters are referred to the general teaching councils or, in England, the National College for Teaching and Leadership. Guidance is available from universities, charities, trade unions, local authorities and central government to support trainee and qualified teachers in implementing their professional duties and knowing the boundaries between appropriate and inappropriate conduct.

## The Equality Act

Teachers need to be mindful of the all-embracing Equality Act (2010), which replaced previous separate legislation on race relations and discrimination. The Act states that schools in Great Britain (see Equality Commission website for Northern Ireland) cannot discriminate against pupils because of their gender, race, disability, religion, belief or sexual orientation. One of the key changes is that schools must take positive action to alleviate disadvantages experienced by pupils with '**protected characteristics**'. Such measures should be proportionate to the relevant aim – for instance providing catch-up classes for Roma children or a project to engage disaffected boys. Previously, schools may have been acting unlawfully by excluding children who did not belong to these groups (University of Bristol, 2013).

**EXTEND YOUR UNDERSTANDING**

Read the NUT guide on the teacher and the law available at: www.teachers.org.uk/files/
the-law-and-you–8857-.pdf (available also in Welsh). Compose a 10-question quiz to ask
colleagues – for example, are teachers required to tell parents about recorded incidents
involving their children or can teachers discipline children who behave badly on the way to
school?

Teachers can only be held responsible for events or accidents that are reasonably
foreseeable. Hence teachers need to undertake appropriate risk assessments to evaluate
potential hazards in relation to pupils' needs and capabilities.

## Educational visits

Risk assessment is particularly important when arranging educational visits and fieldwork.
Guidance is available from the Health and Safety Executive, trade unions, local authorities
and organizations such as English Heritage who have well-established protocols. The
Welsh Government (2010) has published a common framework for educational visits that
includes comprehensive checklists and model forms. It is essential to plan visits carefully
and to ensure that the following factors, though not exhaustive, are considered:

- educational aims;
- appropriate approval granted;
- initial exploratory visit undertaken;
- all relevant parties informed;
- adequate staffing numbers available, taking into account any special needs;
- finance;
- insurance;
- parent/carer information and consent;
- programme content agreed including contingency plans;
- clothing/equipment;
- voluntary helpers;
- medical arrangements;
- transport and accommodation;
- emergency procedures and contacts; and
- post-visit evaluation.

Schools will routinely inform local authorities when arranging visits overseas and residential
visits. Clearly such visits require considerable additional planning in terms of passports,

visas, following child protection procedures and raising awareness of different cultural practices.

## Social networking

Social network sites enjoy huge popularity – it is said that if Facebook had the status of a country it would be the third largest in the world (behind China and India) with over one billion users (Williams, 2012). Unfortunately, more than one in ten teachers accused of misconduct in 2011 forged inappropriate relationships with pupils using social media and emails (Vasagar and Williams, 2012). Teachers have been suspended for posting pictures of themselves drunk or smoking when their accounts lacked sufficient security settings and were easily accessible to pupils. It is fair to assume that if pupils find any amusing, awkward or incriminating material relating to a teacher, it will be circulated. In one case a teacher who attended a hen party had a photograph of herself draped around the shoulders of a naked 'blow up' man posted on Facebook without her knowing. When she arrived at school on the Monday she was unaware of the picture, which had been sent around the whole school community. She was asked to leave the job (Briggs, 2013).

The best advice for teachers is to always err on the side of caution and to avoid the temptation to court popularity through befriending pupils. It is inappropriate to exchange private texts, phone numbers, personal email addresses or photographs of an intimate nature with pupils. Naturally there are times when teachers use their life experiences to enhance children's understanding of topics say in history or geography, for example by showing family album photographs of famous landmarks or museums visited. However, it is important to bear in mind that children are naturally curious about their teacher's personal life outside school and may on their own accord try to find out more.

The charity Childnet, set up in 1995, provides teachers, parents and children with expert online advice and resources on making the most of the Internet. It works in partnership with the UK Safer Internet Centre which also offers guidance on protecting a teacher's professional reputation through practical strategies such as: searching one's own name online to check personal digital identity, establishing private settings, using strong passwords, always logging out, carefully selecting a profile image, responding to allegations, and thinking very carefully about the language used even within private posts. A useful rule-of-thumb is never post anything that would not be said face-to-face to a head teacher or colleague. It is not uncommon for head teachers and school governors to check online what is known about a candidate before conducting any interviews. The General Teaching Council for Scotland (GTC Scotland, 2012b: 5) reminds teachers to think about three questions before posting online entries:

1.  Might it reflect poorly on you, your school, employer or the teaching profession?
2.  Is your intention to post this material driven by personal reasons or professional reasons?
3.  Are you confident that the comment or other media in question, if accessed by others, (colleagues, parents etc.) would be considered reasonable and appropriate?

## Physical contact

Over recent times, the Coalition Government has set out to increase teachers' powers to tackle misbehaviour. For instance, teachers can search for and, if necessary, delete inappropriate images or files on pupils' electronic devices, including mobile phones. Government guidance covers screening, searching and confiscation, preventing and tackling bullying, and the use of reasonable force. Teachers have a right to:

- discipline pupils for breaking school rules, for not following instructions or for other inappropriate behaviour;
- discipline pupils for misbehaviour outside of school, for instance on school visits, if determined by the policy;
- impose detention, if it features within the school's behaviour policy and provided parents are given 24 hours' notice;
- search for and confiscate items;
- use reasonable force to control or restrain pupils where it is necessary to avoid the breakdown of good order;
- have respect shown for their professional role as teachers; and
- operate within a safe working environment.

In a litigious culture, many teachers are naturally nervous over the degree of physical contact with children. But it is unrealistic to suggest that teachers should never touch pupils. The DfE (2013b) non-statutory guidance to schools makes it clear that there are occasions when physical contact may be appropriate, for instance when comforting a distressed pupil, giving first aid or demonstrating techniques in PE lessons. Similarly guidelines for schools in Northern Ireland point out that staff should not feel inhibited in providing a distressed child, especially a younger one, with reassurance involving physical comforting, as a caring parent would provide (DENI, 1999).

In other circumstances teachers have the right to use reasonable force to control or restrain pupils (Crick Report, DfEE, 1998; DfE, 2013b). Teachers can use reasonable force in four contexts:

1   to remove a disruptive child from the classroom where they have refused to follow an instruction to do so;
2   to prevent a pupil behaving in a way that disrupts a school event or visit;
3   to prevent a pupil leaving the classroom where allowing the pupil to leave would risk their safety or lead to behaviour that disrupts the behaviour of others; and
4   to prevent a pupil from attacking a member of staff or another pupil, or to stop a fight in the playground.

One of the less publicized challenges faces young male teachers who teach pubescent girls. Myers (2005) explored these sensitive issues and concludes that they cannot be ignored because this is a disservice to the teaching profession. She refers to the pressures faced by young male teachers most vulnerable to sexual power games by adolescents 'who try out their newfound sexual power on the most powerful adults in their lives' (Myers, 2005, cited by MacBeath, 2012:17). Scottish research also reports male teachers' nervousness about the general public's perception that male child abusers gravitate to schools and discomfiture at being 'mothered' by female colleagues (Hepburn, 2013). Stereotypes about males entering teaching persist – they are seen as 'outsiders', particularly in the Early Years where there remains a serious shortage of male practitioners. Only 3 per cent of nursery teachers in England and Wales are male; while men represent just 12 per cent of the primary school workforce (Paton, 2013).

For trainee teachers, universities have appropriate guidance and regulations relating to appropriate conduct while in school. Typically these should cover the following areas:

- regular attendance;
- punctuality;
- respect for others;
- appropriate use of resources including Internet facilities;
- appropriate behaviour;
- ability to listen and act on feedback and advice;
- taking responsibility for own learning;
- maintaining an appropriate standard of dress and appearance;
- carrying out duties as required by class teachers, mentors, other placement-related staff and tutors; and
- carrying out reasonable instructions as requested by the school and university staff.

It is important for trainees to read and talk through these expectations with the appropriate staff so that there are no misunderstandings. Schools will have particular expectations, for instance regarding dress.

## Safeguarding

Safeguarding has a broader notion than child protection to include enabling children to have optimum life chances and to enter adulthood with confidence. Child protection is the responsibility of all those who work with children. The field – or 'minefield' as Blake (2004) puts it – of child protection is probably the heaviest responsibility for a class teacher. All children, especially young ones, rely on adults to help them meet their physical, emotional and spiritual needs. Sadly, a small number are harmed, injured or occasionally killed. Stories in the media, such as the sexual abuse ring in Rochdale during 2012, are salutatory reminders of what some argue is an endemic problem within the UK (Marley, 2012). In 2010–11, around 346 per 10,000 children were classed as 'in need' (DfE, 2011a). More often, children referred to social services are poorly neglected to the point that their basic needs go unmet. Sometimes this is because carers are indifferent to these needs or simply too preoccupied with their own (Beckett, 2007).

All trainee teachers are required to receive training in child protection. This usually involves specialist input from visiting speakers, such as local authority officers. However, Baginsky (2003) reports considerable variation in the amount of time devoted towards child protection, which in some cases was as little as one hour. Similar concerns have been expressed about the patchy coverage of child protection among those following school-based training routes (Hodgkinson and Baginsky, 2000). Only around 50 per cent of newly qualified teachers feel adequately prepared to handle safeguarding issues (TDA, 2011). Local authorities provide online guidance detailing procedures that teachers need to follow.

Unfortunately, **child abuse** has been around for a very long time. Archaeologists have recently reported the oldest recorded case of child abuse, dating back to ancient Egypt when a three-year-old skeleton showed signs of being repeatedly shaken, causing broken bones (Prigg, 2013). Child abuse includes mental and emotional as well as physical forms. Teachers are especially at risk of their actions being misconstrued in one-to-one situations and during extra-curricular activities. Such misunderstanding can lead to accusations of professional misconduct or even child abuse. In turn, such allegations (founded or otherwise) can destroy family relationships, careers and have a devastating impact on a person's emotional and mental health.

There are many potential signs of child abuse including physical symptoms, attention-seeking, low self-image and truancy. Schools are required to have clear policies and practices relating to child protection. They have duties to cooperate and share information with the local child protection network. Class teachers have key roles to play in child protection in order that all children feel safe, both within school and outside (Sweeney, 1999); hence the importance of being clear over the school's internal procedures.

Suspicions of abuse can be expressed by anyone who is in contact with the school, including children, parents, carers and caretakers. These should be conveyed to the appropriate designated officer within the school, usually the head teacher, recorded in writing, signed and dated. It is particularly important to respond to children who express concerns in a reassuring manner, showing that their views are taken seriously without guaranteeing complete confidentiality.

Organizations such as Barnardo's and the National Society for the Prevention of Cruelty to Children (NSPCC) provide useful guidance on potential signs of neglect and abuse, as well as how to respond to various concerns; for instance, relating to the growing problem of '**sexting**' (NSPCC, 2013). Schools and local authorities should have clear procedures for how teachers should handle disclosures of abuse including allegations against teachers (see also guidance provided by the National Union of Teachers at www.teachers. org.uk/node/18971). Figure 3.3 sets out the information provided by the Scottish government on how to respond to a disclosure.

Children need to know that information may need to be passed on to others in order to keep them safe. It is not the responsibility of teachers to investigate suspected cases of abuse. Local Safeguarding Boards (LSBs), established in 2006, are responsible for monitoring how relevant organizations in each local area cooperate to safeguard and promote the welfare of children. OFSTED (2011) acknowledges that even the best LSBs struggle to show how their work impacts on outcomes for children and families. A government review of child protection (DfE, 2011b) recommends a move away from focusing on targets and processes towards a system centre around the individual needs of children and young people and the extent to which they are being effectively helped.

| | | |
|---|---|---|
| **1** Only ask enough questions to gain basic information. | | |
| **2** Take the allegation seriously and support – do not interrogate! | | |
| **3** Use open-ended questions. (O) | | |
| **4** Do **not** use leading questions. (L) | | |

| When | When did it happen? | O |
|---|---|---|
| | Did it happen last night? | L |
| Where | Where did it happen? | O |
| | Did he/she come into your bedroom? | L |
| Who | Who did it? | O |
| | Was it Daddy/Peter/the babysitter? | L |
| What | What happened? | O |
| | Did such and such happen? | L |
| How Why | Avoid if possible. These questions require a judgement by the child and may also induce self-recrimination. | |

**5** Remember:

☐ Keep the questions open ended.

☐ Do not prompt or suggest to obtain the answer you think you want to hear.

☐ Record, sign and date disclosure or concern on the same day.

☐ If producing the record by computer – print paper copy and sign and date. Do not save copy to hard disk.

**FIGURE 3.3** Checklist for responding when a child discloses abuse

One of the most challenging aspects of the profession is dealing with children who are experiencing distress. There is no 'one size fits all' approach, notwithstanding the need to follow school policies. Getting to know the foibles and idiosyncrasies of individual children is at the heart of pastoral care. Broadly speaking, Packard *et al.* (1997: 54) make the following suggestions for dealing with distressed children:

1    be firm, but gentle;

2    act quickly to settle children who don't want to be left at school by their parents or carers;

3    if a child is upset, don't change your expectations;

4    if an upset child becomes disruptive, send for help;

5    give a child time and space to calm down;

6    keep other children away;

7    your expectation of the children is the most important thing;

8    don't expect children to be able to explain why they are upset;

9    if your discipline of children upsets them, don't let them get away with things for a quiet life; and

10    tell the children: 'You can tell me anything'.

However, classroom life is more complex than following a checklist of recommended techniques. For children, the world can appear to be a harsh and unfriendly place, difficult to cope with on top of their own physical and emotional changes. Teachers need to make responsible decisions on behalf of children, with their best interests in mind (Box 3.2).

---

**BOX 3.2  REAL-LIFE LEARNING CHALLENGE**

Discuss in small groups how you might respond to these situations reported by trainee teachers during their school placements:

■ A 5-year-old regularly looks very tired and lethargic in lessons.

■ A 9-year-old girl does not want to get changed for PE lessons in front of her peers.

■ A gifted footballer in your class is dropped from an important tournament by a colleague and you feel that this is too harsh.

■ A child accuses another child of stealing his lunch money.

■ A 10-year-old boy says that his father hits him.

■ An 11-year-old girl confides in you that she loves another teacher.

■ A child comes to school dirty and dishevelled on most days.

■ You overhear a group of children on the playground describing a graphic video that they had watched at the weekend.

■ A newly arrived child in the class swears at another child.

■ A child is reluctant to go and play at break-time.

---

## Showing tolerance and respect for others

The values of tolerance and respect should permeate everything that the school does, and not be confined to assembly stories or lessons in personal and social education. They should be evident in everyday classroom interactions, the corridors, playground, and out-of-school activities. Schools that take these values seriously plan to promote them through displays, events, curriculum topics and extra-curricular activities. Some schools and local authorities are explicit in their support for the United Nations Convention on the Rights of the Child (UNCRC). For instance they register for the Rights Respecting Schools Award (RRSA). This recognizes schools that model rights and respect in all its relationships. Unicef's own evaluation found that schools that had achieved the RRSA had improved children's decision-making skills (Sebba and Robinson, 2010). This was not just confined to discussions over matters such as playground equipment, lunchtime arrangements and improving toilets. The majority of schools also included pupils on governing bodies, staff appointment panels and evaluations of teaching and learning. Some schools buy into values-based education programmes (Hawkes, 2003; Duckworth and Gilbert, 2009). These claim to develop self-awareness, an understanding of the environment and empathy for others (www.valuesbasededucation.com).

More generally, learner voice should be a strong feature of citizenship education. Unfortunately, a government review of citizenship teaching found very uneven practice (DfES, 2007). This was attributed to a lack of prioritization among head teachers, teachers short on confidence and training, poor community links and insufficient opportunities for pupils to have their say.

Questions about tolerance are often associated with schools of a religious character (commonly known as faith schools). Media reports are often quick to emphasize extremism in Muslim schools, but there are also concerns that some evangelical Christian schools, such as those run by the Accelerated Christian Education movement, preach intolerance (Scaramanga, 2009). The Equality Act makes it clear that it does not permit less favourable treatment of a pupil because they do not (or no longer) belong to the school's religion. For instance, it would be unlawful for a Catholic school to treat a pupil less favourably because he rejected the Catholic faith and declared himself to be a Jehovah's Witness or an atheist. However, faith schools are allowed to give priority in admissions to members of their own religion, but only when the school is oversubscribed.

## British values

The inclusion of 'fundamental British values' within the *Teachers' Standards* (DfE, 2013a) should be set against a background of ongoing concern that extremist views were infiltrating the educational system (Civitas, 2009: Maddern, 2013). Very few would disagree with the need for teachers to support the rule of law, individual liberty, mutual respect, and tolerance of those with different faiths and beliefs. Of course, Britain does not have a monopoly on these values. Respect for diversity, for example, is one of the core values of the United Nations. However, Britain has a proud (if far from perfect) tradition of tolerance. A recent World Values survey ranked Britain as in the top group of the most tolerant of eighty countries. Fewer than 2 per cent of Britons would object to having neighbours from a different faith (Henderson, 2013). This traditionally tolerant outlook has been questioned because of the strains placed on public services such as hospitals and schools as a result of immigration. One poll of 20,000 people by Lord Ashcroft suggests that only 17 per cent of Britons feel, on balance, immigration has been a good thing for Britain (Pearson, 2013).

The Coalition Government is keen to put a British stamp on the National Curriculum introduced in 2014. Hence the history programme of study is strong on British heroes, including creative thinkers (e.g. Isambard Kingdom Brunel and Christina Rossetti), scientists (e.g. Isaac Newton and Michael Faraday) and social reformers (e.g. Elizabeth Fry and William Wilberforce). Learning about what it means to be British is not only about famous people, events, institutions and ceremonies. It should begin with how people behave towards each other – in class, school, neighbourhood and wider community. Primary children should think about their own histories, how they connect to their localities, what makes them different and what they have in common with others and current news relevant to their lives. For children, values can be very abstract and need to be related to real-life contexts. Teachers can refer to the experiences of ordinary Britons in the annual Pride of Britain Awards, displaying the stoicism, courage and neighbourliness that many admire. From a pedagogical view, teachers need to consider how they model values each day.

There are fundamental questions teachers need to consider about identity linked to values: How do they see themselves? What does it mean to be British? How are the British similar to/different from others? Do people hold multiple identities? Do those born in Belfast consider themselves Irish or British? Do third-generation children worshipping in Cardiff mosques regard themselves as Welsh Muslims? Does it matter? What is behind the 'British values' agenda? (Grigg, 2014).

There are many creative approaches to developing children's awareness of British values and heritage. Younger ones can explore issues of identity through their own names, family histories, national icons, images, symbols, landmarks, foods, music, dance, poetry, and stories of heroes and legends. But it is important to take children beyond stereotypes to explore the diversity of Britain. A good starting-point is discussing the 'melting-pot' of Britons in Benjamin Zephaniah's humorous poem 'The British' (in *Wicked World*, Puffin, 2000). Children can discuss the respective relationships between the English, Scots, Irish and Welsh in contexts such as sport, music, language and politics. There are regular discussions in the news about questions of identity, which will interest children. For example, at the time of writing, a storm brews over comments by the England footballer Jack Wilshere, that 'the only people who should play for England are English people' (Fifield, 2013). Britain has always been a multicultural society and so it is important for children to learn about the contribution of ethnic minority groups within their localities and wider national story; for example, through community projects (Grigg and Hughes, 2013).

## Expressing personal beliefs

At a fundamental level, some commentators question whether it is appropriate for primary teachers to impart values. The writer Claire Fox, for instance, argues that there are too many lobbyists and campaign groups pushing agendas in primary schools such as multiculturalism, gay rights and environmentalism. Would all minority groups have a right to voice their beliefs and values? The government announced in 2010 that teachers who were members of the British National Party (BNP), an extremist but legitimate political party, could be dismissed following a case when a BNP activist used a school laptop to post comments describing immigrants as 'filth' (Vasagar, 2010). However, the government has ruled out banning BNP members from teaching because it would be disproportionate (given those likely to be involved) and a significant political act – the BNP is not an illegal organization.

As noted in Chapter 2, it can be difficult for teachers to restrain themselves from expressing personal beliefs on subjects such as politics, sexuality or religion. However, mature teachers want pupils to be able to think for themselves and not to be unduly influenced by their teacher's opinions or values. Nonetheless, occasionally schools are caught in controversy, such as when schools in Lanarkshire were reported to be showing an explicit sex education DVD that had already been banned in England (*Daily Record*, 22 November 2012).

Teachers have a right to express personal beliefs provided that they do so in a professional manner, which is not inappropriate or insensitive to pupils. This can prove challenging in particular aspects of life. Sensitive or controversial issues are defined as those 'that have a political, social or personal impact and arouse feeling and/or deal with questions of value or belief' (Oxfam, 2006: 2).

In terms of expressions of faith, cases have been taken to the European Court of Human Rights on whether Christian employees should be allowed to wear a cross to work, as a symbol of their personal beliefs (Waterfield, 2012). Human rights legislation restricts free speech and religious belief to protect the rights of others. Hence, in a case where a Seventh Day Adventist teacher described homosexuality as 'disgusting' and a 'sin', the teacher was banned indefinitely from teaching on the grounds of unacceptable professional conduct (*The Telegraph*, 12 April 2013). Parliament has discussed cases such as a primary teacher who stopped reading the book *And Tango Makes Three* (Richardson and Parnell, 2005) because it endorsed same-sex relationships in a way that conflicted with her beliefs. When the head teacher discovered this, the teacher was restricted from having her own class because the school policy promoted homosexuality. In terms of political beliefs, there have been calls to ban teachers from membership of right-wing organizations such as the BNP out of fear that they may promote intolerance in schools.

Controversy is part of everyday life. Children need to be equipped with the skills of listening, putting forward their view and being prepared to change their mind, if they are to develop as well-rounded citizens. Knowing how to make sense of arguments and to avoid impulsive reactions are essential skills. It is widely recognized that teaching knowledge and skills divorced from real-world situations can leave children and young people unprepared for the complexities of the modern world (Oxfam, 2006). Outstanding teachers do not shelter children from difficult issues but support them in expressing their feelings in learning to think for themselves. Many children want to know more about issues such as poverty, war, animal rights, global warming, and relationships. Skilfully handled, discussing emotive issues can develop children's reasoning and enquiry skills, mutual tolerance and empathy. Teachers now have access to a growing body of materials to support them in knowing how to share their personal views, tackle controversial issues and respect others (Claire and Holden, 2007).

The legal position on teaching about potentially controversial issues is set out in the Education Act 1996 which requires school governing bodies, head teachers and local education authorities to take all reasonably practical steps to ensure that where political and controversial issues are brought to the attention of pupils, they are offered a balanced presentation of opposing views. This is not straightforward because 'balance' can mean counteracting a one-sided view expressed in the class, community or wider society such as the media.

The Crick Report on Citizenship (1998) notes three possible approaches adopted by teachers in handling controversial matters: the 'neutral' chair in which teachers guide discussions but do not declare their own views; the balanced approach by which teachers encourage discussion of all views, acting as 'devil's advocate' when necessary; and the stated commitment approach that involves teachers declaring their personal views and encouraging children to agree or disagree on the basis of reasoned thinking.

The Citizenship Foundation (Huddleston, 2003: 4) takes this further and provides advice on what this means in practice:

■ giving equal importance to conflicting views and opinions;
■ presenting all information and opinion as open to interpretation; and
■ establishing a classroom climate in which all pupils are free to express sincerely held views without fear.

Outstanding teachers of controversial issues know the importance of establishing clear ground rules, such as the following:

•  only one person to talk at a time – no interrupting;
•  show respect for the views of others;
•  challenge the ideas not the people;
•  use appropriate language – no racist or sexist comments;
•  allow everyone to express his/her view to ensure that everyone is heard and respected; and
•  pupils should give reasons why they have a particular view.

(Oxfam, 2006: 6)

When holding group or class discussions, it is possible for teachers to convey unintentional bias through facial expressions, gestures or tone of voice, or omissions such as failing to challenge a one-sided view.

## Working with school colleagues

Over the past decade or so there has been a significant expansion in the number of adults other than teachers working in primary schools. These include: school business managers (SBMs), cover supervisors, extended schools coordinators, personal tutors, learning coaches, parent support advisers and around 232,000 teaching assistants (TAs), unfairly dubbed the 'mum's army'. This growth was largely in response to government policies including workforce reforms, introduced in 2003 in order to reduce teachers' workload. Teachers were no longer required to routinely undertake numerous administrative and clerical tasks including collecting money, putting up wall displays and stocktaking, although this is currently under review. By 2005 teachers also enjoyed a guaranteed 10 per cent of their timetable set aside for PPA.

Whether the TA workforce as a whole represents value for money has been questioned. Studies suggest that while assistants generally reduce teacher stress levels and improve classroom discipline, they have little impact on pupils' progress or attainment (Friedberg, 2009; Paton, 2011). In most cases, TAs spend too much time on managing group behaviour and completing set tasks, rather than developing pupils' understanding (OFSTED, 2008). One study shows that pupils supported by TAs make less progress than those who are not (Blatchford *et al.*, 2009). This is because teachers are not adequately trained in the management of support staff and groups working with teaching assistants receive less time from their teachers.

In the most effective teams, teachers make time to plan alongside support staff and to provide feedback on their contributions – unfortunately this happens in only one in twenty schools (Blatchford *et al.*, 2009). These planning and review conversations should revolve around questions such as the following:

- Planning and preparation: has the TA had sufficient time to read through and comment upon the planning ahead of the lesson and prepare appropriate resources?
- Learning objectives: is everyone clear about what the pupils should be achieving as part of the TA support?
- Allocated role: does the TA understand the role and how this fits in with the job description? Are support strategies for pupils clearly understood?
- Assessment: does the TA know what is expected in terms of ongoing feedback to pupils and reporting on progress at the end of the session? How will the class teacher monitor the progress of children working with the TA?
- Review: has agreement been reached on the focus and time for reviewing the lesson?
- Feedback to TA: has this been agreed in advance and any targets set?

To make the most of assistants' experience and insight, everyone needs to be clear about what they are meant to do relative to their job descriptions. In some cases TAs support children with special educational needs on a one-to-one basis. Such support might include:

- going over teaching from the earlier part of the lesson;
- revisiting the learning objectives;
- providing audio, tactile or visual cues, e.g. alphabet strip, word-mat, table square, number square, vowel chart, key words/tricky words/new words, taped stories, software, mini-whiteboard, number fans, place-value cards, counters, cubes, shapes;
- scribing responses;
- scaffolding learning through use of the 'mother tongue', writing frames, role play, mind maps, diagrams;
- modelling answers;

- demonstrating and using illustrations;
- using peer tutors;
- conducting further research using the Internet or library;
- rehearsing answers ahead of feedback to the class;
- reminders of targets; and
- feedback on progress.

In one-to-one contexts, TAs also need to understand how to include individuals within group discussions and other tasks if the school is to be truly inclusive.

TAs can also support teachers in undertaking observational assessments, for instance by focusing on the quality of pupils' language skills. Effective teachers fully brief TAs on specific roles, for example encouraging reticent pupils to answer verbally, e.g. 'I think Rosheen has a good idea', or silently, using nods or smiles. They might use question cards or checklists. Many TAs provide specific curriculum or whole-school support, often drawing on particular skills and experiences.

To establish and sustain good working relationships takes effort and sensitivity on the part of all concerned. Teachers need to understand the viewpoints of their assistants and accord them respect that they deserve. Day *et al.* (1987) identified ten key features that characterize effective teamwork:

1   awareness

2   warmth

3   interactions

4   communications

5   intimacy

6   openness

7   authentic behaviour

8   motivation

9   confrontation

10  commitment.

Developing teamwork skills requires commitment from all parties. It often involves working through four stages of skills development:

1   Unconscious incompetence – 'I don't even know that I am no good at this';

2   Conscious incompetence – 'I've realised that I can't do this';

3   Conscious competence – 'I've learned how to do this but I still have to think about it'; and

4   Unconscious competence – 'I can do this without thinking, I can't remember why it was ever a problem'.

(DfES, 2005: 3)

It is important to know the skills and capabilities of others within a team, respecting rather than ridiculing difference and sharing the workload. Trainee and beginning teachers should not feel shy about sharing their skills with more experienced teachers. They may have acquired skills in previous employment, through hobbies or attending university courses. These skills and experiences may include fluency in a foreign language, musical talent, performance and theatre skills, coaching skills, computer know-how, or skills draw from the business sector.

A caring and considerate teacher also takes into account the feelings of colleagues. Teachers experience many interactions in the course of the day, and often it is the brief, informal discussions on the way to a lesson, in the staffroom, on playground duty, or after school, that make all the difference to raising colleagues' spirits. Day *et al.* (1987: 42) note that 'in schools where teamwork is effective, teachers smile at each other, laugh together, take time to listen to each other, and get more involved in each other's work'. Perhaps the most important feature of teamwork is a willingness to be open and honest with each other.

## Working with other professionals

The importance of teachers working closely with other professionals to meet children's needs has long been understood. For example, during times of hardship in the 1930s, teachers teamed up with health workers to provide meals, clothes and shoes. In the 1990s community schools began to offer adult classes in basic skills and other services. The need for professionals to share information and work towards the common goal of supporting children's well-being was tragically highlighted in the case of Victoria Climbié in 2000. Victoria was an 8-year-old girl who died following months of neglect and abuse at the hands of her great aunt. The Laming Inquiry (2003) revealed that social services, the police and the National Health Service missed twelve opportunities to rescue and save her life.

Although the case did not implicate teachers (as Victoria did not attend school in the UK), the government strategy focused on improving the sharing of information across public services. Its *Every Child Matters* (ECM) policy set out five outcomes to be achieved for every child, saying they should be healthy, stay safe, enjoy and achieve, make a positive contribution, and experience economic well-being (DfES, 2003). New Sure Start Children's Centres and 'full service extended schools' opened, providing breakfast and after-school clubs, childcare and health and social services on site. The ECM agenda placed child protection into a broader context of improving the lives of children. A similar model developed in Scotland, *Getting it Right for Every Child* (Scottish Government, 2008). The Children's Act 2004 strengthened the ECM agenda by placing duties on local authorities to better coordinate partnership working. Unfortunately, in 2007 the scenario ECM was designed to avoid happened again when Baby P (Peter Connelly) died after suffering more than fifty injuries.

Critics of ECM argued that it was an excessive response to the Laming Inquiry, adding unnecessary bureaucracy to overstretched schools. Michael Gove, the former Education Secretary, described the ECM agenda as 'meddlesome' (quoted by Stewart, 2012). The five ECM outcomes have since been dropped and replaced by 'help children achieve more' with a focus on standards. Under OFSTED's new inspection framework, schools are no longer graded on promoting pupils' spiritual, moral, social and cultural development, the extentto which pupils 'adopt healthy lifestyles', and 'contribute to the school and wider community'. Although ECM is no longer a government priority, developing effective working relationships with other professionals and parents is clearly beneficial to children.

Studies (Atkinson *et al.*, 2007; Cheminais, 2009) have identified the following characteristics of successful multi-agency partnerships:

- working relationships based on trust and mutual respect;
- distributed leadership providing joint ownership;
- shared common aims and objectives;
- effective communication strategies;
- commitment and involvement of all parties including parents and children themselves;
- joint training events;
- joint review and evaluation; and
- suitable locations for meetings.

## Partnership with parents and carers

There is strong evidence that involving parents in their children's education benefits not only the children and their families but society at large (Desforges and Abouchaar, 2003; Whalley, 2007). The gains for pupils include:

- improved school attendance;
- fewer suspensions;
- increased motivation;
- better self-esteem;
- higher grades, test scores, and qualifications; and
- lower instances of antisocial behaviour.

The earlier in a child's educational process parent involvement begins, the more powerful the impact. Given that children between the age of 5 and 15 spend only 15 per cent of their time in school, the importance of working closely with parents is clear (Scottish Executive, 2003). The quality of education and care is linked directly to the frequency of parent–staff relationships (Papatheodorou and Moyles, 2009).

Parental involvement has two aspects: participation in the life of the school and providing support for children's learning at home. Parents who have high expectations for their children and spend time with them have children who achieve at higher levels than other children. Although this has long been recognized, according to Williams *et al.* (2002) only one in three parents feel involved in their children's schooling while 72 per cent would welcome more involvement. This has since improved – in a 2007 survey around half of parents felt 'very involved' in their child's school life and 92 per cent felt at least 'fairly involved' (DCSF, 2008). OFSTED (2006) found that children strongly value the presence of their parents and carers in schools.

It is important that parents are seen as individuals who could offer a range of skills, energies and ideas to enrich children's education. Parents who come from, or who have lived in, other countries can talk about their experiences. Teachers should be sensitive to the different attitudes, needs and beliefs of parents. As with teaching, there are different parenting styles – some are more authoritarian than others. The Effective Provision of Pre-School Education (EPPE) report concludes: 'what parents do is more important than who parents are' (Sylva et al., 2004: ii). Parental participation increases when schools involve them in planning activities and when teachers recognize the potential of parents to take on responsibilities. Parents should be viewed then as co-educators and efforts made by both parties to establish and sustain a meaningful dialogue.

Good communication between schools and parents depends upon three main factors:

- taking into account the views of parents in identifying priorities for action;
- effective arrangements for meetings and written communications; and
- informing parents of changes and the progress made to improve pupils' education.

(OHMCI, 1998: 9)

Often, the key to overcoming attitudinal barriers is establishing effective communication built on mutual trust and respect. Research reports that many parents face physical and social barriers to becoming more involved in local services, including education. They view schools with suspicion or fear, put off by their hierarchical nature. Parental support can be constructed as a one-sided affair, with teachers perceived as the 'experts' and parents 'in need of help' (Katz et al., 2007: 15).

After their final school placements, a group of postgraduate trainee teachers were asked to draw upon their experiences to consider ways in which schools might work alongside parents. Their ideas are shown in Box 3.3.

---

**BOX 3.3  PGCE TRAINEES' IDEAS ON COMMUNICATING WITH PARENTS**

Tapping into the know-how and specialist skills of parents (e.g. in ICT, business management, painting and decorating, building)

Governing body meetings

Notice boards

Newsletters

Website

Joint school–parent projects (e.g. reading workshops)

Exchange ideas via emails and blogs

Home visits

Parents' evenings

Written reports to parents

Social/fund-raising events

Parent representative bodies

---

Schools approach the question of communicating with parents in different ways. Among the most popular strategies are:

- face-to-face greetings and everyday conversations during drop-off and pick-up times;
- regular meetings with parents;
- newsletters, e-letters and displays;
- curriculum workshops;
- study groups;
- family group meetings;
- home/school diaries;
- invitations to attend and contribute to special assemblies, fetes and shows;
- assisting with educational visits to museums, farms, galleries;
- website information; and
- texting services.

Parents, including foster-parents, under education law have rights to be kept informed of their children's progress in school. The law requires that head teachers of maintained schools provide parents (and pupils if they so request) with:

- a report about the pupil's educational achievements each year;
- access to the educational record for the pupil if they request it in writing; and
- parents may also request, 'at all reasonable times', access to information relating to the school curriculum.

(www.education.gov.uk)

There is a danger of assuming there is only one way of being a good parent – and this tends to have a White, Western, middle-class slant (Shepherd, 2011). Irrespective of their ethnic background and socio-economic status, all parents have the potential to make a difference in the education of their children. Research has shown that where relationships between home and school are strong, teachers avoid making assumptions about parents or assigning 'group characteristics' to any particular community. Knopf and Swick (2007) have explored teachers' common misconceptions of parents, including:

- parents do not care if they do not participate or become involved in their child's school;
- parents do not have time or motivation to be involved; and
- parents are not interested in leadership roles.

In most cases, the realities are very different. The authors point out that most parents who do not participate in school events are constrained by time, resources or competing responsibilities, rather than disinterest. The fact that they are not present at school events does not mean that they do not care about their child's education. Generally, parents from non-White ethnic backgrounds are more involved in their child's school activities, including homework, than parents from White backgrounds (DCSF, 2008).

All parents have rights to participate in certain school-related activities, such as voting in elections for parent governors and the right to be asked to give consent to activities such as school visits. However, the law does not stipulate that schools require the consent of both resident and non-resident parents in circumstances where parents live apart. Parents should be consulted about meetings involving their child, for example a governors' meeting on their child's exclusion. The wishes of parents who do not want to become involved in school life should be respected.

Gaining the trust and respect of parents is one of the core values outlined in this chapter. Teachers need to live by the values associated with teaching as a profession so that they become inspirational role models. In so doing, teachers will help children to understand how their own values are part of who they are and how they might seek fulfilling roles as adults.

## Glossary

**Academies** are schools that follow the National Curriculum but are funded directly by central government, with some private investment.

**Accountability** describes the behaviour and responsibilities of individuals (e.g. teachers) and organizations (e.g. schools) for their actions towards others.

**Augmented Reality** technology superimposes a computer-generated image on a user's view of the real world, providing a form of virtual reality.

**Child abuse** can be defined in different ways and includes physical, mental and emotional abuse or threatened harm of children.

**Knowledge Age** applies to the late twentieth and early twenty-first century when ideas are the main impetus for economic growth, rather than more traditional sources such as land or labour.

**Looked after children** are those in the care of the local authority.

**Massive open online courses** are those available over the Internet without charge and offered to worldwide audiences.

**Protected characteristics** refer to nine specified areas covered by equality and diversity legislation: age, disability, gender reassignment, disability, marriage and civil partnership, race, religion or belief, sex and sexual orientation.

**Role** describes how teachers are expected to behave according to norms.

**Sexting** is 'the exchange of sexual messages and images, creating, sharing and forwarding sexually suggestive nude or nearly nude images through mobile phones and the Internet' (NSPCC, 2013: 1).

**Values** are the fundamental beliefs that people regard as important, right and lasting.

# References

Atkinson, M., Jones, M. and Lamont, E. (2007) *Multi-agency Working and Its Implications in Practice: A Review of the Literature*, Reading: CfBT.

Baginsky, M. (2003) 'Newly qualified teachers and child protection: A survey of their views, training and experiences', *Child Abuse Review*, 12(2): 119–27.

Ball, S. (2008) *The Education Debate*, Bristol: The Policy Press.

Baugh, J. (2010) 'Primary schools must evolve in the 21st century', *The Telegraph*, 20 October.

Beckett, C. (2007) *Child Protection: An Introduction*, London: Sage.

Benn, M. (2011) *School Wars*, London: Verso.

Betts, F. (1992) 'How systems thinking applies to education', *Improving School Quality*, 50(3): 38–41.

Blake, G. (2004) 'The primary teacher's responsibilities for pastoral care', in Brown, A. and Haylock, D. (eds) *Professional Issues for Primary Teachers*, London: Paul Chapman, 102–13.

Blatchford, P., Bassett, P., Brown, P., Koutsoubou, M., Martin, C., Russell, A. and Webster, R. (2009) *Deployment and Impact of Support Staff in School*, London: DCSF.

Briggs, V. (2013) 'Be smart when it comes to using social media', *Times Educational Supplement*, 28 February.

Cheminais, R. (2009) *Effective Multi-Agency Partnerships: Putting Every Child Matters into Practice*, London: Sage.

Civitas (2009) *Music, Chess and Other Sins*, London: Civitas.

Cohen, L., Manion, L. and Morrison, K. (2004) *A Guide to Teaching Practice*, London: RoutledgeFalmer.

Coles, N. (2013) 'Qualified Teacher Status be damned: Children want to be led by talent and enthusiasm', *The Telegraph*, 21 June.

Crick Report (1998) *Education for Citizenship and the Teaching of Democracy in Schools*, London: DfEE.

Day, C., Whitaker P. and Wren D. (1987) *Appraisal and Professional Development in Primary Schools*, Milton Keynes: Open University Press.

DCSF (2008) *The Impact of Parental Involvement in Children's Education*, London: DCSF.

DENI (1999) *Pastoral Care in Schools: Child Protection*, Belfast: DENI.

Dent, H. (1944) *Education in Transition*, London: Kegan Paul.

DES (1967) *Children and Their Primary Schools*, London: HMSO.

Desforges, C. and Abouchaar, A. (2003) *The Impact of Parental Involvement, Parental Support and Family Education on Pupil Achievements and Adjustment: A Literature Review*, London: DfES.

DfE (2010) Teachers' Workload Diary Survey 2010, London: DfE.

DfE (2011a) *Characteristics of Children in Need in England, 2010–11, Statistical Release*, London: DfE.

DfE (2011b) *The Munro Review of Child Protection*, London: DfE.

DfES (2003) *Every Child Matters*, Norwich: The Stationery Office.

DfES (2005) *Extended Schools: Access to Opportunities and Services for All*, London: DfES.

DfES (2007) *Diversity and Citizenship*, Nottingham: DfES.

DfE (2013a) *Teachers' Standards*, London: DfE.

DfE (2013b) *Pupil Behaviour in Schools in England*, London: DfE.

Donaldson, J. (2003) *The Smartest Giant in Town*, London: Macmillan.

Duckworth, J. and Gilbert, I. (2009) *The Little Book of Values: Educating Children to Become Thinking, Responsible and Caring Citizens*, Carmarthen: Crown House.

Eurydice (2008) *Levels of Autonomy and Responsibilities of Teachers in Europe*, Slough: Eurydice.

Evans, D. (2012a) 'Welsh view surveillance culture with suspicion', *Times Educational Supplement*, 24 August.

Evans, D. (2012b) 'Aggressive, struggling to talk and still in nappies', *Times Educational Supplement*, 27 April.

Friedberg, J. (2009) 'Teaching assistants don't boost pupils' progress, report finds', *The Guardian*, 4 September.

Fifield, D. (2013) 'Jack Wilshere enters the Januzaj debate: Keep England for the English', *The Guardian*, 8 October.

Garner, R. (2013) 'Michael Gove creating "neo Victorian" curriculum for primary schools, says professor who led massive review into sector', *The Independent*, 24 September.

Gilbert, I. (2010) *Why Do I Need a Teacher When I've got Google?: The Essential Guide to the Big Issues for Every 21st Century Teacher*, Abingdon: Routledge.

Grigg, R. (2014) 'We're all in this together', *Teach Primary*, 8(1): 41.

Grigg, R. and Hughes, S. (2013) *Teaching Primary Humanities*, Harlow: Pearson.

GTCNI (2004) *Code of Values and Professional Practice*, Belfast: GTCNI.

GTC Scotland (2012a) *The Standards for Registration: Mandatory Requirements for Registration with the General Teaching Council for Scotland*, Edinburgh: GTC Scotland.

GTC Scotland (2012b) *Professional Guidance on the Use of Electronic Communication and Social Media*, Edinburgh: GTC Scotland.

GTCW (2010) *Code of Professional Conduct and Practice for Registered Teachers*, Cardiff: GTCW.

Hargreaves, A. (2000) 'Four ages of professionalism and professional learning', *Teachers and Teaching: Theory and Practice*, 6(2): 151–82.

Hargreaves, A. and Shirley, D. (eds) (2009) *The Fourth Way: The Inspiring Future for Educational Change*, Thousand Oaks, CA: Sage.

Hargreaves, L., Cunningham, M., Everton, T., Hansen, A., Hopper, B., McIntyre, D., Maddock, M., Mukherjee, J., Pell, T., Rouse, M., Turner, P. and Wilson. L. (2006) *The Status of Teachers and the Teaching Profession: Views from Inside and Outside the Profession. Interim Findings from the Teacher Status Project*, London: DfES.

Hawkes, N. (2003) *How to Inspire and Develop Positive Values in Your Classroom*, Hyde: LDA.

Henderson, B. (2013) 'World's most racially intolerant countries mapped', *The Telegraph*, 16 May.

Hepburn, H. (2013) 'Anxious times for male teachers in primary', *Times Educational Supplement*, 16 February.

Hodgkinson, K. and Baginsky, M. (2000) 'Child protection training in school-based initial teacher training: A survey of school-centred initial teacher training courses and their trainees', *Educational Studies*, 26(3): 269–79.

Horn, P. (1989) *The Victorian and Edwardian School Child*, Stroud: Sutton.

House of Commons (2009) *School Accountability*, London: The Stationery Office.

Jeffrey, B. (2002) 'Performativity and primary teacher relations', *Journal of Education Policy*, 17(5): 531–46.

Jones, G. (2003) *A History of Education in Wales*, Cardiff: University of Wales Press.

Katz, I., La Placa, V. and Hunter, S. (2007) *Barriers to Inclusion and Successful Engagement of Parents in Mainstream Services*, York: Joseph Rowntree Foundation.

Kerawalla, L., Luckin, R., Seljeflot, S. and Woolard, A. (2006) 'Making it real: Exploring the potential of Augmented Reality for teaching primary school science', *Virtual Reality*, 10: 163–74.

Laming Report (2003) *The Victoria Climbié Inquiry Report*, London: The Stationery Office.

Levitt, R., Janta, B. and Wegrich, K. (2008) *Accountability of Teachers Literature Review*, Santa Monica, CA: Rand Corporation.

Lightfoot, L. (2009) '"Parents to blame" for problems in UK schools', *The Observer*, 5 April.

Louv, R. (2009) *Last Child in the Woods*, London: Atlantic Books.

MacBeath, J. (2012) *Future of Teaching Profession*, Cambridge: University of Cambridge.

McBer, H. (2000) *Research into Teacher Effectiveness: A Model of Teacher Effectiveness*, London: DfEE.

Maddern, K. (2013) 'Inspectors on the hunt for extremism', *Times Educational Supplement*, 14 July.

Marley, D. (2012) 'A wake-up call for all of us', *Times Educational Supplement*, 6 July.

Mayo, E. and Nairn, A. (2009) *Consumer Kids*, London: Constable.

Mulholland, H. (2012) 'Michael Gove tells academies they can hire unqualified teaching staff', *The Guardian*, 27 July.

Musset, P. (2010) 'Initial teacher education and continuing training policies in a comparative perspective: Current practices in OECD countries and a literature review on potential effects', Education Working Papers, No. 48. Paris: OECD.

Myers, K. (ed.) (2005) *Teachers Behaving Badly?: Dilemmas for School Leaders*, Abingdon: Routledge.

NSPCC (2013) *NSPCC Safeguarding in Education Service Briefing: The Role of Schools, Colleges and Academies in Protecting Children from Sexting*, London: NSPCC.

Oxfam (2006) *Teaching Controversial Issues*, London: Oxfam.

OFSTED (2008) *The Deployment, Training and Development of the Wider Workforce*, London: OFSTED.

OFSTED (2011) *Good Practice by Local Safeguarding Children Boards*, London: OFSTED.

OFSTED (2012) *The Impact of Virtual Schools on the Educational Progress of Looked After Children*, London: OFSTED.

OHMCI (Office of Her Majesty's Chief Inspector in Wales) (1998) *Standards and Quality in Primary Schools: Improving Primary Schools*, Cardiff: OHMCI.

Packard, E., Packard, N. and Brown, S. (1997) *500 Tips for Primary Teachers*, London: Kogan Page.

Papatheodorou, T. and Moyles, J. (2009) *Learning Together in the Early Years: Exploring Relational Pedagogy*, London: Routledge.

Paton, G. (2011) 'Teaching assistants fail to improve school results', *The Telegraph*, 26 May.

Paton, G. (2013) 'Teaching in primary schools still seen as a woman's job', *The Telegraph*, 5 February.

Pearson, A. (2013) 'Mass immigration is testing our tolerance', *The Telegraph*, 4 September.

Philips, H. and McInnes, F. (1950) *Exploration in the Junior School*, London: University of London.

Prigg, M. (2013) 'Archaeologists find "first recorded case" of physical child abuse', *Daily Mail*, 29 May.

Redl, F. and Wattenberg, W. (1951) *Mental Hygiene in Teaching*, New York: Harcourt, Brace World.

Richardson, J. and Parnell, P. (2005) *And Tango Makes Three*, New York: Simon & Schuster.

Scaramanga, J. (2009) 'Fundamental errors with evangelist schooling', *Times Educational Supplement*, 7 August.

Knopf, H.T. and Swick, K.J. (2007) 'How parents feel about their child's teacher/school: Implications for early childhood professionals', in *Early Childhood Education Journal*, 34, 291–6.

Scottish Executive (2003) *Protecting Children: A Shared Responsibility*, Edinburgh: Scottish Executive.

Scottish Government (2008) *A Guide to Getting It Right for Every Child*, Edinburgh: Scottish Government.

Sebba, J. and Robinson, C. (2010) *Evaluation of Unicef UK's Rights Respecting School's Award*, London: Unicef UK.

Shepherd, J. (2011) 'Teachers "expect less" from black, middle-class pupils – study', *The Guardian*, 5 June.

Stewart, W. (2012) 'A dangerous lesson to forget', *Times Educational Supplement*, 31 October.

Sweeney, D. (1999) 'Child protection', in Cole, M. (ed.) *Professional Issues for Teachers and Student Teachers*, London: David Fulton, 38–55.

Sylva, K., Melhuish, E., Sammons, P., Siraj-Blatchford, I. and Taggart, B. (2004) *The Effective Provision of Pre-School Education (EPPE) Project: Findings from Pre-school to end of Key Stage 1*, London: IOE.

TDA (2011) *Results of the Newly Qualified Teacher Survey 2011*, Manchester: TDA.

University of Bristol (2013) *Handbook for Education Professionals*, Bristol: University of Bristol.

Valkenburg, P.M. and Buijzen, M. (2005) 'Identifying determinants of young children's brand awareness: Television, parents, and peers', *Applied Developmental Psychology*, 26: 456–68.

Vasagar, J. (2010) 'BNP Members to be barred from teaching', *The Guardian*, 2 November.

Vasagar, J. and Williams, M. (2012) 'Teachers warned over befriending pupils on Facebook', *The Guardian*, 23 January.

Waterfield, B. (2012) 'Christians should leave their beliefs at home or get another job', *The Telegraph*, 4 September.

Welsh Government (2010) *Educational Visits: A Safety Guide for Learning Outside the Classroom*, Cardiff: Welsh Government.

Whalley, M. (2007) *Involving Parents in their Children's Learning*, London: Sage.

Williams, B., Williams, J. and Ullman, A. (2002) *Parental Involvement in Education*, London: DFES.

Williams, R. (2012) 'Revealed: The Third largest "country" in the world – Facebook hits one billion users', *The Independent*, 4 October.

Withnall, A. (2013) '"Education underclass" of children in the UK still in nappies when they start school', *The Independent*, 3 September.

## Websites

National Union of Teachers is the largest of the teaching unions in England and Wales – www.teachers.org.uk

The National Confederation of Parent Teacher Associations promotes partnerships between home and school – www.ncvo-vol.org.uk

National Parent Forum of Scotland – www.educationscotland.gov.uk/parentzone/getinvolved/forumscotland/index.asp

Childnet seeks to work with parents, teachers and others to make the Internet a safe place for children – www.childnet.com

NSPCC provides resources to support schools in keeping children safe – www.nspcc.org.uk

# 4

# Passionate and creative teachers

## Developing pupils' thinking skills

## Chapter objectives

By the end of this chapter you should be able to:

- Explain what it means to be a passionate teacher and how passion can be developed.
- Describe the notion of creativity and its significance in the primary school.
- Summarize strategies to teach thinking skills.
- Critically reflect upon the contribution of neuroscience to education.

## Introduction

What separates outstanding from good teachers? Many writers suggest that it comes down to passion (Fried, 1995; Liston and Garrison, 2004; Mart, 2013). The common factors among excellent teachers identified in New Zealand, Italy, America, Sweden and France is that they demonstrate a passionate desire for the success of all their students (Day, 2009). This chapter defines passion in the context of teaching. It also considers how teachers might use their passion to develop pupils' creativity and **thinking skills**. Finally, it considers the contribution of neuroscience in understanding how children think and learn.

## What does it mean to be a passionate teacher?

Passion has been defined as 'a strong inclination or desire towards an activity that one likes and finds important and in which one invests time and energy' (Carbonneau *et al.*, 2008: 978). People are passionate about other people, music, food, objects, places, animals, causes, issues, and their jobs. They can feel so strongly about something or someone that they are prepared to experience personal hardship or loss. This reflects the original meaning of the term passion, which was 'to suffer' (Latin *passio*). Such self-sacrifice can result in difficulties in terms of achieving a reasonable work–life balance and maintaining healthy relationships. The danger is that passion can become obsessive and lead to inflexibility, excess and conflict. Those who display obsessive passion feel compelled to work all the time, even when they do not want to, and are driven by words such as 'must', 'need', 'have to' rather than 'want to', 'get to' or 'can't wait to' (Kaufman, 2011). On the other hand, what psychologists call 'harmonious passion' provides purpose, fulfilment and meaning in life. It equates to what Robinson (2009) refers to as 'the Element' or Csikszentmihalyi's (1997) 'state of flow', where someone is so immersed in what they are doing that time recedes into the background.

Neurologically speaking, passion begins in the brain rather than the heart. When a young man had an area of his brain removed to control severe seizures he became completely uninterested in people. Although he could maintain conversations, he preferred to sit alone. He no longer recognized his friends, relatives or even his mother (Goleman, 1996). The surgeon had removed the young man's amygdala (from the Greek word for 'almond'), which controls emotional responses. Yet, the brain is complex and much is still to be understood on how it works. For example, in a similar case of a woman whose amygdala was removed to treat her epilepsy, she developed 'hyper empathy' over 13 years, allowing her to decode other people's feelings. It seems that other parts of the brain worked to compensate for her loss (Gholipour, 2013). Amygdala research may one day provide insight into how children can further develop their emotional competence and control their impulsivity (Blakemore and Frith, 2005).

Writers such as Daniel Goleman (1996) believe that we have two minds: the one that thinks (rational mind) and the one that feels (the emotional mind), commonly referred to as 'heart' and 'head'. When negative emotions, such as anxiety, anger or resentment, take over, rational thinking is inhibited. On the other hand, positive emotions such as joy, hope and love enhance learning experiences. Passion, of course, has both positive and negative aspects. Finding the right balance between emotion and reason is one of life's great challenges.

In the context of teaching, passion is nothing to do with romance, physical attraction or sexual intimacy. Rather, it is concerned with a teacher's love of ideas, subjects and, in a platonic sense, children. There are teachers who are very effective but do not necessarily enjoy what they do. They do not yearn to go to school or derive deep-seated pleasure from teaching others. On the other hand, passionate teachers could not imagine doing anything else than teach. They are risk takers (in the sense of trying to push the boundaries to improve), care deeply about knowledge and ideas, are alive to current news in and out of school, and are drawn to each child's potential (Fried, 1995). Passionate teachers are remembered for different reasons; some for their love of poetry, their passion for the marvels of Space, playing the guitar, their commitment to combating racism or saving the planet. Passion drives teachers to share their love for learning and to think about how to engage young minds as partners in the learning process. This does not mean that passionate teachers are always larger-than-life superheroes, bubbling forth with energy and confidence. Passion can burn in different ways. There are passionate teachers who are quiet, humble and unassuming but who are equally determined to achieve excellence.

## How can passion be developed?

While individuals have different personalities, dispositions and aptitudes, the attributes of a passionate teacher can be cultivated through time, effort and application (Figure 4.1). Studies of world-class performers, for instance in sport, show that they are committed to hours of 'deliberate practice' (Colvin, 2008; Syed, 2011). According to the so-called Ericsson rule, (see Ericsson *et al.*, 2006), to become an expert requires a minimum of 10,000 hours (20 hours for 50 weeks a year for ten years) of well-structured practice. In reality it is not the repetition alone that matters, but acting upon the feedback and reinforcement of improvement. But there is something else. These performers demonstrate mental toughness and authenticity in being true to themselves by following their passions. As Hartley (2012) put it, they work to the simple mantra 'do what you love, and love what you do'. For teachers, Day (2007: 1) notes that 'teaching effectiveness is underpinned by teachers who are able to be at their best emotionally and intellectually'. There are considerable demands on trainee and new teachers in particular, as they face unknown situations – schools vary in their relationships, ethos, physical environments and patterns of behaviour. To become a passionate teacher calls for considerable personal and professional commitment.

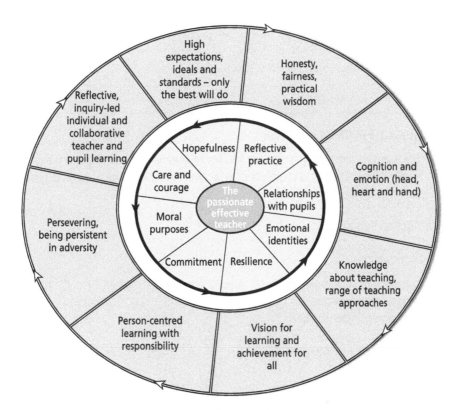

**FIGURE 4.1**  The attributes of the passionate and effective teacher

Source: Day (2007). Reproduced with permission

Teachers can demonstrate their passion through their diligent research when preparing lessons, their animated delivery, interactions with others and the excitement of finding new things out with children. Body language, discussed in Chapter 11, is particularly important in conveying enthusiasm. Neill and Caswell (1993: 101) found that the best teachers looked intently at the class more often than others and used head movements, which are signals of involvement with a speaker. They reported that 'effective teachers smiled more, and used more joking intonation; their lessons were more fun to be in . . . they spent more time discussing hypotheses than the ineffective teachers'. Teachers can show passion through their genuine interest in children – their hobbies, likes, hopes, questions, concerns – and to seek ways of building on this so that lessons are made relevant, enjoyable and meaningful.

The best practitioners know when to use different teaching methodologies to enliven learning. They are soon in tune with how the lesson is unfolding and from observing the learners, sense when to cut short explanations, or when to elaborate further. They also know that children are generally more attentive at the start and end of lessons and the need to capitalize on this (Box 4.1). Research has shown that the brain works in 'prime times', when learning is at its peak, and 'down times', when the brain needs to rest (Sousa, 2003). In a typical 40-minute lesson, prime time equates to 30 minutes and down time 10 minutes. The pattern usually begins with a period of prime time lasting 20 minutes, followed by 10 minutes down time and a second period of 10 minutes prime time. The balance does change depending upon the length of the session – the longer the lesson, the shorter the proportion of prime time. The implications for teachers are that long sessions need to be broken up into smaller blocks of time to maximize learning; activities also need to be varied (Cohen *et al.*, 2004).

---

### BOX 4.1  FOCUS ON PRACTICE

The following table was put together following a seminar discussion with a group of trainees on the approaches they successfully used to inject vitality into each phase of a 'typical' lesson during school placement:

### Section suggestions

### Introduction

Ask quick-fire questions, 'big issue' questions, personal questions,'What if' questions
Pose a problem to resolve
Read a newspaper headline
Tell a joke
Show a picture or object
Set a puzzle
Play a game
Use a puppet
Use mind maps to revise prior knowledge

## Middle

Build a model
Solve a mystery
Take the children outside
Study a painting
Make a frieze
Write a script
Produce a book of calligrams or word pictures
Produce a digital story of a typical day in the school
Devise a speech and record it
Undertake role play with a moral dilemma
Arrange a class museum
Read the start of a story for children to complete
Interview guest speakers
Make a film
Use newspapers to explore bias
Use newspapers to plan a week's television viewing for an elderly person
Engage in a contemporary debate
Draw diagrams, flow charts or posters
Cook food
Open a new 'shop'
Make a board game

## Plenary

Celebrate *any* achievement
Invite pupils to use traffic light cards to demonstrate their level of confidence and understanding
Use a quiz to assess knowledge and understanding
Use Post-it notes to record learning
Ask children to describe the 'missing' learning outcomes
Play 'dumb' – act as if you are unsure about the point of the lesson
Share what they and *you* found difficult about the lesson
Invite pupils to summarize the lesson
Ask peers to comment on the achievement of others
Share your lesson evaluation pro forma with the pupils and ask them to complete it!

Enthusiasm and passion are the most obvious signs of a teacher's commitment. But how are these developed? The starting-point is individual reflection on personal goals and professional responsibilities. What do teachers expect from themselves? What are their aspirations? What does school life mean for them? Unfortunately there are teachers who, for different reasons, have lost the joy of teaching or who are no longer interested in learning. Research indicates that passion can wane during the course of a teacher's career due to a range of factors, such as pupils' behaviour, changes in government policy, and parental demands (Day *et al.*, 2007). While support and professional development might revive a few, passion cannot be forced on teachers who are disengaged.

However, there are also many teachers whose passions are curbed by a standardized culture and who are less effective as a result. Their passions can be developed by school leaders and managers who value their views, encourage initiative and show flexibility, for instance in how the timetable is arranged. According to the National College for School Leadership, outstanding leaders look out for new ideas and allow pupils and staff to experiment, instilling confidence that they will be supported. They model commitment, passion, hard work and energy (NCSL, 2010). They create opportunities to observe and discuss inspirational figures at work. Metcalfe and Game (2006: 59) cite examples of passionate Australian primary teachers who convey energy and invigorate learners, for instance: 'As soon as you walked into Alison's classroom, you could tell it was working. There was lots of movement, lots of different things happening, but there was still a sense of calm. I suppose her passion came through everything that she did.'

While it is a challenge to maintain a passion for teaching day in day out, it is clearly easier to do this in an environment of supportive leadership, and where the demands of bureaucracy are manageable. Like children, teachers are likely to demonstrate their passion and creativity when they feel valued, safe and secure, have access to appropriate resources and are encouraged to take risks. Passion needs to be cultivated in the classroom, school and education at large. A report on the world's best education systems suggests that their central governments provide only loose guidelines on teaching and learning processes 'because peer-led creativity and innovation inside schools become the core driver for raising performance' (Mourshed *et al.*, 2010: 26).

## Passion drives creativity

Passion is often the force that drives individuals to create new ideas. The late Steve Jobs, founder of Apple computers, once told his employees: 'people with passion can change the world for the better' (quoted by Gallo, 2010). He was not passionate about his products in their own right, but the impact they could make on enriching people's lives. Creativity usually follows passion. People are most creative in areas that they feel most passionate about. For example, Google programmers were allocated 20 per cent of their working time to pursue independent projects of their choice. Out of this came Google mail and Google News. The company bosses created a work environment that 'resembles a playground more than a prison camp' (Walker, 2011: 1). One teacher applied the 20 per cent idea to his classroom with the caveats that the time must be used for some type of learning, the work recorded in a homework diary, and the quality should be to a high standard. He provided access to resources (although use had to be justified); the children could choose to work in groups and continue with their projects at home:

> The range of interests in my class included films, cars, animals, console games, sewing, cookery, and so much more. Children have produced books, magazines, websites, guides, film reviews, storybooks, artwork and presentations. And the greatest thing about them all; the content is of an exceptionally high quality
>
> (www.theguardian.com/teacher-network/2012/oct/04/
> google-20-percent-time-schools)

But creativity has its price. By its nature, it is time-consuming, requires space and is difficult to measure or control.

Creativity is an elusive concept and has many definitions (see Box 4.2) – Shaheen (2012) points out that most refer to creative people, aspects of the creative process, products and the environments that promote creativity. Creativity comes in different forms. Big 'C' creativity refers to the contributions of a handful of people who are at the cutting edge of science, social science, art and music, constantly testing the boundaries. Small 'c' creativity refers to ideas or products that are new and meaningful to the individual but only that person – for example, if a child 'discovers' a new colour by mixing two together. In other words, creativity can be seen along a continuum with everyday imagination at one end and the likes of Einstein, Mozart and Da Vinci at the other. Craft (2000) suggests that creativity needs to be broadened as a concept beyond imagination. She uses the term 'possibility thinking' to describe creativity that guides decision making in everyday life. It represents a shift from asking 'what is this and what can it do?' to 'what can I do with this?' and 'what if . . .?'

The process of being creative involves asking questions, making connections, exploring ideas, imagining what might be, and reflecting critically on the outcomes. Sharp (2004: 5) describes the characteristics of creativity as follows:

- imagination;
- originality (the ability to come up with ideas and products that are new and unusual);
- productivity (the ability to generate a variety of different ideas through divergent thinking);
- problem solving (application of knowledge and imagination to a given situation); and
- the ability to produce an outcome of value and worth.

It is easy to become sceptical about originality in schools on the basis that few individuals are ever likely to produce original materials or thoughts. However, Boden (1991) makes

---

**BOX 4.2  KEY CONCEPTS – CREATIVITY, CREATIVE TEACHING AND CREATIVE LEARNING**

Creativity is defined as 'imaginative activity fashioned so as to produce outcomes that are both original and of value' (NACCCE, 1999: 30). It involves fresh thinking, looking at problems and issues from a different angle and making connections. Creative teachers tend to be curious, enthusiastic and have a desire to learn. They make connections and encourage pupils to be creative in their own learning.

Creative learning is about developing children's openness to experiment, take risks and not fear failure. It involves them in collaborating over tasks and critically evaluating their own learning. Wiggins (2011) contrasts creativity with boring and unfruitful learning. He suggests that from the distant past to the present, schools have failed to promote creative learning, preferring studying for recall.

an important observation that originality can be measured in different ways, including how well a person responds to their previous efforts and how the response is viewed by his peers. Finally, the outcome has to be considered valuable in relation to the set purpose – whether a song, painting, poem, sculpture, puzzle, dance routine, line of reasoning or invention.

Sir Ken Robinson describes creativity as the 'genetic code' of education, which is essential for the new economic circumstances of the twenty-first century (Buie, 2005). The worldwide downturn in the economy has highlighted the importance of developing creative thinking in schools, although creativity is subject to cultural and political constraints (Box 4.3).

Creative energy and innovation is not only critical on utilitarian grounds to meet the needs of the economy. It provides each generation with emotional and intellectual satisfaction. At a more conversational level, Wragg (2005: 193) described creative teachers as those who 'go against the flow' or 'row upstream'; but he acknowledged how difficult this could be in a climate of prescriptive practice. Wragg argued that an 'obligation to invent' should reside with all teachers. One of the main obstacles for beginning teachers to overcome is gaining personal confidence in taking risks. 'Playing safe' is an understandable approach for many who have limited pedagogic knowledge and

---

### BOX 4.3 INTERNATIONAL VIEW – CREATIVITY

Creativity is shaped by beliefs, values and customs. In East Asia, Confucianism is the main cultural influence that values silence, humility, conformity, introspection and suppression of emotion – from a Western viewpoint, these appear to block creative thinking as students do not question authority and established thinking. Japanese schools are said to focus on the art of impression over the art of expression (Kim, 2005). In recent years, the Japanese authorities have tried to allow children 'room to grow', for instance through project based learning (McCreedy, 2004). Chinese leaders recognize that a lack of creativity is a barrier to its development as a global and political power. However, its educational reforms, which included giving teachers more scope in the choice of textbooks and the development of the curriculum, have not made headway particularly in remote rural areas. Preparing for examinations, listening to lectures and rote learning characterize Chinese classes (Lockette, 2012). Research shows that creativity differences between Western and Asian students come down to environmental factors and values rather than ethnicity – Kwang (2001) describes this perceived creativity gap in his book *Why Asians are Less Creative than Westerners* (Prentice Hall).

The shortage of resources is a major barrier to teaching creativity in countries such as India. However the Agastya Foundation has used mobile science labs to spark the curiosity of over a million children from poor rural villages. In line with India's philosophical tradition, curiosity for the natural world is linked with curiosity about the self and a holistic conception of the human being. Singapore has a strong commitment to innovation because of its limited natural resources. Hence creative and critical skills have a high priority in the school curriculum (OECD, 2013).

experience. Cremin *et al.* (2009) report that by working alongside non-teacher creative practitioners – website developers, artists, gardeners, architects, photographers, town planners, musicians – teachers' dormant creativity has been awoken. The creative teacher is characterized by an ability to go beyond the usual practice, and is able to generate ideas easily and smoothly. Csikszentmihalyi (1997) draws on 30 years of research to highlight why it so essential to cultivate creativity in school. Young children are particularly creative because they see the world in a fresh, uninhibited way. They are most deeply engaged in tasks when they are allowed to focus on areas of their own individual choice. When they feel at ease and secure emotionally, they become fully involved in their learning, unaware of the passing of time (Basford and Hodson, 2008). The gains in promoting creativity in school should convince teachers of the need to become adventurous in their approach.

Research findings indicate that developing creativity brings benefits in terms of pupil motivation, enthusiasm, independence and enjoyment (Casserley, 2004). However, these benefits accrue because teachers set high expectations and are clear about anticipated outcomes. Promoting creativity in the classroom does not mean providing pupils with free rein in a climate of 'anything goes'. On the contrary, the best teachers recognize that 'higher levels of creativity usually result from an interaction of considerable knowledge and skills with a willingness to innovate and experiment' (HMIe, 2006: 6). The Scottish Inspectorate raises a number of questions about the nature of creativity (HMIe, 2006: 5–6):

1    Is creativity another area of the curriculum?
2    Is creativity promoted only in some subjects or curriculum areas?
3    Is everyone creative?
4    Are younger children more creative?
5    How does creativity relate to thinking skills and to enterprise?

**PAUSE FOR REFLECTION**

How would you respond to the five questions raised by HMIe?

## Creativity in the curriculum

The relative importance of creativity in education has been discussed at length over recent years (Fisher and Williams, 2004; Grainger and Barnes, 2006; Craft, 2011). In England, this has been largely a reaction to perceived shortcomings in successive models of the National Curriculum. The curriculum of the 1990s was seen to be too heavy in content while tightly structured literacy and numeracy lessons failed to give teachers enough scope and time to develop children's creativity. Clegg (1999) argues that there are good reasons why formal education systems don't increase an individual's creativity. Most systems depend on getting through a set curriculum within a set time. Being too creative will only disrupt this. Teachers focus on meeting requirements in a conformist culture. So unless schools are asked to do something else, creativity will always be of secondary importance.

England's most recent National Curriculum, introduced in 2014, has been criticized for continuing to stifle creativity. In the teaching of English, for instance, critics claim that there is too much emphasis on grammar, spelling and punctuation. The children's author Sally Gardner dismisses what she perceives as the government's learning by rote approach to writing, what she calls 'learning by rope ... the gallows for the inquiring mind' (quoted by Garner, 2013). In a letter to *The Telegraph* (20 March 2013), a long list of academics expressed their disapproval of the curriculum's emphasis on rote learning rather than creative thinking. The writer and photographer Roger Mavity (2013) summed up a widely held view:

> Gove's unquestioning respect for the traditional way of doing things would be fine if we were still living in the days of empire, bowler hats and Dixon of Dock Green. But we aren't. In the new order, where globalisation and instant communication have taken over, creativity and ideas have huge value. And that value is not just cultural, but financial, too.

Despite such criticisms, Michael Gove insisted that he supported creativity in schools. The disagreement centres on how creativity is defined and should be developed. Gove believes that *before* children can express themselves they need to acquire basic knowledge and skills. For instance in mathematics, he says, 'unless children are introduced to that stock of knowledge, unless they know how to use numbers with confidence, unless multiplication, long division, become automatic processes, they won't be able to use mathematics creatively' (cited by Robinson, 2013).

Ken Robinson and others argue that although this sounds common sense, in reality life is different. Creativity is a very personal process in which people use their talents and aptitudes in different ways to make meaning. Although creative work does require understanding of basic concepts and skills, it is not a linear process. In other words, a relentless focus on knowledge acquisition and learning skills in isolation does not produce creative thinkers.

Creativity has a higher curriculum profile in other parts of the UK compared to England. In Wales, 'creative development' features as a discrete Foundation Phase (3–7) 'area of learning' for young children. Teachers are expected to build on children's natural curiosity and disposition to learn by providing everyday sensory experiences, both indoors and outdoors. Curriculum guidance for Key Stage 2 gives schools scope to 'make the most' of learning in how they organize and plan the curriculum, with separate guidance on promoting thinking skills (DCELLS, 2008a; WAG, 2010). In Northern Ireland, creativity features within the 'Thinking Skills and Personal Capabilities' framework, while Scottish children are expected to develop their creative ideas and skills in experiences across the curriculum. This is a logical approach in that creativity is a process and disposition rather than a discrete subject (Wyse, 2013).

Teachers need to dispel a number of myths associated with creativity. Creativity should not be seen as confined to special, talented people (Figure 4.2). Nor should it be limited to the arts. Moreover, creativity is not the same as unrestrained 'self- expression'. These are damaging myths because children can be put off learning for life and become disengaged, deskilled and disenfranchised. For example, in mathematics, a quarter of adults in England have the skills of a 10-year-old (Ramesh, 2013). Many adults do not see the beauty in number because, as children, their school lessons amounted to a diet of rote exercises. Yet mathematics can be a very creative subject. Some teachers, despite curriculum prescriptions, inspire children with a love of mathematics by exploring number, shape and patterns. They use children's bodies, toys, board games, local walks, visits, drama, sport, special projects, investigations, the natural environment and technologies to teach mathematics creatively and to show the subject's relevance.

As Sharp (2004: 8) points out, all teachers can promote creativity by:

- asking open-ended questions;
- tolerating ambiguity;

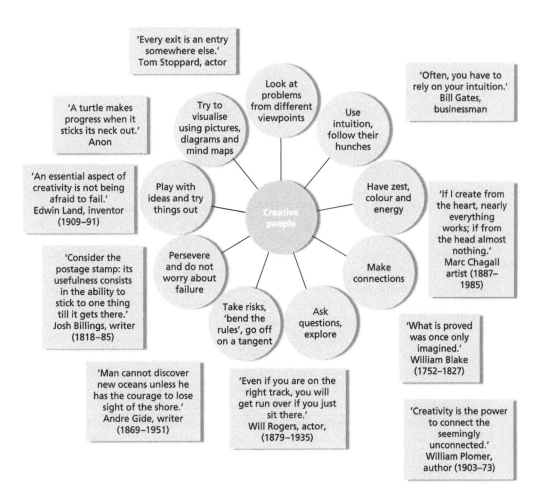

**FIGURE 4.2** Ideas associated with creative people

- modelling creative thinking and behaviour;
- encouraging experimentation and persistence; and
- praising children who provide unexpected answers.

Children and young people want to develop their creativity. In 2008, they voiced their hopes through a 'Manifesto for a Creative Britain', a project carried out by Tate Modern and Creative Partnerships. The Manifesto called for more space in schools to be creative; more access to resources such as musical instruments and paints; opportunities to take risks and try out new things; mentoring to get into the creative industries because they did not know how they worked; and a revised curriculum so that subjects were more relevant to their lives.

If teachers and schools want to improve children's creativity, then no special creativity programmes are needed (Jones and Wyse, 2013). Rather, they need to commit to the belief that it is a basic right of every child to express their thoughts and feelings creatively, whether in poetry, composing music, investigating real-life mathematical problems, painting, programming computer animations, responding to environmental challenges or performing dances. Clearly there are implications here regarding the role of the teacher, resources, timetabling and curriculum planning. But it is possible to develop creative classrooms within National Curriculum frameworks. Creativity is not at the opposite end to achieving high standards in literacy and numeracy. Even in the most standardized of classroom cultures, creative touches and techniques can be introduced to achieve prescribed objectives and make learning more enjoyable.

## Creativity and thinking

One of the key characteristics of creativity is exploring different ways of doing things. This has been variously described as 'possibility thinking', 'divergent thinking', 'lateral thinking', 'astute thinking', 'perceptual thinking' or plain 'creative thinking'. Although there are nuanced differences here, collectively these refer to seeing the world from different perspectives, understanding interpretations, considering the most unlikely scenarios and exploring novel solutions. Divergent thinking seeks to open up the mind often through metaphors, analogies and reframing. For instance, rather than ask children 'What is the sum of 5 plus 5?' they could be asked 'What two numbers add up to 10?'

The importance of teaching divergent thinking from an early age is borne out by research that indicates that this declines, as children get older. When such creativity tests were given to 5, 10 and 15-year-olds, 98 per cent of the 5-year-olds scored at a 'genius' level, but this dropped to 32 per cent for 10-year-olds and only 10 per cent for teenagers (Land and Jarman, 1992). The National Literacy Trust website reports remarkably similar findings from a UK study in 2005. Of 1,600 children aged 3–5, 98 per cent were able to think in divergent ways. By the time they were aged 8–10, this had fallen to 32 per cent and only 10 per cent of 13–15-year-olds could think in non-linear ways. Most alarming, only 2 per cent of 200,000 25-year-olds could think divergently (www. literacytrust.org.uk).

The subject of thinking skills has attracted considerable interest around the world. Governments, employers and educators widely acknowledge that school systems are not preparing children and young people for the demands of twenty-first century work and life. Schools are struggling to keep pace with major social and economic changes, such as the rise in digital lifestyles, environmental challenges and the need to innovate to remain globally competitive. In an international roundtable discussion of how to make school systems great, Michael Barber suggested the following formula for the curriculum:

Well educated = E (K + T+ L)

The letter 'K' stands for knowledge, 'T' for thinking, 'L' for leadership (individual and collective) and 'E' for ethical underpinning (cited by McKinsey, 2009: 12). The shift from knowledge-acquisition to thinking and leadership skills resonates with educational systems such as Singapore and Alberta, Canada, who are trying to develop curricula strong on creative and critical thinking. Effective teaching combines both developing thinking skills with subject content – learners cannot achieve their potential if either is lacking.

The demand for **thinking skills** is evident in employer surveys. Critical thinking is among the essential criteria (along with teamwork, oral and written communication, and work ethic) that American employers look for if young people are to succeed in the workplace (Conference Board, 2006). In the UK, *The Guardian* (22 April 2013) reviewed the top ten desirable skills that featured most in job advertisements and these included thinking flexibly and problem solving.

The modern-day interest in thinking skills can be traced to the influential work of Benjamin Bloom (1913–1999). He was an educational psychologist who was interested in exceptional talent and how high-level thinking could be promoted. He also wanted to know what students thought when they were being taught and so he introduced 'think aloud' protocols. Bloom questioned the existing custom of comparing student performance against each other, preferring to help students focus on achieving curriculum goals. His most famous work was *Taxonomy of Educational Objectives: Handbook 1: The Cognitive Domain* (Bloom *et al.*, 1956). This identified a hierarchy of cognitive thinking skills. It is taxonomic in that each subsequent level depends upon the student's ability to perform at the level or levels that precede it. For example, the ability to evaluate is predicated on the assumption that for the student to be able to evaluate, he or she would need to have the necessary information, understand the information he or she had, be able to apply it, be able to analyse it, synthesize it and then eventually evaluate it (Eisner, 2000). Bloom's work has been subsequently updated by one of his former students and colleagues (Anderson and Krathwohl, 2001; see Table 4.1). The revised taxonomy features verbs rather than nouns, and includes create (rather than synthesis) as one of three higher-order thinking skills.

An indication of Bloom's continued influence can be seen in the planning framework drawn up to accompany the teaching of thinking within the Scottish *Curriculum for Excellence* (Bloomer and McIlroy, 2012). However, Ritchhart *et al.* (2011) point out that in real life thinking is much more fluid than Bloom's taxonomy suggests. A child painting a picture may use knowledge to mix a particular colour, evaluate that the result is not what is desired, tell a friend about the picture or scrap it and create another one. In other words, there is constant back and forth between ways of thinking that leads to learning. While knowledge is the foundation on which skills rest, beyond this everyday thinking draws on different interrelated skills.

**TABLE 4.1** Bloom's original and revised taxonomy

| Level | Original (1956) | Revised (2001) | Features |
|-------|-----------------|----------------|----------|
| Higher order | Evaluation | Creating | Invent, design, construct, blend, set up, produce, improve, organize |
| | Synthesis | Evaluating | Debate, judge, test, conclude, measure, rate, monitor |
| | Analysis | Analysing | Distinguish, question, experiment, inspect, examine, probe, separate, investigate |
| Lower order | Application | Applying | Illustrate, paint, model, interview, adapt, draw, compute, translate, sequence, demonstrate, perform |
| | Comprehension | Understanding | Describe, observe, classify, compare, explain, estimate, define, give main idea, label |
| | Knowledge | Remembering | Listen, group, choose, recite, quote, record, match, sort, underline |

Sources: Bloom (1956); Anderson and Krathwohl (2001)

Nonetheless, taxonomies support teachers in setting work that is appropriately challenging for different pupils (Box 4.4). They also inform planning for progression with words such as 'create' and 'evaluate' usually signposting higher-level thinking. It should be noted that progression also occurs within each level – so, for example, within the skill

---

**BOX 4.4  FOCUS ON PRACTICE**

Examples of work set by trainees at different levels to engage pupils

| Level of thinking | Examples of activities set by trainees |
|-------------------|----------------------------------------|
| Creating | Wrote their own rap song to promote healthy eating (Y6) |
| | Created a new timetable for the week (Y6) |
| | Composed a new advertising jingle for a toy (Y4) |
| Evaluating | Rated the contestants in a school competition (Y5) |
| | Wrote a book review for a magazine (Y4) |
| | Wrote a letter to complain about the litter in the school grounds (Y3) |
| Analysing | Surveyed the views of other children on the use of the playground (Y3) |
| | Made diagrams to show how an electrical circuit could fail (Y4) |
| | Took part in a debate on the closure of small schools (Y6) |
| Applying | Interviewed a visiting speaker (Y5) |
| | Constructed a model of a castle drawbridge to show how it worked (Y5) |
| | Wrote short diary entries for someone during the Great Fire of London (Y4) |
| Understanding | Labelled parts of a sunflower (Y3) |
| | Listed the things needed to make a sandwich (Y2) |
| | Re-told the story of the *Three Little Pigs* in their own words (R) |
| Remembering | Described objects brought back from a visit to the beach (Y1) |
| | Named the main characters in *Toy Story* (R) |
| | Recited the poem 'Lines Written on a Paper Handkerchief' (Y4) |

of historical analysis children might move from studying two pictures and placing them in order of age on a timeline to analyse the causal relationships between the events.

The thinking skills movement is a broad one but shares common principles: intelligence is modifiable; every learner can improve; feedback is essential; learning should be applied to real-life contexts; children should talk about their thinking and discuss their views with others; they need to develop strategies to control how they think (**metacognition**); and deliberately practise their thinking in different contexts. This is in line with a social constructivist approach to learning that values group discussion (Wood, 1998). In short, the focus is very much on *how* rather than *what* to learn.

Thinking skills is not a new phenomenon. Reuven Feuerstein, a child psychologist, developed his instrumental enrichment (FIE) programme while he was working with orphans who survived the Second World War Holocaust. Feuerstein believed that children could develop their intelligence if they were taught how to think. The focus of the programme, which is now global, is on children with learning difficulties and behavioural problems. Extensive evaluations of FIE show positive effects primarily on measures of non-verbal reasoning (McGuinness, 1999). A small-scale study of Scottish border schools using FIE reported improvements in children's confidence, self-belief and perceptions of thinking (Soden *et al.*, 2006).

Since the 1990s governments have included 'thinking skills' in their curricula and invested heavily in support materials for schools. For instance, the Northern Ireland (NI) Curriculum website provides many practical resources for teachers seeking to develop thinking skills, including storybooks, 'thinking cards', posters, whiteboard resources and training activities for teachers (www.nicurriculum.org.uk/TSPC). The Education Scotland website includes Powerpoints, expert videos, case studies from schools, and documentation to show how thinking skills can be promoted in its *Curriculum for Excellence* (www. educatiuonscotland.gov.uk/resources). In Wales, thinking skills feature within the *Skills Framework* (DCELLS, 2008b) and is accompanied by detailed guidance (WAG, 2010). However, evaluation by the inspectorate showed that provision for thinking skills was patchy and few schools used the non-statutory framework effectively (Estyn, 2011).

In Wales, Scotland and Northern Ireland, thinking skills appear explicitly in the curricula documentation. In England, until recently this was the case when schools were expected to teach information processing, reasoning, enquiry, creative thinking and evaluation skills across the curriculum (DfES, 2002). However, Michael Gove believed that thinking skills first require extensive factual knowledge. Others agree that what children need most is a thorough grounding in subject knowledge that will produce good thinkers (Johnson in Johnson and Siegel, 2010). Johnson is critical of those who see thinking as a set of processes to be taught, when in reality thinking is often spontaneous and intuitive: 'A thinking-skills Newton would have said, "curse that apple interrupting my checklist"' (Johnson and Siegel, 2010: 29). He questions the notion of teaching a set of transferable generalized thinking skills – if schools can teach thinking, why do they not teach wisdom? But he does acknowledge that schools should develop Habits of Mind such as openness towards different ideas and concern for accuracy, while maintaining a critical spirit. Willingham (2009) also supports the importance of factual knowledge as the basis of critical thinking. He argues that good teachers are able to use stories to convey essential knowledge and meaning.

**TABLE 4.2** Thinking skills in the curriculum

| Country | Thinking skills |
| --- | --- |
| England | Pre 2014 general skills linked to 2014 subject specific examples:<br>■ Information processing – retrieve and record information from non-fiction (Reading, Year 3–4)<br>■ Reasoning – use logical reasoning to predict the behaviour of simple programs (Computing, Key Stage 1)<br>■ Enquiry – use simple fieldwork and observational skills . . . (Geography, Key Stage 1)<br>■ Creative thinking – perform dances using simple movement patterns (PE, Key Stage 1)<br>■ Evaluation – evaluate and edit by assessing the effectiveness of their own and others' writing and suggesting improvements (Writing, Years 3–4) |
| Wales | *Planning*: activating prior knowledge, skills and understanding; determining the approach/method; determining success criteria.<br>*Developing*: thinking about cause and effect and predicting; forming opinions and making decisions; thinking logically and seeking patterns; thinking critically.<br>*Reflecting*: drawing conclusions on own learning and thinking; determining success; linking and lateral thinking. |
| Scotland | Thinking skills are among the skills for learning, life and work that should be taught across the Experiences and Outcomes of the *Curriculum for Excellence*. For instance within Social Studies, teachers should seek 'to develop the capacity for critical thinking through accessing, analysing and using information from a wide variety of sources' |
| Northern Ireland | 1 *Managing information*: asking, accessing, selecting, recording, integrating, communicating.<br>2 *Thinking, problem solving and decision making*: searching for meaning, deepening understanding, coping with challenges.<br>3 *Being creative*: managing, imagining, generating, inventing, taking risks for learning.<br>4 *Working with others*: being collaborative, being sensitive to others' feelings, being fair and responsible.<br>5 *Self-management*: evaluating strengths and weaknesses, setting goals and targets, managing and regulating self. |

Sources: DfES (2002); DfE (2014); WAG (2010); www.educationscotland/gov.uk; www.nicurriuclum.org.uk/tspc

Such writers would welcome the fact that general thinking skills are no longer part of the curriculum in England. However, teachers are expected to develop children's thinking through subject contexts (Table 4.2). The 2014 curriculum is different in that the subjects are not the 'hooks' by which thinking skills hang. Rather, they are the driving force by which children are to learn skills such as scientific inquiry, geographical fieldwork and understanding mathematical ideas.

## How to promote thinking

Many educationalists agree that children can be taught to improve their thinking. There is less agreement, however, over how best to do this. Some programmes are based on a model where curriculum content is 'infused' with the teaching of thinking skills. Examples include: 'Activating Children's Thinking Skills' (McGuinness *et al.*, 1997) Robert Fisher's approach to 'Philosophy for Children' (Fisher, 1998) and 'Thinking Through Primary Teaching' (Higgins, 2001; Leat and Higgins 2002). There are also stand-alone approaches such as de Bono's CoRT Thinking (Cognitive Research Trust, 1976), Feuerstein's 'Instrumental Enrichment' (Blagg, 1991) and 'Top Ten Thinking Tactics' (Lake and Needham, 1993).

Cognitive acceleration (CA) approaches are among the most effective in raising standards (Adey *et al.*, 2002). Lessons include a challenge ('cognitive conflict'), such as understanding the implied meaning when reading a story. Teachers act as mediators, posing questions to reveal the thinking process. They also bridge children's new learning to existing experiences by seeking out examples in everyday life where new ideas could apply. The authors acknowledge that CA is not a quick fix. They believe that it is not widely adopted in schools because it does not fit in with the features of what many expect from a 'good lesson', such as the setting of clear behavioural objectives and assessed outcomes.

Many programmes advocate the use of visual prompts to support thinking processes. These include timelines, diagrams, charts, concept maps, mind maps (Buzan, 2003), thinking maps (Hyerle, 2011; Grigg and Lewis, 2014) and other 'graphic organizers' such as spider webs, part/whole relationship diagrams and venn diagrams. These cognitive maps can be used in all curriculum contexts and can be added to over time. Many primary schools make effective use of KWHL grids (frames that set out what children 'already Know, Want to know, How we know, and what we have Learnt' − see Figure 4.3) to structure discussion and build on children's prior knowledge. All of these tools should be viewed as supports to promote thinking rather than stand-alone exercises to be completed.

We are learning about: the Romans in Britain

| We know | We would like to know | How will we find out? | What we have learnt |
|---|---|---|---|
| • They lived a long time ago<br>• They wore red coats<br>• There are TV programmes about them<br>• Paul has got a book on the Rotten Romans | • Why they are called Rotten Romans?<br>• What it was like to be a Roman soldier?<br>• What they ate?<br>• Did they go to school?<br>• How did they have fun? | • We could use the internet<br>• Ask Mr Jones (a teacher)<br>• Visit the museum<br>• Read Paul's book<br>• Watch a film<br>• Go to the library | • The army was very tough<br>• Roman soldiers did lots of things as well as fight<br>• The Romans were rotten because of their cruelty<br>• But they were not all bad − they built lots of things, like roads, bridges, gave us new food, clothes and drink<br>• They ate bread, cheese, meat, vegetables and roasted dormice!<br>• The emperor and his friends used a vomitorium when watching bloody games<br>• The internet is a really good place to find information but it sometimes crashes<br>• Archaeologists at Caerleon have found rings, games and coins that tell us about the Romans |

The grid was used by a trainee to structure discussion with a small group of Year 5 pupils with special educational needs. She used the final column to record learning gains by the end of three lessons on the topic

**FIGURE 4.3** An example of a KWHL grid

Creating a thinking school culture is essential if children are to make progress within lessons, through the term and from one class to the next. Ritchhart (2002) identifies the following cultural forces that define classrooms: time, opportunities, routines and structures, modelling, language, interactions and relationships, physical environment and expectations. Each of these can be directed towards purposeful thinking; for instance, by allowing time for children to explore topics in more depth and compose thoughtful responses, and using a thinking vocabulary. Above all, children need to see that their thinking is valued as outcomes as opposed to mere completion of work. Clearly, by its very nature, good classroom teaching should promote effective learning and thinking. The broader school and home culture are also important influences on children's thinking. Organizations such as Thinking Schools International and Expansive Education seek to connect thinking schools through professional networks.

Some writers suggest lesson models for developing thinking skills. For example, Walsh *et al.* (2006) open with a 'tuning in' stage when teachers observe, listen, encourage or show sensitivity as they 'tune in to' children's learning and thinking. The developmental stage is characterized by questioning, modelling, bridging to the real world and giving children time to think. This might spin off to open-ended challenges. At the creative stage teachers encourage autonomy, flair and imagination. They make it clear to children that mistakes are part of learning and introduce ambiguities. The final reflective stage encourages discussion and self-assessment.

By its nature, thinking is 'hidden' and private. However, some writers promote the idea of making thinking visible, verbal and audible so that learners can 'see' and 'hear' how to improve their thinking. Vygotsky (1962), the leading Russian cognitive psychologist, identified 'inner speech' (self-talk) as an important tool to regulating thinking. Young children will often speak out loud while engaged in demanding activity. Inner speech represents an under-used resource in the classroom. Direct modelling and coaching in self-talk strategies can support children's cognitive development and language skills; for instance, when making decisions (How did you . . .? Why did you . . .? What will you . . .?). To support learners and teachers, Zakin (2007) has put forward an Act,

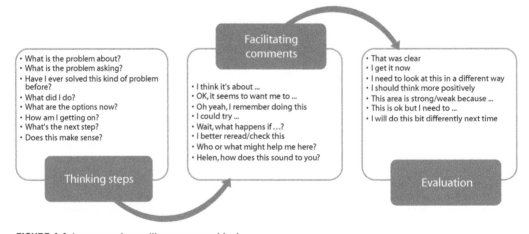

**FIGURE 4.4** Inner speech cognitive assessment tool

Source: Adapted from Zakin (2007)

Reflect and Evaluate (ARE) model (Figure 4.4) comprising three elements: inner speech thinking steps (questions that the learner asks herself); inner speech facilitating comments (inner speech remarks that help the learner to achieve the problem-solving steps); and evaluation of inner speech use (what the learner thinks of her own inner speech comments with regard to task completion).

Visible Thinking Routines (VTRs) are very flexible, powerful and simple ways to encourage pupils to get into the habit of thinking for themselves (Ritchhart *et al.*, 2011). The most popular example is 'Think–Pair–Share', which invites pupils to spend a few seconds reflecting on a question they have been asked before discussing the issue with a partner and then reporting back the gist to the class. Other routines include 'See–Think–Wonder' where pupils are asked to observe closely an object, plant, film, painting or other stimulus, share thoughts with a partner and then identify questions or issues that they are fascinated by. Clearly the teacher needs to choose the stimulus wisely.

Perhaps the most acclaimed proponent of teaching thinking skills is Edward de Bono. According to de Bono, for too long thinking in Western schools has been shaped in the logical, Classical tradition. He simplifies stages of thinking in life as follows:

0–5 years –      the age of 'Why'?

6–12 years –    the age of 'Why not'?

13–100 years – the age of 'Because'

De Bono calls for a move away from the age of 'Because' and return to the ages of 'Why' and 'Why Not' (de Bono Thinking Systems, 2008: 30).

De Bono's CoRT Thinking has been adopted by many different educational and business organisations worldwide (www.edwdebono.com). It consists of numerous 'tools' to promote creative thinking. For instance, 'PMI' (Positive, Minus, Interesting) is used to encourage a less emotive, knee-jerk response to new ideas. PMI works well when reviewing books, planning visits, or making decisions such as which resources to buy. Other tools include 'OPV' (Other People's Views) in which children reflect on how people respond differently when faced with the same circumstances. 'CAF' (Consider all factors) is designed to expand the focus of attention to look beyond the immediate situation. For instance, children might undertake a CAF when making decisions themselves or when reviewing the decisions of others. Supporters point out that these tools need to be used regularly in a deliberate manner and in different contexts if they are to become effective.

De Bono's most famous programme is 'Six Thinking Hats' (de Bono, 2000) devised to develop what he calls 'parallel thinking' rather than argument. At any one time, all members of the discussion group wear the same hat so that they are looking in the same direction. The white hat symbolizes logical thinking and is concerned with what can be proven in a dispassionate way. It is likened to the operation of a computer and the handling of information. By wearing the red hat, pupils are encouraged to express their emotions – what they feel about people, events and situations. The sunny yellow hat is about hope and optimism – looking at the best possible scenario. It should prompt pupils to consider the opportunities that could arise in a given project. The black hat is not only a matter of considering the negative aspects of an idea; it signals caution, risks, the need to play

Devil's Advocate before proceeding. The green hat is associated with growth and conveys creative thinking (Box 4.5). The wearer should think about options, new ideas, interpretations and approaches to a problem. Teachers should prompt pupils into thinking beyond what is known.

The blue hat provides a controlling mechanism to the whole thinking process. By wearing the blue hat, children should think about how they have reached their views. De Bono likens the blue hat to two bookends that bracket the thinking during the lesson. In the analogy of the computer, it represents the software of thinking or the conductor in an orchestra.

Six Thinking Hats has attracted worldwide interest in education and other fields. However, critics such as Bennett (2013) question the evidence that Six Thinking Hats really does what the de Bono Foundation website and supporters claim, namely improve children's behaviour and academic performance (Pugh, 2009). For Bennett, the testimonies from school users are too self-congratulatory and he is right to draw attention to the limited independent research. At best, there are a few small-scale independent international studies that conclude that the use of Six Thinking Hats improves children's skills, for instance in research, organization and questioning (Koh, 2002; Dhanapal and Wern Ling, 2013).

The characteristics of lessons that effectively promote children's thinking include:

- challenging tasks – what Adey *et al.* (2002) refer to as 'cognitive conflict' where teachers set activities that are just beyond pupils' current capabilities but that, with appropriate support from the teacher and more able peers, 'stretch the mind';
- sharing thinking vocabulary, e.g. 'sort', 'reason', 'predict', 'connect';
- encouraging curiosity where learners are not worried about making mistakes, e.g. asking of questions, trying things out;
- focusing on 'how' as well as 'what', e.g. problem-solving strategies compared;
- developing problem-solving strategies, e.g. creating a plan;
- providing opportunities for dialogue, e.g. Why are you doing this? What do you want to find out? ;
- modelling metacognitive strategies, e.g. 'thinking aloud';
- actively listening, e.g. using paraphrases, nodding;
- effectively collaborating with others, e.g. clear roles established for group members;
- cultivating dispositions, e.g. open-mindedness, flexibility, striving for accuracy;
- linking to other subjects and real-world contexts to show relevance of the subject; and
- reviewing and evaluating of thinking using summaries, e.g. Can you say what you now think/know? Would you do things differently? Why? (Box 4.6).

The challenges for the thinking skills movement are to make materials accessible to teachers, continue to draw down firm evidence of what works well and to show that thinking skills can contribute to the priorities of raising standards of literacy and numeracy (Table 4.3).

**BOX 4.5  CREATIVE THINKING IDEAS**

## Using your imagination

What might happen if . . .?
How many kinds of . . . can you think of?
List all . . . that could be used
What might be the arguments for . . . (and against) . . .?

## Experiment with alternatives

How else might you . . .?
Think of five questions you would like to ask . . .
Think of ten things you could use X for
How many words can you make out of . . . (give a starter, e.g. Manchester United)?

## Be original

Design a game for . . . (a blind child, an elderly person, a toddler)
Invent a way to . . . (save water, paint a wall quickly)
Think of a way to improve . . . (an object, game, plan, story)
Create/enter a competition for . . . (the ideal school)

## Changing what we know

What can we add to . . .?
What can we take away from . . .?
What can we replace . . .?
What can we make bigger/smaller . . .?

## Looking at alternatives

Is there another way of doing this?
What choices do we have?
What did X say about this?
How many different pictures can we make from . . . (a sheet of small circles/squares)?
Scatter dots over a page and ask the children to make different pictures.
Use the computer to create different doodles from the same starting point.
Provide four groups of children with a different part of a picture and ask them to guess what is happening elsewhere in the picture. Compare with the original at the end of the lesson.
Give a picture or piece of music a title – compare with others and decide on the most appropriate one.

(Adapted from Fisher, 2005: 84–7)

---

## BOX 4.6 REAL-LIFE LEARNING CHALLENGE

Following a series of lesson observations, the head teacher wants to try and improve the quality of children's creative and critical thinking. 'In too many lessons, the kids are passive and don't ask questions or try things out.' You are responsible for leading learning and teaching in the school and have been asked to recommend five practical whole-school strategies to move things forward. Prepare a briefing for the head.

---

**TABLE 4.3** Overview of some popular thinking skills programmes

| Programme | Key figures | Summary |
| --- | --- | --- |
| Six Thinking Hats | Edward de Bono | Six coloured hats represent different modes of thinking: white (information), red (emotion), yellow (optimism), black (caution), green (creativity), and blue (process). |
| CoRT | Edward de Bono | A set of 60 lessons designed to promote a range of skills through strategies such as PMI (Plus, Minus, Interesting) CAF (Consider All Factors) and OPV (Other People's Views). |
| Thinking Actively in a Social Context (TASC) | Bella Wallace | A creative problem-solving framework applied across the curriculum presented as a TASC wheel. It includes examples of topics, case studies and classroom techniques. |
| Thinking Routines | Ron Ritchhart | Simple classroom procedures used regularly to facilitate the achievement of specific goals or tasks. For instance, 'think–pair–share' is a routine for explanation, 'I used to think . . . now I think' promotes reflection while 'What makes you say that?' focuses on justification. |
| Thinking Maps | David Hyerle | Set of visual tools to support particular thought processes such as a tree map for classifying information or a flow map for sequencing. |
| Philosophy for Children (P4C) or Philosophy with Children (PWC) | Mathew Lipman, Robert Fisher | These interventions are designed to promote multidimensional thinking often using stories and ethical dilemmas as a starting point. |
| Instrumental enrichment | Reuven Feuerstein | The teacher takes the role of mediator and is concerned with how learners approach problems. Paper-and-pencil tasks are provided which focus on skills such as organizing data, comparing, categorizing and analysing. |
| Cognitive acceleration, e.g. CAME, CASE, Let's think | Philip Adey and Michael Shayer | These programmes aim to improve cognitive development and reasoning, originally in secondary mathematics and science. The Let's Think materials apply to 5–6 year-olds, focusing on practical investigations to develop skills such as ordering, classification and causation. |
| Activating Children's Thinking Skills (ACTS) | Carol McGuinness | This infusion programme for Key Stage 2 identified contexts across the curriculum where thinking skills can be developed, e.g. causal reasoning in science or classification of mathematical shapes. |
| Higher Order Thinking Tools (HOT Tools) | Graham Watts | HOT Tools bring literacy and thinking skills together. They are designed to give form and shape to thinking and provide the literacy structures to turn thoughts into extended text. |

Sources: De Bono (1985); www.edwdebono.com; Wallace (2001); Ritchhart *et al.* (2011); Hyerle (2011); Lipman (2003); Feuerstein (1990); Adey and Shayer (1994); McGuinness and Sheehy (2006); http://tomorrowslearning.co.uk/hottools.php

**EXTEND YOUR UNDERSTANDING**

Organizations such as Thinking Schools International and the Thinking Skills Research Centre claim that by explicitly teaching children how to think, schools can raise attainment and engagement. Critics such as Daniel Willingham, American professor of psychology, claim that there is no data showing better outcomes compared with other schools. Can you find any reliable evidence to support the case for teaching thinking skills?

## Neuroscience and active learning

In recent times neuroscience has experienced considerable growth. Developments in scanning technologies have given researchers unprecedented access to brain patterns of healthy children and adults. Organizations such as the Institute of Cognitive Neuroscience undertake extensive research on ways in which educators and neuroscientists might collaborate together. Recent projects include exploring the impact of mobile phone radio wave exposures on children's brain development – given that between 70 and 80 per cent of 11-year-olds own mobile phones this is clearly relevant. Other studies have already shown how excess caffeine (no more than two cans of cola a day) has a negative impact on children's alertness and the importance of regular and sufficient sleep for learning (Howard-Jones, 2011).

However, the extent to which neuroscience can enhance understanding of learning remains controversial. There are serious reservations over the readiness of educational consultants and companies to base practices on wafer-thin 'brain-based learning' research. As Howard-Jones (2011) explains, the journey from 'brain scan to lesson plan' has given rise to a number of myths including:

- fish oils improve brain capacity;
- coordination exercises improve left–right brain functioning;
- sipping water prevents the brain from dehydrating, which therefore improves performance;
- we only use 10 per cent of our brains; and
- boys and girls have different brains.

The most concerning myth is that there are certain periods of childhood after which some things cannot be learned. In fact, the brain's plasticity or ability to change indicates that well-conceived educational interventions can make a difference. But there is no biological reason why children should start formal schooling early. Rather, late starts might be considered more in keeping with natural brain and cognitive development (Blakemore and Frith, 2005).

Busy teachers can easily be lulled into quick-fix ideas to improve pupils' learning and well-being. Approaches such as 'Brain Gym' (Dennison and Dennison, 1992), and accelerated learning (Smith and Call, 2001) have been criticized for lacking rigorous

**PAUSE FOR REFLECTION**

How would you respond if, in 20 years time, the quality of teaching was judged by the measurable impact on pupils' brain development? How might this change your approach to teaching?

scientific evidence. Howard-Jones (2011: 11) is critical of Brain Gym when children are encouraged to drink water while singing (to the tune of 'Frère Jacques'):

> Let's drink water, I love water.
> It gives me En-er-gy.

In fact, drinking water when not thirsty can diminish cognitive ability. From a practical viewpoint, the regular exodus of children to the water dispenser or the swigging of water bottles can be disruptive. Goldacre, doctor and author of *Bad Science*, suggests: 'You can take a perfectly sensible intervention, like a glass of water and an exercise break, but add nonsense, make it sound more technical and make yourself sound clever' (Goldacre, 2009: 18).

Factors such as diet, physical exercise, sleep, social interaction and a stimulating environment, all contribute to all-round healthy development. Over recent years the work of television personalities such as Jamie Oliver has raised public awareness of the need to improve school meals while the government has considered supplementing children's meals with Omega-3 (fish oil) to boost their brainpower, concentration levels and behaviour (Woolf and Lawrence, 2006). Omega-3 is vital to the functioning of the eyes and is used as an effective antidepressant. But Blakemore and Frith (2005) concede that the key is a balanced diet without the need for supplements – while much is known about inadequate diet, little is known about the effects of excess minerals or vitamins. In an entertaining read, Pincock (2009) identifies and rates 100 factors that add to or subtract from brainpower, ranging from breastfeeding to poverty, sunshine to blueberries, and mnemonics to gardening. Top of the positives is infant nutrition while the most damaging factor, as expected, is brain injury followed by sleep deprivation.

Despite reservations, there are some key research findings on children's performance from various disciplines, including neuroscience, that have clear implications for schools:

- sleep – children need regular and sufficient amounts – according to the National Sleep Foundation, children aged five to 12 need 10–11 hours of sleep; napping can improve performance;

- diet – too much fast food has a negative impact on academic ability (Bloom, 2009). The Avon Longitudinal Study of Parents and Children (ALSPAC) shows that toddlers who eat junk food have lower IQ levels than those who eat vegetables (Alleyne, 2011);

- exercise – children who are fit tend to be better at multitasking and performing difficult mental tasks than unfit friends (Gray, 2012);

- music – various sounds can improve well-being but the so-called Mozart effect (which claimed that listening to Mozart made children smarter than those who did not) is a myth;

- emotions – how children feel can impact on how well they think. Negative feelings are detrimental to decision making (LeDoux, 1996). When a person feels content, the brain releases endorphins that enhance memory skills (Jensen 2005);

- environment – children will struggle with learning if they feel afraid because a classroom setting is too restrictive, a home environment is very demanding, or a classmate's behaviour is aggressive;

- over-stimulation – too many new experiences or too much stimulation can cause stress and hinder a child's development. Children need freedom to explore on their own terms and not be exposed constantly to high levels of stimulation;

- abuse – children who are abused can suffer permanent damage in how their brains react to stress (McGowan et al., 2009);

- attention – children are better able to focus on and retain important information when this is presented in small parts; and

- talking – children's cognitive development is aided when they talk about and reflect on what they have been doing (Robson, 2006).

One area of neuroscience described as 'the big hope' (Lee, 2013) is working memory. This allows individuals to hold and process multiple pieces of information in the mind. Companies such as Cogmed develop programmes for schools to improve pupils' retention and concentration (www.cogmed.com). There is no doubt growing popular interest in brain-based learning (Garnett, 2005) and concepts such as **learning styles**.

Numerous writers have advocated that people learn best in different ways and demonstrate preferred styles of learning (Honey and Mumford, 1992; Riding and Rayner, 1998). One of the most popular categorizations of learning styles is the Visual, Auditory and Kinaesthetic (VAK) model (Fleming and Mills, 1992; Smith, 1998; Ginnis, 2002; see Box 4.7). Visual learners might typically say 'I see that now' or 'I get the picture', auditory learners respond with 'That rings a bell' or 'That sounds ok to me' while kinaesthetic learners use phrases such as 'It feels right to me' or 'I can relate to that'. This has since been expanded to VARK to include those reader/writers who have a preference for information presented in words (www.vark-learn.com). According to one survey, 93 per cent of UK teachers said that children learn better if they are taught in a preferred visual, auditory or kinesthetic style (Lee, 2013).

Although VAK has common-sense appeal, research does not suggest that there are any benefits from presenting material according to preferred learning styles. One study described this as 'wasted effort' (Kratzig and Arbuthnott, 2006). It has been rather cruelly dismissed as vacuous learning. Teachers are better off concentrating on learning strategies, rather than styles, given that students can change and learn new ways of thinking. Nonetheless, learning styles has a strong and persistent following. Pritchard (2009: 54) suggests teachers should consider individual learning styles and incorporate these in their plans. He even offers a shorthand way to identify these styles: put simply, visual learners tend to look up (for a mental picture perhaps), auditory learners tend to look to the side and kinaesthetic learners tend to look down.

---

**BOX 4.7  VAK LEARNING STYLES**

*Visual:* those who are visual learners tend to enjoy reading, are good spellers, observe well, are quiet by nature, like to sketch and write, have good handwriting, doodle while listening, but often forget to repeat messages and speak too quickly. They will often plan before doing anything, and like to know the big picture.

*Auditory:* auditory learners will enjoy talking in different contexts, discussing more than writing. They will respond well while working in pairs, small groups and in making presentations, often dominating discussion. They listen carefully, ask questions, can recall tunes with ease, and prefer music to art, but are easily distracted by noise.

*Kinaesthetic:* these learners like to handle and touch things, will move around room, like to make things, will stand very close when talking to someone, and will often play a sport and enjoy sports. Typically, they will swivel on chairs and find it hard to sit still, often fidgeting and tapping. Handwriting is usually poor. Reading habits are usually confined to adventure-style books and they enjoy action films.

---

However, the most comprehensive review of learning style models is generally critical of their reliability (Coffield *et al.*, 2004). An important exception is the research into 'deep' and 'surface' learning undertaken by Entwistle (1981), Marton and others (1997). Essentially, these researchers looked at how students approached learning and found that some saw it as a process of acquiring and reproducing information, while others adopted a deeper approach in trying to make sense of the subject by interacting with the materials in a meaningful way. The main difference lies with the *intention* of the learner. Students who tend to adopt a surface approach look to 'get by', by coping minimally with the curriculum requirements. However, even when students adopt a deep approach to learning they do so in different ways. Some prefer to use facts to build up a picture (a serialist strategy) while others want to see the broad picture by making connections (a holistic strategy). When students adopt these different strategies, they are said to have contrasting learning styles. The argument then runs that those with a holistic style learn more efficiently from reading materials full of pictures, diagrams and examples, while those with a serialist style feel more comfortable with detail and a logical structure. There are also students who adopt a strategic approach, for example in how they manage time and organize their routines, based on their intention to do well in assessments. Entwistle and Walker (2000) caution that it is wrong to put any student wholly into one category; the research describes the relative prominence of each approach.

Despite its popularity among teachers, there is nothing here that good teachers do not already know: children learn through their senses, the environment and motivation are important, children's brains can adapt and process information from everything that they see, hear and do. Clearly then it is important to avoid labelling children as 'auditory' or some other type of learner – styles vary from lesson to lesson, and subject to subject (Kyriacou, 2007; Hewitt, 2008). The idea of matching work to a particular learning style is logistically very demanding in a class of thirty or so children. There is also a strong argument that children should be encouraged to develop their skills to learn through their non-preferred style. Learning is a complex process and rarely relies upon one sense; the most effective learning arguably draws upon the full range of senses and approaches suited to the task in hand. If teachers place too much store in responding to preferences for learning, they may miss the bigger picture of how to encourage pupils to be *flexible* learners, having the capacity to draw upon relevant know-how as required. That said, few would disagree that fostering a love of learning is a primary objective for teachers and to this end pupils need to be motivated, engaged and inquisitive. They need access to various teaching and learning approaches.

The term **active learning** is used to describe learning that 'engages and challenges children's thinking using real-life and imaginary situations' (HMIe, 2007: 5). Active learning is quite different from 'busy work' in that the former is as much to do with quality as quantity (Pollard, 1997: 215). Lessons that feature active learning include a strong focus on reviewing what pupils already know and understand, modelling of listening, and opportunities for children to try out new skills and a review of what has been learned. Brain-based research indicates that active learning approaches are more likely to help individuals retain information than passive ones (Cohen *et al.*, 2004).

In the Early Years, active learning occurs through spontaneous, planned and purposeful play, investigation and exploration, the use of events and life experiences, and focused learning and teaching. The amount of time children spend actively learning is influenced by many factors including motivation and levels of concentration. When the teacher has good classroom organization and management skills, children's wait-time is reduced. Outstanding teachers have clear procedures, for instance when children tidy up, enter and exit the classroom, or when managing playtime, completing the register and changing for physical education lessons. When these procedures are established routines, time is well managed.

Many in the teaching profession believe that children generally remember experiences through 'learning by doing'. This view has been shaped by Edgar Dale's (1969) famous cone of experience, although the figures customarily associated with this have been called into question. Figure 4.5 includes the original cone (right) and an adaptation of the cone of experience (left).

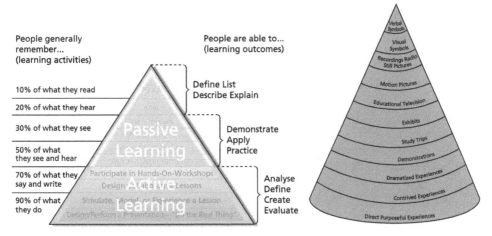

**FIGURE 4.5** Cone of experience

Sources: www.edutechie.ws/.../cone-of-experience-media; Dale (1969)

For teachers, the most important consideration is what works well. The research is clear on this point. Active learning strategies are the most effective (Dunlosky *et al.*, 2013). These can be routinely practised in every lesson, for instance inviting children to explain their views, share ideas, test things out and sum up their thinking. Teachers can incorporate strategies mentioned in this chapter without major adjustments to their planning. The chapter began by highlighting the importance of passion. But this is not confined to teachers. As Fried (2001) points out, children begin life as passionate, curious and powerful learners. Their school experiences should enhance rather than obstruct this journey. Many children continue their passion outside school hours and become skilled in all kinds of hobbies from fishing to computer gaming. The challenge for teachers is to recognize every child's passion and seek to nurture these.

## Glossary

**Active learning** describes when learners are fully involved in acquiring knowledge, skills and understanding.

**Learning styles** have been defined in various ways, including particular approaches, habits or strategies adopted by individuals.

**Metacognition** refers to learners' control of their thinking – whether they are conscious of how well they are learning and what they can do to improve (Flavell, 1976).

**Thinking skills** is a controversial term used to describe general learning strategies such as problem solving and creating ideas.

## References

Adey, P., and Shayer, M. (1994) *Really Raising Standards: Cognitive Intervention and Academic Achievement*, London: Routledge.

Adey, P., Robertson, A. and Venville, G. (2002) 'Effects of a cognitive acceleration programme on Year I pupils', *British Journal of Educational Psychology*, 72: 1–25.

Alleyne, R. (2011) 'Food for thought – diet does boost your intelligence', *The Telegraph*, 8 February.

Anderson, L. and Krathwohl, D.A. (2001) *Taxonomy for Learning, Teaching and Assessing: A Revision of Bloom's Taxonomy of Educational Objectives*, New York: Longman.

Basford, J. and Hodson, E. (eds) (2008) *Teaching Early Years Foundation*, Exeter: Learning Matters.

Bennett, T. (2013) *Teacher Proof*, Abingdon: Routledge.

Blakemore, S.J. and Frith, U. (2005) *The Learning Brain*, Oxford: Blackwell.

Blagg, N. (1991) *Can We Teach Intelligence? A Comprehensive Evaluation of Feuerstein's Instrumental Enrichment Program*, Hillsdale, NJ: Lawrence Erlbaum Associates.

Bloom, A. (2009) 'Fast-food diet can result in slow-brain children', *Times Educational Supplement*, 22 May.

Bloom, B., Englehart, M. Furst, E., Hill, W. and Krathwohl, D. (1956) *Taxonomy of Educational Objectives: The Classification of Educational Goals. Handbook I: Cognitive Domain*, New York, Toronto: Longmans, Green.

Bloomer, K. and McIlroy, C. (2012) *Developing Skills*, Edinburgh: Scottish Government.

Boden, M. (1991) *The Creative Mind: Myths and Mechanisms*, New York: Basic Books.

Buie, E. (2005) 'Creative thinkers wither with age', in *Times Educational Supplement*, 25 March.

Buzan, T. (2003) *Mind Maps for Kids: An Introduction*, London: Thorsons.

Carbonneau, N., and Vallerand R.J., Fernet, C. and Guay, F. (2008) 'The role of passion for teaching in intrapersonal and interpersonal outcomes', *Journal of Educational Psychology*, 100(4): 977–87.

Casserley, M. (2004) 'Developing a creative culture', National Teacher Research Panel, available at: www.ntrp.org.uk.

Clegg, B. (1999) *Instant Brainpower*, London: Kogan Page.

Coffield, F., Moseley, D., Hall, E. and Ecclestone, K. (2004) *Should We Be Using Learning Styles? What Research Has to Say to Practice*, Learning and Skills Research Centre. Trowbridge: Cromwell Press.

Cohen, L., Manion, L. and Morrison, K. (2004) *A Guide to Teaching Practice*, London: RoutledgeFalmer.

Colvin, G. (2008) *Talent is Overrated*, London: Penguin.

Conference Board (2006) *Are They Really Ready To Work? Employers' Perspectives on the Basic Knowledge and Applied Skills of New Entrants to the 21st Century U.S. Workforce*, available at: www.p21.org/storage/documents/FINAL_REPORT_PDF09-29-06.pdf (accessed 22 December 2013).

Craft, A. (2000) *Creativity Across the Primary Curriculum*, London: Routledge.

Craft, A. (2011) 'Approaches to creativity across the UK', in Sefton, J., Thompson, P., Jones, K., and Bresler, L. (eds) *The Routledge International Handbook of Creative Learning*, London: Routledge, 129–39.

Cremin, T., Barnes, J. and Scoffham, S. (2009) *Creative Teaching for Tomorrow: Fostering a Creative State of Mind*, Margate: Future Creative.

Csikszentmihalyi, M. (1997) *Finding Flow: The Psychology of Engagement with Everyday Life*, New York: Basic Books.

Dale, E. (1969) *Audiovisual Methods in Teaching*, 3rd edn, New York: Dryden Press.

Day, C. (2007) 'A passion for teaching', Public lecture for the General Teaching Council for Northern Ireland, 30 April, available at: http://gtcni.openrepository.com/gtcni/ (accessed 16 October 2013).

Day, C. (2009) 'A passion for quality: Teachers who make a difference', *Tijdschrift voor Lerarenopleiders*, 30(3): 4–13.

Day, C., Sammons, P., Stobart, G., Kington, A. and Gu, Q. (2007) *Teachers Matter*, Maidenhead: Open University Press.

DCELLS (2008a) *Making the Most of Learning*, Cardiff: Welsh Assembly Government.

DCELLS (2008b) *Skills Framework for 3 to 19-year-olds in Wales*, Cardiff: Welsh Assembly Government.

de Bono, E. (1976) *Thinking Action: Teacher Handbook – CoRT VI*, New York: Pergamon Press.

de Bono, E. (2000) *Six Thinking Hats*, London: Penguin.

de Bono Thinking Systems (2008) *Six Thinking Hats*, Iowa: de Bono Thinking Systems.

Dennison, P. and Dennison, G. (1992) *Brain Gym*, Ventura, CA: Edu Kinesthetics.

DfES (2002) *The National Curriculum*, London: DfES.

Dhanapal, S. and Wern Ling, K.T. (2013) 'A study to investigate how Six Thinking Hats enhance the learning of environmental studies', *Journal of Research and Method in Education*, 1(6): 20–9.

Dunlosky, J., Rawson, K., Marsh, E., Nathan, M. and Willingham, D. (2013) 'Improving students' learning with effective learning techniques: Promising directions from cognitive and educational psychology', *Psychological Science in the Public Interest*, 14(1): 4 –58.

Entwistle, N. (1981) *Styles of Learning and Teaching: An Integrated Outline of Educational Psychology for Students, Teachers and Lecturers*, Chichester: Wiley.

Entwistle N. and Walker P. (2000) 'Strategic alertness and expanded awareness within sophisticated conceptions of teaching', *Instructional Science*, 28: 335–62.

Eisner, E.W. (2000) 'Benjamin Bloom', *Prospects: The Quarterly Review of Comparative Education International Bureau of Education*, vol. XXX (3): 1–7.

Ericsson, K., Charness, N., Feltovich, P. and Hoffman, R. (eds) (2006) *The Cambridge Handbook of Expertise and Expert Performance*, Cambridge: Cambridge University Press.

Estyn (2011) *The 'Developing Thinking Skills and Assessment for Learning' Programme*, Cardiff: Estyn.

Feuerstein, R. (1990) *Instrumental Enrichment: Intervention Programme for Cognitive Modifiability*, Baltimore, MD: University Park Press.

Fisher, R. (1998) *Teaching Thinking*, London: Cassell.

Fisher, R. and Williams, M. (2004) *Unlocking Creativity – A Teacher's Guide to Creativity Across the Curriculum*, London: David Fulton.

Flavell, J.H. (1976) 'Metacognitive aspects of problem solving', in Resnick, L.B. (ed.) *The Nature of Intelligence*, Hillsdale, NJ: Lawrence Erlbaum, 231–6.

Fleming, N. and Mills, C. (1992) 'Not another inventory, rather a catalyst for reflection', *To Improve the Academy*, 11: 137–49.

Fried, R. (1995) *The Passionate Teacher: A Practical Guide*, Boston, MA: Beacon Press.

Fried, R. (2001) *The Passionate Learner*, Boston, MA: Beacon Press.

Gallo, C. (2010) *The Innovation Secrets of Steve Jobs: Insanely Different Principles for Breakthrough Success*, New York: McGraw-Hill.

Garner, R. (2013) 'Exams, exams, exams': Children's author Sally Gardner says new National Curriculum would stifle classroom creativity', *The Independent*, 19 June.

Garnett, S. (2005) *Using Brainpower in the Classroom*, London: Routledge.

Gholipour, B. (2013) 'Brain surgery to remove amygdala leads to woman's "hyper empathy"', *Huffington Post*, 9 September.

Ginnis, P. (2002) *Teacher's Toolkit*, Carmarthen: Crown House.

Goldacre, B. (2009) *Bad Science*, London: Fourth Estate.

Goleman, D. (1996) *Emotional Intelligence*, London: Bloomsbury.

Grainger, T. and Barnes, J. (2006) 'Creativity in the primary curriculum', in Arthur, J., Grainger, T. and Wray, D. (eds) *Learning to Teach in the Primary School*, London, Routledge, 209–25.

Gray, R. (2012) 'Regular exercise can improve memory and learning', *The Telegraph*, 19 February.

Grigg, R. and Lewis, H. (2014) 'Order your thoughts', *Teach Primary*, 7(8): 57–8.

Hartley, S. (2012) *How to Shine: Insights into Unlocking your Potential from Proven Winners*, Chichester: Capstone.

Hewitt, D. (2008) *Understanding Effective Learning*, Maidenhead: Open University Press.

Higgins, S. (2001) *Thinking Through Primary Teaching*, Cambridge: Chris Kington Publishing.

HMIe (2006) *Emerging Good Practice in Promoting Creativity*, Edinburgh: Scottish Executive.

HMIe (2007) *A Curriculum for Excellence. Building the Curriculum 2*, Edinburgh: Scottish Executive.

Honey, P. and Mumford, A. (1992) *The Manual of Learning Styles*, Maidenhead: Peter Honey.

Howard-Jones, P. (2011) 'Neuroscience and education: Issues and opportunities. A commentary by the Teaching and Learning Research Programme', available at: www.tlrp.org.uk (accessed 16 October 2013).

Hyerle, D. (2011) *Student Successes with Thinking Maps*, Thousand Oaks, CA: Corwin Press.

Jensen, E. (2005) *Teaching with the Brain in Mind*, Alexandria, VA: Association for Supervision and Curriculum Development.

Jones, R. and Wyse, D. (2013) *Creativity in the Primary Curriculum*, Abingdon: Routledge.

Kim, K.H. (2005) 'Learning from each other: Creativity in East Asian and American education', *Creativity Research Journal*, 17(4): 337–47.

Koh, A. (2002) 'Towards a critical pedagogy: Creating "thinking schools" in Singapore', *Journal of Curriculum Studies*, 34(2): 255–64.

Kaufman, S. (2011) 'Increase your passion for work without becoming obsessed', *Harvard Business Review* blog, 21 September.

Johnson S. and Siegel, H. (2010) *Teaching Thinking Skills*, London: Continuum.

Kratzig, G.P. and Arbuthnott, K.D. (2006) 'Perceptual learning style and learning proficiency: A test of the hypothesis', *Journal of Educational Psychology*, 98(1): 238–46.

Kyriacou, C. (2007) *Essential Teaching Skills*, Cheltenham: Nelson Thornes.

Lake, M. and Needham, M. (1993) *Top Ten Thinking Tactics*, Birmingham: Scholastic.

Land, G. and Jarman, B. (1992) *Breakpoint and Beyond: Mastering the Future Today*, Scranton: Harpercollins.

Leat, D. and Higgins S. (2002) 'The role of powerful pedagogical strategies in curriculum development', *The Curriculum Journal*, 13(1): 71–85.

LeDoux, J.E. (1996) *The Emotional Brain*, New York: Simon & Schuster.

Lee, B. (2013) 'Get inside their heads', *Times Educational Supplement*, 1 March.

Lipman, M. (2003) *Thinking in Education*, Cambridge: Cambridge University Press.

Liston, D. and Garrison, J. (eds) (2004) *Teaching, Learning and Loving*, London: RoutledgeFalmer.

Lockette, K. (2012) 'Creativity and Chinese education reform', *International Journal of Global Education*, 1(4): 34–9.

McCreedy, A. (2004) 'The "creativity problem" and the future of the Japanese workforce', in *Asia Special Programme Report*, June, No.121, available at: www.wilsoncenter.org/sites/default/files/asiarpt121.pdf (accessed 23 October 2013).

McGowan, P., Sasaki, A., D'Alessio, A., Dymov, S., Labonté, B., Szyf, M., Turecki, G. and Meaney, M. (2009) 'Epigenetic regulation of the glucocorticoid receptor in human brain associates with childhood abuse', *Nature Neuroscience*, 12: 342–8.

McGuinness, C. (1999) *From Thinking Skills to Thinking Classrooms: A Review and Evaluation of Approaches for Developing Pupils' Thinking*, London: HMSO.

McGuinness, C. and Sheehy, N. (2006) 'Building thinking skills in thinking classrooms', *Teaching and Learning Research Briefing*, 18: 1–4.

McGuinness, C., Curry, C., Greer, B., Daly, P. and Salters, M. (1997) *Final Report on the ACTS project: Phase 2*, Belfast: Northern Ireland CCEA.

McKinsey (2009) *Shaping the Future: How Good Educational Systems Can Become Great in the Decade Ahead*, New York: McKinsey & Co.

Mart, C.T. (2013) 'A passionate teacher: Teacher commitment and dedication to student learning', *International Journal of Academic Research in Progressive Education and Development*, 2(1): 437–42.

Marton, F., Hounsell, D. and Entwistle, N. (1997) *The Experience of Learning: Implications for Teaching and Studying in Higher Education*, Edinburgh: Scottish Academic Press.

Mavity, R. (2013) 'Gove's changes threaten Britain's greatest asset: our creativity', *The Independent*, 28 January.

Metcalfe, A. and Game, A. (2006) *Teachers Who Change Lives*, Melbourne: Melbourne University Press.

Mourshed, M., Chijioke, C. and Barber, M. (2010) *How the World's Most Improved School Systems Keep Getting Better*, New York: McKinsey & Co.

NACCCE (1999) *All Our Futures: Creativity, Culture and Education*, London: DfEE.

NCSL (2010) *How Do School Leaders Successfully Lead Learning?* Nottingham: NCSL.

Neill, S. and Caswell, C. (1993) *Body Language for Competent Teachers*, London: Routledge.

OECD (2013) *OECD-CCE-Singapore International Workshop Educating for Innovation in Asia: The Theory, the Evidence and the Practice*, available at: www.oecd.org/edu/ceri/EDU-CERI-CD(2013)6-ENG.pdf (accessed 7 January 2014).

Pincock, S. (2009) *The Intelligence Equation*, London: New Holland.

Pollard, A. (1997) *Reflective Teaching in the Primary School*, London: Cassell.

Pritchard, A. (2009) *Ways of Learning*, Abingdon: Routledge.

Pugh, R. (2009) 'Put your thinking hat on: How Edward de Bono's ideas are transforming schools', *The Independent*, 29 January.

Ramesh, R. (2013) 'England's young people near bottom of global league table for basic skills', *The Guardian*, 8 October.

Riding, R. and Rayner, S. (1998) *Cognitive Styles and Learning Strategies: Understanding Style Differences in Learning and Behaviour*, London: David Fulton.

Ritchhart, R, Church, M. and Morrison, K. (2011) *Making Thinking Visible*, San Francisco, CA: Jossey Bass.

Ritchhart, R. (2002), *Intellectual Character: What It Is, Why it Matters, and How to Get It*, San Francisco, CA: Jossey Bass.

Robinson, K. (2009) *The Element: How Finding Your Passion Changes Everything*, London: Penguin.

Robinson, K. (2013) 'To encourage creativity, Mr Gove, you must first understand what it is', *The Guardian*, 17 May.

Robson, S. (2006) *Developing Thinking and Understanding in Young Children*, London: Routledge.

Shaheen, R. (2012) 'Creativity', in Arthur, J. and Peterson, A. (eds) *The Routledge Companion to Education*, Abingdon: Routledge, 146–56.

Sharp, C. (2004) 'Developing young children's creativity: What can we learn from research?', *Topic*, 32: 5–12.

Smith, A. (1998) *Accelerated Learning in Practice: Brain-Based Methods for Accelerating Motivation and Achievement*, Stafford: Network Educational Press.

Smith, A. and Call, N. (2001) *The Alps Approach Resource Book*, Stafford: Network Continuum Press.

Soden, R., Kenesson, S., Seagraves, L. and Campbell, D., (2006) *Evaluation of the Scottish Borders Feuerstein Instrumental Enrichment*, available at http://strathprints.strath.ac.uk/37571/1/Soden_et_al_(2006)_Evaluation_of_Scottish_Border_Feuerstein_project.pdf (accessed 16 Ocyober 2013).

Sousa, D. (2003) *The Leadership Brain: How to Lead Today's Schools More Effectively*, Thousand Oaks, CA: Corwin Press.

Syed, M. (2011) *Bounce*, London: HarperCollins.

Vygotsky, L. (1962) *Thought and Language*, Cambridge, MA: The MIT Press.

WAG (2010*) How to Develop Thinking and Assessment for Learning in the Classroom*, Cardiff: WAG.

Walker, A. (2011) 'Creativity loves constraints': The Paradox of Google's twenty percent time', *Ephemera: Theory and Politics in Organization*, 11(4): 369–86.

Wallace, B. (2001) *Teaching Thinking Skills Across the Primary Curriculum: A Practical Approach for All Abilities*, London: NACE/Fulton Publication.

Walsh, G., Murphy, P. and Dunbar, C. (2006) *Thinking Skills in the Early Years: A Guide for Practitioners*, Belfast: Stranmillis University College.

Willingham, D.T. (2009) *Why Don't Students Like School?*, New York: Wiley.

Wood, D. (1998) *How Children Think and Learn*, Oxford: Blackwell.

Woolf, M. and Lawrence, J. (2006) 'Brain food: Why the Government wants your child to take Omega-3, the fish oil supplement', *The Independent*, 11 June.

Wiggins, G. (2011), 'Creative Learning', in Sefton, J., Thompson, P., Jones, K., and Bresler, L. (eds), *The Routledge International Handbook of Creative Learning*, London: Routledge. 320–31.

Wragg, T. (2005) 'Going against the flow: An interview with Ted Wragg', in Wilson, A. (ed.) *Creativity in Primary Education*, Exeter: Learning Matters, 185–93.

Wyse, D. (2013) 'Creativity', in Wyse, D., Baumfield, M., Egan, D., Gallagher, C., Hayward, L., Hulme, M., Leitch, R., Livingston, K. and Menter, I. (eds) *Creating the Curriculum*, Abingdon: Routledge, 117–28.

Zakin, A. (2007) 'Metacognition and the use of inner speech in children's thinking: A tool teachers can use', *Journal of Education and Human Development*, 1(2): 1–14.

## Websites

The Journey to Excellence website includes short videos from leading international figures, such as Edward de Bono and David Perkins, on the teaching of thinking skills – www.journey toexcellence.org.uk/videos/expertspeakers

The website for the Northern Ireland Curriculum and Assessment Arrangements includes stories ('Wise up and Think') for Key Stage 1 designed to develop thinking skills – www.ni curriculum.org.uk/skills_and_capabilities/thinking_skills_and_personal_capabilities/index.asp

The Thinking Schools website operated by Kestrel, a commercial company – www.thinking school.co.uk

Robert Fisher's website on teaching thinking skills – www.teachingthinking.net

The Visible Thinking Routines website includes examples of routines to use in class – www.visible thinkingpz.org

Edward de Bono Thinking Tools website – www.edwdebono.com

# 5

# Professional knowledge and understanding

## Theory, nature and scope of the curriculum

## Chapter objectives

By the end of this chapter you should be able to:

- Reflect upon the nature of knowledge and consider what is worth knowing in the primary school.
- Describe the main learning theories that underpin modern-day practice in the primary school.
- Critically reflect upon the rationale, nature and scope of the primary curriculum.
- Describe the principles and approaches in Early Years provision.

*The notion of a curriculum, an essential body of knowledge, would be absurd even if children remembered everything we 'taught' them. We don't and can't agree on what knowledge is essential.*

*(Holt 1984: 289)*

## Introduction

Becoming an outstanding teacher means more than developing classroom skills and relationships. Understanding the reasons why schools operate in the way they do or why children might respond in a particular manner requires a critical appreciation of educational theory. Teachers who struggle to give confident replies to 'why' questions about their practice are likely to be weak on rationale and therefore more vulnerable to outside pressures. Turner-Bisset (2001: 4) suggests that expert teachers are masters 'over all kinds of knowledge, skills and processes'. All teachers are expected to have a broad professional knowledge of teaching, learning, assessment and behaviour management strategies, a secure grasp of the curriculum that they are to teach, and knowledge of their own professional development needs. But in terms of knowledge and understanding, what sets apart the outstanding teachers? According to OFSTED (2014: 39), 'outstanding teachers 'authoritatively impart knowledge to ensure students are engaged in learning, and generate high levels of commitment to learning across the school.' The emphasis here is on the skill of transferring knowledge and making it accessible to learners so that they develop their own thirst to find out more. Teachers throughout the UK are expected to possess strong subject and curriculum knowledge. This chapter reviews what this means in practice. For instance, can a teacher in Year 6 know enough to teach the full range of curriculum subjects? What does knowledge mean to an Early Years practitioner? How do teachers keep up-to-date with their knowledge? There are also related theoretical questions to explore: Is knowledge hierarchical? Who decides what knowledge children should be taught? Is knowledge as important as skills?

## The nature of knowledge and what is worth knowing

Epistemology is the theory of knowledge that raises questions about the nature of what is known and how knowledge is acquired. A common view is that knowledge is the mix of experiences, values and insights that people have in their heads (**long-term memory**). It can be gained through the senses, language, emotions and reasoning. Since ancient times intellectuals have debated the nature of knowledge and what is worth knowing. Many generations concluded that knowledge of the Bible, or other sacred writings, and living according to its codes was what mattered more than anything else. This was especially so in ages when the heavenly promise of relief from drudgery was perceived as the only real hope that people had. The eighteenth-century Enlightenment witnessed a shift from seeing knowledge based largely on faith to a more rational, scientific and humanist view of how things worked. Gradually the rise in science and medicine coincided with a decline in religious forms of knowledge. Originally writing in the 1960s, the American educationalist John Holt (1984: 288) observed:

> Behind much of what we do in school lie some ideas that could be expressed roughly as follows. (1) Of the vast body of human knowledge, there are certain bits and pieces that can be called essential, that everyone should know (2) the extent to which a person can be considered educated, qualified to live intelligently in today's world and be a useful member of society, depends on the amount of this essential knowledge that he carries around with him (3) it is the duty of schools therefore to get as much of this essential knowledge as possible into the minds of children.

Although this may seem a harsh indictment of (American) schooling, Holt raised questions that are still relevant in twenty-first century Britain (Box 5.1).

Different ways of life and belief systems, gender, family upbringing, social class and language are among the contributory factors that shape how the world is seen and what is held up as significant knowledge. For instance, arguably there has been a longstanding bias against the arts in the school curriculum because those in control have placed a higher value on academic knowledge (Lewis, 1993). Traditionally, the education of girls and boys has differed largely because society assigned different roles to them upon leaving school. Nineteenth-century working-class girls were to be mothers, wives, servants or,

---

**BOX 5.1  QUESTIONS ABOUT KNOWLEDGE IN SCHOOL**

- What should children learn in school?
- Is some knowledge more significant for children to acquire? If so, why?
- What is it appropriate to expect children of different ages to know?
- How should knowledge be organized?
- Who should decide what children are taught?
- To what extent should children direct what they want to know?

---

at best, nurses and teachers. The curriculum was framed accordingly to ensure that they learned needlework, housecraft and basic skills. But what can be said about the content of the modern-day curriculum? Holt pointed out that when he was writing in the 1960s, during the 'Cold War' between East and West, Russian was a popular language to teach in school whereas when he was a boy Latin was seen as a priority by his teachers. The value attached to knowledge changes over time.

Knowledge needs to be viewed as something more than a collection of absolute facts, as Holt warned. Possessing mere knowledge is not enough – students may know a lot of historical facts but that does not make them good historians. Similarly, being able to do something very well is not necessarily a prerequisite to teaching it well. This confuses knowledge of 'doing' with knowledge of 'teaching'. A teacher may be a gifted artist but this does not mean he will make a good art teacher. There is considerable support for the view that knowledge is constructed, shared and modified through interaction with others. Teachers themselves will often comment upon what they have learned from discussions with colleagues as members of professional communities, for example in staff meetings or by attending in-service training events (Stoll and Louis, 2007).

Children need to acquire declarative ('know that'), procedural ('know how') and conditional ('know when and why') forms of knowledge (Table 5.1). For example in mathematics, pupils need to know their number bonds but they also need to know how to apply this knowledge when handling money. They also need to know *when* the use of a calculator or database might be helpful.

**TABLE 5.1**  Types of knowledge

| Type | As when . . . | General example | Specific example |
| --- | --- | --- | --- |
| Declarative ('knowing that') | Recalling facts, dates, figures, symbols, words | Winter follows autumn | Henry VII was the first Tudor king (history) |
| Procedural ('knowing how') | Using problem-solving strategies | How to ride a bicycle | How to calculate the area of a square (mathematics) |
| Conditional ('knowing when and why') | Applying knowledge in contexts | When to ask for help | When it is best to use a database (ICT) |

Teachers also need to promote pupils' awareness of who might furnish answers to their problems beyond those in the classroom. This is especially the case when pupils undertake investigative work. The 'know-who' capability to identify and contact appropriate people is central to personal and social education. It includes the ability to cooperate and communicate with others.

## Teachers' expert knowledge

The educational psychologist, Lee Shulman (1986, 1987), has advanced our understanding of what expert teachers know. He introduced the notion of **Pedagogical Content Knowledge** (PCK) to describe how good teachers are able to represent and make subject content accessible to learners, for instance through explanations, illustrations and metaphors. Shulman and his colleagues found that student teachers with specialist knowledge taught in a manner that encouraged children to reflect and develop complex ideas of their own, rather than 'deliver' prescribed content that relied on children memorizing knowledge (Grossman *et al.*, 1989). For Shulman, the key to understanding the knowledge base of teachers lay at the intersection between content and **pedagogy**. Those teachers with secure PCK (also known as 'craft knowledge') successfully blend the 'what' and 'how' of teaching. Their accumulated wisdom covers pedagogy, learners, subject matter and the curriculum.

In comparison to novices, expert teachers have a larger knowledge base from which to draw; they organize knowledge more efficiently in complex interconnected **schemas** and utilize it more effectively. Research into how experts differ from novices has found that it is not just that the former know more than the latter. Rather, experts in any field structure their understanding around principles or main ideas (Glaser, 1999). This in turn helps them to retrieve knowledge accurately. Experts are familiar with their subject and operate at higher levels in sifting, rearranging, connecting and improving their own knowledge of the world. In one research project, a group of history experts were given the same task as a group of gifted high school students. The task centred on American history, the course followed by the students. This field was outside the expertise of the historians, who specialized in Asian and medieval history. The historians, while lacking the background knowledge of the students, performed better because they were able to apply their know-how or procedural knowledge, for example in what to look for in old documents (Petty, 2006).

Experts possess specialist knowledge that governs their powers of reasoning. They are very good at 'chunking', which is the process by which they remember patterns retained in the permanent memory. This is achieved because of their familiarity with the material, as memory is strengthened through repetition. A simple example might be to consider a regular car journey – while one may not recall the particular names of roads travelled upon, once the route becomes familiar a sense of 'autopilot' kicks in. Recent research suggests that the chunking technique is not just a matter of hard work and is likely to be an innate ability; 14-month-old babies are able to more easily recollect hidden toys and remember greater numbers of toys, if the objects are sorted into groups (Feigenson and Halberda, 2008).

Sometimes experts make things look easy. Becoming an expert takes time and commitment, something that children do not immediately understand. They may become frustrated when they find out they cannot become skilled at something right away. Hence teachers need to encourage them to persevere in building up their knowledge and experience. Experts are able to draw from their memory knowledge, which is well organized, and apply it to the problem in hand, demonstrating focus and clarity of purpose. They are 'self-regulating' in the sense that they are very adept at monitoring their own progress towards a goal, knowing when to step back and reflect on their progress at appropriate points. Experts know the different interpretations of a given problem and usually decide on the right course of action.

Unfortunately it is not clear how novices can best access the knowledge of experts. One of the difficulties is that the procedural knowledge of expert teachers is to a large degree unspoken, tacit in nature and rooted in experience. This raises the importance of making the best use of opportunities to observe in the classroom and developing the principles of reflective practice. According to Ghaye and Ghaye (1998), reflection is seen as a 'conversation' in which the meaning of experience is explored and interrogated. Taken-for-granted values and practices are questioned ('the reflective turn') as teachers seek to describe, explain and justify what they do. In this process of accounting, reflection lends itself to enquiry – an aspect of teaching or learning may be questioned systematically.

## Knowledge transfer

Psychologists have different ways of looking at how knowledge is processed and transferred from the short-term to the long-term memory. 'Short-term memory' refers to the storage of information for a matter of seconds. Once the information is manipulated to complete a task, the individual is using **working memory** that has been likened to a mental jotting pad. It is typically called upon when, for example, calculating change in a supermarket, recalling a new telephone number or remembering ingredients when cooking. But it has limited capacity – the average adult cannot hold more than six or seven units of information for 20 seconds at best. Working memories vary among individual children but improve over childhood. According to Gathercole and Alloway (2007; 2008), if a child is distracted or interrupted while using working memory the process is lost and the child cannot resume from where they were interrupted. The child needs to start the task again. They point out that in a typical class of thirty children aged 7 to 8 years, at least three of them are likely to have the working memory capacities of the average 4-year-old child and three others to have the capacities of the average 11-year-old child, which is quite close to adult levels (Gathercole and Alloway, 2008). Children who have poor working memory capacities generally do not catch up with those of their peers. Working memory is important because it enables children to hold complex information in their mind, such as writing a sentence while trying to spell individual words. Children with poor working memory will forget aspects of the task. This is why effective teachers: monitor children's recall, keep instructions short and simple, frequently repeat the important parts, use accompanying gestures, diagrams and other visuals, break down tasks into smaller components and encourage children to request information when required. Children should also be directed to use memory aids such as wall charts, dictionaries, dictaphones, teacher notes and number lines. Knowledge transferred to the long-term memory is coded according to semantics (meaning) and visuals (images). Hence when ideas are presented in diagrams, tables, maps and charts, learning is made more accessible. This explains why so many books for schools and colleges use a combination of features to 'break up' the text. Knowledge retrieved from the long-term memory is aided by meaning. Children learn when knowledge means something. Hence they often forget sounds learned in isolation because they have no associated meaning.

## Learning theories

The learning journey begins long before children enter formal education. Research suggests that even in the womb the foetus is able to respond to sounds and recognize the mother's voice (*The Telegraph*, 4 January 2013). Babies and young children continue to make sense of their worlds in a wide range of contexts beyond the classroom, from playing on the beach to visiting the supermarket. The core purpose of schools is to promote **learning**. Yet in many classrooms the dominant word is 'work' rather than 'learn': children are told 'Get on with your work' or asked 'Have you finished your work?' They are set 'homework', and teachers plan 'schemes of work'. Watkins (2011) cites the example of a teacher who substituted 'learn' every time she or the class used the word 'work' and found that this led to much higher levels of pupil engagement.

For centuries, children were not seen as active learners. Rather, it was common to liken them to blank pages to be written on or empty vessels to be filled with knowledge. It was the rise in developmental psychology that brought new understanding of how children seek to make meaning in their lives. Many different theorists and researchers have tried to explain how children learn and develop. An understanding of these theories enables teachers to reflect on the rationale of what they see, as well as their own assumptions about how children learn.

### Behaviourism

In the late nineteenth and early twentieth centuries, psychologists such as Sigmund Freud (1856–1939) and Carl Jung (1875–1961) highlighted the importance of understanding the mind and that early childhood experiences were the key to later behaviour patterns. However, reading the mind can be a frustrating business. Hence, during the first half of the twentieth century psychologists began to consider more closely how individuals interacted with their environments. The term 'behaviourism' is derived from the writings of the American psychologist J.B. Watson (1878–1958), who in 1914 wrote a tract called *Behaviour*. In simple terms, **behaviourism** focuses on the connection between stimulus (S) and response (R). Watson introduced the laws of frequency and recency; the former suggested that the more frequently a stimulus and a response are associated, the stronger the habit will become. The second law proposes that the response that occurs most recently after a stimulus is more likely to be associated with it (Jarvis *et al.*, 1998). These laws have implications for teachers who need, for example, to revisit learning objectives and make regular use of mini and full plenaries.

Behaviourists conclude that the learning of a predefined body of knowledge (behaviours) can be promoted through repetition and positive reinforcement. The basic premise of behaviourism is that it is possible to condition behaviour by offering rewards and punishments (Slavin, 2003). The Russian physiologist Ivan Pavlov (1849–1936) provided the most famous experiment (1927) to illustrate behaviourism. When feeding a dog he would ring a bell at the same time. When he stopped feeding the dog but carried on ringing the bell the animal continued to salivate. This reaction was known as *conditional response* and demonstrated learning by association. Despite the unfortunate association of child development with dog training, behaviourism is behind such classroom management practices as 'assertive discipline' (Canter and Canter, 1992), which is characterized by a high level of teacher control where teachers tell the class that they mean what they say and say what they mean. Tests, examinations, repetitive exercises, reviewing techniques, rewards, verbal praise, punishments, and basic question (stimulus) and answer (response) approaches are examples of behaviourism in the classroom.

Classical conditioning focuses on behaviour that invariably follows a particular event. However, psychologists B.F. Skinner (1904–1990) and Edward Thorndike (1874–1949) studied the learning of behaviour that operates on the environment: a person or animal behaves in a particular way to gain something desired or avoid something unpleasant. Skinner (1966) called this operant conditioning, where reinforcement (such as food) increases the probability that a particular response will occur in the future, while punishers (such as scolding) have the opposite effect. According to the law of effect, children are more likely to do something that teachers (or others) want if it leads to a reward and less likely to repeat the action if no reward is forthcoming (or worse, if punishment follows). Behaviour that is consistently rewarded will become 'stamped in' as learned behaviour and behaviour that is consistently punished will be 'stamped out'. Operant conditioning is still behind many programmes designed to help teachers and parents change children's behaviour, including thumb-sucking, dieting, hyperactivity and temper tantrums (Parke and Gauvain, 2009).

Critics of behaviourism maintain that the theory ignores individual free will and does not give enough attention to biological factors, thinking processes and innate feelings. It is too deterministic and reduces behaviour to scientific observation. Some children paint, write poems or read a particular book because they are 'in the mood' to do so and not out of any promised reward. Some studies have shown that if students are rewarded for problem solving they work at a slower rate than those who are not rewarded; while people who are rewarded for sensible behaviour, such as stopping smoking, are less likely to change their behaviour in the long term than those who are not rewarded (Furnham, 2008). Behaviourism also does not account for the creativity and diversity in human behaviour. For instance, on matters such as creative writing or role play behaviourism is less convincing as a theory.

## Humanistic approach

Humanistic psychologists, notably Carl Rogers (1902–1987), reject the deterministic nature of scientific experiments and argue that individuals have free will (personal agency) to make their own decisions in life. The humanistic approach has shaped personal and social education programmes and the teaching of subjects such as sex education, health and citizenship. Children and young people look upon issues in a non-judgemental manner, where notions of 'right' and 'wrong' are suspended so that individuals explore what they want in a guilt-free manner. One of the implications for teachers when creating the learning environment is to consider the whole child, including moods, feelings and thoughts. Moreover, humanistic educators prioritize self-evaluation as a means of assessment rather than tests and grades, which do not contribute to deep learning.

## Cognitive constructivism

According to a constructivist theory of learning, rather than transmit knowledge and be told the 'right' answers, learners need to explore their understanding and draw their own conclusions. Teachers are seen more as facilitators rather than instructors. They support or 'scaffold' learning, for instance by breaking a task down into a sequence of smaller tasks that children can manage. Teachers are likened to 'the guide on the side' rather than 'the sage on the stage' and the emphasis is very much on discovering the skills required to solve problems (Slavin, 2003). But it is a common misunderstanding to think that constructivism means that direct teaching is inappropriate. This confuses a theory of pedagogy with a theory of knowing. Constructivism simply assumes that all knowledge builds on the learner's prior experience and so listening to a teacher can involve active attempts to construct new knowledge. However, on balance, teachers who adhere to constructivist beliefs tend to limit their direct instruction spending more time monitoring and facilitating group discussions.

Cognitive constructivism derives largely from the work of the Swiss biologist and naturalist Jean Piaget (1896–1980). He became interested in children's cognitive development, while working with the French psychologist Alfred Binet (1857–1911), who created the first intelligence test. Piaget concluded that older children think differently to younger ones. It was not simply that they knew more but that they demonstrated qualitatively different thinking as they matured. Whereas young children (2– 7) are egocentric in their thinking, older children (7–11) more readily listen to the ideas of others and recognize that their own ideas are not the only ones; although they are still likely to follow their intuition unless persuaded to do otherwise. Piaget continued with his studies through several decades before proposing a theory of intellectual development over four distinct stages (Table 5.2). His work emphasized the importance of active learning, in which children were free to question, explore and test in the process of constructing their own knowledge. He favoured the expression 'construction rather than instruction' because he was convinced that children learn best when they do things for themselves, rather than receive instructions from adults (Piaget, 1976). Piaget's theory has implications for teachers. To support children's thinking, they should provide props and visual aids, such as models and timelines in history lessons. They should use familiar examples to introduce more complex ideas. Piaget's influence can be seen in most nursery classrooms in which there are play areas, materials for sorting and classifying, sandpits for constructional work, and paints to make symbolic representations of the world. When teaching any topic, most teachers follow the Piagetian principle of moving from the concrete and practical to the more complex and abstract, for instance from discussing a particular poem to poetry in general.

Piaget's stage theory has been criticized on various grounds, including: underestimating children's abilities; assuming that physical manipulation of external objects is essential for normal cognitive development; and underplaying the cultural influences on children's thinking (Child, 2004). Piaget's research methods have also been questioned – for example, he used an unrepresentative sample (based on his three children and others from well-educated backgrounds). Later research studies showed that children's reasoning abilities varied according to how tasks were presented to and understood by them (Donaldson, 1978; Hughes, 1975; Morss, 1991). In sum, teachers need to be mindful of Piaget's 'ages and stages' theory but not interpret this too rigidly.

Among those who challenged Piaget's stage theory was the remarkable cognitive psychologist Jerome Bruner (born in 1915) – who continued to lecture and research at New York University well into his nineties. In contrast to stage theorists, Bruner argued that young children could learn any material so long as the instruction is organized appropriately. He believed that children make sense of their worlds by sorting and arranging ideas. They 'represent' the world through physical actions ('enactive representation'), objects and events ('iconic representation') and symbols such as language ('symbolic representation'). He introduced the notion of 'scaffolding' where pupils are supported to move on in their learning through techniques such as modelling, coaching, reading aloud, use of story, and breaking skills down into separate parts. These 'scaffolds' are temporary measures, taken away once the child succeeds at the task just as stabilizers are removed when a child learns to ride a bicycle independently. Typically in a lesson, a teacher will circulate and through conversation and observation monitor pupils' progress – this is a form of 'soft' scaffolding. Teachers might also plan for the use of particular

**TABLE 5.2** Stages in a child's cognitive development according to Piaget

| Stage | Approximate age | Features |
|---|---|---|
| Sensori-motor | 0–2 | Learns through senses and reflexes e.g. sucking<br>Trial-and-error experimentation e.g. a child tries different sounds or actions as a way of getting attention from a caregiver<br>Begin to develop symbols to represent events or objects in the world |
| Pre-operational | 2–7 | Increasing use of symbols e.g. in role play using a broom as a horse<br>Sees the world through their egocentric perspective rather than others<br>Few children show any understanding of conservation (e.g. of number, length, volume) prior to the age of five<br>Over-generalizes based on limited experience |
| Concrete operational | 7–11 | Begin to think logically about actual (concrete) events, but have difficulty understanding abstract or hypothetical concepts<br>Understand reversibility, or awareness that actions can be reversed e.g. that his or her dog is a Spaniel, that a Spaniel is a dog, and that a dog is an animal |
| Formal operational | 11+ | Ability to think about abstract concepts e.g. love, war, peace<br>Can speculate about the possible<br>Instead of relying solely on previous experiences, children begin to consider possible outcomes and consequences of actions |

'hard' scaffolding strategies such as visual aids, glossaries, questions, prompt cards, help sheets and other additional resources to move the learning forward.

## Social constructivism

One of Piaget's contemporaries, the Russian psychologist Lev Vygotsky (1896–1934), challenged the idea that child development is a universal, natural process. Vygotsky placed much emphasis on the idea that humans develop knowledge, skills and beliefs as a result of social interactions rather than something that happens from *within*. Whereas Piaget focused on the individual, Vygotsky emphasized the social and the central role of language in cognitive development. Of particular significance in education is Vygotsky's notion of the zone of proximal development (ZPD), which described the gap between what a child could *actually* do alone and what he could *potentially* do with the help of someone more knowledgeable, skilled or experienced, whether an adult or another child (Vygotsky, 1978). When a child begins to put together a jigsaw for the first time it is likely to prove very challenging if working alone. But when a parent or more experienced child describes or demonstrates some basic strategies, such as finding all the corner/edge pieces and offers encouragement, the child becomes more competent, confident and independent (Schaffer, 1996). According to Vygotsky, this kind of cooperation and dialogue promotes cognitive development. Because children progress through this zone at different speeds, the implication is that whole-class teaching of the same content using the same approach and at the same time is unlikely to be effective. According to Vygotsky, it is better to have learners working alongside someone at a level slightly above their own. The use of peer tutors, mixed ability groups and **cognitive apprenticeship** models are examples of how Vygotsky has influenced classroom practice.

There are a cluster of theories that support the social aspects of learning including **social constructivism**, **sociocultural theory** and **activity theory**. Although not identical, they all stress that children learn by doing and through interaction with others (Table 5.3). Those who support a social constructivist view of the world play down genetic or biological influences. Although children can learn in solitude and silence, the social occasions of conversations, group projects and debate, also play a key role in learning. Childhood is not seen as a natural stage of development but rather a social construct, subject to different interpretations; for instance, on matters such as how children should be disciplined, when they should start school, the length of their schooling and, more fundamentally, the extent to which they have rights that should be enforced. For social constructivists, children are active agents in making sense of the world around them.

Social constructivist theory has influenced the development of the curriculum. Since the emphasis is on pupils working together to solve problems, this was one of the underlying principles behind the primary literacy and numeracy strategies introduced in English schools in 1998. The theory is also prominent in scientific investigations where children are encouraged to try things out, compare ideas, recheck measurements, question and evaluate. The popularity of constructivism in science education has grown over recent decades, although it is not without challenges in setting up an appropriate learning environment and drawing upon the prior knowledge of thirty or so pupils (Murphy, 2003). The promotion of thinking skills, in which pupils are encouraged to discuss what they

**TABLE 5.3** Overview of learning theories

| School | View of knowledge and learning | Implications for teachers | Key figures |
|---|---|---|---|
| Behaviourism | ■ Behaviour is determined by the environment rather than internal mental processes<br>■ Learning promoted by repetition and reinforcement | ■ Provide initial stimulus<br>■ Use 'feedback sandwich' of positive, corrective and positive comment<br>■ Break down learning into small behaviours to develop into habits<br>■ Model appropriate behaviours | John B. Watson<br>Ivan Pavlov<br>Burrhus Skinner |
| Cognitive constructivism | ■ People are not 'programmed animals' but rational beings<br>■ Learning is an active process<br>■ Knowledge is constructed through enquiry rather than acquiring it passively | ■ Provide problem-solving challenges<br>■ Use errors and misconceptions as teaching points<br>■ Link new learning to pupils' prior knowledge<br>■ Minimize direct teaching 'by telling'<br>■ Model metacognitive strategies such as talking aloud, reviewing, setting goals, predicting | Jean Piaget<br>Jerome Bruner<br>Robert Gagné |
| Social constructivism | ■ Learning depends on social and cultural factors<br>■ Social interaction is essential to learning<br>■ Learning is context specific | ■ Provide opportunities for pupils to collaborate in long-term projects, ask questions and explore<br>■ Promote speaking and listening through debate, discussion, role play<br>■ 'Scaffold' learning through questions, flowcharts, prompts, paired and group work | Lev Vygotsky<br>John Dewey |
| Situated learning | ■ Learning derives from real-life contexts<br>■ Learning occurs within 'communities of practice', which have their own beliefs and practices<br>■ Learners begin on the periphery as novices but move to the centre of the community to become experts | ■ Provide opportunities for pupils to apply their knowledge in real-life contexts<br>■ Create opportunities for social interaction<br>■ Make links with specialists such as geographers, historians, coaches, musicians, artists | Jean Lave<br>Etienne Wenger |

| | | |
|---|---|---|
| Multiple intelligences | ■ Individuals possess distinct multiple cognitive intelligences: linguistic, logic-mathematical, spatial, musical, inter-personal, intra-personal, naturalistic, bodily/kinaesthetic and spiritual | Howard Gardner |
| | ■ Recognize and teach to a broad range of talents and skills beyond verbal and mathematical intelligence<br>■ Draw upon pupils' preferred learning styles when teaching<br>■ Use assessments such as portfolios, journals and independent projects to allow pupils to show their learning using different intelligences | |
| Emotional intelligence | ■ Learning is seen as the ability to understand one's emotions and those of others | Daniel Goleman<br>Peter Salovey<br>Jack Meyer |
| | ■ Recognize and respond to pupils' feelings<br>■ Develop self-awareness<br>■ Promote listening with empathy<br>■ Share feelings with class, where appropriate<br>■ Check non-verbal communication | |
| Experiential Learning | ■ Learning is holistic - involves intellect, senses, personality, feelings<br>■ Experiential learning results from application of knowledge and requires:<br>  – personal involvement<br>  – personal control<br>  – evaluation<br>  – reflection | John Dewey<br>David Kolb<br>Carl Rogers |
| | ■ Begin with pupils' experiences<br>■ Set a positive climate for learning<br>■ Provide stimulating resources<br>■ Clarify purpose of learning<br>■ Feelings and thoughts shared<br>■ Teacher prompts with questions such as 'Did you notice. . .?'<br>■ Assess through self-evaluation | |

already know (activating prior knowledge, identifying key questions and using tools such as mind maps), is underpinned by social constructivist theory.

From this brief overview it is clear that there is no one all-encompassing theory that explains the complexities of learning and child development. But an awareness of theory is needed so that professional practice can be justified and the behaviour of children understood. As Doherty and Hughes (2009: 58) point out: 'Theories are the "kings and queens" of our strategies to safeguard and promote the welfare of children, and to ensure their cognitive, social and psychological development.' Children can learn by sitting still and listening quietly to the teacher. This does not mean that their imaginations are not racing. Similarly, the fact that children appear to be 'active', for instance in group discussion, carrying out an investigation or role play, does not mean that they are learning more effectively.

## Professional knowledge

Teachers need to be actively engaged in creating knowledge as well as benefiting from the sharing of good practice. Hargreaves (2003) suggests that schools start with an audit of staff knowledge using questions such as:

- Which colleagues have helped you improve your teaching?
- What do you think you know or do that others might find interesting?
- Which aspects of your job do you think you are best at?

The desired outcome can take the form of a *Yellow Pages* guide of who to contact for advice on particular issues. Unfortunately the idea of extending this at a local or regional level is not well developed. A survey of more than 4000 primary teachers undertaken by the National Foundation for Education Research (2004: 16) showed that while the vast majority shared their knowledge and expertise within their own schools, only 7 per cent shared good practice with colleagues in other schools on a regular basis. Nonetheless, many trainee and qualified teachers share classroom ideas with their friends and colleagues through discussion forums such as those hosted by the *Times Educational Supplement* or university or local authority intranet systems.

## Curriculum knowledge: rationale and development

There have been many attempts to identify the aims of primary education and the curriculum children should follow in school (Box 5.2). From a government perspective, there has been a considerable degree of consistency in what it expects schools to deliver, ever since the state first became involved in the provision of elementary schooling in the 1830s. The priorities have revolved around producing literate, numerate, morally upright children who upon leaving school positively contribute to (rather than disrupt) society. In 1997 the Secretary of State for Education and Employment at the time declared that 'the first task of the education system is to ensure that every child is taught to read, write and add up' (DfEE, 1997: 9).

---

**BOX 5.2  KEY CONCEPT – THE CURRICULUM**

Latin from *curriculum*, originally applied to a racing chariot, from which is derived racetrack, or a course to be completed; hence a course of study.

The curriculum can be defined in different ways but a starting point is to consider the programme of teaching in school, or the 'formal' curriculum. The way this is 'delivered' affects the 'hidden' curriculum of implicit messages that are conveyed to pupils. Schools also provide many extra-curricular experiences that might be considered as part of an 'informal' curriculum. The 'intended' curriculum is rarely the same as what children are taught in reality (the actual curriculum). The 'experiential' curriculum refers to what children experience in everyday school life. The 'emergent' curriculum is based around the interests and ideas of the learners. The 'negotiated' curriculum refers to teachers and learners co-planning activities, goals and assignments (Boomer *et al.*, 1992). Bruner (1960) advocated a 'spiral' curriculum in which basic ideas were to be revisited and built upon. Wragg (1997) suggested the idea of a 'cubic' curriculum that included all the planned and realized learning incorporating a vision of the future. The debate about what to include in the curriculum, let alone how to describe it, continues as the recent reviews of the curricula for England, Wales, Northern Ireland and Scotland demonstrate.

---

There is no single, uniform history of the primary curricula in the United Kingdom. Raffe *et al.* (1999) have argued strongly for the need to undertake comparative research into educational provision within what they call the four 'home internationals'. The regional stories of Wales, Scotland and Northern Ireland have been shaped by English policy and ideas to varying degrees, but they have retained their distinctive features in educational provision (Lawson and Silver, 1973; Anderson, 1995; Jones, 1997; Jones, 2002). The distinctiveness is shown, for instance, in the statutory inclusion of Welsh in the national curriculum for Wales, and the introduction of **education for mutual understanding** in Northern Ireland. In Scotland, the tradition has been to provide a broad general education under the responsibility of local councils, within national guidelines.

Since the end of the Second World War, there have been a number of changes to the ideological basis of the present-day curricula in the United Kingdom. The 1950s witnessed increasing cultural diversity in Britain and the growth of scientific knowledge, symbolised by the Space Race. Social and educational commentators noted the need for schools to move away from a narrow knowledge base and embrace technology. The government-commissioned report *Children and their Primary Schools* (DES, 1967a) for schools in England, the Gittins Report in Wales (DES, 1967b) and *Primary Education in Scotland* (SED, 1965), endorsed the importance of creativity, exploration and project work (rather than subject-centred study). The child-centred philosophy (see Photos 5.1a–f) was said to make children more self-confident than traditional methods, and 'open-plan classrooms' presented new opportunities for pupils to participate in discovering knowledge, express independence and manage their own learning. Unfortunately, some critics maintain that it also made them 'more self-centred, less disciplined, less literate and less numerate' (Sked, 1997: 159).

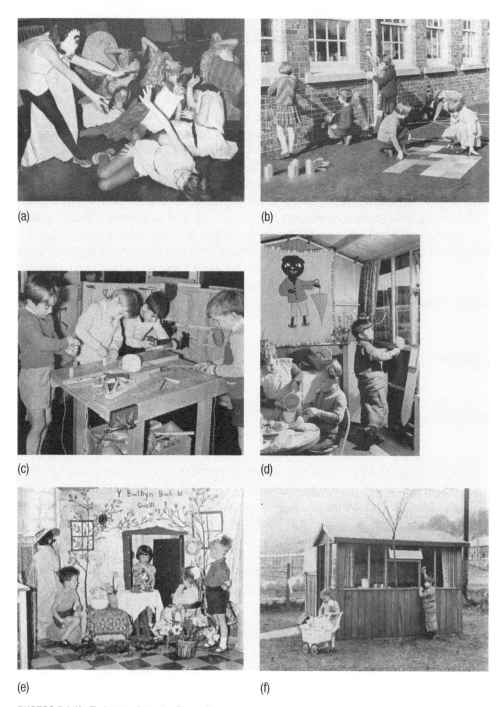

**PHOTOS 5.1 (A–F)**  Images from the Gittins Report

Source: Gittins Report (1967). © Crown Copyright 1967, reproduced under terms of the Click-Use Licence

Right-wing politicians criticized the Plowden Report as being woolly because of its association with vague learning by discovery. Ross (2000: 33) has suggested that the decade between 1976 and 1986 was characterized by 'turmoil in the curriculum' as political wrangling centred over such issues as what knowledge should be transmitted in schools and the emphasis to be given to process (learning by doing). In the wider context of an economic crisis and concerns over how well schools were preparing students for employment, James Callaghan, the Labour Prime Minister, called for a great debate in education in 1976. Debates over child-centred ideology continued through the 1980s. By then the Conservative government under Margaret Thatcher was committed to a policy of accountability and value for money across the public sector. As the influence of child-centred educational philosophy began to diminish, the focus moved towards performance in literacy, numeracy and science. This has been accentuated by perceived underperformance by the UK's 15-year-olds in international tests in reading, mathematics and science. Despite doubts over the reliability of Pisa (Programme for International Student Assessment) tests, the UK has not seen the improvement of other countries and its overall performance is 'stagnant at best' (Shepherd, 2010; Stewart, 2013a). In 2012, performance of pupils in Wales continued to fall significantly below the international average in mathematics, science and reading. This has driven curriculum reforms designed to strengthen learning in literacy and numeracy. Internationally, literacy and numeracy are very much at the core of the curriculum (Box 5.3).

---

### BOX 5.3  INTERNATIONAL VIEW – THE CURRICULUM

Particular ideological, historical, social and cultural forces shape each country's curriculum around the world. For instance, children attending a primary school in rural Africa are expected to 'listen, remember and obey', where the curriculum emphasis is on reading, writing and proving a credit to the family and community (Moyles and Hargreaves, 1998: 91). Most countries include the following in their curricula: first language, mathematics, science, information technology, design, history, geography, PE, art, music, RE, personal and social education, citizenship and the learning of foreign languages (Pepper, 2008). However, there has been a shift towards a skills-based curriculum in many leading countries where the focus is on the development of higher-order thinking skills (Whitby *et al.*, 2006; Bell *et al.*, 2008; Mourshed *et al.*, 2010). John Hattie's conclusion, based on a synthesis of over 6,000 international studies of different aspects of curriculum design, is that 'it is less the content of curricula that is important than the strategies teachers use to implement the curriculum so that students progress upwards through the curricula content' (Hattie, 2009: 156). According to McCulloch (2011), outstanding schools around the world are characterized when:

1    teachers are free to develop their own pedagogies;

2    content is carefully planned around themes rather than discrete subjects;

3    the curriculum does not lead to a neglect of the 'basics';

4    great teachers know their subjects but inspire others to love them too;

5    thinking skills are taught explicitly.

**EXTEND YOUR UNDERSTANDING**

Select a subject's programme of study for the National Curriculum and consider whether the criticisms above hold up to close scrutiny. Find the website of the appropriate professional body that represents the subject and summarize its view of the National Curriculum. If teaching in Scotland, why isn't there a national curriculum and what is the general view among teachers of the *Curriculum for Excellence*?

Although the Education Act (1988) requires schools to offer a broad and balanced curriculum, successful versions of the national curriculum in England have been criticized for failing to do so. For instance, the most recent version in 2014 has drawn the following criticisms from the Association of School and College Leaders (ASCL):

- Art and design, music: so cursory that teachers . . . are at a loss to understand how this is an improvement;

- Citizenship: greatly inferior to the existing programme;

- Computing: so technical and content heavy . . . it almost completely removes all the practical ICT skills that students will need for adult life;

- Design and technology: return to more of a craft-based, maintenance skills approach, which will not prepare students for the real world;

- Geography: too little emphasis on cultural understanding and diversity;

- History: unteachable; will turn students away from history;

- Languages: proper progression between Key Stages 2 and 3 will become impossible for many;

- Physical education: the focus on team games, rather than developing a good understanding of healthy living . . . is a major shortcoming; and

- English, maths and science: unhelpful and potentially damaging imbalance between knowledge and its application.

(Cited by Stewart, 2013b)

## Knowledge of the National Curriculum

The Education Reform Act of 1988 changed the face of primary education in England and Wales. Through the National Curriculum the government imposed its policies on what was to be taught, to whom and when. Since 1988, all state-funded schools are required to provide a broad and balanced curriculum that:

- promotes the spiritual, moral, cultural, mental and physical development of pupils at the school and of society; and

- prepares pupils for the opportunities, responsibilities and experiences of later life

(DfE, 2013)

In England and Wales, the curriculum was divided into core and foundation subjects. Specialist working groups thrashed out the content of each subject's programme of study. The enormity of their tasks should not be underestimated and inevitably there were significant controversies over what they recommended should be taught. Phillips (1998), for instance, recounts the contentions surrounding the revised content of the history syllabus (specifically about British identity and skills versus knowledge), which saw thousands of articles, letters and editorials appear in the press. This was not simply an academic debate, but a political one at the highest level. Margaret Thatcher, as Prime Minister, was at odds with her own education secretary, Kenneth Baker, over what she perceived to be excessive prescription in history and the other foundation subjects.

Through the 1990s the teaching of English, mathematics and science (the core subjects) have had their fair share of controversy. The status of science, for example, has suffered a steady demise as the drive to raise standards in mathematics and English dominated the primary curriculum (Boyle and Bragg, 2005; Tymms *et al.*, 2008). The demands associated with high-stakes testing and assessment meant that the National Curriculum was aptly summed up as 'a dream at conception, a nightmare at delivery' (Campbell, cited in Alexander and Flutter, 2009: 6). But as Davison (2004: 84) notes, the central metaphor of the National Curriculum is 'delivery': a curriculum to be 'delivered' by a teacher is disempowering of pupils and teachers alike. In the opening decade of the twenty-first century, the curricula of the United Kingdom have been subject to major reviews. In England, Sir Jim Rose led the Independent Review of the Primary Curriculum (Rose, 2008). He advocated a reduction in prescribed content by focusing upon 'Essentials for Learning and Life' (literacy, numeracy, ICT capability, learning and thinking skills, personal and emotional skills and social skills). The Rose Review recommended that these skills were to be developed through seven areas of learning, but the Coalition Government rejected this in favour of a subject-based curriculum where essential knowledge is made explicit. The Rose Review acknowledged one of the major difficulties of trying to create a curriculum that is challenging and enriching, where children can apply knowledge and skills learned in one subject to better understand another: 'How can we best help primary class teachers solve the "quarts-into-pint-pots" problem of teaching 13 subjects, plus religious education, to sufficient depth, in the time available?' (Box 5.4). A separate fully independent review of the primary curriculum in England, undertaken by a Cambridge team (2006–09) led by Professor Robin Alexander, questioned the following assumptions:

- knowledge is mere facts or information;
- such facts and information are there to be 'looked up' and 'stored', but never engaged with or questioned;
- knowledge is ineradicably associated with old-fashioned **quasi-Gradgrindian** teaching ('Teach these boys and girls nothing but Facts. Facts alone are wanted in life . . .');
- children may 'access' knowledge but it is no longer necessary for them, or their teachers, to know anything; and
- history is about the learning of dates

(Alexander and Flutter, 2009: 15)

Fundamentally, the Cambridge Primary Review maintained that too many in education misunderstood the meaning of knowledge:

> If the various domains of knowledge are viewed not as collections of inert or obsolete information but as *distinct ways of knowing, understanding, enquiring and making sense* which include processes of enquiry, modes of explanation and criteria for verification which are generic to all content in the domain, then far from being redundant or irrelevant, knowledge provides the means to tackle future problems and needs as well as offering windows of unparalleled richness on past and present.
>
> (Alexander and Flutter, 2009: 16)

Both the Cambridge Primary Review and the Rose Review approved a creative approach to the curriculum, allowing teachers professional autonomy to implement national guidelines to suit their local circumstances. They also called for high quality training in curriculum design and pedagogy. Despite schools gaining greater autonomy in deciding what is taught in areas outside the core subjects, fears remain that breadth and quality of learning in the foundation subjects will be diluted once the National Curriculum for 2014 is established.

In Scotland, the Scottish Executive launched a 'National Debate on Education' in 2002 to explore the purposes and principles of education. Concerns were expressed about an overcrowded curriculum, imbalance in subject coverage and progression in learning. The outcome was the formal launch of *Curriculum for Excellence* (3–18) in 2009 (Table 5.4; Figure 5.1). This represented a shift away from the prescriptive 5–14 curriculum 'guidance' towards more personalized experiences for learners and more professional autonomy for teachers. The emphasis on active learning has been broadly welcomed. However, communicating and implementing the vision are ongoing challenges – as one former director of education put it: 'If you ask 50 head teachers what CfE is about you'll get 50 answers' (cited by Garavelli, 2013). An important distinction is drawn between first-order engagement, when teachers agree in principle with the changes, and second-order engagement, which relates to how the new curriculum is congruent with teachers' deeper

---

**BOX 5.4  REAL-LIFE LEARNING CHALLENGE**

You studied RE as your major subject in university and are a committed Christian writer. You have just been appointed to an inner-city primary school that will be opening next year in a multiethnic community. The majority of parents feel that their particular religion is best dealt with by their own places of worship or inside the family. The Muslim community is worried about the global image of their faith and says they don't want the school to teach religion – their own religion let alone any other religion. Some non-Muslims are also questioning the point of teaching RE. However, others are concerned about a school setting up that may not be teaching RE. One priest calls this 'madness when RE is about open-mindedness and tolerance – and in any case RE is a requirement'. Your head has asked you to prepare some briefing notes on the values that the school hopes to teach through RE and the wider curriculum to share with the community.

**Values**
Wisdom, justice, compassion, integrity

The curriculum must be inclusive, be a stimulus for personal achievement and, through the broadening of experience of the world, be an encouragement towards informed and responsible citizenship.

**The curriculum: 'the totality of all that is planned for children and young people throughout their education'**

- Ethos and life of the school as a community
- Curriculum areas and subjects
- Interdisciplinary learning
- Opportunities for personal achievement

**Learning and teaching**

- Engaging and active
- Setting challenging goals
- Shared expectations and standards
- Timely, accurate feedback
- Learning intentions, success criteria, personal learning planning
- Collaborative
- Reflecting the ways different learners progress

**Experiences and outcomes set out expectations for learning and development in:**

- Expressive arts
- Languages and literacy
- Health and wellbeing
- Mathematics and numeracy
- Religious and moral education
- Sciences
- Social studies
- Technologies

Curriculum levels describe progression and development.

**All children and young people are entitled to experience**

- a coherent curriculum from 3 to 18
- a broad general education, including well planned experiences and outcomes across all the curriculum areas. This should include understanding of the world and Scotland's place in it and understanding of the environment
- a senior phase which provides opportunities for study for qualifications and other planned opportunities for developing the four capacities
- opportunities for developing skills for learning, skills for life and skills for work
- opportunities to achieve to the highest levels they can through appropriate personal support and challenge
- Opportunities to move into positive and sustained destinations beyond school

**Personal support**

- review of learning and planning of next steps
- gaining access to learning activities which will meet their needs
- planning for opportunities for personal achievement
- preparing for changes and choices and support through changes and choices
- pre-school centres and schools working with partners

**Principles of curriculum design:**

- Challenge and enjoyment
- Breadth
- Progression
- Depth
- Personalisation and choice
- Coherence
- Relevance

**Arrangements for**

- Assessment
- Qualifications
- Self-evaluation and accountability
- Professional development

**support the purposes of learning**

**FIGURE 5.1** Values of the Scottish Curriculum

Source: From the curriculum at a glance, Learning and Teaching Scotland (www.ltscotland.org.uk). © Crown Copyright, reproduced under terms of the Click-Use Licence

conceptions about knowledge, learning and assessment (Priestley and Minty, 2013). Teachers in Scotland are very much at the latter stage.

## Knowledge and understanding of the Early Years curriculum

It is important for primary teachers to have a sound knowledge of the principles and practices within the Early Years, given the growing emphasis upon developing dialogue between teachers of different phases. This book can only touch upon these, but there are many informative and up-to-date accounts of Early Years policies and practices across the UK (e.g. Baldock *et al.*, 2013; Palaiologou, 2013). What kind of knowledge do outstanding Early Years practitioners possess? This is perhaps best illustrated by considering

**TABLE 5.4** Primary curricula in the United Kingdom

| Curriculum | England | Wales | Scotland | Northern Ireland |
|---|---|---|---|---|
| Framework | National Curriculum | National Curriculum | Curriculum for Excellence (3–18) | Northern Ireland Curriculum |
| Rationale | To promote the spiritual, moral, cultural, mental and physical development of pupils at the school and of society<br>To prepare pupils at the school for the opportunities, responsibilities and experiences of adult life | To establish a curriculum for the twenty-first century that meets the needs of individual learners while taking account of the broader needs of Wales | To enable all pupils to develop their capacities as: successful learners, confident individuals, responsible citizens and effective contributors to society | To empower young people to develop their potential and to make informed and responsible choices and decisions throughout their lives |
| Ages | Y1–Y2: KS1<br>Y3–Y6: KS2<br>(5–11) | Y3–Y6: KS2<br>(7–11) | P1–P7 (5–12 years):<br>Pre-school and P1 (Early)<br>P2–P4 (First)<br>P5–P7 (Second) | Y3–Y4: KS1<br>Y5–Y7: KS2<br>(5 to 11) |
| Early Years | Early Years Foundation Stage (0 to 5) | Foundation Phase (3–7) | Pre-school and P1 | Y1–Y2: Foundation Stage (3 to 5) |
| Content | Core subjects:<br>■ English<br>■ Maths<br>■ Science<br>Other foundation subjects (KS1/2):<br>■ Art and design<br>■ Computing<br>■ History<br>■ Geography<br>■ Music<br>■ Art and design<br>■ Physical education<br>■ Design and technology<br>■ Foreign language (KS2 only)<br>■ Religious education<br>■ Personal, social, health and economic education (PSHE) | Core subjects:<br>■ English<br>■ Mathematics<br>■ Science<br>■ Welsh (in Welsh-medium schools)<br>Foundation subjects (KS2):<br>■ ICT<br>■ History<br>■ Geography<br>■ Music<br>■ Art<br>■ Physical education<br>■ Design and technology<br>■ Welsh as a second language<br>■ Religious education<br>■ Personal and social education | Curriculum based on experiences and outcomes:<br>■ Sciences<br>■ Languages<br>■ Mathematics<br>■ Expressive arts<br>■ Social studies<br>■ Technologies<br>■ Health and well-being<br>■ Religious and moral education | Areas of learning:<br>■ Language and literacy<br>■ Mathematics and numeracy;<br>■ The Arts (Art and Design, Drama and Music);<br>■ The World around Us (Geography, History and Science and Technology);<br>■ Personal development mutual understanding<br>■ Religious education<br>■ Physical education |
| Other | ■ Language, literacy and numeracy | ■ Curriculum Cymreig<br>■ Education for Sustainable Development and Global Citizenship<br>■ Thinking skills<br>■ ICT | ■ Enterprise<br>■ Citizenship<br>■ Sustainable development<br>■ International education<br>■ Creativity<br>■ Skills for learning, life and work | ■ Communication<br>■ Using mathematics<br>■ Using information and communications technology<br>Thinking skills and personal capabilities:<br>■ Problem solving and decision making;<br>■ Self-management;<br>■ Working with others;<br>■ Managing information;<br>■ Being creative |

Sources: England, see DfE (2013); Wales, see: www.wales.gov.uk; Scotland, see: www.educationscotland.gov.uk; Northern Ireland, see: www.nicurriculum.org.uk

an example. Tina Bruce, a leading author in the Early Years, recalls her inspirational Frobel-trained teacher, Joyce Greaves:

> We did radio plays, pretending to switch her desk off and on like a wireless. We decorated our handwriting books. She read us poetry and played songs on the piano. We used clay, did collage, made models, grew beans in jam jars, found places on a globe and looked at artefacts found in different countries and cultures. We did stories in dance, song and drama, and got in rather a mess making animals out of clay. But perhaps most important, although she had 40 children in her class, we each felt that we mattered to her.
>
> (Bruce, 1999: 35)

Clearly this teacher knew how to connect with each child in her class. This required knowledge not only of their development but how to engage their interests in a broad range of subjects. Moyles *et al.* (2002: 131) report that the best Early Years practitioners bring certain personal qualities and attitudes to the role, which are valued by colleagues and parents alike, for example 'patience', 'tolerance' and 'good humour'. They seek to make young children's first experiences in school memorable, enjoyable and challenging. They know the value of getting to know each child and invest much time and energy in developing relationships.

Global interest in the education of young children has developed considerably in recent years, for instance in New Zealand's pre-school curriculum *Te Whāriki* and *Reggio Emilia* (see Table 5.5), with their emphasis upon community support, providing rich sensory experiences and children taking an active role in their learning. Many practitioners in the United Kingdom have been enthused following visits to Early Years settings in Scandinavia. Despite initial funding difficulties, the Welsh Foundation Phase (DCELLS, 2008) in particular has attracted envy from educationalists that cherish informal, play-centred experiences. The Foundation Phase focuses on active learning, speaking and listening, opportunities for children to become involved in planning and reviewing their work and an emphasis on skills development.

In 2000 the Foundation Stage was introduced in England, seen as a landmark with the education of the under fives officially recognized as important (Basford and Hodson, 2008). However, this has not been without its critics. Many within the Early Years community complained about a government-imposed 'nappy curriculum' where knowledge was divided into six areas of learning, rather than a more holistic and integrated approach as is the case in Wales. There were some concessions presented through the *Curriculum Guidance for the Foundation Stage* (DfEE, 2000), which focused more on describing learning experiences than achievement of outcomes. However, the retention of early learning goals continued to attract criticism on various grounds. Soler and Miller (2008: 58), for instance, claim that the Early Years curriculum prioritized competitiveness: 'The main goal is to support those who can succeed and reach skills-based attainment targets rather than cater for individuality and access for all children.'

More generally, the constant flow of initiatives and policy changes has added to the strain. In England alone, between 1998 and 2008 there have been at least twenty major new policies regarding early childhood education, most notably the *Birth to Three Matters* framework (DfE, 2002), the revised Foundation Stage (in 2007) and the introduction of

Early Years Professional Status (Nutbrown *et al.*, 2008). Since then the Tickell Review (2011) acknowledged the need to simplify the Early Years Foundation Stage, for instance by reducing the number of early learning goals. These recommendations were reflected in the *Statutory Framework for the Early Years Foundation Stage* (EYFS), introduced in 2012. The EYFS is underpinned by the concept of 'school readiness' so that young children are prepared to learn, able to play, make friends and say what is on their minds. The principles are as follows:

- every child is a unique child, who is constantly learning and can be resilient, capable, confident and self-assured;
- children learn to be strong and independent through positive relationships; children learn and develop well in enabling environments, in which their experiences respond to their individual needs and there is a strong partnership between practitioners and parents and/or carers; and
- children develop and learn in different ways and at different rates. The framework covers the education and care of all children in Early Years provision, including children with special educational needs and disabilities.

(DfE, 2012: 3)

There is strong evidence to underpin these principles. For example, the Effective Provision of Pre-School Education (Sylva *et al.*, 2004) research highlighted the importance of engaging with parents and the lasting effects of high-quality pre-school settings on children's well-being. The EYFS is supported by non-statutory guidance, *Development Matters in the Early Years Foundation Stage* (Early Education, 2012), which includes development statements for areas of learning. A sharper focus is placed on the main or prime areas of learning, namely communication and language, physical development and personal and social development (Figure 5.2).

In Scotland, practitioners in the Early Years are expected to work towards the components and principles set out in *Getting it Right for Every Child* (Scottish Government, 2008) and *Pre-Birth to Three: Positive Outcomes for Scotland's Children and Families* (Learning and Teaching Scotland, 2010). Babies and young children should be healthy, achieving, nurtured, active, respected, responsible, included and, above all, safe. These are the outcomes that indicate children's well-being. Provision should be based on four principles:

- rights – to thrive and be nurtured by adults who promote young children's general well-being, health, nutrition and safety;
- relationships – to receive welcoming smiles, hugs, consistency and reassuring comments that build trust; to learn in a safe, secure, loving and familiar environment;
- responsive care – by providing companionship, time and physical affection, which is essential if children are to feel, safe, secure and valued; and
- respect – to be consulted where appropriate, to feel included, to participate and contribute, to express feelings and be listened to.

(Learning and Teaching Scotland, 2010)

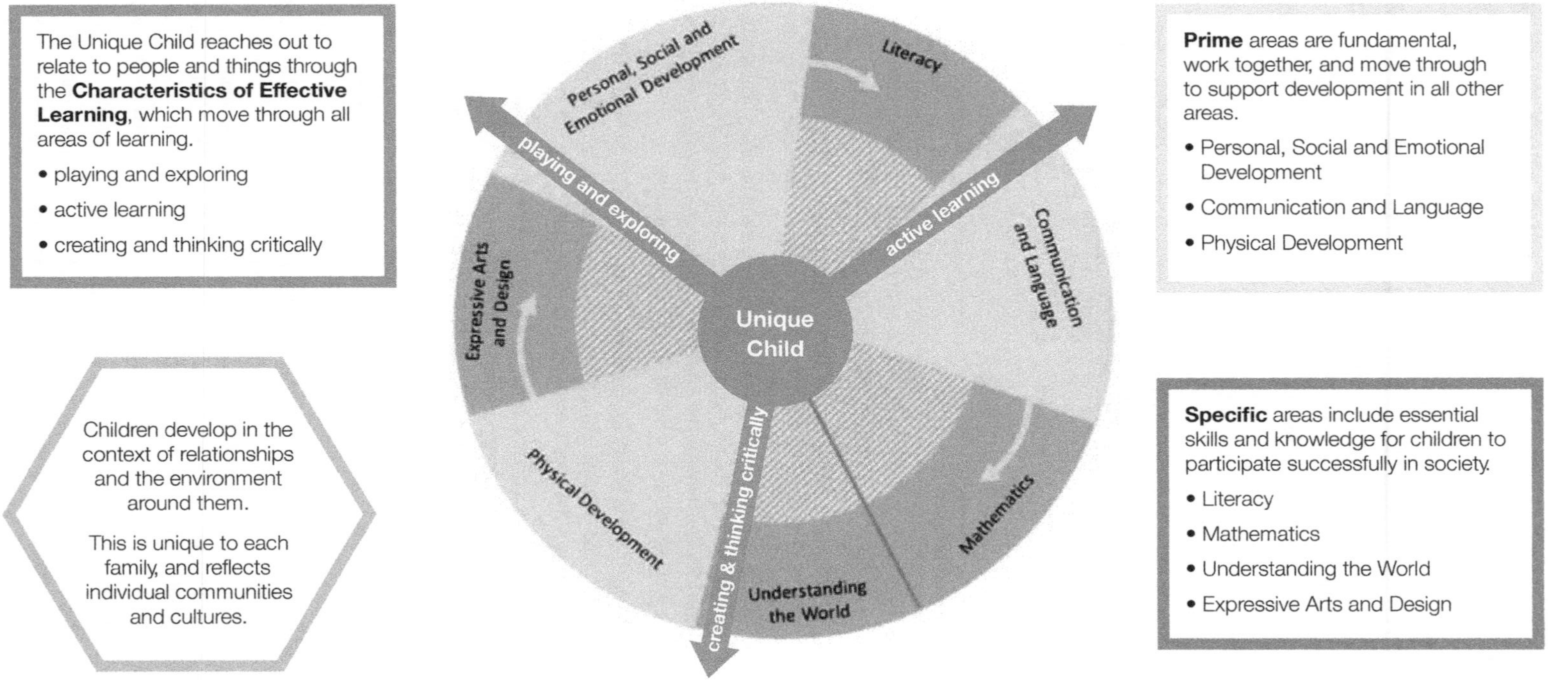
The Unique Child reaches out to relate to people and things through the **Characteristics of Effective Learning**, which move through all areas of learning.
• playing and exploring
• active learning
• creating and thinking critically
Children develop in the context of relationships and the environment around them.
This is unique to each family, and reflects individual communities and cultures.
Personal, Social and Emotional Development
Literacy
playing and exploring
active learning
Communication and Language
Expressive Arts and Design
Unique Child
Physical Development
creating & thinking critically
Mathematics
Understanding the World
**Prime** areas are fundamental, work together, and move through to support development in all other areas.
• Personal, Social and Emotional Development
• Communication and Language
• Physical Development
**Specific** areas include essential skills and knowledge for children to participate successfully in society.
• Literacy
• Mathematics
• Understanding the World
• Expressive Arts and Design

**FIGURE 5.2** Early Years Foundation Stage

Source: Early Education (2012: 4)

Similar principles underpin the Foundation Stage in Northern Ireland (CCEA, 2006) where there is a strong emphasis on providing practical, interactive and enjoyable learning opportunities.

Although there is much common ground in the rhetoric associated with Early Years policy, there are differences in approach adopted by schools (Table 5.5). For instance, Steiner Waldorf Schools seek to provide 'unplugged experiences' by delaying the introduction of complex technologies until the secondary school years. This is based on the view that too much 'screen time' is detrimental to young children's development. This view of technologies does not prevent such schools from receiving outstanding inspection reports (for example, see Wynstones school in Gloucester School Inspection Service (School Inspection Service, 2009)). However, there are commonly held beliefs about the importance of the Early Years of life in enabling children to achieve their potential. The standards-driven agenda in primary education, which has characterized the last few decades, has been criticized on many grounds. One response has been the

**TABLE 5.5** Approaches to the curriculum in the Early Years

| Philosophy | Characteristics |
| --- | --- |
| High Scope | Children are encouraged to choose what materials they would like to use; teachers act as facilitators in supporting and guiding these choices. |
| Steiner schools | Schools based on the ideas of Rudolf Steiner (1861–1925) who advocated a curriculum featuring nature study, a strong spiritual dimension and community focus. |
| Waldorf kintergarten | The name 'Waldorf' refers to the German cigarette company that sponsored the first school in 1919. The education is closely associated with Steiner and focuses on creativity and imagination. Each day is arranged as Head (e.g. mental arithmetic), Heart (e.g. drama) and Hands lessons (e.g. gardening). |
| Montessori schools | An approach to education, derived from Maria Montessori (1870–1952), which has a strong focus on developing the senses and education for peace. One of the key principles is that teachers should 'follow the child'. |
| Te Whāriki | Literally this means 'the woven mat' and derives from the New Zealand Maori community. Five learning strands are woven together to create a learning programme for each child: well-being, contribution, belonging, communication and exploration. |
| Forest schools | Forest school is an innovative approach to outdoor play and learning. It originated in Sweden in the 1950s and was brought over to the UK in the 1990s. Initially, projects run from the school grounds before moving to local woodland where the focus is on developing a range of practical, social and cognitive skills, as well as dispositions. |
| Reggio Emilia | This approach takes its name from a district in northern Italy, where parents rebuilt village schools under the direction of a primary teacher, Loris Malaguzzi (1920–1994), after the destruction of the Second World War. They wanted young children to grow up with democratic values. The approach is based on the belief that children's learning should not be restrained by formal curriculum planning. Their voice should be prominent in deciding what they are learning and where they are heading. |
| Slow Education | Although there are no Slow Schools in the UK, the movement is a reaction to fast-food culture and shares the principles held by Steiner, Montessori and Waldorf. Children grow, prepare and eat their own organic food and are educated to live sustainably. |

emergence of counter-education movements. These include Slow Education, Whole Education and Human Scale Education, all of which share a desire to promote learning in depth rather than a curriculum based on goals, tests and attainment levels (Barker, 2012). Although these movements remain marginal interests, mainstream teachers can benefit from reflecting upon what they are trying to achieve and their underlying philosophy. Making time to talk to young children, finding out their interests and enabling them to try out ideas are important principles of good Early Years practice.

## Playful learning

Many theorists have highlighted the importance of play in young children's learning, including Froebel (see Bruce, 2012), Montessori (1949), Piaget (1976), Vygotsky (1978), Bruner (1986), Gardner (1999) and Laevers (2000). These have provided various models to explore the kinds of environments and strategies that effectively promote play. Most agree that the quality of young children's experiences depends upon committed, enthusiastic and reflective practitioners who demonstrate:

- trusting and caring relationships with children;
- understanding of how young children learn and develop especially through play;
- strong practical knowledge of the curriculum;
- understanding of how to create an indoor and outdoor environment conducive to learning; and
- effective working with parents, carers and the wider community.

There is no shortage of excellent materials explaining the pedagogy of play and why it is fundamental to life (Bishop and Curtis, 2001; Moyles, 2006; Brock et al., 2009). In sum, play enables young children to make sense of their world, to create new ideas, to act out every day experiences, develop self-confidence and social skills and manage their feelings. It provides obvious health benefits at a time when there is growing concern over child obesity levels. Above all, play is important because it is the primary means by which schools can develop children's dispositions to learn, such as resilience in coping with 'not knowing' something for a sufficient length of time without losing confidence.

Wood and Attfield (2005) raise two of the most important questions about play, namely what is it and what does it do for the child? They point out that play is defined in many ways and can, in some cases, be a very traumatic and negative experience for young children – just observe any small child amidst older boisterous children on a hard, cold tarmac playground. Play is a very contextual experience, full of uncertainties – one of its most important features. Often play is defined more in relation to its opposite – serious work (Goodale and Godbey, 1988). Play often involves the blurring of boundaries, so that work and play can become the same activity (Huizinga, 2000). Play is too often associated with young children. Yet adults also play every day of their lives whether through sport, computer games, meeting someone for the first time, or when playing with words.

**PHOTO 5.2** Three-year-olds play with objects hanging from outdoor sound wall

Source: POD/Pearson Education Ltd, Jules Selmes

To be regarded as an outstanding practitioner in the Early Years, it is essential to know how to create opportunities for different forms of play, including:

■ structured play – the adult chooses the activity, provides the materials and organization;

■ spontaneous play – the child plays on the spur of the moment;

■ child-centred play – the child chooses the activity, often from a given choice;

■ heuristic play – objects explored without adult intervention;

■ domestic play – usually in a 'role play' corner, a child or children pretend to carry out household chores;

■ messy play – usually involves water, paint or sand;

■ imaginative play – involves pupils in creative thinking, perhaps role playing a character from a story, nursery rhyme or real-life scenario;

■ repetitive play – sometimes children repeat an activity a number of times until satisfied;

■ outdoor play – can involve games, running, jumping, etc; and

■ creative play – including playing with paint and natural materials.

For many years, leading figures in Early Years have argued that children need to move from symbolic play based on real experience (playing at eating, sleeping etc.) to more complex, abstract forms of play (playing at space ships, worlds under the sea etc.). This is because it is abstract levels of thinking that matter most in developing the kinds of learners society needs (Bruce, 1999). Between the ages of 4 and 7 children should be learning to develop these skills. Playful learning is experiential, active, intrinsically motivated and focuses more on the process rather than the outcomes. Perhaps the greatest challenge for adults working in the Early Years settings is getting the balance between adult-led experiences and children's spontaneous play. This can be shown along a continuum (Figure 5.3).

At one end there is unstructured play, sometimes described as 'pure' play in that adults do not interfere. While children need time for this spontaneous, independent play, this can descend into chaotic and repetitive activity described as 'hands-on, brains-off' (DCSF, 2009: 3). At the other end of the scale, too much tightly directed activity deprives children of the opportunity to explore their own ideas. Best practice involves a precarious balance of time, space and activities. As Moyles *et al.* (2002: 16) cautioned: 'It is imperative that the promotion of "teaching" does not occur at the expense of young children's learning.' This balance cannot be quantified because it depends upon the specific context and children's development. However, in general, studies of excellent pre-schools suggest that children spend two-thirds of time in activities that they have initiated themselves (Coghlan *et al.*, 2010). The role of the practitioner is to provide the necessary structure, or series of steps, for each child to explore new experiences. Many writers refer to this input as 'scaffolding' – but the term can be unhelpful because the metaphor of the building site does not resemble the dynamic interactions of the setting (Moyles *et al.*, 2002). The practitioner's guidance needs to be small enough for the child to gain success, but challenging enough to spur the child's learning forward. Young children need the time, space and freedom to play. Adults themselves should adopt a playful attitude that reinforces the importance of learning through play.

Practitioners in the Early Years need to be very knowledgeable and sensitive when making decisions about the timing and nature of their interventions or interactions. One means of gaining such knowledge is through the use of video-stimulated-reflective-dialogue (VSRD), a research technique that began in the early 2000s (Moyle *et al.*, 2003). It involves replaying filmed episodes of teacher–child interactions, with appropriate permissions. The video footage or still photographs are reviewed, ideally alongside 'a significant other' who is able to support reflection and critical engagement.

Valuing children's contributions, irrespective of whether they provide the 'right' answer, is of particular importance in Early Years practice as young children gain confidence and find their way. During school placement it is a challenge for trainee

| Unstructured | Child-initiated play | Focused learning | Highly structured |
|---|---|---|---|
| Play without adult support | Adult support for an enabling environment, and sensitive interaction | Adult-guided, playful experiential activities | Adult-directed, little or no play |

FIGURE 5.3 Continuum of approaches to learning through play in the Early Years

Source: DCSF (2009: 5)

teachers to establish trusting relationships with children over a short time period. However this can be achieved by talking to them, observing them at play, becoming familiar with their names, noting their interests and by joining in with their activities. During their first few days together many trainees share something about themselves, such as a photograph when they were a child of the same age or other 'icebreakers', to good effect.

The curriculum for the Early Years across the United Kingdom also has a strong focus on children's well-being (Collins and Foley, 2008). This covers both physical (including health care, mental stimulation, access to the outdoors, rest and nutritious food) and emotional aspects (such as making friends, enjoying warm, close and supportive relationships). For young children it is important that they are made to feel safe and secure in their surroundings. In this regard it is useful to ask whether the children are motivated to learn, have the opportunity to share ideas and take responsibility for their learning – or as Carr (2001) put it succinctly, are the children 'ready, willing and able' to learn. Table 5.6 outlines the main areas of the curriculum within the Early Years.

Case studies of good practice in the Early Years are widely available on local authority, school and inspectorate websites (e.g. www.ofsted.gov.uk/resources/goodpractice). These provide opportunities to reflect on how teachers' knowledge informs practice. For example, teachers will often use their knowledge of children's interests gained from discussion and observation to make changes to the environment. In one setting, teachers chose the theme 'Travel and Transport', which particularly appealed to boys. Their interest in the film *Cars 2* led staff to set up an outdoor garage. For one reluctant writer, this led to a significant step forward in attempts to write the names of car parts in his role as mechanic.

**TABLE 5.6** Areas of learning in the Early Years

| Northern Ireland: Foundation Stage (3–5) | Wales: Foundation Phase (3–7) | England: Foundation Stage (0–5) | Scotland Curriculum for Excellence (3–18) |
|---|---|---|---|
| ■ Language and Literacy<br>■ Mathematics and Numeracy<br>■ Personal Development and Mutual Understanding<br>■ The World Around Us<br>■ Physical Development and Movement<br>■ The Arts | ■ Language, Literacy and Communication Skills<br>■ Mathematical Development<br>■ Personal and Social Development, Well-being and Cultural Diversity<br>■ Welsh Language Development<br>■ Knowledge and Understanding of the World<br>■ Physical Development<br>■ Creative Development | Prime areas<br>■ Communication and Language<br>■ Physical Development<br>■ Personal, Social and Emotional Development<br>Specific areas<br>■ Literacy<br>■ Mathematics<br>■ Understanding the World<br>■ Expressive arts and design | ■ Languages<br>■ Mathematics<br>■ Health and Wellbeing<br>■ Sciences<br>■ Religious and Moral Education<br>■ Social Studies<br>■ Technologies<br>■ Expressive Arts |

Sources: Northern Ireland (www.nicurriculum.org.uk/foundation_stage); Wales (http://wales.gov.uk/topics/educationandskills/earlyyearshome/foundation_phase/?lang=en); England (www.foundationyears.org.uk/eyfs-2014); Scotland (www.educationscotland.gov.uk/earlyyears)

In concluding this chapter it is important for prospective teachers not to be dispirited by the volume of what they need to know to become an outstanding teacher. Having a thirst to find out more is a key disposition and one of the joys of teaching is having the opportunity each day to extend not only children's knowledge but also one's own. While strong subject and professional knowledge are important, as the House of Commons Education Committee (2012) report, no one factor (including overall academic ability) correlates to outstanding performance. But what we do know is that the best teachers never stop learning.

## Glossary

**Activity theory** stresses that human behaviour is driven by needs where people use cultural tools, e.g. the Internet, to achieve their objectives.

**Behaviourism** is a theory of learning that stresses that behaviour is acquired and derives from a stimulus–response relationship.

**Cognitive apprenticeship** is a system of modelling where the teacher explains each step in completing a task, which the apprentice (child) imitates while being observed by the teacher.

**Education for mutual understanding** is a cross-curricular theme within the primary curriculum in Northern Ireland, designed to promote better community relations.

**Learning** is a long-lasting change in someone's behaviour, knowledge, skill or understanding acquired through experience (Wallace, 2008).

**Long-term memory** describes knowledge that is permanently held in the mind that is pulled into the temporary working memory as and when needed.

**Pedagogical Content Knowledge** is a blend of subject knowledge and pedagogical strategies that teachers demonstrate to make lessons accessible to learners (Shulman, 1986).

**Pedagogy** can be defined as everything that teachers plan and do to make a difference to children's learning, such as instructing, questioning and explaining as well as implicit behaviours, such as body language.

**Quasi-Gradgrindian** is a reference to Thomas Gradgrind, a notorious head teacher in Dickens's *Hard Times*, who was concerned only with factual knowledge.

**Schemas** are mental representations of the world, for instance how a dog is seen to differ from a cat.

**Social constructivism** assumes that learning occurs when experiences are shared and the participants construct knowledge.

**Sociocultural theory** suggests that people learn through interaction with others, and then by internalizing and transforming knowledge that enables them to solve problems.

**Working memory** describes the ability we have to hold in mind and mentally process information over short periods of time.

# References

Alexander, R.J. and Flutter, J. (2009) *Towards a new Primary Curriculum*, Cambridge: Cambridge Primary Review, available at: www.primaryreview.org.uk/Downloads/Curriculum_report/CPR_Curric_rep_Pt2_Future.pdf (accessed 16 October 2013).

Anderson, R.D. (1995) *Education and the Scottish People*, Oxford: Clarendon Press.

Baldock, P., Fitzgerald, D. and Kay, J. (2013) *Understanding Early Years Policy*, 3rd edn, London: Sage.

Barker, I. (2012) 'Find the time for slow education', in *Times Educational Supplement*, 2 November.

Basford, J. and Hodson, E. (2008) *Teaching Early Years Foundation Stage*, Exeter: Learning Matters.

Bell, M., Cordingley, P., Gibbons, S. and Hawkins, M. (2008) *Building the Evidence Base: Review of Individual Studies from Systematic Research Reviews*, London: QCA.

Bishop, J.C. and Curtis, M. (eds) (2001) *Play Today in the Primary School Playground*, Buckingham: Open University Press.

Boomer, G., Lester, N., Onore, C. and Cook, J. (1992) *Negotiating the Curriculum: Educating for the 21st Century*, London: Falmer.

Boyle, B. and Bragg, J. (2005) 'No science today: The demise of primary science', *The Curriculum Journal*, 16(4): 423–37.

Brock, A., Dodds, S., Jarvis, P. and Olusoga, Y. (2009) *Perspectives on Play: Learning for Life*, Harlow: Pearson.

Bruce, T. (1999) 'In praise of inspired and inspiring teachers', in Abbott, L. and Moylett, H. (eds) *Early Education Transformed*, London: RoutledgeFalmer, 33–40.

Bruce, T. (2012) *Early Childhood Practice: Froebel Today*, London: Sage.

Bruner, J. (1986) *Actual Minds, Possible Worlds*, London: Harvard University Press.

Bruner, J. (1960) *The Process of Education*, Cambridge, MA: Harvard University Press.

Canter, L. and Canter, M. (1992) *Assertive Discipline*, Santa Monica, CA: Canter and Associates.

Carr, M. (2001) *Assessment in Early Childhood Settings*, London: Paul Chapman.

CCEA (2006) *Understanding the Foundation Stage*, Belfast: Early Years Interboard Group.

Child, D. (2004) *Psychology and the Teacher*, London: Continuum.

Coghlan, M., Bergeron, C., White, K., Sharp, C., Morris, M. and Wilson, R. (2010) *Narrowing the Gap in Outcomes for Young Children through Effective Practices in the Early Years*, London: C4EO.

Collins, J. and Foley, P. (2008) *Promoting Children's Wellbeing: Policy and Practice*, Bristol: Policy Press.

Davison, J. (2004) 'Education, culture and social class', in Hayes, D. (ed.) *The Routledge Guide to Key Debates in Education*, London: Routledge, 81–6.

DCELLS (2008) *Framework for Children's Learning for 3 to 7-year-olds in Wales*, Cardiff: DCELLS.

DCSF (2009) *Learning, Playing and Interacting: Good practice in the Early Years Foundation Stage*, London: DCSF.

DES (1967a) *Children and Their Primary Schools*, London: HMSO.

DES (1967b) *Primary Education in Wales*, London: HMSO.

DfE (2002) *Birth to Three Matters*, London: DfE.

DfE (2012) *Statutory Framework for the Early Years Foundation Stage*, London: DfE.

DfE (2013) *The National Curriculum in England*, London: DfE.

DfEE (1997) *Excellence in Schools*, London: HMSO.

DfEE (2000) *Curriculum Guidance for the Foundation Stage*, London: DfEE.

DfES (2007) *The Early Years Foundation Stage*, London: DfES.

Doherty, J. and Hughes, M. (2009) *Child Development Theory and Practice 0–11*, Harlow: Pearson.

Donaldson, M.C. (1978) *Children's Minds*, London: Croom Helm.

Early Education (2012) *Development Matters in the Early Years Foundation Stage*, London: Early Education.

Feigenson, L. and Halberda, J. (2008) 'Conceptual knowledge increases infants' memory capacity', *Proceedings of the National Academy of Sciences*, 105(29): 9926–30.

Furnham, A. (2008) *50 Psychology Ideas You Really Need To Know*, London: Quercus.

Garavelli, D. (2013) 'Comment: Sizing up the curriculum for excellence', *The Scotsman*, 11 August.

Gardner, H. (1999) *Intelligence Reframed: Multiple Intelligences for the 21st Century*, New York: Basic Books.

Gathercole, S. and Alloway, T. (2007) *Understanding Working Memory: A Classroom Guide*, London: Harcourt Assessment.

Gathercole, S. and Alloway, T. (2008) *Working Memory and Learning: A Practical Guide for Teachers*, London: Sage.

Ghaye, A. and Ghaye, K. (1998) *Teaching and Learning through Critical Reflective Practice*, London: David Fulton.

Glaser, R. (1999) 'Expert knowledge and processes of thinking', in McCormick, R. and Paechter, C. (eds) *Learning and Knowledge*, London: Paul Chapman.

Goodale, T.L. and Godbey, G.C. (1988) *The Evolution of Leisure: Historical and Philosophical Perspectives*, State College, PA: Venture Publishing.

Grossman, P.L., Wilson, S.M. and Shulman, L.E. (1989) 'Teachers of substance: Subject matter knowledge for teaching', in Reynolds, M. C. (ed.) *Knowledge Base For The Beginning Teacher*, New York: Pergamon, 159–99.

Hargreaves, A. (2003) *Teaching in the Knowledge Society*, Maidenhead: Open University Press.

Hattie, J. (2009) *Visible Learning*, London: Routledge.

Holt, J. (1984) *How Children Fail*, Harmondsworth: Penguin.

House of Commons Education Committee (2012) *Great Teachers: Attracting, Training and Retaining the Best: Government Response to the Committee's Ninth Report of Session 2010–12*, London: The Stationery Office.

Hughes, M. (1975) 'Egocentricity in children', unpublished PhD thesis, Edinburgh University.

Huizinga, J. (2000) *Homo Ludens: A Study of Play-Element in Culture*. London: Routledge.

Jarvis, P., Holford, J. and Griffin, C. (1998) *The Theory and Practice of Learning*, London: Kegan Paul.

Jones, G.E. (1997) *The Education of a Nation*, Cardiff: University of Wales Press.

Jones, K. (2002) *Education in Britain: 1944 to the Present*, Cambridge: Polity Press.

Laevers, F. (2000) 'Forward to basics! Deep-level learning and the experiential approach', in *Early Years*, 20(2): 20–9.

Lawson, J. and Silver, H. (1973) *A Social History of Education in England*, London: Methuen.

Learning and Teaching Scotland (2010) *Pre-Birth to Three: Positive Outcomes for Scotland's Children and Families*, Glasgow: Learning and Teaching Scotland.

Lewis, T. (1993) 'Valid knowledge and the problem of practical arts curricula', *Curriculum Inquiry*, 23(2): 175–202.

McCulloch, J. (2011) *Subject to Change: Should Primary Schools Structure Learning around Subjects or Themes?* London: Pearson Centre for Policy and Learning.

Montessori, M. (1949) *The Absorbent Mind*, New York: Dell Publishing Company.

Morss, J. (1991) 'After Piaget: Rethinking "cognitive development"', in J.R. Morss and T. Linzey (eds) *Growing Up: The Politics of Human Learning*, Auckland: Longman, 9–29.

Mourshed, M., Chijioke, C. and Barber, M. (2010) *How the World's Most Improved School Systems Keep Getting Better*, London: McKinsey.

Moyles, J. (2006) *The Excellence of Play*, Buckingham: Open University Press.

Moyles, J. and Hargreaves, L. (1998) *The Primary Curriculum: Learning from International Perspectives*, London: Routledge.

Moyles, J., Adams, S. and Musgrove, A. (2002) *Study of Pedagogical Effectiveness in Early Learning*, London: DfES.

Moyles, J. Hargreaves, L. Merry, R. Paterson, F. and Esarte-Sarries, V. (2003) *Interactive Teaching in the Primary School*, Maidenhead: OUP.

Murphy, C. (2003) *Literature Review in Primary Science and ICT*, Bristol: FutureLab.

NFER (2004) *General Teaching Council Survey of Teachers*, Slough: GTCE.

Nutbrown, C., Clough, P. and Selbie, P. (2008) *Early Childhood Education*, London: Sage.

OFSTED (2014) *School Inspection Handbook*, London: OFSTED.

Palaiologou, I. (2013) *The Early Years Foundation Stage: Theory and Practice*, London: Sage.

Parke, R. and Gauvain, M. (2009) *Child Psychology: A Contemporary Viewpoint*, New York: McGraw-Hill.

Pepper, D. (2008) *Primary Curriculum Change: Directions of Travel in 10 Countries*, London: QCA.

Petty, G. (2006) *Evidence Based Teaching*, Cheltenham: Nelson Thornes.

Piaget, J. (1976) *The Child and Reality*, New York: Penguin Books.

Phillips, R. (1998) *History Teaching, Nationhood and the State*, London: Cassell.

Priestley, M. and Minty, S. (2013) 'Curriculum for Excellence: "A brilliant idea, but . . ."', *Scottish Educational Review*, 45(1): 39–52.

Raffe, D., Brannen, K., Croxford, L. and Martin, C. (1999) 'Comparing England, Scotland, Wales and Northern Ireland: The case for home internationals in comparative research', *Comparative Education*, 95(1): 9–25.

Rose, J. (2008) *The Independent Review of the Primary Curriculum*, London: DCSF.

Ross, A. (2000) *Curriculum Construction and Critique*, London: Falmer Press.

Schaffer, R. (1996) *Social Development*, Oxford: Blackwell.

School Inspection Service (2009) *Inspection Report: Wynstones School*, available at: www.schoolinspectionservice.co.uk/docs/Wynstones_2009.pdf (accessed 16 October 2013).

Scottish Education Department (1965) *Primary Education in Scotland (The Primary Memorandum)*, Edinburgh: HMSO.

Scottish Government (2008) *Getting it Right for Every Child*, Edinbugh: Scottish Government.

Sked, A. (1997) *An Intelligent Person's Guide to Post-War Britain*, London: Duckworth.

Skinner, B.F. (1966) *The Behaviour of Organisms: An Experimental Analysis*, New York: Appleton-Century-Crofts.

Slavin, R.E. (2003) *Educational Psychology*, New York: Longman.

Shulman, L.S. (1986) 'Those who understand: Knowledge growth in teaching', *Educational Researcher*, 10(6): 9–10.

Shulman, L.S. (1987) 'Knowledge and teaching: Foundations of the new reform', *Harvard Educational Review*, 57(1): 1–22.

Soler, J. and Miller, L. (2008) 'The struggle for early childhood curricula: A comparison of the English Foundation Stage Curriculum, *Te Whāriki* and Reggio Emilia', in Wood, E. (ed.) *The Routledge Reader in Early Childhood Education*, London: Routledge, 53–66.

Shepherd, J. (2010) 'UK schools slip down world rankings', *Times Educational Supplement*, 7 December.

Stewart, W. (2013a) 'Gove's curriculum could be "chaos", leaders warn', *Times Educational Supplement*, 12 April.

Stewart, W. (2013b) 'Pisa rankings are "utterly wrong"', *Times Educational Supplement*, 14 September.

Stoll, L. and Louis, K.S. (eds) (2007) *Professional Learning Communities*, Maidenhead: Open University.

Sylva, K., Melhuish, E., Sammons, P., Siraj-Blatchford, I. and Taggart, N. (2004) *The Effective Provision of Pre-School Education (EPPE) Project: Findings from the Early Primary Years*, London: EPPE.

Tickell, C. (2011) *The Early Years: Foundations for Life, Health and Learning*, London: DfE.

Turner-Bisset, R. (2001) *Expert Teaching*, London: David Fulton.

Tymms, P., Bolden, D. and Merrill, C. (2008) *Perspectives on Education: Primary Science*, London: Wellcome Trust.

Vygotsky, L. (1978) *Mind in Society*, Cambridge, MA: Harvard University Press.

Wallace, S. (2008) *A Dictionary of Education*, Oxford: Oxford University Press.

Watkins, C. (2011) *Learning: A Sense-Maker's Guide*, London: ATL.

Whitby, K., Walker, M. and O'Donnell, S., (2006) *Thematic Probe: The Teaching and Learning of Skills in Primary and Secondary Education*, London: NFER/QCA.

Wood, E. and Attfield, J. (2005) *Play, Learning and the Early Childhood Curriculum*, London: Paul Chapman.

Wragg, E.C. (1997) *The Cubic Curriculum*, Abingdon: Routledge.

## Websites

Index of Learning Theories and Models – www.learning-theories.com

Department for Education – www.education.gov.uk

The Cambridge-based Primary Review – www.primaryreview.org.uk/index.html

Scotland's Curriculum for Excellence – www.ltscotland.org.uk/curriculumforexcellence/index.asp

Northern Ireland Curriculum – www.nicurriculum.org.uk

The Eurydice (European Commission) website provides information on the curricula across the UK – www.eurydice.org/portal/page/portal/Eurydice

Nursery World includes information on the Early Years Foundation Stage – www.nurseryworld.co.uk/home

Play England and similar organizations around the UK seek to promote freedom to play – www.playengland.org.uk

# 6

# Contemporary issues and best practice in English, mathematics and science

## Chapter objectives

By the end of this chapter you should be able to:

- Critically reflect upon contemporary issues in primary English, mathematics and science (core subjects).
- Explain the nature and scope of the core subjects.
- Identify the features of best practice in teaching the core subjects.

*There is no reading problem. There are problem teachers and problem schools.*

*(Kohl, 1974: 9)*

*In Britain, we're ok at teaching science and maths. Not bad. But certainly not great. This should worry you.*

*(Khan, 2012)*

## Introduction

The scope of this chapter is ambitious. It focuses on the main issues associated with the teaching of primary English, mathematics and science and what the evidence says about outstanding teaching in these subjects. The opening quotes convey something of the longstanding negative tone associated with discussions around literacy, numeracy and science teaching. In recent years the debate has hardened in the light of the mantra that children in the UK are falling behind their international peers in such skills as reading, problem solving and reasoning. Teachers have also experienced national strategies, curriculum reviews and assessment initiatives designed to improve provision and raise standards in the 'core' subjects of English, mathematics and science. Teachers' subject knowledge has been called into question, along with their preparation in teacher-training courses. These are not new issues. But there is a growing sense of urgency, given the disquiet among employers and politicians over how well schools are equipping learners with the skills needed for today's information society. The UK tolerates a long tail of low achievement in literacy, numeracy and technical skills, with 48 per cent of firms putting on basic remedial training for employees (CBI/Pearson, 2013). One survey of 500 firms showed that 42 per cent were dissatisfied with school leavers' use of English and more than a third were concerned about numeracy skills (Vasagar, 2011). Khan (2012), the director of the Campaign for Science and Engineering, argues that if Britain is to compete in a high-skills economy, the profile of science, technology, engineering and mathematics (so-called STEM subjects) needs to be urgently raised. The foundations must begin in the primary school.

## Literacy and numeracy in society

Although being literate and numerate brings social, economic and cultural benefits, many young people leave school without these basic skills. In London alone, an estimated 370,000 parents struggle with literacy – this means that around 1 in 5 may not be able to read confidently with their children (Jama and Dugdale, 2012). The scale and persistence of the problem is illustrated in Figure 6.1, cited by a government report more than a decade ago (DfEE, 1999a). One in sixteen adults could not say where the concert is held in A, while one in four adults could not calculate the change they would receive

(a)                                                        (b)

**FIGURE 6.1** The scale of the literacy and numeracy challenge

Source: DfEE (1999a), available at www.lifelonglearning.co.uk/mosergroup

out of £2 if they bought the goods advertised in B. In sum, one in five adults are functionally illiterate – put simply, if given the Yellow Pages they could not find the page to ring a plumber (DfEE, 1999b). Sir Claus Moser, who chaired the report, attributed the 'shocking situation' to 'past decades of schooling'.

Internationally, an estimated 775 million people cannot read or write. In 2010, the global adult literacy rate was only 84 per cent (www.uis.unesco.org). At all phases of schooling, there are concerns that too many learners are struggling with reading and writing (Box 6.1). In England, only three in every five children reach a good level of development in their communication, language and literacy skills by the age of 5 (OFSTED, 2012b). The Welsh inspectorate, Estyn (2012), note that 40 per cent of pupils arrive at secondary school with reading ages below their actual age. Such figures should not negate the progress over the longer span of time. As the National Literacy Trust, a leading UK charity, points out, current literacy levels represent a significant improvement in children's skills since the mid twentieth century (Jama and Dugdale, 2012). Nonetheless, too many children in the UK leave school without the requisite literacy, numeracy or investigative skills to support their employment. As far as the Westminster government is concerned: 'The truth is, at the moment we are standing still while others race past' (DfE, 2010: 3).

Few stop to question the rhetoric of falling standards in literacy and numeracy. More than a decade ago, Chris Woodhead (2002: 4), former head of OFSTED, described the debate on standards as 'a sham' and seriously questioned the reliability of evidence provided by examinations and inspection reports. He acknowledged that there have been improvements in attainment in literacy and numeracy, but there remained a long tail of underachievement. He argued that many teachers remain confused about how to raise standards. More recently, Michael Barber has called for a cultural change in the UK so that people see educational success as the result of hard work and persistence rather than being born 'bright' or 'smart' (Barber, 2013). The reason why British-Chinese children perform consistently well has been attributed to parental support and an emphasis on practice: 'Children are told: "If you want to learn something, practise, practise and practise it again and you will get better." It may be that this helps to motivate pupils when the rewards can seem a long way away' (quoted by Mansell, 2011).

However, it is easier for politicians to target the curriculum, teacher training and school leadership than the territory of the home. Hence, over recent decades there has been no shortage of initiatives to reform the educational system. In England, the most notable of these comprised the twin National Literacy and Numeracy Strategies, introduced in 1998–99 and which became the Primary National Strategy in 2003. These had mixed fortunes in English schools. OFSTED (2005: 1) initially reported that they had 'a significant positive impact on teaching practice and on pupils' achievement'. Yet the inspectorate identified weaknesses in teachers' subject knowledge and understanding of pupils' progress. Moreover, OFSTED has recently adopted a more cautionary stance. For instance, in its review of mathematics between 2008 and 2011 it concluded that despite huge investment the quality of teaching and planning had not improved (OFSTED, 2012a).

Broader concerns related to the mechanistic nature of literacy and numeracy teaching 'by the clock', with some teachers rigidly following set times for different parts of the lesson. That said, the sessions and guidance did provide necessary structure, particularly

---

**BOX 6.1  INTERNATIONAL VIEW – LITERACY, NUMERACY AND SCIENCE**

Despite previous government investment in the National Literacy Strategy framework and high stakes accountability, England's primary children compare poorly with their international peers. Evidence from PIRLS (Progress in International Reading Literacy Studies, conducted in 2001 and 2006) suggests standards in England and Scotland are behind Singapore, Russia and Canada (Twist *et al.*, 2003; Mullis *et al.*, 2008). The most significant factors affecting reading were high expectations of teachers, positive student attitudes, regular (more than once a week) use of the library/Internet and teaching that promoted independent, strategic and **self-managed learning** (Smith and Ellis, 2005). In contrast, evidence from TIMSS (Trends in International Mathematics and Science Study, 2007) suggests a more positive picture for primary numeracy and science. In mathematics, only three countries, Singapore, Chinese Taipei and Hong Kong, had scores that were statistically significantly higher than England's (Sturman *et al.*, 2008). The weakest area was numeracy although performance in science tests at Year 5 remains strong.

---

for weaker teachers. The Welsh Government has recently introduced the National Literacy and Numeracy Framework and Tests as part of its 'Raising Schools Standards' agenda (Welsh Government, 2012). The Framework serves as the main planning tool from Reception to Year 9 (ages 5–14). In Northern Ireland, an ambitious scheme to raise literacy and numeracy standards includes deploying newly qualified teachers to provide one-to-one tuition for around 6,000 pupils in need (DfE, 2011; Fergus, 2012). Regionally there are also many local authority programmes that prioritized literacy and numeracy, such as Glasgow's 'Literacy and Numeracy for all: Framework for Action' (Glasgow Education Services, 2010). It is clear therefore that there is widespread political will to improve standards.

## Parental engagement

One of the challenges in raising literacy and numeracy standards, particularly for pupils from low-income families, is securing parental engagement. Many such parents themselves have poor literacy skills. However, inspectorates, local authorities and charities (e.g. CfBT Education Trust) regularly report case studies of successful family literacy projects (see also Brooks *et al.*, 2008). Many schools run information evenings and workshops on basic skills for parents. In one school, teachers were concerned that pupils' learning and confidence in applying numerical skills were not being reinforced at home. So the teachers set up a games library in which children could play board games (which promote numeracy skills) and parents invited to attend each week. The games were colour-coded according to age and ability with parents acting as librarians. The initiative brought noticeable improvement in the pupils' skills while they were playing with the parents (OFSTED, 2009). Parents can share their own talents, such as gardening, painting and sport, which can be used as contexts to develop pupils' literacy and numeracy skills. OFSTED (2011b:

18) describe how staff in one outstanding primary school talk about 'catching the children and parents as soon as they come through the door and working to keep them with us, all the way'. Education Scotland's Parentzone provides useful information, ideas and resources for parents to become involved with their children's education (see www.educationscotland.gov.uk/parentzone).

According to Boaler (2009), a professor of mathematics, the biographies of top mathematicians reveal that they were often inspired by interesting problems and puzzles given to them by their parents at home, rather than schoolteachers. To stimulate interest in mathematics, parents can make use of a wide range of everyday objects including: coloured beads, nuts, bolts, washers, dice, sticks, measuring cups, kitchen utensils, word puzzles, newspaper articles, pictures, signs, notices, receipts, pinecones, leaves and other natural resources in everyday interactions. Budgeting pocket money, planning car journeys, visits to shops, the park, the beach or helping out in the kitchen or garden, are all appropriate contexts for promoting positive attitudes to mathematics.

## Teachers' subject knowledge and understanding

The challenges facing schools in raising standards of literacy, numeracy and scientific enquiry are not confined to the children themselves. Unfortunately, too many trainee and serving teachers are not knowledgeable and confident enough in teaching aspects of literacy, numeracy and science (OFSTED, 2008a; The Royal Society, 2010; OFSTED, 2011a; OFSTED, 2011b; OFSTED, 2011c). The knock-on effect is that pupils are switched off subjects. In secondary schools, more than a quarter of mathematics teachers do not possess a relevant degree or postgraduate qualification in the subject (Paton, 2011). Such concerns are not confined to the UK. In a small-scale American study, researchers found that upper elementary-school teachers lacked confidence and knowledge in mathematics, which meant that they were less willing to encourage their pupils to explore mathematical ideas. However, the introduction of two 5-day summer classes, run by a knowledgeable and enthusiastic high-school teacher, brought immediate gains, particularly when teachers took on the role of learners (Feuerborn et al., 2009).

Recently there have been moves to raise entry requirements into teaching training courses. Prospective teachers in England are now required to pass entrance examinations in English, mathematics and reasoning. Similarly in Wales, all trainees need to pass national entry tests in functional literacy and numeracy, as well as possess a minimum GCSE grade B in English and maths or equivalent, rather than a grade C. Such changes are designed to tighten up entry into the profession, although the possession of higher entry grades does not by itself signify stronger teaching potential.

In order to strengthen teachers' professional development in science, in 2004 the government established a network of science learning centres (funded by the Wellcome Trust). The website hosts an e-library of extensive resources, working with the **National STEM Centre**, including video materials on subjects such as space, simple gears, and virtual pets (www.sciencelearningcentres.org.uk).

When teachers lack secure knowledge, children's misconceptions can be left uncorrected. Misconceptions are not always best corrected at the start of a session and can form the basis of enquiry. A popular misconception among children is that they assume that if an object is wrapped up it will keep warm, not understanding that this can also keep objects cool. Children might explore this by wrapping different materials around beakers of cold and hot liquids (Hayes, 2007).

## Curriculum content

Despite concerns over the relative underperformance of English children compared to those in leading educational systems around the world, research suggests that 'most countries teach the same sorts of things as we do' (Ruddock and Sainsbury, 2008: 12). The researchers found that in certain areas, such as number and life processes and living things, the curriculum was less demanding in England for children of similar ages. The most recent National Curriculum (DfE, 2013b) provides schools with added flexibility to introduce content earlier or later than set out in the programme of study. Schools are only required to teach the relevant programme of study by the end of the key stage. The English content is set out for each year in Key Stage 1 (Year 1 and 2). This reflects the rapid pace of development in word reading during these two years. At Key Stage 2 this is based on a 2-yearly model and sub-divided into lower (Years 3 and 4) and upper (Years 5 and 6) stages. All schools must publish their school curriculum by subject and academic year online. Table 6.1 shows an overview of the key components for the English and mathematics programmes of study within the National Curriculum for England.

**TABLE 6.1** Overview of key components within English and mathematics in the National Curriculum for England

| English | Maths |
| --- | --- |
| Reading<br>■ word reading<br>■ comprehension (both listening and reading) | Number<br>■ place value<br>■ addition and subtraction<br>■ multiplication and division<br>■ fractions (including decimals and percentages from Year 5) |
| Writing<br>■ transcription (spelling and handwriting)<br>■ composition (articulating ideas and structuring them in speech and writing) | Measurement<br>Compare, describe and solve practical problems for:<br>■ lengths and heights<br>■ mass/weight<br>■ capacity and volume<br>■ time |
| Spelling, grammar, punctuation and glossary | Geometry<br>■ properties of shapes<br>■ position and direction<br>Statistics |
| Spoken language | |

Source: DfE (2013)

## Literacy and numeracy across the curriculum

In England, the teaching of literacy and numeracy across the National Curriculum has been a requirement for many years. In the 1990s teachers were advised to teach technical and specialist vocabulary and to develop children's understanding of subject language patterns, for instance to explain causality, chronology, logic, exploration, hypothesis, comparison and argument (DfEE/QCA, 1999). The slimmed down National Curriculum of 2014 retains the requirement for children to read and write for a range of purposes and audiences across the curriculum (DfE, 2013b). In Northern Ireland, teachers are expected to promote the cross-curricular skills of Communication (talking and listening, reading and writing) and Using Mathematics (CCEA, 2007). In Scotland, the overarching experiences for literacy and language learning cut across all areas of the curriculum. For instance, learners should have experiences whereby they 'engage with and create a wide range of texts in different media, taking advantage of the opportunities offered by ICT'. Estyn, the Welsh inspectorate, consider the extent to which schools provide evidence of learners applying numeracy and literacy across the curriculum and promote dual (Welsh and English) literacy skills (Estyn, 2013). A lack of reading skills, in particular, can act as a barrier to children's learning in different subjects. Children need opportunities to develop their reading skills through tasks based on literal comprehension, locating facts, analysing and synthesizing. They also need to apply a range of number (e.g. four rules of number, place value, estimation, simple fractions and percentages), measuring (e.g. working with scales, units of measurements, time, temperature) and data handling skills (e.g. gather information in a variety of ways, record, interpret and present it in charts or diagrams, identify patterns in data) – see also Table 6.2.

There is considerable scope to develop pupils' mathematical thinking across subject areas, from planning a garden (design and technology), observing birds at a feeding station (science) or analysing data using ICT. Hansen and Vaukins (2011) show clearly how mathematics underpins everyday life and the considerable cross-curricular potential for teachers to excite pupils' interest in mathematical concepts.

## The nature of primary English and literacy

Traditionally literacy has been seen as the ability to read and write to a level of proficiency that is necessary for effective communication (Box 6.2). However, in more recent times this narrow definition has been extended to cover other forms, such as information (digital) and visual literacy. Information literacy involves skills in evaluating and creating information in digital formats (Lankshear and Knobel, 2008) while visual literacy is concerned with the ability to construct meaning from visual images (Elkins, 2007).

### Speaking and listening

The importance of promoting children's speaking and listening skills is discussed in detail in Chapter 11. The report by the government-appointed Expert Panel (DfE, 2011) on the National Curriculum in England acknowledged that there is compelling evidence to

**TABLE 6.2** Opportunities to develop pupils' understanding of mathematics across the curriculum

| Aspect | Details | Examples |
| --- | --- | --- |
| Managing everyday situations | Using timetables and setting times (video, alarms, cookers, etc.); weighing and measuring (cooking and DIY); taking part in leisure activities using maps, plans, statistical information; buying and selling; borrowing and saving | Organize the school sports day |
| Designing and making | Making containers and wrappers; making displays and models; creating works of art and craft; designing items for personal or household use | Make a box, without a lid, from a square sheet of card or paper |
| Studying aspects of the environment | In the home – personal and family life; in the school – classroom and whole-school features and events; in the immediate environment of the school, built and natural – streets, parks; in the wider environment in space and time – holiday, travel, local history | Observing traffic: sorting, estimating speed; where is the best place for the crossing patrol?; where should visitors park their cars? |
| Investigating in science | Categorizing and identifying; looking for connections; frequency of occurrence; rate of change; observing, comparing and analysing structures | Use a coffee jar lid and some modelling clay to make a device that will measure one minute |
| Investigating areas of mathematics | In sequences; in patterns, shape and number; in properties of shapes and movement; in arrangements and routes; in relationships between sets of numbers or measures | Tessellations using isometric paper; make a book of patterns |
| Play, games and puzzles | Board games, games with cards or other playing pieces; calculator games, computer games and simulations; songs, stories and pictures (especially in the development of early language skills); number and shape puzzles, brain teasers | Design, make and play a mathematical board game, based on a simple journey from home to school |

Source: Adapted from Scottish Office Education Department (1991). © Crown Copyright 1991, reproduced under the terms of the Click-Use Licence

---

**BOX 6.2 KEY CONCEPT – LITERACY**

Literacy derives from the Latin word *litera* (letter) and traditionally describes the ability to read and write. This has since developed a much broader application. The Scottish Government (2009: 10) defines literacy as: 'the set of skills that allows an individual to engage fully in society and in learning, through the different forms of language, and the range of texts, which society values and finds useful.'

---

highlight the link between oral communication, cognitive development and educational attainment. The rationale is not in doubt. The challenge is how to ensure learners make appropriate progress, particularly in cross-curricular contexts. The Communications Trust (2011) is among those bodies that have developed excellent age-appropriate materials to support schools (see www.thecommunicationtrust.org.uk).

## Reading

Perhaps more than any other aspect of the primary curriculum the teaching of reading attracts major controversy (Wray and Lewis, 1997). Few would doubt that without the ability to read for meaning and pleasure, children and young people are seriously disadvantaged in life. There is far less agreement over how children should learn to read. The Bullock Committee, set up by the government to consider language teaching in schools, cautioned that there is no one method, medium or approach that holds the key to the process of learning to read (Bullock Report, 1975; see also Mukherji and O'Dea, 2000). For centuries children were taught to read by using an *alphabetic method* when they learned to name aloud the letters of the alphabet. By the 1900s, this was generally replaced by the *phonic method*, where children were helped to decode words by using sounds. As early as the 1870s the London School Board, responsible for education in the metropolis, set out to raise standards of reading through the 'genuinely synthetic' phonic method. It recognized, however, that it was essential to maintain children's joy of reading. It also acknowledged that it was essential to capture the reading interests of children on the margins of society ('street arabs'); if the authorities could get them into school, then teachers needed to engage them (Galbraith, 1997). A third method known as *look and say* became popular in the 1960s with its emphasis upon learning whole words, often using 'flash cards'. Some schools used a combination of phonics and 'look and say' where the emphasis was on enriching the language experience (Wray and Mallett, 2002). In recent years, phonics has become the preferred method of teaching reading.

## Teaching phonics

According to the government-commissioned Rose Report (DfES, 2006) on the teaching of reading, teachers should focus on developing word recognition knowledge and skills through the teaching of 'synthetic phonics', in which the sounds of letters are blended all through a word in pronunciation. Children are taught all letter sounds, including blends (e.g. 'bl', 'cr', 'st') and **digraphs** (e.g. 'oo', 'ch') in the first few months of school. They are taught to read and spell simultaneously. The Rose Report recommended that high-quality phonic programmes should be followed consistently and carefully, with daily reinforcement and consolidation. Popular schemes include the multi-sensory *Jolly Phonics* and Ruth Miskin's best-selling *Read, Write, Inc.*

The Westminster government sees the systematic teaching of synthetic phonics as the best means of raising standards of reading. In 2012, phonics-screening checks were introduced for six-year-olds and teachers of early reading are required to 'demonstrate a clear understanding of systematic synthetic phonics.'(DfE, 2013a). The government has issued guidance on teaching phonics to 5–7-year-olds through six phases so that children are fluent readers by the age of 7. It is essential to become familiar with the technical language and specific approaches associated with the teaching of phonics, particularly the relationship between **phonemes** and **graphemes** and what this means in practice. The Guardian Teacher Network includes many resources to complement phonics work (Drabble, 2013) while the Department for Education website offers guidance on effective phonics programmes (www.education.gov.uk/schools/teachingandlearning/pedagogy).

OFSTED endorses teaching reading, writing and spelling through systematic phonics. In the best practice, inspectors report:

- teaching letter–sound correspondences (the sounds represented by the letters of the alphabet and the letters used to represent the sounds;
- how to blend (synthesise) individual sounds together to read words; and
- how to break up (segment) the individual sounds in words to spell them.

(OFSTED, 2011a: 25)

Critics of the government approach fear that too much is being made of word recognition at the expense of reading for meaning. The United Kingdom Literacy Association (2010) points out that English is not written in a consistently 'phonic' way, so learning to read phonically will never teach a child how to read everything. Moreover, reading phonically, is not the same as reading. Prominent children's authors such as Michael Rosen, Michael Morpurgo and Philip Pullman call for more emphasis on reading for pleasure and story telling (Henry, 2012). Research suggests that reading for pleasure is more important for children's cognitive development between ages 10 and 16 than their parents' level of education (Sullivan and Brown, 2013). OFSTED (2012b) agrees that schools should develop policies on reading for enjoyment. In essence, phonics programmes are not sufficient by themselves to improve the quality of children's reading. Children need to learn how words are broken down into sounds but they also need to develop language comprehension and a love of reading. While most children learn to read through a synthetic phonics approach, there is a minority for whom this does not work. Intervention programmes such as *Reading Recovery* and *Accelerated Literacy* are designed to support these children with reading difficulties.

## Creating a stimulating reading environment

According to John Holt, the great American educationalist, most children should learn to read in about 30 hours without any formal instruction, provided they are placed in a trusting, comfortable and stimulating environment where they are read to one-to-one by a caring adult (Holt, 1989). Unfortunately, too many children do not develop good reading habits and intervention programmes are needed. Nonetheless, it has been recognized for many years that a literacy rich environment, at home and in school, makes a positive difference to children's attitudes to reading (Figure 6.2). It is good practice to regularly discuss environmental print (such as labels, notices and signs) with learners, as well as creating opportunities for children to make their own signs to be displayed around the class. Popular literacy games to generate interest in the environment include: 'write the room' (where learners use clipboards to write down words featuring a particular letter such as 't'), 'read the room' (where learners read highlighted words) and 'find the word', where the teacher provides a short list of common words for learners to tick off once spotted around the class.

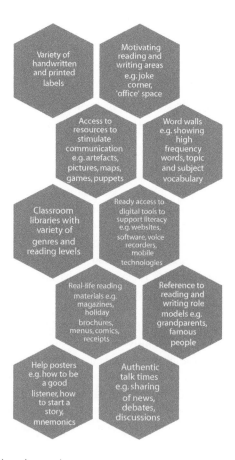

**FIGURE 6.2** Literary-rich environment

## What do good readers do?

Research has shown that good readers employ a range of strategies (Ur, 1996; Vaezi, 2001) highlighted in Box 6.3. It is useful to consider the reading process in three stages: pre, during and after. For each stage, it is important to have clear teaching points in mind. *Before* reading, children need to think about what they *want* from the text. For example, is it to find particular information or to see what happens in the next part of the story? Most teachers will also encourage children to preview the text by looking at the title, any sub-headings, pictures or graphics. Good readers tend to call upon their existing knowledge when reading new materials. *During* reading, children should be invited to question the text, reread parts they are uncertain about, skip forward on minor points and use context to make out the meaning of unfamiliar words. *After* the reading, it is customary practice for teachers to ask children to retell what they have read in their own words, summarizing, reflecting and looking forward to what might be appropriate to read next.

Well-chosen stories and poetry can engage the interests of children from a young age (Photo 6.1). Before children can attempt the first stages of literacy, they need to be exposed to a range of rhymes, poems, stories, traditional tales, fables, playground rhymes, raps, song lyrics, free verse and picture books.

---

### BOX 6.3  STRATEGIES USED BY GOOD READERS

**Making predictions**: predicting what might happen in the text, integrating and combining knowledge.

**Making selections**: focus on what children want to read.

**Skipping insignificant parts**: important bits of the text are highlighted and insignificant pieces ignored.

**Rereading**: read over passages that do not make sense in the first instance.

**Making use of context or guessing**: using context to guess the meaning of unknown words.

**Breaking words into their component parts**: breaking words into their affixes or bases to help guess the meaning of a word.

**Reading in chunks**: groups of words are read together.

**Pausing**: at certain places, pauses help to absorb and internalize the material being read and sort out information.

**Paraphrasing**: sometimes necessary to paraphrase and interpret texts subvocally in order to verify what was comprehended.

**Monitoring**: self-checking to see whether the reading is contributing towards intended purposes.

(Adapted from www.teachingenglish.org.uk/article/theories-reading-2)

---

**PHOTO 6.1** Key Stage 1 children reading

Source: POD/Pearson Education Ltd, Jules Selmes

Research on emergent literacy suggests that certain activities, such as parent–child storybook reading, contribute to a child's readiness to read and write (Roskos and Christie, 2007). Initially young children need to learn how to decode words and extract items of literal meaning. But they also need to use their literacy skills in a range of practical situations – undertaking research, reading the timetable, checking an email or text – if they are to see their value (pragmatic literacy). At a higher level, the ability to question what is said and to consider alternative viewpoints can be taught from an early age (critical literacy). Between the ages of 7 and 11, most children move from 'learning to read' to 'reading to learn'. This process involves progressing from decoding words and making sense of simple texts, to developing a wide vocabulary and reading strategies to understand more complex materials.

## Engaging the reader

Effective reading is not a passive process but an interactive one – children bring their own feelings and thoughts to the text. However, as Waters and Martin (1999: 53) observe: 'Traditionally right through school and into university the focus has been on only one side of the process – the text, thereby ignoring the reader's responses . . . the reader has been forgotten.'

Classroom activities that encourage interaction with texts, such as **directed activities related to texts (DARTs)**, improve children's reading comprehension. These activities either involve children in reconstructing the texts, usually by completing blanks, filling in tables or sequencing pictures or text, or they invite closer analysis – for instance by annotating or summarizing (Table 6.3).

## Reading for enjoyment

Reading for enjoyment involves high levels of choice, satisfaction and interest. Findings from the government's Education Standards Research Team (ESARD, 2012) show that children enjoy reading less as they get older, boys enjoy reading less than girls and children from lower socio-economic backgrounds read less for enjoyment than children from more

**TABLE 6.3** Popular text-related activities used by teachers

|  | Reconstruction activities | Analysis activities |
| --- | --- | --- |
| Definition | Activities that require children to reconstruct a text or diagram | Activities that require children to find and categorize information |
| Texts used | Modified texts | Unmodified texts |
| Types of activities | ■ **Cloze procedure** (fill in missing words, phrases or sentences)<br>■ **Predicting** (anticipating what will happen next)<br>■ **Sequencing** (arrange jumbled segments of text in a logical or time sequence)<br>■ **Comparing** (content, layout of texts)<br>■ **Grouping** (group segments of text according to categories)<br>■ **Table completion** (fill in the cells of a table that has row and column headings, or provide row and column headings where cells have already been filled in)<br>■ **Diagram completion** (complete an unfinished diagram or label a finished diagram) | ■ **Text marking** (find and underline parts of the text that have a particular meaning or contain particular information)<br>■ **Text segmenting and labelling** (break the text into meaningful chunks and label each chunk)<br>■ **Table construction** (draw a table and use the information in the text to decide on row and column headings and to fill in the cells)<br>■ **Diagram construction** (construct a diagram that explains the meaning of the text: for example, draw a flow chart for a text that explains a process, or a branch diagram for a text that describes how something is classified)<br>■ **Questioning** (answer the teacher's questions or develop questions about the text)<br>■ **Summarizing** (key points)<br>■ **Evaluating** (e.g. what they like/dislike; how to improve) |

Source: www.teachingenglish.org.uk. Reproduced with permission

## EXTEND YOUR UNDERSTANDING

Read through Table 6.3 and devise examples of DARTs for a story of your choice.

privileged social classes. Teachers need to provide a wide range of engaging reading materials, read aloud programmes, book discussions and quality time for children to read independently. Choice is important. Books or book vouchers have been found to be effective in motivating readers (Clark and Rumbold, 2006). Moreover, it has long been recognized that children are likely to develop as lifelong readers when parents (and teachers) model a love for reading and books themselves. This means, for example, children seeing adults regularly read for a range of purposes, in different contexts, and to take pleasure from the process. Well-stocked and well-run public and school libraries make a significant difference in motivating young readers. There is a clear link between library use and reading for pleasure; young people that use their public library are nearly twice as likely to be reading outside of class every day (Clark and Hawkins, 2011).

## Grammar

Grammar has been defined by Crystal (1995: 190), a leading authority on language, as the 'rules controlling the way a communication system works . . . it is all to do with making sense'. Knowledge of how sentences are structured allows the reader to make sense of words. Many words in English have different meanings. A word such as 'band' means something different in each of these sentences: 'Robin Hood and his band of followers attacked the castle', 'Pass me the elastic band', and 'Is this the best band of the decade?' Children learn to build sentences to describe events, issue instructions, ask questions, text their friends and do other things. Grammar is simply needed to understand how people express their ideas (Crystal, 2010).

There has been considerable controversy surrounding the teaching of grammar over the years (Beverton, 2001). In analysing educational change in the 1960s and 1970s, Sked (1997) notes that the rise of child-centred learning reduced the role of the teacher to facilitator; there was a corresponding emphasis upon encouraging creativity, at the expense of formal rules such as those required to learn grammar. The traditional view has been that grammar should be prescribed with rules for children to learn and consolidate through exercises. These rules relate to the use of **Standard English** that is sometimes perceived as the 'correct' form of language, for instance 'I did it!' rather than 'I done it!' But one of the difficulties with the traditional 'naming of parts' (this is a noun, verb, adjective) approach to teaching grammar is that there are many exceptions to rules. For instance, the word 'table' can be labelled as a noun. But it can also act as an adjective ('table cloth') or as a verb ('to table a paper at a meeting'). Writers such as Michael Rosen point out that there is no research to suggest that tests in grammar and spelling improve the quality of writing for 10-year-olds but reading for pleasure does – so why not make that a statutory requirement? (Rosen, 2012). A government-funded study concluded that teaching formal grammar, while having some merit in enhancing knowledge of how language works, is not improving writing quality or accuracy (EPPI, 2004). It has been suggested that teaching formal grammar is wasting millions of hours of children's lives and that this is damaging their writing (Kelley, 2008).

However, in England there have been strong government pressures to strengthen grammar lessons with the introduction in 2013 of Key Stage 2 Spelling, Punctuation and Grammar (SPAG) tests. Eleven-year-olds are tested on the correct use of the semicolon and other grammatical features (Bloom, 2012). The *Times Educational Supplement* offers online support materials for teachers struggling to grasp the finer points of the relative pronoun. For children to appreciate the value of grammar, it is important to focus on how different words and phrases are used in sentences to add interest and reflect particular genre features; for instance, writing an effective advertisement requires a catchy slogan, powerful adjectives and hyperbole.

## Punctuation

Punctuation has been likened to the equivalent use of gestures, pauses, intonation and facial expressions when animating spoken language. However, in many cases young readers do not rely on punctuation to make sense of texts because the layout provides clues as to when there is a break or new thought; for instance, a single sentence on each page. The twelve main punctuation marks (capital letters, full stops, commas, semicolons, colons, apostrophes, inverted commas, question marks, exclamation marks, hyphens, dashes and brackets) are important because they assist in conveying the intended meaning in written language. As children mature as readers they encounter variety in punctuation use, such as different conventions for the inverted commas (none, single or double), dash and capital letters. In many cases punctuation seems to depend upon the particular author's style. But the key to teaching punctuation is to encourage children to see its impact on meaning. Myers and Burnett (2004: 86) suggest the following activities to encourage children to see the nature and purpose of punctuation:

- removing punctuation from a text; discussing impact on meaning and then deciding on where punctuating is needed;
- modelling and discussing the use of punctuation marks in shared writing, exploring the impact on meaning when these are omitted or different marks are used;
- using a text as a model for children's own writing;
- collecting examples of the use of a particular form of punctuation;
- investigating ways in which the use of punctuation differs in different kinds of texts; and
- reading aloud extracts to perform.

## Spelling

Vivian Cook's (2004) international best-selling book *Accomodating Brocolli in the Cemetary* shows that there is no shortage of interest in the subject of spelling; he concedes elsewhere that without any major research then it is impossible to say whether standards are indeed falling. Spelling causes problems for many educated and successful people. Former Prime Minister Tony Blair wrote 'toomorrow' three times in a memo, former American vice-president Dan Quayle corrected a child's spelling of potato as 'potatoe', Keats once spelled fruit as 'furuit', Yeats wrote peculiarities as 'peculeraritys', and Hemingway wrote professional as 'proffessional' (Jeffries, 2004). Clearly such mistakes do not signify that someone is unfit to write great literature or run a leading world power. Nonetheless, as the Spelling Society (established in 1908) points out on its website, billions of pounds are spent annually on remedial and spelling classes, all of which could be better used in teaching other subjects in a world that requires a skilled and knowledgeable workforce.

Good practice in the teaching of spelling includes helping pupils to see words within words, placing a lot of emphasis on rhymes and syllables, focusing on the spelling of key words in texts that all the class share, and knowing that spelling rules can be useful (Estyn, 2001). Analogies, mnemonics, word banks, displays and interactive games also have their place. Many teachers expect pupils to use spelling books, encouraging them to 'have a go' before seeking advice. In the best practice, pupils are also taught how to proofread and to correct their own errors. Weekly spelling tests, differentiated for groups of pupils, are also popular. It is important for schools to have a clear long-term plan for developing pupils' spelling that sets out what pupils are expected to do when mistakes are identified by teachers; for instance, to copy the words out a number of times, using the 'look, cover, write, check' approach. Unfortunately, in too many schools there is little consistency in how teachers correct and respond to spelling mistakes. As a result, teachers' comments on spelling often fail to lead to action by pupils (OFSTED, 2012b).

## Using information books

Information literacy skills are high on the educational agenda. A perusal of the curriculum requirements across the United Kingdom shows that questioning, skimming, scanning, selecting, evaluating and locating sources feature extensively. These are among the essential skills for life (Grey, 2008). Being a critical reader means asking searching questions of the text, such as why the author has chosen to use particular words, phrases, techniques or pictures. For a democratic society, developing critical reading habits from an early age is essential.

Research has shown that over 80 per cent of reading time between ages 4 and 7 is spent on reading fiction (Medwell *et al.*, 2007). In the past it has been assumed that children are only able to read non-fiction texts once they have become proficient readers of fiction. However, children are surrounded by information print from the moment they are born and some of the first books that they receive are simple baby albums. The primary curriculum provides many opportunities for teachers to develop children's reference skills such as using contents and index pages, sorting facts from opinions, and locating particular information. Children need to be taught systematically how to read non-fiction (Table 6.4). If children are not taught how to make effective use of a variety of non-fiction texts (for instance, newspapers, diaries, electronic texts, letters, atlases, encyclopaedias, documents, guidebooks and lists), then, ultimately, they are not being adequately prepared for life.

Bielby (1999: 150) advocates a 'search, comprehend and exploit' model for teaching information skills. The search begins by deciding what information is needed, and children will thus need to know how to use the alphabet to look up particular words. On a broader front, children need to be taught how to find their way around a library with their attention drawn to signs, shelf-labels, use of catalogues, subject indexes and digital sources. Particular skills of skimming (to gain an overall idea of content) and scanning (to locate specific words) can be practised using photocopied extracts from books. But to make sense of texts, children need to develop their deeper reading skills so that they

**TABLE 6.4** A model for developing non-fiction reading skills

| Process stage | Questions | Examples of possible strategies |
|---|---|---|
| Activating previous knowledge | What do I already know about this subject? | KWHL grids, mind maps |
| Establishing purposes | What do I need to find out and what will I do with the information? | Brainstorming, KWL grids |
| Locating information | Where and how will I get this information? | Key word searches using the Internet, CD-ROMs, reference books |
| Adopting an appropriate strategy | How should I use this source of information to get what I need? | Cut-and-paste techniques, annotating, highlighting, modelling, thinking aloud |
| Interacting with text | What can I do to help me understand this better? | Cloze procedure, sequencing, text marking (underlining, highlighting or numbering) |
| Monitoring understanding | What can I do if there are parts that I do not understand? | Rereading, ignoring, reading ahead, consulting a dictionary or person who might know |
| Making a record | What should I make a note of from this information? | Writing frames |
| Evaluating information | Which items of information should I believe and which should I keep an open mind about? | Comparing bias sources, such as newspapers |
| Assisting memory | How can I help myself remember the important parts? | Restructuring information into different formats, re-presenting it |
| Communicating information | How should I let other people know about this? | Posters, webpages, emails, notices |

Source: After Fisher and Williams (2006: 197). Reproduced with permission

grasp the meaning of what has been said. To this end, teachers need to draw attention to important clues found in titles, headings, summaries and other organizational features.

# Writing

For many years concerns have been reported about the standards of pupils' writing in primary schools (OFSTED, 2000, 2012b). Writing has been seen as the weakest element of literacy teaching, particularly in relation to the under-performance of boys (Box 6.4). OFSTED (2000) identified the following features in the best teaching of writing:

- a good technical knowledge of literacy;
- the selection of appropriate good quality texts to illustrate the particular writing skills being taught;
- intervention at the point of composition to teach writing skills; and
- the reinforcement and development of writing skills throughout the curriculum.

---

**BOX 6.4  REAL-LIFE LEARNING CHALLENGE**

Your inner-city primary school has recently been inspected and the report recommends raising standards in literacy. In particular, the inspectors found that by the age of seven, boys did not enjoy reading. They also reported that the school had not taken sufficient steps to involve parents. By the age of 11 boys' writing standards were reported to be well below national expectations. Written work was often poorly presented with errors in basic punctuation and grammar. Many boys told the inspectors that they did not enjoy writing. Work with colleagues in drawing up an action plan to respond to the recommendations.

---

Children's writing standards also improve when teachers serve as good role models, for instance sharing their own writings in workshops, providing stimulating tasks and imaginative approaches. Teachers who write with their pupils gain insight into the challenges they face, and develop their own self-confidence. The National Association for the Teaching of English (www.nate.org.uk) runs teacher-writing workshops and groups.

Pupils need to write for a purpose. Younger children might, for instance, write menus for a café role-play area, design signs for a tea party, compose letters after visits and write to other teachers. There is no doubt that children write best when they see the relevance of writing, with a genuine purpose and audience in mind; for example, when writing articles for magazines, pamphlets or creating posters on current affairs, oral presentations and stories, poems and drama scripts that are shared with others (Estyn, 2008; OFSTED, 2012b).

During shared writing sessions, it is useful to have a flipchart or an easel on which to clip large sheets of paper to return to earlier drafts and marker pens in different colours for identifying particular features (such as punctuation, letter-strings or rhymes). Some teachers prefer to use overhead transparencies or the interactive whiteboard. In many classes there are mini-whiteboards and dry-wipe markers shared by children writing in pairs. Children also benefit from clear structure, for example when writing about a character they might be encouraged to think about: looks (facial gestures), sounds (tone of voice), smells (perfume), dress, relationships with other characters, and home background (Iley, 2005).

## The nature of mathematics and numeracy

Mathematics and numeracy are sometimes seen to be synonymous, as was the case in the National Numeracy Strategy (subtitled 'the framework for teaching Mathematics'). Numeracy is too narrowly limited to a study of basic algebra when it also relates to the *application* of other aspects of mathematics, such as shape, space and measures. Mathematics is 'beautiful, intriguing, elegant, logical, amazing and mind-blowing . . . [it can also be] frightening, boring, debilitating and can appear illogical' (Ollerton, 2003: 8).

Mathematics is essentially made up of two branches: arithmetic (numerical thinking) and geometry (spatial thinking). Outstanding teachers regularly seek to make links between these forms of thinking. They seek to promote pupils' understanding of key mathematical concepts, principles and processes. For younger children, practitioners often make use of familiar objects, stories, symbols, language and pictures (Haylock and Cockburn, 2008). This is well illustrated in OFSTED's (2011d) report on *Good Practice in Primary Mathematics*. In one Reception class children were given £1 to spend at the local shop. With help from adults, they produced simple shopping lists to decide what they wanted to buy and what they could afford. Such experience developed children's confidence, understanding and enjoyment of using mathematics in everyday life.

Mathematics suffers a poor image among many who see it as a 'difficult' subject lacking creativity and wrapped up with 'right' and 'wrong' answers. Some perceive mathematics to be about learning a rigid set of rules, rather than a way of thinking and communicating (Cockcroft Report, 1982). One of the major challenges is to help pupils see that mathematics is concerned with understanding and explaining the world around them. Designers, architects, builders, sports coaches and landscape gardeners all employ mathematical thinking. By its nature, mathematics is concerned with describing the workings of the physical and natural world. As Smith (2004: 3) notes, mathematics is important 'for its own sake, as an intellectual discipline; for the knowledge economy; for science, technology and engineering; for the workplace; and for the individual citizen'.

## Problem solving and investigations

Problem solving was defined by the government's Cockcroft Committee, set up to examine the state of mathematics in primary and secondary schools, as 'an ability to apply mathematics to a variety of situations' (Cockcroft Report, 1982: 73). Problem solving is now firmly embedded in the mathematics curriculum and has been given a new lease of life under the thinking skills umbrella. Successful problem solvers use strategies such as checking that they have understood the problem, drawing up a suitable plan and deploying self-monitoring strategies. Outstanding teachers are genuinely committed to fostering a spirit of enquiry. They try to ensure that pupils do not waste time when stuck or doing work that is too easy (OFSTED, 2003). Asking open questions is central to promoting mathematical problem solving.

Pupils should be encouraged to think about alternative ways of working using some of the prompts indicated in Table 6.5. A simple example might be to ask pupils how to make a given number, say 10, using different pairs of whole numbers. Teachers can access many commercial schemes and websites that encourage problem solving through games, puzzles and practical activities. Ollerton (2003) provides examples of 'people math' tasks that are designed to promote active, communal learning. For instance, arranging the class in a circle and providing each child with a number that they have to keep 'secret'; the teacher then asks children to swap places in line with instructions such as 'All those who have a number greater than 5 and less than 10, swap places' or 'All those with a prime number, swap places'.

Such interactive teaching and learning should include constructive dialogue in which children are encouraged to talk about their discoveries, explain their answers, and consider 'what if . . .' scenarios. Discussion is more than a short question-and-answer routine in which the teacher receives the 'required' response. Rather, it involves listening to one another and creating a climate where contributions are made freely without fear

**TABLE 6.5** Prompts relating to mathematical thinking

| Exemplifying, specializing | Completing, deleting, correcting | Comparing, sorting, organizing |
|---|---|---|
| ■ Give me one or more examples of . . .<br>■ Describe, demonstrate, tell, show, choose, draw, find, locate, an example of . . .<br>■ Is . . . an example of . . .?<br>■ What makes . . . an example?<br>■ Find a counter-example of . . .<br>■ Are there any special examples of . . .? | What *must* be. . . added<br>  removed<br>  altered<br>in order to . . .<br>  allow<br>  ensure<br>  contradict?<br>What *can* be. . .<br>  added<br>  removed<br>  altered<br>without affecting . . .?<br>■ Tell me what is wrong with . . .<br>■ What needs to be changed so that . . .? | ■ What is the same and different about . . .?<br>■ Sort or organise the following according to . . .<br>■ Is it or is it not . . .? |
| **Changing, varying, reversing, altering** | **Generalizing, conjecturing** | **Explaining, justifying, verifying, convincing, refuting** |
| ■ Alter an aspect of something to see effect.<br>■ What if . . .?<br>■ If this is the answer to a similar question, what was the question?<br>■ Do . . . in two (or more) ways.<br>■ What is quickest, easiest, . . .?<br>■ Change . . . in response to imposed constraints. | ■ Of what is this a special case?<br>■ What happens in general?<br>■ Is it always, sometimes, never . . .?<br>■ Describe all possible . . . as succinctly as you can.<br>■ What can change and what has to stay the same so that . . . is still true? | ■ Explain why . . .<br>■ Give a reason . . . (using or not using . . .)<br>■ How can we be sure that . . .?<br>■ Tell me what is wrong with . . .<br>■ Is it ever false that . . .? (always true that . . .?)<br>■ How is . . . used in . . .? Explain role or use of . . .<br>■ Convince me that . . . |

Source: Watson and Mason (1998). Reproduced with permission

of someone evaluating and commenting upon everything that is said. Inviting prompts such as 'Can you tell or show us what you mean?' or 'Will it work if . . .?' can result in genuine problem solving. Other useful strategies include encouraging other children to comment with prompts such as 'What do you (a different child) think?' or 'Has anyone an idea of how we check that?' and pursuing an idea irrespective of whether you (as the teacher) know that it will not work. Children need time to *think* about their work, discuss their ideas with others, compare workings and evaluate their progress. The challenge for teachers is to lead pupils gradually away from real-life problem solving to engage with more abstract thinking (OFSTED, 1995). Teachers with good mathematical knowledge deal with children's unexpected questions in a confident manner.

## Knowledge of number

From ancient times, peoples have had high regard for numbers in their association with religious, cultural and political events: 9/11, 666 (the number of the Beast), 24/7, and

1066. Yet numbers are human inventions derived from observing natural phenomena: the number of fingers on the hand, or the number of days and nights that pass between full moons (Glynne-Jones, 2007). As Rooney (2008) notes, people soon started to notice patterns within numbers and their properties can be surprising – for instance, the way in which we can multiply a two-digit number by 11 simply by adding the digits together (providing the two digits add to less than 10) and putting the result in the middle: $63 \times 11 = 693$ (6 + 3 = 9; place 9 between 6 and 3).

Outstanding teachers of mathematics have a deep knowledge of the concepts that underpin division and fractions. Recent research shows that understanding these mathematical operations at the age of 10 is a predictor of future proficiency in mathematics (Maddern, 2012). OFSTED (2009) provide concise examples of how weak teaching can be improved in areas such as knowledge of geometry, the use of unhelpful rules such as 'to multiply by 10 you add a nought' and the need to pick up misconceptions. In a review of twenty successful schools, OFSTED (2011d) also suggest examples of specific techniques to ensure progression from using **number lines** and partition to long multiplication and division.

Research has shown that babies are able to 'recognize' quantities of small amounts and display pre-verbal counting skills (Riley, 2007). By the time they reach school, many young children can count meaningfully, use terms such as 'more' and 'less' appropriately, have a basic understanding of addition and subtraction with small numbers, and invent strategies for solving problems (OFSTED, 1995). Appropriate number activities in the Early Years include collecting natural objects, counting on/backwards, use of number rhymes, activities relating to 'one more/one less', simple number bonds (1 to 5, then 5 to 10), and exploratory activities relating to shapes and measures (O'Hara, 2008).

Like the teaching of reading, schools have their own preferred approaches when teaching numeracy (Frobisher *et al.*, 1999). A constructivist theory of learning suggests that as children seek to make meaning in mathematics they will make mistakes along the way. One of the most important research findings in recent years has been that all pupils constantly 'invent' rules to explain the patterns that they see around them (OFSTED, 1995). For instance, many pupils will acquire the 'rule' that to multiply by 10 it is necessary to add a zero. They then over-generalize these rules to situations that do not work, for example by applying this to decimals.

Many teachers use a range of resources such as number lines, rods, 100-square grids, function-machines, pictures, money and measures. These by themselves are not the answer to effective teaching of number. Rather, the key is to help pupils understand the structure and processes within number operation. Children need to acquire from a young age a *feel* for number. Haylock and Cockburn (1997: 17–19) illustrate how most people carry with them a mental image of numbers. For example if asked to think about the number 3, images might include dots, sides of a triangle, fingers or sweets and less frequently the actual symbol. The idea of a number representing a set of three things is known as the *cardinal* aspect, while the number can also act as a *nominal* label (such as the number 3 bus) and have an *ordinal* aspect, as when used in an order of numbers (for example, page 3 – following page 2 and preceding page 4 of a book). Number lines are often used to demonstrate the ordinal value of numbers.

The ability to count makes use of these various aspects of number. A real challenge for learners is to reach the point of understanding that a number can mean the same thing even though used in different contexts – as when answering the question 'How many pages have you read and which page have you reached?' Children learn best when they see that mathematics is meaningful and relevant. Many have difficulty applying the mathematics they learn in the classroom to everyday contexts outside school. When children have the time to explore, discuss and share ideas, mathematics becomes less 'threatening'. Best practice involves teachers who share the intentions of the lesson, explain mathematical terms clearly and take every opportunity to follow up pupils' ideas (Cockburn and Handscomb, 2006). It is worth keeping in mind that these applications need to be in real-life contexts – a point noted many years ago by Hamilton *et al.* (1947: 50):

There will be some interests, such as transport, newspapers, the Post Office, that will be deepened and enriched if quantitative comparisons are made and experiences requiring measuring, counting, weighing and trading are included.

## Mathematical language

While there are more than 400,000 words in the English language, there are fewer than 1,000 mathematical symbols and these are based on a few principles. Yet in general people seem to make greater progress in English than mathematics (Kelley, 2008). Boaler (2009) points out that one of the major problems in classrooms is that children are not talking enough about mathematics. Leading mathematicians say that being able to talk about problems, rather than listen to others, is at the heart of their understanding. We do not know how many children struggle with mathematics because of the terminology that is used (Durkin and Shire, 1991). Five-year-olds generally experience difficulties whenever phrases such as 'two and one' are not related to specific objects. Young children have to deal with words in the number system that lack logic. For instance, there is no obvious link between the words 'thirteen' and 'twenty-three', as there is when the two numbers are written down in figures. In the main Asian languages, the terms are clear and literal in both formats. The word for 13 is 'one 10 three' and for 23 'two 10 three.' In Welsh, the numbers are written logically – 13 in Welsh is 'one 10 three'. One small-scale study on the English–Welsh border showed that those children whose first language was Welsh were making faster progress in maths than their English counterparts (Loder-Symonds, 2012). Effective teachers include new vocabulary in suitable contexts, for instance by using real and relevant objects, mathematical apparatus, pictures and/or diagrams. It is useful for children to make their own mathematical dictionaries within which they build up their knowledge of specific terms. Pupils should be encouraged to use a combination of symbols, words and pictures to record their work. To promote pupils' confidence in using mathematical language, teachers should make daily use of familiar contexts, such as counting up those having school dinners or talking about absentees. But they should also look for the less obvious opportunities, such as stories in the news, plays, musical charts, anniversaries and current opinion polls. The author's seven-year-old son's interest in mathematics has increased by following his team's (Swansea F.C.) fluctuating fortunes in the premier league, checking their position in the table each week, transfer news and the different formations (e.g. 4–2–3–1, 4–4–2, 4–5–1) in match day programmes.

## Developing positive attitudes

Negative attitudes to maths set in early in the UK – by the age of 7, many children's interest and attainment dip, in most cases never to return. The process then becomes cyclical with some parents (and possibly teachers) passing on their apathy to the next generation. It is not unusual to hear trainee teachers recall their feelings of fear, terror and occasional horror when asked to relate their experiences of being taught mathematics at school (Haylock, 2006: 3). If such attitudes are to be overturned, teachers need to present and believe that mathematics can be a collaborative, stimulating, problem-solving activity, relevant to real life. Positive attitudes towards mathematics will only develop if learners are motivated and this is related to how relevant pupils see their classroom work to their experiences and the real world (Haylock and Cockburn, 1997).

One of the most important aims of teaching mathematics is to help all pupils feel that they can succeed in the subject and that they have the capacity to do so. The focus should be on effort rather than ability, enjoyment and regular practice. Pupils can also develop positive attitudes when they see that mathematics is a powerful tool and an essential form of communication. A poll in 2012 suggests that one in five adults do not believe that the maths they learned in school helped them later in life (www.nationalnumeracy.org.uk/news/10/index.html). Yet teachers can easily demonstrate the relevance of mathematics in everyday life (Box 6.5).

The Cockcroft Report (1982) highlighted the importance of building upon young children's curiosity and uninhibited enthusiasm by developing positive attitudes towards mathematics. Easingwood and Williams (2004: 1) raise the important question: 'Why is it considered socially acceptable to be "not good at maths" when few concede that they are "bad" at English?' The authors attribute this to widespread 'number blindness' among children and the ease by which mathematics could be taught poorly. As with all subjects, attitudes of teachers and learners will have a strong bearing on the quality of teaching and learning in the classroom. Pupils who believe that they are 'no good' at mathematics will generally avoid challenges and lack persistence because they think they are likely to fail and suffer embarrassment. This is known as **learner helplessness**. There has been a longstanding dislike of mathematics as a 'hard' subject among the general population, including teachers and student teachers (Coles and Copeland, 2002). This has been partly attributed to feeble attempts by teachers to show the relevance of the subject. However,

---

**BOX 6.5 KEY CONCEPT – NUMERACY**

The term numeracy was first introduced by the Crowther Report (1959) to represent the mirror of literacy and was applied to sixth-formers' study of solving problems. Since then, numeracy has been described in terms of confidence and competence with numbers and measures. Numerate pupils should be able to process, communicate and interpret numerical information (Askew et al., 1997). Being numerate has been described as 'at home-ness with number' in knowing how numbers relate to each other and having the toolkit of skills to solve problems (Lacey, 1998).

the best teachers develop pupils' interests in mathematics across the curriculum (see Box 6.6). A simple question such as 'How much waste paper is thrown away each day?' or 'How much is the school's heating bill and can this be reduced?' can lead to meaningful enquiries. The author Daniel Tammet (2012) illustrates the imaginative side of mathematics, including stories about the probability of a 45-year-old man seeing his fiftieth birthday, the complexity of snowflakes, counting to four in Icelandic and Shakespeare's first experience with zero.

Research into different attitudes towards teaching numeracy found that children whose teachers held 'connectionist' beliefs made most progress (Askew *et al.*, 1997). Connectionists were described as teachers who valued pupils' methods and teaching strategies with an emphasis on establishing connections within mathematics. So, for instance, they gave greater weight to mental arithmetic over paper and pencil, or practical methods and collaborative working over individual activities. Such connectivity is one of four elements within the Knowledge Quartet model advocated by Rowland *et al.* (2009) as a tool for observing and discussing mathematics teaching. Figure 6.3 includes only a few examples to illustrate each dimension within the Knowledge Quartet.

Outstanding teachers are able to plan coherently, so that learning takes place in a progressive manner. Such planning draws on strong foundations that include understanding the aims of mathematics teaching, familiarity with subject terminology, and an accurate understanding of mathematical ideas and processes. The teacher's ability then to transform such knowledge into accessible forms for children is critical to their success. Such transformation involves using equipment such as **base–10 apparatus** correctly to explain number processes. It also involves effective questioning and illustrations. The best practitioners think flexibly in their teaching. In particular, they are ready to respond to children's ideas and a willingness to move away from the set plan when necessary.

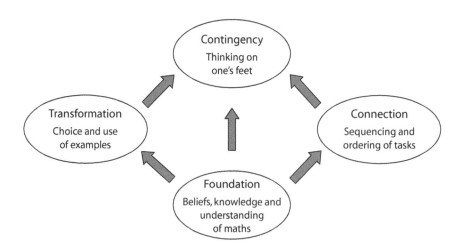

**FIGURE 6.3** Knowledge Quartet

Source: Rowland *et al.* (2009)

## The nature of science

Science education should build upon children's natural curiosity in wanting to know why and how things work. Most children enjoy investigations and working like scientists (Sewell, 2006). It seems that young children can genuinely imitate the practice of real scientists, for instance by identifying clearly what they already know, what they wonder about, and how they might set about exploring their interests (Lunn, 2006). The programme of study for science in England emphasizes the need for teachers to integrate working scientifically across all content areas (Table 6.6).

Like mathematics, science can suffer stereotypes of rather eccentric men in white coats experimenting in a laboratory. Yet, outstanding teachers take every opportunity to dispel such myths and draw attention to how science can legitimately link with multi-sensory dance, poetry, art, design and technology. Any observer in a classroom will relate the excitement that can emerge from children exploring what sinks and floats, observing insects, feeding plants, taking apart a torch to see how it works and seeing how far their model cars will travel. This 'hands-on' element is fundamental to science learning and rooted in the constructivist teaching methodology (Ovens, 2000). The stories associated with great scientists and inventors can be told to illustrate the context within which discoveries occurred and how interests developed; for instance, in Northern Ireland the contributions of John Boyd Dunlop (who founded the Dunlop Tyre Company), Sir Hans Sloane (whose collection formed the basis of the British Museum) and Mary Ward (the first female scientist trying to make her name in a male-dominated world – sadly she became the first fatal victim of a car accident) (Garvin and O'Rawe, 1993).

Although the nature of science is precise and matter-of-fact, it is also provisional and exploratory (Howe *et al.*, 2005). The boundaries of science are constantly under review as new discoveries emerge. Scientists do not all work in the same manner – and they certainly do not reach a consensus on many issues, particularly relating to health, technology and environmental change, as news stories will testify. At a primary level, telling children stories about the lives of famous scientists can be a way into this field of how theories emerge, are challenged, upheld or refuted.

There are many opportunities for children to think about the ethical dimension to science, for instance when discussing the ethics associated with whaling, the use of animal experiments for human purposes, and the eating of animal meat (Reiss, 2008). The demise in the use of classroom pets (on the grounds of expense, health risks and morals) is another example that can engage debate among children and the wider community. Senior *et al.* (2008) argue strongly that the perceived constraints of bringing animals into the classroom should not detract from these valuable and stimulating resources.

### EXTEND YOUR UNDERSTANDING

Read the article by Lunn, S. (2006) 'Working like real scientists', *Primary Science Review*, 94, Sept/Oct, 4–7. Highlight the core features of scientific enquiry undertaken by the case study and consider the use of science 'trees' to aid the process.

**TABLE 6.6** Science programme of study requirements in England

| Phase | Content |
| --- | --- |
| Key Stage 1 | Year 1<br>■ Plants<br>■ Animals, including humans<br>■ Everyday materials<br>■ Seasonal changes<br>Year 2<br>■ All living things<br>■ Habitats<br>■ Animals, including humans<br>■ Uses of everyday materials<br>■ Movement |
| Lower Key Stage 2 | Year 3<br>■ Plants<br>■ Animals, including humans<br>■ Rocks<br>■ Light<br>■ Forces and magnets<br>Year 4<br>■ Plants<br>■ Animals, including humans<br>■ Evolution and inheritance<br>■ States of matter<br>■ Sound<br>■ Electricity |
| Upper Key Stage 2 | Year 5<br>■ All living things<br>■ Animals, including humans<br>■ Properties of everyday materials and reversible change<br>■ Earth and space<br>■ Magnetism<br>Year 6<br>■ All living things<br>■ Evolution and inheritance<br>■ Changes that form new materials<br>■ Light<br>■ Forces<br>■ Electricity |

Working scientifically

Source: DfE (2013b)

## Planning and organizing science investigations

OFSTED (2008b: 11) reports that the most successful schools, in terms of standards, are those where scientific enquiry is at the core of their work. Pupils in these schools are enthusiastic about the subject, confident, and possess the skills to plan investigations and collect, present and evaluate evidence. The rationale for practical science is based on the belief that children learn best by seeing and doing, and are more likely to be motivated and learn through collaborative work. As Woolnough (1994: 25) points out, teachers have almost felt guilty if they had not had their classes engaged in practical tasks. Good teaching of science should provide pupils with the opportunity to pursue enquiries so that they can plan, discuss, predict, share ideas, question and reach conclusions. Loxley *et al.* (2013) advocate the use of scientific ideas to solve theme-based puzzles as part of a storytelling approach. This requires a suitable context and 'hook' to engage interest, such as 'Why was the bird pecking its feathers?'

Common problems associated with practical science relate to the organization of resources, lack of clarity in the objectives and insufficient time set aside for pupils to discuss their findings (Harlen and Qualter, 2009). For younger children, it is more appropriate to speak about exploration rather than formal investigation. In the Early Years, teachers should guide exploration initiated by child or adult, deciding upon appropriate support and intervention strategies (Howe *et al.*, 2005).

There are important points to bear in mind when organizing science investigations that should follow the school's general health and safety policy. The Association for Science Education produces specific safety guidance (2001) covering issues such as the safe storage of equipment and resources, heating and burning, the use of microorganisms, and children working outdoors. Group composition is another important factor when planning science lessons. Groups can be provided with instruction cards or visual prompts to act as reminders of the process of scientific enquiry.

To undertake scientific investigations, children need time and freedom to make decisions – for instance in their choice of resources, or method of recording and presenting findings. They also need to feel confident in using the language to describe their work. Research has shown that children are often unclear about the meaning of terms such as **fair test**, which they apply in an everyday sense of fairness rather than in the restricted sense of controlling variables (AKSIS, 1998). There are different kinds of investigations outlined in Table 6.7.

It is not always necessary for children to undertake their own investigations. Sometimes teacher demonstrations or an observational walkabout can convey new ideas equally forcibly. Of course, the liveliness of the demonstration and the manner in which the audience is engaged are critical in providing unforgettable learning experiences.

Promoting questioning skills is central to effective scientific enquiry. Children need to feel that their questions are taken seriously. Many teachers use question boxes or question walls to this end, from which they collate and prioritize questions in discussion with the class. The children themselves can sort questions according to particular criteria such as habitats and life cycles, before proceeding to think about how they would pursue their lines of enquiry.

Where possible, teachers should try to seize opportunities to promote pupils' understanding and experience of science in out-of-school contexts, such as visits to science museums, wildlife trusts, wetland centres, city farms, supermarkets, parks and National Trust properties (Box 6.7). These can prove valuable opportunities for pupils to take photographs, observe living things, collect leaves, cones and stones, and measure, sample and classify.

**TABLE 6.7** Scientific investigative skills

| Investigation | Examples |
|---|---|
| *Fair testing*: observing and exploring relations between variables | ■ What affects the rate at which sugar dissolves?<br>■ Which is the strongest paper bag?<br>■ Which materials make good raincoats?<br>■ Which parachute falls the slowest?<br>■ Which paper is the strongest?<br>■ What temperature of water dissolves jelly fastest? |
| *Classifying and identifying*: classifying is a process of arranging a large range of phenomena, into manageable sets; identifying is a process of recognizing objects and events as members of particular sets | ■ What is this chemical?<br>■ How can we group these invertebrates? |
| *Pattern-seeking*: observing and recording natural phenomena or carrying out surveys and then seeking patterns in their findings | ■ Where do we find most snails?<br>■ Do people with longer legs jump higher?<br>■ Is there a difference in the cleanliness of leaves found in different places?<br>■ Is there a relationship between height and reach? |
| *Exploring*: careful observations of objects or events, or making a series of observations of a natural phenomenon occurring over time | ■ How does frog-spawn develop over time?<br>■ What happens when different liquids are added together? |
| *Investigating models*: investigations that explore models; incorporates a stage where pupils have to decide what evidence should be collected in order to test a model | ■ How does cooling take place through insulating materials? |
| *Making things*: usually technological in nature | ■ Can you find a way to design a pressure pad switch for a burglar alarm? |

Source: AKSIS (1998). Reproduced with permission

---

**BOX 6.6  FOCUS ON PRACTICE**

A group of very able trainees was asked to submit a brief description of how they developed investigative skills:

'The children in Year 6 followed the fortunes of their chosen football team during the teaching practice and we used this in our numeracy lessons to practise calculations, work on time and predictions.'

(Bethan)

'I set up a "street market" within the Reception class in which children bought and sold groceries and other products at different stalls. They measured and weighed items and each advertised a healthy food such as black-eyed peas!'

(Chris)

'We were doing work on percentages and the Year 4 class were given some flyers that I had picked up from the local supermarket and other shops. We looked at special offers like "Buy one get one free", "Buy 2 and get the cheapest free" and "50% off".'

(Angela)

---

**BOX 6.7  FOCUS ON PRACTICE**

One Year 2 class walked around the school grounds to observe plants growing in different areas. They took photographs of the plants using digital cameras and then brought examples back to the class. They noted what the plants had in common and any differences, recorded on a Venn diagram. Using a digital microscope they examined the plants carefully and could not contain their excitement when they saw tiny insects on leaves. Questions followed, such as 'What are they?', 'Why are they on some plants and not others?' 'Are they eating the plants?'

A trainee who was a specialist in science was eager to demonstrate the relevance of the subject with her Year 6 class by relating each week a story of science in the news.

Another trainee had an 'amazing facts' display board related to her work on the human body and included the following to spark interest and discussion, taken from the Planet Science website:

■ A left-handed person finds it easier to open a jar than a right-handed person.

■ In a lifetime we spend the same amount of time eating as we do blinking.

■ We discard about 10 billion skin flakes every day.

---

## Best practice in teaching science

In general terms, good science teaching is characterized by appropriate pace, challenge, energy and effective feedback to children (Harlen, 2006). Best practice involves teachers making links to children's experiences, providing first-hand opportunities for them to pursue their own ideas, develop enquiry skills and consider alternative viewpoints. A popular strategy is the use of concept cartoons, in which children look at different views expressed by cartoon characters relating to a scientific issue. In groups, children consider who they agree with and why, although often there are no 'right' or 'wrong' answers (Naylor and Keogh, 2000). Genuine scientific enquiries will raise questions, involve mistakes (such as misreading data or miscalculations) and result in revised thinking. As with mathematics, the most successful teaching of science involves pupils in undertaking investigations that they see are relevant to their own lives and experiences. One of the challenges is striking the balance between teacher input and pupil-led enquiry. Outstanding teachers do not overly direct practical work and are eager to give pupils the opportunities to genuinely plan and conduct their own investigations. In so doing children can sometimes discover for themselves that their previously held views need to be modified. Learning through play, when teachers suspend an agenda, is too often confined to the Early Years. Exploratory play has an important function at all levels of scientific enquiry.

As with mathematics, outstanding science teachers motivate pupils by finding links to their everyday lives and preparing engaging materials (Box 6.7). The editorial board of *Primary Science Review* has published a 'Top 20' of activities known to excite and stimulate science enquiry including dandelion parachutes, sticking mouldy bread on the wall, finding iron in Special K cereal, fruit bowl science, and snake charming with a paper clip (PSR, 2007). Teachers can gently encourage children from a young age to begin to explain their answers, and to support what they say with evidence.

However, the challenges teachers face include knowing where to start and how to explain scientific ideas. It is good practice to plan ahead and think about the kinds of explanations and questions that lessons may require. When pupils do ask unexpected questions (and they will), they should be congratulated for working like scientists. At times, the questions may form the basis for further enquiry in a follow-up lesson, or lead to an impromptu demonstration, reference to the Internet or other sources.

Science provides many opportunities to develop key skills in literacy, numeracy and ICT, although too few primary teachers take advantage of these (OFSTED, 2008b). However, examples of excellent practice can be found in government reports and subject association material; for instance, the use of podcasts about the human body, presented in a 'chat show' manner, by P4/P5 classes in Scotland (Rodrigues and Connelly, 2008).

## Glossary

**Base-10 apparatus** refers to the numbering system in common use. Hence in the number 345, base ten refers to the position, the 5 is in the one's place, the 4 is in the ten's place and the 3 is in the hundred's place. Each number is 10 times the value to the right of it, hence the term base ten.

**Digraphs** are a pair of letters representing a single speech sound, such as the ph in pheasant or the ea in beat.

**Directed activities related to texts (DARTs)** are story-related activities to improve learners' reading comprehension. These include sequencing and predicting exercises.

**Fair tests** occur when only one factor (variable) is changed and all other conditions remain the same.

**Graphemes** are written representation of a sound; they may consist of one or more letters; for example the phoneme s can be represented by the graphemes s, se, c, sc and ce as in sun, mouse, city, science.

**Learner helplessness** suggests that some learners have learned to behave inactively and passively, too dependent on others.

**Number lines** are lines with numbers placed in their correct position. They are used for addition and subtraction, and for showing relations between numbers.

**Phonemes** are the smallest unit of meaningful sound, of which there are approximately 44 in English (the number varies depending on the accent).

**The National STEM Centre** provides resources for teachers of Science, Technology, Engineering and Mathematics.

**Self-managed learning** is also known as self-directed learning and involves the learner taking responsibility for their own learning, for instance in deciding on how and when they will acquire the knowledge that they need.

**Standard English** is generally applied to the variety of English most often used by those in educated circles, such as the professions and the media.

# References

AKSIS (1998) Interim Report from the ASE/King's College Science Investigations in Schools [AKSIS] Project, London: University of London.

ASE (2001) *Be Safe! Some Aspects of Safety in School Science for Key Stages 1 and 2*, Hatfield: ASE.

Askew, M. Rhodes, R., Brown, M., Wiliam, D. and Johnson, D. (1997) *Effective Teaching of Numeracy*, London: King's College.

Barber, M. (2013) 'OECD education report: UK needs new "gold standard" to compete with world's best', *The Telegraph*, 3 December.

Beverton, S. (2001) 'Whatever happened to primary English knowledge and understanding?', *Evaluation and Research in Education*, 15(3): 128–35.

Bielby, N. (1999) *Teaching Reading at Key Stage 2*, Cheltenham: Stanley Thornes.

Bloom, A. (2012) 'Do you have the hump with grammar?', *Times Educational Supplement*, 27 July.

Boaler, J. (2009) *The Elephant in the Classroom*, London: Viking Penguin, Souvenir Press.

Brooks, G., Pahl, K., Pollard, A. and Rees, F. (2008) *Effective and Inclusive Practices in Family Literacy, Language and Numeracy: A Review of Programmes and Practice in the UK and Internationally*, Sheffield: CfBT.

Bullock Report (1975) *A Language for Life*, London: HMSO.

Cashdan, A. and Overall, L. (eds) (1998) *Teaching in Primary Schools*, London: Continuum.

CBI/Pearson (2013) *Changing the Pace: CBI/Pearson Education and Skills Survey 2013*, London: CBI.

CCEA (2007) *Northern Ireland Curriculum Primary*, Belfast: CCEA.

Clark, C. and Rumbold, K. (2006) *Reading for Pleasure: A Research Overview*, London: National Literacy Trust.

Clark, C. and Hawkins, L. (2011) *Public Libraries and Literacy: Young People's Reading Habits and Attitudes to Public Libraries, and an Exploration of the Relationship between Public Library Use and School Attainment*, London: National Literacy Trust.

Cockburn, A. and Handscomb, G. (eds) (2006) *Teaching 3 to 11: A Student's Guide*, London: Paul Chapman.

Cockcroft Report (1982) *Mathematics Counts*, London: HMSO.

Coles, D. and Copeland, T. (2002) *Numeracy and Mathematics across the Curriculum*, London: David Fulton.

Cook, V. (2004) *Accomodating Brocolli in the Cemetary*, London: Profile Books.

Crowther Report (1959) *Fifteen to Eighteen*, London: HMSO.

Crystal, D. (1995) *The Cambridge Encyclopaedia of the English Language*, Cambridge: Cambridge University Press.

Crystal, D. (2010) *A Little Book of Language*, London: Yale University Press.

DfE (2010) *The Importance of Teaching*, London: DfE.

DfE (2011) *The Framework for the National Curriculum. A Report by the Expert Panel for the National Curriculum Review*, London: DfE.

DfE (2013a) *Teachers' Standards*, London: DfE.

DfE (2013b) *The National Curriculum in England Key Stages 1 and 2 Framework Document*, London: DfE.

DfEE (1999a) *The National Numeracy Strategy: Framework for Teaching Mathematics: Reception to Year 6*, Sudbury: DfEE.

DfEE (1999b) *A Fresh Start: Improving Literacy and Numeracy*. The report of the Working Group chaired by Sir Claus Moser, London: DfEE.

DfEE/QCA (1999) *English: The National Curriculum for England*, London: DfEE and QCA.

DfES (2006) *Independent Review of the Teaching of Early Reading*, London: DfES.

Drabble, E. (2013) 'How to teach . . . phonics', *The Guardian*, 1 April.

Durkin, K. and Shire, B. (1991) *Language in Mathematical Education*, Maidenhead: Open University Press.

Easingwood, N. and Williams, J. (2004) *ICT and Primary Mathematics: A Teacher's Guide*, London: Routledge.

Elkins, S. (2007) *Visual Literacy*, Abingdon: Routledge.

EPPI (2004) *The Effect of Grammar Teaching (Syntax) in English on 5 to 16 Year Olds' Accuracy and Quality in Written Composition*, London: EPPI.

ESARD (2012) *Research Evidence on Reading for Pleasure*, London, available at: www.eriding.net/resources/pri_improv/121004_pri_imp_reading_for_pleasure.pdf (accessed 6 June 2013).

Estyn (2001) *Raising Standards of Spelling in English in Primary Schools*, Cardiff: Estyn.

Estyn (2008) *Best Practice in the Reading and Writing of Pupils Aged 7 to 14 Years*, Cardiff: Estyn.

Estyn (2012) *Annual Report of Her Majesty's Chief Inspector of Education and Training in Wales 2010–2011*, Cardiff: Estyn.

Estyn (2013) *Supplementary Guidance: Literacy and Numeracy in Primary Schools*, Cardiff: Estyn.

Fergus, L. (2012) 'Thousands of pupils to benefit from literacy and numeracy scheme', *Belfast Telegraph*, 12 October.

Feuerborn, L.L., Chinn, D. and Morlan, G. (2009) 'Improving mathematics' teachers content knowledge via brief in-service: A US case study', *Professional Development in Education*, 35(4): 531–45.

Fisher, R. and Williams, M. (2006) *Unlocking Literacy*, London: David Fulton.

Frobisher, L., Monaghan, J., Orton, A., Orton, J., Roper, T. and Threlfall, J. (1999) *Learning to Teach Number*, Cheltenham: Stanley Thornes.

Galbraith, R. (1997) *Reading Lives*, New York: St Martin's Press.

Garvin, W. and O'Rawe, D. (1993) *Northern Ireland Scientists and Inventors*, Belfast: The Blackstaff Press.

Glasgow Education Services (2010) *Literacy and Numeracy for all: Framework for Action 2010–2012*, Glasgow: Glasgow City Council.

Glynne-Jones, T. (2007) *The Book of Numbers*, London: Arcturus.

Grey, D. (2008) *Getting the Buggers to Find Out*, London: Continuum.

Hamilton, E., Page, A. and Williams, E.M. (1947) *Arithmetic in Primary Schools*, London: Longman.

Hansen, A. and Vaukins D. (2011) *Primary Mathematics Across the Curriculum*, Exeter: Learning Matters.

Harlen, W. (ed.) (2006) *ASE Guide to Primary Science Education*, Hatfield: ASE.

Harlen, W. and Qualter, A. (2009) *The Teaching of Science in Primary Schools*, London: David Fulton.

Hayes, D. (ed.) (2007) *Joyful Teaching and Learning in the Primary School*, Exeter: Learning Matters.

Haylock, D. (2006) *Mathematics Explained for Primary Teachers*, London: Sage.

Haylock, D. and Cockburn, A. (1997) *Understanding Mathematics in the Lower Primary Years*, London: Paul Chapman.

Haylock, D. and Cockburn, A. (2008) *Understanding Mathematics for Young Children*, London: Sage.

Henry, J. (2012) 'Sir Jim Rose criticises children's authors in phonics row', *The Telegraph*, 17 June.

Holt, J. (1989) *Learning All the Time*, New York: Perseus Books.

Howe, A., Davies, D., McMahon, K., Towler, L., and Scott, T. (eds) (2005) *Science 5–11: A Guide for Teachers*, London: David Fulton.

Iley, P. (2005) *Using Literacy to Develop Thinking Skills with Children Aged 7–11*, London: David Fulton.

Jeffries. S. (2004) 'Ooh, I known this one!', *The Guardian*, 18 November.

Kelley, P. (2008) *Making Minds*, London: Routledge.

Khan, I. (2012) 'We need a Kitemark for science and maths', *Times Educational Supplement*, 13 April.

Kohl, H. (1974) *Reading, How To*, London: Penguin.

Lacey, P. (1998) *Building Numeracy*, Trowbridge: Robert Powell Publications.

Lankshear, C. and Knobel, M. (2008) *Digital Literacies: Concepts, Policies and Practices*, New York: Peter Lang.

Loder-Symonds, E. (2012) 'Numeracy campaign: Learning the language of maths', *The Telegraph*, 18 June.

Loxley, P., Dawes, L., Nicholls, L. and Dore, B. (2013) *Teaching Primary Science: Promoting Enjoyment and Developing Understanding*, London: Routledge.

Lunn, S. (2006) 'Working like real scientists', *Primary Science Review*, 94, Sept/Oct: 4–7.

Maddern, K. (2012) 'Fractions and division predict maths success', *Times Educational Supplement*, 17 August.

Mansell, W. (2011) 'Hidden tigers: Why do Chinese children do so well at school?', *The Guardian*, 7 February.

Medwell, J., Wray, D., Minns, H., Coates, E. and Griffiths, V. (2007) *Primary English: Teaching Theory and Practice*, Exeter: Learning Matters.

Mukherji, P. and O'Dea, T. (2000) *Understanding Children's Language and Literacy*, Cheltenham: Nelson Thornes.

Mullis, I.V., Martin, M.O. and Foy, P. (2008) *TIMSS 2007 International Mathematics Report*, Boston, MA: TIMSS and PIRLS International Study Centre.

Myers, J. and Burnett, C. (2004) *Teaching English 3–11*, London: Continuum.

Naylor, S. and Keogh, B. (2000) *Concept Cartoons in Science Education*, Sandbach: Millgate House Publishers.

OFSTED (1995) *Recent Research in Mathematics Education 5–16*, London: OFSTED.

OFSTED (2000) *The Teaching of Writing in Primary Schools: Could Do Better*, London: OFSTED.

OFSTED (2003) *Mathematics in Primary Schools*, London: OFSTED.

OFSTED (2005) *The National Literacy and Numeracy Strategies and the Primary Curriculum*, London: OFSTED.

OFSTED (2008a) *Mathematics: Understanding the Score*, London: OFSTED.

OFSTED (2008b) *Success in Science*, London: OFSTED.

OFSTED (2009) *Mathematics: Understanding the Score: Improving Practice in Mathematics*, London: OFSTED.

OFSTED (2011a) *Excellence in English*, London: OFSTED.

OFSTED (2011b) *Removing the Barriers to Literacy*, London: OFSTED.

OFSTED (2011c) *Success in Science*, London: OFSTED.

OFSTED (2011d) *Good Practice in Primary Mathematics: Evidence from 20 Successful Schools*, London: OFSTED.

OFSTED (2012a) *Mathematics: Made to Measure*, London: OFSTED.

OFSTED (2012b) *Moving English Forward*, London: OFSTED.

Jama, D. and Dugdale, G. (2012) *Literacy: State of the Nation: A Picture of Literacy in the UK Today*, London: National Literacy Trust.

O'Hara, M. (2008) *Teaching 3–8*, London: Continuum.

Ollerton, M. (2003) *Getting the Buggers to Add Up*, London: Continuum.

Ovens, P. (2000) *Reflective Teacher Development in Primary Science*, London: Routledge.

Paton, G. (2011) 'Thousands of school teachers "lack subject expertise"', *The Telegraph*, 20 April.

Primary Science Review (PSR) (2007) 'All change or small change?', 100, Nov/Dec: 9–13, available at: www.ase.org.uk/journals/primary-science/2007/11/100 (accessed 2 February 2014).

Reiss, M.J. (2008) 'Science and ethics: An introduction', *Primary Science*, 104, Sept/Oct: 4–7.

Riley, J. (ed.) (2007) *Learning in the Early Years*, London: Sage.

Rodrigues, S. and Connelly, E. (2008) 'Podcasting in primary science: Creative Science Education', *Primary Science*, 105, Nov/Dec: 33–5.

Rooney, A. (2008) *The Story of Mathematics*, London: Arcturus.

Rosen, M. (2012) 'Michael Rosen's letter from a curious parent', *The Guardian*, 4 June.

Rosen, M. (2012) 'Dear Mr Gove: Michael Rosen's letter from a curious parent', *The Guardian*, 5 November.

Roskos, K. and Christie, J. (eds) (2007) *Play and Literacy in Early Childhood*, New York: Lawrence Erlbaum Associates.

Rowland, T., Turner, F., Thwaites, A. and Huckstep, P. (2009) *Developing Primary Mathematics Teaching*, London: Sage.

Ruddock, G. and Sainsbury, M. (2008) *Comparison of the Core Primary Curriculum in England to those of Other High Performing Countries*, London: DCSF.

Scottish Government (2009) *Curriculum for Excellence: Building the Curriculum 4*, Edinburgh: Scottish Government.

Scottish Office Education Department (1991) *Curriculum and Assessment in Scotland, National Guidelines, Mathematics 5–14*, Edinburgh: SOED.

Senior, R., Hoathe, L. and Ounne, M. (2008) 'You wouldn't teach football without a ball, would you?', *Primary Science*, 101, Jan/Feb: 10–12.

Sewell, K. (2006) 'Why science?', *Primary Science Review*, 95, Nov/Dec: 20–1.

Sked, A. (1997) *An Intelligent Person's Guide to Post-War Britain*, London: Duckworth.

Smith, A. (2004) *Making Mathematics Count*, London: Training and Development Agency for Schools.

Smith, V. and Ellis, S. (2005) *A Curriculum for Excellence Review of Research Literature: Language and Literacy*, available at: www.educationscotland.gov.uk/thecurriculum/whatiscurriculumfor excellence (20 October 2013).

Sturman, L., Ruddock, G., Burge, B., Styles, B., Lin, Y. and Vappula, H. (2008) *England's Achievement in TIMSS 2007 National Report for England*, Slough: NFER.

Sullivan, A. and Brown, M. (2013) *Social Inequalities in Cognitive Scores at Age 16: The Role of Reading*, London: Centre for Longitudinal Studies.

Tammet, D. (2012) *Thinking in Numbers*, London: Hodder & Stoughton.

The Royal Society (2010) *Science and Mathematics Education, 5–14*, London: The Royal Society.

Twist, L., Schagen, I. and Hodgson, C. (2003) *Progress in International Reading Literacy Study (Pirls): Research Summary*, Slough: NFER.

UKLA (2010) *Teaching Reading: What the Evidence Says*, London: UKLA.

Ur, P. (1996) *A Course in Language Teaching: Practice and Theory*, Cambridge: Cambridge University Press.

Vaezi, S. (2001) 'Metacognitive reading strategies across language and techniques', unpublished doctoral dissertation, Allameh Tabataba'i University, Tehran, Iran.

Vaezi, S. (2006) *Reading Tips*, available at: www.the-faculty.org/uploads/documents/Stlg3_Reading_Tips.doc (accessed 2 February 2014).

Vasagar, J. (2011) 'CBI criticises schools over "inadequate" literacy and numeracy', *The Guardian*, 9 May.

Waters, M. and Martin, T. (1999) *Coordinating English at Key Stage 2*, London: The Falmer Press.

Watson, A. and Mason, J. (1998) *Questions and Prompts for Mathematical Thinking*, Derby: Association of Teachers of Mathematics.

Welsh Government (2012) *Improving Schools*, Cardiff: Welsh Government.

Woodhead, C. (2002) *The Standards of Today and How to Raise Them to the Standards of Tomorrow*, London: Adam Smith Institute.

Woolnough, B.E. (1994) *Effective Primary Science Teaching*, Buckingham: Open University Press.

Wray, D. and Lewis, M. (1997) *Extending Literacy: Reading and Writing Non-Fiction in the Primary School*, London: Routledge.

Wray, D. and Mallett, M. (2002) *The Primary English Encyclopedia*, London: David Fulton.

## Websites

The National Association for the Teaching of English provides recent research and recommended readings on literacy – www.ite.org.uk/ite_research/research_primary_focus/005.html

The National Literacy Trust is an independent charity that provides news, research and resources on literacy – www.literacytrust.org.uk

The Spelling Society website – www.spellingsociety.org/kids/index.html

The Association of Teachers of Mathematics aims to promote creative and thinking approaches in the teaching of mathematics – www.atm.org.uk

The Mathematical Association was the first teachers' subject association to be formed in England (1871) and continues to stimulate interest in the subject – www.m-a.org.uk

The National Centre for Excellence in the Teaching of Mathematics focuses upon the continuing professional development of teachers and the sharing of good practice – www.ncetm.org.uk

The Association for Science Teaching includes a link (PrimaryUpD8) to resources for primary classrooms – www.ase.org.uk

The Science Museum has online classroom and homework resources on topics such as forces, electricity and sound – www.sciencemuseum.org.uk

Dr Ben Goldacre's website on Bad Science – www.badscience.net

# 7

# Developing an effective digital pedagogy

## Chapter objectives

By the end of this chapter you should be able to:

- Reflect upon the relationship between modern technologies, education and society.
- Explain what is meant by information and communications technology (ICT), digital literacy and computer science.
- Understand the principles and approaches to develop an effective digital pedagogy.
- Evaluate the evidence for the impact of ICT on pupils' motivation, attainment and behaviour.

*I think it's become accepted that technology is, in itself, a bridge to learning rather than any kind of destination; and that a critical factor to the successful introduction of new learning tools is the intervention and involvement of a brilliant teacher.*

(Lord Puttnam, in Grey, 2005: 61)

## Introduction

This chapter explores technology within the broader context of society and education, to remind teachers of its all-pervasive influence and to point towards the need for a clear **digital pedagogy**. Given the speed of change in the field there is much more to be gained from taking a broader view of how teachers need to adapt their pedagogy to technological change in society. The pace of change is reflected in the language of technology. Black's popular *Dictionary of Computing* (Roseby, 2010) has run through six editions since 1988. It will need another edition soon to include such terms as 'iTods', the generation of toddlers who play regularly on iPads – around 60 per cent of three-year-olds and 40 per cent of two-year-olds (Sanghani, 2013). It is not uncommon to see a toddler who struggles to communicate orally but can easily navigate a smartphone. Older children, young people and adults are described as belonging to different generations of technology (Table 7.1).

**TABLE 7.1** Generations and ICT

| Generation | Born | Characteristics/values |
|---|---|---|
| *Gen Z or Net Generation* | 1995– | Fully integrated technologies within their lives |
| *Gen Y* | 1976–94 | First entirely electronic generation; friends = family |
| *Gen X* | 1965–75 | Use but do not assume technology; brought up on PCs rather than mobiles; friend = not family |
| Baby boomers | 1946–64 | Optimism, personal growth |
| *Silent generation* | 1922–45 | Conformity and sacrifice |

Source: Based on Lichy (2012)

These generational labels are used to illustrate how different age groups use technologies to learn, communicate and build relationships (Lichy, 2012). Often, however, the level of engagement with technology differs *between* rather than across generations. Around a quarter of all Internet users in the UK are 'silver surfers', those aged over 50 (Roberts and Wallop, 2010). One of the most exciting developments here is the diffusion of technological know-how, where younger generations are passing on skills to older ones through schemes such as British Telecom's 'Digital Champions' (btdigitalchampions.com).

## ICT, society and education

The origin of the word 'technology' offers insight into its very nature. It derives from the two-part Greek word *technologia*, meaning skill, art or craft (*techne*) and making sense of things (*logia*). One of the defining characteristics of the human species is the ability to make tools to solve problems. Computers, lasers and electrical appliances all have their origins in the simple tools created by our ancestors. For instance, the ancient portable writing system, the papyrus, was the forerunner of the modern-day tablet. There are also parallels to be drawn between the impact of the fifteenth-century printing press and the development of the Internet. Both have resulted in the free flow of information that transcended borders. Project Gutenberg, named after Johannes Gutenberg who is credited with inventing printing, was the first to produce free e-books and now offers 42,000 classic texts (www.gutenberg.org). The website Cha.Cha.com claims to answer more than a billion questions on a wide range of subjects (www.chacha.com). The developments noted in Table 7.2 have transformed the means by which knowledge is gained, shared and acted upon.

Technology can only be understood fully within its wider social and cultural context. The Internet, for example, is more than the keyboards, dual processors, copper wires and software that make connections possible. It includes the online activities that people engage in and the knowledge that is created and shared. An estimated one in three of the world's population is now online. In many countries, children now spend more time online, texting, watching television and playing video games than they do in school or with their parents (Common Sense Media, 2011). Over the last decade or so, technology has become a driving force in the lives of children across the world. The **digital divide** between the haves and have-nots has been substantially eroded by the speed, flexibility and affordability

**TABLE 7.2**  Key developments in ICT

| Founder | Invention | Date |
|---|---|---|
| Raymond Tomlinson | Email | 1971 |
| Steve Jobs, Steve Wozniak and Ronald Wayne | First Apple computer | 1976 |
| William ('Bill') Gates | Microsoft Operating systems | 1981 |
| Tim Berners-Lee | World Wide Web | 1990 |
| IBM | First smartphone | 1992 |
| Beverly Hills Internet (BHI) | First social media sites – Geocities | 1994 |
| Jeff Bezos | Internet shopping e.g. Amazon, eBay | 1995 |
| Lawrence Page | Google | 1998 |
| Jimmy Swales | Wikipedia | 2001 |
| Mark Zuckerberg | Facebook | 2004 |
| Steve Chen, Chad Hurley and Jawed Karim | You Tube | 2005 |

### PAUSE FOR REFLECTION

Consider what difference the developments in table 7.2 have had on your professional and personal life, as well as society at large. What would life be like without these?

of technology. Poore (2013) points out that the digital divide is becoming more about patterns of *use* rather than patterns of ownership.

The impact of social and economic disadvantage on children's ICT access in the home is a complex subject. According to Ofcom (2012), nine out of ten children aged 5–15 live in a household with Internet access via a PC/laptop. However, children come to school from different experiences in using technologies – as with traditional reading and writing, their competence in digital literacy varies considerably. Although a household may possess ICT equipment this does not mean that everyone in the family makes use of it; nor does lack of ownership mean that children have no access to ICT if they can make use of equipment at school or the public library. Lichy (2011) refers to the development of a 'second-level digital divide' where children and young people's use of technologies are best seen along a continuum, influenced by attitudes, skills, quality of access and social support.

Children grow up surrounded by technologies, beginning with scanned images of themselves before they were born. In a typical day children will encounter the likes of mobile phones, laptops, cash registers, microwaves and barcode readers. Teachers can increase pupils' awareness of everyday technology in the following ways:

- compiling displays from cut-out images showing computer toys, microwaves, televisions and the like from shopping catalogues (older catalogues could be compared to highlight change);
- setting up a technology museum in school showing old phones, video recorders, tape recorders etc;
- marking technological appliances and equipment on house or school plans;

- arranging visits to supermarkets, local business parks, museums, galleries, shopping precincts, science centres, newspaper offices or radio stations to discuss how they use technologies;
- modelling the use of a range of technologies; and
- discussing alternatives to technologies using 'What if . . .?'; scenarios, e.g. 'What if there was no television for a week?' or 'What if there were no computers?'

Although the level of ICT associated with some electronic items is minimal by adult standards, pushing a button or squeezing a toy's body part illustrates the concept of interactivity that is central to ICT (Becta, 2005).

The ways in which children and young people engage with technology out of school often differs from what happens in ICT lessons. In their own time, children learn about technologies by trial and error, messing about and getting 'just-in-time' tips from siblings, friends and adults (Facer, 2011). Famously, in 2001 Dr Sugata Mitra's hole-in-the-wall project in New Delhi showed how children self-educate themselves to a very high level by playing around on a networked computer (www.hole-in-the-wall.com). In school, ICT learning is often controlled, formal and teacher-led. The challenge then for teachers is to consider how best to build on children's informal learning and the playability and sociability of technologies. Put simply, how should schools engage with developments such as virtual worlds, social media and texting that are now so prevalent among children and young people?

The need for educators to rethink how they are preparing students for the twenty-first century is powerfully illustrated in the four-minute slideshow called *Did You Know? Shift Happens*, produced by an American teacher, Karl Fisch. It describes the dramatic changes taking place through technology and **globalization**. Since it was first shown in an American High School, it has been viewed by a global audience in excess of 20 million and adapted for different countries. Among the startling slides are messages such as: 'we are currently preparing students for jobs that don't exist . . . using technologies that haven't been invented . . . in order to solve problems we don't even know are problems yet' (Version 6, 2012; www.shifthappens.wikispaces.com). The amount of new technical information doubles every year. According to Patel (2013) in 1984 there were 1,000 Internet devices, in 1992 a million, and by 2008 a billion. Cisco, the worldwide leader in networking, estimates that by 2016 it will reach 3.4 billion. A 'new educational ecology' is emerging that includes the possibility of schools disappearing and being replaced by a learning *society* (Facer (2011). This is not as radical as it might appear – developments such as 'School of Everything' seek to link up learners and teachers in their locality without the need of a physical school and formal curriculum (www.schoolofeverything.com). The democratization of the Internet has generated thousands of 'folk teachers' (Facer, 2011). These offer their expertise in the form of short videos, available on websites such as YouTube, on subjects such as how to make a timer in Powerpoint, or effective techniques using the smart board.

If teachers are to make the most of technologies for **e-learning**, then they need to understand what Ingram (2000) calls the core structures in education – place, space, time, power and pace (Table 7.3). Supporters of e-learning visualize learners working 'any time, any place, any path and any pace' (so-called 'Martini learning'). As devices such as personal digital assistants (PDAs) and laptop computers become more affordable, the way children

**TABLE 7.3** Traditional versus e-learning

|  | **Traditional** | **E-learning** |
|---|---|---|
| **Place** | ■ Fixed<br>■ In school | ■ Mobile<br>■ Everywhere |
| **Space** | ■ Limited | ■ Unlimited virtual world |
| **Time** | ■ School terms<br>■ Blocks of time | ■ 24/7 Internet access<br>■ Flexible to meet needs |
| **Power** | ■ Teacher as central figure<br>■ Central syllabus | ■ Learner sets goals<br>■ Localised curriculum |
| **Pace** | ■ Set by teacher | ■ Learner controlled |

Source: Adapted from Ingram (2000), cited by National College of School Leadership (NCSL), The e-enabled primary school, available at http://forms.ncsl.org.uk/media/B2D/67/the-e-enabled-primary-school.pdf

learn is changing – instead of having to wait for a timetable slot or room, the technology can be immediately on hand when needed (Selwyn, 2013).

# ICT and the school curriculum

The 'potential' of ICT to transform education has been recognized since computers first appeared in schools in the early 1980s (Barron and Curnow, 1979; HMI, 1985). Although the term IT then applied to any machine that processed information, including video recorders, calculators and telephones, the main application related to the new world of computers (Box 7.1). In a pioneering book *Children Using Computers*, Anita Straker (1989: 7) raised fundamental questions, which remain central in developing a robust digital pedagogy for the twenty-first century:

■ Will the children do and learn things that are worth doing and learning?

■ Is using the computer the most effective way of doing and learning these things? and

■ Is it the most sensible and urgent use of the machine?

Straker highlighted a range of examples where children used computers to develop problem-solving and investigative skills, design programmes, handle historical data, monitor scientific experiments, undertake mathematical calculations and write for a purpose.

Over recent decades, there is no doubt that successive governments in the UK have invested significantly in supporting the development of ICT in the curriculum. Around £5 billion was spent on ICT provision between 1997 and 2009. Government policies during the Labour Government era were highly supportive of technology in schools, and several initiatives ring-fenced funding, such as e-Learning Credits, Curriculum Online and Home Access (Syscap, 2013). The Coalition Government has expected schools to set their own ICT strategies and implementation plans. But it has supported the National Education Network (NEN), which provides schools with broadband services and learning

---

**BOX 7.1  KEY CONCEPTS – IT, ICT, E-LEARNING AND COMPUTER SCIENCE**

The distinction between IT and ICT is likened to English (IT) and literacy (ICT). The former originally referred to information processing through computers and is still used in business circles, but since the 1990s was largely replaced with ICT to reflect communication developments in email, the web, satellites and mobile phones. In practice, the terms are used interchangeably. E-learning has many definitions and synonyms including Internet-based learning, web-based instruction and online learning. Basically these terms refer to any use of web and Internet technologies to create learning experiences (Horton and Horton, 2003). Computer science 'explains how computer systems work, how they are designed and programmed, and the fundamental principles of information and computation' (BCS and Royal Academy of Engineering, 2012: 1).

---

and teaching resources arranged by subjects and phases (www.nen.gov.uk). Regional consortia are linked to this, such as the South East Grid For Learning (www.segfl.org.uk). In 2012 Northern Ireland initiated a five-year plan to equip its 350,000 teachers and students with access to Europe's first Education Cloud environment. **Cloud education** aims to empower students of all ages so that they can learn through mobile devices connected to the 24-hour Internet without such traditional restrictions of space, place, time and authority. Popular examples of 'the cloud' include iCloud, DropBox and Box.Net. Education Scotland has invested heavily in Glow, the national intranet system for its schools while teachers in Wales can share digital practices via the national learning platform, the Hwb (https://hwb.wales.gov.uk).

Such investment has brought improvements in computer–pupil ratio, infrastructure and connectivity. The ratio of computers to children in most primary schools in England has increased from around 1:400 in the 1980s to 1:12 in 2001 and 1:7 in 2013 (Ward, 2011; Syscap, 2013). The British Educational Suppliers Association estimates that children in 51 per cent of primary schools spend more than half their time exposed to technologies such as interactive whiteboards, laptops and other mobile devices (Ward, 2011). But how well such time is used is a moot point. Michael Gove has not been alone in questioning the relevance of the ICT curriculum and the quality of teaching. Green and Hannon (2007) argue that over the last decade despite the staggering change in the amount of hardware in schools, it has not had the expected impact on teaching and learning. However, ICT is changing the relationship between teachers and children. The former are no longer seen as the repository of wisdom. According to a recent survey, only 3 per cent of pupils aged between 6 and 15 would turn to their teachers for information or the answer to a question (Bloom, 2012).

## Computing

Computing is the preferred term used by the Coalition Government in its National Curriculum (DfE, 2013). It revolves around the logical thinking, creativity and problem solving associated with computer science, but is not limited to a study of computers. It raises moral questions about freedom of information (what should remain private or open to the public) and philosophical issues, such as whether machines are intelligent. Computational thinking is transferable to many disciplines, including psychology, economics and statistics. It develops problem-solving skills, an understanding of systems and the relative merits of human and artificial intelligence.

Computer programming may seem rather daunting for primary teachers, especially when a recent review noted that only 22 per cent of ICT teachers (specialists in secondary schools) consider themselves to be good at creating or modifying basic computer programs (Livingstone and Hope, 2011). However, software developments are providing opportunities for primary children to learn basic programming skills. For instance, Scratch visual programming software is designed to create interactive games, stories and music (http://scratch.mit.edu). Codecademy also provides online opportunities to learn coding skills (www.codecademy.com). The Rasperry Pi Foundation seeks to inspire the next generation of coders. It promotes the Rasperry Pi, a cheap, credit-card size computer, which has USB ports for a keyboard and mouse, an Ethernet port, a SD card slot, and an HDMI port for connecting to a monitor or a TV. To make optimum use of this technology, teachers need training, funding is necessary to pay for the essential peripheral equipment, and systematic evaluation is required to measure the impact. But there is no doubt that many children and young people are highly motivated by writing scripts to control robots and other gadgets. There are volunteer network groups such as Code Club and Young Rewired State, which aim to mentor young coders (Stewart, 2012). STEMNET runs a STEM (science, technology, engineering and maths) Ambassador scheme, which takes volunteers into schools and public events to enthuse youngsters in STEM subjects (www.stemnet.org.uk/ambassadors).

The requirements for computing within England's National Curriculum reflect the pressures to ratchet up expectations (The Royal Society, 2012; DfE, 2013). The Key Stage 1 subject content is as follows:

- understand what **algorithms** are; how they are implemented as programs on digital devices; and that programs execute by following precise and unambiguous instructions;
- create and debug simple programs;
- use logical reasoning to predict the behaviour of simple programs;
- use technology purposefully to create, organize, store, manipulate and retrieve digital content;
- use technology safely and respectfully, keeping personal information private; know where to go for help and support when they have concerns about material on the Internet; and
- recognize common uses of information technology beyond school.

By the end of Key Stage 2, pupils should be able to:

- design, write and debug programs that accomplish specific goals, including controlling or simulating physical systems; solve problems by decomposing them into smaller parts;

- use sequence, selection, and repetition in programs; work with variables and various forms of input and output;

- use logical reasoning to explain how some simple algorithms work and to detect and correct errors in algorithms and programs;

- understand computer networks including the Internet; how they can provide multiple services, such as the world-wide web; and the opportunities they offer for communication and collaboration;

- use search technologies effectively, appreciate how results are selected and ranked, and be discerning in evaluating digital content;

- use technology safely, respectfully and responsibly; know a range of ways to report concerns and inappropriate behaviour; and

- select, use and combine a variety of software (including Internet services) on a range of digital devices to accomplish given goals, including collecting, analysing, evaluating and presenting data and information.

(DfE, 2013: 179)

This content represents significantly higher expectations than previous ICT national curriculum requirements. It denotes a shift from software-driven ICT teaching (how to use software), towards computer science (how to create software). Pupils are expected to understand the principles underlying how data is transported on the Internet. For instance, Key Stage 1 pupils should know that each website has a unique name, while older children should learn about the relationship between web servers, web browsers, websites and web pages.

## ICT across the curriculum

The importance of integrating ICT across the curriculum is widely endorsed (Smith, 1999; Leask and Meadows, 2000; Loveless and Dore, 2002; Simpson and Toyn, 2011). When pupils regularly use digital and video cameras in fieldwork, experiment with graphic packages in art lessons, search and evaluate online sources as part of historical enquiries, or create databases to record mathematical investigations, they are beginning to see the rich contribution of ICT to learning in other subjects. Effective use of digital video and photography has been shown to improve performance in physical education, sport and the dramatic arts where performances can be recorded, watched time and again, and improvements of skills targeted (Condie and Munro, 2007). Many children routinely use ICT as a reference source, as well as a means of communication and exploration. Table 7.4 is not exhaustive but illustrates projects where ICT has improved understanding in other areas of the curriculum.

### Digital literacy

One of the key dispositions when working with ICT is for children to strive for accuracy. Knowing how to identify reliable, trustworthy information is an essential life skill. Unfortunately, research suggests that when children and young people use the Internet

**TABLE 7.4** ICT across the curriculum

| Subject/area | Gains |
|---|---|
| Literacy and English language | ■ Writing for a real audience, composing, drafting, revising and presenting<br>■ Understanding of visual narrative using software such as Storybook Weaver<br>■ Understanding the etymology of words and relationship between language, semantics and spelling |
| Mathematics | ■ Using software to manipulate shapes<br>■ Using animations and 'what if . . .?' simulations to enhance understanding of concepts such as probability<br>■ Practising number skills, problem-solving, exploring patterns and relationships |
| Science | ■ Exploring scientific concepts and principles<br>■ Undertaking simulations to aid understanding of scientific decision making in real world e.g. ethics of research biologist working in a rainforest<br>■ Organizing, recording and presenting of results e.g. real-time graphing<br>■ Using dataloggers to measure and control variables e.g. temperatures<br>■ Using spreadsheets for data entry, tabulation and graph production, fair testing and seeking patterns<br>■ Using digital microscopes for close observation<br>■ Comparing results with others using CD-ROMs, databases and the Internet |
| Geography | ■ Using geo-tagging to include photographs of environmental features such as farms on maps<br>■ Communicating with other pupils in different environments via email, webcams, video conferencing<br>■ Using Geographical Information Systems (GIS) to improve geographical enquiry, mapping skills, spatial analysis |
| History | ■ Using databases of census materials to look for patterns and relationships<br>■ Using virtual archives to practice skills of interpretation e.g. Scottish Cultural Resources Access Network, National Archive<br>■ Using digital timelines |
| Religious education | ■ Taking and labelling digital photographs of visits to places if worship<br>■ Filming visitors from faith communities – watching clips, sequencing, making decisions, choosing transitions, and adding titles, credits and sound<br>■ Creating podcasts on themes such as wealth, poverty and justice<br>■ Using databases such as 'What is the Meaning of Life?' (www.natre.org.uk/db) |
| Creative arts | ■ Locating sources of information on artists and designers past and present and from different cultures<br>■ Accessing online galleries and information on art and design movements including new media such as animation, film, interactive websites<br>■ Using a range of software tools to design, edit, manipulate and present both still and moving images and sound<br>■ Exploring different stages in the development of an idea<br>■ Developing an electronic sketchbook - using a scanner or digital camera to collect resources to record observations and ideas<br>■ Using virtual keyboards to compose music<br>■ Using digital sound recorder to record sounds from around the school<br>■ Using music to tell stories and enhancing drama<br>■ Exploring sound patterns and following listening games online |
| Modern Foreign Languages | ■ Communicating through video conferencing and blogging<br>■ Practising language skills through digital video, photographs and online resources |

Sources: The Royal Society (2012); Becta (2009a); Becta (2009b); Murphy (2003)

they tend to believe the first things they find, do not check other sources and do not detect bias (Bartlett and Miller, 2011). Although the effect of this is unknown, the likelihood is that this makes them susceptible to extremist views. The Internet is rife with half-truths, mistakes, propaganda, misinformation and disinformation (Mintz, 2002).

Making sense of online information is often a challenge and calls for high-level **digital literacy**. Initially, digital literacy requires the following:

- basic keyboard and mouse skills;
- the ability to use simple 'office applications' such as word processing, presentations and spreadsheets; and
- technical knowledge of search systems.

Higher levels of digital literacy are demonstrated when learners engage critically with online sources. They do not automatically accept what appears on screen as accurate and reliable information. Children need to recognize that all online material has an author with a particular set of values and priorities. These may be commercial, political or religious and shape the way in which technology is used to convey information and meaning. Digital literacy also includes the ability to communicate knowledge in different contexts and to a range of audiences.

Given the consensus over the need for pupils to develop their digital literacy skills, there is a surprising lack of guidance for teachers. Becta (2009c) produced a *Digital Literacy Planning Tool* to support schools in developing the skills of defining, finding, evaluating, creating and communicating information (Table 7.5).

Defining involves clarifying what information is needed in order to save time and effort. In an age of 'infowhelm' (the exponential growth in information), finding the right material requires skills in sifting, rephrasing and ordering information. These are important so that pupils move away from a cut-and-paste-everything approach. Support is provided through a number of child-friendly search facilities such as 'Ask Jeeves for Kids' (http://uk.ask.com) and Google's 'Safe Search Kids' (www.safesearchkids.org). Evaluating websites includes examining the purpose, format and accuracy of what is on the screen. The pedigree of a website is important and an indicator of this can be found in its address or uniform resource locator (URL). Examples include .gov (government departments), .edu (education institutions), .co (commercial body in the UK), and .org (mostly non-profit organizations).

Once the right information is retrieved, it needs to be reconstructed in a suitable form. Selected text can be re-created in different ways, such as a table, list, diagram or audio. The final skill is learning how to communicate information effectively. This might involve a presentation to an audience, and sub-skills such as timing, voice control and pace should be taught. Buckingham (2007) believes that there is too much emphasis on information retrieval in an age when the boundaries between 'information' and other media have become increasingly blurred. Often, children and young people are able to multitask by watching television, playing computer games, listening to music online and offline, creating their own animations, talking to friends over the Internet, or participating in virtual words such as Disney's Club Penguin, which offers online games and activities within a safe environment. Those who are digitally literate are comfortable with these technologies but also know their limitations, acting sensibly and safely.

**TABLE 7.5** ICT Planning Tool

| Planning stage | Prompts |
| --- | --- |
| **Define**<br>the task and proposed solution | ■ What do you already know about the subject?<br>■ What is the question or key words?<br>■ Are these clear and specific?<br>■ Who is the intended audience? What do they want to know? |
| **Find**<br>information | ■ Have 'rules' of safe online activity been explained?<br>■ Which search engine should be used?<br>■ Are issues of copyright and plagiarism understood?<br>■ Can information be downloaded and stored in appropriate format? |
| **Evaluate**<br>information to match<br>audience/aims | ■ How trustworthy is this information? How do I know?<br>■ Are there contact details for the author?<br>■ Is the information provided in a factual way?<br>■ Is the site easy to use?<br>■ Does the site load quickly?<br>■ Is the material biased?<br>■ Is the content easy to read? |
| **Create**<br>a solution | ■ How should this information be presented (tables, spreadsheets, graphs, reports, posters)?<br>■ What technical support, time and other resources are needed? |
| **Communicate**<br>findings, reflect<br>and improve work | ■ Which is the best format (word, picture, audio file) for the intended audience?<br>■ Can this be improved in its appearance, content, length?<br>■ How should this work be published and shared with others?<br>■ Have all sources been acknowledged? |

Source: Based on Becta (2009c)

The role of the teacher in developing pupils' digital literacy skills depends on the context. In some cases these may be teacher-directed tasks with specified learning outcomes, whereas on other occasions pupils might be afforded more choice – for instance in selecting the questions, topics, websites or how to communicate findings. To be digitally literate means having the confidence, knowledge and understanding to apply technologies in different contexts. Like traditional literacy and numeracy, digital literacy should not be treated as a separate subject. The Cambridge Primary Review (Alexander, 2009: 270) stressed that while ICT should apply across the curriculum, it should receive more explicit attention within the English programme of study: 'It no longer makes sense to attend to text but ignore txt.'

It is now standard practice for young children to use ICT in word processing tasks, to paint using art software, and to learn basic mathematical concepts in number and shape. Many teachers also use a variety of language programmes to reinforce spelling, word patterns and to support story-related activities. Continual advances in digital and video camera technology enable children as young as 3 and 4 to record pre-school events including visits. In the best practice, teachers use digital images to promote oral skills as well as subject knowledge.

## Digital citizenship

Living in a digital world means that children and young people require the skills, attitudes and understanding to ensure that powerful technologies are used responsibly and ethically. Much of the interaction in this digital age occurs remotely and anonymously. This makes it challenging to enforce clear codes of conduct. Digital citizenship is concerned with promoting appropriate behaviour when using technologies. It involves children understanding standards of etiquette (or Netiquette) when communicating information electronically. It requires teachers to provide a safe and secure environment and to raise children's awareness of risks. Digital citizenship is based on fundamental rights and responsibilities. Article 13 of the United Nations Convention on the Rights of the Child (ratified by every country in the world except Somalia and the United States) states:

> The child shall have the right to freedom of expression; this right shall include *freedom to seek, receive and impart information and ideas of all kinds*, regardless of frontiers, either orally, in writing or in print, in the form of art, or through any other media of the child's choice.
>
> (www.ohchr.org/en/professionalinterest/pages/crc.aspx)

The Internet and computers generally have raised wide-ranging concerns among educators, policymakers and parents. Plowman *et al.* (2010a) researched parental attitudes towards 3 and 4-year-olds using technology in the home. Although the authors report some parental disquiet, they conclude that technology is not perceived by parents to be the threat to modern childhood that is often claimed. Publications by the Alliance for Childhood, for example, have called for a refocus in the Early Years on play, reading books and hands-on experiences in nature, claiming that technologies have caused irreversible changes in human biology (Cordes and Miller, 2000; Alliance for Childhood, 2004). The size, design and fixed location of desktop computers do not make them very appropriate technology for young children. Such computers were designed for adults in the workplace rather than young children who lack the fine motor skills to use the mouse effectively. However, there are a growing number of products such as interactive books (e.g. LeapPads), portable laptops and computer-animated toys that are easier to integrate in children's play and learning environment.

Children are exposed to significant levels of screen media. According to Sigman (2012), by the age of 7 the average child will have watched the equivalent of a full year of screen media and by the age of 18 this will have increased to 4 years. Intellectually, it is feared that children's creativity, language and imagination are restricted by such exposure. They are said to suffer social and emotional damage through isolation, exploitation, and weakened relationships with teachers. Physical hazards include visual strain, obesity linked to a sedentary lifestyle and muscular pain. Sigman draws parallels between screen dependency and alcohol and drug addiction. Excessive computer game playing is damaging the brain's reward circuitry in the same way as substance dependence (Sigman, 2012). He warns of the danger of 'passive parenting' as young children are left disconnected in their virtual worlds (Pelling, 2012). There are also moral questions relating to the influence of cyberbullying, violent video games and online pornography (Cordes and Miller, 2000). During the Industrial Revolution, followers of Ned Lud (Luddites) destroyed factory machinery that they perceived to be a threat to their employment and lifestyle (they were proven to be right). Modern-day reference to 'digital or neo Luddites' has become something of a cliché to describe all kinds of protests, including email overload, distractions of mobile phones, students' immediate recourse to Wikipedia and Google and intrusions of surveillance technologies. Digital citizenship is about educating children, young people and teachers in a balanced approach so that they can reach informed decisions about the role of technology in their lives and society at large.

## E-safety

Whenever new technologies are introduced there are concerns over the impact on children's development and well-being. This was the case when the cinema became popular in the 1900s, radio in the 1920s and television in the post-war years. For instance, an American study in 1936 reported widespread parents' complaints about children gulping their meals so as not to miss their favourite radio show and waking with nightmares from listening to 'lurid radio bedtime stories' (cited by Wartella and Jennings, 2000: 33). Despite these longstanding concerns, computer technology raises new challenges. For the first time in history, children can immediately access almost any form of sexual behaviour and violence. With the advent of mobile technologies, no matter what safeguards are built into school IT systems, it is not possible to eliminate all risks. The Byron Review (2008) reported that 57 per cent of 9 to 19-year-olds in Britain had faced online pornography – either through unsolicited email or stumbling across it. They are also exposed to advertisements for all kinds of products and services. Often children access inappropriate material innocently. One trainee teacher experienced embarrassment when allowing a group of children to search for information on female foxes as part of their project on habitats; several images of scantily clad women appeared on screen. There are frequent stories in the media concerning the vulnerability of children and young people to danger – knowingly or unknowingly – when using the Internet and other digital technologies (Dustin, 2012). Arguments persist over the physical, emotional and social dangers related to children's use of technologies (for example, see http://wiredchild.org). Research for the NSPCC (Barter et al., 2009) reports teenage girls are often subject to coercion from partners using online technologies, mobile phones and texting. It is also possible for learners (and teachers) to become inadvertently caught up in illegal activities. Activities such as 'sexting', where sexually explicit messages or photographs or exchanged, mean that teachers need to be clear about their professional responsibilities. Clearly, sex education in teacher training courses needs to include the appropriate use of modern technologies and the adhering to a professional code of conduct for teachers.

Table 7.6 sets out common myths associated with children's online activities, based on a European-wide study. So while there are risks, technologies are such an important part of everyday life children need to be educated in how to make the most of these.

Local authorities provide schools with guidance relating to **e-safety** policy and practices, which should be regularly updated to take into account changes in technology such as issues surrounding use of mobile technologies and 'cloud' storage of data. Lancashire, for example, offers comprehensive Primary eSafety Guidance that schools can adapt, covering matters such as raising awareness with parents, website maintenance, instant

**TABLE 7.6** Myths associated with online activities

| Myth | Survey evidence |
| --- | --- |
| Digital natives know it all | Only 36 per cent of 9–16-year-olds say it is very true that they know more about the Internet than their parents. This myth obscures children's needs to develop digital skills. |
| Everyone is creating their own content | Only one in five children had recently used a file-sharing site or created an avatar, half that number wrote a blog. Most children use the Internet for ready-made content. |
| Under 13s can't use social networking sites | Although many sites (including Facebook) say that users must be aged at least 13, the survey shows that age limits don't work – 38 per cent of 9–12-year-olds have a social networking profile. Some argue age limits should be scrapped to allow greater honesty and protective action. |
| Everyone watches porn online | One in seven children sees sexual images online. Even allowing for under-reporting, this myth has been partly created by media hype. |
| Bullies are baddies | The study shows that 60 per cent who bully (online or offline) have themselves been bullied. Bullies and victims are often the same people. |
| People you meet on the Internet are strangers | Most online contacts are people children know face-to-face. Nine per cent met offline people they'd first contacted online – most didn't go alone and only one per cent had a bad experience. |
| Offline risks migrate online | This is not necessarily true. While children who lead risky offline lives are more likely to expose themselves to danger online, it cannot be assumed that those who are low-risk offline are protected while online. |
| Putting the PC in the living room will help | Children find it so easy to go online at a friend's house or on a smartphone that this advice is out of date. Parents are better advised to talk to their children about their Internet habits or join them in some online activity. |
| Teaching digital skills reduces online risk | Actually the more digital skills a child has, the more risks they are likely to encounter as they broaden their online experience. What more skills can do is reduce the potential harm that risks can bring. |
| Children can get around safety software | In fact, fewer than one in three 11–16 year-olds say they can change filter preferences. And most say their parents' actions to limit their Internet activity are helpful. |

Source: Livingstone et al. (2011)

messaging, incident logs and Acceptable User Policies (Lancashire County Council, 2013). Teachers also need to be mindful of data protection and copyright issues. There are means to address these. For instance, creative content is a 'licence agreement' whereby teachers can protect their materials, such as lesson plans, while allowing colleagues to access these for modification provided these are acknowledged.

One of the challenges for schools that allow children and young people to use mobile phones with 3G capabilities is how to restrict access to approved sites. Schools and universities have various filtering systems and firewalls in place set to prevent user access to unsuitable materials. These can take the form of 'walled gardens' that only allow access to a prescribed list of websites. However, such restrictions mean that much useful content is excluded. A more common approach is to filter pages when users try to open them but, again, this is not perfect. Undesirable content can slip through and useful educational material blocked. However, all schools should have acceptable user policies in place. These set out how adults and children should use the school network. Home–school agreements are also essential, covering matters such as permission to publish photographs of children involved in school projects and uploading materials online.

One emerging trend is for very young children (toddlers and pre-schoolers) to use Internet connected devices, such as touchscreen tablets and smartphones. This raises the likelihood of exposure to inappropriate materials and puts at risk their privacy and safety. Moreover, it is increasingly possible to trace the digital footprints of children left not only by themselves but by friends and family. Parents and grandparents, for instance, regularly post ultrasound scans, pictures and videos of babies and children on social network sites. Eight in ten parents in the UK have uploaded photographs of their children under 2 and one in five have uploaded antenatal scans, figures that are in line with international averages (Holloway *et al.*, 2013: 23). Clearly it is often not possible to gain children's consent but this raises the question of children's future rights to find, reclaim or delete material posted by others (Holloway *et al.*, 2013).

## Towards a robust digital pedagogy

A number of writers highlight the importance of teachers possessing a clear rationale to support the use of ICT (Beetham and Sharpe, 2007; Beauchamp, 2012). Digital pedagogy involves the use of technologies to enhance the experience of education. This can be from a simple PowerPoint to providing online courses. Whether, how, when, where, what and why technologies are used in the classroom are decisions that say something about the pedagogical stance of teachers. Their use of ICT is likely to draw upon the learning theories outlined in Chapter 5. For those who adopt a sociocultural approach, talk and interaction are central to the use of technologies. When children learn how to hold a video camera or take a digital photograph, they understand the importance of cultural tools in society. Most children grow up with such technologies at home and begin to make sense of how they work through listening, observing, playing, imitating and trial-and-error. Often they are able to be powerful learners at home because they benefit from immediate one-to-one interaction and support from parents and siblings in familiar sourroundings. These are the conditions that are conducive to learning. However, it is more challenging for teachers to be as responsive as most parents because they are managing the needs of a group of learners for a limited period of time (Plowman *et al.*, 2010b).

Behaviourism emphasizes stimulus, response and rewards for getting things right. These features stand out in much of the gaming technologies that are proving so popular, as well as computer drill exercises in number bonds or times tables. ICT can provide pre-programmed responses with developments such as voice and gesture recognition, as well as touch sensitive screens. Software, which is branded as age/phase specific, reflects the influence of Piaget and other cognitive theorists. Social constructivism, with its emphasis on collaboration, is evident when pupils engage in activities such as blogging and online discussions. Connectivist theory stresses the importance of how individuals and groups share knowledge through networks (Siemens, 2005). There will be times when teachers draw upon all of these theories. However, most commentators see children taking a more active role in their learning with digital technologies and so a constructivist view is widely endorsed.

Children come to understand their world through historical, geographical, religious, moral, scientific and other lenses. The use of technologies should be seen not only as a means to enable young people to make sense of their surroundings, but also to contribute to more fulfilling lives. As children are already 'digital participants' in society, the question for teachers is usually not the old one of whether or not technologies have a place in education but how these can be used most effectively. Take the example of computer games. These are popular with players of all ages and both genders. But why is it that very young children can sustain concentration over long periods while playing a computer game and yet struggle to stay on task in lessons? Computer games are designed along similar principles that support effective learning: a sense of purpose, clear rules, challenge, resolving conflict and problem solving, interactivity, instant and relevant feedback, a strong social angle, the construction of knowledge and responding to an engaging narrative. Younie and Leask (2013) argue that teachers can build on the strengths of digital games in developing a 'transformative' pedagogy that values active learning over passivity and encourages learners to become personally involved in their learning.

If teachers are to develop a robust digital pedagogy, they need to feel confident in their own technical knowledge and skills. Broadly speaking, teachers need to know how to:

- use common software packages, e.g. word processing, PowerPoint, Excel spreadsheets;
- input, interpret and present data, e.g. analyse trends in the performance of pupils and know where interventions are needed;
- search and evaluate online sources, e.g. websites;
- create digital resources, e.g. multimedia presentations;
- communicate with colleagues, other professionals and parents, e.g. by email and text; and
- use ICT in everyday administrative tasks, e.g. taking registers, timetables, classroom seating plans.

The ICT test for trainee teachers, introduced in England in 2001, was dropped in 2012 because the government no longer had concerns over the ICT skills of newly qualified teachers. Teachers who lack such technical skill or confidence can find out more through subject associations, OFSTED's subject development materials, online professional networks and local authority advisers. However, local authorities and schools are under significant financial constraints to invest in continuing professional development even though teachers need to review and update their knowledge on a regular basis, particularly in ICT (The Royal Society, 2012; Estyn, 2013).

Teachers need to consider how best to support children so that they become informed users, able and confident enough to challenge and question technology rather than accept it passively. Teachers also need to know the principles that underpin the creation of a technology-rich environment. These include:

■    building positive relationships so that technologies are used sensibly and risks managed;

■    establishing and sustaining learning routines that challenge, motivate and relate to real-life contexts;

■    responding to learners' needs, interests, starting-points and perspectives;

■    integrating assessment within learning; and

■    connecting learners to a range of audiences beyond the classroom.

Foremost, teachers should develop positive relationships using strategies that promote children's self-confidence, respect and willingness to take risks with their learning. They need to build on children's prior knowledge and experience, challenge thinking and provide opportunities for children to explore and imagine using the power of technologies. Learners need opportunities to question the merits of particular tools, compared to other resources and approaches.

Outstanding teachers see the importance of building pupils' capacity to connect, select, apply, collaborate and evaluate. They see school communities as having the potential to create knowledge using technologies as well as receive it; they seek to provide challenging learning experiences that encourage children to work in real-life contexts, in which they generate new knowledge as they address authentic problems. Bigum (2003) is critical of what he calls the 'fridge-door' mindset of many schools – the idea that the teacher sets a task, the children complete it, the teacher marks it, and the child takes it home where it might be 'published' temporarily on the fridge door.

Centre to an effective digital pedagogy is being clear over the thinking and learning that the technology seeks to promote. The contribution of Benjamin Bloom's work on educational objectives has been noted in Chapter 4. Anthony Churches has updated Bloom's work to take into account new processes and actions associated with Web 2.0 technologies. The model shows how learners can move towards higher thinking skills, from learning how to send a simple text to creating an animation or podcast (Figure 7.1). This model provides teachers with the confidence to plan challenging activities although it does not mean that all tasks should be completed in digital formats.

Clearly an effective digital pedagogy is largely influenced by a teacher's personal confidence and self-efficacy. Generally, teachers who have little or no confidence in using computers in the classroom will try to avoid them altogether (Becta, 2004). Teacher

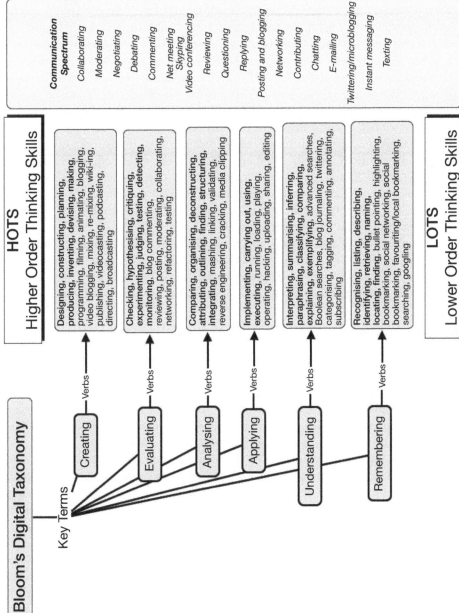

**FIGURE 7.1** Bloom's Digital Taxonomy

Source: Churches (2008)

confidence in using ICT is influenced by many factors, including access to high-quality training and professional development, technical support and connectivity. The Scottish inspectorate suggest that typically in each primary school, one or two teachers lack confidence and do not make effective use of technologies (HMIe, 2007). OFSTED (2011) strikes a more optimistic note, reporting that the teaching of ICT was good or outstanding in nearly two-thirds of English primary schools visited and that confidence is increasing among teachers and assistants. Most newly qualified teachers are confident in the use of ICT to support learning – 86 per cent of those trained in school-based contexts rated this as either good or very good (DfE, 2013). European research concludes that increasing teacher confidence and investing in teacher professional development are the keys to making the most of the significant investments in technologies (European Commission, 2013). Some teachers fear that their own technical skills are not as well developed as their pupils' and therefore have doubts about their teaching. Even if this is the case, teachers should be able to model the critical thinking skills that should underpin effective digital literacy. Monk (2012) argues that teachers who worry over keeping up to speed with the 'technological arms race' need to focus more on what they know about pedagogy rather than ICT. He points out that outstanding teachers use students as resources, encouraging them to become *teachers* themselves.

Outstanding teachers manage their time very effectively. This is particularly important when working with ICT, which can easily consume time rather than save time. Some students and teachers are very well organized and self-disciplined. They efficiently file documents on well-labelled computer folders, providing quick retrieval when needed.

## Interactive whiteboards

Schools in the UK lead the way in terms of interactive whiteboards (IWBs) – 80 per cent of classrooms are equipped with one, compared to only 12 per cent internationally (Hennessy and London, 2013). Most teachers now routinely use interactive whiteboards to illustrate lessons, provide explanations and demonstrate difficult concepts. Specific software is often used alongside a bank of website material including streamed broadband clips (available at websites such as www.bbc.co.uk/learningzone).

For teachers, the advantages of using IWBs include: their flexibility and versatility across age ranges and settings; instant access to a range of materials; opportunities to manipulate content in front of the class; modelling strategies; enlivening lesson delivery by adding colour, music and sound; more professional delivery; and saving of preparation time. For pupils, studies suggest that they find lessons are faster paced, more fun and exciting than lessons without IWBs (Smith *et al.*, 2005). There are also specific learning gains – for instance, young children find it easier to use IWBs than computers because they do not need the fine motor skills demanded by mouse control. IWBs allow teachers and children to adapt what is on the screen using a variety of text, shape, highlighter, pen, spotlight, screen capture, magnifier and fill tools.

However, critics claim that too many teachers use the IWBs as glorified chalkboards and undervalue the key concept of interactivity that covers both technical and pedagogical aspects. The latter involves the balance between teaching and learning using the technology – to what extent do pupils have the opportunity to ask questions, review and evaluate their own and others' understanding? This is not a straightforward matter of allowing pupils more time using the IWB – for example, Smith (2001) suggests that when children come to the IWB during whole-class lessons, this can reduce pace and lead to boredom. Deep learning arises only when pupils are challenged to think carefully about the screen content, to follow their own questions, to justify their decisions and to control the technology to support their learning. Beauchamp and Parkinson (2005) suggest the following progression in how learners interact with technology:

Information presented to the pupils by the teacher

↓

Some class discussion followed by notes on IWB made by the teacher

↓

Sharing of lesson objectives on IWB with class and revisiting them at key points of the lesson

↓

Activities, such as labelling, drawing and constructing graphs, are jointly done on the IWB

↓

A piece of written work, e.g. the conclusion to an investigation, is analysed by the class and suggestions for improvement are made

↓

Arguments and explanations are co-constructed on the IWB by members of the class.

---

**BOX 7.2 FOCUS ON PRACTICE**

Here are two descriptions of outstanding lessons by the inspectorate in Northern Ireland (ETI, 2006: 11):

The IWB was used very effectively in a year 1 class. The teacher was consolidating the children's understanding of initial sounds and reinforcing their knowledge of upper and lower case letters. The programme she devised was linked imaginatively to a topic on 'The Jungle'. The children manipulated graphics on screen and then joined linking lines to match upper and lower case letters. The lesson lasted approximately 40 minutes and the children, especially the boys, were engaged throughout; they responded to the moving stimuli and enjoyed recording their own efforts on screen. The teacher's excellent management of the learning, together with the attraction of the IWB, resulted in an outstanding lesson.

In a year 5 class, the teacher introduced a science lesson using a PowerPoint presentation about sources of energy. One group of children carried out a practical investigation, using a variety of surfaces, to determine differences in how high a ball can bounce. The group used the webcam to record the bouncing ball against a measure chart. They replayed the record and used the 'freeze frame' facility to get an accurate measurement of the height of the ball at the top of its trajectory.

**PAUSE FOR REFLECTION**

Reflect on the two cases of outstanding teaching mentioned in the Focus on Practice box (Box 7.2). Would these still be regarded as outstanding now? Is it more difficult to be rated outstanding when teaching ICT than other subjects?

## Computer suites and mobile technologies

Increasingly, schools are moving away from using desktops in computer suites, where classes are timetabled for the teaching of discrete skills, towards mobile technologies. In some schools, tablets and laptops have replaced the interactive whiteboard and personal computer. By 2015, it is estimated that tablets will form one in five of all computers in primary schools (Syscap, 2013). In England, nearly three-quarters of primary schools want to see research evidence to support the adoption of tablets in the classroom (BESA, 2012). The use of tablet technologies, smart phones and digital cameras is widening the range of learning and teaching approaches. It is also changing the fundamental nature of teaching and making teachers rethink their roles. Pupils become coaches to peers without the need for adult intervention. Self and peer assessment are easily facilitated. The functionality of tablets supports pupils of all abilities.

The Apple iPad, launched in 2010, had dominated the education market although in recent years the Google Android has gained ground (BESA, 2012). The iPad's versatility enables children to take photographs, make and edit films, create music, word process and share ideas. There are many examples of schools making effective use of iPads (Evans, 2012). Research on the effectiveness of ipads in Scottish schools suggests that personal 'ownership' of the device is seen as the single most important gain (Burden *et al.*, 2012). Teachers and children feel this ownership alike. The research found that little formal training or tuition was necessary as learning occurred through play and collaboration. Educational applications ('apps') typically include: encyclopaedias, quizzes, revision aids and animations. Popular examples cover mind mapping (e.g. iThoughtsHD), painting (e.g. Brushes), geography (e.g. Google Earth,) science (e.g. Star Walk), film editing (e.g. iMovie), word processing (e.g. Pages), music (e.g. Garage Band), and publishing (e.g. Book Creator); iTunesU is the world's largest online library of free, educational material.

Funding is an obvious barrier to adopting tablets. Management, security and teacher awareness are further obstacles – more than a third of primary teachers are reported to have no awareness of apps (BESA, 2012). From a technical viewpoint, clearly the convergence of operating systems between mobile and desktop devices is essential. There is also a fundamental issue of 'image-conscious' teachers being seduced by various schemes, such as replacing laptops with the latest iPads. The danger is that schools with their own IT budgets rush to purchase the latest technologies without recognizing their limits – iPads, for example, lack USB connectivity and software such as Microsoft Word and PowerPoint, which causes compatibility difficulties for some teachers (Box 7.3).

---

**BOX 7.3  REAL-LIFE LEARNING CHALLENGE**

You are responsible for ICT within a primary school of 200 pupils. The head teacher wants to raise standards in literacy and numeracy and hopes ICT can support this. He has therefore allocated £10,000 in the ICT budget and has left you to decide how this is spent. There is disagreement among colleagues over whether to continue with the ICT suite (comprising twenty computers) and daily timetabled sessions. Some teachers have expressed a preference for mobile technologies, including providing older pupils with their own iPads. Others are more cautious and are concerned over the cost, safety and training. One colleague has whispered to you that some of the existing technologies are rarely used by a couple of 'dinosaurs'. The Chair of the Governors' Finance Committee is keen for value for money principles to be adopted. He asks 'Why have we got to buy iPads?' Provide clear leadership for colleagues in taking the issues forward by drawing up suggestions on how the money should be spent.

---

## Social media

The rise of **social media** is one of the most noticeable developments in ICT in recent years. For most people who lacked specialist programming knowledge, the early World Wide Web ('Web 1.0') was very much a read-only, one-directional form. However, the Web 2.0 'version' or second generation of the web was introduced around 2005. Its social media tools and services have opened up possibilities for the multiple sharing of information (hence it is also known as the 'read–write web'). Social networking applications are wide-ranging and include:

- communication tools such as blogging (e.g. Blogger, LiveJournal), microblogging (e.g. Twitter, Yammer), social networking (e.g. Facebook, LinkedIn, MySpace) aggregators (e.g. Google Reader, iGoogle), photosharing, slideshows, **clippings**;

- collaboration tools such as conferencing (e.g. GoToMeeting, Skype), **wikis** (e.g. Wikia, PBWorks), social documents (e.g. Google Docs, Dropbox, Zoho), project management (e.g. Bamboo, Huddle), social news (e.g. Digg, Reddit); and

- multimedia tools such as photographs (e.g. Flickr, Picasa), video (e.g. YouTube, Vimeo), live streaming (e.g. Ustream) and presentation sharing (e.g. Scribd, SlideShare).

Social media has attracted criticism on various social, moral and educational grounds. These include concern over misuse of data, a lack of privacy, shallowness, information overload, and a general concern that it damages people's thinking. One poll of 500 British teachers found that seven out of ten believed that children are becoming more and more obsessed with social media; more than half thought that mobile phones and computers had a detrimental impact on pupils' spelling and writing skills (Bloxham, 2010). It also seems that many pupils are more familiar with Web 2.0 applications than their teachers (Becta, 2008). A recent report suggests that one in four children between the age of 8 and 12 had an account on the likes of Facebook, Bebo and MySpace (Ofcom, 2012).

Studies have also shown that through blogging, texting and emailing, children and young people are reading and writing more than previous generations, albeit in different forms. Moreover, text messages demonstrate phonological awareness and manipulation skills, meaning that poor literacy attainment is in spite of 'textism' usage, not caused by it (Plester *et al.*, 2008). Research by the Nuffield Foundation suggests that texting does not damage children's understanding of written or spoken English because they are able to adapt according to the context. However, there is an association between punctuation errors in texts and the spelling ability of primary school children. Those who make fewer punctuation errors when texting tend to be better at spelling and quicker to process writing than those who make more errors in their texts (Smith, 2012). Not everyone agrees. The leading author Sir Terry Pratchett believes that by knocking out half the consonants of our language, texting is restricting children's vocabulary and encourages poor behaviour (Foster, 2012).

A growing number of primary schools around the world are using social media as educational tools. Often their approach focuses on developing the following:

■   positive attitudes to learning;

■   cognitive skills, e.g. identifying patterns, synthesizing ideas, intepreting and evaluating information using wikis;

■   technical know-how, e.g. uploading images, creating usernames, managing a profile;

■   organizational and communication skills, e.g. how to present work to different audiences, setting priorities using to-do lists and other online documents, creating a dialogue with parents and others through the likes of **instant messaging** and Skype;

■   creativity, e.g. publishing ideas in different forms such as slide sharing, **blogs**, audio, animation, comic strips and video;

■   social skills, e.g. team work on a project, peer learning through **social bookmarking**, photosharing or gaming; and

■   appropriate online behaviour, e.g. how to respond to cyberbullying.

Despite these benefits, generally schools have been slow to take up social networking as educational tools. A report by the defunct education body Becta found that only 5 per cent of secondary schools used social networking sites for learning (Greenhough, 2012). However, increasingly schools are seeing the potential to engage learners and are drawing up social networking policies. Typically, these make it clear that school representatives are not to publish any content that may result in actions for defamation, discrimination, breaches of copyright, data protection or other claim for damages. This covers materials that may bring the school into disrepute. It is important for all those who work in schools to know that information they share through social networking applications, even if they are on private spaces, is still subject to copyright, data protection and Freedom of Information legislation, the Safeguarding Vulnerable Groups Act 2006 and other legislation. It is not appropriate to invite pupils under the age of 18 to be a 'friend' to share information with; websites such as Facebook are targeted at older teenagers and adults and have a clear policy not to register younger ones and include systems to report concerns.

The understandable fears relating to social networking should not overshadow its educational potential. The Rose Review (DCSF, 2009) suggested that primary children should be taught about messaging websites, blogs, wikis, webcams and **podcasting**. Mackenzie (2012) argues that there is too much scaremongering about social networking and offers practical advice on how to manage risks. He suggests starting off small with parents and explaining the gains, as well the risks. Social networking has particular potential in strengthening ties with parents. Services such as Scholabo allow schools to create secure, private communities in which teachers can share information with parents and professional colleagues (www.scholabo.com). The environmental savings alone should be noted. An average sized primary school that uses 60,000 sheets of paper per year, just on sending letters home could make significant financial and environmental savings (see http://uk.prweb.com/releases/2011/5/prweb8406739.htm). But social media offers so much more, for instance in terms of its flexibility, participation and creativity.

## ICT, pupils' motivation and attainment

There is considerable evidence to suggest that ICT is making a difference in motivating children, especially in areas such as research, writing, editing, and presentation of work (Passey *et al.*, 2004; Estyn, 2013). The Scottish Inspectorate (2007) report gains in boys' willingness to write, improved perseverance when solving problems and improvements in the readability and presentation of work (HMIe, 2007). Pupils' behaviour is also reported to be better in lessons where ICT is used. Generally, they enjoy lessons more and develop greater independence than in lessons where ICT is not used. Different groups of pupils are reported to be gaining in different ways from the use of ICT including those with special educational needs, disaffected pupils and the more able and talented. In special schools and units, without ICT some children would not be able to communicate with the outside world. They benefit from recognition software and text-to-speech software. Those children who experience dyslexia and dyspraxia can improve academic performance through the use of laptops, voice recognition software and text-to-speech software. Gifted and talented pupils gain particularly from open-ended, problem solving tasks.

Most significantly, there is growing evidence that well-integrated ICT can raise standards. Cox *et al.* (2003) reported positive effects on pupil attainment in almost all national curriculum subjects, notably in the core subjects where there has been greater investment in ICT resources to support learning and teaching. Becta (2009a: 3) highlight gains at all Key Stages, including: equivalent to a term's additional progress in English at Key Stage 2 and 7.5 months' progress for some groups in science through effective use of whiteboards. However, it would be misleading to imply that all learners always benefit from a technology-supported learning experience. Evidence suggests that high-performing girls, for instance, tended to have lower improvement scores while low or underachieving boys showed measurable improvement (Chandra and Lloyd, 2008). Moreover, as Underwood *et al.* (2009) point out, while learners may become motivated by ICT, this does not necessarily lead to improvements in learning if there is a lack of challenge.

There are also methodological difficulties when conducting research in ICT. Simply asking teachers and head teachers how much computers are used, and what difference they make to learning outcomes is not a reliable way of assessing the impact of ICT.

Moreover, it is difficult to establish a direct relationship between ICT use (as cause) and improved performance (as effect) because of the complex nature of teaching, learning and assessment (Rudd, 2000). It should also be noted that schools that use computers a lot are not necessarily more effective than those who do not (Higgins and Packard, 2004).

Nonetheless, there are many case studies of primary and secondary schools that testify to the impact of ICT in developing children's creative and critical thinking (Box 7.4). Primary and secondary schools use laptops to film activities such as making sandwiches and then bluetooth their films for each other to view. Essa Academy (Bolton), for instance, improved GCSE results significantly by personalizing learning through the use of iPod Touch devices (Garner, 2012). Every pupil has their own iPod Touch, which they keep with them day and night. The gadget helps them to do their homework and gives them the opportunity to email their teachers with questions whenever they like. While some tutors set aside a specific time slot to answer pupils' queries, others will fire an answer back within 10 or 15 minutes. The Academy has children from thirty-six language groups. The cost was 7 pence a day over 5 years, with a refresh cost of 18 pence a day. Savings in printing and leasing copiers offset these costs. Such case studies illustrate how cultural changes are often driven from the bottom up rather than determined by government policies.

## PAUSE FOR REFLECTION

At Essa, every pupil is allocated an iPod Touch. In other schools, pupils are encouraged to bring their own devices (BYOD). What are the ethical issues associated with this?

## BOX 7.4  INTERNATIONAL VIEW – THE IMPACT OF ICT ON LEARNING AND TEACHING

A major study of twenty-seven countries reports that effective ICT strategies can improve learning and teaching (STEPs, 2009). In particular, the gains include: learner confidence, motivation, knowledge, creativity, skills, competences and engagement; and teachers' digital competence, access to resources and innovation. The study also reports that teachers generally use ICT well and are optimistic about technologies. However, their knowledge of pedagogy is underdeveloped, assessment remains a challenge and responsibilities can be unclear. Questions persist over the lack of reliable data to measure whether ICT raises standards (Balanskat, 2007; JRC, 2009). A core set of ICT in education indicators has been established by UNESCO (2009) addressing areas such as expenditure on ICT, average number of ICT hours per week and learners-to-computer ratio. It is, however, difficult to isolate a factor such as 'computer use' on student achievement from other variables. Erstad (2005) found in Norwegian schools that the major difference ICT made was in the enlargement of learning space, as students could reach out of the classroom and engage with issues in the wider world.

The extent to which ICT makes a difference to pupils' progress and attainment in school depends on many factors. OFSTED (2009) reports on the characteristics of outstanding lessons using ICT. Aside from general points on meticulous planning, engaging teaching and clear feedback, the inspectorate points out that the best practitioners recognise that the mere presence of a computer is insufficient by itself to sustain motivation. They know, for instance, that pupils' personal ICT equipment is often more appealing than that found in schools.

One of the 'mysteries' of modern education is why technologies have not had the impact once envisaged. Research needs to shed light on the factors that explain why ICT is making a big difference to teaching in some schools but not in others. Clearly, the attitude of teachers towards ICT is a key factor, as with all subjects. When ICT is integrated fully within the learners' experience and not seen as a 'bolt-on', the evidence indicates that it has the greatest impact on academic progress, attitudes, behaviour and motivation (Condie and Munro, 2007).

Although it is foolish to predict the future for technology in education, most experts agree that teaching and learning will become increasingly social and global. It follows that a fast, robust Internet connection is essential as schools (albeit slowly) move towards greater use of cloud computing to set, collect and mark pupils' work. Some educational services, such as Edmodo, already offer this for free (www.edmodo.com). Salman Khan, a former hedge fund analyst, makes remarkable use of educational videos to 'flip the classroom' by inviting pupils to watch videos at home, while doing 'homework' in the classroom with the support of teachers (www.khanacademy.org). The Khan Academy, which has over a million users, aims to provide free, world-class education for anyone, anywhere. It is designed so that peers learn from other peers (as well as teachers) at their own pace and in the comfort of their own environment. Khan believes that technology can humanize education, replacing fear with the joy of learning. As Negroponte (1996: 6) put it, 20 or so years ago: 'Computing is not about computers any more. It is about living.'

## Glossary

**Algorithms** are sets of instructions for achieving goals.

**Blogs** is short for weblogs, which are website diary pages in which individuals express their personal views and experiences.

**Clippings** services such as Clipmarks and Evernote allow users to highlight, clip and save bits of websites in one spot.

**Cloud education** relies on sharing computing resources rather than having local servers or personal devices to handle applications.

**Digital divide** describes the differences between those who have all the necessary resources to participate in current society and those who do not (Eynon, 2009).

**Digital literacy** involves the skills of retrieving, managing, evaluating and presenting electronic information effectively.

**Digital pedagogy** describes the teachers' craft in selecting and using modern technologies to enhance learning.

**E-learning** is electronic learning that uses computers, the Internet and other technologies to deliver part of the curriculum.

**E-safety** describes procedures to protect children and teachers from inappropriate materials, especially on the Internet.

**Globalization** is a process by which the world is becoming increasingly interconnected through trade, technologies and cultural exchange.

**Instant messaging** is a way of using digital text to 'talk' in real time with others, without having to wait for a response.

**Podcasting** refers to creating digital audio media files that are made available for downloading from the Internet, typically available in a series.

**Social media** describes Internet sites where people interact freely, sharing and discussing information about each other and their lives.

**Social bookmarking** is an online service such as Delicious that allows users to add, annotate, edit and share bookmarks of web documents.

**Wikis** allow users to create and edit online content.

## References

Alexander, R. (ed.) (2009) *Children, their World, their Education: Final Report and Recommendations of the Cambridge Primary Review*, London: Routledge.

Alliance for Childhood (2004) *Tech Tonic: Towards a New Literacy of Technology*, Alliance for Childhood: College Park, MD.

Balanskat, A. (2007) 'Comparative international evidence on the impact of digital technologies on learning outcomes: empirical studies'. Paper submitted to the OECD-Keris expert meeting, South Korea, 16–19 October 2007.

Barron, I. and Curnow, R. (1979) *The Future with Microelectronics: Forecasting the Effects of Information Technology*, New York: F. Pinter.

Barter, C., McCarry, M., Berridge, D. and Evans, K. (2009) *Partner Exploitation and Violence in Teenage Intimate Relationships*, London: NSPCC.

Bartlett, J. and Miller, C. (2011) *Truth, Lies and the Internet: A Report into Young People's Digital Fluency*, London: Demos.

BCS and Royal Academy of Engineering (2012) *Draft ICT Programme of Study*, available at http://academy.bcs.org/content/draft-ict-programme-study (accessed 5 April 2013).

Beauchamp, G. (2012) *ICT in the Primary School*, Harlow: Pearson.

Beauchamp, G. and Parkinson, J. (2005) 'Beyond the "wow" factor:developing interactivity with the interactive whiteboard', *School Science Review*, 86(316): 97–104.

Becta (2004) *A Review of the Research Literature on Barriers to the Uptake of ICT by Teachers*, Coventry: Becta.

Becta (2005) *Already at a Disadvantage? ICT in the Home and Children's Preparation for Primary School*, Coventry: Becta.

Becta (2008) *Web 2.0 Technologies for Learning at KS3 and KS4: Learners' Use of Web 2.0 Technologies in and out of School*, Coventry: Becta.

Becta (2009a) *Primary RE with ICT: A Pupil's Entitlement to ICT in Primary RE*, Coventry: Becta.

Becta (2009b) *Primary Music with ICT: A Pupil's Entitlement to ICT in Primary Music*, Coventry: Becta.

Becta (2009c) *The Impact of Digital Technology: A Review of the Evidence of the Impact of Digital Technologies on Formal Education*, Coventry: Becta.

Beetham, H. and Sharpe, R. (2007) *Rethinking Pedagogy for a Digital Age: Designing and Delivering E-Learning*, Abingdon: Routledge.

BESA (2012) *The Future of Tablets and Apps in Schools*, London: BESA.

Bigum, C. (2003) *Knowledge Producing Schools*, Geelong, Australia: Deakin University.

Bloom, A. (2012) 'Flourishing faith in Google for fast facts', *Times Educational Supplement*, 11 May.

Bloxham, A. (2010) 'Social networking: Teachers blame Facebook and Twitter for pupils' poor grades', *The Telegraph*, 16 November.

Buckingham. D. (2007) *Beyond Technology*, Cambridge: Polity Press.

Burden, K., Hopkins, P., Male, T., Martin, S. and Tralai, C. (2012) *iPad Scotland Evaluation*, Hull: University of Hull.

Byron, T. (2008) *Safer Children in a Digital World*, London: DCSF/DCMS.

Chandra, V. and Lloyd, M. (2008) 'The methodological nettle: ICT and student achievement', *British Journal of Educational Technology*, 39: 1087–98.

Churches, A. (2008) *Bloom's Digital Taxonomy*, available at: http://edorigami.wikispaces.com/Bloom%27s+Digital+Taxonomy (accessed 15 September 2013).

Common Sense Media (2011) *Digital Literacy and Citizenship in the 21st Century*, San Francisco, CA: Common Sense Media.

Condie, R. and Munro, B. (2007) *The Impact of ICT in Schools: A Landscape Review*, Coventry: Becta.

Cordes, C. and Miller, E. (eds) (2000) *Fool's Gold: A Critical Look at Computers in Childhood*, College Park, MD: Alliance for Childhood.

Cox, M., Webb, M. and Abbott, C. (2003) *ICT and Pedagogy: A Review of the Research Literature*, London: DfES and Becta.

DCSF (2009) *Independent Review of the Primary Curriculum: Final Report*, London: DCSF.

DfE (2013) *Newly Qualified Teachers: Annual Survey 2013*, London: DfE.

Dustin, H. (2012) 'Sex education can help tackle the abuse of girls. So will the Tories commit to it?', *The Guardian*, 5 October.

Erstad, O. (2005) 'Expanding possibilities: Project work using ICT', *Human Technology*, 1(2): 216–45.

Estyn (2013) *The Impact of ICT on Pupils' Learning in Primary Schools*, Cardiff: Estyn.

ETI (2006) *Information and Communication Technology in Primary Schools*, Bangor: Crown.

European Commission (2013) 'The "teacher effect" on the use of ICT in the classroom', *European Schoolnet Observatory*, Briefing Paper, Issue 1, April, 1–4.

Evans, D. (2012) 'The PC is dead, long live the iPad', *Times Educational Supplement*, 12 October, 4–7.

Eynon, R. (2009) 'Mapping the digital divide in Britain: implications for learning and education', *Learning, Media and Technology*, 34, 277–90.

Facer, K. (2011) *Learning Futures*, London: Routledge.

Foster, A. (2012) 'Texts and Twitter make children behave badly, says Sir Terry Pratchett', *London Evening Standard*, 2 May.

Garner, R. (2012) 'The school where every teacher has an iPad . . . and every student has an iPod', *The Independent*, 20 March.

Green, H. and Hannon, C. (2007) *Their Space: Education for a Digital Age*, London: Demos.

Greenhough, J. (2012) 'Book burning', *Times Educational Supplement*, 1 June.

Grey, D. (2005) *Grey's Essential Miscellany for Teachers*, London: Continuum.

Hennessy, S. and London, L. (2013) *Learning from International Experiences with Interactive Whiteboards: The Role of Professional Development in Integrating the Technology*, OECD Education Working Papers, No. 89, Paris: OECD Publishing.

Higgins, S. and Packard, N. (2004) *Meeting the Standards in Primary ICT*, London: Routledge.

HMI (1985) *The Curriculum from 5 to 16*, London: HMSO.

HMIe (2007) *Improving Scottish Education, ICT in Learning and Teaching*, Livingston: HMIe.

Holloway, D., Green, L. and Livingstone, S. (2013) *Zero to Eight, Young Children and their Internet Use*, London: LSE.

Horton, W. and Horton, K. (2003) *E-Learning Tools and Technologies: A Consumer's Guide for Trainers, Teachers, Educators, and Instructional Designers*, San Francisco, CA: John Wiley & Sons.

Ingram, J. (2000) *Digital Intelligence: The Psychology of Computer Learning and Literacy*, Chicago, IL: Shrew Interactive Multimedia.

JRC (2009) *Assessing the Effects of ICT in Education*, Luxembourg: European Union/OECD.

Lancashire County Council (2013) *Primary eSafety Guidance Document*, available at www.lancsngfl.ac.uk/esafety (accessed 5 April 2013).

Leask, M. and Meadows, J. (2000) *Teaching and Learning with ICT in the Primary School*, London: RoutledgeFalmer.

Lichy, J. (2011) 'Internet user behaviour in France and Britain: Exploring socio-spatial disparity among adolescents', *International Journal of Consumer Studies*, 35: 470–75.

Lichy, J. (2012) 'Towards an international culture: Gen Y students and SNS?', *Active Learning in Higher Education*, 13(2): 101–16.

Livingstone, I. and Hope, A. (2011) *Next Gen*, London: Nesta.

Livingstone, S., Haddon, L., Görzig, A. and Ólafsson, K. (2011) *EU Kids Online II: Final Report*, LSE, London: EU Kids Online, available at: http://eprints.lse.ac.uk/39351 (accessed 15 April 2013).

Loveless, A. and Dore, B. (2002) *ICT in the Primary School*, Maidenhead: Open University Press.

MacKenzie, A. (2012) 'Don't let e-safety worries be a barrier to using social media in school', *The Guardian*, 26 July.

Mintz, A.P. (2002) *Web of Deception: Misinformation on the Internet*, Medford, NJ: CyberAge Books.

Monk, C. (2012) 'ICT teachers need to focus on the teaching, not on the ICT', *The Guardian*, 11 April.

Murphy, C. (2003) *Literature Review in Primary Science and ICT*, Bristol: Futurelab.

Negroponte, N. (1996) *Being Digital*, New York: Vintage Books.

Ofcom (2012) *Children and Parents: Media Use and Attitudes Report*, London: Ofcom.

OFSTED (2009) *The Importance of ICT: Information and Communication Technology in Primary and Secondary Schools, 2005/2008*, London: OFSTED.

OFSTED (2011) *ICT in schools 2008–11*, London: OFSTED.

Passey, D., Rogers, C., Machell, J. and McHugh, G. (2004) *The Motivational Effect of ICT on Pupils*, London: DfES.

Patel, R. (2013) 'The times, are they changing?', *Britain in 2014*, London: The Economic and Social Research Council, 91–3.

Pelling, R. (2012) 'How technology is taking hold of our children's lives', *The Telegraph*, 22 May.

Plester, B., Wood, C. and Bell, V. (2008) 'Txt msg n school literacy: Does texting and knowledge of text abbreviations adversely affect children's literacy attainment?' *Literacy*, 42: 137–144.

Plowman L, McPake, J., Stephen C. (2010a) 'The technologisation of childhood? Young children and technology in the home', *Children and Society*, 24 (1) 63–74.

Plowman, L., Stephen, C. and McPake, J. (2010b) *Growing Up with Technology*, London: Routledge.

Poore, M. (2013) *Using Social Media in the Classroom*, London: Sage.

Roberts, L. and Wallop, H. (2010) 'Silver surfers increase by one million over the last year', *The Telegraph*, 30 June.

Roseby, P. (2010) *Dictionary of Computing*, London: A&C Black.

Rudd, P. (2000) *School Improvement through ICT: Limitations and Possibilities*, NFER, Paper presented at European Conference on Educational Research (ECER) University of Edinburgh, 22 September 2000, available at: www.leeds.ac.uk/educol/documents/00001768.htm (accessed 15 February 2012).

Sanghani, R. (2013) '"iTods" on the rise as 50 per cent of UK toddlers use tablets', *The Telegraph*, 16 October.

Selwyn, N. (2013) *Education in a Digital World*, London: Routledge.

Siemens, G. (2005) 'Connectivism: A learning theory for the digital age', *International Journal of Instructional Technology and Distance Learning*, 2(1), available at: www.itdl.org/Journal/Jan_05/article01.htm (accessed 15 February 2012).

Sigman, A. (2012) 'The impact of screen media on children: A Eurovision for Parliament', in Clouder, C. *et al.* (eds) *Improving the Quality of Childhood in Europe 2012*, Volume 3: *European Parliament Working Group on the Quality of Childhood in the European Union*, Brighton: ECSWE, 88–121.

Simpson, D. and Toyn, M. (2011) *Primary ICT across the Curriculum*, Exeter: Learning Matters.

Smith, H. (1999) *Opportunities for Information and Communication Technology in the Primary School*, Stoke-on-Trent: Trentham Books.

Smith, H. (2001) *Smartboard Evaluation: Final Report*, available at: www.kented.org.uk/ngfl/whiteboards (accessed 20 January 2011).

Smith, H., Higgins, S., Wall, K. and Miller, J. (2005) 'Interactive whiteboards: Boon or bandwagon? A critical review of the literature', *Journal of Computer Assisted Learning*, 21: 91–101.

Smith, R. (2012) 'Text speak does not affect children's use of grammar: study', *The Telegraph*, 5 September.

STEPS (2009) *Study of the Impact of Technology in Primary School*, European Commission, available at: http://insight.eun.org/ww/en/pub/insight/minisites/steps.htm (accessed 17 April 2003).

Stewart, W. (2012) 'A basic approach to programming', *Times Educational Supplement*, 9 March.

Straker, A. (1989) *Children Using Computers*, Oxford: Blackwell.

Syscap (2013) *Report into Changes in Numbers and Quality of School-Owned PCs & Laptops*, Ascot: E-Learning Foundation.

The Royal Society (2012) *Shut Down or Restart? The Way Forward for Computing in UK Schools*, London: Royal Society.

Underwood, J., Baguley, T., Banyard, P., Dillon, G., Farrington-Flint, L. and Hayes, M. (2009) *Impact 2008*, Coventry: Becta.

UNESCO (2009) *Guide to Measuring Information and Communication Technologies in Education*, Montreal: UNESCO.

Ward, H. (2011) 'By the numbers. Use of ICT', *Times Educational Supplement*, 30 September.

Wartella, E.A. and Jennings, N. (2000) 'Children and computers: New technology – old concerns', *The Future of Children: Children and Computer Technology*, 10(2): 31–43.

Younie, S. and Leask, M. (2013) *Teaching with Technologies*, Maidenhead: Open University Press.

## Websites

E-learning Foundation is a charity that seeks to support schools and families so that all children have access to learning technologies – www.e-learningfoundation.com

Futurelab website provides research news and publications – www2.futurelab.org.uk

Hwb, the all-Wales learning platform, provides resources for Welsh schools – https://hwb.wales.gov.uk

The Glow intranet hosted by Education Scotland provides resources for Scottish schools – www.glowscotland.org.uk

Information about Fronter, the developing ICT platform for schools in Northern Ireland – www.nicurriculum.org.uk

Code Club is a nationwide network of volunteers who run after-school computer programming classes for 9–11 year olds – www.codeclub.org.uk

Creative Blogs is the UK's leading supplier of WordPress Multisites blogs for schools – http://creativeblogs.net

iPads in Education explores the use of iPads and e-books in schools and colleges – ipadeducators.ning.com

# 8

# The broader curriculum

## Exploring the humanities and arts

## Chapter objectives

By the end of this chapter you should be able to:

- Explain the distinctive nature of the humanities and arts.
- Argue the case for the contribution of the humanities and arts to children's all-round development.
- Identify the characteristics of best practice in teaching a broad and balanced curriculum.

*We want all schools to be able to offer their pupils a rich and exciting curriculum, in which every subject is taught outstandingly well.*

*(DfES, 2003: 5)*

## Introduction

Is it possible for a single teacher to teach every subject in the primary curriculum outstandingly well? This is particularly challenging with regard to the **foundation subjects**, which have always competed for limited resources and timetable space. As recent curriculum reviews (Rose, 2008; Alexander, 2009) in England have highlighted, there are challenges in providing a 'broad and balanced' curriculum as required by the Education Act (1988). The provision of a two-tier primary curriculum, comprising the undoubtedly essential basics and 'the rest', has a long tradition. It is not only a matter of the number of subjects crammed into the curriculum, but providing stimulating and challenging learning in each subject. As this chapter will show, inspection reports frequently comment on substandard teaching in the humanities and arts. The aspiration for high standards should not be confined to the basics of literacy and numeracy. This chapter points out best practice and challenges in achieving high standards and outstanding teaching across the curriculum.

## The nature of the humanities (history, geography and RE)

In primary schools, the humanities normally embrace history, geography and religious education (Hoodless et al., 2003; Grigg and Hughes, 2013). These are people-centred subjects that focus on the human condition. The essence of the humanities can be illustrated through stories of individuals, events and places. For instance, the lives of Britain's super centenarians (who have lived more than a 100 years) illuminate huge changes in society over a comparatively short time, such as: the rise in technologies, the growth of a consumer society and materialistic values, Christianity's decline, globalization, multiculturalism and the spread of democracy. In 2004, the meeting between Harry Patch (1898–2009) and Charles Kuentz (1897–2005), the last British and German veterans of the World War One trenches, raised fundamental questions about a sense of place, memory, friendship, beliefs, endurance, sacrifice and forgiveness – all central to the humanities. By interviewing their own elderly ones in the local community, children can gain insight into the building blocks of the humanities; such fundamental concepts as change, progress, empathy, power, chronology, place, time, similarity and difference, conflict and consensus, belief, faith and forgiveness.

One of the arguments for planning and teaching history, geography and RE under the humanities umbrella is that they share common elements of learning such as skills in questioning, locating and interpreting sources (Taba, 1962; Hoodless et al., 2003). Enquiry skills run through OFSTED's (2012a) grade descriptors for outstanding teaching in history, geography and RE (Table 8.1).

There are teaching approaches and resources common to history, geography and RE in the use of stories, visits, visitors, artefacts, photographs, group discussion over ethical issues, and locality studies (Box 8.1).

Well-conducted **enquiry-based learning** can stimulate and enthuse pupils' interests as they see the relevance of what they are doing. In one case study of good practice, Year 6 children explored a unit on Climate Change that included strong links with the Glaciology Department at Newcastle University. This resulted in visits to the school by Master's students to present their findings from field trips to Icelandic glaciers and visits by pupils to the university to conduct experiments. The class was introduced to the challenging complexities of glacial movement, the impact of climate change on the Arctic icecap and the wider environment (OFSTED, 2012d). Links with university departments, secondary schools and local organizations are important means of extending pupils' subject knowledge and understanding.

Questioning skills are particularly important although Carter (1998: 155) warns that these should not be overused; as one pupil reportedly advised a newcomer to the class: 'Don't look at anything in the room or she'll ask you a question about it!' Moreover, although most enquiries begin with questions there may be alternative approaches, such as airing a controversial point of view, that prove equally fruitful. There is also the danger of children appearing to be engaged in enquiry learning whereas they are in fact trying to answer questions set by teachers with very little commitment to their personal enquiries (Johnston et al., 2002).

In Scotland's *Curriculum for Excellence* the Social Studies component is organized around three elements:

**TABLE 8.1** Grade descriptors for outstanding teaching in the humanities

| Subject | Quality of teaching |
| --- | --- |
| History | ■ Teachers' practice is informed by excellent knowledge and application of continuing developments in teaching and learning in history<br>■ Learning is rooted in enquiry and teachers routinely promote rigorous historical thinking<br>■ Teachers communicate their passion for history and consistently challenge and inspire pupils to produce the best work they can<br>■ History is very skilfully presented as a dynamic subject to be explored and investigated rather than as a subject to be received, as a result, pupils approach historical enquiries as keen and skilled investigators<br>■ Teachers continuously refine their practice to ensure that teaching promotes excellent progress in history for all groups of pupils<br>■ Teaching makes pupils alive to changing views of the past and helps them to understand how and why interpretations and representations change over time, why history matters and why the particular topics they are taught are worth knowing about<br>■ Teaching ensures that pupils are able to make use of their prior learning in moving their historical understanding forward, as a result, lessons are exciting and often innovative with historical rigour at their core |
| Geography | ■ Communicate enthusiasm and passion about geography to pupils<br>■ Have high expectations and a high level of confidence and expertise both in terms of their specialist and up-to-date knowledge and their understanding of effective learning in the subject<br>■ Use a wide range of innovative and imaginative teaching strategies very effectively to stimulate pupils' active participation in their learning and secure outstanding progress across all aspects of the subject<br>■ Very good use is made of the outside environment and fieldwork to support learning<br>■ Lessons are carefully structured and a range of innovative resources is used regularly and very effectively, with very good use made of multi-media to explore a wide range of geographical issues at a range of scales<br>■ Effective use of a wide range of types of maps is commonplace<br>■ Very effective use is made of ICT and Geographical Information Systems (where relevant) to promote learning and enable pupils to use data and information sources to search and select, organize and investigate and refine and present information skilfully and independently |
| RE | ■ Communicate high expectations, enthusiasm and passion about RE to pupils<br>■ Ensure pupils have a clear grasp of the purpose and direction of their learning<br>■ Strong subject expertise both in terms of specialist knowledge and an understanding of effective learning in RE<br>■ Excellent use of a very wide range of engaging and imaginative resources and teaching strategies to stimulate pupils' active participation in their learning<br>■ Questioning and activities challenge pupils to explore beyond the surface and engage with the deeper meaning and significance of religion and belief<br>■ Encourage pupils to ask their own questions about issues arising from their study, becoming critical enquirers into the world of religion and belief and their personal reflections on issues of meaning and purpose<br>■ Consistently plan and deliver RE very effectively to enable pupils to forge strong links between their study of religion and belief and their personal reflections on issues of meaning and purpose<br>■ Develops pupils' skills of enquiry and reasoned argument effectively<br>■ Assessment and marking engage pupils in dialogue about their progress with the result that pupils know how to extend their understanding and skills<br>■ Planning is skilfully adjusted to meet the pupils' diverse needs |

Source: OFSTED (2012a)

---

**BOX 8.1 FOCUS ON PRACTICE**

During her final school experience, Megan worked with a Year 6 class on a study of a local street. The children devised questions to research and discussed what they wanted to find out. Here are some of the questions the children agreed upon:

■ Where did the street name come from?

■ How has the street changed since it was first named?

■ Which shop sells most goods?

■ How long have the shops been here?

■ Which is the oldest/newest building?

■ When was the church built?

■ Who goes to church?

■ Which is the busiest time for shoppers?

■ Who will do what in our project?

■ How should we tell others about our work?

They sketched out a mental map of the street, which gave Megan an idea of each child's spatial awareness. During the visits, the pupils divided into groups with adult supervision and worked on different tasks; for instance, taking photographs of the buildings and street furniture, interviewing shoppers and annotating maps. As the project unfolded, the pupils looked at a census return for 1901 to see who lived in the street along with trade directories obtained from the local library. They also looked at changes by comparing maps from the 1890s, 1920s, 1960s and today. They practised their mathematical skills by drawing graphs and interpreting their data using the computer.

---

1   people, past events and societies;

2   people, place and environment; and

3   people in society, economy and business.

These are said to recognize the 'special contribution made by each of the social subjects, while enabling them to reflect local contexts'. However, teachers are not bound by these and are encouraged to plan lessons across the curriculum. Religious and Moral Education feature as experiences in which pupils are to learn about Christianity and other world religions, as well as undertake aspects of philosophical enquiry. In Northern Ireland, geography and history are taught as strands in an integrated approach alongside science and technology (CCEA, 2007). This is roughly in line with Blyth's (1990) suggestion that there are three perspectives constituting the humanities, namely historical, geographical and social science.

One of the common challenges in the humanities is teaching children about the need to be cautious when making judgements. Where appropriate, provisional language should be used when describing beliefs, events, peoples and places: for example, '*many* Jews celebrate Shabbat in this manner' or '*some* Victorian teachers were cruel'. Older children should be encouraged to consider counterfactual arguments, again using language such as 'On the other hand . . .', 'However . . .' and 'This is one view, but another is that . . .'.

## Best practice in the humanities

### History

Outstanding teachers of history know that the subject is about people of *all* backgrounds rather than confined to the rich and famous. They avoid a 'top down' approach that tends to exclude women, children and minority groups (Claire, 1996). They are aware of the sensitivities associated with history and the need to develop an open-minded attitude to the past. It is important for learners to gain a sense of how history is 'created' and the use of television programmes, films, re-enactments, visitors and visits can assist in this regard.

Good 'content' starting points for young children are their own personal life stories, family history, changes in the history of the school and immediate locality and stories about famous people and events. The popularity of personal and family history has been heightened on the back of long-running series such as *Who Do You Think You Are?* (BBC, since 2004). Sensitively handled, children can gain considerably from exploring artefacts that belonged to older relatives and asking questions about the lives of those pictured in family albums. One group of postgraduate trainees were asked to plan a history-based project on 'Names' and their suggestions included the following: origins of personal names, surnames, village names (-ton, -wick, -by), street names, pub names, funny names, nicknames, titles, names on gravestones, unnamed soldier, names of peoples and regions (e.g. Saxons, Sussex and Essex), origin of the name England, names of counties, names of towns twinned in Europe, lost names, and longest place-names.

Cooper (2000) suggests that young children can be encouraged to reason about historical sources provided that they have a good structure, for instance by asking three questions:

1   What do you know for certain about this?
2   What can you guess?
3   What would you like to know?

Central to successful history teaching is the development of pupils' enquiry skills, such as observing, questioning and reaching informed conclusions. This is at the heart of the Nuffield Primary History Project (Fines and Nichol, 1997: 3) notion of 'doing history', which is based on five steps:

1   decide on an area of study;
2   frame a key question;
3   find sources to answer the question;

4    ask new subsidiary questions in relation to the key question; and

5    extract, record, analyse, sort and synthesize information to answer the question.

In this regard, teachers testify that the use of evidence bags is an introductory strategy that works well with all ages. A number of objects are placed inside a suitcase or old bag belonging to a real or imaginary person. Working in small groups, the children are challenged to work as detectives to find out what they can from the evidence about the person. Initially the contents of a handbag can be used to develop skills in observation, discussion and reasoning, inferring, questioning and reaching informed conclusions. Table 8.2 shows the responses of a Year 4 class working with a trainee teacher.

There are many variations on this exercise. The trainee featured in Table 8.2 developed this initial idea to consider suitcase evidence that survives for evacuees in the Second World War. She collected a ration book, newspaper cuttings, a diary extract, photographs and an undated map. Another trainee, working with a Year 2 class, brought in objects that she had found in her attic linked to Jane Hissey's story *Old Bear* (Random House, 1993). Artefacts can be taken from different generations, such as parents and grandparents, included to represent a particular time or event in the past. There is also scope for promoting religious and geographical education, for instance by including artefacts for a particular faith or location.

From evidence bags, teachers can introduce children to the work of museum curators and archaeologists. Over recent decades, archaeology has been popularized by the likes of Indiana Jones and other fictional characters and television series such as *Time Team* (Channel 4, 1991–2012). There are frequent newspaper stories, websites and publications reporting new archaeological findings that can be used to stimulate children's curiosity. Ochota (2013) describes eighty of *Britain's Secret Treasures* from the 900,000 finds that are logged on the national Portable Antiquities Scheme. Many of the objects, such as gold coins, axe heads and a witches' bottle, were found by ordinary members of the public going about their everyday lives, walking the dog, digging the garden, farming, building or going on a school visit. Metal detector users unearthed the others intentionally. Organizations such as the Council for British Archaeology (http://new.archaeologyuk.

**TABLE 8.2** Use of a trainee's handbag to introduce historical skills

| Key question: What do we know about the owner? | | |
| Name of the object | What this tells us, e.g. | Our questions |
| --- | --- | --- |
| Purse | Owner is female, where she shops, bank information on credit cards | How old is she? |
| Driving licence | Name of the owner, where she lives | Does she live in a smart house? |
| Car key | Drives a car | Is it her car? |
| Hairbrush | She has blond hair | How tall is the lady? |
| Mirror, lipstick | She cares about her appearance | How much does she spend on make-up? |
| Photograph of two children | She has a family. They look like the person on the driving licence | Are these her daughters? |
| Bottle of mineral water and a cereal bar | She is healthy | What does she weigh? |
| Mobile phone | Who her friends are | Is she a good friend? |

org) and the Young Archaeologist's Club (www.yac-uk.org) are useful contacts for schools.

The relative importance of dates in history lessons has been long debated. Cooper (2006: 35) warns of over-reliance on chronological frameworks such as timelines at the expense of historical enquiries and of the danger of falling back to 'lists of dates' in history lessons. In contrast, the Coalition Government's present national curriculum is strong on the narrative tradition. Inspection reports show that many primary children lack awareness of intervals between the periods they study and the ability to relate what they had learned in one topic to what they discover in another (OFSTED, 2011a). While the progressive use of temporal language in history lessons has merit, it is worth noting that expressions such as 'a long time ago' have very wide meanings for young children – from a few years to billions of years ago (Hodkinson, 2003). Labels, dates and visual prompts can be used to reinforce children's sense of time and chronology. Lomas (1993) discusses the problems and possible solutions in teaching time concepts in school, noting the value of sequencing exercises, family trees, timelines, clock faces, questioning, research tasks and discussions over turning-points in history.

Perhaps the most challenging area to teach is historical interpretations. Historians make inferences or 'best guesses' from the available evidence, but these can differ; for instance, four post-holes in the centre of an Iron Age house plan may be support for the roof, part of a fence to surround animals or a free-standing tower to repair a roof (Cooper, 2000). Anniversaries are reminders of how the past can be interpreted in different ways. Infants are able to make simple deductions and inferences, for instance from studying portraits of Queen Victoria and Elizabeth I (Cooper, 1995). Outstanding practitioners begin to discuss interpretations by using incidents in children's lives, such as a playground squabble that is retold from different points of view. They progress to showing learners a range of modern-day representations of the past, such as films, historical fiction, museum exhibitions, artists' illustrations, and cartoons. YouTube provides a wealth of newsreel, movie extracts and old television commercials. Sometimes popular historical representations are criticized for misleading young people and the general public, such as the 'Blackadder' depiction of the First World War's futility, during the centenary of the war's outbreak (Jeffries, 2014).

History lessons then are excellent contexts for developing thinking skills, such as recognizing that there are different versions of stories (Fines and Nichol, 1997; Wallace, 2003; Hoodless, 2008).

To show that history is relevant and meaningful, many teachers take advantage of anniversaries. These can be intoduced as short five-minute talking points or form the basis for homework or extended investigation. In 2014, as part of the First World War centenary commemorations, the Premier League agreed to donate an artificial football pitch to the Belgian city of Ypres. The Premier League has also been running a Christmas Truce Tournament since 2011, bringing together Under 12 teams from England, Belgium, France and Germany. The prominence of history in television schedules is also a good discussion point. For instance Richard Ernest, a businessman who appeared on the popular entrepreneurial *Dragon's Den* programme (BBC2, since 2005), has created nostalgic pop-up rooms used by doctors to treat early signs of dementia. These Reminiscence Pods (RemPods) engage patients' long-term memory as they recall familiar objects from the 1950s or 1970s, providing much-needed comfort (Reilly, 2013).

## Geography

Of all the curriculum subjects, geography has suffered most from a lack of support, poor teaching and leadership. There are longstanding reports of 'superficial', 'disappointing' and 'inconsistent' teaching in the subject (DES, 1978; HMI, 1989; Walford, 2001; OFSTED, 2011b). In England, geography is more or less disappearing in one in ten primary schools (OFSTED, 2011b). The reasons for the decline are familiar to geography educators: weak teachers' knowledge, insufficient time, blurring of subject content in thematic approaches, lack of quality training and subject leadership. The position of geography is scandalous, given its uniqueness in satisfying children's curiosity about contemporary issues, people and places. Wiegand (1993: 1) put it succinctly: 'Geography is good for you.'

But there is hope. In the same OFSTED (2011b) survey that warns of the loss of geography, provision is outstanding in over a quarter of schools. Here, pupils do well because teachers provide a good range of practical activities to develop their fieldwork and other skills. They have opportunities to debate real issues and are enthused by the regular use of maps, aerial photographs, atlases, charts, diagrams and technologies. Through its website and publications, OFSTED provides case studies of outstanding practice that are useful reference points. These cameos range from a Reception class 'flying' to a Mexican village in a structured play session, comparing what they saw with their own town, to a Year 5 class exploring a treasure map based on a map of the London underground (OFSTED, 2011b). However, the quality of pupils' experience of school geography should not be left to chance. If the standards of geography are to improve, then the following actions are needed:

- the value of geography needs to be fully understood;
- leaders need to further share best practice both *within* and across schools; and
- teachers need support and professional development to improve their expertise.

Optimism is also to be found in the sterling efforts of the Geographical Association. Its comprehensive website offers: guidance for subject leaders, research links, news about projects, teaching tips, cross-curricular materials and updates on the curriculum for teachers throughout the UK (www.geography.org.uk).

The basic content for geography teaching revolves around three interrelated dimensions: environment, place and space (Wiegand, 1993; Carter, 1998). The National Curriculum in England has a strong focus on locational and place knowledge and is specific on what pupils are expected to know; for instance, by the end of Key Stage 1 they should name and locate the world's seven continents and five oceans while 11-year-olds should: 'identify the position and significance of latitude, longitude, Equator, Northern Hemisphere, Southern Hemisphere, the Tropics of Cancer and Capricorn, Arctic and Antarctic Circle, the Prime/Greenwich Meridian and time zones' (DfE, 2013, 199–200). Pupils need to develop their knowledge and understanding of different environments and landscapes, recognizing that there are disagreements over how these are best managed, sustained and improved. They also need to be taught about the distinctiveness of their localities and the diversity of experiences among peoples from around the world. Promoting a deeper understanding of people and places, and the management of an increasingly fragile environment, should be a priority for schools.

Children's understanding of place is obviously influenced by their first-hand experiences as they play, explore and travel around. But they can also benefit from indirect experiences, for instance by seeing webcam images of contrasting localities. Bale (1987) used the term 'private geographies' to describe these emerging ideas. Teachers have an important role to play in exposing children to a wide range of varied places by drawing upon their holiday experiences and highlighting places mentioned in local, national and international news. Asking questions such as 'What is the . . . coldest, hottest, loneliest, highest, busiest, whitest, most colourful, or scariest place in the world?' can spark interest. It is the systematic observation and analysis of places that sets geography apart from other subjects. Pupils should be encouraged to think about the physical and human features that give a place its character and identity.

Geography has direct relevance to pupils' lives because it is concerned with their immediate environments, and helps them to interpret information about peoples and places from around the world. The importance of making geography real to children has been highlighted over many years. Gagg (1951), for instance, put together an impressive list of suggestions: letter writing; making models; starting collections of things like shop packets, tins, labels, postmarks, materials, advertisements, and crops; outside journeys to factories, railway stations, farms, countryside, shops; local observations and records such as traffic census and weather records; use of pictures, charts, maps and reference books; visitors to the classroom, particularly 'foreigners or those who have travelled abroad!' (Gagg, 1951:159). Almost all news stories have a geographical element and teachers should regularly use current affairs to make geography meaningful and relevant. The Royal Geographical Society and National Geographic websites and publications provide reliable, up-to-date and balanced news reports on matters such as changing climatic patterns and global warming. It is worth keeping in mind the positive side of environmental change, for instance in redevelopment of waste land into natural habitats to encourage the return of endangered species (Catling and Willy, 2009). Moreover, planning for environmental education needs to ensure the development of 'personal *concern* for the environment, and the taking of personal *action* in and on behalf of the environment' (Palmer and Neal, 1994: 38).

Perhaps the most important feature of geography is fieldwork. Good planning should ensure that fieldwork and other types of enquiry-based work are regular and important elements of children's experiences (Estyn, 2000). Children enter school with very different experiences of the world. For some children, a walk around a local lake will be a new experience while for others who regularly travel around the country or world a day's walking in a remote and hilly place may be physically challenging and enjoyable (Halocha, 1998). Well-organized walks to places such as a park, garden, shopping precinct, river, beach, high street or fire station can be an ideal context for practising geographical and other skills, such as use of number, as well as developing location knowledge. There are well-established organisations and charities that provide excellent educational sites and support resources for cross-curricular teaching, including: the National Trust, Cadw, English Heritage, Natural England, Historic Scotland, the Wildfowl and Wetlands Trust, Oxfam, the Forestry Commission, the Royal Society for the Protection of Birds and Natural England.

The best practitioners enliven geography teaching through the use of varied and interesting sources such as aerial photographs, plans, rock samples, postcards, newspapers, census materials, sketches and maps of different scales. They also use a range of resources including mobile technologies (M-learning), globes, reference books, models, play mats, wall charts, locality packs, television programmes and websites. As Catling and Willy (2009) point out, whether using sophisticated resources such as geographical information systems (GIS) or the very basic, such as a piece of string and a story book, the aim is to stimulate interest in geography in a creative and open-minded way. The Geographical Association provides an excellent introduction to using GIS systems and other resources. The school grounds can be used as part of the locality study by marking outline maps on the ground, creating sensory trails, setting up a weathervane on a roof, and compass signs on walls. The physical layout of the school and the flow of human traffic can be useful starting points to discuss simple spatial patterns and relationships (HMI, 1986). Through their enquiries, pupils should learn how to formulate questions, collect information in different ways, make decisions, and develop fieldwork skills such as observing, measuring and recording (Box 8.2).

Given the lamentable state of geography in schools, there is a professional duty among all teachers to inject passion into geography lessons. Scoffham (2013) provides guidance on how the subject can be taught creatively, including the use of:

- geographical jokes (e.g. 'what's the fastest country in the world? Russia');
- dingbats (picture puzzles);
- riddles and limericks (e.g. There was an old man of Peru . . .');

---

### BOX 8.2  KEY GEOGRAPHICAL QUESTIONS

#### Places

Where is this place?
What is this place like?
Why is this place as it is?
How is this place connected to other places?
How is this place changing?
What would it feel like to be in this place? (emotional mapping)
How is this place similar/different to?
Do many people visit this place?
How do people use this place?
Has it been modified?

#### Local/global issues

What has happened and where?
Why and how has it happened?
What are the different views?
What action(s) should be taken and by whom?

(After HMI, 1986; Storm, 1989)

- 'guess the flag' games;
- drawing maps from memory;
- monopoly-style board games;
- food, music and artefacts associated with places;
- stories and poems;
- children creating their own photograph packs of the locality; and
- photograph/video games (e.g. 'where is this place?').

## Religious education (RE)

Religious education addresses some of the fundamental questions in life: Where have we come from? Why are we here? What are our responsibilities? What happens after death? In discussing the semantic difficulties associated with the subject, Watson and Thompson (2007: 66) conclude that RE is an 'enquiry into what it means to believe in God and take faith seriously'. The question of whether a teacher of RE is more effective if a believer in God is an interesting one; as the authors add, there is no doubt that a religious (or agnostic) person who is dogmatic and dismissive of others can damage children's sensitivities to religious beliefs and their capacity to think critically.

Most educationalists would argue that teachers can teach RE to a high standard irrespective of their religious affiliation, just as there is no need to be an athlete to teach PE or born in Wales to teach Welsh. However, there is a need to model the kind of enquiry and reflective thinking that lies at the heart of the subject and demonstrate respect for and sensitivity to others. Moreover, teachers need secure subject knowledge and understanding. Yet a report in 2013 by the All Party Parliamentary Group (APPG) on Religious Education found that RE lessons are frequently taught by teachers who lack qualifications in the subject. It also reports that about a half of primary teachers and trainee teachers are not confident in teaching RE and there is wide variation in the quality of initial teacher training (All Party Parliamentary Group on Religious Education, 2013).

Both teachers and pupils have the right to withdraw from RE lessons although in practice few are likely to object to the generally liberal schemes of work taught in primary schools. Daily acts of collective worship are a different matter and should not be confused with RE. Schools are required to conduct daily acts of worship, which should be 'wholly or mainly of a broadly Christian character' unless they have applied and been granted exemption due to their high proportion of children from another religion. In Scotland, non-denominational schools are advised to distinguish between assemblies devised for the purpose of religious observance and assemblies for other purposes such as celebrating success. The form of religious observance is left to the discretion of schools and local authorities. Schools can use the term 'Time for Reflection' if preferred (Scottish Government, 2011).

**PAUSE FOR REFLECTION**

To what extent do you think that religious faith is an asset when teaching RE?

Under the terms of the 1944 Education Act local education authorities in England and Wales had the discretion to establish a Standing Advisory Council for Religious Education (SACRE), but this was made mandatory under the 1988 Education Act. These advise the authorities on the agreed syllabus for RE within **foundation and voluntary controlled schools**. In England, schools are also provided with non-statutory guidance for RE (DCSF, 2010) while in Wales there is a national Exemplar Framework (DCELLS, 2008). Legally, agreed syllabi are required to reflect the fact that the religious traditions in Great Britain are in the main Christian while taking into account the teaching and practices of the other principal religions represented in Great Britain. The presentation, style and content of agreed syllabuses vary but they are not to be designed to convert pupils or impress particular religious beliefs upon them. In voluntary aided and foundation schools with a religious character, RE is taught in accordance with the school's trust deeds and guidelines established by the faith community.

The particular circumstances of teaching in faith schools are described on the websites of organizations such as the Church of England, Northern Ireland's Commission for Catholic Education and the Society of Friends (Quakers). The Church of England is the largest single provider of schools in England with more than 4,800 schools. Church schools face the challenge of being both 'distinctive and inclusive' during a period when the Church of England is concerned that government reforms are undermining the position of RE, for example by cutting funding for training specialist teachers (Church of England, 2012).

The fears are partly supported by OFSTED (2013a) who report that children are leaving school with little knowledge or understanding of different religions – standards of RE are poor in six in ten primary schools, the teaching of Christianity is inadequate in a third of primary schools, while it was 'not uncommon' for RE lessons to be 'almost devoid' of religious content. In these lessons, teachers substitute RE for subjects such as healthy living, charity work, visits to old people's homes, pantomimes and literacy work on topics such as 'feelings'.

The agreed syllabi include a strong emphasis upon providing first-hand experiences in visiting places of worship, observing religious ceremonies, handling artefacts, and expressing emotions through dance, drama and singing. If well managed, pupils can gain considerably from visiting places of worship especially if arrangements can be made for a minister to discuss how the building is used, or for ceremonies to be witnessed. One problem with visiting during the school week is that children often see empty buildings and lose the vibrancy associated with many places of worship. Nonetheless, visits afford opportunities for children to study the architecture (e.g. by observing, sketching or photographing), think about how the furniture is used, talk to the guide or worshippers (if present), look at notice boards to gain a sense of what is happening, and sit quietly to take in the atmosphere. Good religious education features time for reflection and stillness. Reflection tools include the use of calming music, candles, pictures, 'Do Not Disturb' signs and circular seating (White, 2000). Davies (2004) reminds us that giving children the opportunity to be still and quiet so that they can reflect on how the building 'speaks' to them is an invaluable experience. Some children may be awe-struck at the architecture of a cathedral, the details of stained-glass windows or carved sculptures. Others may be intimidated by the vastness or coldness of a place of worship that once accommodated hundreds but is now attended by a handful of elderly worshippers. Clearly, places of worship vary considerably. While decline in Christian religion in the United Kingdom is a historical reality, pupils should be encouraged to consider how people's religious beliefs continue to shape their lives; for instance, in conducting acts of charity in helping the poor and in responding to local and international disasters.

The positive contribution that RE frequently makes to pupils' broad personal development and well-being has been reported to be a major strength in three-quarters of primary schools in England (OFSTED, 2007). However, there is a danger when children learn factual information about religions that they are unable to make connections to their personal lives. Teachers need to consider what opportunities they provide children to learn about their own feelings and how they respond to different situations.

Like all subjects, good planning in RE is essential to successful teaching. McCreery *et al.* (2008: 18–20) point out seven key principles to keep in mind:

1   remember the child;

2   start with the particular and help children see connections;

3   look for similarities between children's experience and the specific religious experience;

4   acknowledge difference;

5   draw out themes for Learning from Religion;

6   seek to engage head, heart and hand; and

7   use as many senses as possible.

With these principles in mind, teachers can plan lessons that can stimulate interest in the subject and promote positive attitudes such as respect, critical awareness, appreciation and open-mindedness. But it is quite easy to gloss over these points. If good RE teaching begins where the children are, it is imperative that teachers find out where the children are in their religious understanding in just the same manner as they would for teaching mathematics. While young children may not be able to say whether they are 'Christians' or 'Sikhs', there are things that they are familiar with that will indicate their identity. A display showing photographs from local places of worship, artefacts, pictures of food items and even the children's names can help confirm this. How well do teachers know what children and their parents believe? This does not have to be intrusive if the motive is to help children in their education. Cole and Evans-Lowndes (1991: 48) illustrate the point by citing their experience of being asked about Jehovah's Witness children: 'Why don't *they* celebrate birthdays?', to which they responded: 'Have we ever invited a local elder of the Jehovah's Witness community into our school to explain those beliefs that it is important for us to know about and to help us respond better to their children?' Those teachers who have done so have been greatly helped by such discussions. The use of visiting speakers is an example of how the subject has moved conceptually away from a study of religious systems towards encounters with religious experiences (Johnston *et al.*, 2002). Meeting and speaking to representatives of faith groups is likely to help bridge the gap between learning from and about religion or between cognitive and emotional learning.

Outstanding teachers of RE know the importance of providing first-hand experiences by visiting places of worship, observing religious ceremonies, handling artefacts, and expressing emotions through dance, drama and singing (Copley and Copley, 1993; Langtree, 1997). They build on children's experiences (Box 8.3). They know that the subject is relevant especially to counter stereotypes and phobias. Best practice in teaching RE includes providing opportunities for:

- exploring controversial religious issues in the modern world – including media misrepresentations of religion;
- representatives of 'seldom heard' religious communities to work with the school and develop confidence that their traditions are respected;
- pupils with strong commitments to share their experience in a safe context and see that their religion or belief is valued and respected;
- learning outside the classroom and inviting visitors to it, giving pupils the chance to interact with different religions and nonreligious groups locally; and
- theme days or assemblies related to, for example, Holocaust Memorial Day – often working in partnership with other subjects, most notably citizenship.

(DCSF, 2010: 32)

In RE lessons, it is important to convey the message that religion matters and affects the way that many people live their lives (Box 8.4). Significantly, the best teachers do not patronize children by ignoring the negative aspects of religion (such as bigotry, narrowness and fanaticism).

---

**BOX 8.3 FOCUS ON PRACTICE**

One trainee planned her RE lessons around the theme of 'babies' with her class of 5-year-olds. Among the activities were:

- observing changes in the growth of a baby from embryo to a one-year-old, using stunning photographs shown on the interactive whiteboard;
- inviting a parent to bring in her baby, who was a younger brother to one of the children in the class;
- discussion about the names given to babies resulting in a simple bar graph of popular names in the school and comparisons with names given to parents and grandparents;
- a visit to the local church to see a real christening;
- selecting favourite lullabies to soothe babies to sleep.

---

**BOX 8.4  INTERNATIONAL VIEW – TEACHING RE**

Historically, where RE has had a prominent place in the curriculum in countries around the world, its aim was to induct pupils into a particular faith. Concerns over such a confessional approach has led countries as varied as Albania, France, America and India to prohibit the teaching of RE in state schools. In these countries, the teaching of RE is limited to faith communities and independent schools. In other countries, such as Germany, Greece and Slovakia, denominational teaching is present in state schools. A more 'neutral' position is adopted in countries such as Denmark, the Netherlands, Norway and Sweden, where the teaching of RE in state schools does not promote one denomination over another. The UK stories reflect a long-standing government commitment to the importance of the subject in school although the details of content and delivery have been highly contested, particularly in Northern Ireland (Copley, 1997).

---

## Creative arts (art, design and technology, music, drama and dance)

### Art

The enriching presence of the arts in children's all-round education has been highlighted despite pressures on schools to focus on literacy and numeracy (Lancaster, 1987; Bloomfield and Childs, 2000). There have been a number of forceful arguments advanced to support the case of increasing time spent on the creative arts. Bloomfield and Childs (2000) call for a change of status for the arts by placing them as the fourth 'R' in the curriculum, after reading, writing and arithmetic. They map out the potential richness of the cultural experiences offered by dance, drama, music and the visual arts, as entitlements for all children. It has also been argued that the arts make a valuable contribution to children's spiritual development for it is 'spirituality that breathes life into a work of art' (Halstead, 1997: 100). The artist's desire to create and express calls upon inner resources and the exercise of the imagination, and results in awe and wonder. In one study at Roehampton University, Watts (2005) reports that pupils listed sixty reasons alone why art is important, including the need to communicate, experiment, have fun, remember things, and make money!

Teachers need to develop carefully pupils' skills in visual literacy. Ward (2003) argues that the experience primary children most miss is that of seeing what is around them. Children need time to practise observation and guidelines on what to look for. As Davidson (1993) points out, what we see depends upon who we are. One outstanding trainee demonstrated this by giving children newspaper photographs to discuss with the accompanying text removed. Small groups had to decide what the images meant and suggest a catchy title before passing on their pictures to others. The images were then mounted for display alongside the suggested titles (Craggs, 1992). Perception is also determined by the intention of the artist. Original paintings often had changes made to them before the final product was complete. Parts of the picture may have been moved around, mistakes covered up and perspectives altered.

The renewed interest in promoting creativity in the curriculum across the United Kingdom has been a major boost for arts education. The ambitions of schools to provide a more thorough arts education has been recognized in strategic publications such as *Excellence and Enjoyment* (DfES, 2003). Schools who achieve high standards in art take opportunities to work closely with specialists such as artists, craftmakers and designers (OFSTED 2009b, OFSTED, 2011c). They follow local and national initiatives and use them to raise expectations. OFSTED defines outstanding teaching of art, craft and design when: 'Teachers are passionate about the subject and creativity in education. They take every opportunity to use visually exciting resources, to give skilled demonstration and to manage materials and workspaces creatively' (OFSTED, 2009b: 67).

On first reading this appears to be very demanding, although many of the skills are generic – such as the use of exciting resources, well-planned lessons, use of first-hand experiences, skilled demonstrations and the ability to reflect critically (Table 8.3). It should also be noted that there is no need for teachers to be talented artists themselves or be formally well qualified in the subject. From the learners' perspective, what matters is the degree to which they are motivated, engaged, and challenged to develop their artistic knowledge, skills and understanding.

Outstanding teachers recognize the cross-curricular appeal of the creative arts. More and more schools now have the confidence to use drama, visual arts, music, movement and dance, as well as the 'new' media of photography, computer art, film, and television to enrich children's experiences in school. Bloomfield and Childs (2000: 5) suggest the model shown in Figure 8.1 to describe the child's role in acquiring and experiencing artistic understanding.

Art has a key role to play in promoting children's personal and conceptual development. It provides contexts for the expression of ideas, feelings and impulses. Successful art lessons occur when teachers plan to develop pupils' appreciation and technical skills while working with a range of media and materials. First-hand experiences can include exploring the elements of colour, line, shape, space, tone, texture and pattern. Pupils can undertake simple explorations such as creating a colour chart using primary colours of blue, red and yellow. Barnes (2001) shows a wide range of starting points in art, from simple doodling to more sophisticated bottle sculptures. As Johnston *et al.* (2002: 188) note: 'if we are to take on board the educational value of art then it must be upgraded from the role of filler activity that it often occupies.' A good education in art will ensure that children see that they can improve their environment through their own artistic endeavour and derive satisfaction from the process (NSEAD, 1987).

## Design and technology

Sir Christopher Wren was one of the world's greatest achitects who designed so much of seventeenth-century London, including St Paul's Cathedral. His son chose the fitting epithet: 'If you seek his monument, look around.' Inspiration for teaching design and technology (DT) can be found all around, from the clothes children wear, school furniture, shopping precincts, housing estates, skin creams, cereals, chocolates, cars and bridges. Sir Norman Foster, famous for designing 'The Gherkin' in London, was

| CHILD's ROLE | |
|---|---|
| **Forming ideas** | **Testing ideas** |
| Personality factors   Sensory perceptual<br>processes | Developing technical skills in dance,<br>drama, music and art |
| Drives, feelings,    Associations,<br>thoughts,        problems, solutions<br>attitudes, values | Physical, intellectual, emotional and<br>social elements |
| Self-expression,    Intelligence,<br>self-discipline,     imagination,<br>self-actualisation,  motivation<br>self-evaluation | Schematic consciousness and non-<br>schematic subconsciousness over a<br>period of time |
| | Through motor skills and cognitive skills<br>of movement, voice, playing instruments,<br>using materials and media |

**Communicating ideas**
Dance   Drama   Music   Art
Integrated Arts

Creating a repertoire of paintings, stories in dance,
dance drama, sound plays, sound pictures, historical
drama, mime, sculptures, puppets, masks, songs,
murals, 3D structures, cantatas, mobiles, and so on

**Responding to the arts**

Critical responses of judgement and appraising artistic achievement of own work through
use of meaningful criteria

Applying criteria to understand selected received works of different world cultures and
historical periods

Examples include paintings, masks, historical dances, musical works, sculptures, plays,
murals, pottery, porcelain, architecture, folk-art as selected and appropriate for
programme of study

**FIGURE 8.1** A model to describe the child's role in developing artistic understanding

Source: Bloomfield and Childs (2000). Reproduced with permission

fascinated as a working-class lad by the trains that passed by his terraced home in Manchester during his childhood in the 1930s and 40s. The built environment is key to stimulating children's interest in how and why structures are made, including the materials, components, mechanisms and control systems used.

Most children enjoy designing and making things (Photo 8.1) and to work with a degree of independence. Defining the nature of design and technology is not straightforward although in education it is seen as 'hands-on problem solving activities that allow learners to grapple with ideas and produce creative solutions' (Hope, 2006: 11). Having a clear grasp of what the subject involves is necessary to teach it successfully. Unfortunately, too many teachers limit DT to making models. Moreover, perhaps more than any other foundation subject, it has suffered from concentration on teaching the basics, a lack of teacher confidence and know-how, and insufficient training and educational research. OFSTED (2011d) acknowledges that the DT curriculum needs modernizing so that pupils develop their knowledge and understanding of electronics, control systems and computer applications to aid designing and making.

Children need opportunities to explore how products are made; for instance, when pupils study a range of torches collected by the teacher, they dismantle them, identify the components and their function, work out how they interact, before starting to design a torch for themselves. In so doing, the best teachers set a design brief that moves pupils away from merely copying an existing solution (OFSTED, 2002). The process of design and technology involves skills of analysis, problem solving, cooperation, practical capability and evaluation, all of which are transferable in other contexts (Tickle, 1996). According to OFSTED (2000), where standards are high pupils have opportunities to creatively apply their knowledge and skills, succeeding in making good-quality products from a range of materials and components. They are able to evaluate as they work, testing products and making necessary modifications.

One of the major difficulties associated with planning DT lessons is the assumption that pupils will begin by drawing up their ideas, followed by making the design and finally evaluating the finished product. This simplistic approach bears little resemblance to the reality of how designers work. It is common practice for ideas to evolve and evaluation to be integrated at all stages. Pupils should be encouraged to make rough scribbles, discuss, list, use ICT, paper, card and other materials when developing their initial ideas. While

**PHOTO 8.1** A child wears a mask that she has designed

Source: POD/Pearson Education Ltd, Mark Bassett

working with materials, children need to be taught how to handle tools safely and how to keep inherent hazards to a minimum. For instance, with food technology children should as a routine wash their hands with germicidal soap before touching foodstuffs.

Numerous organizations have supported teachers over the years in trying to raise the profile of DT in primary schools. The Nuffield Design and Technology Project (2000–2009) provided a range of resources and ideas on topics such as 'Roly Poly' (wheel-based toys), 'Cownet' (making cardboard cows) and 'Shape the Future: The Motor Car' (www.nationalstemcentre.org.uk/elibrary). The Design and Technology Association has worked with the Design Council and the government to introduce a quality standards framework (the Design Mark) to recognize those schools who demonstrate excellence in their teaching (www.thedesignmark.org). The lobbying of the Design Council and others has proved successful. Under the revised DT programme of study in the 2014 National Curriculum, pupils are expected to learn the process skills of designing, making and evaluating, underpinned by technical knowledge. Significantly, pupils should explore DT in a range of relevant contexts, such as the home, playground, gardens, leisure, enterprise, industry and the wider environment (DfE, 2013). DT should be linked to subjects such as mathematics, science, computing and art, to further demonstrate its relevance.

## Music

The place of music in the primary curriculum has been justified on many grounds, including the promotion of social skills, children's spiritual, moral, social and cultural development, a platform for creative thinking and practice, and as a unique form of personal expression (Bigger and Brown, 1999; Jones and Robson, 2008). Music has always made an important contribution in presenting the public face of many schools, through concerts, plays and assemblies. By listening to, composing and performing music from different cultures, children's knowledge of the world widens. Their understanding of different lifestyles is broadened and deepened. From a teacher's viewpoint, music offers so much when planning cross-curricular lessons, particularly by enriching history, geography, dance, drama and RE. There are many exciting possibilities within music education including community projects in which local musicians are encouraged to work alongside children. Knowledge of different styles – jazz, blues, reggae, pop, classical – can be extended in meaningful contexts.

Unfortunately, there is too much variation in the quality of music teaching in primary schools. OFSTED report that music teaching is inadequate in one in five primary schools in England (OFSTED, 2012b). The main weaknesses are that pupils do not spend enough time making music and spend too much time talking and writing. Moreover, too many teachers do not have enough understanding of musical progress. The best teaching occurs when there is a 'joined up' approach to musical learning – where pupils' listening, composing and performing skills complement each other. The inspectorate has produced films to exemplify good practice in a wide range of settings and also highlights case studies of schools that have built very effective partnerships to raise pupils' musical achievement (OFSTED, 2012c).

In response to concerns over patchy provision, the Coalition Government launched a national plan to raise standards in music (DfE, 2011). All children in England have the opportunity to learn a musical instrument; to perform as part of an ensemble or choir;

and to learn to sing. Music education hubs form part of the plan and are designed to improve the quality and consistency of music education, both in and out of school. While in the best practice these hubs are reported to bring energy and vitality to music, early evaluations suggest that they are not achieving their desired aim of reducing the musical divide between rich and poor children. OFSTED (2013b) found only a third of the hubs represented improved provision, compared to support previously given by local authorities. They need to do more to improve the day-to-day musical experiences of all children. Part of the problem is that schools are not required to work with the hubs. Moreover, too many teachers hold low expectations of pupils; for instance in terms of their understanding and use of common musical features such as notation, time signatures, scales, melody shape and chords.

Promoting good listening skills is a central aim of music education. Children live in a world surrounded by sound and background noise. They need to be taught how to listen with discernment and concentration. This requires sensitivity to the needs of others. Outstanding teachers regularly plan opportunities for children to practise listening in contexts such as musical games and group performances when there is a need for individuals to perform at the correct time, at the correct volume and at the right speed. It is important for children to understand that sound is a medium of expression and communication.

To this end, good teachers organize a range of activities including experiments with a variety of musical instruments, use of the voice, and software programs. Developments in music technology – keyboard voices, sampling, processors, sequencers, CD-ROMs – can enhance children's experiences, though research has shown that this can be seen as a male preserve by the time children reach Key Stage 3 (Holt, 1997). Music can be a very rewarding experience for children and does not depend upon having an expert specialist on the staff (Glover and Ward, 2004). However, teachers report that music generates the greatest anxiety concerning lack of expertise or confidence (Downing *et al.*, 2002).

Successful teaching of music depends upon many factors. Secure knowledge and understanding of the four key musical skills is essential: performing, composing, appraising, and listening (DfEE/QCA, 1999). Hennessey (1998) points out that composition is a form of play and teachers need to recognize the need for playfulness in all learners. In line with constructivist theory, she advocates the use of group composition with teachers playing different roles – observing, participating, or offering suggestions and reminders, depending upon the degree of musical learning. The content of the music programme of study has been slimmed down in the 2014 National Curriculum. At Key Stage 1 children are expected to sing, play an instrument, listen and create. At Key Stage 2, playing and performing in solo and ensemble contexts, composition, musical notation, the history of music and appreciation are introduced (DfE, 2013).

In terms of their own subject knowledge, outstanding teachers are conversant with the following elements, which are the building blocks of the subject (Jones and Robson, 2008: 7):

■ duration – short and long notes, pulse, rhythm;

■ dynamics – loud/quiet/silent;

■ tempo – fast and slow;

- timbre – the quality of sound, affected by the way instruments are played and their construction;
- texture – the layers of music, the way sounds are combined;
- structure – the way sounds are organised in time; and
- pitch – high and low, melody.

In the most successful music lessons teachers demonstrate a clear learning focus on the subject, hold high expectations and provide opportunities for pupils to practise their musical skills. Wherever possible, they make reference to real-life musicians and compositions.

The best music teachers are enthusiastic and exhibit a sense of rhythm and pitch, an ability to sing a tune, a willingness to learn and not to be afraid of making mistakes (Barrs, 1994). They should possess a firm conviction that music has an important part to play in children's education. OFSTED (2009a) reports that in the schools where provision for music was outstanding, there is a clear focus on the personal as well as the musical development of children. These schools know why music is important and seek to show its personal value to children. For instance, one primary school provided guitar lessons to a child with serious learning difficulties when he was moving schools. This helped him make the transition more smoothly and gave him a focus, so that he benefited across all his work.

Outstanding teaching in the arts occurs when teachers make use of unexpected opportunities to develop pupils' interests and skills, as reported in Box 8.5.

---

### BOX 8.5  FOCUS ON PRACTICE

This approach was exemplified in 'School Grounds Week', which provided opportunities for pupils of all ages to engage in learning across subjects, making maximum use of the extensive variety of environments available for them to explore. In the woodland walk, for example, they created a sculpture trail, using recyclable materials. As well as producing a giant replica of the Iron Man from netting and cans, they made sculptures of birds, insects and other mini-beasts. They had extensive opportunities to draw and paint on location and were provided with expert support by the teacher, as was illustrated when a Year 6 pupil, struggling to capture the impression of movement and light shining through leaves in the trees, asked for help. Returning to the classroom, the teacher used the Internet to show the work of Impressionist painters and to discuss their use of colour and movement. Back outside, the pupils were encouraged to experiment with making colour patches using felt-tip pens, gradually working up their ideas into a descriptive, emotive scene. The outcomes showed remarkable understanding and originality. The pupils had autonomy to explore and interpret their ideas in their unique style. They used their knowledge of other artists' work to inform but not to constrain their own work. The teacher had skilfully used an unexpected moment to trigger a rich, valuable and unplanned learning experience that led to outstanding results.

(OFSTED, 2009b. © Crown Copyright 2009, reproduced under terms of the Click-Use Licence)

**TABLE 8.3** Grade descriptors for outstanding teaching in art, DT and music

| Subject | Quality of teaching |
|---------|---------------------|
| Art | ■ Exude enthusiasm for the subject and pupils' creativity<br>■ Inspire pupils by taking every opportunity to use visually exciting resources including new technology, create environments that promote curiosity and demonstrate skilfully without inhibiting pupils<br>■ Draw on breadth and depth of subject knowledge to prepare lessons that pupils find informative and interesting<br>■ Regularly refresh knowledge about how and why art, craft, design was and is made to connect with and challenge individual pupils<br>■ Create the conditions that promote pupils' progress while outcomes remain open ended<br>■ Improvise to ensure that no unexpected opportunities for learning are missed<br>■ Use pupils' responses to teaching to inform planning and intervention<br>■ Select from a wide range of teaching styles to deploy strategies that realise subject specific learning objectives<br>■ Use teaching techniques to promote confident, independent and creative learners<br>■ Adapt approaches skilfully to different settings and pupils<br>■ Integrate assessment skilfully into practical elements of lessons, having an evident impact on progress<br>■ Use feedback to pupils to educate, inspire and challenge their creativity<br>■ Use visual exemplification to aid pupils' understanding about how to progress<br>■ Are very well informed about their contribution to pupils' personal development and academic progress, which they promote through the subject<br>■ Show how a professional, personable and inclusive approach enables individuals and groups of pupils to flourish |
| DT | ■ Communicate high expectations, enthusiasm and passion about DT to pupils and challenge their thinking<br>■ A high level of confidence and expertise both in terms of their up-to-date specialist knowledge and their understanding of effective learning in DT<br>■ Employ a very wide range of innovative and imaginative resources and teaching strategies to stimulate pupils' active participation in their learning. This enables pupils to explain their ideas and concepts clearly and apply them with confidence<br>■ Opportunities for pupils to develop and demonstrate their initiative and independence and take responsibility for their learning are thoughtfully planned and secure outstanding progress across all aspects of DT |
| Music | ■ Pupils of all abilities and interests make outstanding progress because teaching focuses in a relentless and coordinated way on their aural development, improving the musical quality and depth of their responses, and high-level or rapidly improving instrumental/vocal techniques (including good attention to posture)<br>■ Music, as the target language, is used to model and explain – confidently, expertly, and musically. Words and notations are used precisely and appropriately to support effective musical learning, rather than drive it<br>■ Pupils' voices are used constantly, not only for discrete singing work but also to help them internalise and understand musical ideas. Similarly, physical movement is used very effectively to help pupils understand and internalise different dimensions of music such as rhythm, tempo and pitch<br>■ Refers to the work of professional musicians and draws knowledgeably on a wide range of historical, social and cultural traditions using a wide range of resources, including new technologies |

**TABLE 8.3** *continued*

| Subject | Quality of teaching |
| --- | --- |
| Music *cont* | ■ Gives pupils the confidence to challenge, ask questions, show initiative and take risks in order to create original, imaginative and distinctive work of high musical quality<br>■ Provides high levels of challenge to pupils with additional musical skills and experience, including taking full account of their musical learning outside of school<br>■ Gives very effective help to pupils who find musical learning and participation difficult, including those with disabilities and special educational needs, and those for whom the Pupil Premium provides support<br>■ While lessons are always planned and structured thoroughly with clear musical learning intentions, teaching responds very positively to pupils' creative, and sometimes unexpected, responses and builds on these to promote outstanding musical learning<br>■ Assessment is outstanding because it focuses relentlessly on the quality and depth of pupils' musical understanding<br>■ Levels and grades are considered thoughtfully over extended periods of time and take a balanced view of pupils' work across a wide range of activities<br>■ Audio and video recordings are used extensively to appraise pupils' work, identify accurately how their musical responses could be improved further, and consistently realise these improvements |

Source: OFSTED (2012a)

# Physical education (PE)

The aim of PE is well expressed by Delaney *et al.* (2008: 7), namely: 'to develop physical competence so that children are able to move efficiently, effectively and safely and understand what they are doing.' The authors point out that the outcome – physical literacy – should be seen as important to children's education and development as numeracy and literacy. The concept of physical literacy owes much to the work of Margaret Whitehead who in the early 1990s argued that PE should create 'a literacy in movement' when individuals 'move with poise, economy and confidence in a wide variety of physically challenging situations' (Whitehead, 2001: 3). Pupils who are physically literate are perceptive in their 'reading' of all aspects of the physical environment, 'anticipating movement needs or possibilities and responding appropriately to these, with intelligence and imagination'. In football it is common for pundits to say how well a footballer 'reads' the game, knowing for instance where to pass or when to move into a space to receive the ball. For children to become physically literate, they need to perform basic movement competencies (within their own physical capacity), apply these in game and other situations, recognize what they need to do to improve and work independently to achieve this. Whitehead's ideas were developed by others including the Association for Physical Education (afPE), the leading UK organization that supports the delivery of PE in schools and the wider community (Whitehead and Murdoch, 2006).

The Department for Education and Science (DfES, 2005: 3) identified ten outcomes that denote high quality PE and school sport (PESS). When pupils experience high quality PE and school sport:

1    they are committed to PE and sport and make them a central part of their lives;

2    they know and understand what they are trying to achieve and how to go about doing it;

3    they understand that PE and sport are an important part of a healthy, active lifestyle;

4    they have the confidence to get involved in PE and sport;

5    they have the skills and control that they need to take part in PE and sport;

6    they willingly take part in a range of competitive, creative and challenge-type activities, both as individuals and as part of a team or group;

7    they think about what they are doing and make appropriate decisions for themselves;

8    they show a desire to improve and achieve in relation to their own abilities;

9    they have the stamina, suppleness and strength to keep going; and

10   they enjoy PE, school and community sport.

It is useful for teachers to reflect upon these ten indicators when evaluating the quality of PE lessons. Questions to consider include:

■    do pupils always remember their PE kit and get ready for lessons on time?;

■    do they help organize lessons? (commitment);

■    do they know how dancers, gymnasts and athletes think differently? (understanding);

■    do they show good body control and movement?;

■    do they have a wide range of techniques they can apply and adapt effectively? (skills);

■    are they happy to work and perform on their own, as well as in groups and teams? (competition);

■    do they ask questions so that they can make progress?;

■    do they react to situations intelligently when performing? (thinking);

■    are they determined to achieve the best possible results? (desire to improve);

■    do they have high levels of concentration and maintain energy levels? (stamina); and

■    do they talk about what they are doing with enthusiasm? (enjoyment).

In recent years, physical education (PE) has attracted increasing government support for various reasons including concerns over rising child and adult obesity levels (HMIe, 2002). For the last decade or so, around 16 per cent of children have been reported to be obese and around a third overweight (Health and Social Care Information Centre, 2012). Evidence indicates that significant numbers of primary school children are concerned about their weight and appearance. By the age of 10, around a third of girls and a fifth of boys cite their bodies as their main sources of anxiety (Hutchinson and Calland, 2011).

Unfortunately, not enough schools have capitalized on the enthusiasm and inspiration generated by sporting events such as the Olympic and Paralympic Games in 2012. OFSTED (2013c) has called upon the Department for Education to introduce a new national strategy for PE and schools to build upon the Olympic legacy and school sport partnerships. One of the worst statistics in British sport, according to Lord Moynihan (the Chair of the British Olympics Association) is the dominance of privately educated sportsmen and women. Four in every ten medal winners at the 2012 Olympics attended independent schools and yet these educate only seven per cent of the nation's children (Paton, 2012). Yet, PE can be a great leveller in bringing together pupils from all backgrounds. It challenges children and young people in a way no other subject can, testing both their physical and mental capabilities. The Coalition Government wants to encourage more competitive sport in schools and to give schools the freedom to concentrate on the improvement of competitive sport provision.

One of the main issues is that insufficient time is allocated to the teaching of PE. A recent survey reveals that 54 per cent of children experience less than two hours a week of PE or games at school (Davies, 2012). Official statistics suggest that in 2007/8, 90 per cent of primary children undertook two hours of sport or physical activity at school, a rise from 62 per cent in 2003/4 (Bardens et al., 2012). The Labour Government had plans to increase the time allocated for PE from 2 to 5 hours, but the Coalition Government has dropped the 2-hour guidance. The Scottish Government has pledged that every pupil in primary school will benefit from at least 2 hours per week of PE as an enduring legacy of the 2014 Commonwealth Games. In 2012, 84 per cent of Scottish primary schools met this target. Quite naturally, the Association for Physical Education has called for longer-term commitment and wants the subject to have the same curriculum status as literacy and numeracy (afPE, 2008).

As with other foundation subjects, many teachers lack confidence and subject expertise in PE – one in three are influenced by their own negative feelings when they were children, impacting on how they teach PE. There is also limited coverage in teacher training – more than 60 per cent of primary trainees receiving less than 6 hours preparation to teach PE (Paton, 2012).

Agencies such as SportScotland, Sport Relief and the Active Schools Network are designed to increase children and young people's activity levels and access to sport. Increasingly, primary schools in England are attracting pupils who are not particularly interested in traditional games by widening the subject's appeal through mountain biking, dance, martial arts and yoga (OFSTED, 2009c).

The importance of PE cannot be overestimated in terms of promoting health, fitness and well-being. In the Early Years, pupils' physical development can be fostered through water and sand play, construction play, musical activities, mark-making and outdoor play – the latter can include climbing and balancing on apparatus, playing on see-saws, building dens, riding bicycles, ball games, and crawling through tunnels (O'Hara, 2008). When taught effectively, PE provides the basis for active living and a life-long interest (Doherty and Brennan, 2008).

Dance is reported to be second only to football as the most popular activity in schools around the country (Higgins, 2008). Its popularity has benefited from television shows such as *Strictly Come Dancing* (BBC1, 2004). Yet in the past it has been regarded as the Cinderella of the arts world, lacking investment and, arguably, any coherent status in the curriculum. Recent changes to the curricula throughout the United Kingdom coupled with government funding have strengthened the position of dance. The subject makes an important contribution to children's physical development. For teachers, dance is a convenient context for cross-curricular activities and can prove an excellent basis for transitional projects, bringing different age ranges together (OFSTED, 2009c). Dance features as the only art form in the physical education curriculum in England, Wales and Northern Ireland, although in Scotland it is grouped together under the Expressive Arts umbrella. The emphasis is very much on creating and performing movements, experiences that generate intellectual and emotional demands. It is also important for learners to appreciate and evaluate performance. Outstanding teachers focus on developing children's enjoyment. One trainee responded to interest from her class of 11-year-olds in the success of dancing protégée George Sampson, winner of the 2008 television show *Britain's Got Talent*. She organized a series of talent contests after school, with a panel of experts drawn from the school offering their views.

Outstanding teachers of PE demonstrate a daily commitment and enthusiasm for the subject (Table 8.4). This can be manifested in many ways, ranging from the way in which they celebrate the achievement of their pupils, to their own determination to improve their expertise. They set positive role models in their manner, dress and attitude (OHMCI, 1997). They provide pupils with sufficient time and opportunities to develop their skills in each aspect of the curriculum, rather than waste time in queues or setting out equipment. Pupils have time to learn from their mistakes and to rehearse techniques in contexts such as games, dances or gymnastic sequences (HMIe, 2002). In sum, the best teachers seek to inspire young people to learn and achieve (DfES, 2004).

## Conclusion

This chapter has demonstrated the value of the foundation subjects. There is clear supporting evidence that providing a rich primary curriculum is not incompatible with achieving high standards in the basic subjects (OFSTED, 2002). However, the evidence from the inspectorate and other sources shows that the quality of teaching in the foundation subjects needs to improve considerably if children's entitlement to a broad, balanced and relevant curriculum is to be achieved.

## Glossary

**Enquiry-based learning** describes an approach when pupils ask and follow up questions, and engage with scenarios or issues in a systematic way.

**Foundation subjects** are studied as part of the National Curriculum comprising in England: history, geography, ICT, physical education, music, art and design, design and technology.

**Foundation schools** are state-funded and run by their own governing body, which employs the staff and sets the admissions criteria. The school can discriminate against all pupils on religious grounds if oversubscribed.

**Voluntary controlled schools** are state-funded in which a foundation or trust (usually a Christian denomination) has some formal influence in the running of the school. Children follow the locally agreed syllabus for religious education.

**TABLE 8.4** Grade descriptors for outstanding teaching in PE

| Subject | Quality of teaching |
| --- | --- |
| PE | ■ Communicate high expectations, enthusiasm and passion about their subject to pupils<br>■ Teachers and external coaches/practitioners have a high level of confidence and expertise both in terms of their specialist knowledge across a range of activities and their understanding of effective learning in the subject<br>■ Use a wide range of innovative and imaginative teaching strategies very effectively to stimulate pupils' active participation in their learning and secure outstanding progress across all aspects of the subject<br>■ ICT is used very effectively to support observation and analysis to improve work further<br>■ Teachers ensure that pupils of all abilities learn new skills, find out how to use them in different ways, and link them to accurately repeat actions, sequences or team tactics<br>■ Pupils are expected to work hard for sustained periods of time and persevere when they begin to tire<br>■ Non-performing pupils are engaged purposefully with other roles, such as observation and feedback, coaching, umpiring and refereeing<br>■ External coaches'/practitioners' and other adults' support is well focused and makes a significant contribution to the quality of learning<br>■ Pupils are given frequent opportunities to assess their own and others' performances and make suggestions for how they could be improved |

Source: OFSTED (2012a)

## References

afPE (2008) *A Manifesto for a World Class System of Physical Education*, Reading: Association for Physical Education.

Alexander, R.J. (2009) *Towards a New Primary Curriculum: A Report from the Cambridge Primary Review. Part 2: The Future*, Cambridge: University of Cambridge Faculty of Education.

All Party Parliamentary Group on Religious Education (2013) *RE: The Truth Unmasked*, London: Religious Education Council for England and Wales.

Bale, J. (1987) *Geography in the Primary School*, London: Routledge and Kegan Paul.

Bardens, J., Long, R. and Gillie, C. (2012) *School Sport*, London: House of Commons.

Barnes, M. (2001) *Staring Points in Art*, Dunstable: Belair.

Barrs, K. (1994) *Music Works*, Twickenham: Belair.

Bigger, S. and Brown, E. (eds) (1999) *Spiritual, Moral, Social and Cultural Education*, London: David Fulton.

Bloomfield, A. and Childs, J. (2000) *Teaching Integrated Arts in the Primary School: Dance, Drama, Music and the Visual Arts*, London: David Fulton.

Blyth, W.A.L. (1990) *Making the Grade for Primary Humanities: Assessment in the Humanities*, Milton Keynes: Open University Press.

Carter, R. (ed.) (1998) *Handbook of Primary Geography*, Sheffield: Geographical Association.

Catling, S. and Willy, T. (2009) *Achieving QTS: Teaching Primary Geography*, Exeter: Learning Matters.

CCEA (2007) *Northern Ireland Curriculum Primary*, Belfast: CCEA.

Church of England (2012) *The Church School of the Future Review*, London: Church of England.

Claire, H. (1996) *Reclaiming Our Pasts: Equality and Diversity in the Primary History Curriculum*, Stoke-on-Trent: Trentham Books.

Cole, W.O. and Evans-Lowndes, J. (1991) *Religious Education in the Primary Curriculum*, Exeter: REM Press.

Cooper, H. (1995) *History in the Early Years*, London: Routledge.

Cooper, H. (2000) *The Teaching of History in Primary Schools*, London: David Fulton.

Cooper, H. (2006) *History 3–11*, London: David Fulton.

Copley, T. (1997) *Teaching Religion: Sixty Years of Religious Education in England and Wales*, Exeter: University of Exeter Press.

Copley, T. and Copley, G. (1993) *Religious Education in Key Stage 1: A Practical Guide*, London: Southgate.

Craggs, C.E. (1992) *Media Education in the Primary School*, London: Routledge.

Davidson, R. (1993) *What is Art?*, Oxford: OUP.

Davies, G. (2004) *Religious Education in the Primary School*, Bangor: University of Wales Bangor.

Davies, G.A. (2012) 'Schools fail pupils' Olympic inspiration', *The Telegraph*, 27 November.

DCELLS (2008) *National Exemplar Framework for Religious Education for 3 to 19-year-olds in Wales*, Cardiff: Welsh Assembly Government.

DCSF (2010) *Religious Education in English Schools: Non-Statutory Guidance 2010*, Nottingham: DCSF.

Delaney, B.J., Donnelly, P., News, J. and Haughey, T.J. (2008) *Improving Physical Literacy*, Belfast: Sport Northern Ireland.

DES (1978) *Primary Education in England: A Survey by HM Inspectors of Schools*, London: HMSO.

DfE (2011) *The Importance of Music: A National Plan for Music Education*, London: DfE.

DfE (2013) *National Curriculum in England*, London: DfE.

DfEE/QCA (1999) *Music: The National Curriculum for England*, London: DfEE/QCA.

DfES (2003) *Excellence and Enjoyment: A Strategy for Teachers in England*, London: DfES/QCA.

DfES (2004) *High Quality PE and Sport for Young People*, Nottingham: DfES.

DfES (2005) *Learning through PE and Sport*, London: DfES.

Doherty, J. and Brennan, P. (2008) *Physical Education and Development 3–11*, London: Routledge.

Downing, D., Johnson, F. and Kaur, S. (2002) *The Arts in Primary Schools*, London: NFER.

Estyn (2000) *Aiming for Excellence in Geography*, Cardiff: Estyn.

Fines, J. and Nichol, J. (1997) *Teaching Primary History*, Oxford: Heinemann.

Gagg, J.C. (1951) *Common Sense in the Primary School*, London: Evans Brothers.

Glover, J. and Ward, S. (2004) *Teaching Music in the Primary School*, London: Continuum.

Grigg, R. and Hughes, S. (2013) *Teaching Primary Humanities*, Harlow: Pearson.

Halocha, J. (1998) *Coordinating Geography Across the Primary School*, Bristol: Falmer Press.

Halstead, J. (1997) 'An approach to the spiritual dimension of primary arts education', in Holt, D. (ed.) *Primary Arts Education: Contemporary Issues*, London: Falmer Press, 96–107.

Health and Social Care Information Centre (2012) *Health Survey for England 2011*, Leeds: Health and Social Care Information Centre.

Hennessey, S. (1998) 'Teaching composing in the music curriculum', in Littledyke, M. and Huxford, L. (eds) *Teaching the Primary Curriculum for Constructivist Learning*, London: David Fulton, 163–72.

Higgins, C. (2008) 'TV dancing craze fuels search for new school stars', *The Guardian*, 18 March.

HMI (1986) *Geography from 5 to 16*, London: DfES.

HMI (1989) *Aspects of Primary Education: The Teaching and Learning of History and Geography*, London: HMSO.

HMIe (2002) *Improving Physical Education in Primary Schools*, Edinburgh: The Stationery Office.

Hodkinson, A. (2003) 'National Curriculum and temporal vocabulary: The use of subjective time phrases within the National Curriculum for history and its schemes of work: effective provision or a wasted opportunity?', *Education 3–13*, 31(3): 28–34.

Holt, D. (ed.) (1997) *Primary Arts Education: Contemporary Issues*, London: Falmer Press.

Hoodless, P. (2008) *Teaching History in Primary Schools*, Exeter: Learning Matters.

Hoodless, P., Bermingham S., Bowen P. and McCreery E. (2003) *Achieving QTS: Teaching Humanities in Primary Schools*, Exeter: Learning Matters.

Hope, G. (2006) *Achieving QTS: Teaching Design and Technology at Key Stages 1 and 2*, Exeter: Learning Matters.

Hutchinson, N. and Calland, C. (2011) *Body Image in the Primary School*, London: Routledge.

Jeffries, S. (2014) 'Blackadder – your country needs you', *The Guardian*, 6 January.

Johnston, J., Charter, M. and Bell, D. (eds) (2002) *Teaching the Primary Curriculum*, Buckingham: Open University Press.

Jones, P. and Robson, C. (2008) *Teaching Music in Primary Schools*, Exeter: Learning Matters.

Lancaster, J. (ed.) (1987) *Art, Craft and Design in the Primary School*, Corsham: NSEAD.

Langtree, G. (1997) *Are You Ready?* Norwich: RMEP.

Lomas, T. (1993) *Teaching and Assessing Historical Understanding*, London: Historical Association.

McCreery, E., Palmer, S. and Voiels, V. (2008) *Achieving QTS: Teaching Religious Education: Primary and Early Years*, Exeter: Learning Matters.

NSEAD (1987) *Art, Craft and Design in the Primary School*, Bristol: NSEAD.

Ochota, M. (2013) *Britain's Secret Treasures*, London: Headline.

OFSTED (2000) *Inspecting Subjects 3–11*, London: OFSTED.

OFSTED (2002) *The Curriculum in Successful Primary Schools*, London: OFSTED.

OFSTED (2007) *Making Sense of Religion: A Report on Religious Education in Schools and the Impact of Locally Agreed Syllabuses*, London: OFSTED.

OFSTED (2009a) *Making More of Music*, London: OFSTED.

OFSTED (2009b) *Drawing Together: Art, Craft and Design in Schools*, London: OFSTED.

OFSTED (2009c) *Physical Education in Schools 2005/08: Working Towards 2012 and Beyond*, London: OFSTED.

OFSTED (2011a) *History for All*, London: OFSTED.

OFSTED (2011b) *Geography Learning to Make a World of Difference*, London: OFSTED.

OFSTED (2011c) *Making a Mark: Art, Craft and Design Education 2008–11*, London: OFSTED.

OFSTED (2011d) *Meeting Technological Challenges?* London: OFSTED.

OFSTED (2012a) *Generic Grade Descriptors and Supplementary Subject-Specific Guidance for Inspectors on Making Judgements during Visits to Schools*, London: OFSTED.

OFSTED (2012b) *Music in Schools: Wider Still, and Wider*, London: OFSTED.

OFSTED (2012c) *Music in Schools: Sound Partnerships*, London: OFSTED.

OFSTED (2012d) *Good Practice Resource – an Enquiry-Based Approach to Learning: St Anne's CofE Primary School*, London: OFSTED.

OFSTED (2013a) *Religious Education: Realising the Potential*, London: OFSTED.

OFSTED (2013b) *Music in Schools: What Hubs Must Do*, London: OFSTED.

OFSTED (2013c) *Beyond 2012: Outstanding Physical Education for All*, London: OFSTED.

O'Hara, M. (2008) *Teaching 3–8*, London: Continuum.

OHMCI (1997) *The Preparation of Physical Education Teachers during Initial Teacher Training*, Cardiff: OHMCI.

Palmer, J. and Neal, P. (1994) *The Handbook of Environmental Education*, London: Routledge.

Paton, G. (2012) 'Olympic chief demands overhaul of PE in state schools', *The Telegraph*, 3 October.

Reilly, P. (2013) 'From vintage shops to old-fashioned pubs: The dementia "pods" that reassure patients in care homes and hospitals – and have now got backing from the Dragon's Den', *Daily Mail*, 27 August.

Rose, J. (2008) *The Independent Review of the Primary Curriculum*, London: DCSF.

Scoffham, S. (2013) *Teaching Geography Creatively*, London: Routledge.

Scottish Government (2011) *Curriculum for Excellence – Provision of Religious Observation in Schools*, Edinburgh: Scottish Government.

Taba, H. (1962) *Curriculum Development*, San Diego, CA: Harcourt Brace.

Tickle, L. (ed.) (1996) *Understanding Design and Technology in Primary Schools*, London: Routledge.

Walford, R. (2001) *Geography in British Schools 1850–2000*, London: Woburn Press.

Wallace, B. (2003) *Using History to Develop Thinking Skills at Key Stage 2*, London: David Fulton.

Ward, B. (2003) *Getting the Buggers to Draw*, London: Continuum.

Watson, B. and Thompson, P. (2007) *The Effective Teaching of Religious Education*, Harlow: Pearson.

Watts, R. (2005) 'Attitudes to making art in the primary school', *International Journal of Art and Design Education*, 24(3): 243–53.

Weigand, P. (1993) *Children and Primary Geography*, London: Cassell.

White, L. (2000) *Reflection Time*, London: National Society.

Whitehead, M. (2001) 'The concept of physical literacy', *British Journal of Teaching Physical Education*, 32(1): 6–8.

Whitehead, M.E. with Murdoch, E. (2006) 'Physical literacy and physical education. Conceptual mapping', *Physical Education Matters*, 1(1): 6–9.

# Websites

## Art

Art on the Net is a website showing the works of a collection of artists – www.art.net

National Portrait Gallery includes an online database of images – www.npg.org.uk

Art in Scotland website provides links to contemporary artists throughout the country – www.zednet.co.uk/artinscotland

Culture Northern Ireland website provides links to literature, heritage, music, visual and performing arts – www.culturenorthernireland.org/index.aspx

National Galleries Scotland provides outreach programmes – www.nationalgalleries.org

## Design and technology

Nuffield Primary Design and Technology website includes examples of pupils' work, classroom materials to download free of charge and other resources for teachers – www.primary dandt.org

The Design and Technology Association website – www.data.org.uk

The James Dyson Foundation includes free resources and ideas for schools – www.jamesdyson foundation.com

## Geography

The primary section of the Geographical Association's website – www.geography.org.uk/ eyprimary

The Ordnance Survey website – www.ordnancesurvey.co.uk/oswebsite

ARKive website contains one of the largest collections of free film footage relating mainly to science and geography subjects – www.arkiveeducation.org

## History

BBC History website contains many sources, ideas and links – http://bbc.co.uk/history

The Historical Association website has a specific section for primary schools – www.history.org.uk

The British Museum Compass website provides useful images of artefacts – www.thebritishmuseum. ac.uk

Nuffield Primary History – www.primaryhistory.org

Gathering the Jewels website contains sources from museums and galleries throughout Wales – www.gtj.org.uk

English Heritage is a large website covering publications for specific sites and an excellent photographic archive called Viewfinder – www.english-heritage.org.uk

Scottish Cultural Resources Across the Network – www.scran.ac.uk

## Physical education

Association for Physical Education provides latest news in the world of PE – www.afpe.org.uk/ public/news.htm

## Music

The Teaching Music website is funded by the Training and Development Agency for Schools (TDA) and aims to help all those involved in music education – www.teachingmusic.org.uk

Music Teachers UK website provides resources including guides for non-specialist teachers – www.musicteachers.co.uk

Online music library allows free previews of classical music – www.naxosmusiclibrary.com

MusicEd website includes a useful links section 'on the web' – www.musiced.org.uk/static/ musiced.html

## Religious education

RE Directory provides useful overview of RE requirements in United Kingdom – www.theredirectory.org.uk

The Professional Council for Religious Education is the subject teacher association for RE professionals in school – www.pcfre.org.uk

*RE Today* has online materials covering different faiths in Britain including free sample pages from the RE journal – www.retoday.org.uk/downloads.htm

The Religious Education Exchange Service has a large database of materials relating to religious education – http://re-xs.ucsm.ac.uk

# 9 Planning and preparation

## Chapter objectives

By the end of this chapter you should be able to:

- Explain the importance of planning within the teaching and learning cycle.
- Distinguish between long, medium and short-term planning.
- Know the characteristics of effective lesson plans.
- Recognize the need to prepare high-quality resources.
- Critically evaluate planning models and approaches.

*Always plan ahead. It wasn't raining when Noah built the ark.*
*(Richard Cushing, 1895–1970, American Cardinal)*

## Introduction

There are not many teachers who become self-made millionaires. But Deanna Jump, an American teacher of 6–7-year-olds, is the only one to make a million dollars on the back of selling 'catchy and creative' lesson plans and units of work (*Daily Mail*, 30 September 2012). She is one of many teachers who sell resources on the American website www.teacherspayteachers.com. UK teachers can exchange free plans on network websites operated by the *Times Educational Supplement* and *The Guardian*. Rather than a potential source of financial prosperity, however, this chapter looks at the importance of planning and preparation as the basis of outstanding teaching. It considers practical matters, such as the nature, content and format of plans, what inspectors and head teachers expect and where to find support to improve planning.

## What is planning and why is it important?

Put simply, planning is deciding what and how to teach. It involves setting goals (aims and objectives), developing strategies and outlining activities to meet these goals. Planning is not a linear process where one step leads smoothly to another. It is part of the dynamic cycle of classroom professional activities that feed into teaching, assessment, evaluation and reporting. Planning begins with having a clear vision as schools and teachers seek to visualize the future, thereby reflecting on basic philosophical questions about what and how children should learn. Inevitably, the vision is informed at a macro level by national policies and guidance, for instance relating to the teaching of literacy and numeracy. It is also shaped by everyday observations of children's learning. These may reveal unexpected learning difficulties or gains experienced by particular children. Such observations should inform future planning. Hence the process is a dynamic one, which calls for regular review and updating of documents.

There are different versions of this cycle that describe practice in many educational systems around the world. The model recommended by the New South Wales Department of Education in Australia (Figure 9.1) clearly conveys the dynamism of planning and its organic relationship with teaching and other key professional duties. The starting point in the cycle is determined by the outcomes of gathering data through teaching, observation and reflection. By considering carefully assessment data from previous lessons, teachers are able to devise plans to meet future needs. The 'How will my students get there?' question prompts teachers to think about teaching strategies, classroom organization and the learning environment. It also focuses attention on what the pupils will do to demonstrate achievement of the intended outcomes, for example what written, oral or artistic 'products' are expected. Teachers need to plan assessment opportunities streamed through the lessons, such as oral presentations, quizzes, journals or practical experiences, so that they can check the progress of pupils *as* learning occurs. Teachers also need to ascertain what the pupils have learned by the end of the lesson to inform future lesson plans so that pupils can move forward in their understanding.

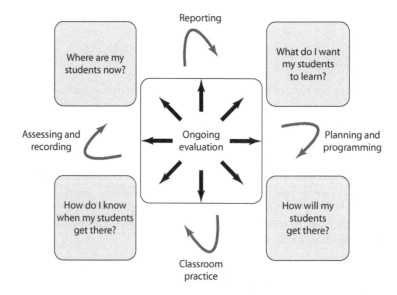

**FIGURE 9.1** Teaching and learning cycle

Source: © State of New South Wales through the NSW Department of Education and Communities (www.curriculumsupport.education.nsw.gov.au/consistent_teacher/tlcycle.htm)

Clear planning is essential because it provides both teacher and learners with a sense of direction and purpose. Without a sound plan, opportunities to develop important knowledge, skills and ideas can be missed. Pupils may become frustrated if they are not sure what they are expected to do and learn, creating potential behavioural difficulties. Stress levels are likely to increase and the general well-being of the class suffer. Another possible scenario is for lessons to drift along, with pupils having a vague sense of the subject and seeing learning as a matter of completing worksheets or 'keeping their head down' in some other way.

Planning is important because it reflects the degree of professionalism demonstrated by teachers. It is not surprising therefore that across European countries teachers are expected to plan effectively (Eurydice, 2002). In England, all teachers are required to 'plan and teach well-structured lessons' as stipulated by the *Teachers' Standards* (DfE, 2013: 8). This includes planning out-of-class activities to consolidate and extend pupils' learning, for instance through visits to museums and galleries, carrying out a street survey or investigations using the school grounds. It also requires the setting of homework and contributing to the design of an engaging curriculum.

Teachers who plan well convey positive messages to a range of audiences including: colleagues, head teachers, parents, governors, local authority advisers and inspectors. They demonstrate care and consideration, for example to visiting supply teachers who need to know pupils' starting points. However, plans are written primarily for teachers' own professional practice and development. Lesson or weekly plans are best seen as 'work in progress' annotated with scribbles and post-it notes rather than beautifully crafted documents.

Planning takes place over three phases: long term, medium term and short term. Over the long term (usually a year) schools identify their aims for all subjects or areas of experience, mapping out topics to be taught through the year and to whom. These long-term plans are usually reviewed once a year or every other year to update them in line with any national changes. In the medium phase (over a half-term or term), the learning objectives are specified along with an outline of activities to achieve these objectives. Short-term planning invariably involves the details of what specific groups of children will do during one lesson or through the day. Details of assessment and resources are also noted. It is important to see the relationship between lesson plans and other documentation. Daily lesson plans should derive from weekly overviews and reflect the school's key policy documents, such as those on teaching and learning. Outstanding teachers are able to make connections between long-, mid- and short-term plans (Figure 9.2).

## Long-term planning

The purpose of long-term planning is to set out how the school meets its curriculum obligations through the year. This includes the requirements set out in each programme of study for the National Curriculum and religious education. Most schools provide a **curriculum map** or overview showing the topics or subjects to be taught in each term for each year group. These can be presented as questions linked to local issues and seasons, as in the case of the school overview shown in Table 9.1. Behind this map sits another layer of subject coverage. With such an enquiry-led, cross-curricular approach, it is important that the curriculum retains its breadth and balance. The appeal of the example

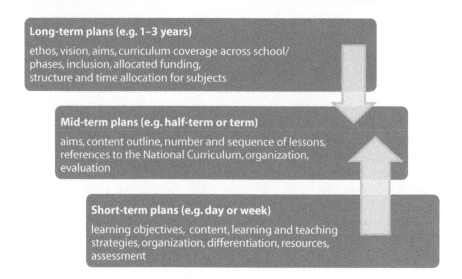

**FIGURE 9.2** Relationship between short-, mid- and long-term planning

**TABLE 9.1** An example of a school's curriculum map

| Year | Autumn | | Spring | | Summer | |
|---|---|---|---|---|---|---|
| 1 | Who am I? | What is it like in Space? | Can we make music? | Do I need a coat today? | Are plants really alive? | Are all animals friendly? |
| 2 | How do we know there was a Great Fire of London? | How can I make my star shine brighter? | How would my uniform be different if I lived in Africa? | Why do we remember Leonardo Da Vinci? | Who lives in a house like this? | Can I make a wheeled vehicle that moves? |
| 3 | Do you know any super heroes? | Would Christmas be different if I lived in France? | Could I become a famous children's author? | How is my daily life different to a child in Tudor times? | What is the life cycle of a coke bottle? | Why do you want to be beside the seaside? |
| 4 | Does every picture tell a story? | | What did the Romans do for us? | | Why should we save the rainforests? | |
| 5 | Why are some cities capitals? | Does everyone celebrate Christmas? | Why did people invade and settle Britain? | | Can I drink a glass of water from the Ingrebourne River? | What makes a champion athlete? |
| 6 | What happened to the children in both world wars? | What does Peace on Earth really mean? | What causes the Earth to get angry? | | What makes a good learner? | What did the Egyptians do for us? |

Source: Mead Primary School (www.mead.havering.sch.uk/curriculum/long-term-plans); Focus Education (UK) Ltd

given is that it features thoughtful questions, builds on prior learning, makes connections, promotes a progressive understanding of topics and seeks to make learning relevant, as with the historical questions.

Practitioners working with young children should base their long-term plans on appropriate national guidance. In England this draws on the four principles of the Early Years Foundation Stage or EYFS (DfE, 2012): responding to the uniqueness of each child, building positive relationships, enabling environments and promoting learning and development. It should also take into account the core statutory framework for children from birth to the end of their reception year. Most local authorities provide planning exemplars for the EYFS, including support for teachers of mixed reception and Key Stage 1 classes, plans for phonics teaching, planning for adult-led and initiated experiences and making the most of outdoor learning opportunities (e.g. www.wiltshire.gov.uk/eyfs-planning-examples-pack.pdf).

Although trainee teachers are unlikely to have much experience of long-term planning, during placement induction meetings it is sensible to gain an overview of where the school is heading. In Scotland, the Education Scotland website provides guidance on how schools can ensure coverage of the key elements in *Building the Curriculum 3* (Scottish Government, 2008). Schools are advised to begin their long-term planning by considering their current position, where they would like to be and how they can get there. The website provides a template for curriculum planning and includes video tutorials on planning. Examples drawn from schools also illustrate different focal points, such as developing cross-curricular links or increasing pupils' say in the curriculum. Teachers in Wales should refer closely to the Foundation Phase, national curriculum subject requirements, the relevant Agreed Syllabus for Religious Education, the National Literacy and Numeracy Framework (Welsh Government, 2013) and the National Support Programme.

## School policies

Long-term planning includes the writing of key policies in school. These provide an overview of how schools operate. Among the most important ones to consider are those covering: learning and teaching, assessment, homework, health and safety, and behaviour management. School policies can vary considerably in detail. Take the example of homework (Box 9.1). In one school, the policy might be that Reception children receive 10 minutes or more homework a day, increasing to two and a half hours a week in Year 6. Another school may not introduce homework until Year 1 and by Year 6 it is less than an hour. Still others have abandoned homework policies and practice altogether (Henry, 2012).

## Cross-curricular planning

Cross-curricular planning and teaching has enjoyed long-standing popularity among primary teachers. In a survey of 311 primary teachers from Northern Ireland, Greenway (2007) reports that 91 per cent favour cross-curricular teaching. The nature and scope of cross-curricular work has been subject to considerable change over recent years reflecting political priorities. In England alone, it has included sustainable development, financial capability, enterprise, values education, citizenship and thinking skills, in addition to six skills identified in the 1999 curriculum: communication, application of number,

---

**BOX 9.1  HOMEWORK**

Government guidelines for England and Wales were introduced in 1998 and stated that children between 5 and 7 years old should receive 20 minutes of homework a night (DfEE, 1998; Estyn, 2004). Feedback from teachers and parents suggests that for many children this is inappropriate because they are too tired to concentrate when they come home from school. The Coalition Government in 2012 duly scrapped these guidelines. In Scotland, homework should not exceed 30 minutes a day by the end of P7 (Medwell and Simpson, 2008). The Scottish government encourages parents to see homework as 'learning out of school'. Research indicates that the value of homework is optimized when it is done in moderate amounts. Most homework takes the form of reading, mathematical games, spelling, multiplication tables, and follow-up work to topics introduced in class.

---

information and communications technology, working with others, improving own learning and performance, and problem-solving. The Coalition Government's National Curriculum has a strong subject focus, rejecting what it saw as the 'woolly, cross-curricular skills' of the Labour regime (Paton, 2013). Only the development of pupils' competence in numeracy and mathematics, language and literacy are identified as areas to be taught across the curriculum (DfE, 2013). However, there is no doubting that many primary schools engage pupils' interests and provide rich, meaningful experiences through a cross-curricular approach (Rowley and Cooper, 2009; Kerry, 2011). Schools retain the professional autonomy in deciding how they are to plan the timetable and arrange the day, providing the content of the programmes of study is covered. Where schools have been very successful in planning in a cross-curricular way there is no reason to change their approach. Barnes (2011) takes the view that cross-curricular work should help children make a positive impact upon the *future*, whereas National Curriculum subjects are designed to help them understand their world *now*. He advocates limiting subjects to a maximum of four rather than try to bend everyone into a particular theme; otherwise there is a danger of making artificial and tenuous links and not developing a depth of learning. He also suggests focusing upon 'powerful experiences' – exploring sites, materials and ideas – asking big questions, and striking a balance between experience, skills and knowledge. In Scottish schools, effective planning for **interdisciplinary learning** includes clarity over what children are to learn based around a few big ideas from different subjects (Education Scotland, 2012). Similarly advice to Welsh schools is to plan cross-curricular topics or themes with clear objectives in mind and to build upon what children already know, understand and can do (Estyn, 2000).

## Medium-term planning

Medium-term plans usually cover a school term or year and provide details regarding the elements of learning to be promoted: knowledge, skills, concepts, attitudes and values. These are sometimes presented as units or **schemes of work**. Resources and teaching strategies should be geared towards maximizing opportunities for pupils to engage in challenging and enjoyable activities.

In England, during the late 1990s and early 2000s many schools adopted wholesale schemes of work introduced by the Qualifications and Curriculum Authority (QCA), a public body set up in 1997 and responsible for maintaining the national curriculum. Some schools valued these non-statutory schemes as planning tools that set out expectations, objectives, activities, resources and intended outcomes for each unit linked to national curriculum subjects. They are still available for reference on the national archives website (http://webarchive.nationalarchives.gov.uk). Although the QCA included examples of annotated schemes, unfortunately, many schools did not adapt the exemplars. This proved detrimental to teachers' creativity and flexibility, as schools throughout the land uniformly learned about the likes of the Indian village of Chembakolli and the paintings of Mondrian rather than developing a curriculum tailored to the needs and interests of children and schools. Moreover, specific criticisms were levied at the conceptual underpinning behind schemes. Hodkinson (2004), for example, was critical of the history schemes, which he considered confusing and ineffective in developing children's understanding of historical time. However, the plans did provide teachers, especially inexperienced and weak ones, with a clear and substantial planning framework – this was particularly so in subjects such as design and technology where curriculum time and training have been squeezed. Figure 9.3 shows part of the design and technology unit for a Year 1 class topic on Homes. The different expectations supported teachers in differentiating their teaching.

There are a number of commercial curriculum programmes used by schools. Chris Quigley Education (2008) focuses on developing subject and 'learning to learn' skills, building on the work of Guy Claxton (2002). Pupils can progress through these skills and achieve bronze, silver and gold levels, for instance in being reflective, resilient and resourceful. Some schools follow the International Primary Curriculum, which is a well-established approach to planning based around exciting themes such as 'Airports', 'Global Swapshop' and 'I'm Alive!" (see www.greatlearning.com/ipc). Similarly the Cornerstones Curriculum seeks to provide teachers with imaginative content linked to the National Curriculum, based around four principles (Engage, Develop, Innovate and Express). Year 3 pupils, for example, follow a unit (Imaginative Learning Project) called 'Scrumdiddlyumptious' (www.cornerstoneseducation.co.uk).

The curriculum planning of schools identified as outstanding by OFSTED shares common characteristics. These include a focus on developing creativity, stimulating the imagination and finding ways of engaging pupils, parents and community to become actively involved in the curriculum. For example, at Cracoe and Rylstone Church of England Primary School in North Yorkshire, every topic has a launch event and a landing. The launch hooks the children into the topic and the landing is a final event to celebrate learning, for instance an assembly or performance where parents are invited in. Between these two events, children and teachers work together on a skills-based curriculum. In another outstanding school, when planning the next curriculum theme, teachers consult their pupils about what it is they know about the theme and what they would like to learn. Pupils are expected to produce something tangible at the end of each theme to show their learning to others. This can include working together on projects and involving parents. Examples include an art gallery replicating the work of a range of artists, a professionally published book on human rights entitled 'Every Child Counts' and a Tudor banquet.

## Unit 1D Homes
### Focus – structures

### ABOUT THE UNIT

This unit gives children opportunities to develop their understanding of structures. Observation of different types of building gives children experience and information to draw on when developing their own ideas. They develop and model their ideas by creating static models from sheet and reclaimed materials and using construction kits. They gain a basic understanding about structures and how these can be made stronger and more stable.

This unit could be adapted by focusing on different types of building or by giving children an opportunity to design and make other static models *eg containers.*

Unit 1B 'Playgrounds' is an appropriate alternative to this unit.

### PRIOR LEARNING

It is helpful if the children have:

- used basic tools safely and appropriately
- discussed ideas
- worked with paper and card – cutting, shaping and joining

This unit builds on experience of play with construction kits and early opportunities for making with reclaimed materials. It also builds on Unit 1A 'Moving pictures'.

### VOCABULARY

In this unit, children will use words and phrases relating to:

- designing *eg choose, try out ideas, discuss, drawing, label, list*
- making *eg join, fix, plan, scissors, hole punch, masking tape*
- knowledge and understanding *eg structure, strong, weak, wall, roof, window, glass, brick, transparent, hinge*
  - mathematical understanding *eg square, rectangle, triangle, cube, cuboid, side, edge, surface, on top of, underneath, smaller than, symmetrical, beside, next to*

### RESOURCES

- pictures/photographs/books showing different types of homes
- construction kits suitable for building walls and shell structures
- sheet materials – card, papers, plastics *eg from tomato containers,* foil, transparent materials *eg acetate, plastic bags*
- range of suitable reclaimed materials for making buildings
- joining materials *eg glue, masking tape*
- finishing materials *eg collage materials, paint, fabric pieces*
- scissors, snips, hole punch, stapler

### EXPECTATIONS

**at the end of this unit**

*most children will:*

have constructed a model home, incorporating the main features of windows and doors, which shows evidence of understanding different types of buildings and their main features

*some children will not have made so much progress and will:*

have built a model from construction kit components and attached features to the model *eg roofs and windows using sheet or reclaimed materials* or, with support, have built a model from reclaimed materials

*some children will have progressed further and will:*

have added more details and features *eg stairs, interior rooms, cut-out windows, curtains, gutters* and be able to say why they have included them; have used a basic understanding of structures to make their models strong and stable

**FIGURE 9.3** Part of the scheme of work for a DT topic

Source: http://webarchive.nationalarchives.gov.uk

## Short-term planning

Planning over the short term covers what is to be taught during the day or week. For trainee teachers, training providers usually expect separate lesson plans on the basis that the trainees need to gain experience in the process of thinking through what they are going to do. John (2006) argues that trainee teachers should not be expected to follow a common planning format because this constricts their creativity and does not give due regard to the uncertainties of the classroom, such as time-pressures, attitudes and moods. Instead, he supports a dialogical model where trainee teachers focus on those aspects of planning that are most significant to their particular circumstances and needs.

Research shows that more experienced teachers, including outstanding ones, do not use written lesson plans but are able to give clear mental plans when asked (McCutcheon, 2002). They may draw up aide mémoires for themselves, noting key teaching points or resource issues. But the key planning strategy involves mentally rehearsing the sequence of the lesson before delivery, 'running through' in their heads possible difficulties and practical considerations, such as when to give out materials. Experts tend to leave detailed decision making to the time prior to starting the lesson or to various points in the lesson itself (John, 2006). Whereas experienced teachers engage in long-range planning, the thinking of beginners is more short term. For many teachers, lesson plans are presented as weekly overviews or highlighted half-term plans.

In England and Wales despite the introduction of guaranteed time for planning, preparation and assessment (PPA time) in 2005, which was welcomed by the teaching profession, around half of primary teachers acknowledged that this did not result in improvements to their planning (DCSF, 2009). This is partly because PPA time is used in many different ways, other than to plan lessons. Planning, especially in the light of frequent curriculum change, continues to cause teachers stress. In some schools, planning is seen as a heavy, formulaic burden and, more generally, a factor why some teachers leave the profession (Vasagar, 2011). However, planning does not have to be like this. There are legitimate ways to reduce planning and preparation time. Plans can be streamlined, shared and adapted. ICT can be utilized and additional adults deployed effectively in preparing materials. The Department for Education, OFSTED and the QCA (DfES, 2002) reassure inspectors are not looking for a particular model of planning, provided lesson objectives were clear. The preparation of overly detailed lesson plans, running to 3 or 4 pages and typically including 500-word descriptions of activities, has been criticized by OFSTED (2012) as being counter-productive, inflexible and not necessarily focused. Sir Michael Wilshaw, head of OFSTED, acknowledges that 'there should be no prescription about lesson structure' (quoted by Ward, 2012b: 4). The most recent inspection handbook elaborates:

> Inspectors will not expect teachers to prepare lesson plans for the inspection. However, they will use the evidence gathered from lesson observations to help judge the overall quality of the school's curriculum planning ... inspectors must not advocate a particular approach to teaching or planning lessons. It is for the school to determine how best to teach and engage pupils to secure their good learning.
>
> (OFSTED, 2013: 11–12)

There are similar reassurances from the other inspectorates in the UK, whose main focus is on the impact of planning rather than any particular format that will vary according to school context. As a general principle, plans for younger children tend to be more open-ended to build on their interests and respond to their changing needs, whereas Key Stage 2 plans adopt a more formal structure. Most teachers working within the 3–11 age range will use weekly overviews containing objectives or key questions, summaries of the session content and group activities, a list of resources, the roles of additional adults and assessment strategies.

There are different models of lesson planning but the most prevalent are based on a long-standing interest in achieving set objectives. John (2006) traces this to the influence of Tyler (1949), Bloom (1956) and Gagné (1970), and their interest in a rational, efficient system of instruction. They advocated a linear process of planning, which begins with the specification of objectives and ends with a lesson evaluation. Bloom's taxonomy has been criticized, for example because it implies pupils need to start with recall and description and progress towards analysis and synthesis. Instead, Sherborne (2013) argues that these higher-order processes should be used from the beginning to facilitate understanding. Interestingly, McCutcheon (1980) found that American elementary teachers rarely planned lessons on the objectives-first model. Rather they chose the activities first and then planned around the students. However, Bloom continues to underpin curricula planning and sets out levels of learning used by many teachers. Gershon (2013) argues that even in its original form, Bloom's Taxonomy should still be part of a teacher's planning (Box 9.2). He advises teachers to be more proactive in displaying the verbs associated with the revised model with related questions and challenges. Hence, using the top two levels of the Taxonomy, pupils could be arranged in groups to devise an advertising campaign to sell what they have learned during the lesson (synthesize) and then to present their campaign so the class can judge how well they have synthesized the learning.

---

**BOX 9.2  PLANNING QUESTIONS TO CONSIDER BASED ON BLOOM'S REVISED TAXONOMY OF OBJECTIVES**

**Remembering** – what essential knowledge and skills are to be covered?

**Understanding**– what do I intend the pupils to understand?

**Applying** – what opportunities will pupils have to use their knowledge? How will I make reference to real-life contexts?

**Analysing** – how will pupils think about the content? Can I create activities in which they summarize what they have learned?

**Evaluating** – what will I do to check the progress of pupils against the learning objectives? How will I encourage pupils to evaluate themselves and see the value of the lesson?

**Creating** – what opportunities will pupils have to create, plan or combine ideas?

(Adapted from Anderson and Krathwohl, 2000)

---

**BOX 9.3  THE MADELINE HUNTER MODEL OF LESSON PLANNING**

1   **Anticipatory set** (introduction) – a snappy 'wake-up' activity to gain attention and interest, setting the stage for the lesson; seeking ways to activate learners' prior knowledge and experience to help them relate to the lesson.

2   **Objectives** – telling pupils what they'll be able to do as a result of the lesson.

3   **Input** – giving out instructions, communicating key knowledge.

4   **Model** – demonstrate what might be the intended outcome and explain the process.

5   **Check for understanding** – ask questions, look at faces and other body language cues.

6   **Guided practice** – helps pupils to start summarizing new skills, applying new knowledge under supervision and direction.

7   **Independent practice** – allows pupils opportunity to work on their own, without teacher input, to summarize new skills.

8   **Closure** – sum up learning and next steps.

---

The introduction of standardized curricular and a greater focus on meeting targets in many countries has meant that teachers have been more conscious of planning with clear objectives in mind. Many American students make use of the Madeline Hunter model for lesson planning (Hunter, 1982). Hunter's research into effective teaching found that irrespective of the teacher's style or background, or the abilities of the class, lessons were planned around common elements that enhanced learning. An adapted version is noted in Box 9.3. The eight-step model does not include self-assessment and evaluative elements, although both of these can be integrated through the whole process. There are variations on this model and in some cases not all steps are present in every lesson. It was not designed as a rigid model but to guide trainee teachers in thinking about what is necessary when planning.

Petty (2009) advocates an alternative model of lesson planning known as Present, Apply and Review (PAR). Typically in a one-hour lesson the teacher begins by presenting new material (15 minutes) and then sets activities for the pupils to apply the knowledge, theories or skills that have just been presented (40 minutes). The learning is then summarized and clarified, with an emphasis on the key points (5 minutes). Most teachers use variations on the traditional three-part lesson based on a starter, where the teacher introduces a topic, followed by the middle part when children undertake activities and the conclusion, when there is discussion and assessment of what has been learned.

## Characteristics of effective short-term plans

There is always a danger that prescribed lesson planning formats dictate teachers' thinking processes. It makes sense therefore to focus on the key features of effective plans as borne out by research, practice and general educational consensus (DfES, 2002). These can be expressed as responses to simple questions (Figure 9.4):

- Why is this lesson being taught?
- What will the pupils do?
- How will you know what they have learned?
- What are the next steps to improve learning?

## Why? (Learning objectives)

Short-term planning begins with trying to explain the purpose of the lesson and what teachers hope children will take away. Slavin (2003) refers to the concept of 'intentionality', by which he means doing things for a reason; the intentional teachers are constantly thinking about the outcomes they want their students to achieve and about how each decision they make moves children towards those outcomes. However, all teachers make changes to their short- and medium-term plans. In the hands of the effective teachers, lesson plans are not used as rigid structures. As Leaman (2006: 9) points out: 'Planning should inform and direct what happens in the classroom, not prescribe it.' That said, it is very challenging for trainee teachers with limited experience to implement a *major* change of direction during the flow of a lesson. There are times, however, when astute teachers recognize the need to redirect, pause, reflect (with the children), and perhaps abandon the planned lesson altogether. This should not be seen as an admission of failure. Rather, it can be seen as an indicator of a mature and reflective practitioner.

Most lesson plans feature one or more of the following: aims, goals, **learning objectives**, learning intentions or intended learning outcomes. Teachers should consider the following key question: 'At the end of the lesson/session/term/year, what do I want my students to know, to do or to understand which will take their learning on from where it is now?' (Kerry, 2002: 1).

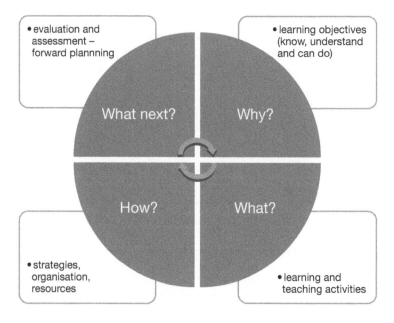

**FIGURE 9.4** Planning questions

Learning objectives can be framed in terms of knowledge and understanding, concepts, skills, values and attitudes. Objectives are often classified as behavioural and non-behavioural. The former have been variously described as measurable objectives, instructional objectives and performance goals. They all focus on what learners are able to do after a set period of time and hence the intended behaviour needs to be explicit – for instance, to explain how evaporation works, to list three reasons why the Romans invaded Britain, to construct an electrical circuit. There are times when objectives need to be less precise and measurable, for example when seeking to develop learners' appreciation of a painting or poem, sensitivity to other people's feelings or sense of awe associated with a particular place or object. Although difficult to measure, these non-behavioural objectives are appealing because they are more flexible and 'open up' access to higher-level thinking – they are often expressed through infinitives such as *to appreciate*, *to be aware of* or *to understand* (Cohen *et al.*, 2004: 120). To plan for deep learning, by which pupils apply their knowledge and reflect on what they know, requires an understanding of the key concepts that underpin each subject (Erickson, 2007).

The customary advice to beginning teachers is to write learning objectives and improvement targets with the acronym SMART (Specific, Measurable, Achievable, Realistic, Time-related) in mind (Hughes, 2002; Petty, 2009; Cockburn and Handscomb, 2006). It is important to focus on pupil achievement rather than teacher performance and the outcome rather than the process. Learning objectives should contain verbs (Table 9.2) that focus on what pupils will do (rather than the teacher). The choice of verb is important because this will form the basis of assessment. Hence, if a teacher writes 'by the end of the lesson, pupils will plan a journey to a local museum', then the pupils will need to have the opportunity to plan out the route and the plan will provide the evidence of their learning. These can be easily converted into pupil-friendly target cards, e.g. 'to describe . . .' or 'to list . . .'.

Technically speaking, there is a difference between learning objectives and learning outcomes. Learning objectives cover what teachers would *like* pupils to learn by the end of the session, whereas learning outcomes refer to what pupils have actually learned. It is therefore more accurate to write learning objectives or *intended* learning outcomes on lesson plans.

Learning objectives should relate closely to the relevant curriculum requirements. Trainee teachers sometimes refer to a long list, whereas the skill is to focus on two or three specific references. Hence, rather than aiming to develop pupils' speaking skills it

**TABLE 9.2** Useful words when writing learning objectives

| Recall | Reorganize | Apply |
|--------|------------|-------|
| Repeat | Describe | Use |
| Define | Plan | Analyse |
| Identify | Review | Compare |
| Name | Explain | Calculate |
| List | Translate | Interpret |
| | Tabulate | Solve |
| | | Demonstrate |

is better for teaching and assessment purposes to hone in on particular aspects, say 'speak audibly and fluently' or 'logically argue a case'.

It is common in many schools for teachers to express objectives as TIB ('This is because . . .'), WALT ('What Are We Learning Today'), or OLI ('Our Learning Intention is . . .') along with success criteria expressed as WILF (What I'm Looking For is . . .), terms popularized by Shirley Clarke in the late 1990s and conveyed by some teachers through comic or animal characters. However, Clarke herself admits that WILF in particular has not had the desired impact. Pupils tend to give back to teachers what they think they want and WILF only served to reinforce this, rather than children devising their own success criteria. Even worse, using animals meant some young children say, 'We're learning this for the dog' (Ward, 2012a). In many schools, older pupils themselves record learning objectives in their books and use them as a basis for assessing their progress during the lesson. There are times when teachers decide *not* to share the learning objectives with the children and instead encourage the class to suggest what these could have been at the end of the session.

Many teachers write learning objectives on the board. But as Walker (2008) points out, merely writing the learning objectives for pupils to read and copy does not mean that they understand them. Moreover, as guidance to teachers in Northern Ireland (CCEA, 2002) makes clear, teachers should not confuse what pupils are doing with what they are learning. Hence learning objectives need to focus on the learning rather than the activities. Knight (2011) suggests using learning questions with pupils such as: 'Do I know how to write open and closed questions?'

Learning objectives are often *differentiated* to meet the needs of different learners. The 'must/should/could' formula was advocated by the QCA schemes of work widely used in the 2000s. Some schools think this shows a lack of sensitivity to lower achievers and demotivates them. Others use the differentiated objectives as targets. With such an approach there is a danger of setting groups of pupils up for a limiting experience and creating a culture of low expectations. It is important therefore to be flexible (by encouraging individuals to move on to reach more demanding objectives) and not to 'box in' particular learners.

## What? (Learning and teaching)

When planning lessons, it is sometimes easy to lose sight of the fact that the focus should be on what children will learn and what teachers intend to teach. In reality, learning and teaching are rarely neat and tidy. Much learning takes place in an unplanned, spontaneous manner. The challenge for new teachers is to accept that carefully devised activities can constrict (as well as enable) learning. The word 'activities' is derived from the Latin *activus*, meaning a 'state of being active, briskness, liveliness'. In schools that follow philosophies that promote active learning, such as Reggio Emilia and High/Scope, children are reported to be more confident and reflective in their decision making, self-motivated, expressive and energetic (Williams, 2003). Some challenges are also noted, including managing time and space (Whitebread, 2007). Teachers should try and plan a range of stimulating activities including: reading and writing for different purposes and audiences, investigations, games, debate, listening, discussion, designing and making things, drama, art work, composition and performance. As one of the fundamental aims of education is to promote independent learning, activities need to be devised to encourage pupils to explore, question, think and try things out. There are various ways of encouraging independence. These include:

- allowing children opportunities to plan some of the activities themselves;
- giving children a 'planning board' on which they note their tasks and allow them choice of when they do particular activities;
- using a variety of visual prompts to remind pupils of 'how to' tackle problems;
- use of **peer tutoring**;
- providing open-ended tasks and questions e.g. 'What would you think about . . .?';
- allowing children opportunities to access, use, organize and manage resources; and
- use of peer and self-assessment (see Chapter 13).

Time needs to be planned for children to exercise responsibilities, for example in sorting and tidying their areas. It is also important to reduce the likelihood of minor interruptions, such as when children ask to sharpen a pencil.

Making activities interesting is not straightforward despite the oft-quoted advice to do so. There is a plethora of tips available to trainees on how to spice up introductions, sustain interest during the middle section of lessons and reach a rousing conclusion (Best, 2003; Cohen *et al.*, 2004). Teachers need to find out through discussions and observations what individual pupils are interested in, how they relate to others and how they respond to different subjects. Chasty (1997) put it succinctly in pointing out that 'If a child does not learn the way you teach, then teach him the way he learns.' While some children prefer reading, others prefer to listen or to find out things by working with others. It is important to take into account the different starting points of learners. Wilson (2000) discusses the difficulties of 'dressing up' subjects without losing their essence. His unusual answer is to think of subjects as 'forms of life' and not just a mix of knowledge and skills. Rather, he asks teachers to consider questions such as 'What would a school look like if it devoted itself entirely for (say) a month to immersing pupils in literature/science/ music/French etc?' or 'How can pupils be given permanent and habitual responsibility for pursuing the subject?' These philosophical questions may seem of little practical value to teachers eager to capture the interest of thirty 11-year-olds on a wet Friday afternoon. But some schools have responded creatively to the timetable by planning 'blocks' of time for teaching particular subjects or themes.

### How? (Strategies)

Lesson plans need to note logistical information, such as the number of learners in the class, those with special or additional needs, the nature of the groupings, approximate timings for each stage of the session and the duration of the session. It can be a useful exercise to allocate an approximate time to each part of a lesson plan and this is an expectation among some teacher training providers. Broadly speaking, in a three-section lesson plan, the introduction may last up to 10 minutes, the main body cover 30–40 minutes, concluding with a 10-minute plenary. Some trainees build into their lessons time for pupils to ask questions as a regular feature. Those who prefer to plan more open-ended lessons have called the three-part structure into question. As the popular writer and consultant Pie Corbett explains: 'Some sessions may not start with teaching at all. The children might enter the room to find there are floury footprints everywhere and the bin has been turned over – what has happened?' (cited by Ward, 2012b).

Questioning is a key teaching strategy that is discussed in detail in Chapter 11. For planning purposes, some teachers record one or two key questions to 'anchor' the lessons against the learning objectives and subject coverage. The questions can stem from what the pupils have already asked in previous lessons. This has the advantage of using pupils' own interests to structure the session and, in theory, they should be motivated to want to find out more. Effective practice involves high-quality adult–child interactions or **'sustained shared thinking'** (Siraj-Blatchford *et al.*, 2002). Table 9.3 illustrates the variety and challenging nature of questions, taken from the Northern Ireland curriculum. American research shows that teachers who are unfamiliar with lesson content tend to plan low-level tasks and questions and discourage learners from asking questions themselves (Kauchak and Eggen, 2007).

One of the challenges when planning is how to engage the 'invisible pupils', who are often overlooked. They rarely cause disruption or participate. They appear to be present in body but not in mind. Practical strategies to engage such pupils include encouraging the class to answer, not by raising hands but by writing answers on mini boards. Research by the Nuffield Foundation in primary science lessons found the use of puppets, animated by teachers, helped shy pupils open up. The puppets provide pupils with a reason to talk by posing questions using simple vocabulary, whereas talking to an adult can be intimidating (see www.puppetsproject.com). Effective teachers inevitably draw upon children's experiences and interests in everyday school life. They may do this by finding out, before a lesson starts, common points of interest or recalling pupil ideas from other lessons. Martin (2012) suggests that teachers make use of 'personal bests' (PBs) to challenge learners and improve enjoyment of learning. According to Hattie (2012), these relate to setting goals that are competitive (relative to previous bests) and self-improving (success leads to enhanced performance).

Beginning teachers are often advised to plan work at three levels: lower, mid and higher ability. In a sense this is a rather arbitrary convention but it is a reminder not to treat the class as one homogenous unit. One of the common experiences when planning is the tendency to pitch work at the needs of the broad middle ability range within the class and to provide additional material, demands or help for those at the extremes (Kyriacou, 2007). The difficulty with this approach is that the higher-attaining pupils tend to be given more work in the form of extension sheets, rather than stimulated to learn at a deeper level. Many studies have indicated that devising tasks so that they are well matched to pupils' needs is a very demanding aspect of teaching (McNeil and Sammons, 2006). Much is made of setting challenging tasks for all learners.

**TABLE 9.3** Key questions relating to 'The World Around Us' featured in the Northern Ireland curriculum

| Question | Concept | Subject |
| --- | --- | --- |
| Why do people and animals move? | Movement and energy | Science |
| Where do we live? | Place | Geography |
| How has this place changed? | Change | History |
| Am I the same as everyone else? | Interdependence | Science |

The concept of 'challenge' is a complex one. It relates to what learners already know and is highly individual. Teachers tend to see challenge in the task set whereas pupils see challenge in the struggle to complete the activity. Hattie (2012: 51) points out that 'in most school tasks, we need to already know about 90 per cent of what we are aiming to master in order to enjoy and make the most of the challenge'. In reading, this prior knowledge is more like 95–99 per cent – if learners know less than 50 per cent of what is being taught, they are not likely to be engaged in the task. This can lead to feelings of boredom, self-doubt and fear. This raises important implications for lesson planning. Highly skilled teachers find out what children know prior to introducing new ideas and are able to set tasks that are moderately challenging but not so demanding that they are beyond the grasp of learners. They create a climate in which feedback is a matter of routine and focuses on the strategies used by learners, the nature of misconceptions and the value of errors. As teachers gain experience and know-how, most widen their approaches to differentiation beyond the customary graded worksheets or ability groups, both of which have their critics (Box 9.4). There is flexibility to draw upon content from earlier or later key stage programmes of study, provided this is appropriate to the needs of individual pupils. Rose and Howley (2007: 19) warn that 'simply giving a pupil with SEN work that is less demanding than that given to others is not adequate'.

Kerry (2002) reports on the relative merits of various differentiation strategies and concludes that the nature of the group/class should be considered carefully in deciding on the most appropriate form. Above all, it is important to reflect upon the purpose of differentiation. For instance, is it to increase knowledge and understanding, to set challenges or to sustain interest? Differentiation has to be 'for' the pupils in the sense that it is a means to remove potential barriers to learning and to open up opportunities for all pupils to achieve.

Planning for differentiation requires a detailed understanding of individual pupils, for instance those identified with additional learning needs, new arrivals, those for whom English is an additional language, and those who may have missed previous related lessons. Such knowledge can be acquired through regular conversations with colleagues and

---

**BOX 9.4  KEY CONCEPT – DIFFERENTIATION**

Kerry (2002: 81) defines differentiation as 'the process whereby the levels of tasks set to students in class or for homework are matched to the known levels of performance and potential of the individual students involved'. The ideas of curriculum access and entitlement that underpin differentiation are not new. The Hadow Report (1931: 151) pointed out that 'the teacher's method must be elastic enough to meet the needs, often widely divergent of all the children'. Differentiation gained popularity in the 1980s with for example a government *White Paper* (DES, 1985) explaining that it was one of the key principles upon which the curriculum should be based. Differentiation requires teachers to have a strong awareness of individual needs and an ability to adjust the curriculum to these needs. Research points to using a range of classroom strategies, including grouping, questioning, varying objectives, recording methods, time and pace, and exploiting pupils' interests (Lance and Hill, 1995).

parents, as well as through observing and talking to the children. One danger for teachers is going through the motions when planning for different abilities. Rose and Howley (2007: 19) warn that: 'At times, what passes for differentiation is no better than discrimination. If all that is achieved is the presentation of work to pupils, that keeps them occupied but does not advance their learning, we are not providing an adequate service to the individual.'

There is a tendency sometimes for teachers to think that only the more able pupils need to be challenged. All pupils should find learning challenging but within their grasp. Taking different groups into account, it is possible to vary the lesson pace, content, structure and time as part of balanced differentiation. In some cases, work needs to be planned for an individual pupil because of specific learning difficulties. However, no individual pupil should ever feel isolated in the classroom. The overall aim is to involve all pupils in the lesson and so different work should not exclude pupils from key elements in the lesson, such as discussing what has been achieved against the learning objectives.

## Deployment of additional adults

It is important to plan also for the contribution of other adults, noting how they will support children's learning. These may include: learning support assistants, parents, other students and voluntary helpers. Vincett *et al.* (2005) discuss models of teamwork in classrooms and how teacher assistants can be deployed most effectively. It's possible, under the 'zoning model', to allocate assistants to particular areas of the classroom in which different activities will occur such as painting and cooking. The zoning method also involves adults taking responsibility for pupils passing through their areas, not dissimilar to zonal marking in football matches.

Workforce reforms and curriculum changes, especially in the Early Years, have meant that the number of teacher assistants has increased dramatically in recent years (Sage and Wilkie, 2004). Islington Early Years Foundation Team (2009) suggests the following guidelines for deploying adults over the course of a week:

- two fifths of their time supporting child-initiated play and learning;
- two-fifths of their time leading adult-guided activities (including opportunities for guided work in literacy, group and circle times for children aged 3–5); and
- one-fifth of their time observing children.

An assistant's job description might mean that she is expected by the school to work alongside a particular child, a group or more generally to act in a monitoring role. For instance, in an outdoor session an additional adult might be asked to observe closely the play of boys and girls, given the research evidence that boys tend to dominate outside play and the use of equipment (Hobart and Frankel, 2005). The teacher assistant might support pupils working on the computer, or in reading. In many cases the assistant will be delegated by the school to support an individual with additional learning needs. This should be noted in the session plan. Communication between the supporting adult, children, class teacher and the trainee is particularly important. Where this is not clear, there is potential for role conflict within the team and associated stress. Managing people involves many skills that may not be at the forefront of teacher education courses. Vincett *et al.* (2005) point out that team work that swept through schools in the 1970s was abandoned due to complex factors, not least the teacher's need for privacy and independence. The authors add that the rhetoric for the benefits of additional support is so strong that little thought has been given to the changing dynamics within the classroom and how the potential support of additional adults can be maximized. For trainee teachers, there is often the challenge of working alongside older, more experienced support assistants. Moreover, from a child's perspective, the impact of the growing number of adults in the classroom in terms of constraining their initiative has not yet been fully explored.

## What next? (Assessment to inform planning)

Lessons should feature opportunities to review pupils' progress against the learning objectives. This does not always have to occur at the end of the lesson. Brief mini-plenaries, at appropriate points, enable pupils to explain or show what they are learning and any difficulties encountered. Traditionally the term 'progression' has been taken to mean 'getting through' topics. But planning for progression involves taking into account children's starting points in learning (DCSF, 2007). It is about the *rate* of progress for each learner. Popham (2011) distinguishes between 'upper case' and 'lower case' learning progressions. In the former, the teacher focuses on pupils' understanding of 'big or rich' ideas, how their learning of particular things develops over a period of time, and judgements on progression are based on solid evidence. With 'lower-case' progression, teachers consider what pupils have learned over a relatively short period of time, as a result of their instruction. In order to achieve this, teachers need to establish what pupils know, do and understand at given points. This is informed by various sources including: what they have learned from evaluations of previous learning, discussions with the class teacher, and mapped content within mid-term plans and curriculum guidance. The skilled teacher then adapts the lesson according to how the pupils are progressing. By observing children at work, asking questions, holding brief discussions, listening to children's responses and marking work, it is possible to build up an understanding of how well children are doing within a session. It may be the case that the pupils need more (or less) time to come to terms with the material. This assessment of learning demands secure subject knowledge, awareness of pupils' individual needs, together with the confidence to change track in the lesson. Collecting information on how well pupils learn can be obtained in many forms – oral, written, pictorial and practical evidence – but should relate to the objectives for each session and lead into future plans (feed forward). A broad range of work examples will contribute to a solid base for making judgements on pupils' progress and as a result report the extent of pupil achievement (Nicholls, 2004).

In terms of planning for progression, it is important to consider how the tasks set are likely to move pupils forward in their learning by:

- working in increasingly analytical ways (e.g. making a summary of learning);
- handling more complex material and ideas (e.g. comparing different interpretations);
- constructing their own enquiries (e.g. formulating questions on a given topic); and

- with encouragement, exploring content areas that technically lie outside the curriculum as defined (e.g. exploring content from a higher phase).

In the past, planning for progression has meant getting through topics rather than progression in children's learning (DCSF, 2007). Lessons can be learned from those working in other fields. For example Andy Banks, who coached the Olympic medal-winning swimmer Tom Daley, explains that he helps him understand why and where he had gone wrong, focusing on process and ignoring everything else. They discuss planning backwards, thinking through 'this is where he needs to be, this is where we are now, so what are we going to do now to achieve that?' (Cited by Lucas and Claxton, 2012: 28).

Planning should take into account how pupils' progress will be monitored and assessed. This should include details of strategies and anticipated evidence of achievement. It is common practice to note within lesson plans that children's prior knowledge and understanding will be reviewed at the outset. This diagnostic approach can provide useful information and questions such as 'Who can tell me what we did in our last music lesson?' or 'Can anyone show us how to . . .?' link teacher assessment and pupil learning (Brown and Wragg, 2001). Outstanding teachers encourage learners to think about how well they are doing in progressing towards the learning objectives and share success criteria (what needs to be done to achieve the objectives) to this end. Self- and peer assessment can be implemented from an early age through the use of simple visual and verbal instructions. For older children the use of written checklists or reminders on the wall serves to focus their attention on whether they have completed the tasks required. A 'yes/no' or 'tick/cross' entry keeps this manageable and provides children with the beginnings of self -review prior to handing in work (Briggs et al., 2008).

There are times when learning objectives may apply to particular parts of lessons or group activities and not others. For instance, during a numeracy session the learning objectives may vary for the mental warm-up, directed group activities and the whole-class plenary. Moreover, in some cases learning objectives might be tailored to individual children in the form of personalized targets. More generally, the use of self-review questions tied to the learning objectives is an important assessment strategy. These can include:

- What did you find difficult about learning to . . .?
- What are you very pleased with about learning to . . .?
- Can anyone remember what we were trying to learn today?
- What have you learned new today that you didn't know before?
- What do you think you need to do next to improve your learning about . . .?
- If you tell someone else what this lesson was about, what would you say?

## Planning in the Early Years

Many of the key principles for planning in the Early Years apply to older children. All children should feel included, secure and valued. Effective practice also needs to build on what children can already do and their prior experiences and interests. Teachers should involve children, whatever their age, in planning lesson content so that they gain a sense of ownership. Planning should maximize opportunities to work closely with parents, carers and the wider community, which includes out-of-class learning. Particularly with young children, practitioners should understand that all areas of learning – physical, personal, social, emotional and intellectual – are interrelated and interdependent (QCA, 2000). For instance, when a child broke an arm and brought in her X-ray, staff in one school responded by opening a 'hospital'. The class discussed the needs of hospitals, including a reception with a telephone, appointments book and patient records. They set up role-play opportunities that involved attending to patients, measuring temperatures and 'writing' prescriptions. A parent, who works as a nurse, visited the class to talk about her work.

In the Early Years, teams usually hold a weekly planning review meeting attended by all practitioners working on a day-to-day basis with the children. Records or field notes of children observed should form the starting point for the meeting, to identify and plan for individual children's interests, learning and developmental needs. In Wales, Foundation Phase practitioners plan for continuous, enhanced and focused provision. Continuous provision gives children access to dedicated areas (e.g. sand/water, construction, mark-making) set up within their classroom and outdoors that they can choose to work/play in when they are not engaged in focused tasks. Enhanced provision is based on adjusting plans to enrich children's experiences, such as adding a challenge to water or sand play. Adults usually lead focused tasks, such as direct teaching of number bonds. The balance of activities is left to practitioners to decide. In England, the guidance for the Foundation Stage is around 50/50 in terms of the balance between child initiated and adult-led activities.

Practitioners need to take into account how inside and outside daily routines offer children opportunities for development and learning across the areas of learning. Such planning for 'continuous' learning could include a breakdown of the kinds of routines children enjoy and a map of the environment showing where a range of knowledge, skills and concepts can be developed through regular engagement. These might include areas for sand and water play, exploring books, sound making, role-play, and construction. Planning through topics is not appropriate for children under the age of 3 who lack the maturity to make connections. Rather, planning needs to focus heavily on the Prime Areas of Learning – personal, social and emotional development (PSED), communication and language (C&L) and physical development (PD). For children aged 3–5, mid-term plans should reflect a more equal focus on all areas of learning as children gain confidence and ability. Local authority advisory teams often provide clear guidance for teachers including planning templates (Figure 9.5).

It is not possible to plan learning objectives or intentions for activities that children choose but it is necessary to observe their learning to inform future planning. Planning for adult-guided sessions should include learning intentions (Figure 9.6).

## Involving children in planning

There is a growing emphasis upon involving pupils in the planning process, derived from a constructivist learning theory (Littledyke and Huxford, 1998; Fisher, 2002; see Box 9.6). In many respects this reflects the learner-centred notions that permeate government

| Islington's EYFS Medium Term Planning for Fictional 3-5s Setting | | Date: Autumn Term 1 | |
|---|---|---|---|
| **Main focus/Theme: Settling in** | **Personal, Social and Emotional Development** | **Communication and Language** | **Physical Development** |
| **Displays:** Children's photographs, names Tidy-up board and visual timetable Area signs and how to use them (for parents as well as children) Displays that show routines Displays of children's self-portraits for welcome board | Developing independence in using the provision Focus on self-help skills: dressing, undressing, using the toilet, etc Establish routines for children Helping children and parents to make friends Start to develop profile books for new children and use regularly as focus activity Develop familiarity of the school environment/staff – small group tours of the school taking photos of some key people e.g. FS staff, head teacher, secretary, premise manager, cook etc Opportunities for older children to support younger children | Supporting children in developing listening and attention skills Opportunities for children to talk with adults on one-to-one and small group basis Daily story sessions to encourage increasing attention and recall Set up a listening area where children can listen to stories and rhymes Regular Phase 1 activities to develop phonological awareness | Provide lots of opportunities for large, physical movement, e.g. climbing equipment, wheeled toys, balancing equipment, large construction equipment, hoops, tyres, etc Provide physical activities which will support children's friendships/co-operation skills, e.g. throwing and kicking balls to each other, using large boxes to make a construction together etc Working alongside children to develop tool use, eg: spreaders, scissors, stapler |
| **Maths** | **Literacy** | **Understanding the World** | **Expressive Arts and Design** |
| Begin to develop a repertoire of number rhymes and songs Focus on rich mathematical environment, especially outside Focus on numbers personal to children, their age, house number, telephone, siblings age etc Provide activities which develop counting skills up to 10 | Working alongside children to develop confidence in emergent writing (graphics area) Focus on a rich literacy environment, especially role play and outside Focus on meaningful print such as children's names, labels in the environment Model oral blending of sounds to make words in everyday contexts Introduce daily phonics session for those who are ready | Local trips in small groups to shops, park etc to provide opportunities for talk about who we are, where we come from and to get to know one another Provide stories that help children to make sense of different environments | Encourage and support small world and role play Ensure workshop areas for children to express themselves creatively are set up and children know how to use them (painting, music, technology, malleable etc) Begin to learn a range of familiar songs and rhymes |
| **Characteristics of Effective Learning** | **Assessment** | **Environment/Resources** | **Parents** |
| **Playing and Exploring:** Encourage children to 'have a go' and explore their new environment  **Active learning:** Encourage children to learn together and from each other Encourage children to persist with an activity even when it is challenging  **Creating and Thinking Critically:** Encourage open ended thinking Model being a thinker, showing that you don't always know | Narrative observation and discussion with parents and child to be completed for all children by half-term Providing appropriate support and differentiation for ...... (children with SEND, or EAL | Listening and responsive adults Organisation inside and out of workshop areas Resources accessible and labelled Use outside to provide/support all areas of learning | Develop relationship with parents/carers Invite parents on local trips to shops, park etc, invite parents to story time at the end of the session Plan parent/child breakfast morning – aim to introduce new parents to existing parents and build up familiarity of setting and how children learn through play |

**FIGURE 9.5** An example of a mid-term planning framework for Early Years

Source: © Islington Early Years Foundation Stage Team (2012)

| | |
|---|---|
| Date:   5th March 2012 | Name of staff:  Marian |

**Area of learning:**
Communication and Language
Physical Development
Literacy
Understanding the world

**Experience/activity:**

Can you make a plasticine boat that floats? Have water in large sink inside as well as water tray.  Let the children make guesses about whether their boat is likely to sink or float; make a chart for children to note this down

**Learning intentions:**

Describe and talk about what they see
Show curiosity about why things happen
Talk activities through and reflect on and modify what they are doing

**Targeted children:**  Nuray, Salma, Josh

**Opportunities for assessment:**

Is Nuray able to ask and answer questions?
Josh – what are his skills in manipulating the plasticine?

**Resources:**

Plasticine, wooden clay tools, rolling pins. Pictures of different boats: easel and paper for noting children's guesses about sinking and floating.

**Adult input (including language to be introduced, questions to be asked):**

Why do you think your boat sank?
How could you make it different?/What can you try now?
How did you make your boat look like that?/What happened?
You thought really hard about that.
Sink/float/top/bottom/heavy/roll

**Differentiation (how will you adapt this activity to meet all children's needs?):**

Josh- allow him to spend time manipulating plasticine, labelling his actions.
Nuray – model more complex language and encourage  himto ask questions and record info. on sheet

**Evaluation to inform future planning (in addition to individual observations):**

The activity was very popular so was continued in the afternoon. I added 2 smaller trays for children to have their own ones or work in pairs – Josh spent ages playing by himself with the boat that he had made. Nuray helped Melissa to make a boat that floated and was able to describe to me how she had made it. The plasticine got quite slimy and was hard to get off fingers.

**FIGURE 9.6** An example of a short-term plan for Early Years

Source: © Islington Early Years Foundation Stage Team (2012)

curriculum documentation especially relating to the Early Years. One of the intended outcomes of *Every Child Matters* (DfES, 2003a) was that learners should make a positive contribution to their school lives; children and young people are entitled to have ownership of their learning (Cheminais, 2006). Natural anxieties among teachers include the fear that the curriculum will not be covered if they digress in response to children's ideas. In part this is largely due to the culture in classrooms created by a national curriculum driven by tests and where pupil attainment is held as the benchmark of a teacher's success. However, the Coalition Government maintains that the National Curriculum provides the essential content, freeing teachers to spend time on a broader curriculum. Katz's view that teachers should seek to *uncover* rather than cover the curriculum (see Fisher, 2002: 38) suggests involving children more fully in the planning of sessions. In the High/Scope pre-school approach, practitioners identify five categories of 'key experiences' within which children can demonstrate independence:

1. Creative Representation (to draw, paint, role play, pretend, make models);

2. Language and Literacy (to talk about personally meaningful experiences, describe, write, have fun with language);

3. Initiative and Social Relations (to make plans, decisions, solve problems encountered in play, express feeling, be sensitive to others);

4. Movement and Music (to feel and express steady beat, move in various ways and with objects, explore the singing voice, develop melody); and

5. Logical Reasoning (to classify – explore and describe similarities, differences, and attributes of things; to seriate – comparing, arranging and fitting and ordering things by attributes; to develop number – comparing, one-to-one correspondence, counting; to be aware of space – changing shape, experiencing different play spaces, and interpreting special relations; to be aware of time – starting and stopping, time intervals, anticipating and describing sequences of events).

(OECD, 2004: 9)

The need to build on pre-school experiential learning in the primary years is now widely endorsed (HMIe, 2007a; CCEA, 2007; Stephen *et al.*, 2010). For instance, the curriculum for Northern Ireland refers to the 'Plan, Do and Review' process, which is designed to foster children's engagement in their own learning (Box 9.5).

**PAUSE FOR REFLECTION**

In some schools, children form part of interview procedures in the appointment of new teachers. One secondary school has created a student inspection team called 'Insted' – the student inspectors observe 200 lessons across all departments and write a report on their findings (Morrison, 2009). Is too much being made of pupil or student voice? Do these initiatives raise the standard of teaching or are they additional work for teachers and little more than political gimmicks?

## BOX 9.5  THE 'PLAN, DO AND REVIEW' PROCESS

**Plan**

- Clarify tasks.
- Generate ideas.
- Design ways of approaching tasks or problems.

**Do** (carry out the plan and communicate findings):

- Find and analyse relevant information.
- Create, trial or test out possible solutions.
- Make decisions.
- Draw conclusions.
- Present ideas, opinions or outcomes.

**Review** (both the process and outcomes of their work and their learning):

- Evaluate progress throughout and make improvements when necessary.
- Reflect on their thinking and the learning.
- Transfer thinking and learning to other contexts.

(CCEA, 2007: 9–10)

## BOX 9.6  REAL-LIFE LEARNING CHALLENGE

Mr Swift is a new head teacher who has been appointed to your school. He has monitored lesson plans and has called a staff meeting to review the school's approach to short-term planning because there are too many inconsistencies for his liking. Mrs Khan, a Foundation Stage teacher, includes lots of children's questions in her plans and wants to see children's voices heard more in the school especially at Key Stage 2. Mr Neil, the Special Educational Needs Coordinator, is concerned about the lack of planning by classroom colleagues to support the needs of individuals in class. Ms Lewis is looked upon by colleagues as an excellent teacher and about to retire. She thinks that too much is made of what is written on a plan and says that the details should be left to the professional discretion of each class teacher. She does not think that planning should be formulaic. In your role as Leader of Learning, the head has asked you to prepare a briefing paper setting out the way forward for the school. He specifically wants a recommended lesson plan format.

## Planning out-of-class learning

There is a well-established tradition of primary school teachers making regular and productive use of the outdoors as a learning environment. Gardening and nature study, for instance, became popular in the late nineteenth century. Interest in outdoor learning has been renewed following regular reports of modern life producing a generation of unfit children. Studies show clearly the all-round benefits of learning outdoors, including knowledge retention, critical thinking, enjoyment, physical development and improved behaviour (Beames *et al.*, 2011). Developments such as **Forest Schools** have attracted considerable support. For many schoolchildren, typical outdoor experiences include using the school grounds, local studies and residential stays, some of which involve visits abroad. Logistical planning needs to consider contingencies for changes in the weather, organizing resources, transport, risk assessment, group management and communication. Children should be proactively involved in such planning discussions.

Teachers can benefit from expert planning advice from a range of organizations including Natural England, the National Trust and the Council for Learning Outside the Curriculum. In terms of national policy, Scotland has led the way within the UK and outdoor learning is integrated throughout its *Curriculum for Excellence* (Figure 9.7). Its guidance has emphasized the need to bridge indoor and outdoor learning – as one

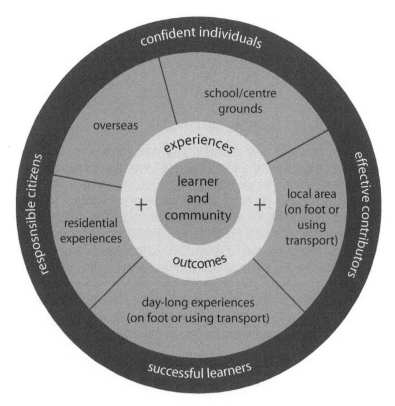

**FIGURE 9.7** Planning outdoor learning within *Curriculum for Excellence*

Source: Learning and Teaching Scotland (2010: 12)

**EXTEND YOUR UNDERSTANDING**

Read the following research report on Forest Schools and evaluate their impact:

www.forestschools.com/forest-schools-research

lecturer put it: 'We are not saying "goodbye" to our classrooms, we are opening them up' (Education Scotland, 2009: 5).

## Evaluating lessons

The importance of evaluation has grown over recent years, for example because inspectors look to test the accuracy of a school's evaluation as the basis of inspections. Inspectors are concerned with how well leaders know the current performance of pupils, the quality of learning and teaching within the school and whether improvement planning is appropriate to take the school forward. Individually, trainee and serving teachers need to reflect each day on the quality of their teaching – evaluation should be seen as a process rather than an event. Those responsible for initial teacher training, such as higher education institutions or school-based providers, expect trainee teachers to follow guidance on the format (e.g. narrative, tabular, mind map), frequency (e.g. daily, weekly) and focus (e.g. learning objectives, whole-school target, teacher's professional development goal) of evaluations. Typically these include prompts and questions relating to the learning objectives, subject content, teaching approaches, classroom organization and management, and progress in learning. One university proforma asks trainee teachers:

- to comment on how well the learning objectives were met. Identify children or groups who experienced difficulties and those who exceeded expectations and analyse why;
- to reflect and comment on what aspects of the lesson went well and why;
- to analyse and comment upon what aspects of the lesson need to be improved upon; and
- What do you need to do to address the points made above and how will you implement these action points?

The purpose of evaluation is to weigh up the value of the lesson for learners as well as the teacher. It should, therefore, move beyond description towards analysing the reasons behind what has been achieved (or not achieved) and what needs to be done next (by both learners and teacher). Most evaluations are based on an objectives model that begins with reflection on whether pupils have achieved the intended learning outcomes. This model has pros and cons – it offers potential clarity, structure and focus, but takes little or no account of matters not stated in the lesson objectives (Cohen *et al.*, 2004). Unexpected learning gains often occur in lessons, for instance following spontaneous discussion. Evaluations should look beyond lessons to consider pupils' progress against the overall aims set out in mid-term plans. Pupils themselves should contribute towards the evaluation process and good teachers regularly draw on their views. The best lesson evaluations are characterized by:

- clarity, analysis and succinctness – significant issues are identified ahead of minutiae;
- focus on outcomes – achievements of individuals and groups of learners; and
- improvements in pupils' experiences and teacher input.

## Preparation of resources

Resources serve the main purpose of supporting teaching and learning. They should not dictate the learning. The quality and deployment of resources can have a major impact on the classroom experience. It is important to do the mundane things well, such as checking that basic resources (such as pencils, paper and rubbers) are set out or readily available for the lesson so that time is not wasted. Pupils themselves can be actively involved here by taking responsibility to distribute and store away resources.

Effective teachers have, as a matter of course, always planned lessons with variety to engage interest. But the wealth of resources now available to teachers means that it is reasonably straightforward to plan opportunities to develop the full range of senses. Hence, in a numeracy lesson a teacher might plan to do the following:

- use the interactive whiteboard to share learning objectives and capture interest with a number game;
- use 100-square and number fans to consolidate learning;
- allow pupils a few minutes to talk over their work in pairs;
- encourage individuals to record their answers on mini white-boards;
- ask pupils to use their own number fans or empty number lines;
- display a poster showing common symbols and words used in the lesson;
- provide multi-link cubes to investigate patterns; and
- ask pupils to use *Post-it* notes to record answers for discussion in plenary.

## Evaluating resources

Teachers are prime targets for commercial companies who produce an amazing range of products, as a perusal through a set of education catalogues in the staffroom will reveal. Hence an important skill that teachers need to develop is the ability to evaluate resources, especially when operating within a personal or school budget where 'value for money' is critical. The starting point for evaluating resources is whether they are 'fit for purpose' and how well they meet the requirements of the curriculum (Table 9.4). Trainee teachers should always check with their placement school the range and availability of its resources. Inventories may be provided, for instance detailing CD-ROMs or 'big books' intended

**TABLE 9.4** Questions to consider when evaluating resources

| Type of resource | Possible questions to consider |
| --- | --- |
| Visual (e.g. pictures, photograph packs, posters, paintings, maps, artefacts, sketches, cartoons) | Can I prepare this visual aid on my own?<br>Is this visual resource user-friendly and likely to motivate learners?<br>Can the children produce an image such as this as part of their learning?<br>How expensive is this visual resource?<br>Can I get a free digital version of this resource? |
| ICT resources (e.g. websites, scanners, videos, cameras, CD-ROMs) | Will this digital resource work in the classroom (according to the operating system)?<br>Is the software easy to follow, engaging and inclusive?<br>Is the content accurate?<br>How much time will I need to devote to this before I am familiar with its functions and capabilities?<br>What are the implications for differentiation?<br>Can the children use these resources independently? |
| Reading books (e.g. textbooks, stories, information books) | What are the readability levels?<br>Are the subjects likely to motivate boys and girls?<br>What is the quality of the pictures?<br>Is the vocabulary too demanding?<br>Is there a good quality glossary or index?<br>Is the text challenging? |

for each class or phase. It makes sense to read reputable reviews beforehand and websites such as Schoolzone (www.schoolzone.co.uk) are helpful in this regard. Moreover book suppliers such as Amazon allow viewers to 'look inside' sections of particular texts and stories online before purchasing.

Most publishers are very conscious of the potential impact of their resources in the classroom and society at large. It is important to select resources that are not likely to cause offence. In the context of promoting an **anti-bias curriculum**, several companies have taken the lead in producing some first-class resources for schools, ranging from puppets to subject-based books for teachers. For instance, there are many ways in which history can be made inclusive through the use of stories of migration, oral testimony and first-hand sources such as maps and census returns (Clarke, 1996). The Institute of Race Relations is a good starting point in finding examples of resources that could be used to promote anti-racism.

## Worksheets

Worksheets remain a popular resource among trainees and teachers, despite concerns over their educational value especially with younger children. Museums, galleries and gardens are also concerned about the value of worksheets in developing learners' appreciation of their collections. As with all resources, trainee teachers should consider carefully the purpose and merits of using worksheets: What are they for? Who are they for? Are there better ways of recording ideas? Are they used to 'occupy' the children, consolidate knowledge or extend thinking? What will happen to these worksheets? Can they be recycled? Worksheets can serve different purposes, including sharing information, asking questions, prompting research, revising knowledge or simply keeping learners busy. OFSTED (2008) reports that while many educational sites provide free worksheets, teachers often use these uncritically without ensuring that they are relevant to the particular learning needs of the class. There is plenty of practical advice on how to design quality worksheets (Grey, 2005: Cohen *et al.*, 2004). Design should be clear and attractive, while spelling and grammar are particularly important for trainees to get right – it is surprising how many simple errors appear on trainee resources. Content, of course, has to be at an appropriate level and the potential problem that this can cause should not be underestimated. One teacher (merrily) reminded a Year 5 class on a worksheet that only young children believe in Santa Claus and their task was to write a letter, working for the Post Office, to explain to them that he did not exist, the outcome of which were national headlines as parents complained about having to deal with upset children at home (*London Evening Standard*, 2006).

Several websites provide frames that can be easily adapted by teachers. For instance, the National Association of Advisors for Computers in Education (www.naace.co.uk) website provides templates and a broad range of resources including digital stories to support learning across the curriculum. Resources produced by the BBC and other television companies are usually of a high standard and many of these are available digitally.

## The learning environment

It is widely recognized that the school environment can have a significant impact on children's learning (Box 9.7). In Victorian times, inspectors reported upon the cubic space in classrooms and the unhealthy consequences of unopened windows and cramped writing conditions. Any space that is uncomfortable, psychologically unfriendly or threatening is not conducive to good learning. Attentiveness is linked to temperature and lighting (Jensen, 2000). If children feel cold or too warm, cannot see clearly or sit for too long in uncomfortable places, they are less likely to show interest in the lesson. There is strong evidence for the effect of basic physical variables such as air quality, temperature and noise on learning (Higgins *et al.*, 2005). 'Ownership' of space and equipment by both teachers and learners is important. Clark (2010) describes how very young children can play an active role in developing the design of learning environments. Through discussion, photographs, maps and drawings, 4-year-olds are able to say what they think about light, colour, texture, as well as specific physical spaces and features. Younger children prefer bright colours and patterns while adolescents prefer more subdued colours (Higgins *et al.*, 2005). Some studies suggest that cool colours permit concentration (Brubaker, 1998).

### Seating and furniture

Classroom fixtures and furnishings should be designed with children in mind. If the chairs are too big, the ceilings too high and the displays above their eye level, children can feel less confident in the classroom. On the other hand, if they can look out of windows, reach storage areas, and sit on suitable chairs, they will feel more 'at home' and can be encouraged to take responsibility in their learning. There is no 'right' seating plan although

---

## BOX 9.7  INTERNATIONAL VIEW – THE LEARNING ENVIRONMENT

Designing school buildings to reduce heat loss is one thing. It is quite another to prevent 'learning loss'. Yet research shows that involving learners, teachers and other users of school buildings in the design process brings major benefits in terms of motivation, behaviour and well-being (Higgins *et al.*, 2005). From a study of thirty primary schools in five countries, Alexander (2001) reports some broad consistencies. Children's work is more prominently displayed in American and British schools, children sit as individuals in rows in India, rows of pairs in Russia and around work 'centres' in America. Russian classrooms tend to have 'a great deal of (natural) light' whereas many British and American classrooms depend on artificial light throughout the day. One international report concludes that investment is needed to develop teachers' and pupils' 'spatial literacies and spatial vocabularies so that learning environments they spend so much time in can become more relevant to the events occurring within' (Fisher, 2005: 166). Technologies are transforming learning environments in many different ways. The Dissolving Boundaries project, for example, brings Protestant, integrated and Catholic schools in Northern Ireland together with those in the south. Pupils investigate joint projects such as the Irish famine, healthy eating and learning French (Lightfoot, 2012).

---

teachers should review regularly the layout of the class. Table arrangements include columns, rows, an E, F, V or U-shape, the horseshoe and a semi-circle. Research suggests that children are often given tasks to do as individuals and yet they sit within group arrangements, where friends often distract them (Maddern, 2011). The most effective approach is to move furniture to suit the circumstances of the lesson (task, time of day, group size, ability, behaviour) although teachers can be dogged about classroom layout despite spending many hours planning lessons.

It is something of a myth to say that moving furniture disrupts lessons. Often this can be done at break times. Moreover, it signals a clear start to lessons, as children know the type of activity that they are going to do once they see the layout. Effective teachers ensure smooth transitions through the use of phrases such as 'we are going to do quiet working now' when arranging tables in rows. Where possible, the arrangement of furniture needs to give individual children a sense of private space. Children with Asperger's syndrome will find issues of space very important and they will need to know that their space will be respected. They will find an uninvited intrusion into their space very threatening. Teachers working in open-plan classrooms will face different challenges to those in the more traditional settings. Keeping distractions from other classes to a minimum will be one of these. Teachers need to consider carefully the classroom layout, how best to organize spaces for learning – for instance, how to facilitate quiet reading, music making or designing. Research comparing seating arrangements (rows and tables) shows that 'less attentive and less successful pupils are particularly affected by the desk arrangement, with their on-task behaviour increasing very significantly when seated in rows instead of at tables' (Higgins *et al.*, 2005: 25–6). Generally, pupils who sit near the front and in the middle of the class hear better and have greater opportunities to communicate with teachers than those who sit at the back or side of the classroom.

## Displays

Displays are also an important consideration when planning and preparing the learning environment. Smawfield (2006) highlights the inventiveness of classroom displays from around the world, where teachers make use of windows, ceilings, the backs of bookcases, tables, boxes, 'string' washing-lines, shelves, floors, and public places, such as libraries and hotels. Displays can take many forms, including models, exhibitions, role-play, collections and the customary wall panels. Displays should be interactive – prompting children to observe, explore, question and reflect. They should reflect the learning process in different curriculum areas and include questions and prompts. Learners can play a key role in selecting and organizing materials for displays, given that one of the purposes is to celebrate their achievements. Teachers need to ensure that displays reflect children's home and community experience so that they feel valued. Hegarty (1996: 77) raises some questions for reflection over such issues as ownership, clarity and involvement:

- What is the display for?
- In what ways will it support learning?
- Is it the best way of achieving the purposes?
- Has it got an element of openness?
- Is it pitched at a level that is meaningful for all the children?
- Can the children produce it in part or wholly?
- Will the process of producing the display support the children's level of responsibility, confidence, collaboration and risk taking?

Space can be kept in the display for exhibiting material that relates to weekly lessons. Space can also be set aside to show progression in particular skills during the year – for instance by showing handwriting extracts for each child each term. Whole-class displays convey the message that everyone is valued.

While displays can enrich a classroom environment, there are warnings that they can result in 'visual overload' that distracts pupils from concentrating on important tasks. Jarman suggests that walking into some classroom is 'like entering a bright, noisy shopping mall or supermarket packed with colours and shapes coming at you from all directions' (quoted by Lightfoot, 2006). She advocates de-cluttering environments and creating flexible spaces – for example, through screens, drapes and panels hung from the ceiling that can roll up and down to make a screen.

## Maximizing the use of ICT

Twenty-first-century teachers are in the privileged position of having immediate access to knowledge hitherto unheard of and few would disagree that ICT has revolutionized lesson planning and preparation. The advent of digital resources has meant that teachers can access, adapt and prepare economical, environmentally friendly, lasting, attractive and engaging resources to support all subject areas (Barber *et al.*, 2007; see Box 9.8). The annual BETT show (previously known as the British Educational Training and

BOX 9.8 FOCUS ON PRACTICE

A group of trainees and lecturers was asked to name top websites that they use to acquire high quality images. The results are as follows:

- www.freefoto.com
- www.bigfoto.com
- www.jupiterimages.com
- http://pics4learning.com
- www.clipart.com/en
- http://animationfactory.com
- www.educationscotland.gov.uk/earlyyears/resources

Technology Show) remains the most useful source of the latest technologies. It is also worthwhile reading product reviews and examples of classroom applications in popular magazines such as *Teach Primary* (Maze Media), *Child Education* (Scholastic) and *SEN Magazine* (SEN Magazine Ltd).

Many universities and schools have resource areas within their own intranet systems in which trainees and serving teachers can share resource and planning ideas. There are some excellent grids for learning made available by local authorities (although many have password protected areas) and the respective national governments. Audio and visual sources, such as online video extracts, can enliven lessons. The best trainees are conscious of the need to select carefully resources for the lesson in hand. Occasionally too many resources can be used in a session, which can be distracting and does not allow sufficient time to focus on the key teaching points.

Most teachers prepare resources for use on the IWB, largely in the belief that this will improve presentation, engage learners and generally make the lesson more enjoyable. However, the evidence of IWB's impact on pupils' motivation and attainment is mixed. One key finding is the need for pupils themselves to become more involved in using interactive technologies. There are signs that future learning will increasingly involve the use of table-top interactive boards and displays that allow collaborative activities, software that enables the transfer of data from individual technologies to central boards and video-conferencing facilities across sites (Rudd, 2007).

## Keeping planning in perspective

While planning should not be underestimated, in recent years concerns have been expressed over the amount of paperwork that teachers are expected to complete. In 2006 primary schoolteachers spent on average more than 8 hours a week in lesson planning and preparation. In total, around 30 per cent of time is spent on preparation and assessment (Angle *et al.*, 2009). The PricewaterhouseCoopers study of *Teacher Workload* (PwC, 2001) found that most teachers would like to spend less time on planning. It also noted that teachers produce more documentation than is necessary in the (mistaken) belief that inspectors demand it.

In response to such surveys, the government has provided guidance in an effort to 'set the record straight about what is expected by national authorities' (DfES, 2003b). The introduction of planning, preparation and assessment (PPA) time for all teachers in England and Wales has been widely welcomed by the profession. Since 2005 all teachers have had an entitlement to a guaranteed minimum of 10 per cent of their timetabled teaching commitment for PPA. In Scotland, the McCrone Agreement (2001) also provided teachers with non-teaching preparation time each week.

## Glossary

**Anti-bias curriculum** is a curriculum in which forms of prejudice are actively addressed including racism, homophobia and sexism.

**Curriculum maps** are visual means of showing what is taught, say through the year.

**Interdisciplinary learning** is a planned approach to learning that uses links across different subjects or disciplines to enhance learning (Education Scotland, 2012).

**Forest Schools** offer children a range of learning experiences in a local woodland setting.

**Learning objectives** are statements that specify what the learner should know, understand or do usually by the end of a session.

**Peer tutoring** is a system of instruction in which learners help each other and learn (themselves) by teaching.

**Schemes of work** correspond to a medium-term plan setting out the content to be covered along with aims, support resources and assessment opportunities.

**Sustained shared thinking** refers to an episode in which two or more individuals 'work together' in an intellectual way to solve a problem, clarify a concept, evaluate activities, or extend a narrative (Siraj-Blatchford *et al.*, 2002: 8).

## References

Anderson, L. and Krathwohl, D. (eds) (2000) *A Taxonomy for Learning, Teaching, and Assessing: A Revision of Bloom's Taxonomy*, New York: Longman.

Angle, H., Fearn, A., Elston, D., Bassett, C. and McGinigal, S. (2007) *Teachers' Workloads Diary Survey*, BMRB Social Research, available at: http://dera.ioe.ac.uk/11063/1/DCSF-RR159.pdf (accessed 20 January 2011).

Barber, D., Cooper, L. and Meeson, G. (2007) *Learning and Teaching with Interactive Whiteboards*, Exeter: Learning Matters.

Barnes, J. (2011) *Cross-Curricular Learning 3–14*, London: Paul Chapman.

Beames, S., Higgins, P. and Nicol, R. (2011) *Learning outside the Classroom: Theory and Guidelines for Practice*, London: Routledge.

Best, B. (2003) *Accelerated Learning Pocketbook*, Alresford: Teachers' Pocketbooks.

Bloom B.S. (1956) *Taxonomy of Educational Objective, Handbook I: The Cognitive Domain*, New York: David McKay.

Briggs, M., Woodfield, A., Swatton, P. and Marton, C. (2008) *Achieving QTS: Assessment for Learning and Teaching*, Exeter: Learning Matters.

Brown, G.A. and Wragg, E.C. (2001) *Questioning in the Primary School*, London: Routledge.

Brubaker, C.W. (1998) *Planning and Designing Schools*, New York: McGraw-Hill.

CCEA (2002) *Assessment for Learning for Key Stages 1&2*, Belfast: CCEA

CCEA (2007) *Northern Ireland Curriculum Primary*, Belfast: CCEA.

Chasty, H. (1997) *Children with Special Needs: Assessment, Law and Practice – Caught in the Act*, London: Jessica Kingsley Publishers.

Cheminais, R. (2006) *Every Child Matters: A Practical Guide for Teachers*, London: David Fulton.

Chris Quigley Education (2008) *Planning a Skills-based Curriculum*, Newcastle upon Tyne: Chris Quigley.

Clark, A. (2010) *Transforming Children's Spaces*, London: Routledge.

Clarke, H. (1996) *Reclaiming our Pasts*, Stoke-on-Trent: Trentham Books.

Claxton, G. (2002) *Building Learning Power: Helping Young People Become Better Learners*, Bristol: TLO.

Cockburn, A.D. and Handscomb, G. (eds) (2006) *Teaching Children 3 to 11*, London: Paul Chapman.

Cohen, L., Manion, L. and Morrison, K. (2004) *A Guide to Teaching Practice*, London: RoutledgeFalmer.

DCSF (2007) *Personalised Learning: A Practical Guide*, London: DCSF.

DCSF (2009) *Aspects of School Workforce Remodelling*, London: London Metropolitan University.

DES (1985) *Better Schools: A Summary*, London: HMSO

DfE (2012) *Statutory Framework for the Early Years Foundation Stage*, London: DfE.

DfE (2013) *Teachers' Standards*, London: DfE.

DfEE (1998) *Homework: Guidelines for Primary and Secondary Schools*, London: DfEE.

DfES (2002) *Planning Guidance for Primary Teachers*, London: DfES.

DfES (2003a) *Every Child Matters*, London: HMSO.

DfES (2003b) *Raising Standards and Tackling Workload: A National Agreement*, London: DfES.

Education Scotland (2009) *Outdoor Learning: Practical Guidance, Ideas and Support for Teachers and Practitioners in Scotland*, Glasgow: Education Scotland.

Education Scotland (2012) *CfE Briefing: Interdisciplinary Learning*, Glasgow: Education Scotland.

Erickson, H.L. (2007) *Concept-Based Curriculum and Instruction for the Thinking Classroom*, Thousand Oaks, CA: Corwin Press.

Estyn (2000*) Planning Through Topic Work in Key Stages 1 and 2*, Cardiff: Estyn.

Estyn (2004) *Homework in Primary and Secondary Schools*, Cardiff: Estyn.

Eurydice (2002) *The Teaching Profession in Europe: Profile Trends and Concerns. Report 1: Initial Training and Transition to Working Life*, Brussels: European Commission.

Fisher, J. (2002) *Starting from the Child*, Maidenhead: Open University Press.

Fisher, K. (2005) *Research into Identifying Effective Learning Environments*, Paris: OECD.

Gagné, R. M. (1970) *The Conditions of Learning*, New York: Holt, Rinehart, & Winston.

Gershon, M. (2013) 'Still blooming after almost 60 years', *Times Educational Supplement*, 25 October.

Greenway, R. (2007) 'Geography teaching in Northern Ireland primary schools: A survey of content and cross-curricularity', *International Research in Geographical and Environmental Education*, 16(4): 380–98.

Grey, D. (2005) *100+ Essential Lists for Teachers*, London: Continuum.

Hadow Report (1931) *The Primary School*, London: Board of Education.

Hattie, J. (2012) *Visible Learning for Teachers*, Abingdon: Routledge.

Hegarty, P. (1996) 'Quality on display', in Cooper, H. , Simco, N., Hegarty, P. and Hegarty, P. (eds) *Display in the Classroom*, London: David Fulton, 60–77.

Henry, J. (2012) 'Michael Gove scraps homework rules', in *The Telegraph*, 3 March.

Higgins, S., Hall, E., Wall, K., Woolner, P. and McCaughey, C. (2005) *The Impact of School Environments: A Literature Review*, Newcastle: University of Newcastle.

HMIe (2007) *A Curriculum for Excellence: Building the Curriculum 2*, Scottish Executive: Edinburgh, available at www.educationscotland.gov.uk (accessed 20 July 2013).

Hobart, C. and Frankel, J. (2005) *A Practical Guide to Activities for Young Children*, Cheltenham: Nelson Thornes.

Hodkinson, A. (2004) 'Does the English Curriculum for history and its schemes of work effectively promote primary-aged children's assimilation of the concepts of historical time? Some observations based on current research', *Educational Research*, 46(2): 99–117.

Hughes, P. (2002) *Principles of Primary Education*, London: David Fulton.

Hunter, M. (1982) *Mastery Teaching*, El Segundo, CA: TIP Publications.

Islington Early Years Foundation Stage Team (2009) *Good Practice Guidelines: Planning*, Ealing: Islington Early Years Foundation Stage Team.

Jensen, E. (2000) *Brain-Based Learning*. San Diego, CA: The Brain Store.

John, P. (2006) 'Lesson planning and the student teacher: Re-thinking the dominant model', *Journal of Curriculum Studies*, 38(4): 483–98.

Kauchak, D.P. and Eggen, P.D. (2007) *Learning and Teaching: Research-based Methods*, New York: Pearson.

Kerry, T. (2002) *Learning Objectives Task Setting and Differentiation*, Cheltenham: Nelson Thornes.

Kerry, T. (ed.) (2011) *Cross-Curricular Teaching in the Primary School*, Abingdon: Routledge.

Knight, S. (2011) 'AfL for inclusive, differentiated learning: Benefiting all students in a class', *Practical Research for Education*, 44: 57–63.

Kyriacou, C. (2007) *Essential Teaching Skills*, Cheltenham: Nelson Thornes.

Lance, A. and Hill, M. (1995) *Differentiation in Practice*, Oxford: National Primary Centre.

Leaman, L. (2006) *The Naked Teacher*, London: Continuum.

Lightfoot, L. (2006) 'Tear down your distracting classroom displays, skills agency tells teachers', *The Telegraph*, 18 November.

Lightfoot, L. (2012) 'Laying the world at their feet', *Times Educational Supplement*, 13 April.

Littledyke, M. and Huxford, L. (1998) *Teaching the Primary Curriculum for Constructivist Learning*, London: David Fulton.

*London Evening Standard* (2006) ' "Santa Claus does not exist" school tells stunned kids', 20 December.

Lucas, B. and Claxton, G. (2012) 'Why we should all be hands-on', *Times Educational Supplement*, 9 November.

McCutcheon, G. (1980) 'How do elementary school teachers plan? The nature of planning and influences on it', *The Elementary School Journal*, 81(1): 4–23.

McCutcheon, G. (2002) *Developing the curriculum: Solo and Group Deliberation*, New York: Educator's International Press.

McNeil, F. and Sammons, P. (2006) *Improving Schools*, London: Routledge.

Maddern, K. (2011) 'Seats in groups, columns or rows', *Times Educational Supplement*, 21 October.

Martin, A.J. (2012) 'Goal setting, personal best (PB) goals, and academic achievement', in Hattie, J. and Anderman, E. (eds) *International Guide to Student Achievement*, Oxford: Routledge, 356-8.

Medwell, J. and Simpson, F. (2008) *Successful Teaching Placement in Scotland, Primary and Early Years*, Exeter: Learning Matters.

Morrison, N. (2009) 'Right to be heard', *Times Educational Supplement*, 23 January.

Nicholls, G. (ed.) (2004) *An Introduction to Teaching*, London: RoutledgeFalmer.

OECD (2004) *Starting Strong Curricula and Pedagogies in Early Childhood Education and Care*, Paris: OECD.

OFSTED (2008) *Learning Outside the Classroom – How Far Should You Go?*, London: OFSTED.

OFSTED (2012) *Moving English Forward*, London: OFSTED.

OFSTED (2013) *School Inspection Handbook*, London: OFSTED.

Paton, G. (2013) 'Coalition attacked over "atomised" National Curriculum', *The Telegraph*, 16 April.

Petty, G. (2009) *Teaching Today: A Practical Guide*, London: Nelson Thornes.

Popham, W. J. (2011) *Transformative Assessment in Action*, Alexandria, VA: SCD.

PwC (2001) *Workload Study Final Report*, London: DfEE, available at: www.davidsmawfield.com/assets/img/classroom-display-handbook.pdf (accessed 5 October 2013).

QCA (2000) *Curriculum Guidance for the Foundation Stage*, London: QCA.

Rose, R. and Howley, M. (2007) *The Practical Guide to Special Educational Needs in Inclusive Primary Classrooms*, London: Paul Chapman.

Rowley, C. and Cooper, H. (eds) (2009) *Cross-Curricular Approaches to Teaching and Learning*, London: Sage.

Rudd, T. (2007) *Interactive Whiteboards in the Classroom*, Bristol: Futurelab.

Sage, R. and Wilkie, M. (2004) *Supporting Learning in Primary Schools*, Exeter: Learning Matters.

Scottish Government (2008) *Curriculum for Excellence: Building the Curriculum 3*, Edinburgh: Scottish Government.

Sherborne, T. (2013) 'Why Bloom's Taxonomy is in need of pruning', *Times Educational Supplement*, 1 November.

Siraj-Blatchford, I., Sylva, K., Muttock, S., Gilden, R. and Bell, D. (2002) *Researching Effective Pedagogy in the Early Years*, Nottingham: DfES.

Slavin, R. (2003) *Educational Psychology: Theory and Practice*, London: Longman.

Smawfield, D. (2006) *Classroom and School Display: A Guide for Teachers and Teacher Training*, available at: www.davidsmawfield.com/assets/img/classroom-display-handbook.pdf (accessed5 October 2013).

Stephen, C. (2010) 'Taking active learning into the primary school: A matter of new practices?', *International Journal of Early Years Education*, 18(4): 315–29.

Tyler, R. W. (1949) *Basic Principles of Curriculum and Instruction*, Chicago, IL: University of Chicago Press.

Vasagar, J. (2011) 'Stress drives teachers out of schools', *The Guardian*, 25 April.

Vincett, K., Cremin, H. and Thomas, G. (2005) *Teachers and Assistants Working Together*, Maidenhead: Open University Press.

Walker, L. (2008) *The Essential Guide to Lesson Planning*, Harlow: Pearson.

Ward, H. (2012a) 'Assessment for Learning has fallen prey to gimmicks, says critic', *Times Educational Supplement*, 15 July.

Ward, H. (2012b) 'Is it time to ditch the rule of three?', *Times Educational Supplement*, 4 May.

Welsh Government (2013) *National Literacy and Numeracy Framework*, Cardiff: Welsh Government.

Whitebread, D. (2007) 'Developing independence in learning', in Moyles, J. (ed.) *Early Years Foundations: Meeting the Challenge*, Maidenhead: Open University Press.

Williams, J. (2003) *Promoting Independent Learning in the Primary School*, Buckingham: Open University Press.

Wilson, J. (2000) *Key Issues in Education and Teaching*, London: Cassell.

## Websites

Tesconnect, from the Times Educational Supplement, contains around 700,000 free teaching resources – www.tes.co.uk/teaching-resources

Association of Teachers' website contains sites referred to by expert teachers, includes approved sites covering all curriculum areas and key stages – www.byteachers.org.uk

The National Archives hosts the old QCA schemes of work – http://webarchive.nationalarchives.gov.uk/20090608182316/standards.dfes.gov.uk

# 10

# Promoting inclusive practice

## Meeting the needs of learners

## Chapter objectives

By the end of this chapter you should be able to:

- Explain the development and concepts of special educational needs and inclusion.
- Identify common barriers to learning and how these might be overcome.
- Know how to find specialist support in terms of providing for children with additional learning needs.

*What makes a school accessible? 'Let out that it's okay to be different and you don't need to be a certain someone to fit in.'*

*(P6 pupil quoted in Children in Scotland, 2007: 10)*

## Introduction

Over recent years, teachers have had to deal with an increasing diversity of children's needs. Around one in four primary school pupils are from an ethnic minority background and one in six do not have English as their first language. More than a million children between 5 and 18 years old in UK schools speak in excess of 360 languages between them (www.naldic.org.uk). The relevance of SEN to *all* teachers is borne out by statistics. Around one in five children – a total of 1.9 million – have **special educational needs** (SEN) in England and Wales. Controversially, OFSTED (2010) report that up to a quarter of these children are wrongly diagnosed and this disguises the need to improve the quality of teaching. There are claims that schools misdiagnose difficulties in order to attract more resources.

Unfortunately, the term SEN has become so broad it has been difficult to distinguish between 'deserving' and 'undeserving' cases (Gilbert, 2012). Some fear that parents and schools are quick to latch on to the additional resources associated with SEN provision (Gilbert, 2010). Nonetheless, the key messages for pre and serving teachers are: (1) to move away from viewing SEN as associated with a distinct group whose care and teaching responsibility rests with others, (2) to develop teaching strategies and networks to meet the needs of a range of learners. This chapter outlines the historical and political context for such diversity and how effective schools and teachers meet the challenges that this brings.

The good news is that the quality of pre-service training in diversity issues is improving. Surveys of newly qualified teachers show that they are more confident now than ever before to meet the needs of different learners. In 2003, only 22 per cent of newly qualified teachers in England rated training to teach pupils with English as an additional language to be good or very good; this rose to 58 per cent in 2013. Similarly, improvements are peceived in preparing to teach pupils from ethnic minority backgrounds, from 29 per cent rated good or very good in 2003 to 64 per cent in 2013 (DfE, 2013: 20).

## From special educational needs to inclusion

The origins of special education in the United Kingdom can be traced to the opening of the first schools for blind children, for example in Liverpool, Edinburgh, Bristol and London, at the end of the eighteenth century (Pritchard, 1963). Separate institutions for a few of the most serious 'physically handicapped' and 'mentally defective' children existed but the majority fared as best they could in a mixture of workhouses, asylums, ordinary elementary schools or at home. Government support for special education began in the 1890s and by 1918 legislation provided for the compulsory education of 'physically defective and epileptic' children.

The different needs of children were recognized in the 1944 Education Act under its slogan 'education for all'. The Act established the principle that any child considered educable would have access to schooling. Where there were concerns over the educability of children, parents were required to submit them for medical examination. The uneducable became the responsibility of the health authorities. Similar arrangements were introduced in Scotland, under the Education (Scotland) Act 1945. The Handicapped Students and School Health Service Regulations 1945 in England and Wales developed a framework of eleven categories of handicap: blind, partially sighted, deaf, partially deaf, delicate, diabetic, educationally subnormal, epileptic, maladjusted, physically handicapped and those with speech defects. The regulations required blind, deaf, epileptic, physically handicapped and aphasic children (those with communication disorders) to be educated in special schools. Other handicapped children could attend mainstream schools if there was adequate provision. At the time it was estimated that up to 17 per cent of the school population might be expected to receive special educational 'treatment' (Wearmouth, 2012). In reality, for most mainstream teachers, disability was a matter for special schools.

This segregated picture remained largely unchanged until the 1960s and 1970s when the human rights movement gave a voice to marginalized groups. For those with disabilities, frustrations were aired over the perceived weaknesses of a segregated educational system; for instance, it was argued that young people left special schools stigmatized and the educational outcomes were no better than mainstream schools (Hodkinson and Vickerman, 2009). Moreover, concerns were expressed over the inequalities associated with a tripartite system of selection whereby children were filtered into grammar, technical or secondary modern schools, depending upon their success at eleven-plus examinations. As a result, increasingly through the 1970s comprehensive schools were established to provide secondary education for all pupils in their area, although selection lingered on in Northern Ireland and parts of England.

In this wider context of demands for equality of opportunity, a review of provision for handicapped children in Britain was published as the Warnock Report (1978). It introduced the concept of special educational needs to replace previous labels. This moved the discourse away from a medical model, with its emphasis on individual limitations, towards seeing disability within a social and educational context. In particular, mainstream schools had a key role to play in shaping attitudes, values and beliefs that contributed towards disability. Based on teacher perceptions, it was estimated that 20 per cent of children experienced greater difficulties in learning than their peers. The Warnock Report reinforced the notion that the majority of these could be met in the mainstream and receive legal protection in the form of a statement. It was no longer a matter of medical care but social integration.

Since the early 1980s, UK and international legislation has strengthened the rights of children with SEN to be educated in mainstream schools (Box 10.1). In particular, the United Nations Convention on the Rights of the Child (United Nations, 1989) and the Salamanca Statement (UNESCO, 1994) promoted the concept of **inclusion** in mainstream education.

During the 1990s the philosophy of inclusion challenged schools to move beyond cosmetic integration by breaking down barriers to learning. In short, rather than the children 'fitting' into the school system, inclusive practice requires teachers to adapt to meet the needs of all learners. In 1994, the government published a Code of Practice to offer statutory guidance to schools in England and Wales on supporting those with learning difficulties (DfE, 1994, subsequently revised in DfES, 2001 and National Assembly for Wales, 2004). This stipulated that children should receive an individual education plan (IEP) and the most severe needs would be supported externally. As part of the National Curriculum in England and Wales, a statutory inclusion statement required schools to set suitable learning challenges, respond to pupils' diverse needs and overcome potential

---

### BOX 10.1  KEY CONCEPTS – SEN AND INCLUSION

In England, a child or young person has SEN if they have significantly greater difficulty in learning than the majority of others of the same age, or have a disability that prevents or hinders them from making use of educational facilities of a kind generally provided for others of the same age in mainstream schools or mainstream post-16 institutions (DfE, 2013). In Wales, Scotland and Northern Ireland the broader terms Additional Learning Needs (ALN), Additional Support Needs (ASN) and Additional Educational Needs (AEN) are preferred to what has been seen as the outdated and limited terminology of SEN. The term inclusion has been interpreted in different ways (Daniels, 2000). It was once common to see inclusion as synonymous with special educational needs and how well SEN pupils were 'integrated' into mainstream schools. It now extends to diverse groups who are at risk of underachievement, marginalization or exclusion.

barriers to learning and assessment (DfEE, 1999). Scottish legislation in 2004 adopted a wider view of inclusion through the concept of 'additional support for the learning'. This sees all pupils potentially requiring some form of additional support, for a variety of reasons at some point in their school career. Such a broad view has been criticized for ignoring the needs of specific groups (Farrell, 2004). The Westminster government's *Removing Barriers to Achievement* strategy (DfES, 2004a) made it clear that all teachers are teachers of pupils with SEN. In 2010, the Equality Act replaced all previous equality legislation. It reinforced that schools cannot discriminate against pupils because of their sex, race, disability, religion, belief or sexual orientation.

Over the past 30 or so years, underpinning the integration of children with SEN into mainstream schools in many countries has been the assumption that this has been the right thing to do (Box 10.2).

For organizations such as the Centre for Studies on Inclusive Education, it makes social sense for all children to learn together (CSIE, 2002). It argues that only inclusion has the potential to reduce fear and prejudice, and promote friendship, respect and understanding. European research suggests that education that is good for students with special needs, benefits *all* students in the same school setting (European Agency for Development in Special Needs Education, 2003).

Physical integration into schools does not, however, automatically lead to participation and therefore may not be inclusive. In 2005 Baroness Warnock herself called for a rethink on the subject of SEN, suggesting that inclusion could be taken 'too far', resulting in the closure of special schools to the detriment of children with SEN. She argued that inclusion should mean that 'all children should be included under the common educational project, not that they should be included under one roof' (Warnock, 2005: 37). Around 1 per cent of children are educated in special schools, the vast majority (97 per cent) allocated statements (DfE, 2010). Warnock made some disturbing claims:

- bullying of children with SEN is inevitable especially in mainstream secondary schools;
- children with SEN increasingly tend to be lumped together indiscriminately;

---

**BOX 10.2 INTERNATIONAL VIEW – INCLUSION**

The development of inclusive education in many countries originates with the adoption of the United Nations Convention on the Rights of the Child (United Nations, 1989), the most ratified international treaty in history. This was followed by the Salamanca Statement (UNESCO, 1994: 11), which makes it clear that 'all children should learn together, wherever possible, regardless of any difficulties or differences they may have'. However, most countries of the former Soviet Union support segregated practices, whereas all European Union countries now have policies in place to promote inclusion. In Italy, children are regarded as having Special Rights (rather than Special Needs). The emphasis is on listening to the voices of all children. The Pedagogical Centre of Montenegro has developed a range of inclusive education programmes, for instance to support equal education for Roma children. Organizations such as Enabling Education Network and the European Agency for Development in Special Needs Education highlight examples of good practice from around the world.

■ children with similar needs may get entirely different provision as the number of children issued with statements varies enormously from one local authority to another; and

■ too often children with special needs in mainstream schools have been taught almost entirely by teaching assistants who are not fully qualified, and therefore they have not benefited from the best teaching.

Warnock's comments triggered widespread debate. There are regular stories in the press featuring campaigns to keep special schools open, parents lobbying to get their child into (or back into) mainstream schools or fighting to get them transferred to special schools. In its review of provision, OFSTED (2010) found that no one model – special schools, full inclusion in mainstream classes or special units – was more effective than any other. It added, however, that 'more good or outstanding provision existed in resourced mainstream schools'.

Most recently, the Coalition Government has aimed to transform SEN provision by developing a 'family centred system' in which parents and young people have greater say in the decisions that affect their education. Numerous studies have reported the strain on parents raising a child with a disability (European Commission, 2013). Many feel isolated and overwhelmed by the time-intensive demands required to care for many children with disabilities. Involving parents of children with SEN is central to inclusive schooling. Under the government arrangements, local authorities provide a 'local offer' containing details about specialist support, training, arrangements for travel to and from school, identification and assessment procedures, and information about the quality of its education, health and care provision for children and young people with SEN. A new Code of Practice, effective from 2014, replaced the graduated model of 'school action', 'school action plus' and 'statements' with combined education, health and care plans for individuals. The government also reiterates the commitment to children and young people with SEN being educated in mainstream settings and the expectation that 'all teachers are teachers of children with special educational needs'.

Over three centuries, disability issues have moved from the shadows of hidden history to the forefront of the political and educational agenda. This transition reflects different ideological perspectives on inclusion, summarized in Table 10.1.

Presently, inclusion is part of a broad social agenda that covers health, welfare, vocational training and employment. In this sense disability is seen as socially constructed

**TABLE 10.1** Ideological perspectives on SEN and inclusion

| Model | Characteristics |
|---|---|
| Medical | ■ Disability is innate<br>■ The remedy is to treat the condition or syndrome |
| Social | ■ Disability is a reflection of how the able-bodied see disability<br>■ The remedy is to develop stronger relationships between the disabled and the non-disabled |
| Political | ■ Disability is caused by societal structures, the environment, institutions<br>■ Full inclusion requires valuing the rights of disabled people and prosecution of those who discriminate against the disabled |

and the key is how well society adapts the environment to suit the individual, rather than the person's condition (Hickman and Jones , 2009).

This is not to deny the continuing influence of the medical model. Babies born even a week early have a greater propensity to develop special needs. Overall, eight out of ten severely premature babies go on to have learning difficulties, with two out of ten having a severe disability. Only a decade ago, many of these would have died but now grow up to enter the education system (Gilbert, 2010). The medical view also shapes discussion over dyslexia. Lewis (2001) suggests that some parents, teachers and children find learning difficulties easier to 'accept' if a 'medical' label is applied. She adds the obvious benefit for drug companies if medication is adopted as the main prescription for a particular 'condition'. The use of Ritalin as treatment for attention deficit hyperactivity disorder (ADHD) is controversial. Singh (2012), a bioethics researcher for the Wellcome Trust, found that most of the children prescribed the drug valued the medication for giving them control over their decisions. Singh argues that it is stigma rather than drugs that is holding them back. Others, such as the creativity guru Sir Ken Robinson, are sceptical over the readiness to prescribe Ritalin sweeping (American) schools (see 'Changing Education Paradigms', available on www.youtube.com).

## Approaching inclusion

As teachers, a good starting point to inclusion is to consider one's own attitude towards those with SEN. It is not unusual to feel anxious, uncomfortable or unsure when interacting with children with SEN. One survey suggested that around two-thirds of newly qualified teachers did not feel that their initial training prepared them sufficiently in the area of SEN (Jerome and Shilela, 2006). There have been regular calls (OFSTED, 2006; OFSTED, 2008b) to improve the initial training and continuing professional development of all teachers in the field of learning difficulties and disabilities (LDD). Training and experience are critical in shaping positive attitudes.

## Overcoming barriers to learning: planning and teaching

The *Teachers' Standards* (DfE, 2013) expect teachers to 'have a secure understanding of how a range of factors can inhibit pupils' ability to learn and how best to overcome these'. Within school, these include issues relating to the leadership, teaching and the environment. By law, every school must have an accessibility plan, showing how they intend to improve accessibility for disabled pupils. Unfortunately, it is easier for a disabled person to be 'socially invisible' because of the barriers they face in accessing the environment built by the able-bodied (Dare and O'Donovan, 2002; Save the Children, 2002).

Individuals themselves create their own barriers to learning. These can include low expectations, a shortage of confidence, or negative thinking. Relationships are central to learning and teaching. Sometimes it is 'how' something is said or done that prompts a defensive reaction rather than lesson content. Barriers to learning are most effectively addressed when mainstream teachers establish a rapport with individual learners and work closely with parents. This means getting to know whether there is anything in school that makes children feel anxious, such as the curriculum, teaching methods, other pupils, areas of the building or times of the day. For example, research has shown that formal tests cause considerable stress and anxiety among pupils (Lord and Jones, 2006).

There are also barriers to learning that operate within society at large that are beyond the control of teachers. Children's attendance at school can be affected by many factors and in extreme cases this can include violence, the need to work or poverty. Malala Yousafzai's story of being shot by the Taliban for attending school in northern Pakistan has become a modern symbol of a girl's universal right to education (Yousafzi and Lamb, 2013). In many developing countries, girls must work instead of attending school. High costs, discrimination, poverty and conflict have denied education to around 100 million children – 60 per cent of whom are girls (*The Independent*, 5 September 2005). Irregular and non-attendance at school have also been longstanding problems in the UK. Inclusive programmes have been developed for well-defined groups such as Looked After Children, Travellers' Children and School Age Mothers. A recent review in Northern Ireland reports that attendance incentive schemes are widespread and include small prizes for excellent attendance, such as a pencil case, day trips for year groups with the highest attendance rate and certificates (DoE, 2012). The involvement of Education Welfare Services, strong communication with parents, breakfast clubs, and afterschool activities are among the most effective management strategies.

In recent times, psychologists have seen an increase in referrals for school phobia (Tickle, 2009). School phobia or refusal is already estimated to affect one in every 20 children. Physical symptoms include vomiting, headaches, fatigue and panic attacks with a risk of sufferers carrying anxiety phobias into adulthood. One lad explains: 'I felt allergic to the building. I didn't want to kill myself or anything, but I didn't want to go to school. It's like you just can't, my legs wouldn't work and it made me sick' (quoted by McVeigh, 2008). It should not be underestimated that schools face significant challenges in trying to engage those disaffected children and parents who appear apathetic and even hostile to the educational system. At a secondary level, studies show that schools that have successfully reintegrated disaffected pupils have done so through a coordinated approach working with multi-agency services to ensure that pupils' needs are met (OFSTED, 2008a).

OFSTED (2006) identify the characteristics that enable pupils with learning difficulties and disabilities (LDD) to make outstanding progress: ethos, specialist staff and focused professional development. The inspectorate reports that there are no differences in the quality of teaching for pupils with LDD or teaching in general. However, specialist teachers possessed greater knowledge and skill in assessing and planning when the needs of pupils were more complex. Those teachers who lack experience of LDD can, inadvertently, focus too much on social integration at the expense of learning.

It is widely acknowledged that careful planning is essential in meeting the needs of learners. The most successful teachers hold high expectations of everyone in the class and make learning accessible to all. Richards and Armstrong (2011) use the 'community of learners' idea to remind teachers that planning activities should not separate into those with and without special educational needs. The authors argue that traditional planning for different groups of learners, labelled as 'SEN', 'gifted' or 'EAL' is not helpful in meeting the individual needs of learners. They support mixed-ability groups, team teaching, using a range of differentiation strategies and, most important, embracing the concept of diversity.

Pupils who have complex needs are likely to benefit from particular approaches to teaching and learning, such as Braille or sign language in the case of children with visual or hearing impairments. Similarly, distinctive teaching approaches are used with children with autism. However, in a review of teaching strategies for pupils with SEN, Davis and Florian (2004) concluded that a combination of approaches often produces more powerful effects than any single strategy. Further research indicates that approaches for teaching pupils with difficulties in learning are 'not distinctively different, although the knowledge that underpins their use may be' (Hall, 2004; Daniels and Porter, 2007: 17). The kinds of issues to consider when planning for inclusive teaching are noted in Table 10.2.

## Deployment of additional adults

It is common practice to deploy additional adults to support pupils with SEN. There has been a huge increase in the number of teaching assistants in UK schools over the past two decades. These additional adults comprise about a quarter of the workforce in English and Welsh maintained schools. Reforms in school workforce remodelling during the late 1990s have meant that support staff have taken on duties such as supervising the reading of small groups of pupils. While caring and knowledgeable teacher assistants often carry out day-to-day support for children with SEN, such practice has been seriously questioned. On average, children with SEN spend more than a quarter of their time away from a qualified teacher and roughly half as much contact with their classmates (Maddern, 2013).

Many assistants are seen as 'experts' by teachers, despite their lack of formal training and qualification. According to a report by the Institute of Education, children with SEN supported on a one-to-one basis make less academic progress in the core subjects, calling into question the rapid growth in teacher assistant numbers. The challenge is striking a balance between the need for pupils to learn alongside pupils without SEN while, at the same time ensuring that pupils learn at a different pace and often in a different manner (OFSTED, 2006).

Outstanding mainstream teachers work flexibly with colleagues in responding to individual needs. They seek out ways to include children with SEN, ensuring that their views are respected. While they recognize that there will always be children who require specialist input, they focus on the process of learning (what and how) and their responsibility in moving this forward. In the best practice, additional adults are very well briefed by the teacher and know their particular roles. They contribute to high-quality interactions. Teacher assistants need to know whether to play the part of listener, observer, friend, initiator, mediator, responder or guide (Johnston and Nahmad-Williams, 2008). They need to be briefed each day on their role. Additional adults can play a key part in assisting pupils overcome barriers to learning by teaching what Gross (1996) referred to as 'bypass' strategies – enabling pupils with SEN to circumvent difficulties, such as language, to access the curriculum. For instance, on occasions they might scribe or tape answers from a child who struggles with writing. However, there are a number of writers who question the assumption that learners with SEN should be taught by support staff (Webster and Blatchford, 2012). Moreover, Wedell (2005: 5) warns that 'the velcroing of LSAs [Learning Support Assistants] to pupils sometimes actually becomes a form of within-class segregation'. The development of 'personalised learning' is intended to encourage teachers to become more responsive to individual needs and interests.

**TABLE 10.2** Issues to consider when planning for pupils with SEN

| Consideration | Key questions |
| --- | --- |
| Learning objectives | ■ How do the learning objectives relate to the needs in the IEPs?<br>■ How can I personalise or modify class learning objectives?<br>■ What are the cognitive, emotional, physical and sensory needs of the individuals? |
| Content (ideas, skills, values) | ■ Is the content exciting and relevant?<br>■ Does it build on previous learning?<br>■ How will I communicate the content?<br>■ How can I break the content down into small sections?<br>■ Will I adopt a different style for different learners? |
| Vocabulary | ■ Have I simplified the language?<br>■ Is my oral language clear and concise?<br>■ Have I used clearly structured language and simple sentences on worksheets?<br>■ Have I broken up large amounts of text (e.g. with sub-headings, visuals, bullet points)?<br>■ Have I provided subject-specific visual dictionaries?<br>■ Have I prepared key word lists? |
| Environment | ■ Is there sufficient light in the room?<br>■ Have I opened the window if it is too warm?<br>■ Has each learner sufficient personal space?<br>■ Is there enough space for all learners to move around?<br>■ Are the seating arrangements conducive to good viewing and hearing?<br>■ Where will I stand so all can see me?<br>■ How can I ensure that any physical or sensory-impaired pupils have full access in the lesson? |
| Teacher's role | ■ Can I set aside a few minutes one-to-one time with individuals?<br>■ Can I use eye contact and other non-verbal means to involve pupils with SEN? |
| Resources | ■ Will key resources be to hand?<br>■ If I use PowerPoint, is there too much text on the slides?<br>■ Are my visual aids bright, bold and colourful?<br>■ Can SEN pupils use ICT to enhance their learning?<br>■ Are sensory-impaired pupils using their equipment (e.g. hearing aids or microphones) correctly?<br>■ Are resources clearly labelled so all pupils can locate them? |
| Additional adults | ■ Are these well briefed on their roles?<br>■ Is the amount of time they spend supporting pupils monitored and compared to the degree of teacher support? |
| Social and emotional issues | ■ How can I help this child feel involved?<br>■ Who will be sitting next to pupils with SEN?<br>■ Have I established clear boundaries on acceptable behaviour?<br>■ Have I anticipated possible difficulties or triggers and what will I do to alleviate these? |
| Assessment | ■ How can I ensure that every child feels a sense of worth at the end of the lesson?<br>■ What am I looking for in this particular child's work/behaviour?<br>■ How can I involve the pupils in their assessment? |

## Differentiation

Teachers have always taught mixed ability classes although setting work appropriate to the needs of each child remains a major challenge. Differentiation focuses on meeting the needs of individual learners. While dated, research by Bennett *et al.* (1984) found that 60 per cent of Year 2 children and 70 per cent of Year 3 children in a range of settings were seen to be working at tasks that were either much too easy or much too hard for them. OFSTED has no qualms about telling parents, children and teachers when the work set is not sufficiently challenging as this letter extract to a school in Leicester illustrates: 'Unfortunately, we found that you are not learning enough. Lots of the work is too easy for you' (*The Daily Telegraph*, 2008). According to Tomlinson and Strickland (2005), teachers usually differentiate instruction by adjusting one or more of the following:

- the content (what they learn) e.g. use of multiple texts;
- the process (how they learn) e.g. in groups, independently, with additional adult support; and
- the product (how they demonstrate their learning) e.g. through text, visual or oral forms.

Research shows that lower ability pupils are particularly at risk of demotivation once they realize that certain 'grades' are beyond them – a 'thickie' and 'boffin' culture can emerge (cited by Lord and Jones, 2006: 71). Rose and Howley (2007) suggest, where possible, to give the same piece of work to several pupils in order that they can discuss, support and even coach each other. The authors add that in such circumstances more able pupils benefit in thinking through their explanations and instructions. Table 10.3 and Box 10.3 provide examples of strategies that have proven effective in supporting children with particular learning difficulties (see also Box 10.4).

Scottish researchers suggest that learners with SEN favoured small group work and one-to-one opportunities and believe that this makes a significant difference to their school experiences (Children in Scotland, 2007). This research also noted that pupils could talk about:

- how to improve accessibility (by installing stair lifts, ramps or providing communication boards);
- the use of peer supports, such as circles of friends, buddy systems, and specific projects; and
- innovative solutions to help children feel more involved and valued: for example, developing a spade-like attachment for wheelchair users so they could join in ball games.

Peer tutoring has also brought social and academic benefits to pupils with SEN. Peer tutoring involves children of the same age helping their peers (one child acts as the tutor while the other is the learner or tutee), while cross-age tutoring involves students from older classes helping younger children. This approach has well documented academic and social benefits for both the tutor and the learner (Fuchs and Fuchs, 1998).

**TABLE 10.3** A summary of support strategies

| Strategies | Will help with |
|---|---|
| Task-boards:<br>■ detailing sequence of activities, groups<br>■ help to keep track of what the child or group has to do | All conditions |
| Personal written instructions:<br>■ enlarged text<br>■ font size 14 on non-white paper<br>■ good spacing and chunking of information | Dyslexia<br>Irlen syndrome<br>Dyspraxia<br>Hearing impairment |
| Coloured markers/symbols against text: particularly on the board when viewed from a distance but also useful on individual texts so that children can locate their place again | Irlen syndrome<br>Dyslexia<br>ADHD<br>Visual impairment |
| Lighting: natural light or ordinary tungsten lighting/lamps rather than fluorescent strip lighting; personal lamps in study coves are ideal | Hearing impairment<br>Visual impairment<br>Irlen syndrome |
| Sloping surfaces for writing | ADHD<br>Dyspraxia<br>Dyslexia |
| Sticking paper to the surface at the correct angle | ADHD<br>Dyspraxia<br>Dyslexia |
| Seating: children with particular difficulties may need to sit near the front but not necessarily at a 'low-ability' group table | Hearing impairment<br>Visual impairment<br>ADHD |
| Tape presentations giving content and instructions: no adult needed | Hearing impairment<br>Visual impairment<br>Dyslexia, Irlen syndrome<br>Dyspraxia |
| Small group/one-to-one: some children need the adult to moderate their behaviour and help them with work | Down Syndrome<br>Various conduct disorders |
| Use of computers: many activities can be adapted for use on personal computers (PCs), including cloze procedure activities, matching activities as well as specifically designed programs such as 'Wordshark' | Will help most children but need to change background, font type and size, resolution and colour for dyslexia, Irlen and visual impairment<br>Use of speaking programmes good for hearing-impaired (with headphones), visual impairment, dyslexia/Irlen and dyspraxia |
| Use of tape-recorders to record activities | Good for all children who have difficulty with writing, composing and recording<br>Those with ADHD may be impulsive and not want to wait their turn |
| Large egg timers as a visual time scale | Helps time organisation for dyslexic/ADHD |
| Use of modified equipment (e.g. special rulers with handles) | Dyspraxic children, children with grip problems |
| Personally addressing children: using signals, be explicit about actions, give time to prepare an answer | Visual impairment, ADHD |

Source: Bold (2004). Reproduced with permission

---

**BOX 10.3  FOCUS ON PRACTICE**

A group of outstanding postgraduate trainees was asked for their suggestions of how they supported pupils with SEN. Their answers included:

- sitting alongside a particular child or group;
- allocating additional time to complete activities;
- allocating an additional adult or more able peer to act as 'coach';
- setting timed targets for particular learners;
- setting tasks with added structure (e.g. writing frames or simplified sequence of instructions);
- reading aloud pieces of text;
- making a conscious effort to talk to them on a one-to-one basis for a minute or so each day;
- supplying visual or auditory cues to assist with writing;
- using ICT such as language or mathematics programs and tape recorders;
- in literacy lessons, focusing on word families (e.g. book, took, look, etc.);
- asking pupils to repeat what they have been asked to do;
- demonstrate and model correct procedures;
- providing oral alongside written instructions, delivered one at a time;
- using attractive, accessible resources – font size, simplified words, visual cues.

---

**BOX 10.4  REAL-LIFE LEARNING CHALLENGE**

Julie is eight years old and has Asperger's Syndrome. In school, she has the support of a teaching assistant (TA). She is liked by most of the class. Julie becomes distressed by the behaviour of her peers. How can the class teacher include her more in lessons?

---

## Participating in extra-curricular activities

Pupils with SEN should have opportunities to participate in appropriate extra-curricular provision. Lewis *et al.* (2006: 6) report how extra-curricular activities were important in boosting disabled children's self-esteem and confidence: 'They matter in their own right but also because they encourage children to take risks, and so to escape from overprotection, and mature.' Outstanding teachers seek out opportunities to involve children through building on their interests and strengths, as well taking into account their difficulties.

## Children with disabilities

Put crudely, by the end of our lives almost half of us will be disabled (www.scope.org.uk). Over recent years, there has been significant progress in highlighting the achievements of disabled people, for instance through the much-viewed and celebrated Paralympics of 2012. Disability Discrimination legislation has also established clear rights for disabled people, requiring employers (including schools) to make 'reasonable adjustments' so that disabled people can work effectively alongside able-bodied colleagues. However, insensitivity, prejudice and ignorance remain widespread. Normality is too readily associated with the able-bodied. It is not uncommon for people with a disability to be stared at, pitied ('you poor thing'), or patronized. As Clements and Spinks (2010) point out, those with a disability may become more disabled by the attitudes that others hold about them and by the environment in which they live and work, rather than the disability itself. The important point is to focus on the real person – their capabilities, interests and ideas, rather than only their disabilities.

Families with disabled children want the same things as other families. They want their children to be included and accepted by the community; they want them to enjoy school and make progress in their learning. As the charity Save the Children (2002) point out, the priorities for disabled children are not 'special', they are basic. Disabled children need food, shelter, love, care, protection and education. Yet according to one survey, around 25 per cent of disabled people (compared to 20 per cent of non-disabled people) said they had a negative experience of schooling. In part this was attributed to disruptions, for example because of hospital treatments. But it was also due to a lack of facilities, low expectations held by others, and inappropriate labelling such as 'lazy' or 'slow' (Grewal *et al.*, 2002).

## Groups of learners

One of the major challenges schools currently face is trying to ensure that a child's chances of success are not related to ethnicity, socio-economic background or gender. In England, the McBer Report (2000) concluded that the 'star teachers' of the future 'will be those who work to make what is now the best become the standard for all'. Unfortunately, there is a long tail of underachievers in school. Marshall (2013) estimates that this is between 20 and 30 per cent of children and argues that inspections should focus on what schools do to improve their progress and move children off the SEN register. This next section considers how outstanding teachers respond to the needs of particular groups of learners:

- those from low-income families;
- those from specific ethnic minority backgrounds;
- boys;
- looked after children;
- gifted and talented; and
- newly-arrived children.

## Children from low-income families

There is compelling evidence to show that poverty has a negative impact on children's educational achievement and quality of later life (DCSF, 2009a). Children who struggle at school are more likely to suffer poor diet, reduced life expectancy and low-paid employment or unemployment, compared to those who achieve well. Publications from organizations such as the Joseph Rowntree Foundation regularly highlight the multiple effects of deprivation on individuals, families and society (Hirsch, 2008). Working-class pupils are less likely to achieve 5+ A★–C passes at GCSE than their middle class peers and are less likely to go on to higher education (Demie and Lewis, 2010). Research has increasingly moved away from understanding why working-class children underachieve, to what can be done to address this. Although successful schools vary in their character, they share the following characteristics:

- strong, inspirational leadership by the head teacher supported by a capable management team;
- close links with parents and increasing community support, which earn the schools the trust and respect of parents;
- detailed, rigorous examination of performance undertaken regularly and followed by action that leads to improvement;
- teaching and learning of a high quality informed by assessment of performance;
- a broad curriculum that incorporates aspects of pupils' own culture and adds relevance and self esteem to pupils' view of themselves;
- teachers and staff from ethnic minority backgrounds who provide role models for pupils and who understand their needs; and
- a strong commitment to equal opportunities and a clear stand on racism.

(Demie and Lewis, 2010: 8)

There is widespread political agreement that social class remains the strongest predictor of educational achievement in the UK. In other words, children's success at school is shaped largely by factors such as parental occupation, income and qualifications. Unfortunately efforts to close the gap between children from materially poor and rich backgrounds have been generally unsuccessful. As Education Secretary Michael Gove bluntly put it to a Commons education committee: '"rich, thick kids" do better than "poor, clever" children, even before they start school'(Shepherd, 2010). There has been little sustained improvement in the educational outcomes for disadvantaged groups, such as white working-class boys. Perry and Francis (2010) call for greater value being placed on what children and young people bring from working-class backgrounds as a group, rather than selective targeting of high achieving individuals. Recent central policies have focused on raising aspirations among working-class children and families. However, critics argue that this approach tends to stigmatize individuals who are left believing that hard work combined with talent will automatically bring social and economic rewards (Perry and Francis, 2010). As part of its social justice agenda, the Coalition Government have adopted a Pupil Premium as policy (Higgins et al., 2013). Additional funding is available to schools to close the gap between disadvantaged pupils and their peers (in 2014–15,

£1300 for primary-aged pupils and £1900 for all looked after children, adopted children and children with guardians).

## Learners from ethnic minority backgrounds

Inequalities in the educational outcomes of children from ethnic minority backgrounds have been well documented for many years. Early explanations suggesting biological reasons have long been discredited although occasionally resurface within a 'racist' discourse (Archer and Francis, 2006). Generally speaking, Indian and Chinese pupils are more likely to achieve better examination results at school than other ethnic groups. On average, Black, Bangladeshi and Pakistani pupils perform less well than White pupils. Socio-economic factors are largely behind the differences. Many children from minority ethnic groups are from lower socio-economic groups: around a third of Pakistani and Black pupils are eligible for free school meals, while more than half of Bangladeshi, Gypsy/Roma and pupils of Travellers of Irish heritage are entitled to free school meals (Bhattacharyya, 2003).

Schools that are most successful in raising the attainment of pupils from ethnic minority backgrounds share common characteristics. They accept no excuses, take time to talk to children, value cultural diversity and explicitly challenge racism. Their tracking and target setting systems enable them to identify needs early on and divert resources accordingly. They routinely celebrate success. These schools have strong leadership and inclusive policies and practices, close links with parents, a culture of achievement with high expectations and focused support for pupils in need.

Over the last decade or so successive governments, local authorities and organizations have provided practical guidance on how to improve outcomes for ethnic minority groups at all phases of education (DCSF, 2009b). It is worth considering case studies that have been published from initiatives such as the Black Children's Achievement Programme (Demie et al., 2006; DCSF, 2010). Effective approaches to raise the reading attainment of Black Caribbean boys include:

- the use of Black African-Caribbean male learning mentors;
- making the curriculum more culturally relevant and accessible;
- developing a stock of appropriate reading and other resources; and
- enhancing speaking, listening, reading and writing/vocabulary and skills through using African-Caribbean heritage literature.

However, an evaluation of the government's Black Children's Achievement Programme (launched in 2005) found that there remained a lack of awareness or concern among staff about Black children's underachievement and the need to address it (Maylor et al., 2009). The best practitioners build upon children's natural curiosity about differences, for example by using artefacts, images, music, dance and visits from a variety of traditions. There are many excellent resources to support planning and teaching multicultural issues. For instance, the Real Histories Directory (www.realhistories.org.uk) provides online resources on subjects such as 'Black History Month', 'Migration', 'Religious Festivals', 'Slavery' and 'Identity'. Many schools organize international evenings, establish links with schools abroad, and invite visiting speakers from different religious and/or ethnic groups within the community.

## Boys

There is a deep-seated and international concern over the gender gap in literacy, with girls consistently reaching higher standards than boys. Evidence indicates that girls outperform boys in areas such as spelling, reading and writing by the end of the primary school (Maynard, 2002; Campbell, 2002). The problem of boys' underachievement is neither new nor confined to Britain. The 1868 Taunton Commission mentioned concern about the standards of boys' work. It remains an international problem with girls doing better than boys in reading and writing, for example in the United States, Australia, Scotland and Holland.

Pedagogical approaches that are reported to reduce the gender gap include:

- a greater emphasis on paired and group talk;
- the use of short, specific focused activities and, when appropriate, more sustained, ongoing activities;
- more integrated use of ICT;
- clear, realistic and challenging target-setting; and
- paired reading schemes, with 'experts' supporting 'novices'.

However, it is important to note that the strategies that appeal to boys are equally 'girl-friendly'. Younger and Warrington (2005: 15), who conducted research on behalf of the government, could not support the notion of 'boy-friendly pedagogies', pointing out that it is simply a question of quality teaching. Children's writer Anthony Horowitz (2012) suggests that discussions along the lines of boys not reading as much as girls are as valuable as thinking about 'tall versus short' children.

The cross-party Boys' Reading Commission (National Literacy Trust, 2012) reiterate familiar advice for teachers to build on boys' interests, promote reading for enjoyment and to reach out to fathers to get involved in reading projects. It also suggests setting up a universal advisory service for teachers to improve their knowledge of children's books. Using male role models, such as footballers and other sportsmen, can foster boys' interests in books. Freedman (2012), author of the Jamie Johnson series and former football journalist, regularly shares his passion for reading and writing with primary children. Many of the top football and rugby teams have education community officers. Promoting education and inclusion through football are among the key themes of the Football League Trust and its seventy-two clubs.

Language is often a gateway (or barrier) to educational achievement. In one Early Years setting, staff identified 'communication hot spots' where children spoke more, and also areas where children rarely spoke. They found that boys often engaged more in physical activities that demanded little talk. As a result, the staff redesigned areas to encourage collaboration and talk. For instance, they set up activities for water play that required groups of children to collect and direct the flow of water. Construction activities were also provided that captured the imagination of the boys. The successful completion of these tasks depended upon communication with one another.

One of the difficulties associated with general discussions over the 'gender gap' – the relative attainment of boys and girls – is that some of the key questions are overlooked; for instance, which boys underachieve and when? Gender is complicated by other factors such as ethnicity and social class in understanding how children fare in school. For example, some working-class boys are less academically successful than middle-class girls while some Asian boys may outperform some groups of Asian girls. There is some evidence to suggest that class and level of parental education are the most reliable predictors of children's success in school (Smith, 2004).

Research cited by Tomlinson (2005: 198) showed that although both middle- and working-class boys demonstrated the same stereotyped male behaviour, the middle-class boys achieved well: 'It was acceptable for middle class, and some Asian boys, to be both masculine and studious, in ways that had never been available to working class or black boys.' Contributory factors to boys' underachievement can include school-related issues such as tasks set, groupings, resources, assessment strategies and teaching styles. But attitudes of boys and girls towards education are also influenced by factors largely beyond the control of teachers, such as expectations at home and employment prospects in the community (Arnot *et al.*, 1998). Other points to consider include the 'crisis of masculinity' and whether the shortage of decent male role models has any bearing on boys' underachievement (Browne, 2004). Some writers (Hannan, 1999; Noble and Bradford, 2000) argue that boys and girls have different learning preferences and schools need to adjust their teaching approaches accordingly. Davies (2006) provides a useful introduction to the subject (Table 10.4).

Brain-based research has established that, developmentally, boys talk later than girls and are less able than girls when it comes to multi-tasking; boys also have a higher tolerance of pain (Moir and Jessell, 1993). To generalize, it is argued that female brains communicate more effectively than boys (Banks and Shelton Mayes, 2001). These generalizations are worth keeping in mind, but there is a danger that if they are too rigidly applied they

**TABLE 10.4** Gender differences

| The average boy | The average girl |
| --- | --- |
| Likes data, systems and facts | Is more organized |
| Is more likely to read non-fiction than fiction | Plans out tasks |
| Has a shorter concentration span and is easily bored | Has better listening and oral skills |
| Is a risk taker and doer | Dislikes taking risks |
| Requires more space | Likes relationships and people |
| Is more likely to be disruptive | Is less likely to take up teacher time or receive praise in the classroom |
| Learns by doing and by experience | Learns by adopting a step-by-step approach |
| Likes maths, technology, IT and PE | Likes English, drama, dance, art, music |

Source: Davies (2006). Reproduced with permission

reinforce stereotypes. For instance, Connolly (2004) is dismissive of paying too much regard to gender differences in learning style and the tips provided to teachers on how to make their lessons 'boy friendly'. For one thing, some girls are likely to be alienated; for another, schools should focus on aspects of learning that boys find difficult, especially working with open-ended tasks.

Pollard *et al.* (2008: 437) point out that many differences that are usually associated with gender are socially constructed through 'socialization, the pressure of expectation and culturally ascribed roles'. There remains a tendency in society at large to think of occupations that best fit men or women and within education itself; male students who opt to teach in Early Years settings still encounter prejudice. Primary teachers have too readily seen boys as 'livelier, adventurous, boisterous, self-confident, independent, energetic, couldn't-care-less, loyal and aggressive' while girls are 'obedient, tidy, neat, conscientious, orderly, fussy, catty, bitchy and gossipy' (cited by Martin, 1999: 108). In turn, this can result in boys and girls being channelled into particular classroom activities. Ironically, the school system tends to frown upon the very qualities that many parents and society at large encouraged in boys from infancy. On the other hand, girls are generally better behaved than boys and experience greater acceptance from primary teachers who are mainly female (Parke and Gauvin, 2009). In everyday practice teachers can avoid stereotypes by assigning jobs without regard to gender, for instance in role play avoiding automatically allocating a girl to the part of a secretary or nurse and persuading boys and girls to take on leadership roles. Boys and girls can also be encouraged to work and sit together.

Schools most successful in reducing the gender gap have modified their teaching strategies to suit boys and girls although what has worked well in one context, such as breaking lessons down into smaller units, has not necessarily been successful in another. It is known that boys tend to dominate space and talk in primary schools and this clearly has implications for teachers when asking questions, inviting responses and arranging groupings. Cohen *et al.* (2004) continue to provide the most succinct advice to trainee teachers including practical suggestions on how to raise boys' achievement and caution on the language model set for all children. Seating plans need to be considered carefully so that boys and girls both have equal opportunities to contribute. As part of a literature review in Northern Ireland, Lloyd (2011) reviews effective strategies in the school and community to engage boys including: carefully structured work, the use of discussion frames, focused praise, 'boyzones' in libraries and involving fathers.

## Looked after children

Several projects have proved successful in offering looked after children the same access to books and reading as their peers. These included *Reading Rich*, funded by the Scottish

**EXTEND YOUR UNDERSTANDING**

Ask a colleague to focus during one lesson observation on the extent to which you:

- direct questions at boys and girls;

- ask boys and girls a balance of lower and higher-order questions;

- invite boys and girls to carry out different tasks (both formal and informal);

- involve boys and girls in discussions;

- expect girls to be better behaved;

- generally ask boys before girls;

- expect boys to be noisy and disruptive;

- set tasks that engage the interests of boys and girls;

- encourage boys and girls to work together and take turns;

- expect girls to be more sensible and responsible;

- expect boys to be stronger and more assertive.

Government, between 2004 and 2007, and the National Literacy Trust's *Young Readers* Programme that aims to motivate disadvantaged children and young people to read for pleasure. National policy frameworks such as 'Children's Homes: National Minimum Standards/National Care Standards' (DfE, 2011) make it clear that children's needs should be at the centre of their care. There are significant challenges relating to the transience and disruptions that children in care face, which can affect attitudes to reading and learning. Nonetheless, suggestions from looked after children on what support might assist their educational progress include opportunities to choose and purchase their own books (Poulton, 2012). An evaluation of *Reading Rich* found that meeting writers was a major factor in motivating looked after children to read more (Finn, 2008). More generally, researchers report that strategies that work well with looked after children are the same for all learners, including: maintaining a rapid pace of instruction, assessment for learning, using frequent questioning in which pupils know they may be called upon to respond, focusing upon developing metacognitive (thinking) skills, and making use of cooperative learning (Sharples *et al.*, 2011).

## Gifted and talented pupils

Authors use a variety of terms to describe those pupils who do exceptionally well at school: 'more able', 'very able', 'gifted', 'highly able' and 'gifted and talented' are among the most commonly used expressions. The latter is currently popular although it covers a wide range of possible gifts and talents. The official line endorsed by the Qualification and Curriculum Development Agency (QCDA) is as follows:

- 'gifted' learners as those who have abilities in one or more subjects in the statutory school curriculum other than art and design, music and PE;

- • 'talented' learners as those who have abilities in art and design, music, PE, or performing arts such as dance and drama.

(www.qca.org.uk/qca_6402.aspx)

These rather limited definitions are reinforced with the idea that they apply to the top 5–10 per cent of a school population. Wallace (2000) suggests that gifted children typically show above-average ability, creativity and task commitment. It is important to bear in mind that some gifted children may have special educational needs, and this is an area that the government itself is keen to research further (DfES, 2004a). There are also subject-specific characteristics of exceptional ability. Some pupils can demonstrate exceptional performance in language, for instance creative writing, use of extensive vocabulary and depth of understanding. In science, individuals may quickly spot patterns in their observations or show innovative practice while exploring. Gifted mathematicians are able to generalize, use mathematical symbols confidently and work logically (Haylock, 2004).

There are school-wide strategies that are deployed to identify and assess able pupils. These include nomination by the teacher, peer recommendation, test results, screening, parental identification, discussion with children and referrals from the community. Smith (2007: 15–17) provides a useful though not exhaustive checklist to identify gifted and talented children, namely those who:

- ■ possess a wide vocabulary;
- ■ ask lots of questions;
- ■ have a very retentive memory;
- ■ are extremely curious and able to concentrate for longer periods of time;
- ■ have a wide general knowledge;
- ■ enjoy solving problems;
- ■ show strong feelings and emotions;
- ■ have an unusual and vivid imagination;
- ■ have an odd sense of humour; and
- ■ set high standards and can be perfectionists.

However, identification is not straightforward. As the Northern Ireland Council of Curriculum, Examinations and Assessment (CCEA, 2006: 6), in its excellent literature review of provision for gifted and talented children, point out:

> The typical picture of the highly able child is of a hard-working pupil who diligently completes work, and is perhaps known as the class 'swot' or 'brain box'. In reality the picture is much more complex than that. Alongside the gifted achievers are those who – despite their gifts and talents – persistently underachieve due to boredom, lack of interest, or crippling perfectionism; young children who are cognitively advanced enough to play games with complex rule structures and yet not socially mature enough to deal with the frustration that occurs when their peers cannot grasp the game; children whose giftedness may be masked by the fact that they are not being educated in their first language or who also have a disability.

Gifted pupils generally absorb information quickly and demonstrate knowledge well beyond what might be expected from children of their age. They are not simply recognized by their success in examinations. For example, gifted and talented learners may demonstrate leadership qualities, high-level practical skills or a capacity for quick thinking. Some gifted pupils underachieve due to various factors, such as low expectations held by teachers, boredom, a lack of motivation or self-esteem on behalf of the pupils, or because potential is masked by learning difficulties. West (1991) examined the lives of famous thinkers, including Einstein, Edison and Churchill, all of whom had 'underachieved' at school. He concluded that there was an association between visual talent and verbal difficulty and suggested that the visually talented can encounter particular learning problems in a normal classroom where teaching is linear (one fact following another in a specified order).

Stephen Tommis, former director of the National Association for Gifted Children, pointed out:

> There's a perception that gifted children don't need help, they'll rise to the top anyway. This perception shows a lack of understanding of the problems associated with giftedness for children and parents. A seven-year-old gifted child may have the intellect of a 12-year-old but in terms of social and emotional development they are still seven.

But what can be done in order to recognize and challenge gifted and talented pupils? Lee-Corbin and Denicolo (1998) suggest that what matters most (as with all children) is the quality of interaction with their teachers. Smith (2005) reminds teachers of the importance of skilful questioning when teaching gifted and talented pupils. Outstanding teachers probe children's understanding by using open-ended prompts, especially 'how' and 'why' questions such as the following:

- How are you planning to do this?
- Why did you decide to start like this?
- How do you know?
- How can you be sure?
- Why are these answers different?
- How many ways can you . . .?

Gershon (2013) draws on the questioning skills of the ancient Greek philosopher, Socrates, to challenge more able pupils. He argues that teachers should flit between different roles in order to question pupils' assumptions:

> **The gadfly** – by mimicking the gadfly, which nips away at larger animals, teachers can ask lots of small questions to check thinking e.g. 'What do you mean by that?', 'But, what if . . .?', 'Does that always apply?', 'How can you be certain that is true?'

> **The stingray** – in the same way that a stingray unleashes its sting, teachers can 'shock' pupils to review their thinking with questions such as 'Imagine if X was not the case,

what then?', 'What if you lost your memory?' or 'What if we ran out of petrol (or some other great change)?'

**The midwife** – questions can prompt the 'delivery' of new ideas e.g. 'That's an interesting thought; could you explain it a bit more?', 'How might that affect things?', or 'What made you think of that idea?'

**The ignoramus** – playing dumb is a useful strategy to elicit explanation, using questions such as: 'What do you mean?', 'I'm sorry I don't understand can you help me?', 'Can you show me?', 'Can you start from the beginning?', or 'Are you saying that . . .?'

These Socratic questioning techniques should form part of the teacher's everyday repertoire.

The key to meeting the needs of all pupils, including the more able, is meticulous planning. Lessons should feature opportunities for pupils to evaluate their learning. Gifted and able pupils should become familiar with words such as 'argue', 'judge', 'justify' and 'defend'. They should develop habits of rereading their work with a critical eye – for example by using a highlighter to identify evidence to support what they say or generate questions on their work for others to answer. Content needs to be planned so that all pupils are working at the edge of their capabilities. Gifted and talented pupils need to be encouraged to analyse problems, ask questions themselves, compare views and not take for granted what they read. For some very able children, their level of thinking is well beyond the vocabulary that they possess and so teachers need to support them with prompts such as 'Are you thinking . . .?' or 'Am I right to say that you think . . .?' Freeman (1998), on behalf of OFSTED, reviewed the international research on provision for 'highly able' children. She noted that the best practice enriched the curriculum by encouraging creative thinking, independent activities, making connections, playing with ideas so as to come up with new ones, and making contacts with other professionals, such as artists, performers, agricultural and industrial scientists, scholars and craftspeople. Many schools run additional sessions for gifted and talented pupils, where for instance they work on open-ended tasks based on real-world problems and encourage children to enter particular competitions. Close working relationships with parents is also critical – in one study, fewer than one in seventeen parents said they had been given enrichment activities to do at home with their children (NAGC, 2006).

There is debate over whether gifted children are better off following **accelerated learning** programmes, where they for example work with an older age range (class), or whether for social and emotional reasons they should stay with their peers. Research suggests that gifted learners tend to prefer the company of older playmates and can suffer extreme boredom and misery if kept with children of their own age (Woolfolk *et al.*, 2008: 177).

## Newly arrived children

The UK has a very long history of immigration. In the summer 2013 archaeologists reported their findings from studying the skeletons of twenty-five people, aged between 6 and 55, at a Bronze Age burial site in Kent. Isotopes, which are derived from drinking water, can be used to identify where the individual was living at the time their tooth enamel formed. While nine of the group lived locally, eight came from Norway or Sweden, and five from Spain or possibly North Africa (Philipson, 2013). Today, London is the most culturally diverse place – with 37 per cent of residents from ethnic minorities. In the boroughs of Tower Hamlets, Brent and Newham, there are ethnic majorities, particularly of Pakistani and Bangladeshi origin (Lydall, 2004).

Since 2004 many schools have had to adjust to significant changes in pupil mobility with the increasing numbers of newly arrived children entering the United Kingdom from the new member states of the European Union. This has resulted in considerable strains in some areas as schools working with local authorities endeavour to meet new social and linguistic needs. In Wales, for example, demand for ESOL (English for Speakers of Other Languages) exceeds capacity, raising equal access issues (Estyn, 2008). The National Association for Language Development in the Curriculum (NALDIC) points out on its website that although the number of EAL learners in schools has risen by over 50 per cent since 1997, specialist teacher expertise in schools is becoming increasingly rare. In general, high mobility rates are found in schools within areas of serious economic and social deprivation indicated by the large proportions of pupils eligible for free school meals (Dobson and Henthorne, 2000). Teachers also face the challenge of responding to the needs of children who enter their classes through the year, having moved from other schools within the country.

Despite these challenges, there is a range of support for teachers to help meet the needs of newly arrived children. Much of the expertise emanates from specialist teams in local authorities. These teams can include English as an Additional Language and Ethnic Minority Achievement consultants, bilingual teaching assistants and learning mentors. For those teachers without expert support, the DfES (2004b) recommends strategies such as the following: use of visual and auditory cues, modelling, role play, involving the pupil in routine tasks such as giving out books and equipment, creating listening opportunities and wherever possible, making curriculum links to the culture and language of newly-arrived pupils. Outstanding teachers build into their planning reference points that are familiar to newly arrived children, such as different kinds of housing, shops, food and drink, music or places of worship not confined to RE lessons. They are also highly sensitive to individual contexts. They do not assume that all newly arrived children are familiar with their family's country of origin or heritage country. While some children are likely to respond well to an invite to become an 'expert' on another country they know well, others may react negatively due to recent painful memories, e.g. as refugees. Teachers need to plan lessons collaboratively with any additional adults, such as a language support teacher, so that roles are agreed – for instance, whether it will be a team teaching session, or focused support for a particular child or group.

## Gaining help as a non-specialist teacher

The field of SEN is an emotive and complex one. It is essential, therefore, that those new to the profession take time to develop knowledge and understanding by reading some of the high quality support materials that have been produced in recent years. Inclusive education has formed a major market for publishers and there are a number of useful introductory books available (Tilstone and Layton, 2004; Mitchell, 2008; Briggs, 2012; Wearmouth, 2012). Westwood (2013) focuses on meeting the challenges of diverse classrooms and Farrell (2012) provides a comprehensive account of best practice in relation to various disabilities and disorders. The complexities of SEN are well handled by Cline and Frederickson's (2009) 650-page tome. The authors demonstrate how an integrated approach, particularly multidisciplinary work, is essential to promoting effective education. There are also dedicated periodicals, such as *SEN Magazine* and the *British Journal of Special Education*.

Trainee teachers can benefit from specific online guidelines, for instance the Training Development Agency's (TDA) SEN toolkit (available on the Digital Education Resource Archive, www.dera.ioe.ac.uk/13765), a commissioned guide by Peacey and Wearmouth (2007) and in-depth modules covering planning, teaching and assessment issues.

Useful starting points include guidelines from the respective inspectorate bodies on matters such as promoting equal opportunities (Estyn, 2005), and resources generated by organizations such as the Dyslexia Association, the National Autistic Society and the Tourette Syndrome (UK) Association. One child in a hundred is thought to have Tourette Syndrome (TS), also known as multiple tic disorder and tic spectrum disorder. In SEN populations, the proportion is much higher – 25 per cent has been suggested (Ball and Box, 2008). Involuntary tics include eye blinking, repeating words (including bad language), head jerking, cartwheeling and touching other people's genitals. With the child's consent, raising whole-class awareness of TS can minimize potential bullying while seating the child at the back of a class near a door appears to work. This means that the child is not being watched by everyone, and can leave the classroom if necessary.

There are also some first-class Internet-based materials devoted towards special and inclusive education (see the website list at the end of this chapter). In particular resources produced by the National Association of Special Educational Needs (NASEN) and government-related materials should be consulted. While it is important to keep up to date with current guidance, there is much to be gained from considering older materials. For instance, the National Archives hosts the government's formal *Inclusion Development Programme*, which has training resources covering such areas as speech, language and communication needs, as well as dyslexia and autism.

Subject-specific guidance is available on websites such as the Geographical Association, which features 'think pieces' on questions such as 'Does SEN mean differentiation or does SEN mean inclusive teaching?' (www.geography.org.uk). The Mathematical Association publishes *Equals* for ages 3–18 (www.m-a.org.uk) devoted to promoting inclusive mathematics teaching. Robbins (2000) draws attention to 'high-energy' classrooms in which mathematics lessons are characterized by pace, know-how, investigation and challenge for all learners. The last point is particularly important because it might be assumed that only the high attaining pupils should be stretched – 'In the high-energy classroom the child with individual learning difficulties will not have the burden of low expectations' (Robbins, 2000: 78).

Outstanding teachers create inclusive classrooms in which all children feel accepted. This is very challenging, given the wide range of needs in the school population. It requires team work to implement effective early intervention and support. It takes time and application to differentiate effectively and to get to know pupils as individuals – their home lives, languages, cultures and strengths. But the best practitioners see such diversity

**PAUSE FOR REFLECTION**

Simon Baron-Cohen (2012), the UK expert on autism (and brother of comedian Sacha Baron-Cohen!), suggests that people on the autistic spectrum are more likely to be attracted to science, maths and technology – and parents who are scientists are more likely to have children who have autism. Reflect on the science and maths teachers you know – do you feel that certain personality types are attracted to science and maths? If so, what do you think are the implications for how those subjects should be taught in the primary school?

as a resource that enriches school life. They are not naïve over prejudice, cultural stereotyping, social injustice and inequalities, but they demonstrate a 'can do' attitude and seek to promote success for all learners.

This chapter has highlighted some disturbing facts about educational inequalities. Children growing up in poorer families do not achieve as well as those who come from more prosperous backgrounds (Goodman and Gregg, 2010). Particular groups, such as Black Caribbean and gypsy, Roma and traveller children, have underachieved for many years (DCSF, 2008; OFSTED, 2011). Too many children are wrongly labelled as having special educational needs, when they are held back for other reasons, such as teachers' low expectations (OFSTED, 2010). Improving the quality of teaching in each of these three cases can make a difference. The much-respected Effective Pre-School, Primary and Secondary Education (EPPSE) 3–16 project considered how disadvantaged children succeeded against the odds. The researchers found that it was due to the combined efforts of parents, teachers, networks of family and friends and children themselves. The most effective teachers were those who explained clearly and were approachable when things were difficult to understand. The research highlighted the importance of recruiting the best teachers to schools in disadvantaged communities (DfE, 2010). Schemes such as **Teach First** are designed for this purpose and there is some evidence that its teachers are making a difference (OFSTED, 2008c).

The EPPSE report also highlighted the determination and self-belief of children themselves. When faced with a problem they would persevere by 'having a go at it', looked to others for help or used books and computers. When faced with negative life events such as divorce, serious illness or loss of a loved one, they showed resilience and looked upon school as a distraction and focus for learning. Similar findings are reported in America. In his best-selling book, *How Children Succeed*, the journalist Paul Tough (2013) concludes that they do so through grit, curiosity and 'conscientiousness', shaped by caring teachers, social workers, parents and others. Much of this is common sense. Children do well at school when they apply themselves, enjoy supportive families and are taught by effective teachers.

## Glossary

**Accelerated learning** covers a range of approaches designed to improve the speed and quality of learning, such as mind maps.

**Inclusion** is underpinned by the principle that all children have the right to be educated together regardless of any special need or disability.

**Special educational needs** refer to learning difficulties or disabilities that call for special educational provision.

**Teach First** is a charity-run programme, where high achieving graduates are selected and trained in schools in 'challenging circumstances' for a period of two years.

## References

Archer, L. and Francis, B. (2006) *Understanding Minority Ethnic Achievement*, London: Routledge.

Arnot, M., Gray, J., James, M., Rudduck, J. and Duveen, G. (1998) *Recent Research on Gender and Educational Performance*, London: OFSTED.

Ball, C. and Box, H. (eds) (2008) *Education Issues and Tourette Syndrome: An Introduction For Parents and Schools*, London: Tourette Syndrome (UK) Association.

Banks, F. and Shelton Mayes, A. (2001) *Early Professional Development for Teachers*, London: David Fulton.

Baron-Cohen, S. (2012) 'Autism and the technical mind', *Scientific American*, 307(5): 72–5.

Bhattacharyya, G., Ison, L., Blair, M. (2003) *Minority Ethnic Attainment and Participation in Education and Training: The Evidence*, London: DfES.

Bennett, N., Desforges, C., Wilkinson, B. and Jackson, D. (1984) *The Quality of Pupil Learning Experiences*, Hillsdale, NJ: Lawrence Erlbaum Associates.

Briggs, S. (2012) *Inclusion and How to Do It: Meeting SEN in Primary Classrooms*, London: David Fulton.

Browne, N. (2004) *Gender Equity in the Early Years*, Maidenhead: Open University Press.

Campbell, R. (2002) *Reading in the Early Years*, Buckingham: Open University Press.

CCEA (2006) *Gifted and Talented Children In (and Out) of the Classroom*, Belfast: CCEA.

Children in Scotland (2007) *Access All Areas: What Children and Young People Think about Accessibility, Inclusion and Additional Support at School*, Edinburgh: Children in Scotland/Scottish Borders Council.

Clements, P. and Spinks, T. (2010) *The Equal Opportunities Handbook*, London: Kogan Page.

Cline, T. and Frederickson, N. (2009) *Special Educational Needs, Inclusion and Diversity*, Maidenhead: Open University Press.

Cohen, L., Manion, L., Morrison, K. (2004) *A Guide to Teaching Practice*, London: RoutledgeFalmer.

Connolly, P. (2004) *Boys and Schooling in the Early Years*, London: RoutledgeFalmer.

CSIE (2002) *Ten Reasons for Inclusion*, London: CSIE.

Daniels, H. (ed.) (2000) *Special Education Re-formed: Beyond Rhetoric?* London, Falmer Press.

Daniels, H. and Porter, J. (2007) *Learning Needs and Difficulties among Children of Primary School Age: Definition, Identification, Provision and Issues* (Primary Review Research Survey 5/2), Cambridge: University of Cambridge.

Dare, A. and O'Donovan, M. (2002) *Caring for Young Children with Special Needs*, Cheltenham: Nelson Thornes.

Davies, S. (2006) *The Essential Guide to Teaching*, Harlow: Pearson.

Davis, P. and Florian, L. (2004) *Teaching Strategies and Approaches for Pupils with Special Educational Needs*, London: HMSO.

DCSF (2008) *The Inclusion of Gypsy, Roma and Traveller Children and Young People*, Nottingham: DCSF.

DCSF (2009a) *Deprivation and Education*, Nottingham: DCSF.

DCSF (2009b) *Building Futures: Believing in Children*, London: DCSF.

DCSF (2010) *Making an Impact on Black Children's Achievement: Examples of Good Practice from the Black Children's Achievement Programme*, London: DCSF.

Demie, F. and Lewis, K. (2010) *Raising the Achievement of White Working Class Pupils: School Strategies*, London: Lambeth Research and Statistics Unit.

Demie, F., McLean, C. and Lewis, K. (eds) (2006) *The Achievement of African Heritage Pupils: Good Practice in Lambeth Schools*, Lambeth: Lambeth Research and Statistics Unit.

DfE (1994) *Code of Practice on the Identification and Assessment of Special Educational Needs*, London: DfE.

DfE (2010) *Performing Against the Odds: Developmental Trajectories of Children in the EPPSE 3–16 Study*, London: DfE.

DfE (2011) *Children's Homes: National Minimum Standards*, London: DfE.

DfE (2013) *Draft Special Educational Needs (SEN) Code of Practice: for 0 to 25 years*, London: DfE.

DfEE (1999) *The National Curriculum: Handbook for Primary Teachers in England*, London: DfEE.

DfES (2001) *Special Educational Needs Code of Practice*, Nottingham: DfES.

DfES (2004a) *Removing Barriers to Achievement: The Government's Strategy for SEN*, Nottingham: DfES.

DfES (2004b) *Aiming High: Understanding the Educational Needs of Minority Ethnic Pupils in Mainly White Schools*, Nottingham: DfES.

Dobson, J. and Henthorne, K. (2000) *Pupil Mobility in Schools – Final Report*, London: University College.

DoE (2012) *Research into Improving Attendance in Schools Serving Deprived Areas*, Belfast: DoE.

European Agency for Development in Special Needs Education (2003) *Special Education Across Europe in 2003*, Odense: Denmark.

European Commission (2013) *Support for Children with Special Educational Needs (SEN)*, Brussels: European Commission.

Estyn (2005) *Equal Opportunities and Diversity in Schools in Wales*, Cardiff: Estyn.

Estyn (2008) *A Review of English for Speakers of Other Languages (ESOL) Provision*, Cardiff: Estyn.

Farrell, M. (2004) *Inclusion at the Crossroads: Special Education – Concepts and Values*, London: David Fulton.

Farrell, M. (2012) *Educating Special Children: An Introduction to Provision for Pupils with Disabilities and Disorders*, Abingdon: Routledge.

Finn, M. (2008) *Evaluation of Reading Rich*, Edinburgh: Scottish Government Social Research.

Freedman, D. (2012) 'Pitch-perfect male role models for boys', *Times Educational Supplement*, 24 August.

Freeman, J. (1998) *Educating the Very Able: Current International Research*, OFSTED Review of Research, London: HMSO.

Fuchs, D. and Fuchs, L.S. (1998) 'Researchers and teachers working together to adapt instruction for diverse learners', *Learning Disabilities Research and Practice*, 13, 126–37.

Gershon, M. (2013) 'Elongate their learning', *Times Educational Supplement*, 15 February.

Gilbert, F. (2010) 'Special needs is a fad that harms children', *The Telegraph*, 22 July.

Gilbert, F. (2012) 'The special needs system is open to abuse', *The Guardian*, 15 May.

Goodman, A. and Gregg, P. (2010) *Poorer Children's Educational Attainment: How Important Are Attitudes and Behaviour?*, York: Joseph Rowntree Foundation.

Grewal, I., Joy, S., Lewis, J., Swales, K. and Woodfield, K. (2002) *'Disabled for Life?' Attitudes Towards, and Experience of, Disability in Britain*, London: Department for Work and Pensions.

Gross, J. (1996) *SEN in the Primary School: A Practical Guide*, Buckingham: Open University Press.

Hall, W. (2004) 'Inclusion: special needs' in Bold, C. (ed.) *Supporting Learning and Teaching*, London: David Fulton, 137–50.

Hannan, G. (1999) *Improving Boys' Performance*, Oxford: Heinemann Education Publishers.

Haylock, D. (2004) 'Gifted and talented pupils in primary schools' in Brown, A. and Haylock, D. (eds) *Professional Issues for Primary Teachers*, London: Paul Chapman, 150–65.

Hickman, C. and Jones, K. (2009) 'Inclusive practice for children with special educational needs', in Waller, T. (ed.) *An Introduction to Early Childhood*, London: Sage, 126–36.

Higgins, S., Katsipataki, M., Kokotsaki, D., Coleman, R., Major, L.E. and Coe, R. (2013) *The Sutton Trust-Education Endowment Foundation Teaching and Learning Toolkit*, London: Education Endowment Foundation.

Hirsch, D. (2008) *Estimating the Costs of Child Poverty*, York: Joseph Rowntree Foundation.

Hodkinson, A. and Vickerman, P. (2009) *Key Issues in Special Educational Needs and Inclusion*, London: Sage.

Horowitz, A. (2012) 'How can we stop killing the love of reading?', panel discussion at the London Festival of Education, 17 November.

Jerome, L. and Shilela, A. (2006) *The Role of Local Authorities in the Delivery of Qualified Teacher Status Standards in Diversity*, Cambridge: Anglia Ruskin University.

Johnston, J. and Nahmad-Williams, L. (2008) *Early Childhood Studies: Principles and Practice*, Harlow: Pearson.

Lee-Corbin, H. and Denicolo, P. (1998) *Recognising and Supporting Able Children in Primary Schools*, London: David Fulton.

Lewis, A. (2001) 'Charlotte's Web: Special educational needs in mainstream schools', in Richards, C. (ed.) *Changing English Primary Education*, Stoke on Trent: Trentham Books, 79–93.

Lewis, A., Parsons, S. and Robertson, C. (2006) *Survey of Parents and Carers of Disabled Children and Young People in Great Britain*, Birmingham: University of Birmingham.

Lloyd, T. (2011) *Boys' Underachievement in Schools Literature Review*, Belfast: CYMS.

Lord, P. and Jones, M. (2006) *Pupils' Experiences and Perspectives of the National Curriculum and Assessment*, Slough: NFER.

Lydall, R. (2004) 'London is capital of diverse cultures', *London Evening Standard*, 29 September.

McBer, H. (2000) *Research into Teacher Effectiveness: A Model of Teacher Effectiveness*, London: DfEE.

McVeigh, T. (2008) 'Pupils suffer "school phobia" as term starts', *The Observer*, 7 September.

Maddern, K. (2013) 'Pupils with special needs "separated" from teachers and peers', *Times Educational Supplement*, 8 February.

Marshall, P. (ed.) (2013) *The Tail: How England's Schools Fail One Child in Five: And What Can Be Done*, London: Profile Books.

Martin, J. (1999) 'Gender in education', in Matherson, D. and Grosvenor, I. (eds) *An Introduction to the Study of Education*, London: David Fulton, 103–16.

Maylor, U., Smart, S., Kuyok, A. and Ross, A. (2009) *Black Children's Achievement Programme Evaluation*, London: DCSF.

Maynard, T. (2002) *Boys and Literacy: Exploring the Issues*, London: RoutledgeFalmer.

Mitchell, D. (2008) *Contextualizing Inclusive Education*, London: Routledge.

Moir, A. and Jessell, D. (1993) *Brain Sex: The Real Difference Between Men and Women*, London: Penguin.

NAGC (2006) *Neglected Voices? Engaging Parents in the Education of Their Gifted and Talented Children. Executive Summary*, Milton Keynes: NAGC.

National Assembly for Wales (2004) *Special Educational Needs Code of Practice for Wale*, Cardiff: Crown.

National Literacy Trust (2012) *Boys' Reading Commission: The Report of the All-Party Parliamentary Literacy Group Commission*, London: National Literacy Trust.

Noble, C. and Bradford, W. (2000) *Getting It Right for Boys . . . and Girls*, London: Routledge.

OFSTED (2006) *The Logical Chain: Continuing Professional Development in Effective Schools*, London: OFSTED.

OFSTED (2008a) *Good Practice in Re-engaging Disaffected and Reluctant Students in Secondary Schools*, London: OFSTED.

OFSTED (2008b) *How Well New Teachers are Prepared to Teach Pupils with Learning Difficulties and/or Disabilities*, London: OFSTED.

OFSTED (2008c) *Rising to the Challenge: A Review of the Teach First ITT programme*, London: OFSTED.

OFSTED (2010) *The Special Educational Needs and Disability Review*, London: OFSTED.

OFSTED (2011) *Removing the Barriers to literacy*, London: OFSTED.

Parke, R.D. and Gauvin, M. (2009) *Psychology: A Contemporary Viewpoint*, London: McGraw-Hill.

Peacey, N. and Wearmouth, J. (2007) *A Guide to Special Educational Needs For Trainee Teachers*, London: TDA.

Perry, E. and Francis, B. (2010) *The Social Class Gap for Educational Achievement: A Review of the Literature*, London: RSA Projects.

Philipson, A. (2013) 'Britain was a nation of immigrants even in the Bronze Age', *The Telegraph*, 5 June.

Pollard, A., Anderson, J., Maddock, M., Swaffield, S., Warin, J. and Warwick, P. (2008) *Reflective Teaching*, London: Continuum.

Poulton, L. (2012) *Looked-After Children and Literacy: A Brief Review*, London: National Literacy Trust.

Pritchard, D. (1963) *Education and the Handicapped, 1760–1960*, London: Routledge.

Richards, G. and Armstrong, F. (eds) (2011) *Teaching and Learning in Diverse and Inclusive Classrooms*, London: Routledge.

Robbins, B. (2000) *Inclusive Mathematics 5–11*, London: Continuum.

Rose, R. and Howley, M. (2007) *The Practical Guide to Special Educational Needs in Inclusive Primary Classrooms*, London: Paul Chapman.

Save the Children (2002) *Schools for All*, London: Save the Children.

Sharples, J., Slavin, R., Chambers, B. and Sharp, C. (2011) *Effective Classroom Strategies for Closing the Gap in Educational Achievement for Children and Young People Living in Poverty, Including White Working-Class Boys*, London: C4EO.

Shepherd, J. (2010) 'Rich, thick kids achieve much more than poor clever ones, says Gove', *The Guardian*, 28 July.

Singh, I. (2012) 'Why are so many adults convinced that Ritalin does children harm?', *The Telegraph*, 15 October.

Smith, C. (2005) *Teaching Gifted and Talented Pupils in the Primary School: A Practical Guide*, London: Paul Chapman.

Smith, J. (2004) 'Gender issues in education', in Browne, A. and Haylock, D. (eds) *Professional Issues for Primary Teachers*, London: Sage, 166–80.

Smith, R. (2007) 'The kid's got talent, you know', in *Junior Education*, 15–17.

Tickle, L. (2009) 'Tears for Fears', *The Guardian*, 3 March.

Tilstone, C. and Layton, L. (2004) *Child Development and Teaching Pupils with Special Educational Needs*, Abingdon: RoutledgeFalmer.

Tomlinson, S. (2005) *Education in a Post-Welfare Society*, Maidenhead: Open University Press.

Tomlinson, C.A. and Strickland, C.A. (2005) *Differentiation in Practice: A Resource Guide for Differentiating Curriculum, Grades 9–12*, Alexandria, VA: ASCD.

UNESCO (1994) *The Salamanca Statement and Framework for Action on Special Needs Education*, Salamanca: UNESCO, available at: www.unesco.org/education/pdf/SALAMA_E.PDF (accessed 20 October 2013).

United Nations (1989) *United Nations Convention on the Rights of the Child*, London: UNICEF, available at: www.unicef.org.uk/Documents/Publication-pdfs/UNCRC_PRESS200910 web.pdf (accessed 20 October 2013).

Wallace, B. (2000) *Teaching the Very Able Child*, London: David Fulton.

Warnock Report (1978) *Report of the Committee of Enquiry into the Education of Handicapped Children and Young People*, London: HMSO.

Warnock, M. (2005) *Special Educational Needs: A New Look, Impact No 11*, London: Philosophy of Education Society of Great Britain.

Wearmouth, J. (2012) *Special Educational Needs: The Basics*, Abingdon: Routledge.

Webster, R. and Blatchford, P. (2012) 'Supporting learning?: How effective are teaching assistants?, in Adey, P. and Dillon, J. (eds) *Bad Education*, Maidenhead: Open University Press, 77–92.

Wedell, K. (2005) 'Dilemmas in the quest for inclusion', *British Journal of Special Education*, 32(1): 3–11.

West, T. (1991) *In the Mind's Eye*, Buffalo: Prometheus.

Westwood, P. (2013) *Inclusive and Adaptive Practice: Meeting the Challenge of Diversity in the Classroom*, Abingdon: Routledge.

Woolfolk, A., Hughes, M. and Walkup, V. (2008) *Psychology in Education*, Harlow: Pearson.

Younger, M. and Warrington, M. (2005) *Raising Boys' Achievement*, London: DfES.

Yousafzi, M. and Lamb, C. (2013) *I am Malala: The Story of the Girl Who Stood Up for Education and Was Shot by the Taliban*, London: Weidenfeld & Nicolson.

## Websites

The government websites are a useful starting point for information on SEN:

England – www.education.gov.uk

Wales – www.wales.gov.uk

Scotland – www.educationscotland.gov.uk

Northern Ireland – www.nicurriculum.org.uk

National Association for Special Educational Needs is the leading organisation in the UK dedicated to providing information relating to SEN – www.nasen.org.uk

Every Disabled Child Matters campaigns to get rights and justice for every disabled child – www.edcm.org.uk

National Association for Language Development in the Curriculum website – www.naldic.org.uk

The SEN Teacher website contains free resources for teachers – www.senteacher.org

National Association for Able Children – www.nace.org.uk

# 11

# Language, literacy and communication skills

## Chapter objectives

By the end of this chapter you should be able to:

- Reflect critically on the question of raising standards of literacy and communication.
- Explain the characteristics of effective verbal, nonverbal and paraverbal forms of communication.
- Identify effective strategies for teaching English as an additional language and modern foreign languages.
- Reflect upon personal communication skills and how these might be improved.

*When you have kids who show up to school late from being up all night, hungry cuz [sic] mom can't be bothered to buy food, and various 'uncles' dealing drugs from the apartment where they live, it's no wonder reading just isn't a priority*

*(MacLeod, 2007)*

## The question of standards

At all levels of education, concerns about standards of language, literacy and communication have been raised periodically since formal schooling and teacher training began in the nineteenth century. For instance, employers in the 1920s bemoaned the difficulty in finding school leavers who could 'speak and write English clearly and correctly' while a survey of fifty-two university lecturers reported in the 1970s that all their students 'were illiterate to some degree' (DES, 1975: 10). As Chapter 6 noted, a view on standards is shaped by how competence in language, literacy and communication is defined and measured. In fact, the longer historical perspective suggests an improving trend in standards of basic literacy: before 1500, only 10 per cent of English adults could sign their names, whereas by 1900, virtually all brides and grooms could do so. Since then, standards of functional literacy have, on balance, steadily improved (Mitch, 1992; Brooks, 1997; Tymms and Merrell, 2007; Oxford Economics, 2010; DBIS, 2012).

However, there is no escaping the fact that a significant proportion of the UK population continues to demonstrate poor literacy skills. Most concerning is reports for each phase of schooling that point out that too many children and young people struggle with basic language and literacy. The Bercow Report (2008) estimated that 7 per cent of 5-year-olds (around 40,000) enter school with significant difficulties with speech and/or language, requiring specialist support. By the end of Reception, 12 per cent of children cannot write their own names and 19 per cent cannot link sounds to letters (Centre for Social Justice, 2013). One in five eleven-year-olds are not reaching expected levels for their age, amounting to 100,000 pupils in 2011 alone (OFSTED, 2012). The proportion of 16–65-year-olds who read on a daily or near-daily basis has fallen since 2003, along with the proportion that own twenty-five books or more. Frequency of reading is linked to literacy levels, with those who read the most in their everyday lives achieving the highest scores and those who never read achieving the lowest (DBIS, 2012). The fundamental challenge is how to support the significant minority of children and adults who still read below the level the National Curriculum expects of 11 year olds.

There is no single factor that explains the perceived decline in children's language competency. Traditional causes have included television, aspects of the home environment, parenting skills and shortcomings in teacher training. Some of the more unusual suggestions include: the widespread use of buggies, which face away from the pusher and therefore impede conversation, unlike the more sociable but old-fashioned prams with seats at front; and the development of central domestic heating systems that have encouraged family members to disperse to their own space to do their own activities, instead of staying in a single, family room where social interaction is more likely (National Literacy Trust, 2005). Technology based materials are the most frequently read among children and young people; nearly two-thirds read websites every week, and half read emails and blogs/networking websites (such as Bebo, MySpace) every week (Clark *et al.*, 2009). Yet Close (2004) argues that children are suffering from a limited attention span due to activities such as television viewing and computer games. These technologies tend to promote a 'scan and shift' viewing rather than a 'focused' attention. For some commentators, the key issue is how children use such technologies rather than the length of time for which they are exposed to them (Law *et al.*, 2013).

American research has highlighted the significant difference in the number of words spoken to children from different social classes. Beginning in the 1980s, Hart and Risley (2002) studied forty-two pre-school children from professional, working-class and poorest families in Kansas City. By the age of 3, children brought up by professional parents had heard around 50 million words, compared to 30 million for working-class children and just 12 million among the poorest ('welfare') families. Moreover, children of professional parents had heard about 700,000 encouragements and only 80,000 discouragements. On the other hand, children in welfare families had heard only 60,000 encouragements, but twice as many discouragements. Most disconcerting was that, by their third birthday, the average vocabulary level of children from professional families was higher than that of the parents in the welfare families. Hart and Risley calculated that in order to close the vocabulary gap between children from very poor families and working-class children, the former needed an additional 41 hours language instruction each week.

Studies in the United Kingdom raise similar concerns (Law *et al.*, 2013). In London alone, it is estimated that one in five mums and dads do not have the skills to read confidently to their children (Jama and Dugdale, 2012). Unfortunately, a minority of parents, from all social classes, neglects their responsibilities. They see education as the sole remit of schools or opt out of spending time with their children by 'buying' them with expensive presents that do not need their involvement. The upshot of this is that pupils' language skills are perceived to be so poor that their learning is hindered. Hence on both sides of the Atlantic numerous programmes (such as Head Start and Sure Start) have been introduced to raise standards of literacy and improve home–school communication, especially among children living in socially disadvantaged homes. Law *et al.* (2013) have reviewed the most significant recent programmes designed to address young children's language delay, such as Bookstart, the Nuffield Early Language Intervention and Talk of the Town. They call on policymakers to direct resources to roll out the most effective practices.

There is no doubt that effective, targeted language support in the pre-school years can have a positive impact on children's later progress in the primary years. It's claimed that if parents engage with their child's education, their attainment increases by 15 per cent, regardless of the family's social background (Centre for Social Justice, 2013). When parents or carers regularly read, teach songs and nursery rhymes, attend the library, play with letters, paint and draw with children, and take them on visits, they provide secure foundations for cognitive, social and emotional development. The key is what parents do with the children when at home rather than who they are (Sylva *et al.*, 2004). Young children's development is enhanced when parents talk regularly to them and in an elaborative style (for example, by varying intonation, explaining why things happen, discussing motives and describing objects). Hamer (2012: 17) highlights the value of reminiscing about events as a particularly effective way of helping young children understand, and use, words. A reminiscing style includes:

- asking 'Wh-questions' (who, what, where, etc.);
- making associations (linking the event to the child's prior knowledge);
- using 'follow-ins' (encouraging aspects of the conversation that the child is interested in);
- evaluations; and
- praise.

Hamer concludes that the communication environment is a more dominant predictor of early language than social background. Dockrell *et al.* (2012) have produced a Communication Supporting Classrooms (CSC) Observation Tool, one of many useful publications arising from the government-funded Better Communication Research Programme. The CSC Observation Tool is aimed at Reception and Key Stage 1 classes and is based on an extensive review of relevant research. Practitioners are invited to spend an hour observing three dimensions:

- language learning environment (e.g. some classroom displays include items that invite comments from children, there is good light, role play is available);
- language learning opportunities (e.g. small group work, use of talking partners, structured conversations with adults); and

**EXTEND YOUR UNDERSTANDING**

If working with an Early Years setting or at Key Stage 1, download a copy of the CSC Tool, read the rationale and discuss with colleagues whether and how it could be used in your setting. See www.gov.uk/government/collections/better-communication-research-programme

■ language learning interactions (e.g. adults get down to the child's level when interacting with them, use children's names, pausing).

Findings from a pilot study revealed high scores on the environmental factors, but less evidence for quality interactions and structured language learning.

## Raising standards

The most important school influence in raising standards of pupils' language, literacy and communication is the quality of teaching. Excellent teaching in these skills is characterized by:

■ providing challenging tasks with high levels of pupil engagement;
■ flexible classroom organization – pairs, groups, whole-class activities, chosen to fit purpose of lesson;
■ tasks matched to abilities;
■ deliberate modelling of desired behaviour, e.g. writing processes, scanning a text, speaking on a formal occasion;
■ demonstrating a personal passion for writing and reading;
■ appropriate pace linked to pupil capabilities and responses;
■ strong teacher–pupil interaction; and
■ careful monitoring and constructive, timely feedback.

Research on effective teaching of literacy (effectiveness was judged by pupils' learning gains) has shown that effective Key Stage 1 teachers tended to use published schemes only to consolidate points already taught (Wray *et al.*, 2000). They were also less reliant on decontextualized exercises, deriving most of their teaching of word and sentence features from whole texts. The observers noted that the use of time was closely monitored with teachers setting time limits for particular sub-tasks, such as planning within a lesson on writing story beginnings. Above all, the most effective teachers modelled reading and writing extensively. They used blackboards, flip charts, posters and whiteboards to demonstrate not only what was to be produced in the lesson but also the desired processes. Hence they would write letters, skim texts, make notes, and demonstrate intonation when reading aloud, sing nursery rhymes, select words from a vocabulary list, model informal and formal speech, and punctuate text. The authors concluded that the most effective teachers encouraged a 'mindful' approach to the learning of literacy in their pupils.

Recently, there has been no shortage of government effort and investment to raise standards, given UK pupils' poor international performance in reading tests. The National Literacy Trust website provides a useful summary of 'regional' developments designed to raise standards in literacy. In Scotland, there has been much publicity associated with highly successful local literacy programmes in West Dunbartonshire and Clackmannanshire. These are based on the teaching of reading through synthetic phonics, discussed in Chapter 6. In West Dunbartonshire it was claimed that pupil illiteracy was eradicated, while by the end of primary school Clackmannanshire pupils were three-and-a-half years ahead of their peers in reading and almost two years ahead in their spelling (Scott, 2010).

These programmes shaped policy in England, where approaches to reading have become politicized in a more centralized educational system. The Rose Review's *Independent Review of the Teaching of Early Reading Final Report* (DCSF, 2006) endorsed synthetic phonics and the government followed up with support for practitioners through the Communication, Language and Literacy Development Programme (CLLD). While this increased teachers' confidence, knowledge and skills in teaching early reading, concerns continue to be expressed over a decline in young children's speaking and listening skills on entering school (The Centre for Social Justice, 2013).

The respective balance between speaking, listening, reading and writing within the curriculum has been questioned (Alexander, 2012). The Expert Panel appointed to review the National Curriculum in England concluded that discrete strands for speaking and listening should be retained within the programme of study for English (as in the 2007 and 1999 National Curriculum documents) and feature in all other subjects. However, the final English programme of study has attracted widespread criticism. The United Kingdom Literacy Association (UKLA) argues that the content is not challenging or expansive enough to raise standards (www.ukla.org). It sees the government defining literacy too narrowly with an emphasis on dictation and sentence construction rather than compositional skills in Key Stage 1. Many young children write at length and with meaning, before they are able to spell conventionally, because they want to say something. Spelling, grammar and punctuation skills are most effectively taught in the real context of stories, information texts and letters. The overemphasis on synthetic phonics is also criticized because it is seen to restrict children's independent reading.

The debate over synthetic phonics has rumbled on for many years. The poet Michael Rosen is among those who fear that children, who in England are subjected to a phonics test by the age of 6, may learn to decode words but lack the passion for reading, thereby developing a 'can read, won't read' culture. His suggestions include giving every 5-year-old a local library card. Most commentators agree that systematic phonics instruction should be part of every teacher's repertoire, which in England is a requirement within the *Teachers' Standards* (DfE, 2013). There is no reason why the development of reading comprehension should not go hand in hand with the teaching of decoding skills. Research is clear that dialogic reading – when adults ask children questions about stories or picture books and provide feedback through repetitions, modelling and expanding upon answers – is more effective than less interactive forms of shared reading (Kennedy *et al.*, 2012).

Throughout the UK government policies focus on raising literacy standards. The Welsh Assembly has recently introduced a National Literacy (and Numeracy) Programme and a system of national testing (Welsh Government, 2013). This sets out annual national expectations for learners (5–14) with three literacy strands (oracy across the curriculum, reading across the curriculum and writing across the curriculum). In Northern Ireland, teachers have been relieved from the pressure of preparing pupils for a transfer test to concentrate on developing teaching strategies to meet the needs of all learners (Department of Education, 2011). The Scottish Government's Literacy Action Plan (Scottish Government, 2010) seeks to raise literacy standards through early intervention strategies and a strong focus on literacy and language development in *Curriculum for Excellence*.

## Barriers to effective literacy and communication skills

The first principle of communication is that people respond to what they think was said or meant, and not necessarily to the speaker's intended message or actual words (Woolfolk *et al.*, 2008). This is why one of the key challenges in overcoming communication difficulties is narrowing the gap between what is said and what is understood. One very effective way for teachers to do this is to make daily use of summaries. Paraphrasing what someone has said creates a time frame in which both the speaker and listener can reflect on what has been said. If the summary is inaccurate, then at least the speaker has a chance to correct it and the respondent can offer a new summary. Summaries refine and clarify messages and reduce the risk of misunderstanding.

In the classroom, there are a number of 'roadblocks' to effective communication (Gordon, 2003; Table 11.1). These can include poor teaching emanating from a tendency to judge, criticize, blame, order, threaten and label. Even praise can be counter-productive if it denies that a pupil has a learning difficulty; for instance, saying something such as, 'You are really clever. Work it out for yourself' may not be the most appropriate feedback. Perhaps the most damaging comments are those in which teachers are sarcastic at the expense of the pupil, or inherently biased in what they say.

**TABLE 11.1** Barriers to effective communication skills in school

| Barrier | Description |
| --- | --- |
| Environmental | Layout of the classroom, background noise, poor lighting; limited resources |
| Attitudinal | Personality differences, the learner's feelings at the time |
| Physical | Hearing and speaking impediments |
| Psychological | The learner's state of mind |
| Cultural | Learners may address other learners and adults differently according to their customs, upbringing, and religion |
| Physiological | Personal discomfort resulting from, for instance, ill health, poor eye sight or hearing difficulties |
| Linguistic | Learners may know little of the main language of the classroom; difficulties in understanding key words |
| Pedagogic | Poor quality explanations and presentation of materials; misunderstanding of children's needs |

The quality of communication in the classroom is also hindered when the teacher provides too much information, lacks clarity, demonstrates negative body language, interrupts too often, ignores important physical distractions, chooses the wrong medium to communicate and generally fails to engage the interest of pupils.

Excellent teachers combine different forms of communication (non-verbal, paraverbal and verbal) to ensure that messages are clear, accurate and understood.

## Non-verbal communication

Non-verbal communication amounts to communication without words and has been likened to the submerged part of an iceberg. It includes facial expressions, gestures, eye contact, touching, tone of voice, and less obvious signals such as dress, posture and spatial distance. Children generally use gesture to communicate before they use words. Their first gestures, such as reaching, clapping and waving 'bye bye', typically begin between 9 and 12 months of age. Researchers have shown that 5-week-old babies can engage in conversational-type activities, indicated by their eye gazing, chuckling and mouth movements (Riley, 2006). These activities are precursors to speech in that they confirm the mutually supportive roles that speaker and listener need to sustain meaningful communication. As babies develop, their initial interactions with others lead to games of peek-a-boo, throwing and retrieving, handling of books with sounds, textures and colours, and other contexts for genuine communication.

There has been some limited research that indicates that smiling, touching, and close body distance with young children can aid their learning significantly (Bevan, 1985; Baringer and McCroskey, 2000). For young children, touch is a key means of exploring the world around them. As children grow older, however, touch becomes less fitting. The most pervasive type of non-verbal message is body language with research suggesting that it accounts for between 50 and 70 per cent of total information communicated (Mukherji and O'Dea, 2002). It's possible to say how someone is feeling within the first 7 seconds of meeting them, based on facial expression and body language (Kuhnke, 2012).

Body language is divided into two forms: kinesics (facial expression, gestures and body movement) and proxemics (touch, position, posture and distance). Every day, teachers use a combination of both – smiles, stares, grimaces, raised eyebrows, outstretched arms, finger pointing, finger tapping, shaking and nodding of the head and hand movements – to convey particular messages (see Photo 11.1). Even babies can read adult facial expressions and recognize parental emotions such as fear. Eye contact is the most powerful tool for communication. According to Marland (1975: 74):

> The key is the communication with the eyes. Feel the sectors of the room, and underline the structure and sequence of your remarks by directing your phrases to the different sectors . . . Within each group, look at only one pupil, a different one each time you return to the sector, and cast your remarks to him. Feel that you are communicating personally with that individual: look him or her in the eyes, and be aware of his or her expression.

**PHOTO 11.1** An enthusiastic and animated teacher talks to a group of children

Source: POD/Photodisc

Ancient Chinese traders were experts in watching their buyers' eyes when negotiating prices. If the pupils dilated, which is the sign of a favourable response, the trader knew that the offer was too generous and had to renegotiate.

The power of genuine smiles in everyday life and the classroom should not be underestimated. Smiling generates much higher levels of stimulation to the brain and the heart than being given money or having a cigarette, according to clinical tests (*The Scotsman*, 4 March 2005). Smiles are very contagious – like yawns, if a person smiles, the other person usually smiles back. White and Gardner (2012) cite research to show that student teachers that smiled more often and for longer periods of time, conducted classes where their children spent more time thinking, answered questions more often and discussed topics more readily. They also claim that male teachers have an advantage over female teachers because pupils are pre-programmed to pay more attention to male smiles. Clearly, context should determine when it is appropriate to smile. Teachers also need to: reflect on who they smile most at; try smiling at those who would not normally give cause to smile; and guard against the tendency to smile more at higher attaining pupils.

Teachers should try and avoid staring too closely at an individual pupil for any protracted time (a recommended time is 5 seconds out of every 30) because this can create a feeling of unease. Beattie (2003) explains that non-verbal behaviour is a major form, in which emotion is expressed, as well as how relationships are built and attitudes negotiated. Moreover, teachers' clothes and general posture can create lasting impressions in the minds of children.

Cognitively, gestures operate to clarify, contradict, or replace verbal messages. When telling stories, they can express the dimensions of objects or characters. Gestures also serve an important function with regard to regulating the flow of conversation. For example, if a pupil is talking in class, single nods of the head from the teacher are likely to encourage the child to continue and perhaps elaborate. Teachers who regularly use gestures are more effective in communicating messages than those who do not (White and Gardner, 2012). Beats, for example, are very effective to emphasize the message. Typically a teacher might wag a finger for each word when giving an instruction. It is worth noting, however, that inappropriate use of gestures can hinder performance.

Teachers need to be careful when using body language because it can convey different meanings to children from various cultural backgrounds. Take a few of the most common gestures: the thumbs-up signal in Sardinia is an obscene insult, the V-sign in Sicily is seen as a 'victory' sign, the 'wave goodbye' in Argentina can mean 'please stay', while the 'okay' sign is a rude sexual gesture in Arab countries. Neill and Caswell (1993) discuss the cultural differences and problems that arise from simple non-verbal signs, such as a downcast expression. While this carries a universal meaning of being submissive, Western teachers prefer to see the faces of children they are reprimanding (Neill and Caswell, 1993). The way a person stands when talking to others, the avoidance of eye contact, the relative distance between two people, and the use of touch all have cultural meanings. The cultural backgrounds of some children mean that they may appear to be shy and withdrawn. On the other hand, among Black Americans a child returning the teacher's gaze is seen as a defiant response. Unfortunately, there is little research on cultural differences in non-verbal communication among children in British schools. Despite this, the high publicity surrounding the case of a Muslim learning support assistant who was suspended in 2006 by the governors of a primary school for refusing to remove her veil highlights the potential cultural tensions associated with dress and body language (Hilborne and Paton, 2006).

Teachers need to respond appropriately to other people's non-verbal communication, including that demonstrated by colleagues and the pupils themselves. The facial expressions of pupils can determine when teachers should slow down, speed up or in some cases redirect the lesson. Children are quick to pick up on the mannerisms of teachers, which can prove distracting. These could vary from sitting on the table at the start of the lessons, fiddling with an ear or overuse of particular phrases or tags at the end of sentences.

## Paraverbal communication

Paraverbal communication in the classroom is concerned with such matters as orientation (e.g. where the teacher and pupils sit), interaction (e.g. the degree of separation between teacher and pupils, whether physical or in terms of gaze or attitude, with respect to the class), movement (e.g. when the teacher moves around or stands still) and support (e.g. the extent that the teacher maintains a support posture by leaning against or on a structure, material or person). Although it is unclear why, novice teachers tend to use a greater number of gestures and make more kinesic demonstrations when teaching than do expert teachers (Castañer *et al.*, 2010). This may well reflect a novice's uncertainty over subject knowledge.

By nature, humans are territorial creatures – people often mark their space by leaving items on chairs or towels around the swimming pool. Teachers 'mark' their territories when they move around the classroom. In a classic work, the anthropologist Edward Hall (1966) suggested that there are four 'reaction bubbles' (Figure 11.1). The first intimate one extends from 15 cm to 46 cm and is occupied by those who know each other very well. The second personal zone extends to 1.2 metres; those who feel comfortable with each other's presence occupy this. It is the recommended distance for a teacher and pupil to discuss matters, such as feedback, behaviour or personal problems. A third zone covers social contexts such as parties, while the fourth relates to meeting strangers and public events. On a typical school day teachers tend to occupy the personal and social zones. Significantly, they also determine who 'enters' these zones. White and Gardner (2012) suggest teachers tend to preserve more distance between themselves and students they dislike. They also note that reprimands are more effective when delivered from a close distance (within a metre) than those delivered from a long distance. Confident teachers move around the classroom to address children from different places. This is different from walking around as they speak, which can prove distracting and create a 'moving target'.

At another level, vertical distances exist between individuals. In the classroom, effective teachers will often lower themselves to a child's eye level. This is said to be less intimidating for small children who feel more comfortable interacting with an adult on the same level. In this sense, making use of vertical distance can aid the quality of communication. On the other hand, the disciplinarian can put this information to use in order to gain psychological advantage over an unruly pupil.

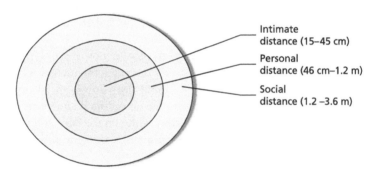

**FIGURE 11.1** Distances in the classroom

Source: Pease and Pease (2004)

### EXTEND YOUR UNDERSTANDING

Studies (cited by White and Gardner, 2012) have shown that when trainee teachers wear suits to school they feel more confident in dealing with pupils. The flip side, however, is that such confidence related only to the trainee teachers' perceptions and made no difference to the behaviour of pupils. Michael Gove supported a dress code for teachers, saying that it makes schools more professional and commands more respect from pupils (see www.tes.co.uk/article.aspx?storycode=6049355). What evidence is there for such a claim and does it matter whether a teacher wears jeans and flip-flops, or tight clothes?

# Verbal communication

The quality of teacher talk is claimed to be the most important factor in effective teaching (Anderson, 1991). Given that many teachers spend so much of their time talking to pupils, it makes sense that training programmes should include guidelines on how to do this well. Teacher success in creating a rich and vibrant classroom language, hinges largely on the quality of explanations, questions and discussions.

## Explaining

Explanations enable children to 'see' or understand how and why something should be done or the meaning behind things. This can apply to a procedure, such as how to print off a document from a computer, to a concept such as 'evaporation' or 'bias'. Teachers also explain objectives, such as the purpose of a visit, how people relate to each other (as in stories), why there are differences and inconsistencies and the reasoning behind decisions. Clarity is the key to successful explanations. Kyriacou (1998) points out that the most important aspect of explaining is the skill in deciding the next step that pupils can take in going from what they know at the beginning of the lesson, to the intended learning by the closure of the session. However, measuring the quality or level of explanation itself is not a straightforward task. Explanations can be influenced by a number of factors, including a teacher's prior knowledge, expressiveness and personality. The ability to explain goes beyond mere description; the key aspect is an emphasis on *why* things happen (Box 11.1).

Explanations are about causes and pursuing understanding. They are at the core of critical thinking. Given the importance of explanations, there is surprisingly little research on what constitutes high-quality work in this field and there is no commonly accepted typology (Cohen *et al.*, 2004). One study suggests that higher-order explanations offer reasons or causes (Why is . . .?) while at a mid level there is a tendency to describe a process or structure (How is . . .?) and at a low level explanations involve clarifying the meaning of terms (What is . . .?).

## Questioning

Those aspiring to be excellent teachers will take time to become familiar with the significance, nature and range of questioning. Questions can be asked for many reasons, including a desire to stimulate interest in a topic, check understanding, model enquiry

---

**BOX 11.1  CHARACTERISTICS OF GOOD QUALITY EXPLANATIONS**

| | |
|---|---|
| Simple | Simple, short and grammatically correct sentences |
| Explicit | Open and clear purpose stated e.g. 'I want to explain how . . .' |
| Eye contact | Keep audience in view and interact with them |
| Links | Use key words to connect thoughts such as 'because', 'so' and 'why' |
| Examples | Illustrate what is said or written, e.g. with reference to pupils' own experiences, or current affairs |

skills or to show a genuine interest in what is being said. However, Delamont (1976) pointed out that 'cross-questioning', checking up and interrogating are frowned upon in everyday life but are the staple diet of classrooms. Some questions may leave children feeling very positive and empower them in their learning. In a typical day it is estimated that teachers pose between 30 and 120 questions each hour, amounting to a staggering 1.5 million questions in a career (Woolfolk *et al.*, 2008: 597). The majority of these are of a managerial type while higher-order, open-ended questions concerned with thinking do not feature as much as experts would like. The majority of teachers' questions – up to 80 per cent – require only factual recall from pupils. In part, this has been attributed to a lack of understanding among teachers about the significance of higher-order questioning. Although there is some debate about the distinction between higher and lower order questions, good teachers know that questions should be chosen to fit the type of learning that they intend to promote.

There are a number of common errors in questioning that teachers should avoid. Often teachers pose questions that are in reality instructions, for instance: 'Will you get your books out please?' Teachers are among the few professional groups who ask questions to which they already know the answers. Cohen *et al.* (2004: 237) cite the anecdote of a 6-year-old child not answering a teacher who asked what '8 + 4 made' because 'the teacher already knew, and I already knew, so I don't know why she asked the question'. If teachers are genuine about developing open-mindedness, they should ask questions they cannot immediately answer correctly. Once a question is asked there is a tendency among some teachers to either answer it or lead pupils to the answer. Pupils may view some questions as threatening and intrusive, causing unnecessary tension in the classroom. Sometimes teachers ask too many questions (particularly of a closed nature) in a machine-gun manner without giving children enough time to reflect on their responses. In the best practice teachers use a full range of questions, match questions to individual needs, mentally note responses, assess whether a follow-up question is necessary and generally are mindful of the need not to over-play questioning so that pupils have the chance to think and discuss themselves. Fisher (2005b) suggests that teachers are likely to get a better response when they:

■ ask fewer but better questions;
■ seek better answers; and
■ encourage children to ask their own questions.

Questioning is very much a matter of quality rather than quantity (Box 11.2). By reducing the number of questions, it is possible to make more time for children to respond and to focus on helping them to improve their answers.

Outstanding teachers demonstrate the ability to ask a range of questions to challenge pupils and extend thinking (Box 11.3, Table 11.2). They are also adept at involving shyer pupils, for instance by using strategies such as prompt Q-cards distributed beforehand.

Questions have been classified in different ways. Wragg (1993) studied more than 1,000 lessons and divided teachers' questions into three main areas:

■ managerial questions related to running the class (e.g. 'Who's finished all the problems?');

---

**BOX 11.2  CHARACTERISTICS OF GOOD QUESTIONING**

- Use a variety of questions (closed, open, focused, viewpoint)
- Select questions to fit particular pupils' needs
- Allow pupils sufficient time to think and answer
- Frame questions with clear objectives in mind
- Use language that is simple, short and understood
- Follow a logical order
- Deliver in a warm, interesting manner
- Rephrase when necessary

---

**BOX 11.3  FOCUS ON PRACTICE**

The following question board can be used in many contexts and take different formats. For instance, a 30-minute discussion with trainees produced the following suggestions: this could be converted into a floor mat, dice or wall chart and used as a basis for reviewing a story, scientific investigation or historical enquiry. It could form the basis of a quiz to check knowledge and understanding, a game board, a pathway for the outdoor area, prompts for role-play or interactive digital resource (e.g. pictures revealed behind the questions).

| What? (What if . . .?) | Who? | Where? |
|---|---|---|
| When? | Why? | How? |
| | | (How much . . .?) |

---

- information/data questions that involved the recall of information (e.g. 'How many legs does an insect have?'); and
- higher order questions associated with analyzsing or making generalizations (e.g. 'Why is a bird not an insect?').

His findings revealed that 57 per cent of questions were of a managerial type, 37 per cent were based on information recall and only 8 per cent were concerned with higher order thinking. Another way to categorize questions is in terms of convergent questions (limited to one right answer) and divergent questions (with many possible answers). Table 11.2 sets out different types of questions used by teachers.

The majority of teachers will be familiar with closed questions, which tend to elicit a narrow range of answers and open questions that encourage a broader response. Both forms can be equally effective, depending upon the context. Research seems to suggest that there are patterns of appropriate questioning for different groups of pupils (Woolfolk *et al.*, 2008). Lower-ability pupils seem to benefit more from knowledge-based and

**TABLE 11.2** Types of questions

| Type of question | Rationale | Examples of questions asked by trainees |
| --- | --- | --- |
| Open questions | Often used to invite viewpoints on subjects, to seek out new ideas and consider alternatives | What do you think about . . .? What questions do you have? How can we solve this? |
| Big questions | Develop profound thinking about moral issues | Is it wrong to ever steal? What happens when we die? |
| Fat questions | Develop extended answers with pupils not allowed to answer using less than so many words | How would you describe what happened? [using no less than 15 words] |
| Closed (factual) questions | Useful for checking factual knowledge and understanding | When did Queen Victoria die? What happened in the story? |
| Probing questions | Useful to explore particular subjects, characters or issues, although these need to be used sensitively | Was the Big Bad Pig *really* that bad? |
| Hypothetical questions | Pose a theoretical situation in the future to which children might be invited to offer their views | What would you do if you were head teacher for the day? |
| Reflective questions | Encourage children to think over what might have been done or said as part of a review | How could we improve yesterday's dance? |
| Leading questions | Used to gain acceptance for a particular view | Fox-hunting is wrong, isn't it? |

comprehension-style questions that allow for a high proportion of correct answers, and plenty of encouragement. Higher-attaining pupils respond more to harder questions (closed and open-ended) and more critical feedback.

As a planning tool, it is good practice for teachers to use key questions to 'anchor' their lessons. But, as Hayes (1998) points out, for novice teachers it is very difficult to develop verbal questioning as a form of differentiation. This can be achieved by linking questions to a hierarchy of thinking, such as Bloom's well-established Taxonomy (Bloom, 1956). Teachers move their questioning from the 'What?' and 'How?' descriptive types to the 'Why?' and 'What for?' which call for more complex reasoning (Table 11.3).

Higher-order thinking skills are best learned when pupils begin to take responsibility for their own learning. Teacher-dominated lessons prohibit this and squeeze out time and energy needed to pursue enquiries that are at the heart of critical and creative thinking. Table 11.4 sets out in more detail examples of challenging questions that can be asked, although context will determine which are appropriate.

## Responding to pupils

It is important for beginning teachers to develop the habit of pausing after asking questions so that pupils are accustomed to having time to think about what is being asked. In the

**TABLE 11.3** Questions linked to Bloom's original Taxonomy

| Purpose | Examples |
|---|---|
| Knowledge | Can you tell me what . . .?<br>Can you remember . . .?<br>What is the name of . . .?<br>What do you know about . . .?<br>Can you (list, tell, show, describe, identify) . . .? |
| Comprehension | How does this work . . .?<br>Can you describe for me . . .?<br>What does the evidence suggest?<br>What is your interpretation of . . .? |
| Application | Can you show me how . . .?<br>Where else might we see this?<br>Can you give examples? |
| Analysis | Why did this happen?<br>Can you explain . . .?<br>What caused . . .?<br>What caused . . .?<br>Can you compare and contrast . . .? |
| Synthesis | What if we . . .?<br>How would you (create, plan, generalize) . . .?<br>How else might we (combine, formulate, arrange, write) . . .? |
| Evaluation | Why do you think . . .?<br>How would you (assess, rank, measure, convince) . . .?<br>How do you discriminate between . . .? |

early 1970s research conducted in elementary science classes in American schools indicated that on average teachers waited less than a second for a response before saying something else (Rowe, 1974). More recent research suggests that when wait time is increased pupils are more confident in responding (Black *et al.*, 2003). Recommended 'wait' times are between 3 and 5 seconds for a closed question and up to 15 seconds for an open-ended question (Cohen *et al.*, 2004: 241). Pupils' short answers can be extended by: 'echoing' what they say, inviting further comment (e.g. 'Can you give an example?'), adding a personal experience, or asking others to comment. American research indicates that the most common teacher response to pupils' answers is a simple acceptance statement such as 'OK' or 'Uh-huh'. Teachers need to move this on by making it clear to pupils why they respond the way they do. Everyone should be expected to contribute and the answers, right or wrong, used as a basis for discussion. The aim is to improve thinking rather than getting things right straightaway. Teachers use a range of techniques to enhance the quality and richness of children's responses (Figure 11.2).

Good teachers use the following kinds of responses:

- repetitions, e.g. 'Yes, the pig was prowling outside';
- reformulations, e.g. 'So, you're saying that life was not so bad then after all?';

**TABLE 11.4** Questions for higher-order thinking

| Question frame | Thinking |
|---|---|
| **1. Questions that probe reason and evidence** | |
| Why do you think that . . .? | Forming an argument |
| How do we know that . . .? | Assumptions |
| What are your reasons . . .? | Reason |
| Do you have evidence . . .? | Evidence |
| Can you give me an example/counter example . . .? | Counter example |
| **2. Questions that explore alternative views** | |
| Can you put it another way . . .? | Restating view |
| Is there a different point of view . . .? | Speculation |
| What if someone were to suggest that . . .? | Alternative views |
| What would someone who disagreed with you say . . .? | Counter argument |
| **3. Questions that seek clarification** | |
| Can you explain that . . .? | Explaining |
| What do you mean by . . .? | Defining |
| Can you give an example of . . .? | Giving examples |
| How does that help . . .? | Supporting |
| Does anyone have a question to ask . . .? | Enquiring |
| **4. Questions that test implications and consequences** | |
| From your ideas, can we work out if . . .? | Implications |
| Does it agree with what was said earlier . . . ? | Consistency |
| What would be the consequences of that . . .? | Consequences |
| Is there a general rule for that . . .? | Generalizing |
| How could you test to see if . . .? | Testing for truth |
| **5. Questions about the question/discussion** | |
| Do you have a question about . . .? | Questioning |
| What kind of question is this . . .? | Analysing |
| How does what was said help us to . . .? | Connecting |
| So where have we got to with this problem . . .? | Summarizing |
| Are we any closer to answering the problem . . .? | Drawing conclusions |

Source: Adapted from Fisher (1998; 2005a)

■ rejections, e.g. 'No. You better check this again'; and

■ recaps, e.g. 'Fine. Do you remember what we did first?'

There is a danger of providing excessive praise, regardless of the quality of pupils' answers. Grosz (2013) points to the danger of overpraising rather than trying to build confidence gently. Comments such as 'You're so clever' and 'You're such an artist' can mask an adult's inability or unwillingness to engage with children as individuals, listening to what they want to say, their interests and passions. How teachers respond to pupils' answers can have an important bearing on the classroom ethos and relationships. For years, teachers have suffered from the 'answer-pulling' syndrome as they draw children towards particular ideas. One 5-year-old Travellers' child inquired of his teacher. 'Why do you keep asking the kids questions when you knows [sic] all the answers? Like . . . like . . . what colour

## Pause, prompt, praise

### Pausing

This includes allowing thinking time. Sometimes a minimal encouragement will prompt further thinking – 'Hmmm', 'Uh huh', 'Yes', 'OK', 'I see'.

Non-verbal encouragement includes eye contact, facial signals such as smiling, and body gestures.

### Prompting and probing

This involves giving verbal encouragement, for example by checking whether we have understood what the child has said and giving opportunities for rethinking and restating an idea – 'Can you explain?', 'Tell us again'. Probing questions include: 'Why do you think that ...?', 'How do you know ...?', 'What do you mean by ...?', 'What if ...?', 'Is it possible that ...?'

### Praising

This is giving positive feedback. Being specific and personal with praise – 'That's an interesting answer', 'I like the way you ...' – can foster general participation by supporting the hesitant, rewarding risk-takers and valuing contributions.

**FIGURE 11.2** Pause, prompt and praise technique

Source: DfES (2004a: 66)

is it then? You can see for yourself it's red . . . so why do you keep asking them?' (Scott, 1996: 36). This raises a significant point about the need for genuine enquiry in which pupils (and teachers) are not afraid to face uncertainty. A group of trainees, when asked what they feared most about teaching history, said not knowing the answers to questions raised by pupils. Children who provide (sensible) wrong answers can easily lose confidence unless they learn within a climate of reassurance and support. One pupil, referring to answering a question, said 'It's like walking a tightrope' (Dean, 1992: 95).

Children enter school full of questions and should be encouraged to continue to do so as they progress through school. At the start of topics, their questions can be regularly displayed and sorted into categories such as those that can be answered immediately or need further research. The nature of a good question can be discussed. There are many activities that promote children's questionings skills, including 'hot-seating', generating question boxes and books, interviews, question games and examining stimulating visual sources.

## Discussing

Outstanding practitioners are able to sustain high quality discussions at individual, group and whole-class level. Realistically, however, eliciting good oral contributions from *every* child on a daily basis is a significant challenge for the most experienced of teachers. Partin (2009) likens the role of the teacher to a moderator in whole-class discussions in trying to ensure that all have the opportunity to participate. Over the years, the UK government has supported resources to promote pupils' speaking and listening skills. In England, these included the Citizenship scheme of work (QCA, 2002) and professional development materials (DfES, 2004b). However, the traditional pattern of whole-class interaction has

# PAUSE FOR REFLECTION

Use the following checklist to reflect upon the quality of your explanations, questioning and responses:

## Questions

- Could all the children hear the questions?
- Did I direct questions at different ones?
- Did I ask a variety of closed and open-ended questions?
- Did I give children enough time to answer?
- Did I ask the questions in a sensible, logical order?
- Did I encourage children to ask their own questions?
- Do I ask questions that pupils can answer successfully?
- Do I always praise or otherwise acknowledge correct responses?

## Explanations

- Are my words clearly spoken?
- Do I speak too slowly or too fast?
- Do I look at the person who is speaking to me?
- Do I go over and display key terms, discussing their meaning?
- Are the main ideas linked together?
- Are my sentences brief and to the point?
- Do I use gestures and facial expression well?
- Do I change my intonation and pace to good effect?
- Do I use real-life, meaningful examples to illustrate the points?
- Is there anything that might detract from my explanations (e.g. dress, posture)?

## Responses

- Do I always acknowledge what children say?
- How well do I paraphrase what children say?
- Do I ask probing follow-up questions?
- How well do I build upon what children say?
- Do I provide regular praise for effort?
- Do I pick up and correct misunderstandings?
- Do I use pupils' names when replying?
- Do I challenge pupils to consider alternative views when appropriate?
- Do I say too much when responding?
- How well do I encourage pupils to explain their answers?

persisted in many schools (Edwards and Westgate, 1994; Hardman *et al.*, 2003). Too many teachers continue to confine classroom exchanges to questions posed by themselves in which they seek out the 'right' answer, rather than opening up discussions. According to Hargreaves *et al.* (2002), only one in ten of the spoken contributions that children made during the national literacy hour exceeded three words – only 5 per cent were longer than five words. In part the problem derives from the pressures teachers feel to 'cover everything' and the misconception that discussion is inferior to written work (Black, 2004).

There are times when whole-class discussions are appropriate. In such cases, teachers:

- develop pupils' opinions and motivation for discussion;
- structure the physical space of the classroom;
- bring learners' ideas to the forefront of discussion;
- create reasons for listening; and
- encourage learners to question and respond to each other (McGraw, 2002).

It is essential for teachers to create an environment that is conducive to productive speaking and listening – see Figure 11.3.

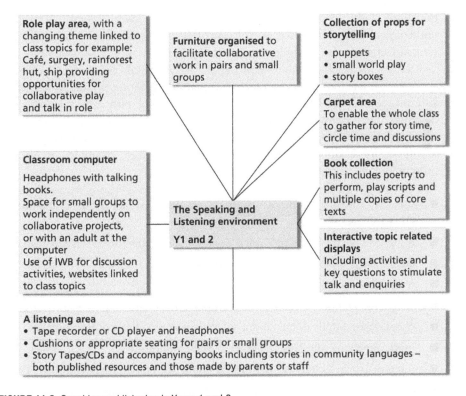

**FIGURE 11.3** Speaking and listening in Years 1 and 2

The practicalities begin by having a clear focal point for discussion, perhaps shared on the board as a question, problem or scenario. The form of discussion needs to be chosen, such as small-group discussion or a full class debate, and the room set up accordingly (circle or horseshoe formats work well). Procedures for discussion need to be clear, such as whether questions need to be directed through the teacher. The use of a soft ball or another object can help with the management of whole-class discussion, as only the pupil holding the ball speaks. In order to prevent some pupils dominating the discussion, some teachers have allocated three tokens to each pupil who hands one in after each comment. Once all three tokens have been used, the pupil is no longer allowed to contribute. At the end of discussions, it is important to summarize key points. Mini plenaries during lessons can also take the form of brief oral presentations with feedback (from teacher and peers) focusing on the quality of the speaker's talk and the listening skills of the audience.

Much of the research that supports classroom discussion is based on constructivist beliefs that talk is a powerful means of learning. The best teachers are able to do this by initiating discussions using open-ended queries, such as 'What's going on here?' and extending discussions through follow-up prompts such as 'That is what the author said, but what did the author mean?' The effective use of a range of verbal and non-verbal prompts is central to facilitating discussions. Kelly (2007: 5) reminds teachers that they are likely to get a greater response from pupils if they make it clear that 'questions are aimed at *how* they think about a problem rather than *what* the right answer might be'. This philosophy underpins developments such as thinking skills and assessment for learning across the United Kingdom (for example, see DCELLS, 2009).

Outstanding teachers model speaking and listening skills in a range of contexts, such as formal presentations, playground talk and when greeting visitors. Such teachers are also in tune with the kind of specialist language used by historians, scientists, artists and designers. They know, for example, that historians often couch their conclusions with word such as 'However, . . .' or 'In general'. They model social protocols when listening to others, for example by not interrupting the speaker. Examples of how teachers promote pupils' speaking skills include:

- using stimulating resources – puppets, artefacts, music, speakers and the outdoor environment;
- using ICT such as tape and video diaries, videoconferences, paired computer work;
- encouraging cross-curricular applications;
- setting homework tasks that involve talking;
- using real context and audiences for tasks – fetes, showing new ones around etc;
- encouraging pupils to talk about what they know ahead of written tasks;
- using interactive displays, 'feely bags' and exhibitions;
- using dramatic techniques (e.g. freeze frame, forum theatre, role play);
- using talking partners so that pupils can share ideas and interview one another; and
- allowing pupils thinking time to rehearse what they will say.

# Listening

Listening is a deliberate activity and differs from hearing, which is an automatic process of turning sound waves into sensations. **Active listening** involves the construction of meaning from all the verbal and non-verbal signals that a speaker communicates (Hennings, 1992). It requires an understanding of the message and not just the words actually spoken. Listening is shaped by many factors. According to Brown and Wragg (1993: 20) 'our capacity to listen diminishes with anxiety' – when teachers are uncertain over their subject knowledge, they can become anxious and reluctant to engage in discussion.

Listening is the least taught language skill in school and yet it is the most prevalent in society (Jalongo, 2007). As a result, listening has been known as the neglected or forgotten language art for more than 50 years (Tompkins, 2002). Although children are expected to spend around 50 per cent of their time listening in school, disappointingly there is very little direct teaching of listening skills (Berg, 1987; Jalongo, 2007). This is surprising given the frequency of comments such as: 'Three, two, one . . .', 'It's your time that you are wasting', 'I don't mind waiting', 'Well, you'll have to stay in at break time if you continue', or simply 'Sssshhh'. The intention is to attract attention and refocus minds. It should not be assumed that children have the same attitude towards listening as adults. While it is instinctive to be sociable with others, children lack understanding of the social etiquette associated with ending their own conversations and immediately tuning into what others have to say. Allen (2013) points out that it is important for teachers to be explicit about developing listening skills – when to listen, how to listen and how to process information. This requires an informative rather than a patronizing approach so that pupils see silence as a useful and pleasurable, rather than punitive, experience.

This is not to underestimate the challenge in promoting a listening culture. It's estimated that typically around 50 per cent of children find listening difficult, preferring noise and the sound of their own voices, described by the Myers-Briggs Type Indicators as falling within the category of 'extroversion' (Allen, 2013). These children, in particular, need support in controlling their natural urge to speak out. In many classrooms, concentrating on one particular sound is made difficult because there are so many competing noises. Concerns are not only expressed about children's listening skills. American studies indicate that adult listening skills are poor. Typically, most adults only listen attentively to about 12 per cent of what they hear and tend to listen in short 30-second bursts before being distracted (Sage and Wilkie, 2004).

It is actually very difficult to ensure that all children are listening at the same time, for instance when providing a key instruction or offering collective feedback. Audiologists recommend that the average classroom noise levels should not exceed 35 dBA (decibel A filter), whereas typical classroom noise levels range from 41 to 51 dBA (Crandell and Smaldino, 1994). It is important to create a physical and social environment that supports and values listening. Teachers should regularly evaluate the school's listening culture – case studies and ideas are supplied by organizations such as the Young Children's Voice Network (www.ncb.org.uk).

Teachers can deploy a range of strategies to develop active listening skills in the classroom (Box 11.4). These include mentally repeating what someone says (a child, parent or another teacher) to help focus the mind and refraining from interrupting. Another

---

**BOX 11.4  FOCUS ON PRACTICE**

A Year 1 trainee reflected on what she considered to be an excellent model for listening demonstrated by her class teacher: she would always make time for children to speak and never rush them, even when one or two struggled to get out what they wanted to say. Sometimes she would say: 'Shall we come back to you in a minute?' The thing that most impressed me was the way that she involved the other children in listening to a particular child speaking. She did this in lots of ways, such as asking someone to help her to remember what was said, or using Mr Forgetful (a puppet) who had 'a bad memory'.

---

useful strategy is to summarize the oral contribution of pupils during a natural break in the conversation, allowing individuals the opportunity to correct any potential misunderstanding in a climate of mutual respect. Sincerity is a key element in active listening. Good listeners do not go through the motions, but show through verbal and non-verbal cues their desire to understand the message. Strategies to improve active listening include:

- acknowledging what the child says with a word, simple 'uh huh' or gesture (e.g. nod of the head);
- asking occasional questions for clarification or extension of what is said;
- recapping on what you think has been said;
- maintaining eye contact with the children;
- avoiding being distracted by environmental factors;
- allowing the speaker to finish;
- showing awareness of non-verbal messages (both of the speaker and listeners); and
- providing brief and constructive feedback.

## Promoting effective classroom talk

The promotion of pupils' oracy skills in the classroom has to contend with a long tradition in which children were to be silent unless spoken to in the classroom. Children's talk was often valued only in terms of how they responded to what adults said. Yet, nearly all children enter school as effective talkers (Eke and Lee, 2009). They use talk to make meaning of the world around them but find some school talk is very different from their own experiences. It is always a worthwhile exercise to ask children what they think makes a good speaker. Tann (1991) reported children believed it was someone who talked a lot, who talked loudly or who wasn't boring.

Speaking and listening have tended to be the poor relatives of language. The Primary Strategy provided detailed objectives for the teaching of speaking and listening, and suggested how these skills could be incorporated across the curriculum (DfES, 2003).

Palmer (2004) provides a range of speaking frames to help pupils move on from the restricted patterns of spoken language to more complex ones, in much the same way as the widely used writing frames support the development of writing. For example, those for Year 3 include 'show and tell' (personal treasures) frames for individual use, 'We're thinking of . . .' (objects, animals or places) frames for paired tasks and 'How to . . .' frames (making something, following rules, using your imagination) for group work.

To engage reluctant speakers, teachers have used a range of strategies including: puppets, artefacts, photographs, song lyrics, jokes, moral dilemmas, newspaper headlines, poetry reading, choral recitations, visits, visitors, 'Ask the Expert' question-and-answer sessions, 'This is Your Life' presentations, role-play, games, museum displays and sports reports. Fisher and Williams (2006) recommend the use of talk diaries to raise the profile of speaking and listening. These are effective when related to children's own interests, recognizing that language operates in different contexts outside the school. In the Early Years, teachers should make particular use of nursery rhymes and stories, sensory play, puppets and visual sources to develop children's imagination.

Many schools use Circle Time and variations on news time as popular contexts for developing talk. Grugeon *et al.* (1998) warn that these well-used strategies may not be as effective as commonly thought as teachers often dominate discussions. In some cases children have allocated 'My Talk Time' slots of 5–10 minutes to talk about subjects that interest them. They may bring along objects, pictures, toys and books to illustrate their talk. These occasions provide teachers with insights into what matters to children, many of whom respond to the occasion with some relish. There are times when children might be encouraged to provide more formal presentations in which they are given set speaking guidelines and brief feedback for them to improve.

The use of drama has long been recognized as an educationally valuable means of communication, with seminal contributions from Dorothy Heathcote (Woolland, 1993; Wagner, 1999; Fleming, 2001). Drama contributes to children's moral and social development, providing opportunities to improve behaviour and inter-personal relationships (Dickinson and Neelands, 2006). Good Early Years' practitioners make use of a rich variety of props, masks, puppets, costume, plays, movement and settings to enhance children's experiences and aid their communication. Drama is an integral part of life in many primary schools and offers every child opportunities to succeed (Scrivens, 1994).

Studies show that teachers talk for between 75 and 90 per cent of classroom time, which significantly reduces opportunities for children to develop their own language skills (Arnold, 1999; Hayes, 1998; The Communication Trust, 2013). More than 40 years ago, the Bullock Report (DES, 1975) calculated that pupils had on average a 20-second window to each contribute verbally in a 45-minute lesson. Recent research suggests little improvement, putting the average length of a pupil's contribution to class discussion at just four words (The Communication Trust, 2013). Even when teachers are not actually talking, they can exercise control over the subject discourse, for example by directing what pupils say. Teachers usually tell pupils when to talk, what to talk about, when to stop talking and, to a lesser extent, how well they talked. Interestingly, one survey found that 18 per cent of primary-aged children had a conversation of over 30 minutes in average length compared to 1 per cent of adults (Keep, 2005).

**TABLE 11.5** Dos and Don'ts relating to the teaching of talk

| Do | Don't |
|---|---|
| ■ Choose questions and topics that are likely to challenge children cognitively. | ■ Merely ask children to guess what you are thinking or to recall simple and predictable facts. |
| ■ Expect children to provide extended answers that will interest others in the class. | ■ Tolerate limited, short answers that are of little interest to other children. |
| ■ Give children time to formulate their ideas and views. | ■ Hope for high quality answers without offering preparation or thinking time. |
| ■ Provide models of the patterns of language and the subject vocabulary to be used. | ■ Expect children to formulate well thought out answers without the language to do so. |
| ■ Expect children to speak for all to hear. | ■ Routinely repeat or reformulate what children have said. |
| ■ Vary your responses to what children say; debate with children; tell and ask them things in order to extend the dialogue. | ■ Just ask questions. |
| ■ Signal whether you want children to **offer** to answer (hands up) or to prepare an answer in case you invite them to speak. | ■ Habitually use the competitive 'hands up' model of question and answer work. |
| ■ When children give wrong answers ask them to explain their thinking and then resolve misunderstandings. | ■ Praise every answer whether it is right or wrong. |

Source: DfES (2003). © Crown Copyright 2003, reproduced under terms at the Click-Use Licence

It does not have to be this way (Table 11.5). Schools that are successful in developing children's language and communication skills (sometimes from very low starting points) share characteristics: they are well led, place a high priority on language development, draw on children's own language experiences, include daily activities to promote talk, provide excellent role models and take professional development seriously. School leaders play a proactive role in establishing a whole-school language policy that all teachers follow in areas such as grammatical skills, vocabulary and narrative. These schools take full advantage of materials and resources to make the curriculum accessible to all learners. Individual teachers can reflect on their own language models. Their input can be video recorded and reviewed in terms of 'events' such as pauses, interjections by children, and pupils' responses.

## Promoting meaningful group speaking and listening

Well-planned group discussion can help pupils understand different viewpoints, justify their views, and enable pupils to speak who do not usually do so in whole-class contexts. However, there are disadvantages – group work can easily deteriorate into low-level chat about pet rabbits and pencil cases that have nothing to do with the set tasks. Moreover, a few pupils can easily dominate group discussion. Numerous studies (for example, Hastings and Chantrey Wood, 2002) have suggested that there is a significant difference between children sitting around a table and genuine collaborative work. When children sit in groups, they are usually asked to work in pairs, which do not require group seating. Moreover, the fact that children sit in groups does not mean that they will work well together. Howe and Mercer (2007) note 'merely providing opportunities for children to work and talk together has no discernible benefit for learning'. They need to be taught communication and social skills including how to resolve differences, reach considered group decisions and avoid petty disputes. Tasks that include an element of controversy, such as debates over moral issues, are most likely to lead to productive interactions. This is especially so when the tasks extend understanding and cannot be completed by individuals working independently. Mercer (2000) suggests that teachers should develop opportunities for 'exploratory talk' in which pupils share, challenge and evaluate their views. By justifying what they say, children get into the habit of making their reasoning visible in the talk, which represents a distinctive social mode of thinking. It is important therefore for teachers to ask probing questions and to encourage pupils to think aloud.

There are many practical guidelines available for teachers to follow in promoting effective group talk (Box 11.5). It is important to remember that not every piece of work needs to have a written outcome. Group talk requires ground rules to be made clear at the outset, such as one person speaking at a time, providing a reason for what is said and respecting what others say.

---

### BOX 11.5  PROMOTING EFFECTIVE GROUP TALK

- Ensure that the group is well motivated by a chosen topic to discuss and clear about the purpose of their talking: is it to persuade someone to do something or to inform others about a news item?

- Make it clear how much time pupils have to talk and encourage them to work to deadlines (e.g. when to feed back).

- Use Post-it notes to help pupils arrange and rearrange their ideas.

- Use prompts such as starter phrases to help pupils: I wonder if . . . What if . . . Would it work if . . . What about . . .?

- Discuss with pupils who will do what within the group (e.g. chairperson, minute-taker, timekeeper, observer, supporter/critic of a view, spokesperson).

- Provide some form of oral framework linked to the purpose for talking: e.g. for persuasive talk something like 'We believe strongly that . . .', 'We feel this for two reasons. One . . . . Two . . .', 'We think you should . . . because . . .'

- To ensure fair time for individual group members to talk, consider providing an 'entitlement to speak' by handing out equal numbers of counters to each person: each time they speak, they use one counter. This allows the teacher to monitor contributions from members in all groups.

- Feedback on discussion should be structured to allow talk to be redrafted and built upon: e.g. pairs could feed back in fours, then build up to whole-class discussion.

- Consider the role of the teacher within the class – will the teacher join the group and, if so, contribute? How might this influence the dynamics and tone? Will the teacher monitor from a distance or play an active part as a group member?

---

**BOX 11.6  REAL-LIFE LEARNING CHALLENGE**

You saw a news report claiming that shy children can develop social phobias and mental disorders. You have several shy children in your class who have rarely said anything since the start of term, 6 weeks ago. How are you going to respond to this?

---

One of the dangers with group discussion is that teachers can easily underestimate the value of pauses, laughter, disagreement and the space to think about what to say. It requires a highly trained practitioner to know when children should be given the freedom to argue and go off track, in the confidence that they are still learning through talk.

It is challenging for teachers to strike the right balance between intervening and taking a 'back seat' during discussions with children. The skills of questioning, prompting, probing and elaborating are all required, especially with shy children (Box 11.6). One of the difficulties in managing classroom discussion is that children can sometimes reject an idea on the basis of *who* contributed it, perhaps because they have a low opinion of the contributor. Although there has been a significant increase in the materials available to support children's listening and speaking skills, sometimes children do not see discussion as 'real' work. This is not helped when trainee teachers say to children following a whole-class discussion: 'Right, let's get on with some work', or 'OK, I've got some work for you to do now.'

## Teaching English as an additional language

The linguistic profile of the UK's educational system has become increasingly diverse. In 2012, just over 1 million primary and secondary children spoke a first language other than English compared to around 800,000 in 2007 (Barkham, 2013). According to the National Association for Language Development in the Curriculum (NALDIC), the number of learners for whom English is an additional language (EAL) is increasing; in 2011, it was 16.8 per cent of primary pupils while in 2009 it was 15.2 per cent (www.naldic.org.uk). In Bradford primary schools, 43 per cent of children speak English as a second language. Almost 140 different languages are represented, led by Urdu, Chinese and Filipino. Significant numbers also speak Eastern and Northern European languages such as Polish, Latvian and Russian (Baker, 2012).

Children with EAL are not a homogenous group – their needs, family circumstances, achievements and interests vary. Their presence in school adds a new, exciting dimension for all children while presenting additional challenges for teachers. At the outset it is important to find out children's attitudes towards their home language – some may feel embarrassed or uncomfortable about using it in school. Parents may also share the same view.

If teachers truly value an inclusive learning environment, they should adopt a positive attitude towards children's first language. They can do so by taking on the role of language learner, learning a few words and phrases of the children's mother tongue. When children for whom English is an additional language see teachers taking risks and making mistakes, the tone is set for genuine discussion about language and collaborative learning. Much can be learned from colleagues who have considerable experience in multilingual schools.

Bilingualism is more than having the ability to speak two languages fluently. It involves understanding the cultures within which the languages are rooted. In a genuinely bilingual educational context, students are expected to read and write in two or more languages at an age-appropriate level. In other words, they become 'biliterate'. However, the benefits of bilingualism are far reaching and include personal relations, health, travel opportunities and employment prospects. Bilingualism brings benefits to society in terms of tourism, social cohesion and national security. Research is clear that learning two or more languages does not disadvantage children and many countries support bilingual education (Box 11.7). Proficiency in a second language depends upon substantial quality exposure to the language (Mehisto, 2012).

There is a growing body of materials available to help teachers communicate with pupils who are not fluent in English. Resources provided by organizations such as NALDIC, the inspectorates and government websites should be consulted. A series of professional development modules *Excellence and Enjoyment: Learning and teaching for bilingual children in the primary years* (DfES, 2006) provided comprehensive guidance as part of the Primary Strategy and is now available on the National Archives website. The Education Scotland website includes case studies of best practice. In one nursery school in Glasgow, parent volunteers (past and present) and bilingual students produced a welcome DVD in Mandarin, Polish and Urdu. The school has also introduced language communication folders, containing photographs and names of members of staff, and simple entries in English alongside home languages. These cover learning, routines and health issues. Specialist teaching support for newly arrived asylum-seeking children can vary considerably depending on local authority resources. Pupils' exposure to Standard English can be developed in a range of contexts such as art, drama, numeracy and science, as well as specific resources such as dual language materials, visual aids and talking books.

---

## BOX 11.7 INTERNATIONAL VIEW – BILINGUALISM

Many countries around the world support the development of bilingual education. But there are differences over when and how children should be introduced to another language. Total immersion programmes focus only on the target language for either the first few years or the whole period of schooling; dual language programmes use both languages as media for instruction; while transitional bilingualism uses the mother tongue as a means to improving the target language, often English. On balance, research tends to support the effectiveness of dual language programmes (Cummins, 2000). In Wales, all children are required to learn Welsh when they enter school. In Welsh-medium schools, English is only introduced at the age of 7. Bilingual education attracts considerable political interest and is not always seen in a positive light. Since 1998 in California, for example, all non-English speaking students are required to be placed in a special one-year class where instruction must be overwhelmingly in English, except with a written request from parents.

Classroom teachers are also expected to take responsibility for meeting the linguistic needs of bilingual children by demonstrating a commitment to their participation in lessons (DfES, 2004b). Box 11.8 sets out some examples of recommended ideas that classroom teachers and trainees could use to help newly arrived children who are not fluent in English. Group work can provide good opportunities for such pupils to develop their

---

### BOX 11.8  SUGGESTED STRATEGIES FOR PUPILS WHO ARE NOT FLUENT IN ENGLISH

- Make sure you pronounce their names properly, and try to greet them in every lesson.

- Make sure students know your name: introduce yourself and write down your name for them.

- Sit the students next to sympathetic members of the class, preferably those who speak the same language and can translate.

- Try to encourage students to contribute to the lesson by using the home language.

- Do not worry if beginners say very little at first, as plenty of listening time is important when starting to learn a new language.

- Try to teach beginners some useful basic phrases such as yes, no, miss/sir, thank you, please can I have . . . , I don't understand.

- Encourage them to help give out equipment and collect books, so they have to make contact with other children. However don't treat them as the class dogsbody!

- Encourage them to learn the names of equipment, symbols or terms essential for your subject.

- Use pictures and labels. They can make their own 'dictionaries' for key words for your subject.

- Short vocabulary lists can be provided for each lesson.

- Ask pupils for their 'home language equivalents' of English words.

- If pupils/students are literate in their first language, try to obtain bilingual dictionaries, and encourage their use. They may have their own dictionaries at home.

- If pupils/students are literate in their home language, teachers can use books in it for initial reading lessons.

- Visual cues are extremely helpful, for example videos, slides, pictures, diagrams, flash cards and illustrated glossaries.

- Reading material can be made easier by oral discussion, relating it to a pupil's own experiences. If reading material is recorded on cassette, a pupil can listen and read simultaneously.

(DfES, 2005. © Crown Copyright 2005,
reproduced under terms of the Click-Use Licence)

English, but culturally this is likely to be a new experience for many children who have left countries where the educational system is more formal than in the United Kingdom. Further practical advice aimed at trainee teachers who work with EAL children is offered by Hughes (2008). She suggests seating the children near the teacher, where directions can be given with fewer instructions, avoiding asking such children for lengthy responses and trying to gain a sense of the local socio-linguistic experience, for example by walking around the neighbourhood.

## Teaching modern foreign languages

There is long-standing support for the teaching of foreign languages in the primary school. Of the 6,000 or so languages spoken around the world, the Coalition Government wanted schools to choose from French, Spanish, German, Italian or Mandarin. These five are widely agreed to be the key languages that will help young people succeed in later life. Mandarin, in particular, is held as essential to economic prosperity, given the rise of the Chinese economy. Currently, around one in ten state primary schools offer no language lessons at all and a further 20 per cent only offer it to some year groups (Henry, 2012). Following consultation, the National Curriculum in England gives schools more flexibility in deciding on the foreign language to be taught at Key Stage 2 – this can include any modern or ancient foreign language (e.g. Latin or Greek) and should focus on enabling pupils to make substantial progress in one language.

By learning a foreign language, children improve their conversation skills and literacy in English, as well as broaden their understanding of other cultures. Planning for MFL at primary level should build upon the four language skills (listening, speaking, reading and writing) to reinforce cognitive development. One of the challenges for primary schools who use specialist visiting teachers is to build upon their input in literacy, numeracy and other subject areas – the 'Spanish and vanish' effect.

Although it is something of a cliché, all teachers should see themselves as language teachers. Outstanding teaching of a modern foreign language is characterized by pace, challenge and interest (OFSTED, 2011). Mainstream teachers can learn techniques and approaches from specialist language teachers. One of their challenges is not to rely too much on teacher talk and 'over-modelling' (Tsui, 2003). When teaching a target language, such as French or Spanish, experts recommend the following:

- providing learners with opportunities to speak for a real purpose;
- developing learner independence as linguists;
- displaying 'chunks' of useful language in the classroom and around the school; and
- building intercultural knowledge and understanding into lessons.

European studies highlight the importance of focusing upon oral skills, the use of ICT and extra-curricular activities to stimulate interest in modern foreign languages (Eurydice, 2012).

## Glossary

**Active listening** seeks out the meaning of what is said by taking into account words and non-verbal cues.

## References

Alexander, R. (2012) 'Neither national nor a curriculum?', *Cambridge Primary Review*, available at: www.primaryreview.org.uk/downloads_/news/2012/06/2012_06_29NC_review_SoS_letter.pdf (accessed 20 September 2013).

Allen, V. (2013) 'Prepare them for a life of listening', *Times Educational Supplement*, 8 February.

Anderson, L.W. (1991) *Increasing Teacher Effectiveness*, Paris: UNESCO.

Arnold, J. (1999) *Affect in Language Learning*, Cambridge: Cambridge University Press.

Baker, H. (2012) '140 languages spoken by pupils in district bring classroom challenges', *Bradford Telegraph and Argus*, 27 February.

Baringer, D.K. and McCroskey, J.C. (2000) 'Immediacy in the classroom: Student immediacy', *Communication-Education*, 49: 178–86.

Barkham, P. (2013) 'The school where they speak 20 languages: A day at Gladstone Primary', *The Guardian*, 28 February.

Beattie, G.W. (2003) *Visible Thought: The New Psychology of Body Language*, Hove: Routledge.

Bercow Report (2008) *The Bercow Report: A Review of Services for Children and Young People (0–19) with Speech, Language and Communication Needs*, London: DCSF.

Berg, F.S. (1987) *Facilitating Classroom Listening: A Handbook for Teachers of Normal and Hard of Hearing Students*, Boston, MA: College Hill Press.

Bevan, L. (1985) 'A touching way to teach: Nonverbal communication in the primary school classroom', *Early Years*, 6(1): 18–33.

Black, L. (2004) 'Teacher–pupil talk in whole-class discussions and processes of social positioning within the primary school classroom', *Language and Education*, 18(5): 347–60.

Black, P., Harrison, C., Lee, C., Marshall, B. and William, D. (2003) *Assessment for Learning: Putting it into Practice*, Maidenhead: Open University Press.

Bloom, B. (1956) *Taxonomy of Educational Objectives*, Boston, MA: Allyn & Bacon.

Brooks, G. (1997) 'Trends in standards of literacy in the United Kingdom, 1948-1996', available at: www.leeds.ac.uk/educol/documents/000000650.htm (accessed 20 January 2014).

Brown, G. and Wragg, E.C. (1993) *Questioning*, London: Routledge.

Castañer, M., Camerinoa, O., Anguerab, M., Gudberg K. and Jonsson, C. (2010) 'Observing the paraverbal communicative style of expert and novice PE teachers by means of SOCOP: A sequential analysis', *Procedia Social and Behavioral Sciences*, 2: 5162–7.

Centre for Social Justice (2013) *Requires Improvement*, London: The Centre for Social Justice.

Clark, C., Osborne, S. and Dugdale, G. (2009) *Reaching out with Role Models: Role Models and Young People's Reading*, London: National Literacy Trust.

Close, R. (2004) *Television and Language Development in the Early Years: A Review of the Literature*, London: National Literacy Trust.

Cohen, L., Manion, L. and Morrison, K. (2004) *A Guide to Teaching Practice*, London: Routledge.

Cummins, J. (2000) *Language, Power and Pedagogy: Bilingual Children in the Crossfire*, Clevedon: Multilingual Matters.

Crandell, C. and Smaldino, J. (1994) 'An update of classroom acoustics for children with hearing impairment', *The Volta Review*, 96: 291–306.

DBIS (2012) *The 2011 Skills for Life Survey: A Survey of Literacy, Numeracy and ICT Levels in England*, London: Department for Business, Innovation and Skills.

DCELLS (2009) *Developing Thinking: Optional Assessment Materials*, Cardiff: Welsh Assembly Government.

DCSF (2006) *Independent Review of the Teaching of Early Reading Final Report*, London: DCSF.

Dean, J. (1992) *Organising Learning in the Primary School Curriculum*, London: Routledge.

Delamont, S. (1976) *Interaction in the Classroom*, London: Methuen.

Department of Education (2011) *Count, Read: Succeed*, Belfast: Northern Ireland.

DES (1975) *A Language for Life*, London: DES.

DfE (2013) *Teachers' Standards*, London: DfE.

DfES (2003) *Speaking, Listening, Learning: Working with Children in Key Stages 1 and 2*, London: DfES.

DfES (2004a) *Excellence and Enjoyment: Learning and Teaching in the Primary Years*, London: DfES.

DfES (2004b) *Speaking, Listening, Learning: Working with Children in Key Stages 1 and 2, Professional Development Materials*, London: DfES.

DfES (2005) *Aiming High: Meeting the Needs of Newly Arrived Learners of English as an Additional Language*, London: DfES.

DfES (2006) *Excellence and Enjoyment: Learning and Teaching for Bilingual Children in the Primary Years*, London: DfES.

Dickinson, R. and Neelands, J. (2006) *Improve Your Primary School Through Drama*, London: David Fulton.

Dockrell, J., Bakopoulou, I., Law, J., Spencer, S. and Lindsay, G. (2010) *Developing a Communication Supporting Classrooms Observation Tool*, London: DfE.

Edwards, A. and Westgate, D. (1994) *Investigating Classroom Talk*, London: Routledge.

Eke, R. and Lee, J. (2009) *Using Talk Effectively in the Primary Classroom*, London: David Fulton.

Eurydice (2012) *Key Data on Teaching Languages at School in Europe 2012*, Brussels: European Commission.

Fisher, R. (1998) *Teaching Thinking: Philosophical Enquiry in the Classroom*, London: Continuum.

Fisher, R. (2005a) *Teaching Children to Think*, Cheltenham: Stanley Thornes.

Fisher, R. (2005b) *Teaching Children to Learn*, Cheltenham: Stanley Thornes.

Fisher, R. and Williams, M. (eds) (2006) *Unlocking Speaking and Listening*, London: David Fulton.

Fleming, M. (2001) *Teaching Drama in Primary and Secondary Schools*, London: David Fulton.

Gordon, T. (2003) *Teacher Effectiveness Training: The Program Proven to Help Teachers Bring Out the Best in Students of All Ages*, New York: Crown Publishing Group.

Grosz, S. (2013) *The Examined Life: How We Lose and Find Ourselves*, London: Chatto & Windus.

Grugeon, E., Hubbard, L., Smith, C. and Dawes, L. (1998) *Teaching Speaking and Listening in the Primary School*, London: David Fulton.

Hall, E. (1966) *The Hidden Dimension*, New York: Garden City.

Hamer, C. (2012) *NCT Research Overview: Parent–Child Communication Is Important from Birth*, London: NCT.

Hardman, F., Smith, F., Mroz, M. and Wall, K. (2003) 'Interactive whole-class teaching in the national literacy and numeracy strategies', Paper presented at the British Educational Research Association Annual Conference, Heriot-Watt University, Edinburgh, 11–13 September.

Hargreaves, L., English, E. and Hislam, J. (2002) 'Pedagogical dilemmas in the National Literacy Strategy: Primary teachers' perceptions, reflections and classroom behaviour', *Cambridge Journal of Education*, 32(1): 9–26.

Hart, B. and Risley, T.R. (2002) *Meaningful Differences in the Everyday Experience of Young American Children*, Baltimore, MD: Brookes Publishing.

Hastings, N. and Chantrey Wood, K. (2002) 'Group seating in primary schools: An indefensible strategy?' Paper presented at the annual conference of the British Educational Research association, 12–14 September 2002.

Hayes, D. (1998) *Effective Verbal Communication*, London: Hodder & Stoughton.

Hennings, D.G. (1992) *Beyond the Read Aloud: Learning to Read Through Listening to and Reflecting on Literature*, Bloomington, IN: Phi Delta Kappa International.

Henry, J. (2012) 'Foreign languages to be compulsory from age seven', *The Telegraph*, 9 June.

Hilborne, N. and Paton, G. (2006) 'Aishah's dream is to teach', *Times Educational Supplement*, 20 October.

Howe, C. and Mercer, N. (2007) *Children's Social Development, Peer Interaction and Classroom Learning* (Primary Review Research Survey 2/1b), Cambridge: University of Cambridge.

Hughes, P. (2008) *Principles of Primary Education*, London: Routledge.

Jalongo, M.R. (2007) *Early Childhood Language Arts*, New York: Pearson.

Jama, D. and Dugdale. G. (2012) *Literacy: State of the Nation: A Picture of Literacy in the UK Today*, London: National Literacy Trust.

Keep, G. (2005) *Talking Families Talking Communities*, Warwick: Calor Gas Limited.

Kelly, S. (2007) 'Classroom discourse and the distribution of student engagement', *Social Psychology of Education*, 10: 331–52.

Kennedy, E., Dunphy, E., Dwyer, B., Hayes, G., McPhillips, T., Marsh, J., O'Connor, M. and Shiel, G. (2012) *Literacy in Early Childhood and Primary Education*, Dublin: NCCA.

Kuhnke, E. (2012) *Body Language for Dummies*, Chichester: John Wiley.

Kyriacou, C. (1998) *Essential Teaching Skills*, Cheltenham: Nelson Thornes.

Law, J., Todd, L., Clark, J., Mroz, M. and Carr, J. (2013) *Early Language Delays in the UK*, London: Save the Children.

McGraw, R. (2002) 'Facilitating whole-class discussion in secondary mathematics classrooms', PhD thesis, Indiana: Indiana University.

MacLeod, F. (2007) 'Scotland's ranking in child literacy falls', *The Scotsman*, 29 November.

Marland, M. (1975) *The Craft of the Classroom*, London: Heinemann.

Mehisto, P. (2012) *Excellence in Bilingual Education*, Cambridge: Cambridge University Press.

Mercer, N. (2000) *Words and Minds: How We Use Language to Think Together*, London: Routledge.

Mitch, D.F. (1992) *The Rise of Popular Literacy in Victorian England*, Philadelphia, PA: University of Pennsylvania.

Mukherji, P. and O'Dea, T. (2002) *Understanding Children's Language and Literacy*, Cheltenham: Nelson Thornes.

National Literacy Trust (2005) *Why Do Many Young Children Lack Basic Language Skills?*, London: National Literacy Trust.

Neill, S. and Caswell, C. (1993) *Body Language for Competent Teachers*, London: Routledge.

OFSTED (2011) *Modern Languages: Achievement and Challenge 2007–2010*, London: OFSTED.

OFSTED (2012) *Raising Standards in Literacy Speech*, London: OFSTED.

Oxford Economics (2010) *Study to Identify How 'Literacy' Levels Have Developed over Time*, Lisburn: Oxford Economics.

Palmer, S. (2004) *Speaking Frames*, London: David Fulton.

Partin, R. (2009) *The Classroom Teacher's Survival Guide*, San Francisco, CA: Wiley.

Pease, A. and Pease, B. (2004) *The Definitive Book of Body Language*, London: Orion.

Qualifications and Curriculum Authority (2002) *Citizenship: Assessment at Key Stages 1–4*, London: QCA.

Riley, J. (2006) *Language and Literacy 3–7*, London: Sage.

Rowe, M.B. (1974) 'Wait time and rewards as instructional variables, their influence on language, logic and fate control', *Journal of Research in Science Teaching*, II: 81–94.

Sage, R. and Wilkie, M. (2004) *Supporting Learning in Primary Schools*, Exeter: Learning Matters.

Scott, K. (2010) 'Phonics: Lost in translation', *The Guardian*, 19 January.

Scott, W. (1996) 'Choices in learning', in Nutbrown, C. (ed.) *Children's Rights and Early Education*, London: Paul Chapman, 34–43.

Scottish Government (2010) *Literacy Action Plan*, Edinburgh: Scottish Government.

Scrivens, L. (1994) *Drama in the Primary School*, Harlow: Pearson.

Sylva, K., Melhuish, E.C., Sammons, P., Siraj-Blatchford, I. and Taggart, B. (2004) *The Effective Provision of Pre-School Education (EPPE) Project: Final Report*, London: DfES.

Tann, S. (1991) *Developing Language in the Primary Classroom*, London: Cassell.

The Centre for Social Justice (2013) *Requires Improvement*, London: The Centre for Social Justice.

The Communication Trust (2013) *A Generation Adrift*, London: The Communication Trust.

Tompkins, G. E. (2005) *Literacy for the 21st Century: A Balanced Approach*, Upper Saddle River, NJ: Prentice Hall.

Tymms, P. and Merrell, C. (2007) *Standards and Quality in English Primary Schools Over Time: The National Evidence*, Cambridge: University of Cambridge Faculty of Education.

Tsui, A. (2003) *Understanding Expertise in Teaching: Case Studies of Second Language Teachers*, Cambridge: Cambridge University Press.

Wagner, J. (1999) *Dorothy Heathcote: Drama as a Learning Medium*, Santa Barbara, CA: Greenwood Press.

White, J. and Gardner, J. (2012) *The Classroom X-Factor*, London: David Fulton.

Woolfolk, A., Hughes, M. and Walkup, V. (2008) *Psychology in Education*, Harlow: Pearson.

Woolland, B. (1993) *The Teaching of Drama in the Primary School*, London: Longman.

Wragg, E.C. (1993) *Questioning in the Primary School*, London: Routledge.

Wray, D., Medwell, J., Fox, R. and Poulson, L. (2000) *The Teaching Practices of Effective Teachers of Literacy*, Educational Review, 52(1): 75–84.

## Websites

The National Literacy Trust provides news and many resources on all aspects of literacy teaching – www.literacytrust.org.uk

BT's education website includes a range of activities to help children develop their speaking and listening abilities – www.bteducation.org

National Association for Language Development in the Curriculum has a very good document archive – www.naldic.org.uk

UNICEF has some resources that can be used to promote purposeful speaking and listening activities, linked to the rights of children to be heard – www.unicef.org.uk/tz/resources

The ican charity contains resources to support schools in becoming 'communication friendly' – www.ican.org.uk/talkingpoint

# 12

# Behaviour management

By the end of this chapter you should be able to:

- Define children's behaviour and explain why it matters to so many people.
- Critique models and theories of behaviour management.
- Explain the main types and causes of misbehaviour.
- Understand teachers' powers, rights and responsibilities.
- Reflect on how to respond to inappropriate behaviour.

*We live in a decaying age. Young people no longer respect their parents. They are rude and impatient. They frequently inhabit taverns and have no self-control.*

*(6,000-year old Ancient Egyptian tomb inscription)*

*Young people today think of nothing but themselves. They have no reverence for parents or old age. As for the girls, they are forward, immodest and unladylike in speech, behaviour and dress.*

*(Attributed to Peter the Hermit, 1274)*

## Introduction

The opening quotes illustrate that, for thousands of years, adults have been anxious over young people's behaviour. Byron (2009) argues that in the modern age this has created a culture of ephebiphobia (fear of young people) and paedophobia (fear of children) as powerless teachers struggle to keep order. The Education Minister, Elizabeth Truss, has spoken out about toddlers unable to sit still and running amok in nurseries causing chaos (Williams, 2013). In reality, such antisocial and violent conduct is limited to a minority. However, there is no doubt that those entering the profession, whether teaching in the Early Years or in the primary or secondary school, face considerable challenges in maintaining high standards of behaviour. This chapter sets classroom behaviour in the wider social and historical context. It also explores the key theories that underpin best practice. How teachers respond to children, including their misbehaviour, partly depends upon what they value and believe about the purpose of education, relationships with children and their behaviour. In other words, teachers have their own theories. By comparing these to what researchers and educationalists say, teachers can enhance their understanding of the complexities associated with behaviour.

## What is behaviour and why does pupils' behaviour matter?

Psychologists define 'behaviour' as all aspects of observable human activity (Child, 2004). An everyday scenario where a child hits another, resulting in a public outcry and one running away in tears, illustrates three key aspects of behaviour: action, reaction and movement. Each of these can be observed. Modern-day educational psychology recognizes that behaviour is also about mental processes, how and what children think and the memories they hold. The 'behaviour' of the brain has attracted considerable interest in recent years, with numerous myths emerging discussed in Chapter 4. Nonetheless, understanding non-observable behaviour, i.e. children's thoughts, is clearly important when responding to their outward behaviour.

Many diverse parties are interested in children's behaviour, including teachers, parents, children's services, psychologists and other professions, the commercial world, the food and health industries, governments, children's rights groups, and children themselves. The multi-billion pound behaviour industry includes: 'agony aunt' columns in newspapers, guidance from government departments, parenting bodies, religious and self-help groups, charities, major organizations such as the National Health Service and the National Society for Prevention of Cruelty to Children, television programmes such as *Supernanny* (Channel 4 since 2004), websites, books, magazines, training courses and conferences. Why is there so much interest in children's behaviour?

Clearly most of those in the teaching profession care about how children behave because they know this has a bearing on how well they learn. When children misbehave, they learn less and prevent their peers from learning. Teachers want orderly classes so that they can teach without disruption. Some teachers and others also feel that poor behaviour reflects on the quality of teaching. They may feel anxious that colleagues, head teachers, local authority advisers or inspectors will conclude that they are not good teachers if they cannot keep control of their class. This may result in a reluctance to discuss disruptive behaviour even though all teachers experience this at some points in their careers.

Modern-day governments recognize the important link between discipline and learning. When the House of Commons Education Committee recently discussed behaviour it noted: 'Good order is essential in a school if children are to be able to fulfil their learning potential' (House of Commons, 2011: 3). The government also has a duty of care to children as part of its commitment to the United Nations Convention on the Rights of the Child. Article 28 states: 'Discipline in schools should respect children's human dignity.'

At the most serious level, children who are excluded from school because of their behaviour underachieve and this has a high cost to the individual, families and society at large. Those who underachieve at primary school often fail to 'catch up'. They are more likely to become disengaged from education and alienated from society. Educational underachievement is strongly linked to poverty, crime and economic underperformance (The Prince's Trust, 2007).

In simple terms, the government needs to ensure that it has enough teachers. Hence its concern when surveys repeatedly show that teachers are quitting the profession because of children's poor behaviour (Smithers and Robinson, 2003; Teacher Support Network, 2010). Disruptions add considerable stress to fellow pupils and teachers alike. Poor behaviour is also a disincentive for those applying to the teaching profession.

The UK government interest in behaviour has been reflected through recent reviews, task groups and strategies (DCSF, 2009; Scottish Executive, 2001, 2006 and 2009; DENI, 1996). There have been different emphases in government policy illustrated in the titles of publications, from the Conservative government's *Pupils with Problems* (DfEE, 1994) to New Labour's *Social Inclusion: Pupil Support* (DfEE, 1999). The latter represented a policy shift towards combating social exclusion. The Behaviour for Learning materials (EPPI Centre, 2004) encouraged teachers to consider a solutions-based approach to behavioural problems. The emphasis was on moving away from a 'blame' culture to seeing behaviour in the context of social interactions – misbehaviour is seen not in isolation but as part of a chain of actions and reactions. This approach attempted to shift teachers' thinking away from labelling children as 'troublesome' or 'naughty' towards understanding or visualizing improved behaviour. However, the training materials did acknowledge that behaviour is complex and shaped by wider influences such as the family and relationships with the community (Visser and Raffo, 2005).

The Coalition Government's White Paper on *The Importance of Teaching* (DfE, 2010) has sought to strengthen the authority of teachers and head teachers, for instance by extending their powers to issue detentions and to search pupils. Head teachers have also been advised on the powers teachers have for discipline and the need for a robust behaviour policy (DfE, 2013b). The *Teachers' Standards* (DfE, 2013a) focus on teachers setting high expectations and improving the quality of the learning environment. In 2009 the government appointed its own behaviour guru, Charlie Taylor, to offer advice drawing on his experiences as a head of a challenging London primary school; when he took up the headship, thirty-six children aged 11 and under had been excluded by mainstream schools. Taylor's unconventional approach to behaviour management – he used everything from massage to tea and toast – was designed to 'put something back in the tank'; in other words to raise pupils' self-belief in a 'war zone' (O'Hara, 2010). Taylor has since drawn up a rather banal behaviour checklist (Box 12.1) on the basics of classroom management for schools to adapt (DfE, 2011b).

The commercial and business world recognizes the economic potential of shaping children's behaviour. UK children watch on average 10,000 television adverts each year. Although it is difficult to measure the impact of this on children's behaviour, many would argue that such viewing has resulted in a rise in pester power, direct copying of behaviour, and a more subtle and gradual effect on attitudes (Hanley, 2000). The Advertising Association (2011) argues that the real issue is children's unsupervised access to media rather than the nature and content of advertisements. Nonetheless, as testified in shops every day, children have acquired a socially acceptable right to want things that many parents loathe to refuse, in fear of disappointing children or facing the inevitable tantrum.

## BOX 12.1  BEHAVIOUR CHECKLIST FOR TEACHERS

### Classroom

- Know the names and roles of any adults in class.
- Meet and greet pupils when they come into the classroom.
- Display rules in the class – and ensure that the pupils and staff know what they are.
- Display the tariff of sanctions in class.
- Have a system in place to follow through with all sanctions.
- Display the tariff of rewards in class.
- Have a system in place to follow through with all rewards.
- Have a visual timetable on the wall.
- Follow the school behaviour policy.

### Pupils

- Know the names of children.
- Have a plan for children who are likely to misbehave.
- Ensure other adults in the class know the plan.
- Understand pupils' special needs.

### Teaching

- Ensure that all resources are prepared in advance.
- Praise the behaviour you want to see more of.
- Praise children who are doing the right thing, more than criticizing those who are doing the wrong thing (parallel praise).
- Differentiate.
- Stay calm.
- Have clear routines for transitions and for stopping the class.
- Teach children the class routines.

### Parents

- Give feedback to parents about their child's behaviour – let them know about the good days as well as the bad ones.

(DfE, 2001b)

---

### PAUSE FOR REFLECTION

How might you adapt the checklist in Box 12.1 to your teaching context?

From another perspective, controlling wayward children is big business for pharmaceutical companies working in partnership with psychiatrists. Critics claim that the number of children diagnosed with depression, anxiety and other mental health problems is a shocking indictment of child exploitation and modern psychiatry. Gosden (2009) questions the criteria used to diagnose children; for example those with hyperactivity are said, over a 6-month period, to fidget, talk excessively or run about – but which children would not meet these criteria? Davies (2013) believes the astonishing rise in children diagnosed with ADHD (from around 1 per cent in the 1950s to 25 per cent in 2013) is due to the lack of objective, scientific testing in psychiatry. This is relevant to the teaching profession because of the general readiness to accept labelled children and to see their mental disorders as medical rather than educational problems. In other words, the 'treatment' is deferred to psychiatrists and the medical world rather than seen as a teaching and parenting responsibility. In some cases, the extensive use of drugs such as Ritalin to control children's behaviour may mask poor parenting.

On the other hand, Singh (2012) interviewed children about their experiences of ADHD and found that most valued the medication in controlling their impulsiveness. She argues that it is not the drugs that hold children back, but low expectations when adults believe such children are incapable of good behaviour. Children with ADHD would like more strategies to help them control their behaviour; they would like more friends, more time outdoors and less shouting in the classroom. She concludes:

> On school playgrounds, a bullying culture identifies them as targets. Other kids think it's fun to wind them up to see them lose control. Even well intentioned teachers don't know what to do. A child with ADHD will use his diagnosis as an excuse for bad behaviour because he knows he can.

Finally, but above all, children's behaviour matters to themselves. They understand the value of rules to protect them from harm and to promote their well-being. Research (Office of the Minister for Children and Youth Affairs, 2010) on behalf of the Irish government shows that children can identify the key principles for effective discipline:

- loss of privilege (being deprived of something that was of value to the child);
- instructional value (affording the child an opportunity to learn about the consequences of their behaviour);
- consistency (delivering discipline in a consistent manner and following through with appropriate action); and

### EXTEND YOUR UNDERSTANDING

Watch the TED talk delivered by Sir Ken Robinson on 'Changing education paradigms'. Make notes on the trends that he identifies as 'troubling', particularly the rise in the number of children diagnosed with ADHD (www.ted.com/talks/ken_robinson_changing_education_paradigms. html). Try to find sources that challenge this view and come to your own conclusion about the implications for you as a teacher.

---

**BOX 12.2  INTERNATIONAL VIEW – BEHAVIOUR AND CULTURE**

How children are expected to behave and how adults respond to this varies according to social and cultural values. Religious beliefs among fundamentalist Christians, Jews and Muslims, for example, have shaped and continue to influence the use of physical force along the lines of 'Spare the rod, spoil the child'. Among the Rwala Bedouin tribes, adolescent boys were punished with a dagger to harden them for their adult lives while at the other extreme Eskimo parents ignored their children even if they hit or swore at them (Konner, 2010). Removing a child from adults or peers for a period of time (commonly referred to as 'time-out') is often seen in Western cultures as an acceptable way to help young children avoid antisocial or difficult behaviour. However, many parents who belong to collectivist cultures (e.g. Asia, Africa and Latin America) see the use of time out as very harsh (Rogof, 2003; Wise and da Silva, 2007). Globally, according to a United Nations investigation, between 80 and 90 per cent of children experience physical punishment at home (Pinheiro, 2006). Corporal punishment has been banned in schools throughout Europe except France and the Czech Republic, although in a recent UK poll half of parents would like to revive this (Stewart, 2011). From a Western perspective, children's rights are ignored frequently in the Middle East, Africa and South America, but these are very different cultures. Pupils in Ghana told a head teacher who wanted to stop using the cane: "Master, if you do not punish us, we will not behave and we will not learn" (cited by MacBeath, 2012). Anglo-American and Canadian parents tend to reason with children from a young age, as they believe children have a capacity to control their own behaviour. In contrast, African-American and Hispanic parents tend to exercise parental control over the child's environment and the way he or she behaves until middle childhood.

---

- fairness (adopting discipline strategies that reflect fair-mindedness and a sense of justice).

Children's behaviour is very much shaped by social and cultural contexts (Box 12.2). There is a danger, however, of perpetuating stereotypes. In Japan, for instance, there are doubts over the picture of well-controlled classrooms and self-disciplined students. Observers believe that Japanese children spend too much time playing computer games and arrive at school without knowing the most basic of social skills. One study found that it was not uncommon for Japanese children to sleep through lessons uninterrupted (MacBeath, 2012). The development of multicultural schools has also raised its own challenges as teachers resolve tensions between different ethnic minority groups.

## Standards of behaviour in school

What do we know with confidence about children's behaviour in school? The Steer Report (2009) controversially concluded that standards of behaviour in schools were good and had improved in recent years. However, there are evidential difficulties in trying to establish a consistent view on standards of behaviour. Data from inspection reports, teacher and pupil surveys and parental opinion varies. According to OFSTED (2013), around 700,000 pupils attend schools where behaviour needs to improve. The Education Committee of the House of Commons (House of Commons, 2011) was so frustrated at the lack of accurate data, for instance on serious incidents in schools, it was unable to give a decisive view on the state of behaviour in schools or whether there had been an improvement over time. The Committee heard from witnesses who questioned the validity of judgements made by inspectors and in official documents such as the Steer Report. During inspections some schools were said to suspend the worst behaved pupils, while some head teachers allegedly underplayed discipline problems when giving evidence to the Steer Report because they had 'a lot to lose'.

The following summary of what is known about standards of children's behaviour is based on a review of key literature (OFSTED, 2001, 2012; Munn *et al.*, 2004; Scottish Executive, 2006; Paton, 2012; NFER, 2012; DfE, 2012; Scottish Government Social Research, 2012):

■ around 9 in 10 pupils behave well in primary schools;

■ pupils' behaviour is generally seen to be better in primary than secondary schools;

■ 'low-level' frequent disruption, such as talking out of turn or fiddling, is the most common form of pupil misbehaviour;

■ extreme acts of violence in schools are very rare;

■ between 20 and 25 per cent of pupils experience bullying;

■ teachers' unions and the education media frequently express concern over pupil indiscipline;

■ although still rare, extreme violence against school staff is on the increase;

■ pupil misbehaviour is a major source of teacher stress; and

■ the misbehaviour of a minority of pupils has a damaging impact on teachers' well-being and the learning of other pupils.

In the pre-school years, research indicates that older children, girls, and heavier birth weight babies achieve higher cognitive test scores and display fewer behavioural problems than other children (Cullis and Hansen, 2007). The level of the mother's education (but not her ethnicity) is a strong factor in the behaviour patterns of the under-fives. Family income also plays a key role – positively with cognitive outcomes and negatively with problem behaviour. Young children brought up by lone parents are also more likely to demonstrate behavioural problems than those who live with both parents. The government has been advised to target support to 'mothers who suffer from depression as well as poorly educated mothers, boys, younger children and low birth weight babies' (Cullis and Hansen, 2007: 9).

It is important to dispel myths associated with behaviour because these can damage a new teacher's self-confidence and belief in children, which are essential to establishing successful relationships (Table 12.1).

**TABLE 12.1** Myths and truths about behaviour

| Myths | Truths |
|---|---|
| Teachers who have problems with behaviour are poor teachers | All teachers experience problems with behaviour |
| Teachers are responsible for classroom order | Positive pupil behaviour is a shared responsibility held by many, including: teacher assistants, head teachers, parents and children themselves |
| Teachers should not 'smile before Christmas' | A sense of enjoyment when learning is important at all times of the year. Humour can be a very effective discipline strategy. |
| Standards of pupils' behaviour in schools are poor | The vast majority of pupils behave well in school. |
| Some children will always prove troublesome | Behaviour is learned. Therefore it can be improved. |
| Carrying knives, assaults and other serious behaviour problems are on the increase | There are concerns about a growing culture of violence among young people, but this is confined to a minority of schools and colleges. Most disruption in school is of a low-level nature. |

**PAUSE FOR REFLECTION**

Reflect on the myths and truths (Table 12.1) associated with children's behaviour. How do these relate to your own personal experiences both as schoolchild and teacher?

## Types and causes of misbehaviour

Low-level disruptive behaviour is most common in schools. Although what counts as 'low-level' may vary from one teacher to the next, generally this is behaviour that distracts from the lesson, such as fidgeting, whispering, giggling, or shouting out. As Cox (2008) observes: 'It's the tap tap of the pen on the desk, the swinging on the back of chairs, the inability to comply with the simplest request, the mobile phones that wear us down.'

There are five broad categories of minor misbehaviour (Table 12.2). Such behaviour can escalate into more serious disorder if unchecked. High-level disruptions include challenging the authority of the teacher, verbal and physical abuse, or damaging property. Such actions can sap the energies of teachers and leave them disillusioned.

According to Johnston *et al.* (2007) children misbehave for many reasons ranging from too many food additives to boredom. However, there are also children who are diagnosed as having specific behavioural, emotional and social difficulties (BESD).

### Children with behavioural, emotional and social difficulties (BESD)

In England the old SEN Code of Practice (DfES, 2001: 87) defined children and young people who demonstrate BESD as: 'Withdrawn or isolated, disruptive and disturbing,

**TABLE 12.2** Types of misbehaviour

| Low level categories | High level |
|---|---|
| Talk e.g. whispering in assembly | Frequent verbal abuse |
| Movement e.g. out-of-seat behaviour | Refusal to obey rules |
| Time e.g. not putting away resources in time | Truancy |
| Pupil–pupil relations e.g. distracting a peer | Bullying |
| Teacher–pupil relationships e.g. shouting out when asked not to | Challenge to authority |

hyperactive and lack concentration; those with immature social skills; and those presenting challenging behaviours arising from other complex special needs.' Hence, the term BESD is a broad one and can include children and young people who present less obvious behaviours such as depression, anxiety, and school phobia. There are also children with specific conditions. These include those who experience Tourette Syndrome (named after a French doctor who first described patients with physical and verbal tics), Asperger's Syndrome (named after the Austrian paediatrician who described children who lacked non-verbal communication skills) and other psychiatric disorders.

It is very difficult to gauge how many children experience BESD at any given time because of their wide-ranging and organic needs. In general, such needs are often met through a safe and supportive environment that may include: counselling, specialized behavioural and cognitive approaches, flexible teaching arrangements, positive and regular interactions with peers and adults, access to alternative forms of communication, and the provision of particular aids, equipment and resources.

## Mental health issues

One area of growing concern is the 10 per cent of children and young people reported to have clinically diagnosed mental health problems, but this can be as high as 45 per cent of looked after children (www.mentalhealth.org.uk). A report on the Targeted Mental Health in Schools programme (2008–11) recommended that primary schools should prioritize mental health work because this has a direct bearing on behavioural problems (DfE, 2011a). The kind of support that proves effective includes:

- a focus on emotional skills;
- creative and physical activities;
- peer support;
- individual consultations;
- group therapy;
- information, training and counselling for parents; and
- training and counselling for staff.

There is a range of psychotherapies designed to support children and young people experiencing mental health problems. In short, the focus is on developing conversations with individual children to overcome problematic thoughts or behaviours. The humanistic approach focuses on building children's confidence in their own ability and potential. Specialist therapists contribute to a global mental health industry that includes:

- colour therapists who advocate wearing yellow clothes and accessories as yellow is associated with sunshine, light and joy;
- psychotherapists who recommend using visualization; techniques to create 'internal' sunshine pictures;
- nutritional therapists who suggest boosting serotonin levels in the brain by eating high-protein foods such as chicken, turkey, quorn and tofu;
- music therapists who advocate singing, song writing, listening and movement;
- art and drama therapists who value creative processes to increase self-esteem, self-awareness and general well-being;
- light therapists who believe that adding blue light to indoor atmospheres, as opposed to the standard yellow lights typically used, helps boost mood and productivity year-round, especially during the winter;
- hydro therapists who value the healing properties of water; and
- play therapists who use play to prevent or resolve psychosocial difficulties.

Many primary schools have set up multisensory rooms and have long recognized the value of music, art and nature as a means to calm and refocus children.

Evaluations indicate that successful mental health promotion programmes are, essentially, based on good teaching practices, such as fostering warm relationships, developing pupil autonomy and promoting a clear understanding about boundaries, rules and expectations (DfE, 2011a). But this should not undermine the challenges in responding to specific emotional and psychological difficulties. These include a lack of shared language across mental health and education services and a shortfall of confidence and training among mainstream teachers.

Children with BESD are at significant risk of underachievement and can disrupt the learning of others. As a result there has been a long-standing (and ongoing) debate over whether they should be taught in separate special schools, units or within mainstream classes. As OFSTED (1999) acknowledged, children with BESD are among the most difficult pupils to teach. Early identification and intervention have proven to be particularly successful. The Good Behaviour Game (GBG), first used in 1967, has proven to be very effective in reducing inattentive, disturbing and destructive behaviours. Teams compete for prizes, privileges and special activities as they comply with set rules (the GBG manual can be freely downloaded on the Internet).

Nurture groups have proven to be popular in providing a structured and predictable environment in which children who show signs of BESD begin to establish trusting relations with adults. Educational psychologists train nurture group teachers and assistants while parents are brought in regularly and children encouraged to participate in many mainstream school activities including lessons, assemblies and playtimes. OFSTED (2011) report that nurture groups can make a significant difference to the behaviour and social skills of children who might otherwise be at risk of exclusion. However, nurture groups are limited in their effectiveness unless the whole school community creates a supportive ethos and builds close ties with parents.

The roots of serious emotional and behavioural problems can be complex. Early relationships developed within the family are the foundations of learning. Bowlby's (1969) attachment theory suggests that young children instinctively seek attachment when threatened, for instance by separation, insecurity and fear. He thought that if there were a breakdown in the maternal attachment within the first 2 years of life, this would lead to serious cognitive, behavioural and emotional problems. The long-term consequences could include depression, increased aggression and delinquency.

One useful model to help teachers understand such complexities was provided by the psychologist Urie Bronfenbrenner (1917–2005). Born in Russia and educated in America, Bronfenbrenner was fully aware of the differences in children's upbringing. He suggested that each child was like a small doll stacked within many Russian dolls, each representing different social levels:

- the microsystem of familiar experiences, such as the family or classroom;
- the mesosystem where two microsystems interact, such as relations between parents and teachers;
- the exosystem of external environments that have an indirect influence on development, for instance where a parent works;
- the macrosystem that represents the influence of society at large, for example laws, traditions, social mores or cultural values; and
- the chronosystem representing the passage of time that shapes child development, such as anniversaries.

The ecological model has been adapted in many contexts. For instance, the Centre for Excellence and Outcomes in Children and Young People's Services (C4EO) uses Bronfenbrenner's perspective to demonstrate the importance of bringing children's services together (Figure 12.1).

The theory is well supported by evidence that clearly shows how parent care for children is influenced by their own commitments, the support of local services and wider beliefs about childcare. In turn, children's behaviour is shaped by many experiences including: the death of a parent, moving house (chronosystem), the birth of a baby brother (microsystem), the work promotion of a father (exosystem) or changes to uniform regulations (macrosystem). Bronfenbrenner made parental involvement the cornerstone of Head Start, the American pre-school programme, which since 1965 has supported more than 30 million low-income children and their families.

Thirty or so years later, Bronfenbrenner's views about the family have grown in significance. For instance, one in two children in Europe and the USA now experience parental separation (Amato, 2010). This cannot be seen in isolation from other social processes, such as financial hardship, longer working hours and usually less contact time for fathers, all of which have a negative impact on children's behaviour. Parental conflict is the most accurate predictor of a child's adjustment and this continues long after the actual separation (Lewis et al., 2014).

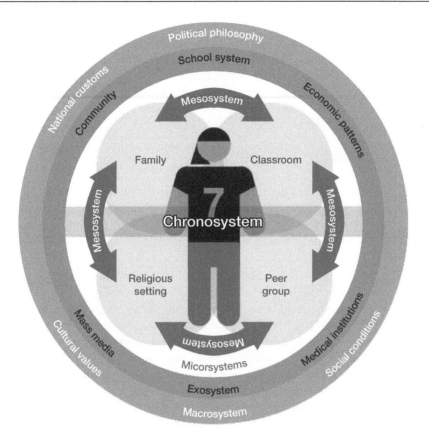

**FIGURE 12.1** Bronfenbrenner's ecological model

Source: www.c4eo.org.uk/themes/earlyyears/eresource/assets/pdfs/ecologicalmodel.pdf

In 2007 Cambridge University published a report on primary education. The team listened to the views of children, moving out from the classroom to the school and wider community. There was remarkable agreement among those interviewed within the eighty-seven 'Community Soundings':

- children are under intense and perhaps excessive pressure from the policy-driven demands of their schools and the commercially driven values of the wider society;
- family life and community are breaking down;
- there is a pervasive loss of respect and empathy both within and between generations;
- life outside the school gates is increasingly insecure and dangerous; and
- the wider world is changing rapidly and in ways which it is not always easy to comprehend though on balance they give cause for alarm, especially in respect of climate change and sustainability.

(Cited by MacBeath, 2012: 22)

Such pressures have meant that the task facing teachers and other professionals in maintaining order to ensure effective learning is more demanding than a generation ago. There is no doubt that the home learning environment plays a key role in children's cognitive and behavioural development. However, some children succeed in school despite living in materially unpromising circumstances while others struggle despite a comfortable material home environment (Desforges and Abouchaar, 2003).

## What is behaviour management?

Behaviour management seeks to create a school climate in which positive behaviour is encouraged, while opportunities for poor and antisocial behaviour are reduced. To be effective, it involves not just teachers, but also parents, head teachers and other professional colleagues. It requires a whole-school commitment to promoting responsible and respectful behaviour.

More than a hundred years ago a teachers' manual advised that good discipline depended upon four factors: the parent, the class teacher, the head teacher and the architect of the school (Collar and Crook, 1902). Parents were expected to train their children in habits of obedience and truthfulness, send them to school regularly and support teachers' efforts. For their part, teachers were expected to demonstrate specific skills such as voice control, deliver lessons that interested pupils, and arrange well-organized classrooms. Head teachers were expected to set the lead by providing a fair and clear system of rewards and punishments, while developing a sense of duty among children. Finally, the school architect was held up as essential in planning the school environment so that teachers and children did not suffer from poor ventilation, lighting and heating.

Although much has changed in the last century or so, there are constants to effective behaviour improvement: teachers' maintaining high expectations, establishing fair and consistent discipline, parental support and the creation of an environment conducive to learning. The Steer Report (2005) recommended that school architects pay close attention to acoustics and lighting in classrooms, so that pupils, wherever they sit, are able to participate fully in classroom activities.

Modern-day behaviour management programmes draw on different theories (Table 12.3). Assertive discipline, for example, is based on the behaviourist theory that children's behaviour can be conditioned or modified through reinforcement, particularly rewards and sanctions. Cognitive behavioural programmes emphasize how children think about their behaviour as well as the actual behaviour itself. Hence, they focus on self-regulation techniques such as talking to oneself, defining problems and evaluating possible solutions. Children might be asked to log incidents on 'trouble cards', noting trigger points, along with actual and future responses (Evans et al., 2003). Possible topics might include lessons in controlling anger, relaxation techniques and problem-solving skills.

Systematic programmes seek to develop whole-school solutions-focused approaches to behaviour management. For example, Quality Circle Time is a popular approach where children have the opportunity to contribute to open, free discussion to solve problems and set targets (Mosley, 1993). The teacher acts as a facilitator encouraging cooperation. However, critics have argued that Circle Time is too much of a gimmick (Housego and Burns, 1994). Miller and Moran (2005), on behalf of the National Foundation for

Educational Research (NFER), provide a balanced assessment suggesting that there are modest gains in pupils' self-esteem but that approaches such as Circle Time are only part of the answer. Teachers need to work together to embed Assessment for Learning strategies, such as peer feedback and target setting, discussed in Chapter 13. Children need to learn the social value of 'being honest and fair' and adopting a 'can-do' attitude.

The humanistic approach to behaviour management has been reflected in the focus on promoting children's emotional well-being over the past decade or so. Examples include the development of the Social Emotional Aspects of Learning (SEAL) programme in primary and secondary schools (DCSF, 2007), the UK Resilience Programme (UKRP) for secondary pupils, and controversial lessons in happiness designed to 'immunise youngsters from becoming miserable' (Martin, 2008). In Scotland, children's well-being is central to *Getting it Right for Every Child* (GIRFEC), where every child has a named person, usually a teacher or health visitor, who acts as the point of contact for the child and family (Scottish Government, 2008). Online resources and case studies illustrate how GIRFEC works in practice (www.scotland.gov.uk/Topics/People/Young-People/gettingitright/resources/using-girfec-approach).

Although there are many different approaches to behaviour management, most are based around the following Rs:

- rules (and consequences) – clear, positively worded (dos rather than don'ts), displayed, discussed, reviewed and revised when necessary;

- rewards – proportionate to behaviour, relational (e.g. providing attention) as well as material (e.g. prizes, money);

- routines – clear arrangements for movement during lessons, transition points, collecting and putting away resources; use of time signals, music, sounds, pictures to aid routines;

- rights and responsibilities – teachers, pupils and parents all share these; and

- relationships – these are at the heart of behaviour management; good behaviours need to be modelled; teachers who are authoritative but approachable in speech and body language; pupils who are encouraged to work together as teams and solve their own problems; building trust and confidence.

Many of their differences revolve around specific elements such as the effectiveness of praise and, more generally, the balance of responsibilities between teachers and children. At one extreme there are schools, such as those run on the Sudbury model in America, in which children are fully involved in the running of the school and where the voice of a 5-year-old counts as much as the head teacher's. Summerhill in Suffolk is the most famous example in England, founded by A.S. Neil in the 1920s (Wilby, 2013). Inspectors have commended the school's powerful and effective behaviour management approaches where all established and followed 'community laws' (OFSTED, 2007).

The theoretical underpinning for such models draws on democratic principles and the contributions of psychologists such as William Glasser (1989; 2012). In his 'Quality School' model, teachers focus on developing caring rather than 'deadly habits' (Table 12.4) through weekly meetings, role-play, team projects and cooperative learning.

**TABLE 12.3** Summary of major behaviour theories

| Theory | Summary | Practical implications |
|---|---|---|
| Behavioural | Behaviour is the result of learning from the environment rather than cognitive processes. | ■ Use rewards to reinforce good behaviour and sanctions following poor behaviour<br>■ Impose rules consistently and objectively |
| Cognitive – Behavioural | Behaviour is determined by thinking patterns, beliefs, self-confidence, attitudes and expectations. | ■ Involve pupils in setting and monitoring their own behaviour targets through individual plans<br>■ Use self-regulation strategies such as visualisation, talking aloud, exploring options |
| Humanistic | Behaviour is established through relationships and responding to the emotional needs of each individual. | ■ Listen carefully to what pupils say<br>■ Establish one-to-one dialogue<br>■ Support peer-to-peer relationships<br>■ Use counsellors<br>■ Use nurture groups<br>■ Distinguish between poor behaviour and the child – don't blame the latter<br>■ Use children's first names |
| Psychodynamic | Behaviour is linked to early childhood experiences and attachment patterns developed in infancy. | ■ Therapists use metaphor in artwork, drama, play and stories to 'unlock' conflicts<br>■ Adults act as substitute attachment figures |
| Biological | Behaviour is a result of biological processes. | ■ Schools work closely with health professionals such as psychiatrists.<br>■ Drugs may be prescribed |
| Ecological | Behaviour is influenced by physical-spatial and social environments | ■ Architects, teachers and others seek to create attractive buildings and learning environments<br>■ Consider seating plans, lighting, heating, and furniture within classroom, corridors and wider school environment<br>■ Consider use of behaviour contracts working in partnership with parents/carers |
| Systemic | Behaviour is linked to the school ethos and wider social and cultural norms | ■ Walk around the school and see it through the eyes of a child – what are the potential learning experiences, joys, hazards and behaviour 'hot points'?<br>■ Following this, review school policies and practices<br>■ Establish open and frequent communications with parents/carers<br>■ Be aware of the wider community and cultural impact on the individual child. |
| Social learning | Behaviour is influenced by observing the actions of others | ■ Use of 'buddy' system<br>■ Model good behaviour throughout school |

Source: Adapted from www.youngminds.org.uk

**TABLE 12.4** Glasser's habits

| Seven caring habits | Seven deadly habits |
| --- | --- |
| Supporting | Criticizing |
| Encouraging | Blaming |
| Listening | Complaining |
| Accepting | Nagging |
| Trusting | Threatening |
| Respecting | Punishing |
| Negotiating differences | Bribing or rewarding to control |

Some behaviour management models focus on children's interaction with the environment; for instance, the 'Learning Zone Model' was originally conceived within the context of outdoor adventure education (Senninger, 2000). It is seen as a way of understanding how people behave when faced with risky activities, such as rock climbing, but has been adapted to school contexts as follows:

- Safety Zone – where learners feel physically and emotionally secure;
- Learning Zone – where learners are challenged and supported to learn;
- Anxiety Zone – where learners begin to experience negative stress and as a consequence demonstrate low levels of misbehaviour; and
- Stress Zone – where learners react badly to situations.

(Best and Thomas, 2007)

The model seeks to equip teachers with an understanding of how to move learners away from the anxiety and stress zones, where learning suffers, towards the other two zones. Teachers should make it clear, for instance, that risk taking is a good thing and support this in practice. They should recognize that there will be times when children are stressed about lessons and offer reassurance to return to their safe zone before they re-enter the learning zone. In practice this might mean offering a time-out break or a change of activity.

What do we know about the effectiveness of different behaviour management programmes? Evans *et al.* (2003) provide a synthesis of research findings. They conclude that behavioural strategies using rewards and sanctions are effective in reducing disruptive behaviour in the short term. However, evidence is lacking to say whether these make a difference over the longer term. For individual children who prove disruptive in the mainstream class, there is also evidence that they can benefit from a short focused cognitive programme where they are withdrawn and trained in self-instruction. Finally, research shows that young children can respond positively when asked to monitor the behaviour of peers and this can reduce disruptive behaviour.

Each of the popular models outlined in Table 12.5 have been critiqued and the main concern relates to a lack of reliable research to demonstrate sustained effectiveness (Edwards and Watts, 2010). Specific elements are also debated. For instance, Kohn (1999) sees the use of praise as destructive to motivation. He also believes that too much attention is given to developing children's self-control, arguing this stifles their curiosity and spontaneity.

**TABLE 12.5** Popular behaviour management models

| Model and key figures | Characteristics |
|---|---|
| Withitness, Jacob Kounin | **Withitness** - the teacher needs to be with it to know what is going on everywhere in the room at all times<br>**Alerting** – optimal learning takes place when teachers keep pupils alert and held accountable for learning<br>**Transitions** - smooth transitions between activities and maintaining momentum are key to effective group management<br>**Ripple effect** – how a teacher handles one child's misbehaviour will have an impact on others, whether encouraging or reprimanding |
| Congruent communication, Haim Ginott | **Modelling** – adults should model desired behaviour<br>**Co-operation** – should be invited rather than demanded<br>**Discipline** – should be used instead of punishments<br>**Feelings** – teachers should calmly express how behaviour makes them feel<br>**Praise** – only used if warranted and authentic<br>**Self-management** – teachers need to build self-esteem and trust<br>**Communication** – the words teachers use should fit feelings. 'I' statements should replace 'you' statements, to avoid criticizing the child; teacher should ignore common four-letter words rather than make an issue; 'sane' messages should focus on behaviour and not the child's character<br>**Comments/rules** – should be attached to objects e.g. 'the pencil is not for throwing' |
| Choice theory, William Glasser | **Choice** – emphasis should be on children making good choices<br>**Meetings** – weekly discussions where group diagnoses the problem and seeks solutions<br>**Consequences** – should always follow good and bad behaviour<br>**Rules** – must always be enforced |
| Discipline without tears, Rudolph Dreikurs | **Discipline** – emphasis on developing self-discipline and self-imposed limits, rather than punishment<br>**Goals** – misbehaviour follows mistaken goals e.g. attention seeking, revenge, power grabbing<br>**Belonging** – children need to belong and so behaviour should work towards this<br>**Effort** – should be encouraged but praising of work and character avoided |
| Assertive Discipline, Lee and Marlene Canter | **Assertive discipline** – teachers should insist on responsible behaviour (assertive rather than hostile or passive approach)<br>**Rights** – teachers have basic rights to expect appropriate behaviour and support from parents and others; children have basic rights to receive help and support, to choose how to behave knowing the consequences<br>**Planning** – a discipline plan is needed to meet these rights; teachers should anticipate and practice verbal responses<br>**Expectations** – need to be stated, followed and repeated every time<br>**Communication** – use of 'I' messages e.g. 'I need you to . . .', 'I like that'; 'I understand what you are saying but . . .'; eye contact and use of names essential when speaking; use gestures and other non-verbal cues; no shouting<br>**Misbehaviour** – should never be ignored; follow through natural consequences<br>**Positive assertions** – awards, personal attention, phone calls to parents, special privileges, home and group rewards |
| Positive classroom discipline, Fred Jones | **Maximizing classroom time** – to reduce lost time due to misbehaviour teacher should make more use of (a) body language – eye contact, signals, gestures, physical proximity (b) incentives (c) individual help<br>**Incentives** – stars, grades, work displays have limited impact because they motivate only the achievers; group or class incentives build cooperation and reduce need for teacher effort<br>**Back-up systems** – for inside and outdoors<br>**Rules** – must be taught, visible, few, simple and clear; consequences of breaking rules followed |

Sources: Kounin (1970); Ginott (1972); Jones (1987); Dreikurs (2004); Canter and Canter (2009)

**EXTEND YOUR UNDERSTANDING**

Explore further one of the models outlined in Table 12.5. Identify criticisms of the model and any research to support its impact.

Some approaches to behaviour emphasize the need for teachers to take control as strong disciplinarians. The government's Troops to Teaching (T3) programme is seen by its supporters as a necessarily tough response to the culture of youth violence affecting a minority of inner-city schools, including knife crime, drugs and assaults (Burkard, 2008). Critics argue that such military discipline is inappropriate for school life (Gilbert and Sarwar, 2010). The Canter model of assertive discipline has a strong focus on the rights, feelings and needs of teachers to teach without interruption by children misbehaving.

## Responding to pupils' behaviour

It is important to approach behaviour management from a positive mindset. For example, parents can be contacted when their children behave well and not just when there are problems. The old saying 'catch them when they are being good' is an important one. Children's efforts need to be celebrated and shared in the school and wider community. Many schools hold special achievement assemblies to which they have invited parents and other relatives.

Behaviour requires a graduated response depending upon the seriousness of the incident (Box 12.3). Wragg's (1993: 65) study of misbehaviour found that the outcome of teachers' responses was pupils' silence in 90 per cent of cases and that only in 5 per cent of cases does the misbehaviour continue. Interestingly, the teachers remained calm in nine out of every ten observations. Relatively few pupils openly challenged teachers.

---

**BOX 12.3 BEHAVIOUR MANAGEMENT LADDER**

- Child reminded of expectations for proper behaviour in school (school rules).
- Discussion between adult and child about his or her behaviour leading to a verbal apology.
- Loss of privilege for the child (for example, 5 minute blocks of Golden Time).
- Issues explored through a class discussion or Circle Time.
- Child receives a written warning and a loss of a playtime.
- Interview with the assistant head and a loss of free time or privilege.
- Interview with the head teacher with possible communication with child's parent/carer.
- Involvement of outside personnel.
- Suspension.

(www.constantine.cornwall.sch.uk/home/home.htm)

---

nt to choose the appropriate response and not to overreact to or minimize
Box 12.4). The response may work well for one child but not another.
chers make when responding to pupils' behaviour can influence how pupils
ers shout, display anger or argue, then they are less likely to secure the
vant compared to teachers who are calm, proactive and follow the school's

---

**BOX 12.4  FOCUS ON PRACTICE**

A group of trainee teachers was asked to reflect upon their experiences of managing behaviour in the classroom:

'I found that as long as I kept them interested I didn't have too many problems. They were a busy class of 5-year-olds and so they needed lots of hands-on stuff. I set up areas where they could touch and look at things (objects, photographs), and used Sam the puppet policeman to have a word when someone stepped out of line.'

*Matthew*

'The best thing that worked for me was music. I used it for transitions in lessons and as background sounds to calm the class.'

*Rhian*

'Routine was the key . . . this sounds mundane but 4-year-olds need a sense of order in the day; but I did find that the children responded well to using the choice board for role play, blocks, etc.'

*Sam*

'I tried to make references to real-life experiences in lessons – you know, newspaper stories, what was on the TV, cartoons, shopping receipts, places the children knew, last night's football scores – to trigger lessons. Whenever interest waned a bit, I would try and drop in a relevant anecdote.'

*Mike*

'This lad was autistic and to be honest I knew hardly anything about autism before the practice. So during preparation week I spoke to his adult support, the class teacher and the special educational needs coordinator to improve my understanding of what to do. I also spoke to Stephen (the child) about his interests and watched his behaviour when the class teacher was teaching. I think all of this helped me not overreact when Stephen hid under the table or when he kept talking about his pet gerbil. I also found the Asperger syndrome material on the National Autistic Society website really helpful.'

*Lauren*

'I have to say I found this practice difficult because of the behaviour of a few. It was not that I didn't prepare well. I spent hours getting together some exciting stuff but these three children usually spoiled things – like when I brought in some frogspawn and they ended up throwing it around. I felt at the end of the day I'd have been better off giving them some exercise in a book on the cycle of a frog.'

*Tom*

policy. Beadle and Murphy (2013) highlight the futility and counter-productiveness of shouting at children.

One of the challenges for teachers is to remain emotionally objective when responding to a range of situations (Box 12.5). Outstanding teachers do not take pupils' misbehaviour personally because they know that they are more likely to become angry, upset, resentful or depressed. Rather, they treat incidents in a professional matter-of-fact manner, which may include explaining how the misbehaviour has impacted on the feelings of others. The most effective interventions are subtle, brief and often semi-private – for instance, moving close to a child and having 'a quiet word.' The power of silence should not be ignored. Lees (2013) shows that 'strong silence' is one of the most important and yet neglected cost-free tools to enhance learning. Deliberate stillness enables children to focus and reflect, thereby improving behaviour and concentration. A growing number of primary schools are using quiet spaces, silent moments and techniques such as meditation to create a calm learning environment. In some cases, children have difficulty in getting a night's sleep because of poor diet, too much exposure to late-night television, and a lack of exercise. Teaching them relaxation techniques has increased their alertness (Paton, 2011). Planned periods of silence should not be confused with the old adage 'children should be seen and not heard'. Rather, silence is seen through a positive rather than punitive lens. OFSTED (1999) noted the value of quiet spaces, such as a supervised library area, where pupils could be guaranteed time to themselves; or rooms acting as 'social havens' for deeply troubled children to go to at break times (OFSTED, 2001). Observational research has shown that where schools provide facilities for children to sit down and chat at playtime this has reduced bullying and aggressive confrontations (Lloyd-Bennett and Gamman, 2000). Many schools provide 'cooling off' areas or appropriately staffed time-out rooms (Daniels *et al.*, 1998; Scottish Executive, 2001; Educational Institute of Scotland, 2003). The reality of many school environments with scattered buildings makes supervision challenging, and as a consequence this can exacerbate behaviour problems. One suggestion is for pupils to create a map of hot spots on the school grounds, featuring a traffic light system in which green marks an area that they feel is safe; red is unsafe; and amber is where they usually feel safe with rare incidents of trouble. The school then uses this information to discuss what can be done to make the environment safer.

Teachers also use a range of non-verbal signs, such as raised eyebrows or a finger to the lips, to reinforce expectations. At times, however, verbal intervention is unavoidable. This is often the stage that trainees struggle with by not thinking enough about the choice and delivery of language. Short and clear commands are often sufficient to redirect attention, with a focus on the positive behaviour desired, such as, 'Tom, remember how well you sat for the story last time'. Some children will shout out answers, especially young ones, and it can feel a long haul to encourage them to put their hands up before answering. But it is important to praise the content of the answers while highlighting what is expected.

Questioning is an important strategy in encouraging pupils to think about what is socially acceptable behaviour. Galvin (1999) suggests avoiding the 'why' question because this can prolong and complicate problems. Rather, he lists the following:

- What should you be doing?
- What did we agree about that?

---

**BOX 12.5  REAL-LIFE LEARNING**

In groups, consider how you might handle the following scenarios and what further information you might need:

1    responding to a pupil who refuses to leave his seat;

2    two children are arguing in the playground. One calls the other a racist name;

3    a child is chewing gum in assembly;

4    a timid boy comes to see you after the lesson and says he is being beaten at home;

5    you observe on repeated occasions another colleague shouting loudly at the same child;

6    a parent comes into your class and complains about another child bullying her daughter.

---

- What's the rule?
- What do you need to do?
- What do you think about what you are doing now?
- Is that reasonable or fair?
- Will that work be finished by break time?
- Do you think this is fair to . . . me, your parents, or the rest of the class?

## Responding to more serious misbehaviour

It is important to respond to behaviour in a consistent manner, where pupils know exactly what the consequence of their actions is likely to be depending upon the seriousness of their behaviour. Clearly behaviour that affects the safety and well-being of pupils (e.g. bullying or violence) or criminal activity falls within the serious category and should involve discussions with parents. The fundamental importance of establishing working relationships with parents/carers to ensure children's good behaviour has been recognized for some time (Elton Report, 1989; Kendall-Seater, 2005). This is not always straight-forward. Communities do not always agree with the school's values and approach to discipline. One study of Pakistani youngsters aged between 16 and 25 found that three-quarters had been physically chastised as a child at home and 72 per cent agreed that this was an appropriate form of discipline; 42 per cent reported being hit with a shoe by the mother and yet 27 per cent considered that this was not abusive behaviour (Irfan and Cowburn, 2004). In some cases children may pick up negative attitudes to school from parents. However, there are a number of innovative schemes designed to support parents in the upbringing of their children and to forge close working relationships with schools; for instance, Parent Support Advisers working with the most disengaged or troubled pupils and parents (Steer Report, 2008). The importance of building a strong sense of community has been shown where children are more likely to benefit from effective pastoral care.

## Bullying

Bullying can take many forms beyond physical aggression. Pupils can be bullied because of their disability, race, faith or sexuality. Cyber bullying has become a growing concern, with children and young people suffering from abusive emails, instant messaging and phone bullying by text message. The extent of bullying in primary schools is difficult to gauge, but according to a national survey in 2006, carried out by the charity Bullying UK, 69 per cent of 4,772 pupils complained that they had been bullied and, alarmingly, 34 per cent needed to see a doctor. Moreover, 85 per cent of pupils said that they had seen bullying in school (www.bullying.co.uk/index.aspx). The most frequent form of bullying is name-calling aimed at children's weight and appearance. Nearly one in three incidents of bullying occur on the playground, while corridors, dining halls and toilets also feature as potential danger zones.

The distress caused by bullying should never be underestimated, with some victims suffering long-term effects into their adult years. Major heartache and tragedy can beset families of victims and no accusation of bullying should be ignored. Unfortunately, bullies do not wear labels for ease of detection. The 2006 survey revealed that 48 per cent of pupils had told their teacher more than five times that they were being bullied while 60 per cent did not feel that their complaints were taken seriously. In some cases, children may not understand that they are involved in bullying either as a perpetrator or victim. Hence it is important to make explicit and model desirable behaviours in contexts such as personal and social education lessons as well as through informal interactions in everyday contexts. Trainee teachers should report any concerns about bullying to the class teacher or senior member of staff.

Government guidance on preventing and tackling bullying sets out the powers schools have, the principles they should follow and specialist resources available to staff (DfE, 2012). All schools in the United Kingdom are required to have an anti-bullying policy, although these vary in detail and effectiveness. Most schools deploy a range of preventive strategies including Circle Time, counselling, peer mediation and **restorative justice**. An important element in dealing with bullying is involving bystanders – these are the very ones who know what is happening. To this end, there are attempts by charities such as Bullying UK to develop a 'telling school' culture in which pupils feel comfortable talking about unacceptable behaviour without fear of reprisal from bullies. The key here is to discourage pupils from seeing themselves as 'telling tales' but rather acting as 'good guys' in the school community.

In serious cases teachers will often work as part of a network of professionals including health and social workers. Inter-agency cooperation is high on government agendas throughout the United Kingdom. While teachers play a central role in keeping order, they cannot do so alone. They need the support of colleagues, specialists, head teachers, parents and the wider community in establishing and maintaining a calm and purposeful classroom atmosphere.

## Glossary

**Restorative justice** derives from the criminal justice system and is based on trying to repair the damage done to individuals (victims) and build relationships, rather than punish offenders.

## References

Advertising Association (2011) *Parents, Children and the Commercial World: Facts, Issues and Solutions*, London: Advertising Association.

Amato, P.R. (2010) 'Research on divorce: Continuing trends and new developments', *Journal of Marriage and Family*, 72: 650–66.

Beadle, P. and Murphy, J. (2013) *Why Are You Shouting at Us?: The Dos and Don'ts of Behaviour Management*, London: Bloomsbury.

Best, B. and Thomas, W. (2007) *Everything You Need to Know About Teaching*, London: Continuum.

Bowlby, J. (1969) *Attachment: Attachment and Loss*: Vol. 1. Loss. New York: Basic Books.

Burkard, T. (2008) *Troops to Teachers*, London: Centre for Policy Studies.

Byron, T. (2009) 'We see children as pestilent', *The Guardian*, 17 May.

Canter, L. and Canter, M. (2009) *Assertive Discipline: Positive Behavior Management for Today's Classroom*, Santa Monica, CA: Canter and Associates.

Child, D. (2004) *Psychology and the Teacher*, London: Continuum.

Collar, G. and Crook, C. (1902) *School Management and Methods of Instruction*, London: Macmillan.

Cox, T. cited by Harrison, A. (2008) 'Teachers stressed by behaviour', available at: http://news.bbc.co.uk/1/hi/education/7316505.stm (accessed 20 May 2013).

Cullis, A. and Hansen, K. (2007) *Child Development in the First Three Sweeps of the Millennium Cohort Study*, London: DCSF.

Daniels, H., Visser, J., Cole, T. and de Reybekill, N. (1998) *Emotional and Behavioural Difficulties in Mainstream Schools*, Research Report RR90. London: DfEE.

Davies, J. (2013) *Cracked*, London: Icon Books.

DCSF (2007) *Primary Social and Emotional Aspects of Learning (SEAL)*, London: DCSF.

DCSF (2009) *Delivering the Behaviour Challenge: Our Commitment to Good Behaviour*, London: DCSF.

DENI (1996) *Promoting and Sustaining Good Behaviour: A Discipline Strategy for Schools*, Belfast: DENI.

Desforges, C. and Abouchaar, A. (2003) *Parental Support and Family Educationon, Pupil Achievement and Adjustment: A Literature Review*, London: DfE.

DfE (2010) *The Importance of Teaching*, London: DfE.

DfE (2011a) *Me and My School: Findings from the National Evaluation of Targeted Mental Health in Schools 2008–2011*, London: DfE.

DfE (2012) *Behaviour and Discipline in Schools: A Guide for Head Teachers and School Staff*, London: DfE.

DfE (2013a) *Teachers' Standards*, London: DfE.

DfE (2013b) *Pupil Behaviour in Schools in England*, London: DfE.

DfEE (1999) *Social Inclusion: Pupil Support*, London: DfEE.

DfES (2001) *Special Educational Needs: Code of Practice*, London: DfES.

Dreikurs, R. (2004) *Discipline Without Tears: How to Reduce Conflict and Establish Cooperation in the Classroom*, Toronto: Wiley.

Educational Institute of Scotland (2003) *Social, Emotional and Behavioural Difficulties: School Survey, May 2003*, Edinburgh: EIS.

Edwards, C. H. and Watts, V. J. (2010) *Classroom Discipline and Management*, Milton, Qld: John Wiley & Sons.

Elton Report (1989) *Enquiry into Discipline in Schools*, London: HMSO.

EPPI Centre (2004) *A Systematic Review of How Theories Explain Learning Behaviour in School Contexts*, London: EPPI Centre.

Evans, J., Harden, A., Thomas, J. and Benefield, P. (2003) *Support for Pupils with Emotional and Behavioural Difficulties (EBD) in Mainstream Primary School*, London: EPPI/NFER.

Galvin, P. (1999) *Behaviour and Discipline in Schools*, London: David Fulton.

Gilbert, F. and Sarwar, A. (2010) 'Should more ex-soldiers become teachers?', *The Guardian*, 24 November.

Ginott, H. (1972) *Teacher and Child: A Book for Parents and Teachers*, New York: Avon Books.

Glasser, W. (1989) *Control Theory in the Practice of Reality Therapy*, New York: Harper & Row.

Glasser, W. (2012) *Choice Theory in the Classroom*, New York: HarperCollins.

Gosden, R. (2009) 'Controlling wayward children', in Beder, S., Varney, W. and Gosden, R. (eds) *This Little Piggy Went to Market: The Corporate Capture of Childhood*, London: Pluto Press, 205–21.

Hanley, P. (2000) *Copycat Kids? The Influence of Television Advertising on Children and Teenagers*, London: ITC.

House of Commons (2011) *Behaviour and Discipline in Schools*, London: House of Commons.

Housego, E. and Burns, C. (1994) 'Are you sitting too comfortably? A critical look at "Circle Time" in primary classrooms', *English in Education*, 28(2): 23–9.

Irfan, S. and Cowburn, M. (2004) 'Disciplining, chastisement and physical child abuse: Perceptions and attitudes of the British Pakistani community', *Journal of Muslim Minority Affairs*, 24(1): 89–98.

Johnston, J., Halocha, J. and Chater, M. (2007) *Developing Teaching Skills in the Primary School*, Maidenhead: Open University Press.

Jones, F. (1987) *Positive Classroom Discipline*, New York: Fredric H. Jones & Associates.

Kendall-Seater, S. (2005) *Reflective Reader: Primary Professional Studies*, Exeter: Learning Matters.

Kohn, A. (1999) *Punished by Rewards: The Trouble with Gold Stars, Incentive Plans, A's, Praise, and Other Bribes*, New York: Mariner Books.

Konner, M. (2010) *The Evolution of Childhood*, Cambridge, MA: Harvard University Press.

Kounin, J. (1970) *Discipline and Group Management in Classrooms*, New York: Holt, Rinehart & Winston.

Lees, H. (2013) *Silence in Schools*, Stoke-on-Trent: Trentham Books.

Lewis, C., Miell, D. and Coiffait, F.M. (2014) 'Children's relationships and the family', in Holliman, A.J. (ed.) *Routledge International Companion to Educational Psychology*, London: Routledge, 117–26.

Lloyd-Bennett, P. and Gamman, R. (2000) 'Whole-school policy reviews and projects', *Educational and Child Psychology*, 17(1): 20–32.

MacBeath, J. (2012) *Future of Teaching Profession*, Cambridge: University of Cambridge.

Martin, N. (2008) 'Happiness lessons to be given to schoolchildren', *The Telegraph*, 7 September.

Miller, D. and Moran, T. (2005) 'Time to change the perspective on self-esteem? Circle Time and beyond', NFER Topic 34, November, 12–18.

Mosley, J. (1993) *Turn Your School Round*, Wisbech: LDA.

Munn, P., Johnstone, M. and Sharp, S. (2004) *Discipline in Scottish Schools: A Comparative Survey over Time of Teachers' and Headteachers' Perceptions*, Edinburgh: Scottish Executive.

NFER (2012) *NFER Teacher Voice Omnibus February 2012 Survey: Pupil Behaviour DFE Research Report DFE-RR219*, available at: www.nfer.ac.uk/teachervoice (accessed 20 November 2013).

Office of the Minister for Children and Youth Affairs (2010) *Children's Perspectives on Parenting Styles and Discipline: A Developmental Approach*, Dublin: Minister for Health and Children.

O'Hara, M. (2010) 'Headteacher Charlie Taylor's unconventional approach pays off', *The Guardian*, 23 August.

OFSTED (1999) *Principles into Practice: Effective Education for Pupils with EBD*, London: OFSTED.

OFSTED (2001) *Improving Attendance and Behaviour* (HMI 242), London: OFSTED.

OFSTED (2007) *Inspection Report: Summerhill School*, London: OFSTED.

OFSTED (2011) *Supporting Children with Challenging Behaviour through a Nurture Group Approach*, London: OFSTED.

OFSTED (2012) *Official Statistics: Maintained School Inspections and Outcome*, London: OFSTED.

OFSTED (2013) *The Annual Report of Her Majesty's Chief Inspector of Education, Children's Services and Skills*, London: OFSTED.

Paton, G. (2011) 'Silence is golden: How keeping quiet in the classroom can boost results', *The Telegraph*, 21 October.

Paton, G. (2012) 'Bad behaviour in schools "fuelled by over-indulgent parents"', *Times Educational Supplement*, 30 March.

Peter the Hermit, cited by Byron, T. (2009) 'We see children as pestilent', *The Guardian*, 17 March.

Pinheiro, P.S. (2006) *World Report on Violence Against Children*, Geneva: United Nations.

Prince's Trust (2007) *The Cost of Exclusion*, London: The Prince's Trust.

Rogof, B. (2003) *The Cultural Nature of Human Development*, Oxford: Oxford University Press.

Scottish Executive (2001) *Better Behaviour – Better Learning: Summary Report of the Discipline Task Group*, Edinburgh: Stationery Office.

Scottish Executive (2006) *Behaviour in Scottish Schools: Insight 34*, Edinburgh: Scottish Executive.

Scottish Executive (2009) *Promoting Positive Outcomes: Working Together to Prevent Antisocial Behaviour in Scotland*, Edinburgh: Scottish Executive.

Scottish Government (2008) *A Guide to Getting It Right for Every Child*, Edinburgh: Scottish Government.

Scottish Government Social Research (2012) *Behaviour in Scottish Schools 2012: Final Report*, Edinburgh: Scottish Government.

Senninger, T. (2000) 'The Learning Zone Model', available at: http://social-pedagogy.co.uk/concepts_lzm.htm (accessed 20 May 2013).

Singh, I. (2012) 'Why are so many adults convinced that Ritalin does children harm?', *The Telegraph*, 15 October.

Smithers, A. and Robinson, P. (2003) *Factors Affecting Teachers' Decisions to Leave the Profession*, Liverpool: University of Liverpool.

Steer, A. (2005) *Learning Behaviour: The Report of the Practitioners' Group on School Behaviour and Discipline*, Nottingham: DfES.

Steer, A. (2008) *Behaviour Review Part 3*, Nottingham: DfES.

Steer, A. (2009) *Review of Pupil Behaviour Interim Report 4*, Nottingham: DfES.

Stewart, W. (2011) 'Parents dust down the cane', *Times Educational Supplement*, 18 September.

Teacher Support Network (2010) *Teacher Support Network and Family Lives Behaviour Survey 2010*, London: Teacher Support Network.

Visser, J. and Raffo, C. (2005) *Behaviour and Attendance Materials for Primary Initial Teacher Training Tutors*, Northampton: University of Northampton.

Wilby, P. (2013) 'Summerhill school: These days surprisingly strict', *The Guardian*, 27 May.

Williams, M. (2013) 'Childcare minister Elizabeth Truss attacks unruly nurseries', *The Guardian*, 22 April.

Wise, S. and da Silva, L. (2007) *Differential Parenting of Children from Diverse Cultural Backgrounds Attending Child Care*, Australian Institute of Family Studies, available at: www.aifs.gov.au/institute/pubs/rp39/rp39.pdf (accessed 20 November 2013).

Wragg, E.C. (1993) *Primary Teaching Skills*, London: Routledge.

## Websites

Department for Education advice and guidance on behaviour management including reasonable force – www.education.gov.uk/schools/pupilsupport/behaviour/behaviourpolicies

Scottish Government's advice on behaviour – www.scotland.gov.uk/Topics/Education/Schools/HLivi/behaviour

Teacher Support provides practical and emotional support for teachers – www.teachersupport.info/

National Union of Teachers, the largest teachers' union, provides guidance on behaviour management and the law – www.nut.org.uk/node/16381

Kidscape has a wide range of anti-bullying publications for young people, parents and teachers – www.kidscape.org.uk

# 13

# The art of juggling

## Monitoring, assessment, recording and reporting

By the end of this chapter you should be able to:

- Describe classroom monitoring and observation strategies.
- Explain the purposes and nature of assessment.
- Critically reflect upon the impact of Assessment for Learning.
- Explain the importance of record keeping and reporting.

*Low achievement in schools may have much less to do with a lack of 'innate' ability than with pupils' lack of understanding of what they are meant to be learning and what counts as quality.*

*(James et al., 2007: 10)*

## Introduction

Monitoring, assessment, recording and reporting are probably among the most uninspiring words in education. Their historic association with authority figures such as judges and tax inspectors do little to enthuse. However, they are key responsibilities in the life of a teacher and have a direct bearing on the quality of pupils' experiences in school. Since formal schooling began, huge sums of money have been spent on finding ways to reliably test what children know, understand and can do, to report this information to others and to decide what pathway learners take as a result. For a long time, underpinning this has been a debate about whether children's intelligence is inherited or learned, whether it could and should be measured and, if so, how. Today, most psychologists tend to think that both genetics and the environment influence children's intelligence in about equal amounts (Woolfolk *et al.*, 2008). Children's cognitive abilities, just like other skills, can be improved. To do so, teachers need to regularly observe and monitor children closely so that they can build up a reliable picture of their interests, needs and capabilities. They then need to provide pupils with clear feedback so that they can improve their performance.

## Monitoring

Monitoring can serve different purposes. In the National Curriculum era, schools have become familiar with regular monitoring of the quality of teaching, planning and deployment of resources (Tymms and Merrell, 2007). The best teachers know what is happening in their classrooms, even when they may not actually be facing the children. In this regard Kounin (1970) suggested the important idea of 'withitness' to describe those teachers who were able to discern the underlying tone of the lesson. With-it teachers often seem to have very good 'presence' in the classroom. They are also able to multitask or what Kounin called 'overlapping'; for example sitting alongside a small group and keeping an eye on what is happening in the background. They pick up signals from the pupils and can see potential problems that may arise, almost as if they know what is going to happen before it does.

Effective teachers use a range of monitoring strategies including the following:

- *standing back* – once the activities have been set up to see which groups seem to be working;
- *listening in* – briefly checking to see that each group is on the right track;
- *reviewing* – with either a group or whole-class if it is clear that there are misunderstandings or uncertainty regarding the learning objectives;
- *focus group* – monitoring and assisting a particular group for a set time, say ten minutes;
- *making notes* – collecting data on what pupils are doing and how they approach the task; Post-it notes are useful in this regard.

While working with a particular group, skilled practitioners are also able to look up and see what is happening around them. When monitoring the responses of the whole class, where a teacher sits or stands is important to maximize eye contact. For younger children, much of this will occur when reading a story on the carpeted area. When given a choice, it is nearly always the case that a handful of pupils will regularly choose to sit as far away from the teacher as possible (Hayes, 2006). Research into where children sit and what constitutes the optimum visibility for teachers has resulted in a 'triangle' (Figure 13.1) by

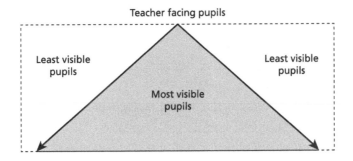

**FIGURE 13.1** The visibility triangle

Source: After Pye (1989)

which children on the teacher's left and right (outside the triangle) are least visible and less likely to interact with the teacher (Pye, 1989). The implication for teachers is to make a conscious effort to include all children when monitoring, for instance by focusing systematically on children to the left, right and middle.

Most classes will include 'invisible children' – the quiet and undemanding ones who don't ask for help and for long periods wait patiently for the teacher's attention. It is possible to 'draw out' these children by setting aside time for paired and small group work, effectively deploying support assistants and through the use of personalized targets. Generally speaking it is best to stand still when delivering brief instructions because too much movement can be distracting.

Box 13.1 includes examples of monitoring questions to reflect upon. Many of these kinds of questions become second nature to excellent teachers, who seem to have the knack of knowing what to ask and when. Effective monitoring can result in changes to planning, teaching and classroom management. For instance, if having reviewed the written work of particular children the teacher may feel that they are not working well enough. This might lead to further monitoring (perhaps through observation and talking to pupils) to find out why this might be the case. Perhaps the seating arrangements or group composition are explanatory factors and these may need to be modified. Good quality monitoring covers not only how well pupils do in relation to achieving the learning objectives but also how well children relate to each other and the adults around them. Well-briefed additional adults have an important monitoring role to play as extra pairs of ears and eyes.

One of the main challenges associated with observing young children and adults is to step aside from personal values, beliefs and cultural norms and to become truly objective

---

### BOX 13.1  MONITORING QUESTIONS

■ Do the children look interested or bored?

■ Do the children know what they should be doing?

■ Are any pupils 'hiding'?

■ How many children are on task?

■ Can the pupils see what they should see (e.g. the interactive whiteboard)?

■ Are the resources on hand if needed?

■ What is the general noise level?

■ Are the support assistants well deployed?

■ Are the pupils working together?

■ Which individuals need additional help, challenge or consolidation?

■ Are pupils putting their hands up a lot? If so, why?

■ Is a queue forming before me? If so, how can I prevent this?

■ Are there any obvious health and safety issues?

**PHOTO 13.1** A nursery worker allocated a role to support the learning of 3–4 year olds.

Source: POD/Pearson Education Ltd, Jules Selmes

**EXTEND YOUR UNDERSTANDING**

Look carefully at Photo 13.1 and write down what you see. Then show the picture to a colleague and compare views. How could this scene be interpreted in different ways?

when reaching a conclusion. Equally, the behaviour of the observed is influenced by whether they know they are being observed, by whom, and other contextual factors. Observational experiences can be charged with underlying emotions and assessment must make allowances for this. People readily jump to conclusions about the behaviour of others. This is well illustrated by an old television commercial in which a smart-looking businessman was walking along the pavement. From behind, a scruffy youth jumps on him, but this was no mugging; rather the youth saved the man from a falling object that would have killed him. As Hopkins (2008: 75) points out, poor observation is characterized by moving to judgements too quickly. In Photo 13.1, is the nursery worker acting unprofessionally by speaking to a friend about personal matters on her mobile phone? Or is her conversation (mock or real) part of the learning experience for the children?

## Observation

Observation involves a process of carefully watching children, listening to what they have to say and making a note of the findings. Hopkins (2008) reminds us of the principles of observation: the need to establish a climate of trust between observer and observed; to agree on a focus; to agree 'ground rules'; to establish criteria; to give appropriate feedback as part of a two-way discussion; and to see observation closely linked to planning and assessment. Observation can serve several purposes in assessing children's development, shedding light on the teacher's practice and providing information for reporting to parents. It is of particular importance in the Early Years settings where 'hard' written evidence for children's achievements is limited. Observing children is equally instructive whether it occurs indoors or outdoors.

Observation is a highly skilled business. It has been described as 'the only true test of the quality of a practitioner's work' (MacLeod-Brudenell, 2004: 294). The best observers are constantly taking mental notes of how well children interact with others, the extent to which they persevere when working alone, how they express their views or feelings, when they show initiative and independence or take an interest in something. They plan systematic opportunities to regularly observe each child in their care, although much of their observation is of an informal (spontaneous) nature. Critically, they are able to undertake observations without recourse to preconceived views about the child's capabilities. They take into account the views of the child, parents and others in reaching an overall assessment. Although observation is complex and time-consuming, it is an essential process. It is possible to improve the quality of observational skills through practice, discussion and critical reflection. Palaiologu (2008: 50) suggests that to become a skilful observer teachers need to 'develop objectivity and absence of emotional bias by stepping out of the role that you normally hold'.

There are several observational techniques. Within Early Years settings, *participant observation* is widely undertaken as part of the daily routine and takes advantage of events as they occur. It involves the adult taking some part in the activities but makes quick notes at a convenient break or shortly afterwards. In effect, the teacher becomes an 'inside' observer who acts spontaneously. Critics point out that it can be difficult to manage (Devereux and Miller, 2003). On other occasions, for instance when not teaching, it would be possible to become a *non-participant observer*. Here, the observation adopts an 'outsider' role. The observer refrains from interfering (unless children's safety is an issue) and discreetly observes what is happening. Sometimes it is worth observing closely an individual child or a pair of children for a sustained period. This so-called 'pupil pursuit' technique involves logging the child's activities and movements with the aim of capturing a flavour of what the experience means to children, without making them too self-conscious. Some questions to consider when observing children are shown in Box 13.2.

Wood (2008: 116) advocates 'a pedagogy of listening to inform assessment' across a range of contexts and activities. There are ethical considerations to listening carefully and responding to what pupils have to say, but Wood is keen to support a 'credit-based' model of assessment in which children's perspectives are duly acknowledged. Evidence from recorded observations, video and still images, and children's own representations should inform judgements.

## Pupils' progress

Monitoring the progress thirty or so pupils make in lessons is particularly challenging. Community websites such as those operated by the *Times Educational Supplement* contain

---

**BOX 13.2  QUESTIONS TO CONSIDER WHEN OBSERVING CHILDREN**

■  Are the activities too easy or too difficult?

■  How are the children using the resources?

■  Is there anything missing that the children need?

■  Is sufficient time/space provided for the experience and consolidation?

■  Are the children fully involved in the activity – if not, why not?

■  How independent are the children in their learning?

■  Are the children able to work/play alongside/in cooperation with other children?

■  Do the children need practitioners' intervention?

■  Has there been opportunity for sustained thinking?

■  What needs to be done to move the learning on?

■  Is there a balance of activities over time (indoor/outdoor, individual/group, etc.)?

(DCELLS, 2008. © Crown Copyright 2008,
reproduced under terms of the Click-Use Licence)

---

examples of innovative resources made by teachers anxious to 'prove' that the children are moving forward. These include variations on success ladders (candles, footprints), upon which children visibly mark their progress at set times towards achieving the lesson's learning objectives. The danger is that children spend too much time colouring in charts and not enough time learning. The challenge is to integrate assessment for learning strategies so that they become routine, for instance when pairs review each other's progress using a rubric or checklist. A simple thinking routine such as 'I used to think . . . now I think . . .' can also be effective in reflecting upon new thinking. Technologies can play an important role in monitoring progress during lessons; for example, in a PE lesson pupils can film themselves to see skill development, while interactive games and quizzes can be used to rehearse mathematical vocabulary or mental arithmetic. Teaching assistants and more able pupils (acting as peer tutors) can contribute towards gathering evidence for progress. Above all, if pupils are to progress in lessons they need to be reminded of their starting points (their prior knowledge), know what is expected of them (the goals) and how they can show progress (meeting the success criteria). In other words, learning needs to be made visible, which is the central theme of John Hattie's much-publicized work.

It is easier to demonstrate pupils' progress over an extended period of time, such as a term. The concept of progress, as defined by inspectors, focuses largely on progress over an extended period of time gauged by examining children's books, talking to children and teachers and considering data (OFSTED, 2013). So, if lessons considered 'good' or even 'outstanding' do not lead to good or better progress over time, then it follows that the quality of teaching is likely to require improvement. The flip side to this is that if a lesson is observed that requires improvement but the progress is good, then the judgement on the quality of teaching over time will be good.

## What is the nature and scope of assessment?

Perhaps the one word that has caused more heated debate than any other in the history of education is 'assessment' (Box 13.3). It is a subject that interests governments, local authorities, inspectors, parents, teachers, employers, and the learners themselves – all have a vested interest in the outcomes. In the nineteenth century, elementary school teachers were paid partly according to pupils' success in examinations. Today, school managers track the performance of pupils over time and are accountable to parents, governors, local authorities and inspectors for such trends. The proportion of pupils who pass certain tests, rightly or wrongly, effectively judges the worth of a school.

Too readily, however, the term 'assessment' is associated with marking and grading pupils' work and success (or otherwise) in tests or examinations. Assessment has a wider remit than measuring learning. One of the key principles of assessment is that it should serve the purpose of improving as well as proving learning. Learners need to know what they need to do to become better, whether this be as writers, speakers, spellers, artists, musicians, problem solvers, map-readers or team players. Hence assessment should be seen as a formative process, used by both teachers and learners, through which changes can be made to teaching and learning so that pupils achieve desired goals.

Outstanding teachers understand and adhere to the principles that underpin effective assessment. There should be no hidden agendas. Assessment should be tied to objectives shared with learners. All learners should have the same opportunity to achieve and not be discriminated against. Assessments should be valid and reliable, which means that they measure what is intended and that there is consistency in the marking. From a practical viewpoint, assessments need to be manageable in terms of time and resources, but they also need to be challenging so that learners have the opportunity to demonstrate their achievement.

Assessment involves deciding upon what evidence to use and collect, and how this should be collected, interpreted and reported (Harlen, 2007). Essentially, effective assessment focuses upon one or more of the following:

■    knowledge and application (e.g. facts, concepts, names, ideas, relationships);

---

### BOX 13.3  KEY CONCEPT – ASSESSMENT

**From the Latin *ad* = besides and *sedere* = to sit down.**

Literally applied, assessment therefore means to sit down beside a pupil and suggests discussion, working together and offering help to improve. Assessment is effective when it involves early and perceptive feedback to learners so that they know what they have to do to improve and have time to make any changes. In recent years, primary schools have responded to Assessment for Learning defined as 'the process of seeking and interpreting evidence for use by learners and their teachers to decide where the learners are in their learning, where they need to go next, and how best to get them there' (Assessment Reform Group, 2002).

- skills (e.g. communication, use of number, manipulative skills, working with others); and

- attitudes and values (e.g. enjoyment of learning, respect, sensitivity).

Hence, in assessing pupil responses to a lesson on making an electrical circuit, a teacher might look for whether the pupils: *know* the names of the components (bulb, switch, buzzer, battery, and so forth); are able to *apply* this knowledge (e.g. by explaining everyday appliances that use electricity); demonstrate *cooperative skills* in working together to make the bulb light or buzzer sound; and show *enjoyment* in seeing their circuit work.

Although assessment is undertaken for a variety of purposes, teachers are mostly concerned with providing feedback on pupils' work. Assessment can also be used to compare how well individual pupils, groups or classes have performed against set standards (criterion-referenced tests) or compared to the results of others (norm reference comparison).

Assessment takes on many formats including reviews, reports, tests, portfolios, presentations, practical work, projects, performances and exhibitions. There are variations within each of these, such as open-book, unseen or oral examinations (Race *et al.*, 2005). Sometimes assessment takes on a formal nature, while on other occasions it is integral to discussion with pupils. In the short term, over the course of a lesson, teachers want to check the progress pupils make in meeting the learning objectives. They may begin by reviewing what pupils already know from previous work, perhaps through summaries using mind maps or whole-class question-and-answers (Figure 13.2). During the lesson activities, teachers will often sit alongside a group or groups to check what the pupils are thinking, doing, saying or feeling. In the lesson closure, it is customary for teachers to return to the learning objectives and invite comments from pupils on how they have worked towards achieving these. At different times in the lesson effective teachers will seek to diagnose any misconceptions and work out how best to deal with these. It is clear then that assessment should be integral to the teaching process.

## Assessment for Learning

Over the last decade or so 'Assessment for Learning' (AfL) has dominated the assessment landscape. The architects, Paul Black and Dylan Wiliam (1998), publicized the concept in their influential report *Inside the Black Box* that summarized 9 years of international research comprising more than 250 studies. AfL was seen as a major means of raising standards, especially for lower-attaining pupils. The authors concluded that too much teaching time was given over to teacher-led instruction at the expense of encouraging reflection among pupils. Too often, pupils did not receive constructive feedback that set out clearly what they needed to improve their work and how this could be achieved. The authors made four key recommendations:

1   make more time for pupils to think and answer questions in class;

2   provide constructive comments (rather than marks) for homework;

3   encourage pupils to assess each other; and

4   involve pupils in the design of assessments and mark schemes.

| Traffic lights  | Thumbs up/thumbs down  |
|---|---|
| Red – doesn't understand<br><br>Amber – not quite there<br><br>Green – got it!<br><br>**Uses:**<br>Individuals indicate their level of understanding or feelings by showing the appropriate coloured card.<br>Useful at various stages in the lesson – but particularly in mini-plenaries and plenaries. | **Uses:**<br>Similar to Traffic Lights in that it can be used at any point to ascertain understanding or feelings. |
| **Teacher benefit:**<br>• Gives an immediate indication of pupils' understanding and/or feelings<br>• Teacher is able to tailor support and amend plans | **Pupil benefit:**<br>• Allows pupils to give an immediate response in a secure environment<br>• Avoids trials of writing self-assessments. More fun! |

| Talk partners  | Post–its  |
|---|---|
| **Uses:**<br>Pupils share with a partner:<br>• three new things they have learnt<br>• what they found easy<br>• what they found difficult<br>• something they would like to learn in the future. | **Uses:**<br>Groups, pairs, individuals evaluate learning on post-it notes<br>• What have I learnt?<br>• What did you find easy?<br>• What did you find difficult?<br>• What do I want to know now? |
| **Teacher benefit:**<br>• Gains an overview of learning that has taken place<br>• Has an opportunity to change the focus of teaching – if necessary | **Pupil benefit:**<br>• Focuses on thinking about learning<br>• Encourages them to think 'beyond' to the next step. |

**FIGURE 13.2** Examples of self-assessment strategies

Source: Association for Achievement and Improvement through Assessment (www.aaiaorg.uk). Reproduced with permission

The rationale behind AfL focuses on using evidence and discussion to find out where pupils are in their learning, where they need to go and how best to help them get there. In 2002 a follow-up report *Working Inside the Black Box* elaborated further on techniques to improve the quality of pupil responses, such as extending the 'wait time' given to pupils to several seconds so that they have time to think (Black *et al.*, 2002). Since then Black and Wiliam have regretted using the word 'assessment' because of its association with tests and exams rather than better teaching (Stewart, 2012).

## Sharing learning objectives or intentions

In Chapter 9 the importance of writing clear learning objectives was discussed. Another way of expressing this is to use the more open-ended term, 'learning intentions'. Kerry (2002) suggests that learning objectives have two essential components: an intention on the part of the teacher and a learning outcome to be gained by the pupil. An objectives-led model of teaching and learning needs to take into account the realities of how children learn in the primary classroom. Flexibility is needed because young children naturally want to explore their own worlds, follow their own intentions, and respond best when well motivated. Children are capable of learning many things not prescribed by learning objectives. However, learning objectives provide a useful means of monitoring pupils' progress and coverage of the curriculum. Moreover, pupils who understand the learning objectives and assessment criteria and have opportunities to reflect on their work show greater improvement than those who do not (Fontana and Fernandes, 1994).

Pupils need to understand the goals of their learning so that they can judge whether they have achieved them. Hence it is important to share objectives or intentions in a child-friendly, meaningful language. Box 13.4 shows a trainee teacher's example working with a Year 2 class.

While it makes sense to be explicit with pupils by explaining the purpose of the lesson, in practice this can be challenging. Video analysis of lessons (James and Pollard, 2008) has shown how difficult it can be for teachers to shift from writing learning objectives on the board (the letter of AfL) to practices based on deep principles integrated into the flow of lessons (the spirit of AfL). Sharing learning objectives does not have to be a mechanistic process. There are many different ways of doing this so that pupils feel fully engaged. Teachers might:

- share some words or phrases related to the content of the lesson and ask the pupils to determine the learning objectives;

---

**BOX 13.4 SHARING INTENDED LEARNING OUTCOMES AND SUCCESS CRITERIA**

| | |
|---|---|
| Intended learning intention | to draw a bar graph of our favourite animals |
| Success criteria | we will use different colours to help us read the graph |
| | we will use a key |
| | we will give the graph a title |
| | some of us will use the computer |

- offer the learning objective as an anagram for pupils to rearrange words;
- share the learning objective orally using directed questions to check understanding;
- share a picture relevant to the learning objective;
- use software such as Phrasr which is an interactive web-based application that uses Flickr images to illustrate phrases that users submit (www.pimpampum.net/phrasr);
- provide pupils with the key words only from the learning objective and ask them to suggest connected words;
- ask pupils to highlight the most important words in the objective;
- leave some words out of the objective and ask pupils to complete;
- invite pupils to create their own learning objective, using key words, as they are the learners;
- reveal the learning objective at the end of the lesson but encourage pupils to think what it might be during the lesson
- refer to some websites that create visual representation of objectives e.g. www. jigsawplanet.com creates a jigsaw puzzle, or www.wordle.net produces a word cloud. Websites such as www.xtranormal.com or www.goanimate.com allow users to create text to animated clips;
- display the learning objective in another language, slowly revealing a few English words and asking pupils to work this out;
- display a 'map' of the lesson through key words and images. From this, pupils can be invited to work out the objective.

Sharing implies a two-way process. Hence pupils should have opportunities to discuss learning objectives, negotiate what they would like to explore further and share their own intentions. In some lessons, it may be appropriate to have multiple learning objectives for different groups of learners (Box 13.5). For instance, a group learning objective can be placed on different tables with appropriate resources. Learners can decide which task

---

**BOX 13.5  FOCUS ON PRACTICE**

In a history lesson, one trainee explained to a Year 5 class what she was looking for in their study of the Tudor period in responding to the question: *How do we know about life in Tudor times?*

- You must be able to . . . name different sources we have used in the lesson.
- You should . . . ask a 'hard' question about each source for a friend to answer.
- You could . . . use the sources to explain what they tell us about life for rich and poor people at that time.

At the end of the lesson the pupils then discussed and recorded their success against these criteria using a simple traffic light system.

to undertake and set about planning to meet the objective. In the plenary, groups can share their work and guess each group objective.

## Clear success criteria

It can be a sobering experience to ask children *why* they are learning what they are learning. The purpose of sharing the success criteria is to make it clear and open to learners what will be looked at when deciding whether they have met the learning objectives. Sharing success criteria is designed to help pupils become independent and confident learners. Children will offer their own ideas of what criteria are used to measure success in school – writing a sufficient amount, producing what was wanted, having things neat and tidy, getting the answers right. Pollard *et al.* (2000) have shown that pupils' explanations for their attainment are complex and draw upon such factors as home, family, the nature of the subject and whether they liked the work or not.

Clarke (2001) argues that while intended learning outcomes and success criteria should be noted in teachers' plans, only the intended learning outcomes should be shared in advance of the lesson. She suggests that the teacher waits to see how children respond to the task and writes their suggested words in speech bubbles towards the end of the lesson. In this way, the children are becoming actively involved in determining the success criteria. Simply asking children to comment on how they would know whether a piece of work is good can generate interesting dialogue – whether commenting upon a dance routine, model castle or creative writing. On the other hand, there are times when teachers decide to set the criteria up front with the class. These can be at three different levels (must, should, could) to cater for different abilities.

## Self-assessment and evaluation

One of the aims of primary education is to foster pupils' independence. Hence excellent teachers take every opportunity to promote independent learning. Such independence involves trying out ideas, taking risks, learning to make decisions and reflecting on personal effort and achievements. Both self-assessment and self-evaluation are important skills in becoming an independent learner. Self-assessment occurs when individuals make judgements about their own achievements and reflect over *what* they have learned. Self-evaluation is concerned with thinking about *how* they have worked. Both are important reflective elements within Assessment for Learning.

Several studies have reported learning gains by those pupils who have been involved in self- and peer assessment (Black and Wiliam, 1998; Assessment Reform Group 1999). Hattie (2008) has ranked pupil self-assessment as one of the top factors in raising standards. Black (1998) reports, however, that it takes time for children to overcome their fear of tests and understand the criteria before they embrace self-evaluation. James *et al.* (2007) argue strongly that strategic and reflective thinking is essential to the development of learning autonomy. It is the 'stepping back' from the learning, where learners discuss how they are working with others, that needs to be taught alongside the 'step back in' process in order to restructure (improve) learning. The 'prize', the authors argue, is learning autonomy when children are no longer dependent upon the teacher.

The curriculum offers many opportunities for learners to develop self-reflective skills – for instance when evaluating a product in design and technology, reviewing a piece of writing or assessing a performance in dance or games. There are many practical resources that can be made to aid children's reflective thinking. Wilson and Murdock (2008) provide examples of charts, 'know-feel-do-wonder' wheels, thinking bookmarks, 'stepping stones' and starter questions. They recommend the use of sentence strips such as 'This is important to me because . . .', to stimulate individual, small group tasks or whole-class reflective discussions. Some schools use **rubrics** as a form of self- and group assessment linked to challenges, such as designing a poster (Fleming, 2008). Rubrics can take the form of tables with the criteria listed down the left-hand side and levels of performance listed across the top (Box 13.6). The rubrics can be modified depending on the task and the pupils' abilities. Some schools use debriefing techniques in which pupils are encouraged to look at particular 'challenge' events, such as investigations or design briefs, from the perspective of what happened and what do we do with what we have learned. The review may take various forms such as journal writing or group discussion. A simplified three-step action research model of 'What?; So what?; and Now what?' is used to help structure and move learning forward.

Across the curriculum, pupils should get into the habit of explaining how they arrived at answers and to justify their choices. This can be achieved orally within a group setting, or on a one-to-one basis. The plenary is a good opportunity to review progress against the learning objectives and to give pupils time for silent reflection before sharing with a partner what they have learned. However, pupils can demonstrate negative attitudes, or are content to 'get by', if they feel that assessment concentrates on comparing their performance against others (Murphy, 1998: 125). On the other hand, assessment that encourages learners to think about their own performance and is based on the assumption that *every* learner can succeed builds up personal confidence and self-belief. American studies have shown that pupils with learning difficulties who have been taught to use self-monitoring strategies related to their understanding of reading and writing tasks have shown performance gains (McCurdy and Shapiro, 1992).

In Scotland, *Curriculum for Excellence* (Scottish Executive, 2004) has a strong focus on involving pupils in their own learning through its 'experiences and outcomes' model. Schools are encouraged to make use of online self-assessment toolkits to audit the extent

---

**BOX 13.6  EXAMPLES OF A YEAR 2 RUBRIC USED BY A TRAINEE FOR SELF-ASSESSMENT**

What we are trying to do: To write a thank you letter to Farmer Jones.   How did I do?
I put the address in the right place
I included the date
I used Dear Mr Jones
I said why I was writing
I signed the letter
I checked the letter for mistakes
I checked my friend's letter for mistakes

to which they have incorporated the principles of Assessment for Learning into their practice. The Framework for Assessment (Scottish Government, 2011) sets out expectations in terms of progress defined in terms of 'how well' and 'how much' pupils learn.

Self-assessment helps pupils take more responsibility for their own learning. One simple but effective approach used in many schools is a traffic-light system (Photo 13.2) whereby pupils indicate their level of confidence and understanding – red for uncertainty, amber for partial understanding and green for full understanding. The icons are recorded in written work and used as show-cards following teacher explanation to indicate their comprehension. The teacher acts upon this by pairing up greens and ambers to deal with problems between them and targeting the reds for teacher support. In this way, the teacher is responding directly to individual needs.

There are a number of prompts that can be displayed around the classroom to create a reflective ethos. The Partnership Management Board (PMB, 2007) for Northern Ireland suggests the following:

- The most important thing I learned was . . .
- What I found difficult was . . .
- What I enjoyed most was . . .
- What I want to find out more about is . . .
- What I need more help with is . . .
- What still puzzles me is . . .
- What surprised me was . . .
- What I have learned that is new is . . .
- What helped me when something got tricky was . . .

**PHOTO 13.2** Scottish children in class using circular green and red cards to indicate understanding

Source: POD/Pearson Education Ltd, Ann Cromack, Ikat Designs

- What really made me think was . . .
- Right now I feel . . .
- I might have learned better if . . .
- What I would change about this activity to help another class learn is . . . .

## Peer assessment and tutoring

Peer assessment, when pupils assess the work of their contemporaries, has been justified on the grounds that peers usually possess more detailed knowledge of the work of others than their teachers. Research suggests that peer assessment improves pupils' motivation to work more carefully and can 'help you think more' (Stefani, 1994). A major review of research into the use of peer and self-assessment in secondary schools reported gains in attainment, self-esteem and learning how to learn (Sebba *et al.*, 2008). Peers tend to use the same language and can model achievement, while children generally accept criticisms more readily from their peers than from their teachers. Peer assessment can take place in pairs or groups. In the case of the latter, the focus may be on assessing how well pupils worked together rather than on individual skills.

The success of peer assessment depends upon two main factors. First, how well pupils understand what they are looking for and what needs to improve. Second, how well the teacher creates a climate of mutual support and openness so that pupils feel safe to share thoughts without fear that these may upset others. Practical resources, such as rubrics, can be created to support the process of peer assessment. Examples can be found on the Education Scotland and local authority websites.

Numerous schools use the long-standing idea of peer tutoring by which a child helps another. This approach provides mutual social and intellectual benefits for both the helping child and the recipient. These include consolidating knowledge and skills, finding new meanings, modelling desired behaviour and social bonding (Fisher, 2005). Numerous research projects have reported significant benefits from peer tutoring. One study in Fife found that if teachers use weaker readers or less well-behaved pupils as tutors rather than the 'good' pupils, there are particular benefits provided the pairing is done according to ability (most able readers from different ages paired together and less able readers from different ages paired together). Tutors improve their self-confidence and specific skills, such as pausing, questioning and reading aloud (Belgutay, 2011).

## Feedback

One of the mantras in contemporary education comes from John Hattie's best-selling book on *Visible Learning* (2008), namely that the single most effective way to improve education is to focus on the quality of feedback pupils receive. Effective feedback is:

- simple – deals with one point at a time;
- evidence-based – linked to a piece of work;
- timely – immediate;
- personal – tailored to the individual; and
- forward-looking – tells the learner what to do to improve.

Most primary school children seem to prefer oral to written feedback. Although ticks, gold stars, merit awards, smiley faces and 'good work' comments express approval, they do not help children to 'bridge the gap' between present performance and future goals (Briggs *et al.*, 2008: 83). For effective learning to take place, Murphy (1998: 125) points out that it does make a difference if pupils believe that their efforts are more important than 'ability'; that they will inevitably make mistakes as part of learning and that they are in control over their own learning. Tunstall and Gipps (1996) refer to a conceptual progression from giving personal, evaluative comments for motivational or control reasons to inviting pupils to suggest how they might improve. The end of the spectrum that outstanding teachers want to move towards involves encouraging pupils to monitor or regulate their own learning using metacognitive strategies, thereby becoming less dependent upon teachers in evaluating the worth of their work. The overall message here is the manner in which feedback is delivered – 'how' as well as 'what' is said – and the importance of creating a climate of mutual trust.

The psychology of feedback is particularly important. Research in the 1990s had suggested that children often worried when teachers asked to look over their work and this anxiety increased with age. They also felt guilty and uncertain over whether they had done what the teacher had asked (Pollard *et al.*, 2000). Since then there have been reports of an increase in test-induced stress among pupils in the primary school (Harlen and Deakin Crick, 2002). Motivation is a key factor in educational achievement. Pupils are often motivated when teachers have high expectations. Pupils' progress is linked to their own beliefs about what teachers think about their potential to improve (Jarvis, 2005). Hence, teachers need to consider carefully when and how they talk to pupils (alone or within a group), where (at the teacher's desk or alongside the pupil) and what they are going to say or write. The feedback 'sandwich' of a positive comment, followed by an area for development and concluding with an upbeat remark (or symbol) is characteristic of good practice. Overuse of praise can be counter-productive. In many classrooms, teachers routinely praise children for their achievements. The emphasis is on getting things right and achieving high scores. However, Black and Wiliam (1998: 8–9) point out:

> Where the classroom culture focuses on rewards, 'gold stars', grades or place-in-the-class ranking, then pupils look for the ways to obtain the best marks rather than at the needs of their learning, which these marks ought to reflect. One reported consequence is that where they have any choice, pupils avoid difficult tasks. They also spend time and energy looking for clues to the 'right answer'.

Torrance and Pryor (2001) observed teachers giving 'protective care at the expense of helping a child to learn'. While well intentioned, teachers need to move away from focusing feedback on the self and more towards the strategies used to address the task in hand. Some teachers deploy counterfactual arguments as a technique to encourage pupils to think about the legitimacy of their answers and the logical nature of their thinking.

Pupils respond to feedback in different ways. As noted in Chapter 4, those with a growth mindset look to use feedback as a basis for improvement. Unfortunately, many pupils do not understand what teachers are trying to tell them and marking is of limited value (Box 13.7).

---

**BOX 13.7  HOW PUPILS RESPOND TO FEEDBACK**

'A tick means he probably likes it.' (Year 6)

'He wrote on it so it must be good.' (Year 3)

'If it's a tick I'm quite happy because it means it's good work, but if it's two sentences at the bottom it means it's quite bad.' (Year 6)

'Good doesn't help much – he's just saying that it's not really very good. I'd like it if he just told the truth.' (Year 3)

'It's one of my best because my handwriting is joined up neat.' (Year 3)

'Smiley faces are for working hard, neat handwriting, spelling, the date right.' (Year 3)

(Weeden *et al.*, 2000)

---

Teachers should try and model what they expect from pupils. This is often achieved by reading out examples from pupils' written work during the lesson, but there is a danger of failing to comment about how the quality of work can improve. The 'show and tell' approach has limited assessment value unless teachers engage pupils in thinking about why work is considered good (or otherwise) and whether the success criteria have been met. While there is a danger that pupils will tell teachers what they think they want to hear, generally speaking primary schoolchildren are likely to provide honest, genuine comments especially if they are confident that the teacher is committed to improving their learning.

## Marking

There are three key points to consider when marking children's work, namely, how well they have done in relation to the set task, whether there are any particular strengths and what they need to know to improve. Teachers have traditionally marked children's work through a combination of ticks, crosses, grades and comments. One of the dangers is to slip into writing general comments such as 'Well done', 'Good effort', and 'Try harder'. Even specific comments need to be made based on knowledge of individual learning needs (Box 13.8). A pupil who was told to 'use paragraphs' responded: 'If I'd known

---

**EXTEND YOUR UNDERSTANDING**

Read Hattie and Timperley's (2007) article on the power of feedback, available at: http://education.qld.gov.au/staff/development/performance/resources/readings/power-feedback.pdf

Reflect on how well you use feedback to improve the quality of the learning experience.

---

**BOX 13.8  KEY CONCEPT – MARKING**

The word 'marking' is derived from an old German word macron that meant to set out a boundary. This involved drawing a line in the ground, or placing stones to show where one territory ended and another began. While marking takes on a broader meaning today, the idea of deciding boundary lines remains, for instance in determining which candidates fall within particular degree classifications.

---

how to use paragraphs, I would have done' (Mansell *et al.*, 2009:11). Pupils need to know *how* to improve.

Research indicates that the most effective marking is based only on high-quality comments, even though a comments-only marking policy is likely to encounter opposition (Black *et al.*, 2003: Gardner, 2012). Most classroom practitioners accept that periodic use of grades can be helpful in order to reach a summative judgement – perhaps on a couple of pieces of work a term, indicating progress. When pupils' work is marked there is a tendency for pupils to focus on the grades or marks rather than what the teacher writes. It is essential that time is set aside to discuss with children pointers for improvement and to allocate sufficient time for them to address these. There are times when it is better to talk sensitively to children rather than write comments; for instance, when there is uncertainty over what the child knows or intended to say, or when the work is well above or below expectation.

Some teachers use a code to save time when marking work, which is shared with pupils. Many schools operate a policy of 'two stars and a wish' (stars indicating good features and the wish relating to what the teacher would like to see improve). Some teachers use symbols to indicate whether the comments are intended for audiences other than pupils, such as parents, the head teacher or inspectors.

The key question for teachers to consider is: 'Do these comments help pupils move forward in their learning?' (Box 13.9). Effective teachers follow up their comments and

---

**BOX 13.9  FOCUS ON PRACTICE**

A Year 4 class worked on a newspaper project with a trainee teacher who focused on developing persuasive writing. Her comments included the following:

- 'This is a great advert. It really makes me want to buy the coat.'
- 'Great offer – 2 for 1. But you should include the contact details.'
- 'Good choice of font size and colour to attract my eyes!'
- 'Love the combination of text and image – did you forget the price on purpose?'
- 'I think you could have spent more time on the presentation – this means a lot in advertising!'

create opportunities for pupils to respond, for instance through a short dialogue, and also encourage children to read each other's work to see how well they have responded. Teachers should acknowledge when children have met a particular target, but also return to it from time to time to check the achievement has been sustained. Comments can be made at interim stages when children are working to indicate emerging strengths or areas for development, and need not always be at the end of a piece of work. If pupils record learning objectives in their books, marking can indicate the extent to which these have been achieved by highlighting relevant sections. When marking work in particular subject areas, such as history or religious education, it is important to write subject-specific comments, rather than general remarks on language use, spelling and presentation. This will help children to consider how they might make progress in these subjects. Generally speaking, principles for effective marking are set out in Box 13.10.

## Questioning

During their everyday interactions teachers should use a range of questions, as discussed in Chapter 10. One of the priorities for teachers when using questions in an assessment context is to try and prompt children to talk, become involved in the lesson and explain their ideas. A popular whole-group strategy is Pose–Pause–Pounce: a question is posed to the whole group; the teacher then waits to allow children time to think, before naming someone to answer. The process becomes inclusive by asking other children to contribute, for example 'Mia, can you give an example of what Tom means?' In order to gauge understanding, it is important to set questions at different cognitive levels; from initial knowledge recall ('How many areas of the castle can you name?) to higher-order skills such as evaluation ('Do you think the castle is a good symbol for the Welsh Tourist Board? Why?').

---

**BOX 13.10  PRINCIPLES WHEN MARKING PUPILS' WORK**

- Provide guidelines on the layout and presentation of work *before* submission.
- Make it clear to children how well they have done in relation to achieving the learning objectives.
- Make expectations clear. Some trainees use the WILF acronym of 'What I Look For' so that children know what is expected.
- Acknowledge progress (however slight).
- Personalize comments by using children's names.
- Write clear and brief comments.
- Comment upon what has been done well and what still needs improvement.
- Tell pupils when you will discuss and follow up comments.
- Date and initial comments.

## Target setting

Target setting operates at all levels, from the individual child to the teacher, class, school, local authority and nationwide. On the whole, targets should be short, realistic and quantifiable, such as 'to begin my next story with a dramatic opening'. There are times when pupils work towards broader targets, for instance 'to make greater use of connectives'. Many schools use target cards to record individual or group targets (Clarke, 2001). Targets can be turned into 'I can' statements and form the basis of an ongoing record of achievement for individuals. Target setting can be a significant strategy for improving the achievement of children. Targets need to be challenging, but relate to each child's starting point for learning. One of the reasons behind target setting is to develop pupils' decision making about their own learning. In the best practice, schools link their School Improvement Plan directly to the targets for pupils (OFSTED, 2004). Class targets should be displayed as visual reminders for lessons and individual targets are often noted inside pupils' books. The TES Connet website has examples of free downloadable targets, for instance linked to each National Curriculum level for writing.

## The impact of Assessment for Learning

Despite the widespread endorsement of AfL (DCSF, 2007a; PMB, 2007; DCSF, 2008), in practice there have been mixed reports on how well teachers have implemented the recommended strategies. One of the explanations has been that teachers have been too pressurized to improve students' results in externally set tests and examinations to fully implement AfL strategies (Black and Wiliam, 2004). In Northern Ireland, while there have been reported improvements in pupils' motivation and self-esteem, teachers also identified challenges such as the demands of marking, time pressure, increased noise levels in classroom activities and the difficulty of implementing AfL across the curriculum (Leitch, 2006). In Scotland, while there has been an increase in the range of assessment methods used to monitor and record pupils' achievements, teachers are not clear about the principles of assessments (George St Research, 2007). Black and Wiliam believe this is also the case in England where many teachers know the terms but do not understand or follow the underlying principles: 'The problem is that government told schools that it was all about monitoring pupils' progress; it wasn't about pupils becoming owners of their own learning' (Stewart, 2012). According to OFSTED (2008), the impact of AfL in the teaching of English and mathematics is limited because teachers do not review learning effectively during lessons; neither do they provide enough opportunities for pupils to assess their own work or that of their peers.

One of the dangers with AfL is that teachers become cosmetic in its application. They may, for example, regularly share learning objectives at the start of lessons but fail to break these down so that pupils understand the ideas. Sharing learning objectives can become mechanistic. In the best practice, teachers integrate AfL strategies as part of their everyday teaching. For instance, research on behalf of the National Literacy Trust identifies twelve classroom strategies used by teachers to embed formative assessment within the teaching of writing (Rooke, 2012). These included:

- the use of a washing line to display emerging notes, sentence starters and key vocabulary;
- children giving a written response about their partner's writing;
- peers using three colour-coded highlighter pens to review each other's writing; and
- children writing a sentence or two evaluating their own writing, identifying which parts they felt worked best and which parts they felt needed further work. The teacher then used these as a starting point for her comments.

## Assessment of learning

Formal testing has been a long-standing feature of Britain's educational system. School managers and governments have always been interested in test scores. Concerns are expressed over the levels of anxiety among pupils taking tests, a narrowing of the curriculum as teachers teach to tests, negative impact on low-achieving pupils, and the administrative workload for teachers, pulling them away from teaching.

The distinction between formative and summative assessment is not always clear-cut. Formative assessment evidence can be included in summative reports. For example, pupils can choose their best pieces of work for a portfolio and add an updated commentary. Moreover, summative test results can be used formatively if teachers discuss these and explore how pupils' answers could be improved. 'Formative' and 'summative' should not then be seen as labels for different types of assessment but rather should be used to describe how assessments are used (Table 13.1). An activity is not formative unless the information it provides is used to take learning forward (Mansell *et al.*, 2009).

Teachers are required by law to undertake a range of assessments although these vary across the UK (Table 13.2). Over the last decade or so, government policy towards assessment in English primary schools has focused strongly on measuring and publicizing

**TABLE 13.1** Two main uses of assessment

|  | Assessment for learning (formative) | Assessment of learning (summative) |
|---|---|---|
| What? | Assessment that supports on-going learning | Assessment that summarises learning at particular points in time |
| When? | Short term – integrated within the learning process (e.g. start, middle and end of lessons) | Usually long term – often at the end of a stage in learning (e.g. the completion of a unit of work) |
| Why? | To improve learning | To report findings to audience such as parents, next teacher or school<br>To set targets<br>To track pupil progress<br>To evaluate and plan |
| Who? | Pupils involved in self- and peer assessment | Teacher-led assessment |
| How? | Formative comments and questions linked to how well pupils have progressed against learning objectives (learning valued for itself) | Summative marks, grades, certificates or prizes, which indicate standard reached by pupils |

**TABLE 13.2** Assessment requirements in primary schools in the UK

| | Early Years | KS1 | KS2 |
|---|---|---|---|
| England | EYFS Profile for each child in Reception, describing attainment against 17 early learning goals | Phonics screening check in Y1<br>Tasks and tests at any time in Y2 as part of normal classroom activity, inform teacher assessments in English, mathematics and science at end of Y2<br>Local authority moderation | Statutory test in grammar, punctuation and spelling at end of Y6<br>Teacher assessments in English, mathematics and science at the end of Y6, reported to the Standards and Testing Agency and parents<br>English and mathematics tests at end of Y6<br>Optional tests (internally marked) in English and mathematics for years 3–5, for higher-attaining pupils<br>Local authority moderation |
| Wales | Foundation Phase on-entry assessment<br>End of Foundation Phase teacher assessment of:<br>■ Personal and Social Development, Well-being and Cultural Diversity<br>■ Language, Literacy and Communication Skills<br>■ Mathematical Development | | Statutory national reading and numeracy tests<br>End of KS2 teacher assessments in:<br>■ English<br>■ Welsh first language (if the learner has followed the Welsh programme of study) or Welsh second language,<br>■ Mathematics and<br>■ Science<br>Internal and cluster school moderation |
| Scotland | | *Curriculum for Excellence* (3–18) experiences and outcomes at five levels with pupils progressing at their own pace<br>Teachers complete assessments based on a range of evidence rather than single tests<br>Pupil profile of best achievements completed at end of P7 (age 11)<br>On-going process of dialogue and reflection for all learners from 3 to 18, informing profiles at any significant time | |
| N. Ireland | Foundation Stage – Teacher Observation | In Y3–Y7 teachers assess pupils using Levels of Progression, in:<br>■ Areas of learning<br>■ Thinking Skills and Personal Capabilities<br>■ Cross-Curricular Skills<br>Teacher assessments based on:<br>■ Classroom observation<br>■ Discussion and questioning<br>■ Monitoring<br>At end of KS1 and KS2, levels given to pupils.<br>Computer-based assessments in literacy and numeracy for Year 4 to 7 pupils | |

Sources: www.nicurriculum.org.uk; www.educationscotland.gov.uk; www.wales.gov.uk/educationandskills; www.education.gov.uk

performance. Schools have been subjected to external testing, league tables that rank them according to the pupils' test results and requirements to report their results publicly.

Following an independent review of Key Stage 2 assessment led by Lord Bew (DfE, 2011), the importance of public accountability was endorsed provided that it gives a fair and representative picture of the school's performance. The report calls for inspectors to give equal weighting to pupil progress as well as attainment in coming to an overall judgement on a school. The panel also recommends greater use of teacher assessment while retaining external tests. The Westminster government accepted all of the Bew recommendations. Recently, schools in England have been given scope to devise their own assessments and the use of 'levels' scrapped on the basis that it was too narrow a definition of what children can do as well as being too complicated, especially for parents. However, schools are still required to report at the end of each key stage and benchmark their performance against national tests – the assessment load in England is heavy compared to other countries (see Box 13.11).

The assessment requirements in Wales, Scotland and Northern Ireland tend to rely more on teachers' professional judgements rather than external assessments. Teachers are expected to make best-fit judgements drawing on a range of evidence and contexts including:

- practical and oral work;
- written work completed in class;
- homework; and
- school-based assessments.

In Scotland, the National Assessment Resource supports assessment approaches within *Curriculum for Excellence*. It includes examples of how practitioners are interpreting the curriculum standards and expectations across ages, subjects and qualifications. Teachers are expected to support learners in producing profiles of their best achievements by the end of the primary school. The profile is effectively a record of achievements and, unlike the report to parents, does not include any detailed points for development.

---

### BOX 13.11 INTERNATIONAL VIEW . . . ASSESSMENT

It is very common practice for governments to specify expected outcomes or competences for different ages. Some countries, such as South Korea, Japan, New Zealand and Spain, limit external assessments by only requiring pupil samples rather than a full population to be assessed. Literacy and numeracy are subjects for compulsory assessment in many countries, including: Australia, Canada, France, Hungary, Japan, Korea, New Zealand and Spain. It is rare for countries to publicize individual school results in the form of league tables in the national media. In their review of assessment systems in twenty-two countries, Hall and Øzerk (2008) conclude that the English system is the most intrusive and comprehensive, internationally.

In Northern Ireland, Levels of Progression replaced Levels of Attainment with a stronger emphasis on skills, in addition to knowledge and understanding. The expectation is that they will be more challenging to achieve. In Years 4 and 7, teachers are required to tell parents the numerical level along with a comment for communication, mathematics and ICT. Moderation includes teachers meeting in local cluster arrangements and external checks by the Council for the Curriculum, Examinations and Assessment (CCEA). At the end of KS1 (Year 4) pupils are expected to achieve level 2 and at the end of KS2 (Year 7) pupils are expected to achieve level 4. Pupils are expected to progress at least one level between each key stage.

## Assessment in the Early Years

The assessment of young children has been a controversial issue in recent years. International research has shown that very few countries use formal assessments of 3- and 4-year-olds, which are seen as being premature and potentially harmful (Bertram and Pascal, 2002). Rather, there is almost universal support for the use of ongoing assessments of children by class teachers and carers. The idea of measuring young children's attainment through scores and the use of such data in the context of teachers' performance management has raised concerns (Edgington, 2004). At the end of the Foundation Stage, some summer-born children will be only 4 years old while others born in September are nearly 6. This significant age difference makes it unrealistic to expect these children to achieve similar standards.

To assist teachers in making assessments, in England the DCSF published *The Early Years Foundation Stage Profile Handbook* (DCSF, 2007b). A revised framework was introduced in 2012 designed to reduce paperwork and simplify reporting and assessment arrangements (DfE, 2012). When a child is aged between 2 and 3, practitioners are required to review their progress and provide parents and/or carers with a short written summary of their child's development in the prime areas: communication and language, physical development and personal, social and emotional development. Practitioners may add any other relevant information that highlights the child's strength and that might identify areas for development. The progress check is completed in partnership with parents. At the age of 5, children are to be assessed against seventeen **early learning goals**.

Practitioners indicate whether children are meeting expected levels of development, or if they are exceeding expected levels, or not yet reaching expected levels ('emerging'). The Department of Education provides exemplification on its website to establish the national standard for the level of learning and development expected for each of the seventeen ELGs (www.education.gov.uk/assessment). Practitioners need to be familiar with each area of learning, the level of development expected and the developmental continuum leading to each ELG. When completing the Profile, they should make a best-fit judgement for each ELG (Standards &Testing Agency, 2013).

As the two statutory assessments on entry to the nursery and at the end of the Foundation Stage are summative in nature, it is important for practitioners to collect evidence of a wide range of achievements to show progression. Montessori settings use Learning Journey portfolios, which contain observations, anecdotes and reflections, together with

| Area of learning | | Aspect | Emerging | Expected | Exceeding |
|---|---|---|---|---|---|
| Communication and language | ELG 01 | Listening and attention | | | |
| | ELG 02 | Understanding | | | |
| | ELG 03 | Speaking | | | |
| Physical development | ELG 04 | Moving and handling | | | |
| | ELG 05 | Health and self-care | | | |
| Personal, social and emotional development | ELG 06 | Self-confidence and self-awareness | | | |
| | ELG 07 | Managing feelings and behaviour | | | |
| | ELG 08 | Making relationships | | | |
| Literacy | ELG 09 | Reading | | | |
| | ELG 10 | Writing | | | |
| Mathematics | ELG 11 | Numbers | | | |
| | ELG 12 | Shapes, space and measures | | | |
| Understanding the world | ELG 13 | People and communities | | | |
| | ELG 14 | The world | | | |
| | ELG 15 | Technology | | | |
| Expressive arts and design | ELG 16 | Exploring and using media and materials | | | |
| | ELG 17 | Being imaginative | | | |

**FIGURE 13.3** Extracts from the Early Years Foundation Stage profile

Source: Standards and Testing Agency (2013: 49–50)

| | Prime areas of learning |
|---|---|
| | **Communication and language** |
| 01 | **Listening and attention:** Children listen to instructions and follow them accurately, asking for clarification if necessary. They listen attentively with sustained concentration to follow a story without pictures or props and can listen in a larger group, for example, at assembly. |
| 02 | **Understanding:** After listening to stories children can express views about events or characters in the story and answer questions about why things happened. They can carry out instructions which contain several parts in a sequence. |
| 03 | **Speaking:** Children show some awareness of the listener by making changes to language and non-verbal features. They recount experiences and imagine possibilities, often connecting ideas. They use a range of vocabulary in imaginative ways to add information, express ideas or to explain or justify actions or events. |
| | **Physical development** |
| 04 | **Moving and handling:** Children can hop confidently and skip in time to music. hold paper in position and use their preferred hand for writing, using a correct pencil grip. They are beginning to be able to write on lines and control letter size. |
| 05 | **Health and self-care:** Children know about and can make healthy choices in relation to healthy eating and exercise. They can dress and undress independently, successfully managing fastening buttons or laces. |
| | **Personal, social and emotional development** |
| 06 | **Self-confidence and self-awareness:** Children are confident to speak to a class group. They can talk about the things they enjoy, and are good at, and about the things they don't find easy. They are resourceful in finding support when they need help or information. They can talk about the plans they have made to carry out activities and what they might change if they were to repeat them. |
| 07 | **Managing feelings and behaviour:** Children know some ways to manage their feelings and are beginning to use these to maintain control. They can listen to each other's suggestions and plan how to achieve an outcome without adult help. They know when and how to stand up for themselves appropriately. They can stop and think before acting and they can wait for things they want. |
| 08 | **Making relationships:** Children play group games with rules. They understand someone else's point of view can be different from theirs. They resolve minor disagreements through listening to each other to come up with a fair solution. They understand what bullying is and that this is unacceptable behaviour. |

**FIGURE 13.3** *continued*

samples of work and photographs charting the child's progress (Montessori Schools Association, 2012). Throughout the United Kingdom there is a strong emphasis on teachers using their professional judgements and using a range of evidence to support assessment. Accurate assessment inevitably draws upon a range of viewpoints including what the child thinks, additional supporting adults and parents/or other primary carers.

Sir Michael Wilshaw, head of OFSTED, has called for earlier and more focused assessment of children in the Foundation Stage. Wilshaw believes that by waiting until the end of the Reception year it is too late to provide the support some children need in communication, language and literacy, particularly those from poorest families (Ross, 2013).

## Assessment of personal and social development

The formal assessment of pupils' personal and social development has always been problematic and in many cases tends to be confined to the acquisition of knowledge and understanding (OFSTED, 2002). Schools are required to keep records on all aspects of pupils' development. Assessment practice in personal and social education has been weak for many years (OFSTED, 2005; OFSTED, 2013). The challenge of assessment is exacerbated by disagreements over the content and purposes of personal and social development (Inman *et al.*, 1998). But there is general agreement that by the time young people conclude their schooling they should be able to: function independently, make informed choices and decisions, express themselves clearly, use their initiative to tackle problems, apply what they know, understand and can do in different situations, and establish and maintain positive relationships (DfES, 2003).

Many primary schools use observation and discussion of pupils' work, along with self-assessment, as their main strategies (Estyn, 2001; Lee and Plant, 2000). Non-threatening approaches using quizzes, word searches and games can be used to assess knowledge of topics such as safe use of medicines or the effect of drugs. Role-play is a popular means of assessing knowledge and understanding of health and safety issues. This can include peer assessment with children offering feedback on the decisions taken by their peers; for instance, in deciding what to do if lost on a school visit abroad or how to behave on the school bus.

When it comes to assessing the personal development of pupils there is widespread opposition to the use of any grades (Browne and Haylock, 2004). The Scottish guidelines on personal and social education make it clear 'when assessing pupils' personal and social development, personal rates of development are not and cannot be standardised' (Scottish Office Education Department, 1993). Some aspects of personal and social development are not linear; for example, self-esteem can fluctuate according to circumstances. Self-assessment therefore takes on a central role in allowing pupils time to pose their own questions, compare their personal values to those held by the school and society at large and to reflect on what happens when such values are challenged. Eaude (2008) feels strongly that it is inappropriate to use levels or scores to measure the outcomes associated with personal development. This is not to say that there is no place for summative and formative assessment in these areas of a child's development. For instance, reporting back to parents on their children's personal development is an obvious time for summative assessment. Many parents are more interested in the personal and social development of their children than their academic progress. They are keen to know whether their children are sociable and responsible.

While the assessment of knowledge, understanding and skills in personal and social education can be treated in much the same way as other parts of the curriculum, the difficulty with assessing values and attitudes is the assumption that there is common agreement over what should be demonstrated. Values are shaped by many factors. Noble and Hoffmann (2002: 205) point out:

> We cannot tell pupils what attitudes they should have, even if we wanted to . . . pupils need to be given time and space to explore their own attitudes, to compare and contrast their own with others', and be given permission to amend, adjust, change or confirm their attitude as they mature.

OFSTED point out that in the best assessment practice the pupils are aware of the learning outcomes and are encouraged to assess themselves and to record their own progress. Evidence can be obtained from a range of activities including:

- pupils' participation in debates and Circle Time;
- writing letters to and replies from agony aunts or uncles;
- exploring stereotypes in the media, fiction and non-fiction;
- telling stories with dolls or puppets;
- visits to places of worship; and
- looking after the school grounds.

## Record keeping

Accurate record keeping is essential in teaching. In the best practice recording is clear, manageable and covers all subjects and aspects of the curriculum. Records should note what has been achieved as well as what has been experienced, contain examples of pupils' work that illustrates their level of achievement, and include opportunities for pupils to select their own work against agreed criteria (OHMCI, 1998). Records should form the basis of forward planning and accurate reporting to parents. The importance of accurate record keeping has been highlighted by OFSTED (2006) in cases that have undermined procedures for safeguarding children in school. Decisions about the format of records and the retention of evidence are left to the discretion of schools (Headington, 2000). Keeping up-to-date and accurate records is necessary to ensure that assessment, reporting and subsequent planning are effective.

Teachers typically keep a range of records such as the following:

- a record of pupil attendance;
- a class list;
- a group list noting particular abilities or difficulties;
- records relating to pupils' reading, language and mathematics;

- observational notebook including comments on pupils' all-round development; and
- a portfolio of sampled work relating to the achievements of individual pupils.

Outstanding trainees keep detailed records, containing accurate and useful assessments of individuals as well as analyses of the performance of groups or whole classes (OFSTED, 2005). Records that require only a tick/cross or yes/no can provide trainees with a quick overview of pupils' learning. But they are crude indicators and usually do not give sufficient detail about the context of assessment or how pupils' learning can be moved on. Portfolio evidence can be more rigorous especially if selected pieces of work are annotated, noting for instance the degree of independence shown by the pupil. Many schools keep exemplar group or class portfolios to build up evidence for standards (levels) in a particular subject or area of experience. These are often used for moderating meetings or as a basis for discussions with parents and other interested parties. In some schools, pupils choose what work to place in their record of achievement to denote the progress that they have made. In order to promote independence and a shared responsibility, it is desirable to encourage pupils to become involved in the business of recording. For example, pupils might enter information into their reading records such as the titles of books read, the names of authors, dates of reading and a simple evaluation of the texts.

There are a number of statutory record-keeping duties placed on schools throughout the United Kingdom. They are required to keep records on every child, including information on academic achievements, personal development and progress through the school. Such records should be updated annually. In the United Kingdom, schools are also required to put in place systems for handling and recording race-related incidents. Under the terms of the Education Act 2005, schools must evaluate the extent to which learners feel safe and adopt safe practices. The reasoning behind keeping records is essentially three-fold: to ensure that sufficient information on children's progress is passed to parents, teachers and other professionals; to ensure that there is continuity in providing services to children if staff leave or are temporarily unavailable; and to keep an account of how the school is undertaking its responsibilities in supporting learners.

There are different ways of recording children's achievements and progress. Among the most frequently used by schools include: notebooks, diaries, Post-it notes, index cards, record sheets, digital photographs, videos and audiotapes. There are many examples of observation record sheets available through publishers, the Internet, colleges, schools and local authorities. These typically include such details as: the name of the observer, name of the child, date of observation, starting and finishing times, number of adults present, description of the activity, area of observation, and additional contextual comments.

## Reporting

Teachers report to different audiences including fellow colleagues, governors, parents, guardians, other professionals and the pupils themselves. Many schools invest in software programmes, such as *ReportBox*, *SIMS Teacher Comments* and *The Report King*, to generate quick reports. The software draws on stock phrases linked to the curriculum and in this sense provides consistency and saves significant time. While the use of computer-generated reports is supported by trade unions, some commentators believe that parents are short-changed in not receiving enough personalized comments. Seldon (2010) claims the art of report writing has suffered with the advent of uniform and bland reports. One of the dangers of cutting and pasting banked comments when writing reports is that parents soon pick up on those teachers who really know their children, for instance during discussions at parents' evenings.

The best practice in reporting occurs when teachers provide a clear and detailed account of achievements and offer practical suggestions for improvement. Teachers should balance comments on effort and attitude with those relating to achievement. There is a need to avoid over-praising pupils' achievements, at the expense of noting areas for development, because this can create a false impression of children's progress. OHMCI (1998: 14) reported that this was the tendency in around 10–15 per cent of schools. When providing oral or written reports, it is useful to bear in mind the following points:

- prepare well – give sufficient time for reporting. If using software, get to know its limitations. When speaking to parents/carers, have to hand pupils' work for them to review and reread any written comments beforehand;

- focus on the individual pupil – refer to his/her personal strengths, interests and areas for development;

- keep it simple – use language that is straightforward and free of jargon but without patronizing parents;

- avoid over-generalizations – while comments such as 'she is doing well' are likely to be welcomed, parents are entitled to know more details, e.g. relating to targets in reading and numeracy;

- double check everything for accuracy – misspellings or factual errors convey a poor professional image; accuracy also needs to be evident in areas such as attendance records;

- present reports in a positive spirit – there should be something to celebrate for all children, e.g. contributions to wider school life, extra-curricular activities, kindness, otherwise questions will be asked about the quality of teaching; and

- discuss with senior colleagues how to deliver 'difficult' messages beforehand – criticisms should never be levelled at individuals and assumptions/value judgements avoided, e.g. he spends too much time playing on the computer at home.

Some schools provide trainee teachers with opportunities to write 'mock up' reports to parents based on their assessment of pupils in their class. In the best practice, they are able to attend a parents' evening to 'shadow' a qualified teacher. This provides experiences in seeing how reports are delivered and in time management.

## PAUSE FOR REFLECTION

Try to dig up one of your old school reports when you were a child. How accurate do you think it was and how have you changed? What would the report say now?

## Glossary

**Early learning goals** are collections of statements in England that set out the expected level of attainment at the end of the EYFS. There are seventeen ELGs drawn from seven areas of learning.

**Rubrics** are tools that describe the parts and levels of performance of a particular task.

## References

Assessment Reform Group (1999) *Assessment for Learning: Beyond the Black Box*, Cambridge: Cambridge University Press.

Belgutay, J. (2011) 'Peer tutoring works best with age gap', *Times Educational Supplement*, 15 April.

Bertram, T. and Pascal, C. (2002) *Early Years Education: An International Perspective*, London: QCA.

Black, P. (1998) *Testing: Friend or Foe?*, London: Falmer Press.

Black, P. and Wiliam, D. (1998) *Inside the Black Box: Raising Achievement through Classroom Assessment*, London: King's College.

Black, P., Harrison, C., Lee, C., Marshall, B. and Wiliam, D. (2003) *Assessment for Learning: Putting It into Practice*, Maidenhead: Open University Press.

Black, P. and Wiliam, D. (2004) 'Teachers developing assessment for learning: Impact on student achievement', *Assessment in Education*, 11(1): 49–65.

Black, P., Harrison, C., Lee, C., Marshall, B. and William, D. (2002) *Working Inside the Black Box: Assessment for Learning in the Classroom*, Windsor: NFER Nelson.

Briggs, M., Woodfield, A., Martin, C. and Swatton, P. (2008) *Assessment for Learning and Teaching in Primary Schools*, Exeter: Learning Matters.

Browne, A. and Haylock, D. (eds) (2004) *Professional Issues for Primary Teachers*, London: Sage.

Clarke, S. (2001) *Unlocking Formative Assessment*, London: Hodder Murray.

CWDC (2009) *The Common Assessment Framework for Children and Young People: A Guide for Practitioners*, London: CWDC.

DCELLS (2008) *Observing Children*, Cardiff: Welsh Assembly Government.

DCSF (2007a) *The Children's Plan*, London: DCSF.

DCSF (2007b) *Early Years Foundation Stage Profile Handbook*, London: DCSF.

DCSF (2008) *The Assessment for Learning Strategy*, Nottingham: DCSF.

Devereux, J. and Miller, L. (2003) *Working with Children in the Early Years*, London: David Fulton.

DfE (2011) *Independent Review of Key Stage 2 Testing, Assessment and Accountability*, London: DfE.

DfE (2012) *Statutory Framework for the Early Years Foundation Stage*, London: DfE.

DfES (2003) *Explaining Personal and Social Development*, London: DfES.

Eaude, T. (2008) *Achieving QTS: Children's Spiritual, Moral, Social and Cultural Development*, Exeter: Learning Matters.

Edgington, M. (2004) *The Foundation Stage Teacher in Action*, London: Sage.

Estyn (2001) *Standards and Quality in Personal and Social Education in Primary and Secondary Schools in Wales*, Cardiff: Estyn.

Fisher, R. (2005) *Teaching Children to Learn*, Cheltenham: Nelson Thornes.

Fleming, G. (2008) *Rubrics: A Self-evaluation Tool that Supports Children's Learning*, Coventry: National Teacher Research Panel.

Fontana, D. and Fernandes, M. (1994) 'Improvements in mathematics performance as a consequence of self-assessment in Portuguese primary school pupils', *British Journal of Educational Psychology*, 64(3): 407–17.

Gardner, J. (ed.) (2012) *Assessment and Learning*, London: Sage.

George Street Research (2007) *Evaluation of the Status of Assessment of Learning in Scotland 2006–07*, Edinburgh: Learning and Teaching Scotland.

Hall, K. and Øzerk, K. (2008) *Primary Curriculum and Assessment: England and Other Countries (Primary Review Research Survey 3/1)*, Cambridge: University of Cambridge Faculty of Education.

Harlen, W. (2007) *The Quality of Learning: Assessment Alternatives for Primary Education*, Cambridge: University of Cambridge.

Harlen, W. and Deakin Crick, R. (2002) *A Systematic Review of Summative Assessment and Tests on Students' Motivation For Learning*, London: EPPI-Centre.

Hattie, J. (2008) *Visible Learning*, Abingdon: Routledge.

Hattie, J. and Timperley, H. (2007) 'The power of feedback', *Review of Educational Research*, 77(1): 81–112.

Hayes, D. (2006) *Inspiring Primary Teaching*, Exeter: Learning Matters.

Headington, R. (2000) *Monitoring, Assessment, Recording and Reporting*, London: David Fulton.

Hopkins, D. (2008) *A Teacher's Guide to Classroom Research*, Maidenhead: Open University Press.

Inman, S., Buck, M. and Burke, H. (eds) (1998) *Assessing Personal and Social Development*, London: Falmer Press.

James, M. and Pollard, A. (2008) 'Primary Review Research Survey: 2/4 Learning and teaching in primary schools: Insights from TLRP', Cambridge: University of Cambridge.

James, M., McCormick, R., Black, P., Carmichael, P., Drummond, M-J., Fox, A., Frost, D., MacBeath, J., Marshall, B., Pedder, D., Procter, R., Swaffield, S. and Wiliam, D. (2007) *Improving Learning How to Learn: Classrooms, Schools and Networks*, London: Routledge.

Jarvis, M. (2005) *The Psychology of Effective Learning and Teaching*, Cheltenham: Nelson Thornes.

Kerry, T. (2002) *Learning Objective, Task Setting and Differentiation*, Cheltenham: Nelson Thornes.

Kounin, J. (1970) *Discipline and Group Management in Classrooms*, New York: Holt, Rinehart & Winston.

Lee, J. and Plant, S. (2000) *PASSPORT: A Framework for Personal and Social Development*, London: Calouste Gulbenkian Foundation.

Leitch, R. (2006) 'Assessment for learning. Keynote presentation', 12 January, CCEA Conference: Assessment for Learning.

McCurdy, B.L. and Shapiro, E.S. (1992) 'A comparison of teacher monitoring, peer monitoring, and self-monitoring with curriculum-based measurement in reading among students with learning disabilities', *Journal of Special Education*, 26(2): 162–80.

MacLeod-Brudenell, I. (ed.) (2004) *Advanced Early Years Care and Education*, Oxford: Heinemann.

Mansell, W. (2008) 'AfL critics vindicated by research', *Times Educational Supplement*, 21 November.

Mansell, W., James, M. and the Assessment Reform Group (2009) *Assessment in Schools. Fit for Purpose? A Commentary by the Teaching and Learning Research Programme*, London: Economic and Social Research Council.

Montessori Schools Association (2012) *Guide to the Early Years Foundation Stage in Montessori Settings*, London: Montessori Schools Association.

Murphy, P. (1998) *Learners, Learning and Assessment*, London: Paul Chapman.

Noble, C. and Hoffman, G. (2002) *The PSHCE Co-Ordinator's Handbook*, London: RoutledgeFalmer.

OFSTED (2002) *Personal, Social and Health Education and Citizenship in Primary Schools*, London: OFSTED.

OFSTED (2004) *Setting Targets for Pupils with Special Educational Needs*, London: OFSTED.

OFSTED (2005) *Handbook for the Inspection of Initial Teacher Scottish Government (2011) Training for the Award of Qualified Teacher Status 2005–2011*, London: OFSTED.

OFSTED (2006) *Safeguarding Children: An Evaluation of Procedures for Checking Staff Appointed by Schools*, London: OFSTED.

OFSTED (2008) *Assessment for Learning: The Impact of National Strategy Support*, London: OFSTED.

OFSTED (2013) *Not Yet Good Enough: Personal, Social, Health and Economic Education in Schools*, London: OFSTED.

OHMCI (1998) *Assessment, Record-Keeping and Reporting in KS1 and KS2*, Cardiff: OHMCI.

Palaiologu, I. (2008) *Childhood Observation*, Exeter: Learning Matters.

PMB (2007) *Assessment for Learning for Key Stages 1 and 2*, Belfast: CCEA.

Pollard, A., Triggs, P., Broadfoot, P., McNess, E. and Osborn, M. (2000) *What Pupils Say: Changing Policy and Practice in Primary Education*, London: Continuum.

Pye, J. (1989) *Invisible Children*, Oxford: Oxford University Press.

Race, P., Brown, S. and Smith, B. (2005) *500 Tips on Assessment*, London: RoutledgeFalmer.

Rooke, J. (2012) *Transforming Writing Interim Evaluation Report*, London: National Literacy Trust.

Scottish Executive (2004) *A Curriculum for Excellence*, Edinburgh: Scottish Executive.

Scottish Government (2011) *Curriculum for Excellence: Building the Curriculum 5: A Framework for Assessment*, Edinburgh: Scottish Government.

Scottish Office Education Department (1993) *Personal and Social Development: 5–14 National Guidelines*, Edinburgh: Scottish CCC.

Sebba J., Deakin Crick, R., Yu, G., Lawson, H. and Harlen, W. (2008) *Systematic Review of Research Evidence of the Impact on Students in Secondary Schools of Self and Peer Assessment*, London: EPPI-Centre.

Seldon, A. (2010) 'School reports in a class of their own', *The Telegraph*, 5 April.

Standards & Testing Agency (2013) *Early Years Foundation Stage Profile Handbook*, London: Standards & Testing Agency.

Stefani, L.A.J. (1994) 'Peer, self and tutor assessment: Relative reliabilities', *Studies in Higher Education*, 19(1): 69–75.

Stewart, W. (2012) 'Think you've implemented Assessment for Learning?', *Times Educational Supplement*, 13 July.

Torrance, H. and Pryor, J. (2001) 'Developing formative assessment in the classroom: Using action research to explore and modify theory', *British Educational Research Journal*, 27(5): 615–31.

Tunstall, P. and Gipps, C. (1996) 'Teacher feedback to young children: A typology', *British Educational Research Journal*, 2(4): 389–404.

Tymms, P. and Merrell, C. (2007) *Primary Review Research Report 4/1 Standards and Quality in English Primary Schools Over Time: The National Evidence*, Cambridge: University of Cambridge.

Weeden P., Winter, J. and Broadfoot, P. (2000) *The LEARN Project Phase 2: Guidance for Schools on Assessment for Learning: Project Report*, Bristol: University of Bristol.

Wilson, J. and Murdock, K. (2008) *Helping Your Pupils to Think for Themselves*, London: Routledge.

Wood, E. (2008) 'Listening to young children: Multiple voices, meanings and understandings', in Paige-Smith, A. and Craft, A. (eds) *Developing Reflective Practice in the Early Years*, Maidenhead: Open University Press, 108–21.

Woolfolk, A., Hughes, M. and Walkup, V. (2008) *Psychology in Education*, Harlow: Pearson.

## Websites

Assessment Reform Group provides information on ten principles of AfL – www.assessment-reform-group.org

NFER – the NFER has published twelve excellent leaflets to support good assessment practice in primary schools – www.nfer.ac.uk/gripping-assessment-primary

The Association for Achievement and Improvement through Assessment (AAIA) – www.aaia.org.uk

The National Assessment Resource provides support for Scottish teachers – www.education scotland.gov.uk/learningteachingassessment/assessment/supportmaterials/nar

The Council for the Curriculum, Examinations and Assessment in Northern Ireland advises on what should be taught and monitors standards – www.ccea.org.uk

# 14

# Continually learning

## Teachers as researchers

## Chapter objectives

By the end of this chapter you should be able to:

- Define educational research and explain why it should matter to teachers.
- Describe the stages in the research process.
- Evaluate different research methodologies and approaches.
- Understand the nature of Master's level work in education as an evidence-based profession.
- Recognize the importance of continuing professional development.

*Teachers often leave a mark on their students, but they seldom leave a mark on the profession.*
*(Wolfe, cited by Beverly, 1993: 4)*

## Why educational research matters

Lawrence Stenhouse (1926–1982), one of the great British educationalists, defined research as 'systematic, critical and self-critical enquiry that aims to contribute to the advancement of knowledge' (Bassey, 1995: 2). Educational research is largely derived from the social rather than the physical sciences and has an emphasis on seeking new insights, rather than finding absolute truths (Box 14.1). It aims to inform judgements made by teachers and policy makers to improve the experiences for learners. People use research for different reasons. Market researchers seek to find out what consumers think about products and services, writers of historical fiction quarry primary sources to give their stories an authentic feel, while scientists seek to explain natural phenomena through experimentation and observation. In everyday life, people research all sorts of things, from house prices to holiday venues and building regulations.

Teachers should show an interest and participate in research for several reasons. For example, research can:

- increase teachers' knowledge and understanding of particular aspects of learning and/or teaching;

- empower them to generate their own knowledge rather than wait for someone else to tell them what to do;

- improve teachers' skills, self-confidence and dispositions;

- add weight to their professional viewpoints in discussions with parents, colleagues and managers;

- put teachers in contact with other professionals to gain different perspectives;

- provide opportunities to step back and reflect on their own practice and professional development;

- result in qualifications or publications to add credibility to their standing; and

- ultimately, result in improvements in the quality of teaching and learning.

The immediate availability of so much information via the Internet has raised concerns that students and teachers are not developing rigorous research skills. There is widespread concern that children are over-dependent on search engines, struggle to judge the reliability of online information and find it too easy to copy the work of others (Purcell et al., 2012). A survey of Internet use in 2004 warned that the major challenge for UK educators by 2014 was to move children on from going online for ready-made entertainment and information, towards developing opportunities for critical engagement, the generation of content and active participation (Livingstone and Bober, 2004). Progress has been slow. In a European study of 25,000 children and young people, including those in the UK, less than half of 11–13-year-olds were able to compare websites to decide whether information is true (Sonck et al., 2011, 2, 4). The problem of too readily accepting online information extends to higher education. One study suggests that half of university students are prepared to submit essays bought off the Internet (Williams, 2010). There are regular stories of academics, popular writers and politicians accused of plagiarism – even a new book for law students on how to write papers properly was plagiarized (www.bbc.co.uk/news/18962349).

The demands on teachers' time in planning lessons, teaching, monitoring, assessing, writing reports, meeting parents and working with other professionals, mean that engaging with research can be, understandably, challenging. According to Hancock (2001), there are several factors that explain why teachers are reluctant to undertake research. First, he suggests that there has never been a public expectation that teachers would write about the theories that underpin what they do. Their 'craft' is not seen as something that merits research and high-profile discussion because there is a common perception that anyone can teach young children. Second, teachers' working conditions militate against anything that does not directly bear on classroom practice. Third, Hancock argues that the profession has been disorientated by one government reform after another. In effect, this has sapped their confidence and dignity.

In recent years, attempts have been made to make education research more accessible to teachers because of criticisms that much of it has been irrelevant, costly and limited in scope (Tripp, 1993). One report on behalf of OFSTED found that much educational research was undertaken 'in a vacuum, unnoticed and unheeded by anyone else' (Tooley,

---

**BOX 14.1  KEY CONCEPT – RESEARCH**

**Old French, recercher – to seek, or search again**

The term 'research' has many meanings and forms. Originally used in the sixteenth century, it conveyed the idea of 'intensive searching, an investigation directed towards discovery' (Onions, 1966: 759). At a simple level, research effectively involves asking a question, seeking out answers and then presenting findings to others. The exploratory nature of research involves quantitative (numbers) and qualitative (text and images) ways of capturing evidence, such as the use of surveys and interviews. Research serves different purposes, including satisfying personal professional development, meeting wider political needs and bringing about changes in schools

---

1998: 6). In reviewing 241 articles in leading education journals, only one was written by a serving teacher working as a researcher. Since then, there have been improvements in the reporting of educational research. The Department for Education (DfE) website reports recent research and links to the National Archives for older publications. In Northern Ireland, the Access to Research Resources for Teachers (ARRT) Space is an educational research database designed to promote evidence-informed practice to support policymakers. Its e-resources include research dissertations by students who have completed a Master's education programme on subjects such as the deployment of classroom assistants, the management of children with ADHD and trainee confidence in teaching science. The General Teaching Council for Northern Ireland publishes a *Professional Update* for teachers and schools, which provides readable summaries of important research relating to teaching, learning and assessment. Since 1928, the Scottish Council for Research in Education (SCRE) Centre has been supporting Scottish education through research. Based at the University of Glasgow, the Centre focuses on key themes such as Creativity, Culture and Faith, exploring questions such as 'does religious education work?' (Conroy *et al.*, 2013).

The Teaching and Learning Research Programme (TLRP) was the largest programme of educational research in the UK. Over 10 years (1999–2009), the TLRP included 700 researchers and 100 projects clustered around these topics:

- learning in specified curriculum areas;
- learning across the curriculum;
- the use of ICT to enhance learning;
- environments for better learning; and
- schools and improvement.

The TLRP research outcomes can be accessed via the British Education Index (https://bei.leeds.ac.uk/freesearch/TLRP/BEISearch.html). Its website provides summaries of research and publications relating to Early Years, primary education and other phases.

There are useful research briefings on varied subjects such as 'Factors that make teachers more effective across their careers' (TLRP, 2006) and 'Towards Evidence-based Practice in Science Education' (TLRP, 2004). For research to make a difference in the classroom, findings need to be translated into understandable, tangible outcomes, such as classroom materials. School leaders also need to create a culture in which research is valued.

## Evidence-based practice

The possibilities of teaching as a research-based profession have been debated at length and are well outlined by Hammersley (2007). For many years teaching has been some way behind other professions, such as medicine, in exploiting the potential of research to improve practice. In an important speech to the Teacher Training Agency, David Hargreaves (1996) argued that teachers should follow the example of medical practitioners, who combined their own personal, clinical experiences with the best available research evidence when treating patients. Hargreaves (1996: 12) pointed out: 'Expertise means not just having relevant experience and knowledge but having *demonstrable* competence and clear *evidence* to justify doing things in one way or another.' Petty (2006: 3) expands on this: 'We are knee deep in strategies that could improve things for our students, so the question is not "will this strategy work?" but "*which* are the most productive strategies to adopt?"'

**Evidence-based practice** had been very much the focus of New Labour since Tony Blair's election in 1997. The commitment was to move away from politics guided by ideology towards, in Blair's words, 'what counts is what works' (Bochel and Duncan, 2007: 90).

In education, the principles of evidence-based practice include the need to make decisions based on sound evidence, the importance of reviewing teaching constantly in the light of evidence, and exploring why something works well. While Petty (2006: 4) draws heavily on international research to highlight the most effective teaching methods, he concludes that academic research is not the 'final court of judgement, but what works in your classroom'. This has now been expanded to what works best. The development of Teachers' TV (with 3,500 programmes available on the *Times Educational Supplement* website) and other online video exemplification has helped trainee and experienced teachers see effective classroom practice in action.

However, evidence-based practice is not without its critics. While well-conducted and relevant research can *inform* the work of teachers, to suggest that teaching should be *based* on evidence is problematic. Simply presenting teaching with evidence and then expecting teachers to modify their practice is a rather naïve and unrealistic assumption. Discussions with experienced teachers who have attended in-service courses may reveal that even when 'new' ideas are logically presented and personally well received, for a variety of reasons they are not always adopted at school level. The resource and planning implications, anticipated parental objections, or concerns over staff engagement may account for this. It is also the case that teaching is a complex business in which decisions are made based on values and perceptions as well as 'facts', rather like refereeing in games. As Wellington (2006: 99) points out: 'The key factors affecting teaching style and approach on a particular day are numerous and not always based on educational criteria, e.g. safety or classroom behaviour may take priority in some situations.'

More fundamentally, research is often contested – even within the fields of medicine and science, as illustrated with the debates over the MMR jab and autism, the health risks associated with mobile phones or genetically modified foods. Ben Goldacre, a doctor and academic, writes about how the media promotes public misunderstanding of science. He highlights wacky stories masquerading as science, where scientists have reportedly 'found' the formula for something, such as the perfect boiled egg, the most depressing day, or the perfect way to eat ice cream (Goldacre, 2009). Goldacre is concerned that teachers are being duped by commercial interests and in the process are being disempowered. He wants teachers to become better informed through the use of **randomized controlled trials**, so that they know which classroom strategies work best.

> We need a group of schools, teachers, pupils, or parents, who are able to honestly say: 'we don't know which of these two strategies is best, so we don't mind which we use. We want to find out which is best, and we know it won't harm us.'
>
> (Goldacre, 2013: 12)

### EXTEND YOUR UNDERSTANDING

Explore what the use of randomized control trials might mean in schools, as suggested in Goldacre's paper on *Building Evidence into Education*, available at: www.gov.uk/government/news/building-evidence-into-education

## Teachers as researchers

The link between teacher and researcher is not a new one. Originally, Lewin (1946) envisaged teachers working alongside researchers in a cycle of planning, action, observation and reflection. Lawrence Stenhouse (1975) developed the 'teacher-as-researcher' model in the context of advocating curriculum change. He suggested: 'A research tradition that is accessible to teachers and which feeds teaching must be created if education is to be significantly improved' (Stenhouse, 1975: 165).

Stenhouse believed the teacher could act as an agent for change by challenging practice and, temporarily, by looking upon the world of the classroom through the eyes of a stranger. Research was seen as a means of empowering teachers to develop their expertise.

In simple terms, **action research** is essentially about studying and seeking to improve some aspect of classroom practice. Stenhouse argued: 'It is teachers who, in the end, will change the world of the school by understanding it' (cited by Rudduck, 1988). The focus is very much on the teacher designing, controlling and reflecting upon the process and in this sense serves as a democratic counter to research led by expert academics. It is research 'carried out by the actors themselves' (Bassey, 2007: 148). Figure 14.1 shows the basic action research cycle (Kemmis and McTaggart, 1982):

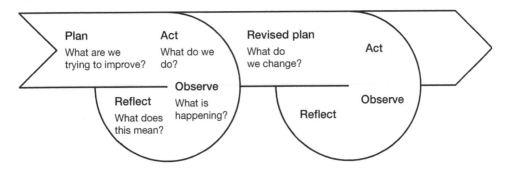

**FIGURE 14.1** Action research cycle

Action research is an 'inside-out' model of professional development through which teachers serve a dual role as practitioners and researchers. Action research should be a model that appeals to trainee and newly qualified teachers keen to investigate classroom issues that interest them. The model can operate at different levels. In the first instance this may take the form of a mini-research project based on an aspect of classroom practice, such as investigating the variety of questions asked by a teacher through the course of a week. This can then be taken a stage further by involving fellow class teachers in a parallel study and finally broadened to include teachers in other school contexts, such as those who work in a networked or twinned school. Lankshear and Knobel (2004) argue that teachers should not feel restricted to conducting research in their own classrooms, but should consider the wider community, studies of policies, social class, and engage with a variety of anthropological, sociological and historical materials. In terms of the latter, Derek Gillard's website on the history of education in England is an excellent starting point, providing first-hand documentary evidence along with commentaries (www.educationengland.org.uk).

There is no shortage of up-to-date advice for teachers on how to conduct action research and set this within a contextual framework (e.g. McNiff and Whitehead, 2006; Noffke and Somekh, 2009). The international journal *Educational Action Research* has provided scholarly articles since the early 1990s. The reality is, however, that despite the hype critics argue that few teachers appear to be using action research on a regular basis as a tool to help them improve the quality of teaching and learning (Burgess, 2001). One of the major criticisms of action research projects is that they are very often 'all action and no research' (Godfrey, 2004: 207).

The contribution of action research in developing knowledge and new theories has been underplayed, according to McNiff and Whitehead (2009: 2), with too much emphasis given over to professional development where: 'Practitioners are encouraged to "tell their stories", but are not required to offer explanations and critical analyses of those stories.'

The authors believe that teachers are too reluctant to engage seriously with theories but that their voices are critical to social and cultural change. Engaging in research should be regarded as a valid form of professional development, especially when teachers work alongside expert researchers and colleagues in other schools.

There are a number of informative guides on different aspects of the research process (Denby *et al.*, 2008; Bell, 2010; Thomas, 2013; see also the NFER website). Typically these provide guidance on formulating research questions, drawing up a research plan, following the process and working within an ethical framework. Arthur *et al.* (2012) provide guidance on more recent research methodologies such as using blogs, as well as specifics such as effect size, conducting meta analysis and using statistical packages such as SPSS (Statistical Package for the Social Sciences). Most University websites and student support services also offer advice on how to retrieve information, take notes, interrogate databases and structure reports. Plymouth University has one of the most comprehensive education research websites that includes advice on questionnaires, interviews and case studies (www.edu.plymouth.ac.uk/resined/resedhme.htm). The University of Manchester includes a helpful academic phrase bank (www.phrasebank.manchester.ac.uk).

## Teachers' own frame of reference

The term **paradigm** frequently occurs in research literature and refers to a way of seeing the world based on philosophical assumptions about how to investigate problems. When researchers conduct research they draw upon their own values, beliefs and prior knowledge. They are also shaped by prevailing views in society at the time. Hammersley (2012) raises a number of questions researchers need to consider including: should research aim to produce knowledge or improve practice? Should it be politically neutral or seek to challenge inequalities? Can it demonstrate 'what works' in terms of policy and practice, or is it limited to providing broad understandings for indirect use to policymakers, practitioners, and others? Should researchers use a variety of methods? What criteria should be used to judge the quality of research? Given the wide range of approaches and perspectives, it is difficult to determine what constitutes good research. There are a number of factors to consider when judging research, including the clarity of aims, definitions and questions, the reliability of evidence, the representative nature of any sample and ethical matters, such as any potential conflicts of interest. Above all, research should be judged by the extent to which it has been conducted in a balanced, sensitive and critical manner to produce results that potentially can make a difference in education.

The two main paradigms that underpin educational research are the positivist and naturalistic (interpretive) approaches. Positivism is rooted in the physical sciences and seeks to predict and explain why things happen, often using statistical tools, such as surveys and questionnaires. The typical scientific method begins with a hypothesis, which is then tested, with subsequent results considered as to whether they support an existing theory. The research involves observing and collecting data and looking for patterns. Up until the 1980s positivism held sway in educational research, but attempts to 'scientifically' measure teaching effectiveness encountered criticisms. There are too many variables in any teaching situation, critics maintain, to control with any degree of reliability. That said, as Pollard (2008) points out, in recent years the scientific model has attracted renewed interest from policymakers keen to improve the quality of their decisions. This is illustrated through the use of pupil and school performance data and longitudinal studies of large cohorts of pupils. The Centre for Longitudinal Studies, based at the Institute of Education in London, is responsible for running three of Britain's internationally renowned birth cohort studies: the 1958 National Child Development Study, the 1970 British

Cohort Study and the Millennium Cohort Study (MCS). The MCS tracks 19,000 children born in 2000–1 and covers such topics as: parenting; child behaviour and cognitive development; health; income and poverty; neighbourhood and ethnicity (www.cls.ioe. ac.uk).

One of the difficulties with scientific research in educational contexts is that the views of the individual can be ignored. This led to the development of a more flexible interpretive model, by which the subjective views of teachers, pupils and others are given due attention. Interpretivism seeks to understand how different people see, think, and feel about the world. Experienced teachers know that classroom events can be interpreted in different ways. For example, when children sit quietly in a classroom this does not necessarily mean that they are attentive or well behaved. Or the fact that children answer teachers' questions successfully does not mean that they understand the teaching points.

Interpretive researchers are mindful of different perspectives and how 'reality' can be perceived. Gage (2007) uses the analogy of 'spin doctoring', where an event is turned to the advantage of a particular political group. Hence the losing of an election might be presented in a positive light if the low turnout was highlighted. What matters here is a readiness to accept different meanings to an event. The interpretive model favours qualitative research because this focuses on case studies rather than measuring variables. In summary, Kvale (1996) provides two useful metaphors to explain the differences between qualitative and quantitative research: the former is likened to a traveller on a journey wandering through the landscape, striking up conversations with people on the way, visiting new places, and returning home to tell a tale; the latter is seen as a mining operation, in which knowledge is understood to be buried metal to be uncovered and untainted by the miner.

On balance, most trainee and serving teachers are likely to focus on their immediate worlds using qualitative research questions. Both the scientific and interpretive paradigms share the goal of describing and analysing classroom practice. The teacher generally takes a passive role as the subject of study – the researchers collate the data through observations, questionnaires or interviews. Action or teacher research, as an alternative model, places the practitioner at the heart of the research process. Hargreaves (1996) sees action research as a means of giving control to teachers and new insights into 'taken-for-granted' aspects of their everyday work.

# Research stages

## 1 Identifying the research topic

There is no shortage of topics to research in education. These can relate to: classroom management, patterns of teacher or pupil behaviour, the progress made by particular groups of learners (e.g. boys, girls, Black Caribbean, gifted and talented pupils), motivation, barriers to achievement, subject-specific aspects of learning, questions about leadership, use of resources, relationships with parents, governors and others, transition, pupils' attitudes towards school, behaviour, truancy, use of the outdoor environment, and a wide range of assessment issues. These can tie in closely with priorities identified within school development plans; for instance, a school might be seeking to raise standards in writing and eager to find out the impact of a particular scheme or strategy. Ideas for research can be gleaned from conversations with colleagues, reading professional literature or lesson observations. Research topics need to be clearly defined and interest the researcher. But above all, a topic should be selected where there is a possibility of advancing knowledge and understanding in the profession and where the subjects of research are likely to benefit.

In terms of action research, there is a need to identify an area for improvement or change. This could relate to weaknesses in teaching or learning noted in an inspection report or arising from self-evaluation. Test results might prompt questions about the achievements of particular groups of pupils that warrant research. Peer observation might reveal inconsistencies in the use of resources, such as the interactive whiteboard, that raise questions such as whether this makes any difference to pupils' motivation.

## 2  Posing research questions or hypotheses

The aims of the research project should be clearly stated and can be expressed in terms of questions, hypotheses or propositions, all of which indicate the direction and scope of study. Bordage and Dawson (2003: 378) suggest that 'the single most important component of a study is the research question. It is the keystone of the entire exercise.' The characteristics of good research questions include whether they are:

- feasible – achievable within time, location and resources;
- interesting – personally, to colleagues and the wider profession;
- clear – understandable and unambiguous;
- authentic – teachers need to 'own' the questions;
- significant – to learners as well as teachers;
- ethical – within established code of ethics and professional values; and
- relevant – to the aims of the educational research.

Inevitably, questions will evolve as research develops. If undertaking qualitative research, it is customary to ask open-ended questions or use statements. These are more likely to prompt a rich response, for instance from interviewees sharing their life experiences, say in teaching.

Finding the right questions to ask is not straightforward. It is helpful to review existing research questions to understand how they are framed. There are different kinds of research questions. Initially a general question may guide the research but then be supplemented with specific ones that can be answered through the collection of data, observation or some other procedure. Research questions are intended to keep the researcher focused, especially given the tendency to become sidetracked through a project. It is always useful to refer back to the research questions if in doubt over the direction of the inquiry. That said, research questions could be refined as new data and issues surface. Action research is, by nature, a recursive, iterative and organic process. Examples of research questions asked by teachers include:

- What will happen to the quality of Year 6 writing if we implement peer editing?
- How might pupils' behaviour change if we introduce 10-minute silent reading periods after lunchbreak?

- How can we use children's feedback to improve the quality of our instructions?
- How can we improve pupils' punctuality?
- How much time do children spend discussing their learning as as a group during the week?

Hypotheses have been defined as 'predicted answers to research questions' (Punch, 2009: 65). These are used instead of questions when the researcher has an explanation or theory in mind and wants to test it out. For instance, a trainee who found the behaviour of her class 'difficult' during her first week of a placement discussed this with her tutor and believed that by modifying her voice control it would make a positive difference during the remainder of the placement. She asked the class teacher to monitor this, although her conclusion was that there were other factors that accounted for improvements in behaviour including the use of rewards and the absence of a particularly disruptive child.

## 3  Background reading

Throughout a project, effective researchers read a range of sources (particularly articles in peer-reviewed journals) to find out what others have already concluded and to critique existing findings. A literature search or review is a well-established part of any research proposal, dissertation, paper or thesis. Literature reviews tend to run throughout action research projects, rather than form a discrete section or chapter. Thorough literature reviews seek to engage with previous and existing theories, interpretations and models. Researchers need to justify why their study is necessary – perhaps there is a gap in existing knowledge, some new policy has been introduced and responses are sought, or previous research in the subject was many years ago. It is not necessary to read everything that has been written on a topic but it is essential to focus on relevant major works. One of the common pitfalls is namedropping or what has been called 'king making' and 'sandbagging' (McNiff and Whitehead, 2009:117). Here, writers may operate under the illusion that by simply referring to many authors, this demonstrates an impressive breadth and depth to their reading. The key to successful reviews is to select and prioritize only relevant sources and to show a critical understanding of what others have said.

Many of the following sources will be available on the Internet but web-based research should supplement rather than replace study of first-hand sources and original use interviews, observations and surveys:

- academic texts and articles in refereed journals such as the *British Educational Research Journal*;
- HMI reports and publications;
- government publications including Parliamentary papers (http://parlipapers. chadwyck.co.uk), national strategies and other documents held at the National Archives (www.nationalarchives.gov.uk);
- data, e.g. primary school performance tables, National Curriculum results, outcomes for particular groups such as children looked after (see www.gov.uk), international comparative data such as PISA (see www.oecd.org/pisa);

- school-level documentation including lesson plans, self-evaluation documents, strategic plans, assessment data, prospectus;

- children's work, e.g. stories, poetry, art, performances, music;

- local authority materials, e.g. schemes of work; policies; guidance on health and safety;

- surveys by YouGov, Ipsos Mori and other market researchers;

- trade union publications, e.g. guidance on the law;

- research produced by established organizations such as the Economic and Social Research Council (www.esrc.ac.uk) and the National Foundation for Educational Research (www.nfer.ac.uk);

- conference papers, e.g. those produced for BERA;

- international studies such as those produced by UNESCO (United Nations Educational Scientific and Cultural Organisation) or OECD (Organisation for Economic Cooperation and Development);

- newspapers, e.g. online newspaper archives such as the British Newspaper Archive (www.britishnewspaperarchive.co.uk) and Welsh newspapers online (http://papuraunewyddcymru.llgc.org.uk/en/home);

- artefacts including toys, books, magazines, school objects and childhood memorabilia, e.g. see Museum of Childhood collection at: www.museumofchildhood.org.uk;

- sounds and oral history, eg. British Library collection at www.bl.uk/oralhistory;

- photographic archives, e.g. Getty Images (www.gettyimages.co.uk); SCRAN (www.scran.ac.uk); digital gallery of the National Library of Scotland (http://digital.nls.uk);

- film and recorded materials such as the BFI Archive (www.bfi.org.uk); Internet Archive (https://archive.org);

- subject association publications e.g. Geographical Association resources;

- publications by charities, e.g. Joseph Rowntree Foundation, the Sutton Trust and Oxfam;

- dissertations – see Index to Theses in the UK;

- databases and digital library collections, e.g. EPPI-Centre database of education research; the American-based Education Resources Information Center (ERIC);

- reference works, e.g. on research methods, action research, ethnography, learning and teaching; and

- indexes, e.g. United Nations Human Development Index comprising the Life Expectancy Index, Education index and Income Index; the UK indices of multiple deprivation.

Fortunately, a growing number of educational publications are now available on the Internet and there are many established and reliable websites, including gateways and portals, that focus on bringing research findings to the attention of busy teachers. The American-based ERIC provides a digital library of research sponsored by the United States Department of Education (http://eric.ed.gov) while EBSCO Information Services runs the British Education Index, which covers articles published in UK journals from 1976 onwards and UK theses (www.ebscohost.com/discovery).

There are numerous online research tools and specialized searches available, such as Google Scholar, and Noodle Tools (www.noodletools.com). The growth of e-journals and e-books has made research easier and less costly. University libraries will hold collections and databases. Typically, these include book and journal titles and possibly dissertations, technical reports and working papers. Most journals will feature an abstract at the beginning of the article that provides an overview of the research.

## 4  Devise a research plan

Having identified the area for research and 'read around' the subject, the next stage involves drawing up a research plan or design. In effect, this provides an overview of the research process and can take the form of a series of questions (Table 14.1). The plan needs to say what research tools are needed to collect data to address the questions. These can include quantitative (numerical) and qualitative methods. The latter might include interviews, observational field notes or tape-recorded lessons. In many cases, researchers favour a mixed approach. So, for instance, a trainee whose dissertation focused on teacher

**TABLE 14.1**  Research design

| Main question | Sub questions |
| --- | --- |
| What are the purposes of the research? | Who decides? |
| Who owns the research? | Who controls the data? |
| What are the costs? | Human, material, physical, administrative? Who will carry out the research? |
| How will the data be gathered? | What methods of data collection will be used: surveys, questionnaires, ethnography? What format will be followed (e.g. for questionnaires or observations)? |
| What is the time-scale? | How frequently will the data collecting occur? |
| What are the ethical considerations? | Will participants be identified? What editing should occur? |
| Where will the research take place? | Whole school? Classroom? Playground? |
| How will the data be analysed? | Will ICT software be used? What statistical tests will be needed? Who will process the data? What data protection issues arise? How will the data be validated? |
| How will the findings be presented? | Orally? Online? Journal? Who will be the audience? |
| What format will this take? | Will tables be used? How will the data be made accessible and 'reader friendly'? |
| Who will read/wants this research? | Will the material appear in the public domain? |

Source: Adapted from Cohen *et al.* (2007). Reproduced with permission

stress utilized a questionnaire circulated among teachers, observations and interviews. Ultimately, successful research often hinges on the clarity of purpose, as manifested in the quality of questions, and the choice of methodology. A research plan needs to consider practical matters such as the time available to undertake the research, how to arrange visits or interviews and balancing other work/life commitments. By setting and achieving mini-goals, set as milestones, the research journey becomes less daunting.

## 5 Choose and use appropriate research tools

Effective researchers consider carefully the methods (*how* of research), so that they most closely match the aims (*why*) of the project. Table 14.2 outlines some of the basic research tools but serious researchers would also consider more sophisticated methods mentioned in recommended readings (Lankshear and Knobel, 2004; Cohen *et al.*, 2011). Research journals are a popular means of collecting and recording evidence in action research projects. Observational notes can be made 'on the spot' and entered in the journal immediately or later using Post-it notes. The immediacy of the journal means that feelings and beliefs can be recorded without the haziness of recollecting events at a later time.

Interviews are another key method of gaining research information. These can be structured and carefully planned or quite spontaneous, informal and conversational. Interviews offer a platform for intimate discussion and the opportunity for interviewees to speak candidly about their preferences, dislikes, hopes and fears, but ultimately the interviewer may only find out what the speaker is prepared to say. Interviewing children raises particular ethical issues and is affected by the kind of relationship established with the teacher. One trainee who interviewed a group of more able pupils as part of her dissertation on differentiation was told by one 10-year-old: 'I thought that's what you wanted me to say.'

Observation is an important means of monitoring and assessment, especially in the Early Years. In terms of research, child observation can furnish valuable evidence, particularly if sustained systematically over a period of time. Observing children in their everyday environments (home, classroom, day-care setting, or playground) can reveal information on the physical environment (e.g. use of resources) and aspects of children's developments, such as communication skills, patterns of play, and physical development. There are different degrees of structure to observation and researchers need to decide exactly what they are looking for and how to record data. Options include:

■ simple jotting on Post-it notes or in a diary;

■ describing events at specified times;

■ rating scales or checklists;

■ pen portraits of those observed;

■ field notes related to a theme, such as pupils' independence; and

■ sketches, diagrams or photographs.

If working alongside children as a participant observer, there are practical problems to overcome such as making notes without arousing curiosity and dealing with distractions. Observation schedules can be useful aids, for example in noting pupils' responses to questions, behaviour or the quality of teaching. The times and frequency of behaviours

**TABLE 14.2** Common data collection methods

| Type | Method | Advantages | Challenges |
|---|---|---|---|
| Quantitative | Questionnaires, surveys, checklists | ■ Low cost<br>■ Possibility of gaining a lot of data quickly<br>■ Option to complete anonymously<br>■ Good for comparisons<br>■ Possible to adapt existing questionnaires for particular research<br>■ Analysis helped by ICT software | ■ Questioning can be misleading<br>■ Completion is impersonal<br>■ Response rates can be disappointing<br>■ Statistics are often open to interpretation |
| Qualitative | Interviews | ■ Opportunity to gain detailed information from knowledgeable respondent<br>■ Scope to gain different perspectives on same questions | ■ Time-consuming (e.g. to transcribe tape-recorded interviews)<br>■ Requires high-level skills (e.g. questioning, reading non-verbal cues, sensitivity)<br>■ Logistical issues (e.g. where and when) |
| | Documents | ■ Low cost<br>■ Many available online and easily accessible<br>■ Possible to read wider historical, political and educational contexts | ■ Possible data restrictions applied to certain documents<br>■ Written from particular perspectives and are not 'value neutral' |
| | Observation | ■ Most practitioners will have experience in observation<br>■ Options to tape/video record and view later<br>■ Option to tape/film 'secretly'<br>■ Able to record 'as it happens' | ■ Those observed can change their behaviour if observation is known<br>■ Ethical issues with 'secret' observation<br>■ Difficult to interpret seen behaviours<br>■ Recording can be time-consuming |
| | Diaries and journals | ■ Personal insights over a period of time<br>■ Good basis for follow-up interviews | ■ Subjective and may not be representative<br>■ Legibility |

should be noted. A simple coding system helps to record quickly what is observed (Box 14.2).

**Ethnography** involves researchers trying to understand a culture by sharing the experiences of the community, sometimes over several months or years, keeping notes as they go along. This can be challenging and requires researchers to break free from their own assumptions as they endeavour to look at life from the viewpoints of others. That said, it is possible to adopt a reflexive approach by including evolving personal experiences,

## BOX 14.2 FOCUS ON PRACTICE

A trainee undertook observations of small groups to find out the extent to which girls in her class made verbal contributions to discussion. The following is an example of a simple recording chart that she used.

| | Time in one minute intervals | | | |
|---|---|---|---|---|
| Pupil | 1 | 2 | 3 | 4 |
| Paul | 5 | 5 | 5 | 5 |
| Joshua | 5 | | 5 | 5 |
| Katie | | 5 | 5 | |
| Mia | | | | 5 |
| Hannah | 5 | | | |

This exercise was repeated with the same group on ten occasions through the week with similar results. They confirmed the trainees' perception that Paul dominated the group talk although she was surprised to see how little Mia and Hannah said. Among the questions for further observation were the reasons why these two girls did not talk much, what part non-verbal communication played and why the boys tended to initiate discussion. As a consequence of these observations, the trainee changed the composition of the group for language lessons and subsequently noted that the girls' oral contributions increased.

attitudes and responses as part of the research itself, perhaps recorded in a journal. For example, one researcher spent time with young males in south London and discusses his growing abhorrence at what he discovered (cited by Breakwell *et al.*, 2008).

Ethnography is particularly valuable when seeking to find out more about groups who are often on the periphery of society or whose voices are seldom heard, such as children living on the streets or Travellers' children. Those pursuing feminist research often make use of ethnography as a means of empowering women. Examples of ethnographic studies that have extended our understanding include insights into the challenges faced by minority ethnic groups living in multicultural societies, and school achievement as a factor of parental education and income (cited by Doherty and Hughes, 2009). In some American teacher education programmes students are set assignments in which they are expected 'to understand and interrogate oppression in order to act against it in their classrooms . . . teachers need to be allied with marginalised communities in the fight for social justice' (King, 2008: 1117). They are asked, for example, to develop a working

### EXTEND YOUR UNDERSTANDING

Read K. Bhopal (2004) 'Gypsy travellers and education: changing needs and changing perceptions', in *British Journal of Educational Studies*, 52(1): 47–64. How effectively does the author give 'voice' to an under-represented community?

relationship with a community member and to collaborate on a lesson that uses his or her perspective, life history, knowledge, talents or interests.

Davis *et al.* (2008) provide a fascinating account of how a researcher attempted to understand the lives of children with multiple impairments in a Scottish special school. He admitted that he did not have a clue about how he was expected to behave by staff and children and found it very difficult to understand whether the children were happy with his presence in the class:

> This led to a lot of standing around, getting in the way of children and staff, until my role in the class developed. This uncomfortable experience was compounded by my academic related fear that I would be unable to fulfil the requirements of my post – to develop interactions with disabled children in order to understand their social worlds.
>
> (Davis *et al.*, 2008: 221)

There are important lessons to be learned from his perseverance in handling various research pressures, such as overcoming negative staff views, coming to terms with his own cultural assumptions and the need to adopt imaginative fieldwork notes in learning to interpret and record non-verbal language.

## 6  Collect and record data

Researchers collect data or information through measurement, observation, interviews and experiences (Box 14.3). They might count the number of times boys answer questions, observe how children use particular areas of the playground, discuss with pupils or teachers their views on a topic, or participate in the learning experience themselves. Sometimes it is impossible to access the subjects of research, for instance when undertaking historical study. It is also not always necessary to engage directly with people. For example, researchers may use data from documents, newspapers and magazines, diaries, images, government publications and official statistics.

All sources, whether first-hand (primary) or secondary (which interpret primary data), should be treated with caution. The researcher needs to weigh up the relative value of sources considering the following points:

- authenticity – can the source be verified by others?
- credibility – what are the qualifications/reputation of the author? are opinions well supported with reliable evidence?

---

### BOX 14.3  REAL-LIFE LEARNING CHALLENGE

You have seen research on body language that suggests that children are very good at interpreting nonverbal cues (e.g. gestures) and that these are very powerful influences on their learning. You want to know what kind of messages you convey in the classroom and how children respond to these. Two other colleagues are willing to help out. How would you set out planning a small-scale research project?

- currency – how up to date is the source?
- audience – who is the intended audience?

When using first-hand data, researchers are also keen to ensure that it is reliable and valid using a range of techniques (Table 14.3). Reliability is about the consistency of results, so for instance pupils given the same spelling test by different teachers close in time should attain similar scores. Validity refers to the measurement of data – the extent to which the different parts (variables) of the research 'fit together' to make a valid argument. Linked to this is the notion of 'member checking', by which the researcher checks the emerging analysis with the subjects if appropriate and possible to do so. For example, a transcript of an interview with a teacher might be taken back to be checked for accuracy before or after analysis – when shown afterwards, the idea is to check the reasonableness of the explanations. A wider circle of 'critical friends' can be invited to participate in the analysis, thereby offering a degree of moderation to the research process.

Findings can be recorded in many ways including diagrams, charts, tables and other visual means, such as concept maps and timelines. In written formats, a personal journal can be useful to record feelings, including frustrations, about the research. Sound recordings of interviews or observations can be made using a digital or video camera. For instance, an edited video recording of lessons can be made using appropriate software such as Windows Moviemaker. It is also possible to produce audio recordings in which the researcher summarizes findings, for instance through podcasts. In such cases one minute or less is a good limit to ensure the sound files are small enough in size for webpages.

Taking field notes is an important skill, particularly for qualitative researchers. Hoffmann (2001: 31) draws attention to the key principles of note taking during research: copy accurately; check, double-check and, if in doubt, triple-check all facts; keep a note of all sources. The format for note taking can include concept maps, timelines, flow charts, as well as keyword notes. Some note takers organize everything around 'headings and points'.

**TABLE 14.3** Research techniques

| Technique | Description |
|---|---|
| Triangulation | Consider the research question from at least three separate pieces of data or three points of view |
| Sampling | Process of selecting a portion of the population to enable the researcher to make generalizations |
| Categorizing and sorting | There are many software applications that can assist in the management of data, removing the manual burdens of classifying and sorting qualitative data: this allows the researcher to explore patterns and trends, as well as test out theories |
| Ordering | The data can be ordered in different ways, such as by chronology, significance or frequency |
| Comparing and contrasting | Consider similarities and patterns in the data; also what stands out as different |
| Conferring | Check data analysis with others, such as fellow teachers or learners themselves – their views may validate or challenge your emerging findings |

Numbering points, using abbreviations, headings, colours, arrows and boxes, can all help make notes memorable.

During research mistakes can easily occur during the early stages of background reading and recording. For instance, the date '1998' can be recorded as '1989' perhaps because the writer is tired or has been distracted. When taking notes it is important to record the exact references (author, title, date and relevant page number), which will prove particularly useful if queries arise at a later time. It is also imperative that figures are verified wherever possible.

## 7 Analyse findings

When analysing data, researchers look out for patterns or trends and how the findings compare with those in the research literature. Quality analysis is characterized by clear exposition of complex issues, identification of causal relationships, comparison, sustained logical arguments and the challenging of assumptions (Burton *et al.*, 2008). The key question for analysis is whether the data answers the research question. ICT software such as Microsoft Excel and more sophisticated programs, for example SPSS, offer detailed analysis.

Content analysis is used by quantitative researchers when they count how often something appears in particular media, such as magazines, newspapers, television advertisements, radio programmes, pictures, or interviews. The data can be recorded and compared using a coding schedule and presented in tables. Adams *et al.* (2011) revisited previous research on the way fathers were under-represented in picture books. The authors found a significant shift from invisible to involved fathers in the care of their young children. Haggarty (1995) has used content analysis to explore conversations between teachers and student teachers on predetermined issues. She discovered that mentors were reluctant to move beyond 'politeness' to explore any disagreements between themselves and the student teachers.

Providing teachers are clear about directions, children themselves can undertake content analysis; for instance by recording specific entries in their favourite magazines, television schedules or sports pages in newspapers.

## 8 Communicate findings

When summarizing research findings, it's useful to think about three questions:

- What did you do?
- What did you find out?
- What might you change as a result?

The first question is a useful prompt to review what was done (e.g. interviewed teachers, surveyed parents, observed ten Year 4 mathematics lessons) to see through the aims. The second question focuses on the research outcomes, for example in terms of discovering what the subjects think about something, their disposition or how well they learned a skill. The final question focuses on the impact of the research, particularly on the researcher; for instance, it could lead to changes in practice or attitude.

The ultimate goal of any investigation is, as Wolcott (1994) puts it, to tell a story. In academic circles, the traditional way of communicating these stories is through conferences, peer-reviewed journals such as *The British Journal of Educational Research*, books or more recently through blogs, social media or online communities such as academia edu (www.academia.edu). Unfortunately academics sometimes fail to communicate their key research findings clearly and succinctly. Consider this example, taken from an abstract of a paper intended for teacher educators:

> Using the literature from critical pedagogy and cultural studies, this paper argues that teacher education's focus on pedagogical content knowledge should move beyond the idea of teaching students how to pedagogize pedagogically free content to helping them recognize the inherently pedagogical nature of content and its implications for (and in) teaching.
>
> (Segall, 2004: 489)

Even a well-informed lecturer is likely to struggle to understand what is meant by 'pedagogize pedagogically free content'. While it is important to learn how to write in a formal style, ideas must be communicated clearly. Most universities provide guidance to support students on how to improve their written and oral communication skills. Table 14.4 offers a summary of key points to bear in mind. The Plain English Campaign offers free online guides as well as an A–Z of alternative words (www.plainenglish.co.uk).

Despite major advances in the field of communicating research findings, there remain concerns that 'education researchers don't know how to disseminate their results to practitioners' (Kaestle, 1993: 28). Collaborative research projects enable schools to share findings locally and contribute to the building up of necessary networks of support. As Dadds (2001: 134) notes, exceptional teachers of the future will need not only to maintain their excellent standard of teaching but also to *share* their practice and *influence* colleagues. Teachers, acting as researchers, may communicate their findings through staff meetings, training workshops or in research assignment submissions for particular courses. The format of the communication can vary, from presenting a 10-minute synopsis to fellow students or conference delegates to submitting a 100,000-word dissertation.

One of the major difficulties in education is implementing the change associated with research recommendations (Wallace *et al.*, 2008). There is something of a 'denial of change' that operates in some schools, where there is a prevailing scepticism over new ideas. Resistance is usually linked to technical, cultural or political reasons – teachers may lack the expertise to carry through changes, feel that the ideas are not appropriate to the school context or perhaps see a 'hidden' agenda. When research points to changes in teaching or learning, these may run contrary to deeply held – even unspoken – views about how schools should function and how teachers should be free to 'do their jobs'. Local authorities have a key role to play in acting as *mediators* between research, policy and practice and to encourage teachers to become involved in research themselves. Advisers, for instance, can act as 'brokers' between schools with similar research interests to promote evidence-informed practice (Wilson *et al.*, 2003).

The successful introduction of new ideas, whether in the classroom or whole institution, requires careful planning, vision, commitment and perseverance. Kotter (1998), a leading

**TABLE 14.4** Communication aide-mémoire

| Aspect | Pointers for writing |
| --- | --- |
| Audience | Focus on the intended audience – most readers or listeners have limited time and so need to know the key messages in a direct, concise and engaging manner. |
| Conciseness | Use short sentences – most experts suggest on average 15–20 words.<br>Avoid clichés e.g. 'last but not least' (finally). |
| Clarity | Use examples, real-life experiences or illustrations for main points. Avoid jargon and explain technical terms and abbreviations. |
| Objectivity | Avoid personal bias and prejudice.<br>Personal pronouns i.e. 'I, me, you, we, us' are generally avoided in academic writing in favour of an impersonal style e.g. 'There are . . .', 'It is . . .', but this depends on the context e.g. reflective journal writing, lesson evaluations. |
| Active voice | Generally use the active rather than passive voice, where the subject performs (rather than receives) the action e.g.<br>Active – OFSTED inspected the school.<br>Passive – the school was inspected by OFSTED. |
| Structure | Introduction – share aims and focus.<br>Main body – present arguments with examples, one key point per paragraph.<br>Conclusion – summarise evidence, state overall viewpoint.<br>Use sub-headings, tables, graphs, and other visuals to organise and enliven content. |
| Content | Demonstrate good content knowledge and understanding by engaging with theories, offering alternative views, questioning points, reference to latest research and discussing implications for teaching and learning.<br>Show classroom applications, where appropriate. |
| Style | Use signpost words to change direction e.g. 'On the other hand. . .'<br>Follow any publisher or University guidelines to ensure grammar, style and punctuation are in line with the recommended 'house' style. |
| References | Cite full sources to support arguments and set these out as recommended e.g. following Harvard style. Consider using software such as Refworks to generate citations and bibliographies.<br>See also: Pears, R. and Shields, G. (2010) *Cite Them Right*, London: Palgrave. |
| Proofread | Always proofread – mistakes are more easily noticed when re-reading at a later date. Use computer spellchecks and search facilities. |
| Editing | Be ruthless in cutting out 'empty' words and phrases. |

| | Pointers for oral presentation |
| --- | --- |
| Voice | Vary tone, pace, pitch and power.<br>Pause.<br>Do not become tied to notes (avoid a 'reading' voice).<br>Check all can hear. |
| Structure | Share purpose at the outset.<br>Present points in a logical sequence.<br>Use a timer for each section but show flexibility and 'think on your feet'. |
| Content | As per content guidance for written presentation.<br>Keep to 4 or 5 key points.<br>In conclusion reinforce these. |
| Resources | Use ICT and other resources to enhance rather than detract from the key messages.<br>Check all is working beforehand.<br>Keep text in PowerPoint slides to a minimum – key words.<br>Share hand-outs if appropriate. |
| Body language | Use gestures to emphasize points.<br>Dress appropriately.<br>Smile and try to look relaxed but not over-confident. |
| Audience | Try to engage the audience through eye contact, references to their experience, humour, questions and mini tasks (if appropriate). |
| Time | Keep to allocated time in oral presentations – audiences and organizers do not like speakers who go over time. |

American writer on change, advocates the importance of clear communication and good role models so that colleagues can see that useful change is possible.

## Ethical considerations

Researchers should always act with honesty or integrity. An ethical framework should encase all stages of research, from the drawing up of aims and questions through to collating, storing and presenting data. The overriding principle is to cause no harm to the participants and, where possible, produce benefits for them and the wider educational community.

The ethical dimension in research is particularly important when working with young learners. These revolve around preventing harm to children, gaining informed consent (parents and children), avoiding deception, and respecting privacy and confidentiality of data (Punch, 1994). On no account should there be any coercion for participants to behave in a certain manner. In the context of children's rights, there is now a strong lobby advocating that children should make informed choices about such matters as deciding whether to participate, and having a say in the direction and use of the research (Hill, 2005). While the 'listening to learners' agenda has become popular in recent years, Roberts (2008) distinguishes between 'listening' to children and 'hearing' what they say, arguing that researchers and practitioners may not have 'heard' children. She maintains that children are experts on their own lives and researchers need to find meaningful ways to interact and engage with them during research. Policy and practice is shifting towards involving children themselves in research and consultation through imaginative contexts and approaches (Alderson, 2008). For instance, in one community project children aged 3 to 8 years used cameras and conducted surveys and interviews about children's views on improving their housing estate. They produced an illustrated report that they presented to local authority officers at a council meeting. Some of the recommendations, such as locating the playground at the centre of the estate, were adopted.

In terms of photographing and recording children, schools, universities and other teacher education providers will have guidelines that should be consulted. Organizations such as the British Educational Research Association (BERA, 2004) also publish codes of ethical conduct for research. One key consideration is the future use of any material and whether it will be available within the public domain, such as featuring on a school website.

## Research at master's level

In the UK over recent years the notion of 'master's-level profession' has gained widespread support. Bodies such as the Universities Council for the Education of Teachers (UCET) argue that this would raise the status of the profession, bringing benefits to individual teachers as well as schools and the pupils themselves. In particular, teachers need space to undertake in-depth investigations, reflect on their own teaching practices and improve their techniques.

Government interest has been shown in practice-based master's programmes, as opposed to the more traditional university-centred ones. In England, the government initially funded the development of the Master's in Learning and Teaching programme under the direction of the Training and Development Agency (TDA, 2009) but the funding (but not the programme) was subsequently cut. The Welsh Assembly launched its Masters in Educational Practice in 2012, focusing on the national priorities of literacy, numeracy and reducing the impact of poverty on attainment. Similarly, the Scottish government has outlined plans for its own Masters of Education (National Partnership Group, 2012). These programmes are designed to show the relevance of theory to everyday practice.

Although master's degrees vary from one university to another, they share the following characteristics:

- an in-depth knowledge and understanding of the discipline informed by current scholarship and research, including a critical awareness of current issues and developments in the subject;
- the ability to study independently in the subject; and
- the ability to use a range of techniques and research methods applicable to advanced scholarship in the subject (QAA, 2010).

The programmes are also designed to promote a range of generic skills such as solving problems in a creative way and communicating effectively. Those who achieve a master's qualification are expected to convey a sense of authority derived from extensive background reading coupled with the ability to synthesize and challenge views (Box 14.4).

---

### BOX 14.4 INTERNATIONAL VIEW . . . A MASTER'S PROFESSION

The inspiration for teaching as a master's-level profession comes from Finland, the country that often scores highest in international comparisons. All Finnish teachers follow a 5-year master's degree. As part of their study, students are required to spend one year in a model or training school associated with the university. Teacher education has a strong research base. Teachers must combine the roles of researcher and practitioner. They write a research-based thesis as the final requirement for the master's degree. In America, around half of all teachers hold a master's degree, and the number of teachers with advanced degrees has nearly doubled in the last 50 years. According to the National Council on Teacher Quality, however, holding master's degrees does not make teachers more effective. In fact, the Council believes that some studies have shown that master's degrees have a slightly negative impact on student achievement (NCTQ, 2004). In a comparative study of teacher qualifications in six nations, Ingersoll (2007: 9) found that only 16 per cent of elementary teachers in South Korea and only 2 per cent of elementary teachers in Singapore held master's degrees. Both South Korea and Singapore are among the highest-performing educational systems in the world. The master's programme is similar to the graduate training scheme in Boston (USA) which combines a one-year (4 days' each week) apprenticeship in schools with one day a week doing coursework that contributes towards a master's degree qualification.

The research component of a master's programme usually takes the form of an action research project, extended essay or dissertation. A dissertation might be typically structured as shown in Box 14.5. University guidance on the writing of these assignments should be followed. Often, universities provide clear and practical advice on how to manage time, the use of library services, location of key sources, referencing, word counts, layout, submission, avoiding plagiarism and where to turn for support.

M-level work demands engagement with complex issues, autonomous planning and implementation of tasks and an understanding of 'a complex body of knowledge, some of which may be at the *current boundaries of education*' (Sewell, 2008: 9, emphasis in original). Those who qualify with a Postgraduate Certificate in Education (M-level) should be prepared to *lead* practice in the future. In the process of becoming an outstanding teacher there is a need to develop an understanding of research, theory and practice. This is an ongoing process through your career.

---

**BOX 14.5  THE TYPICAL CONTENTS OF A RESEARCH DISSERTATION**

Title – title should reflect focus of study, name and date.

Acknowledgements – lists those who have helped during the research.

Contents – chapter headings and page references.

Abstract – describes briefly what the project aimed to achieve, methods employed and conclusions reached.

Introduction – includes rationale for choosing the subject and methodologies; selected research questions, potential value and relevance of research should be noted.

Literature review – draws attention to existing evidence relating to subject, including views of experts.

Methodology – sets out the qualitative and/or quantitative processes by which the researcher collected data.

Analysis – data is interrogated, compared and analysed for patterns.

Findings – evaluates the results of the research. These can be presented in different ways, for instance charts, diagrams and tables.

Conclusion – includes a summary of the research, the extent to which research questions have been answered and recommendations as to how this might be developed further.

References – this includes details of sources referred to in the text, using the Harvard system.

Bibliography – sets out all sources consulted.

Appendices – can include raw data, consent forms and templates.

## The importance of continuing professional development

Professional knowledge never remains static because it changes in the light of new research and reflection on experience. One of the greatest challenges facing teachers and schools is how to keep their knowledge up to date. Historically, much continuing professional development (CPD) has revolved around teachers attending courses and conferences as individuals. Ideally, they would then return to school suitably inspired to enthuse others, reflect with colleagues over existing provision and implement changes designed to improve practice. However, teachers' professional development has been described as 'erratic, poorly planned and poorly evaluated', characterized by 'passive learning' (Cordingley *et al.*, 2005). Only 7 per cent of schools follow up to see whether there is any impact on children's attainment and only 1 per cent of training is said to be transformative (Featherstone and Pyle, 2009). In a telephone survey of 825 teachers and managers by the Wellcome Trust (2006), 38 per cent expressed a positive attitude towards CPD, dubbed 'believers', and rated content covering subject updates and teaching most valuable. However, 33 per cent were 'agnostics', believing in the principle of CPD but doubting much of its quality and relevance, while 12 per cent thought that CPD focused too much on government initiatives rather than their own professional needs. The remaining 16 per cent were described as 'seekers' who valued CPD but found opportunities in school were limited. The most effective CPD involves a process of collaboration, sustained implementation, evaluation and reflection. Evaluation is the weakest element with many teachers confusing this with dissemination (Goodall *et al.*, 2005; Cordingley, 2013).

Much of the CPD activity over recent decades has been based on an 'input' model where success was measured by teacher attendance at workshops, conferences and courses. Gradually CPD has shifted towards an 'output' model with an emphasis on trying to gauge what differences have been made to teaching and learning.

These important questions are deceptively complex and may take several years to fully answer. They reflect a move towards whole-school research and CPD through the development of **Professional Learning Communities** (PLCs).

The impact of PLCs is well documented internationally and is central to the Welsh Government's *School Effectiveness Framework* (Harris and Jones, 2010), which is designed to raise standards and improve the quality of learning and teaching. Research shows that

---

**PAUSE FOR REFLECTION**

How would you answer the four questions posed by Kelly (2013: 12)?

1   What professional development activities have you undertaken this year?

2   Have you reflected on the learning gained from carrying out these activities?

3   Have the activities and the reflection combined made a difference to what and how you teach or train?

4   Can you show evidence of what the difference has been and the impact it has made on your learners, colleagues or the organization in which you work?

teachers who are part of a PLC tend to be more effective in the classroom and achieve better student outcomes than those who work alone (Lewis and Andrews, 2004). Teachers who receive and act upon high-quality CPD make a difference to children's learning – their rate of progress improves twice as fast as those in other classes. This improvement is most noticeable for those described as 'less able' (Timperley *et al.*, 2007). PLCs have proven effective in all school contexts and secured improvements irrespective of the socio-economic backgrounds of pupils (Verscio *et al.*, 2008). The most effective PLCs have a relentless focus on improving pupil achievement (Bolam *et al.*, 2005). Networks of PLCs (between and across schools) enable teachers to widen their expertise and to share their most effective practice.

The Institute for Learning (IfL) and the Centre for the Use of Research and Evidence in Education (CUREE) have produced a route map to assist practitioners in finding the right CPD resources and opportunities. Although designed with further education audiences in mind, the route map is a useful resource to trigger discussion and reflection over the possibilities for CPD among primary teachers and trainees.

Choosing the right CPD to meet the needs of the school is particularly important in cash-strapped times. Leaders have to balance the developmental needs of individual teachers, school priorities and investment to prepare for national changes. Professional development needs to focus on improving learning, rather than seeking to change teaching practice. Hence the starting point has to be identifying the potential learning gains associated with CPD (Weston, 2013a). Schools can draw on a growing body of resources to support their CPD provision. These include the Sutton Trust's Pupil Premium Toolkit, the York Informed Practice Initiative (YIPI) and the Teacher Development Trust's Good CPD Guide website. The Sutton Trust's toolkit evaluates different CPD-related content on the basis of cost, known impact, and reliability of evidence (Higgins *et al.*, 2013). Training on developing teachers' effective feedback, for example, scores well as a 'high-impact, low-cost, moderate evidence' investment. The Trust points out that the starting point should be the school's own evaluation of its priorities.

The world's best performing educational systems are based on strong professional development for teachers. In Singapore, the government funds 100 hours of professional development for every teacher each year. Yet in England, there is no expectation that teachers should undertake a structured programme of accredited continuing professional development. Schools most commonly rely on five whole-school training days, first introduced in 1988 as part of curriculum reforms. These 30 or so hours compare to 1,100 hours that students spend in a typical classroom during the year (Weston, 2013b). The emphasis in government policy over recent years is to see the most valuable CPD and research as narrowly focused on what works well in school (McLaughlin, 2013). Developments such as **School Direct** and **Teaching Schools** illustrate such localism. The latter are designed not only to serve as beacons of excellent practice, but to work

## EXTEND YOUR UNDERSTANDING

Visit the IfL's interactive route map and consider where you are on your professional journey: www.ifl.ac.uk/newsandevents/latest/routemap

closely with other schools to coach and support leaders, trainees and serving teachers, given that the differences in pupil attainment are far greater *within* schools in England than between them. It is self-evident that teachers can benefit from developing their knowledge of their practices in their schools. However, they can also gain much from looking outside to other schools, as well as listening to the views of external critical friends. The General Teaching Council for Scotland has led the way in the UK through the introduction of a Professional Update system to 'support, maintain and enhance' teachers' continued professionalism. Teachers are expected to develop their skills and evidence this in a formal, supportive setting (General Teaching Council for Scotland, 2013).

It is widely agreed that the UK needs to learn from the world's leading education performers if it is to improve the quality of its teachers and schools. In the realm of CPD this is difficult because governments rarely state the form and content of CPD activity (Whitehouse, 2011). However, if CPD is to have the kind of impact in UK schools as in countries with leading educational systems, there needs to be similar investment, clear strategic leadership and the support of teachers who see the value in what they are learning.

## Glossary

**Action research** involves teachers participating fully in the cycle of planning, conducting and evaluating a project.

**Ethnography** involves researching a culture *in situ*.

**Evidence-based practice** as applied to teaching, involves the use of the best research to inform decisions in the classroom and profession.

**Paradigm** is a model or way of seeing the world based on a set of assumptions and values.

**Professional Learning Communities** are groups of practitioners who collaborate on a particular enquiry with the aim of improving pupils' learning and raise standards.

**Randomized controlled trials** (RCTs) are experiments where subjects are allocated at random to receive a particular intervention or serve within a control group. RCTs then measure and compare the outcomes from the trial.

**School Direct** is a school-led training path where graduates can apply to train as a teacher with the expectation of employment once they qualify.

**Teaching Schools** are outstanding schools who take a leading role in the training and professional development of teachers.

## References

Adams, M., Walker, C. and O'Connell, P. (2011) 'Invisible or involved Fathers? A content analysis of representations of parenting in young children's picturebooks in the UK', *Sex Roles*, 65(3–4): 259–70.

Alderson, P. (2008) 'Children as researchers', in Christensen, P. and James, A. (eds) *Research with Children: Perspectives and Practice*, Abingdon: Routledge, 276–90.

Arthur, J., Waring, M., Coe, R. and Hedges, L.V. (eds) (2012) *Research Methods and Methodologies in Education*, London: Sage.

Bassey, M. (1995) *Creating Education through Research: A Global Perspective of Educational Research for the 21st Century*, Newark: Kirklington Moor Press, in association with the British Educational Research Association.

Bassey, M. (2007) 'On the kinds of research in educational settings', in Hammersley, M. (ed.) *Educational Research and Evidence-based Practice*, London: Sage, 141–50.

Bell, J. (2010) *Doing Your Research Project: A Guide for First-Time Researchers in Education, Health and Social Science*, Maidenhead: Open University Press.

BERA (2004) *Revised Ethical Guidelines for Educational Research*, available at: www2.le.ac.uk/institution/committees/research-ethics/resources-and-links/EDUCATIONALRESEARCH.pdf (accessed 17 February 2014).

Beverly, J. (1993) 'Teacher-as-researcher', ERIC Digest, available at: http://files.eric.ed.gov/fulltext/ED355205.pdf (accessed 10 December 2013).

Bhopal, K. (2004) 'Gypsy travellers and education: Changing needs and changing perceptions', *British Journal of Educational Studies*, 52(1): 47–64.

Bochel, H. and Duncan, S. (eds) (2007) *Making Policy in Theory and Practice*, Bristol: The Policy Press.

Bolam, R., McMahon, A., Stoll, L., Thomas, S., Wallace, M., Greenwood, A., Hawkey, K., Ingram, M., Atkinson, A. and Smith, M. (2005) *Creating and Sustaining Effective Professional Learning Communities*, London: DfES.

Bordage G. and Dawson B. (2003) 'Experimental study design and grant writing in eight steps and 28 questions', *Medical Education*, 37: 376–85.

Breakwell, G., Hammond, S., Fife-Schaw, C. and Smith, J.A. (eds) (2008) *Research Methods in Psychology*, London: Sage.

Burgess, H. (2001) 'Sustaining improvement through practitioner action research', in Banks, F. and Shelton Mayes, A. (eds) (2001) *Early Professional Development for Teachers*, London: David Fulton, 332–44.

Burton, N., Brundrett, M. and Jones, M. (2008) *Doing Your Education Research Project*, London: Sage.

Cohen, L., Manton, L. and Morrison, K. (2007) *Research Methods in Education*, Abingdon: Routledge.

Cohen, L., Manton, L. and Morrison, K. (2011) *Research Methods in Education*, 7th edn, Abingdon: Routledge.

Conroy, J., Lundie, D., Davis, R., Baumfield, V., Barnes, P., Gallagher, T., Lowden, K., Bourque, N. and Wenell, K. (2013) *Does Religious Education Work?*, London: Bloomsbury.

Cordingley, P., Thomason, S., Saunders, L., Haggar, H., Sturgis, J. and Robinson, K. (2005) *The Impact of Collaborative CPD on Classroom Teaching and Learning*, London: TDA.

Cordingley, P. (2013) *The Contribution of Research to Teachers' Professional Learning and Development*, London: BERA.

Dadds, M. (2001) 'Teacher professional development and the sound of a handclap', in Richards, C. (ed.) *Changing English Primary Education*, Stoke-on-Trent: Trentham Books, 123–38.

Davis, J., Watson, N. and Cunningham-Burley, S. (2008) 'Disabled children, ethnography and unspoken understandings', in Christensen, P. and James, A. (eds) (2008) *Research with Children: Perspectives and Practice*, Abingdon: Routledge, 220–38.

Denby, N., Butroyd, R., Swift, H., Price, J. and Glazzard, J. (2008) *Master's Level Study in Education*, Maidenhead: Open University Press.

Doherty, J. and Hughes M. (2009) *Child Development Theory and Practice 0–11*, Harlow: Pearson.

Featherstone, G. and Pyle, K. (2009) *NFER Teacher Voice Omnibus: November 2009 Survey. Continuing Professional Development*, Slough: NFER.

Gage, N. (2007) 'The paradigm wars and their aftermath', in Hammersley, M. (ed.) *Educational Research and Evidence-based Practice*, London; Sage, 151–66.

General Teaching Council for Scotland (2013) *Professional Update: A Positive Innovation in Scottish Schools*, Edinburgh: General Teaching Council for Scotland.

Godfrey, R. (2004) 'Can everyone be a researcher?' in Hayes, D. (ed.) *The Routledge Guide to Key Debates in Education*, Abingdon: Routledge, 207–10.

Goldacre, B. (2009) *Bad Science*, London: Fourth Estate.

Goldacre, B. (2013) *Building Evidence into Education*, available at: www.gov.uk/government/news/building-evidence-into-education (accessed 10 December 2013).

Goodall, J., Day, C., Lindsay, G., Muijs, D. and Harris, A. (2005) *Evaluating the Impact of Continuing Professional Development*, London: DfES.

Haggarty, L. (1995) 'The use of content analysis to explore conversations between school teacher mentors and student teachers', *British Educational Research Journal*, 21(2): 183–97.

Hammersley, M. (ed.) (2007) *Educational Research and Evidence-based Practice*, London; Sage, 151–66.

Hammersley, M. (2012) 'Methodological paradigms in educational research', British Educational Research Association online resource, available online at: http://www.bera.ac.uk/wp-content/uploads/2014/03/Methodological-Paradigms.pdf (accessed 10 December 2013).

Hancock, R. (2001) 'Why are class teachers reluctant to become researchers?', in Soler, J., Craft, A. and Burgess, H. (eds) *Teacher Development*, London: Sage, 119–32.

Hargreaves, D. (1996) 'Teaching as a research-based profession: Possibilities and prospects', in Hammersley, M. (ed.) *Educational Research and Evidence-based Practice*, London: Sage, 18–42.

Harris, A. and Jones, M. (2010) 'Professional learning communities and system improvement', *Improving Schools*, 13(2): 172–81.

Higgins, S., Katsipataki, M., Kokotsaki, D., Coleman, R., Major, L.E. and Coe, R. (2013) *The Sutton Trust-Education Endowment Foundation Teaching and Learning Toolkit*, London: Education Endowment Foundation.

Hill, M. (2005) 'Ethical considerations in researching children's experiences', in Green, S. and Hogan, D. (eds) *Researching Children's Experiences: Approaches and Methods*, London: Sage.

Hoffmann, A. (2001) *Research for Writers*, London: A&C Black.

Ingersoll, R.M. (2007) *A Comparative Study of Teacher Preparation and Qualifications in Six Nations*, Philadelphia: CPRE.

Kaestle, C.F. (1993) 'The awful reputation of educational research', *Educational Researcher*, 22: 23–31.

Kelly, J. (2013) *IfL Review of CPD*, London: Institute for Learning.

Kemmis, S. and McTaggart, R. (1982) *The Action Research Planner*, Geelong, Australia: Deakin University Press.

King, J.E. (2008) 'Critical and qualitative research in teacher education', in Cochran-Smith, M.,Lytle, S.L., FeimanNemser, S. and McIntyre, D.J. (eds) *Handbook of Research on Teacher Education*, London: Routledge, 1094–135.

Kotter, J.P. (1998) 'Leading change: Why transformation efforts fail', in *Harvard Business Review on Change*, Boston, MA: Harvard Business School Press, 1–20.

Kvale S. (1996) *Interviews: An Introduction to Qualitative Research Interviewing*, Thousand Oaks, CA: Sage.

Lankshear, C. and Knobel, M. (2004) *A Handbook for Teacher Research*, Maidenhead: Open University Press.

Lewin, K. (1946) 'Action research and minority problems', *Journal of Social Issues*, 2(4): 34–46.

Lewis, M. and Andrews, D. (2004) 'Building sustainable futures: Emerging understandings of the significant contribution of the professional learning community', *Improving Schools*, 7(2): 129–50.

Livingstone, S. and Bober, M. (2004) *UK Children Go Online: Surveying the Experiences of Young People and Their Parents*, London: LSE Research Online.

McLaughlin, C. (ed.) (2013) *Teachers Learning: Professional Development and Education*, Cambridge: Cambridge University Press.

McNiff, J. and Whitehead, J. (2006) *All You Need to Know About Action Research*, London: Sage.

McNiff, J. and Whitehead, J. (2009) *Doing and Writing Action Research*, London: Sage.

National Council on Teacher Quality (2004) *Increasing the Odds: How Good Policies Can Yield Better Teachers*, Washington: NCTQ.

National Partnership group (2012) *Teaching Scotland's Future: National Partnership Group*, Edinburgh: Scottish Government.

Noffke, S. and Somekh, B. (eds) (2009) *The SAGE Handbook of Educational Action Research*, London: Sage.

Onions, C.T. (ed.) (1966) *Oxford Dictionary of English Etymology*, Oxford: Oxford University Press.

Petty, G. (2006) *Evidence-based Teaching*, Cheltenham: Nelson Thornes.

Pollard, A. (2008) *Reflective Teaching*, London: Continuum.

Purcell, K., Rainie, L., Heaps, A., Buchanan, J., Friedrich, L. and Jacklin, A. (2012) *How Teens Do Research in the Digital World*, Washington, DC: Pew Research Center's Internet and American Life Project.

Punch, K. (2009) *Introduction to Research Methods in Education*, London: Sage.

Punch, M. (1994) 'Politics and ethics in qualitative research', in Denzin, N.K. and Lincoln, Y.S. (eds) *Handbook of Qualitative Research*, Thousand Oaks, CA: Sage, 83–104.

QAA (2010) *Master's Degree Characteristics*, Gloucester: QAA.

Roberts, H. (2008) 'Listening to children: And hearing them', in Christensen, P. and James, A. (eds) *Research with Children: Perspectives and Practice*, Abingdon: Routledge, 260–75.

Rudduck, J. (1988) 'Changing the world of the classroom by understanding it: A review of some aspects of the work of Lawrence Stenhouse', *Journal of Curriculum and Supervision*, 4(1): 30–42.

Segall, A. (2004) 'Revisiting pedagogical content knowledge: The pedagogy of content/the content of pedagogy', *Teaching and Teacher Education*, 20: 489–504.

Sewell, K. (ed.) (2008) *Doing Your PGCE at M-Level*, London: Sage.

Sonck, N., Livingstone, S., Kuiper, E. and de Haan, J. (2011) *Digital Literacy and Safety Skills*, London: EU Kids Online.

Stenhouse, L.A. (1975) *An Introduction to Curriculum Research and Development*, London: Heinemann Education Books.

TDA (2009) *The National Framework for Masters in Teaching and Learning*, London: TDA.

Thomas, G. (2013) *How to Do Your Research Project: A Guide for Students in Education and Applied Social Sciences*, London: Sage.

Timperley, H.S., Wilson, A., Barrar, H. and Fung, I. (2007) *Teacher Professional Learning and Development: Best Evidence Synthesis Iteration*, Wellington, New Zealand: Ministry of Education.

TLRP (2004) TLRP Briefing 4, 'Towards evidence-based practice in science education', available at: www.tlrp.org/pub/research.html (accessed 10 December 2013).

TLRP (2006) TLRP Briefing 20, 'Factors that make teachers more effective across their careers', available at: www.tlrp.org/pub/research.html (accessed 10 December 2013).

Tooley, J. (1998) *Educational Research: A Critique*, London: OFSTED.

Tripp, D. (1993) *Critical Incidents in Teaching*, London: Routledge.

Verscio, V., Ross, D. and Adams, A. (2008) 'A review of research on the impact of professional learning communities on teaching practice and student learning', *Teaching and Teacher Education*, 21: 80–91.

Wallace, F., Blase, K.A., Fixsen, D.L. and Nadom, S. (2008) *Implementing the Findings of Research: Bridging the Gap Between Knowledge and Practice*, Alexandria, VA: Educational Research Service.

Wellcome Trust (2006) *Believers, Seekers and Sceptics*, London: Wellcome Trust.

Wellington, J. (2006) *Secondary Education: The Key Concepts*, London: Routledge.

Weston, D. (2013a) 'Seven deadly sins of teacher development', *Times Educational Supplement*, 21 June.

Weston (2013b) 'Putting professional and personal development at the heart of school activities', 15 February, blog available at: www.teacherdevelopmenttrust.org (accessed 10 December 2013).

Whitehouse, C. (2011) *Effective Continuing Professional Development for Teachers*, London: Centre for Education Research and Policy.

Williams, R. (2010) 'Internet plagiarism rising in schools', *The Guardian*, 20 June.

Wilson, R., Hemsley-Brown, J., Easton, C. and Starp, C. (2003) *Using Research for School Improvement: The LEA's Role* (LGA Research Report 42). Slough: NFER.

Wolcott, H.F. (1994) *Transforming Qualitative Data: Description, Analysis and Interpretation*, Thousand Oaks, CA: Sage.

## Websites

The Institute of Education in London hosts the Digital Education Resource Archive, a treasure trove of UK documentation for researchers – http://dera.ioe.ac.uk

The Evidence for Policy and Practice Information and Coordinating Centre (EPPI-Centre), hosted by the Institute of Education, University of London – www.eppi.ioe.ac.uk/cms

The Centre for the Use of Research and Evidence in Education (Curee) provides research reports and digests – www.curee.co.uk/our-projects/research-informed-practice-site-trips

The British Education Index supports the professional study of education and includes conference papers – www.leeds.ac.uk/bei

The British Education Research Association provides an overview of some of the activities and aims of BERA – www.bera.ac.uk

The Nuffield Foundation, set up in 1943, funds research in many areas – www.nuffield foundation.org

The National Foundation for Educational Research carries out research projects each year across all sectors of education and includes online 'How to . . .' research guides – www.nfer.ac.uk

Access to Research Resources for Teachers Space (ARRT Space) is part of the website of the General Teaching Council for Northern Ireland – http://arrts.gtcni.org.uk/gtcni

The Teacher Development Trust seeks to improve educational outcomes for children by raising the quality of teacher professional development – www.teacherdevelopmenttrust.org

The GoodCPDGuide is a free database of high-quality professional development resources for education – http://goodcpdguide.com

The Sutton Trust operates a Teaching and Learning toolkit that summarizes research findings on different topics – http://educationendowmentfoundation.org.uk/toolkit/about-the-toolkit

Scotland's Journey to Excellence website includes research summaries, CPD resources and improvement guides – www.journeytoexcellence.org.uk/index.asp

# Index